Classic Writings on Poetry

Classic Writings on Poetry

Edited by William Harmon

COLUMBIA UNIVERSITY PRESS

NEW YORK

Columbia University Press
Publishers Since 1893
New York   Chichester, West Sussex
Copyright © 2003 Columbia University Press
All rights reserved

Library of Congress Cataloging-in-Publication Data
Classic writings on poetry / edited by William Harmon.
        p. cm.
    ISBN 0–231–12370–1 (cloth : alk. paper)—0–231–12371–X (pbk. : alk. paper)
    1. Poetry—History and criticism. 2. Poetics. I. Harmon, William, 1938–

    PN1016.C53 2003
    809.1—dc21

                                                        2003040917

∞

Columbia University Press books are printed on permanent and durable acid-free paper.
Printed in the United States of America
c 10 9 8 7 6 5 4 3 2 1
p 10 9 8 7 6 5 4 3 2 1

CONTENTS

INTRODUCTION

1

In the beginning, let us say, people used language for practical purposes exclusively. Then these literal ancestors of ours discovered that they could augment the practical with the aesthetic, and poetry was born—poetry defined loosely as language used in a special way and for a special purpose beyond immediate practicalities. It remains possible, however, that the order of evolution was reversed, and that poetry came first and practicality second; some speculate that even pottery was first ornamental or ritual in purpose and only later found to be useful for cooking and storage.

Whatever the order of the first two stages—communication then poetry, poetry then communication—it is likely that the third stage involved reflection on poetry, which we usually call criticism. Early in these early days, a poet wrote something like

> Perhaps in this neglected spot is laid
> Some heart once pregnant with celestial fire . . . ,

at which any normal, intelligent reader might bridle. One would have to note, first, that it is not one's heart that becomes pregnant; second, that what something gets pregnant *with* is not fire; third, that fire is not normally described as celestial—quite the contrary, fire is often considered *infernal*. One might demand, "Is this surrealist? Or just nonsensical?" A scholar would have to answer, "No, it's just conventional mid-eighteenth-century poesy." In fact, it is Thomas Gray's "Elegy Written in a Country Churchyard," a mine of clichés for almost three centuries: "short and simple annals of the poor," "paths of glory," "far from the madding crowd," "purest ray serene." These questions and objections mark the point where the immediate, practical use of language gives way to some use beyond the immediate or the practical—such as education—and seems to exist at least in part for itself. And it is here that criticism becomes interesting and valuable and vexed.

Poetry resists absolute definitions. Something that seems inseparable from and vital to poetry in one culture will be unintelligible or ridiculous in another. Rhyme, for example, has been an incidental blemish of prose in many literatures, especially those of classical antiquity (Sanskrit, Greek, Latin); in time, however, in the poetry of Europe, rhyme turned into an ornament so important that "rhyme" itself virtually came to mean "poem," as in Coleridge's "The Rime of the Ancient Mariner." During the Middle Ages, when unrhymed quantitative verse still persisted from antiquity, particularly in the language of the Christian church, which was dedicated to the preservation of Latin, rhymed accentual verse was introduced for certain religious texts set to music, but rhyme was so alien to true poetry, according to many conservatives, that such texts were called"proses." The honorific term "verse" was kept for old-fashioned poems (for example, "Adeste Fideles," still sung today, does not rhyme in Latin or English). Accordingly, in the early fifteenth century, "in prose" could mean "in rhyme." (To insult a kind of verse by calling it prose persisted for centuries, as when in 1880 Matthew Arnold delivered a famous verdict, "Dryden and Pope are not classics of our poetry, they are classics of our prose.")

Sound effects do not constitute the only slippery characteristic of poetry. Rhetorical devices, so crucial to much Western poetry, also contribute to incomprehension. The English poet George Barker taught in Japan just before World War II. As Barker's fellow poet John Heath-Stubbs tells it:

> George had some difficulty in getting the Japanese students adequately to understand English poetry. He set them for comment a poem of A. E. Housman . . . beginning "The chestnut casts its flambeaux." The students came to him in a body and said: "We find this poem extremely obscure. We have looked up the words in the dictionary, and it appears to say that the chestnut tree is throwing away torches. We cannot comprehend how a chestnut tree can have torches to throw away." The reason for this

misunderstanding was that classical Japanese poetry makes no use whatsoever of metaphor or simile.

> John Heath-Stubbs, *Hindsights: An Autobiography* (London: Hodder and
> Stoughton, 1993), 147; also recounted in Robert Fraser, *The Chameleon Poet:*
> *A Life of George Barker* (London: Jonathan Cape, 2001).

That account may not accurately register the entire truth about Japanese language and literature, but the general experience will be familiar.

Beyond the levels of sound and rhetoric, between different poetics there may
also be incomprehension or miscomprehension of language and concept. Ancient Hebrew poetry seems to have relied more on grammatical patterns than
on any conceptual or acoustic patterns that would be familiar to speakers of an
Indo-European language. Translators of the Bible have recognized that parts of
it are poetry, but it is usually printed as prose. Even so, the standard subdivisions,
which have been used for almost five hundred years, suggest prose and poetry
together: chapters as in prose, verses as in poetry, even though the verses are
printed as prose.

Since the criticism of literature is itself a species of literature, complications
become exponential and controversy begins almost immediately. Among many
other causes of conflict, poets and the critics of poetry disagree about diction and
rhetoric. Seldom has a poem sounded remotely like real speech, but seldom has
a poet failed to claim that he or she writes the way normal people talk. Everybody
professes an earnest preference for the simple and direct, but any writer coming
even close to simple and direct is quickly forgotten, while those who are most
complex and indirect—Shakespeare, Milton, Wordsworth, Whitman, Dickinson,
Eliot—command respect. Even the celebrated minimalist Thoreau had to say,
"Simplicity, simplicity, simplicity!" and "Simplify, simplify," which are practically
contradictions in terms—likewise, Blake's "To generalize is to be an idiot."

But the definitions of both generalization and idiocy change with time; the
hits of one age become the laughingstock of the next. Samuel Johnson tears
Milton's "Lycidas" to pieces for its inconsistency and presumed insincerity.
William Wordsworth likewise flays Johnson's "The Vanity of Human Wishes"
for its pompous redundancy. According to William Hazlitt's description of
Wordsworth:

> Nothing . . . can be fairer, or more amusing than the way in which he
> sometimes exposes the unmeaning verbiage of modern poetry. Thus, in
> the beginning of Dr. Johnson's "Vanity of Human Wishes"—

> > Let observation with extensive view
> > Survey mankind from China to Peru—

he says there is a total want of imagination accompanying the words; the same idea is repeated three times under the disguise of a different phraseology. It comes to this: "let observation with extensive observation observe mankind"; or take away the first line, and the second, "Survey mankind from China to Peru," literally conveys the whole.

It does not matter much that Johnson's satirical poem imitates a precursor by Juvenal that mocks pompous diction. Eighteenth-century satirists seem to have experimented with maximal redundancy, the prize going to one of Pope's couplets: "Or alom-stypticks with contracting pow'r / Shrink his thin essence like a rivelled flow'r," which says the same thing at least five times over.

Johnson tore Milton, Wordsworth tore Johnson, and Wordsworth himself came in for all sorts of tearing from later poets, including Byron, Hartley Coleridge, Robert Browning, James Kenneth Stephen, Ezra Pound, T. S. Eliot, and Aldous Huxley—all of whom, in their turn, have been torn, ad infinitum. It remains obvious, as it was obvious in the dim days of the evolution of language, that poetry is a most engaging thing. It is there; it exists necessarily, as does its criticism.

2

This sampling starts with a few pieces from classical antiquity and extends its reach to the early twentieth century. Out of the thousands of things written on poetry, these have kept their freshness and pertinence for modern readers of English. The answers and solutions change from age to age, but the questions and problems persist, often in much the same form as that employed by Aristotle or Horace. As later critics return to the perennial puzzles addressed by the Greeks and Romans, there may be some danger of reinventing the wheel. But wheels need to be reinvented now and again, lest they lose their shape. In none of the documents is poetry as such distinguished very crisply from prose. Aristotle's *Poetics* has to do with much besides poetry itself, however defined, and many of his observations would apply to works in prose as well those in verse. That flexibility may have something to do with the origin of the words *poem* and *poetry*.

Poem seems to begin as a past participle of a Greek verb meaning "to make," so that a poem is rather vaguely construed as a product, and poetics is the study of how such a product is produced. Possibly the meaning of *poem* has always been evasive and figurative—the sort of usage that we reserve for special subjects, such as religion and emotion, about which it is impossible to be precise. A poem is anything composed, so that John Milton, in one of his prose pamphlets of the 1640s, could suggest, "He who would not be frustrate of his hope to write well hereafter in laudable things, ought him selfe to be a true Poem, that is a composition and patterne of the best and honourablest things."

3

I hope to show that while poetry has been many things to many sorts of people, it has not been remote from the daily lives and work of ordinary people. That is by no means to say that poetry itself is ordinary or simple; it isn't. But if you stay alert, you can hear poetry in many places besides a classroom. You probably heard poetry on the day you were born, even though you could not comprehend it; after you pass away, poetry may be spoken over your remains, even though you will not hear it. We have always reserved poetry for the special things and occasions. It means so much to us that we believe poetry comprises some of the best works ever produced by the species. Poetry allows the ordinary to become extraordinary for a time; some people, possibly not model family members or citizens or scholars or even warriors, have touched sublime genius thanks to poetry. If you cannot believe that enterprises such as Comedy and Tragedy, the love lyric, the epic, and Choric songs are superintended by the great goddesses who are the very daughters of Memory and Zeus himself, then you are in for a revelation and maybe a conversion. The heights of expression have been reached in poetry, and poetry therefore commands some of our best attention. It remains a mystery; even the mechanical aspects are mysterious. But we have never stopped thinking about it.

Classic Writings on Poetry

1

PLATO (?427–348 B.C.)

Plato's work survives chiefly in the form of dialogues involving Socrates and other citizens of Athens interrogating each other about the nature of truth, love, justice, education, and other topics that continue to engage us. The Socratic dialogue, whatever the topic, is a demonstration, first, of a brilliantly effective educational device, wherein the teacher leads the pupil by a series of questions in a discussion, and, second, of an equally brilliant rhetorical device, wherein one makes a point by step-by-step reasoning and not by mere assertion.

Plato's complex philosophy usually assumes that we live in a layered world, with mutable material reality at the bottom, experienced by the fallible senses, and some kind of immutable immaterial reality at the top, experienced by the intellect. The world of bodily experience is so conditional, subjective, changeable, and temporary that Plato dismisses it and concentrates instead on the superior reality of forms and ideas. Since our perceptions necessarily involve images of approximations of reality, art is even further removed from the real, since it comprises fictional and even fabulous imitations of images, which are themselves perversions of an approximate reality. Thus seen as radically fictional and unreal, art becomes a seducer and a betrayer, distracting the mind by lies from its efforts to know the truth.

Such a stance toward literary art seems inherently paradoxical, since all who argue along such lines—including Boethius and Tolstoy as well as Plato—must do so in a work that is itself a piece of literature: maybe not overtly labeled fiction, but still a work that must use language, however feeble and fickle that instrument must be.

A dialogue on the general problem of truth was inaugurated by Plato more than 2,000 years ago, and its importance and interest are undiminished today. Plato's *Republic* concerns itself with the ideal state and includes a consideration of the role of poetry in education. This dialogue condemns poetry because it corrupts youth—yet another Socratic irony, since it was on charges of introducing new deities and corrupting youth that Socrates was tried and executed. The irony may need to be deciphered or resolved, since it seems that Socrates (at least in Plato's account) was punished for the same crime that poetry in general was guilty of. If nothing else, the case shows that Athenians cared about the corruption of their youth. These very topics are at the center of some of Plato's dialogues—especially the *Apology*—but not in ways that pertain to poetry or criticism.

THE REPUBLIC (CA. 360 B.C.; EXCERPT)

Benjamin Jowett (1817–1893) was an Anglican clergyman and educator. His translations of Plato's *Dialogues* appeared in 1871. The translations from poetry come from Jowett's translations of both Plato and Plato's quotations from others. The numbers in brackets following quotations refer to book numbers.

BOOK III

[participants] SOCRATES–ADEIMANTUS

[Socrates narrates:]

Such then, I said, are our principles of theology—some tales are to be told, and others are not to be told to our disciples from their youth upwards, if we mean them to honor the gods and their parents, and to value friendship with one another.

Yes; and I think that our principles are right, he said.
But if they are to be courageous, must they not learn other lessons besides these, and lessons of such a kind as will take away the fear of death? Can any man be courageous who has the fear of death in him?

Certainly not, he said.

And can he be fearless of death, or will he choose death in battle rather than defeat and slavery, who believes the world below to be real and terrible?

Impossible.

Then we must assume a control over the narrators of this class of tales as well as over the others, and beg them not simply to but rather to commend the world below, intimating to them that their descriptions are untrue, and will do harm to our future warriors.

That will be our duty, he said.

Then, I said, we shall have to obliterate many obnoxious passages, beginning with the verses,

> I would rather he a serf on the land of a poor and portion-
>   less man
> than rule over all the dead who have come to nought.
> [*Odyssey*, 11]

We must also expunge the verse, which tells us how Pluto feared,

> Lest the mansions grim and squalid which the gods abhor
> should he seen both of mortals and immortals. [*Iliad*, 20]

And again:

> O heavens! verily in the house of Hades there is soul and
>   ghostly form
> but no mind at all! [*Iliad*, 23]

Again of Tiresias: —

> [To him even after death did Persephone grant mind,] that
>   he alone should
> be wise; but the other souls are flitting shades. [*Odyssey*, 10]

Again: —

> The soul flying from the limbs had gone to Hades, lament-
>   ing her fate,
> leaving manhood and youth. [*Iliad*, 16]

Again: —

> And the soul, with shrilling cry, passed like smoke beneath
> the earth. [*Iliad*, 23]

And, —

> As bats in hollow of mystic cavern, whenever any of them has dropped
> out of the string and falls from the rock, fly shrilling and cling to one
> another, so did they with shrilling cry hold together as they moved. [*Od-
> yssey*, 24]

And we must beg Homer and the other poets not to be angry if we strike out
these and similar passages, not because they are unpoetical, or unattractive to
the popular ear, but because the greater the poetical charm of them, the less
are they meet for the ears of boys and men who are meant to be free, and who
should fear slavery more than death.

Undoubtedly.

Also we shall have to reject all the terrible and appalling names which describe
the world below—Cocytus and Styx, ghosts under the earth, and sapless shades,
and any similar words of which the very mention causes a shudder to pass
through the inmost soul of him who hears them. I do not say that these horrible
stories may not have a use of some kind; but there is a danger that the nerves
of our guardians may be rendered too excitable and effeminate by them.
There is a real danger, he said.
Then we must have no more of them.
True.
Another and a nobler strain must be composed and sung by us.
Clearly.
And shall we proceed to get rid of the weepings and wailings of famous men?

They will go with the rest.
But shall we be right in getting rid of them? Reflect: our principle is that the
good man will not consider death terrible to any other good man who is his
comrade.

Yes; that is our principle.
And therefore he will not sorrow for his departed friend as though he had
suffered anything terrible?

He will not.

Such an one, as we further maintain, is sufficient for himself and his own happiness, and therefore is least in need of other men.

True, he said.

And for this reason the loss of a son or brother, or the deprivation of fortune, is to him of all men least terrible.

Assuredly.

And therefore he will be least likely to lament, and will bear with the greatest equanimity any misfortune of this sort which may befall him.

Yes, he will feel such a misfortune far less than another.

Then we shall be right in getting rid of the lamentations of famous men, and making them over to women (and not even to women who are good for anything), or to men of a baser sort, that those who are being educated by us to be the defenders of their country may scorn to do the like.

That will be very right.

Then we will once more entreat Homer and the other poets not to depict Achilles [*Iliad*, 24] who is the son of a goddess, first lying on his side, then on his back, and then on his face; then starting up and sailing in a frenzy along the shores of the barren sea; now taking the sooty ashes in both his hands and pouring them over his head, or weeping and wailing in the various modes which Homer has delineated. Nor should he describe Priam the kinsman of the gods as praying and beseeching,

> Rolling in the dirt, calling each man loudly by his name.
> [*Iliad*, 22]

Still more earnestly will we beg of him at all events not to introduce the gods lamenting and saying,

> Alas! my misery! Alas! that I bore the harvest to my sorrow.
> [*Iliad*, 18]

But if he must introduce the gods, at any rate let him not dare so completely to misrepresent the greatest of the gods, as to make him say —

> O heavens! with my eyes verily I behold a dear friend of
>   mine chased round and round the city, and my heart is
>   sorrowful. [*Iliad*, 22]

Or again:—

> Woe is me that I am fated to have Sarpedon, dearest of
>   men to me, subdued at
> the hands of Patroclus the son of Menoetius. [*Iliad*, 16]

For if, my sweet Adeimantus, our youth seriously listen to such unworthy representations of the gods, instead of laughing at them as they ought, hardly will any of them deem that he himself, being but a man, can be dishonored by similar actions; neither will he rebuke any inclination which may arise in his mind to say and do the like. And instead of having any shame or self-control, he will be always whining and lamenting on slight occasions . . . .

And therefore let us put an end to such tales, lest they engender laxity of morals among the young.

By all means, he replied.
But now that we are determining what classes of subjects are or are not to be spoken of, let us see whether any have been omitted by us. The manner in which gods and demigods and heroes and the world below should be treated has been already laid down.

Very true.
And what shall we say about men? That is clearly the remaining portion of our subject.

Clearly so.
But we are not in a condition to answer this question at present, my friend.

Why not?
Because, if I am not mistaken, we shall have to say that, about men, poets and story-tellers are guilty of making the gravest misstatements when they tell us that wicked men are often happy, and the good miserable; and that injustice is profitable when undetected, but that justice is a man's own loss and another's gain—these things we shall forbid them to utter, and command them to sing and say the opposite.

To be sure we shall, he replied.
But if you admit that I am right in this, then I shall maintain that you have implied the principle for which we have been all along contending.

I grant the truth of your inference.
That such things are or are not to be said about men is a question which we

cannot determine until we have discovered what justice is, and how naturally advantageous to the possessor, whether he seems to be just or not.

Most true, he said.

Enough of the subjects of poetry: let us now speak of the style; and when this has been considered, both matter and manner will have been completely treated.

I do not understand what you mean, said Adeimantus.

Then I must make you understand; and perhaps I may be more intelligible if I put the matter in this way. You are aware, I suppose, that all mythology and poetry is a narration of events, either past, present, or to come?

Certainly, he replied.

And narration may be either simple narration, or imitation, or a union of the two?

That again, he said, I do not quite understand.

I fear that I must be a ridiculous teacher when I have so much difficulty in making myself apprehended. Like a bad speaker, therefore, I will not take the whole of the subject, but will break a piece off in illustration of my meaning. You know the first lines of the *Iliad*, in which the poet says that Chryses prayed Agamemnon to release his daughter, and that Agamemnon flew into a passion with him; whereupon Chryses, failing of his object, invoked the anger of the God against the Achaeans. Now as far as these lines,

> And he prayed all the Greeks, but especially the two sons of
> Atreus, the chiefs of the people,

the poet is speaking in his own person; he never leads us to suppose that he is any one else. But in what follows he takes the person of Chryses, and then he does all that he can to make us believe that the speaker is not Homer, but the aged priest himself. And in this double form he has cast the entire narrative of the events which occurred at Troy and in Ithaca and throughout the *Odyssey*.

Yes.

And a narrative it remains both in the speeches which the poet recites from time to time and in the intermediate passages?

Quite true.

But when the poet speaks in the person of another, may we not say that he assimilates his style to that of the person who, as he informs you, is going to speak?

Certainly.

And this assimilation of himself to another, either by the use of voice or gesture, is the imitation of the person whose character he assumes?

Of course.

Then in this case the narrative of the poet may be said to proceed by way of imitation?

Very true.

Or, if the poet everywhere appears and never conceals himself, then again the imitation is dropped, and his poetry becomes simple narration. However, in order that I may make my meaning quite clear, and that you may no more say, 'I don't understand,' I will show how the change might be effected. If Homer had said, 'The priest came, having his daughter's ransom in his hands, supplicating the Achaeans, and above all the kings'; and then if, instead of speaking in the person of Chryses, he had continued in his own person, the words would have been, not imitation, but simple narration. The passage would have run as follows (I am no poet, and therefore I drop the meter), 'The priest came and prayed the gods on behalf of the Greeks that they might capture Troy and return safely home, but begged that they would give him back his daughter, and take the ransom which he brought, and respect the God. Thus he spoke, and the other Greeks revered the priest and assented. But Agamemnon was wroth, and bade him depart and not come again, lest the staff and chaplets of the God should be of no avail to him—the daughter of Chryses should not be released, he said—she should grow old with him in Argos. And then he told him to go away and not to provoke him, if he intended to get home unscathed. And the old man went away in fear and silence, and, when he had left the camp, he called upon Apollo by his many names, reminding him of everything which he had done pleasing to him, whether in building his temples, or in offering sacrifice, and praying that his good deeds might be returned to him, and that the Achaeans might expiate his tears by the arrows of the god,'—and so on. In this way the whole becomes simple narrative.

I understand, he said.

Or you may suppose the opposite case—that the intermediate passages are omitted, and the dialogue only left.

That also, he said, I understand; you mean, for example, as in tragedy.

You have conceived my meaning perfectly; and if I mistake not, what you failed to apprehend before is now made clear to you, that poetry and mythology are, in some cases, wholly imitative—instances of this are supplied by tragedy and comedy; there is likewise the opposite style, in which the my poet is the only speaker—of this the dithyramb affords the best example; and the combination of both is found in epic, and in several other styles of poetry. Do I take you with me?

Yes, he said; I see now what you meant.
I will ask you to remember also what I began by saying, that we had done with the subject and might proceed to the style.

Yes, I remember.
In saying this, I intended to imply that we must come to an understanding about the mimetic art—whether the poets, in narrating their stories, are to be allowed by us to imitate, and if so, whether in whole or in part, and if the latter, in what parts; or should all imitation be prohibited?

You mean, I suspect, to ask whether tragedy and comedy shall be admitted into our State?

Yes, I said; but there may be more than this in question: I really do not know as yet, but whither the argument may blow, thither we go.

And go we will, he said.
Then, Adeimantus, let me ask you whether our guardians ought to be imitators; or rather, has not this question been decided by the rule already laid down that one man can only do one thing well, and not many; and that if he attempt many, he will altogether fall of gaining much reputation in any?

Certainly.
And this is equally true of imitation; no one man can imitate many things as well as he would imitate a single one?

He cannot.
Then the same person will hardly be able to play a serious part in life, and at the same time to be an imitator and imitate many other parts as well; for even when two species of imitation are nearly allied, the same persons cannot succeed in both, as, for example, the writers of tragedy and comedy—did you not just now call them imitations?

Yes, I did; and you are right in thinking that the same persons cannot succeed in both.

Any more than they can be rhapsodists and actors at once?
True.
Neither are comic and tragic actors the same; yet all these things are but imitations.

They are so.
And human nature, Adeimantus, appears to have been coined into yet smaller pieces, and to be as incapable of imitating many things well, as of performing well the actions of which the imitations are copies.

Quite true, he replied.
If then we adhere to our original notion and bear in mind that our guardians, setting aside every other business, are to dedicate themselves wholly to the maintenance of freedom in the State, making this their craft, and engaging in no work which does not bear on this end, they ought not to practice or imitate anything else; if they imitate at all, they should imitate from youth upward only those characters which are suitable to their profession—the courageous, temperate, holy, free, and the like; but they should not depict or be skilful at imitating any kind of illiberality or baseness, lest from imitation they should come to be what they imitate. Did you never observe how imitations, beginning in early youth and continuing far into life, at length grow into habits and become a second nature, affecting body, voice, and mind?

Yes, certainly, he said.
Then, I said, we will not allow those for whom we profess a care and of whom we say that they ought to be good men, to imitate a woman, whether young or old, quarrelling with her husband, or striving and vaunting against the gods in conceit of her happiness, or when she is in affliction, or sorrow, or weeping; and certainly not one who is in sickness, love, or labor.

Very right, he said.
Neither must they represent slaves, male or female, performing the offices of slaves?

They must not.
And surely not bad men, whether cowards or any others, who do the reverse of what we have just been prescribing, who scold or mock or revile one another in drink or [not] in drink or, or who in any other manner sin against themselves and their neighbors in word or deed, as the manner of such is. Neither should they be trained to imitate the action or speech of men or women who are mad or bad; for madness, like vice, is to be known but not to be practiced or imitated.

Very true, he replied.

Neither may they imitate smiths or other artificers, or oarsmen, or boatswains, or the like?

How can they, he said, when they are not allowed to apply their minds to the callings of any of these?

Nor may they imitate the neighing of horses, the bellowing of bulls, the murmur of rivers and roll of the ocean, thunder, and all that sort of thing?

Nay, he said, if madness be forbidden, neither may they copy the behavior of madmen.

You mean, I said, if I understand you aright, that there is one sort of narrative style which may be employed by a truly good man when he has anything to say, and that another sort will be used by a man of an opposite character and education.

And which are these two sorts? he asked.

Suppose, I answered, that a just and good man in the course of a narration comes on some saying or action of another good man,—I should imagine that he will like to personate him, and will not be ashamed of this sort of imitation: he will be most ready to play the part of the good man when he is acting firmly and wisely; in a less degree when he is overtaken by illness or love or drink, or has met with any other disaster. But when he comes to a character which is unworthy of him, he will not make a study of that; he will disdain such a person, and will assume his likeness, if at all, for a moment only when he is performing some good action; at other times he will be ashamed to play a part which he has never practiced, nor will he like to fashion and frame himself after the baser models; he feels the employment of such an art, unless in jest, to be beneath him, and his mind revolts at it.

So I should expect, he replied.

Then he will adopt a mode of narration such as we have illustrated out of Homer, that is to say, his style will be both imitative and narrative; but there will be very little of the former, and a great deal of the latter. Do you agree?

Certainly, he said; that is the model which such a speaker must necessarily take.

But there is another sort of character who will narrate anything, and, the worse lie is, the more unscrupulous he will be; nothing will be too bad for him: and he will be ready to imitate anything, not as a joke, but in right good earnest, and before a large company. As I was just now saying, he will attempt to represent the roll of thunder, the noise of wind and hail, or the creaking of wheels, and pulleys, and the various sounds of flutes; pipes, trumpets, and all sorts of instruments: he will bark like a dog, bleat like a sheep, or crow like a cock; his entire art will consist in imitation of voice and gesture, and there will be very little narration.

That, he said, will be his mode of speaking.
These, then, are the two kinds of style?
Yes.
And you would agree with me in saying that one of them is simple and has but slight changes; and if the harmony and rhythm are also chosen for their simplicity, the result is that the speaker, if he speaks correctly, is always pretty much the same in style, and he will keep within the limits of a single harmony (for the changes are not great), and in like manner he will make use of nearly the same rhythm?

That is quite true, he said.
Whereas the other requires all sorts of harmonies and all sorts of rhythms, if the music and the style are to correspond, because the style has all sorts of changes.

That is also perfectly true, he replied.
And do not the two styles, or the mixture of the two, comprehend all poetry, and every form of expression in words? No one can say anything except in one or other of them or in both together.

They include all, he said.
And shall we receive into our State all the three styles, or one only of the two unmixed styles? or would you include the mixed?

I should prefer only to admit the pure imitator of virtue.
Yes, I said, Adeimantus, but the mixed style is also very charming: and indeed the pantomimic, which is the opposite of the one chosen by you, is the most popular style with children and their attendants, and with the world in general.

I do not deny it.
But I suppose you would argue that such a style is unsuitable to our State, in which human nature is not twofold or manifold, for one man plays one part only?

Yes; quite unsuitable.
And this is the reason why in our State, and in our State only, we shall find a

shoemaker to be a shoemaker and not a pilot also, and a husbandman to be a husbandman and not a dicast also, and a soldier a soldier and not a trader also, and the same throughout?

True, he said.

And therefore when any one of these pantomimic gentlemen, who are so clever that they can imitate anything, comes to us, and makes a proposal to exhibit himself and his poetry, we will fall down and worship him as a sweet and holy and wonderful being; but we must also inform him that in our State such as he are not permitted to exist; the law will not allow them. And so when we have anointed him with myrrh, and set a garland of wool upon his head, we shall send him away to another city. For we mean to employ for our souls' health the rougher and severer poet or story-teller, who will imitate the style of the virtuous only, and will follow those models which we prescribed at first when we began the education of our soldiers. . . .

BOOK X

SOCRATES–GLAUCON

[Socrates narrates:]

Of the many excellences which I perceive in the order of our State, there is none which upon reflection pleases me better than the rule about poetry.

To what do you refer?
To the rejection of imitative poetry, which certainly ought not to be received; as I see far more clearly now that the parts of the soul have been distinguished.

What do you mean?
Speaking in confidence, for I should not like to have my words repeated to the tragedians and the rest of the imitative tribe—but I do not mind saying to you, that all poetical imitations are ruinous to the understanding of the hearers, and that the knowledge of their true nature is the only antidote to them.

Explain the purport of your remark.
Well, I will tell you, although I have always from my earliest youth had an awe and love of Homer, which even now makes the words falter on my lips, for he is the great captain and teacher of the whole of that charming tragic company; but a man is not to be reverenced more than the truth, and therefore I will speak out.

Very good, he said.

Listen to me then, or rather, answer me.

Put your question.

Can you tell me what imitation is? for I really do not know.

A likely thing, then, that I should know.

Why not? for the duller eye may often see a thing sooner than the keener.

Very true, he said; but in your presence, even if I had any faint notion, I could not muster courage to utter it. Will you enquire yourself?

Well then, shall we begin the enquiry in our usual manner: Whenever a number of individuals have a common name, we assume them to have also a corresponding idea or form. Do you understand me?

I do.

Let us take any common instance; there are beds and tables in the world — plenty of them, are there not?

Yes.

But there are only two ideas or forms of them — one the idea of a bed, the other of a table.

True.

And the maker of either of them makes a bed or he makes a table for our use, in accordance with the idea — that is our way of speaking in this and similar instances — but no artificer makes the ideas themselves: how could he?

Impossible.

And there is another artist, — I should like to know what you would say of him.

Who is he?

One who is the maker of all the works of all other workmen.

What an extraordinary man!

Wait a little, and there will be more reason for your saying so. For this is he who is able to make not only vessels of every kind, but plants and animals, himself and all other things — the earth and heaven, and the things which are in heaven or under the earth; he makes the gods also.

He must be a wizard and no mistake.

Oh! you are incredulous, are you? Do you mean that there is no such maker or creator, or that in one sense there might be a maker of all these things but in another not? Do you see that there is a way in which you could make them all yourself?

What way?

An easy way enough; or rather, there are many ways in which the feat might be quickly and easily accomplished, none quicker than that of turning a mirror round and round—you would soon enough make the sun and the heavens, and the earth and yourself, and other animals and plants, and all the other things of which we were just now speaking, in the mirror.

Yes, he said; but they would be appearances only.

Very good, I said, you are coming to the point now. And the painter too is, as I conceive, just such another—a creator of appearances, is he not?

Of course.

But then I suppose you will say that what he creates is untrue. And yet there is a sense in which the painter also creates a bed?

Yes, he said, but not a real bed.

And what of the maker of the bed? Were you not saying that he too makes, not the idea which, according to our view, is the essence of the bed, but only a particular bed?

Yes, I did.

Then if he does not make that which exists he cannot make true existence, but only some semblance of existence; and if any one were to say that the work of the maker of the bed, or of any other workman, has real existence, he could hardly be supposed to be speaking the truth.

At any rate, he replied, philosophers would say that he was not speaking the truth.

No wonder, then, that his work too is an indistinct expression of truth.

No wonder.

Suppose now that by the light of the examples just offered we enquire who this imitator is?

If you please.

Well then, here are three beds: one existing in nature, which is made by God, as I think that we may say—for no one else can be the maker?

No.

There is another which is the work of the carpenter?

Yes.

And the work of the painter is a third?

Yes.

Beds, then, are of three kinds, and there are three artists who superintend them: God, the maker of the bed, and the painter?

Yes, there are three of them.

God, whether from choice or from necessity, made one bed in nature and one only; two or more such ideal beds neither ever have been nor ever will be made by God.

Why is that?

Because even if He had made but two, a third would still appear behind them which both of them would have for their idea, and that would be the ideal bed and the two others.

Very true, he said.

God knew this, and He desired to be the real maker of a real bed, not a particular maker of a particular bed, and therefore He created a bed which is essentially and by nature one only.

So we believe.

Shall we, then, speak of Him as the natural author or maker of the bed?

Yes, he replied; inasmuch as by the natural process of creation He is the author of this and of all other things.

And what shall we say of the carpenter—is not he also the maker of the bed?

Yes.

But would you call the painter a creator and maker?

Certainly not.

Yet if he is not the maker, what is he in relation to the bed?

I think, he said, that we may fairly designate him as the imitator of that which the others make.

Good, I said; then you call him who is third in the descent from nature an imitator?

Certainly, he said.

And the tragic poet is an imitator, and therefore, like all other imitators, he is thrice removed from the king and from the truth?

That appears to be so.

Then about the imitator we are agreed. And what about the painter?—I would like to know whether he may be thought to imitate that which originally exists in nature, or only the creations of artists?

The latter.

As they are or as they appear? You have still to determine this.

What do you mean?

I mean, that you may look at a bed from different points of view, obliquely or directly or from any other point of view, and the bed will appear different, but there is no difference in reality. And the same of all things.

Yes, he said, the difference is only apparent.

Now let me ask you another question: Which is the art of painting designed to be—an imitation of things as they are, or as they appear—of appearance or of reality?

Of appearance.

Then the imitator, I said, is a long way off the truth, and can do all things because he lightly touches on a small part of them, and that part an image. For example: A painter will paint a cobbler, carpenter, or any other artist, though he knows nothing of their arts; and, if he is a good artist, he may deceive children or simple persons, when he shows them his picture of a carpenter from a distance, and they will fancy that they are looking at a real carpenter.

Certainly.

And whenever any one informs us that he has found a man knows all the arts, and all things else that anybody knows, and every single thing with a higher degree of accuracy than any other man—whoever tells us this, I think that we can only imagine to be a simple creature who is likely to have been deceived by some wizard or actor whom he met, and whom he thought all-knowing, because he himself was unable to analyze the nature of knowledge and ignorance and imitation.

Most true.

And so, when we hear persons saying that the tragedians, and Homer, who is at their head, know all the arts and all things human, virtue as well as vice, and divine things too, for that the good poet cannot compose well unless he knows his subject, and that he who has not this knowledge can never be a poet, we ought to consider whether here also there may not be a similar illusion. Perhaps they may have come across imitators and been deceived by them; they may not have remembered when they saw their works that these were but imitations thrice removed from the truth, and could easily be made without any knowledge of the truth, because they are appearances only and not realities? Or, after all, they may be in the right, and poets do really know the things about which they seem to the many to speak so well?

The question, he said, should by all means be considered.
Now do you suppose that if a person were able to make the original as well as the image, he would seriously devote himself to the image-making branch? Would he allow imitation to be the ruling principle of his life, as if he had nothing higher in him?

I should say not.
The real artist, who knew what he was imitating, would be interested in realities and not in imitations; and would desire to leave as memorials of himself works many and fair; and, instead of being the author of encomiums, he would prefer to be the theme of them.

Yes, he said, that would be to him a source of much greater honor and profit.
Then, I said, we must put a question to Homer; not about medicine, or any of the arts to which his poems only incidentally refer: we are not going to ask him, or any other poet, whether he has cured patients like Asclepius, or left behind him a school of medicine such as the Asclepiads were, or whether he only talks about medicine and other arts at second hand; but we have a right to know respecting military tactics, politics, education, which are the chiefest and no-blest subjects of his poems, and we may fairly ask him about them. 'Friend Homer,' then we say to him, 'if you are only in the second remove from truth in what you say of virtue, and not in the third—not an image maker or imita-tor—and if you are able to discern what pursuits make men better or worse in private or public life, tell us what State was ever better governed by your help? The good order of Lacedaemon is due to Lycurgus, and many other cities great and small have been similarly benefited by others; but who says that you have been a good legislator to them and have done them any good? Italy and Sicily boast of Charondas, and there is Solon who is renowned among us; but what city has anything to say about you?' Is there any city which he might name?

I think not, said Glaucon; not even the Homerids themselves pretend that he was a legislator.

Well, but is there any war on record which was carried on successfully by him, or aided by his counsels, when he was alive?

There is not.

Or is there any invention of his, applicable to the arts or to human life, such as Thales the Milesian or Anacharsis the Scythian, and other ingenious men have conceived, which is attributed to him?

There is absolutely nothing of the kind.

But, if Homer never did any public service, was he privately a guide or teacher of any? Had he in his lifetime friends who loved to associate with him, and who handed down to posterity an Homeric way of life, such as was established by Pythagoras who was so greatly beloved for his wisdom, and whose followers are to this day quite celebrated for the order which was named after him?

Nothing of the kind is recorded of him. For surely, Socrates, Creophylus, the companion of Homer, that child of flesh, whose name always makes us laugh, might be more justly ridiculed for his stupidity, if, as is said, Homer was greatly neglected by him and others in his own day when he was alive?

Yes, I replied, that is the tradition. But can you imagine, Glaucon, that if Homer had really been able to educate and improve mankind—if he had possessed knowledge and not been a mere imitator—can you imagine, I say, that he would not have had many followers, and been honored and loved by them? Protagoras of Abdera, and Prodicus of Ceos, and a host of others, have only to whisper to their contemporaries: 'You will never be able to manage either your own house or your own State until you appoint us to be your ministers of education'—and this ingenious device of theirs has such an effect in making them love them that their companions all but carry them about on their shoulders. And is it conceivable that the contemporaries of Homer, or again of Hesiod, would have allowed either of them to go about as rhapsodists, if they had really been able to make mankind virtuous? Would they not have been as unwilling to part with them as with gold, and have compelled them to stay at home with them? Or, if the master would not stay, then the disciples would have followed him about everywhere, until they had got education enough?

Yes, Socrates, that, I think, is quite true.

Then must we not infer that all these poetical individuals, beginning with Homer, are only imitators; they copy images of virtue and the like, but the truth they never reach? The poet is like a painter who, as we have already observed, will make a likeness of a cobbler though he understands nothing of cobbling; and his picture is good enough for those who know no more than he does, and judge only by colors and figures.

Quite so.

In like manner the poet with his words and phrases may be said to lay on the colors of the several arts, himself understanding their nature only enough to imitate them; and other people, who are as ignorant as he is, and judge only from his words, imagine that if he speaks of cobbling, or of military tactics, or of anything else, in meter and harmony and rhythm, he speaks very well—such is the sweet influence which melody and rhythm by nature have. And I think that you must have observed again and again what a poor appearance the tales of poets make when stripped of the colors which music puts upon them, and recited in simple prose.

Yes, he said.

They are like faces which were never really beautiful, but only blooming; and now the bloom of youth has passed away from them?

Exactly.

Here is another point: The imitator or maker of the image knows nothing of true existence; he knows appearances only. Am I not right?

Yes.

Then let us have a clear understanding, and not be satisfied with half an explanation.

Proceed.

Of the painter we say that he will paint reins, and he will paint a bit?

Yes.

And the worker in leather and brass will make them?

Certainly.

But does the painter know the right form of the bit and reins? Nay, hardly even the workers in brass and leather who make them; only the horseman who knows how to use them—he knows their right form.

Most true.

And may we not say the same of all things?

What?

That there are three arts which are concerned with all things: one which uses, another which makes, a third which imitates them?

Yes.

And the excellence or beauty or truth of every structure, animate or inanimate, and of every action of man, is relative to the use for which nature or the artist has intended them.

True.
Then the user of them must have the greatest experience of them, and he must indicate to the maker the good or bad qualities which develop themselves in use; for example, the flute-player will tell the flute-maker which of his flutes is satisfactory to the performer; he will tell him how he ought to make them, and the other will attend to his instructions?

Of course.
The one knows and therefore speaks with authority about the goodness and bad-ness of flutes, while the other, confiding in him, will do what he is told by him?

True.
The instrument is the same, but about the excellence or badness of it the maker will only attain to a correct belief; and this he will gain from him who knows, by talking to him and being compelled to hear what he has to say, whereas the user will have knowledge?

True.
But will the imitator have either? Will he know from use whether or no his drawing is correct or beautiful? Or will he have right opinion from being com-pelled to associate with another who knows and gives him instructions about what he should draw?

Neither.
Then he will no more have true opinion than he will have knowledge about the goodness or badness of his imitations?

I suppose not.
The imitative artist will be in a brilliant state of intelligence about his own creations?

Nay, very much the reverse.
And still he will go on imitating without knowing what makes a thing good or bad, and may be expected therefore to imitate only that which appears to be good to the ignorant multitude?

Just so.
Thus far then we are pretty well agreed that the imitator has no knowledge worth mentioning of what he imitates. Imitation is only a kind of play or sport,

and the tragic poets, whether they write in iambic or in Heroic verse, are imitators in the highest degree?

Very true.

And now tell me, I conjure you, has not imitation been shown by us to be concerned with that which is thrice removed from the truth?

Certainly.

And what is the faculty in man to which imitation is addressed?

What do you mean?

I will explain: The body which is large when seen near, appears small when seen at a distance?

True.

And the same object appears straight when looked at out of the water, and crooked when in the water; and the concave becomes convex, owing to the illusion about colors to which the sight is liable. Thus every sort of confusion is revealed within us; and this is that weakness of the human mind on which the art of conjuring and of deceiving by light and shadow and other ingenious devices imposes, having an effect upon us like magic.

True.

And the arts of measuring and numbering and weighing come to the rescue of the human understanding—there is the beauty of them—and the apparent greater or less, or more or heavier, no longer have the mastery over us, but give way before calculation and measure and weight?

Most true.

And this, surely, must be the work of the calculating and rational principle in the soul.

To be sure.

And when this principle measures and certifies that some things are equal, or that some are greater or less than others, there occurs an apparent contradiction?

True.

But were we not saying that such a contradiction [in] the same faculty cannot have contrary opinions at the same time about the same thing?

Very true.

Then that part of the soul which has an opinion contrary to measure is not the same with that which has an opinion in accordance with measure?

True.

And the better part of the soul is likely to be that which trusts to measure and calculation?

Certainly.

And that which is opposed to them is one of the inferior principles of the soul?

No doubt.

This was the conclusion at which I was seeking to arrive when I said that painting or drawing, and imitation in general, when doing their own proper work, are far removed from truth, and the companions and friends and associates of a principle within us which is equally removed from reason, and that they have no true or healthy aim.

Exactly.

The imitative art is an inferior who marries an inferior, and has inferior offspring.

Very true.

And is this confined to the sight only, or does it extend to the hearing also, relating in fact to what we term poetry?

Probably the same would be true of poetry.

Do not rely, I said, on a probability derived from the analogy of painting; but let us examine further and see whether the faculty with which poetical imitation is concerned is good or bad.

By all means.

We may state the question thus:—Imitation imitates the actions of men, whether voluntary or involuntary, on which, as they imagine, a good or bad result has ensued, and they rejoice or sorrow accordingly. Is there anything more?

No, there is nothing else.

But in all this variety of circumstances is the man at unity with himself—or rather, as in the instance of sight there was confusion and opposition in his opinions about the same things, so here also is there not strife and inconsistency in his life? Though I need hardly raise the question again, for I remember that all this has been already admitted; and the soul has been acknowledged by us to be full of these and ten thousand similar oppositions occurring at the same moment?

And we were right, he said.

Yes, I said, thus far we were right; but there was an omission which must now be supplied.

What was the omission?
Were we not saying that a good man, who has the misfortune to lose his son or anything else which is most dear to him, will bear the loss with more equanimity than another?

Yes.
But will he have no sorrow, or shall we say that although he cannot help sorrowing, he will moderate his sorrow?

The latter, he said, is the truer statement.
Tell me: will he be more likely to struggle and hold out against his sorrow when he is seen by his equals, or when he is alone?

It will make a great difference whether he is seen or not.
When he is by himself he will not mind saying or doing many things which he would be ashamed of any one hearing or seeing him do?

True.
There is a principle of law and reason in him which bids him resist, as well as a feeling of his misfortune which is forcing him to indulge his sorrow?

True.
But when a man is drawn in two opposite directions, to and from the same object, this, as we affirm, necessarily implies two distinct principles in him?

Certainly.
One of them is ready to follow the guidance of the law?
How do you mean?
The law would say that to be patient under suffering is best, and that we should not give way to impatience, as there is no knowing whether such things are good or evil; and nothing is gained by impatience; also, because no human thing is of serious importance, and grief stands in the way of that which at the moment is most required.

What is most required? he asked.
That we should take counsel about what has happened, and when the dice have been thrown order our affairs in the way which reason deems best; not, like children who have had a fall, keeping hold of the part struck and wasting time in setting up a howl, but always accustoming the soul forthwith to apply

a remedy, raising up that which is sickly and fallen, banishing the cry of sorrow by the healing art.

Yes, he said, that is the true way of meeting the attacks of fortune.

Yes, I said; and the higher principle is ready to follow this suggestion of reason?

Clearly.

And the other principle, which inclines us to recollection of our troubles and to lamentation, and can never have enough of them, we may call irrational, useless, and cowardly?

Indeed, we may.

And does not the latter—I mean the rebellious principle—furnish a great variety of materials for imitation? Whereas the wise and calm temperament, being always nearly equable, is not easy to imitate or to appreciate when imitated, especially at a public festival when a promiscuous crowd is assembled in a theatre. For the feeling represented is one to which they are strangers.

Certainly.

Then the imitative poet who aims at being popular is not by nature made, nor is his art intended, to please or to affect the principle in the soul; but he will prefer the passionate and fitful temper, which is easily imitated?

Clearly.

And now we may fairly take him and place him by the side of the painter, for he is like him in two ways: first, inasmuch as his creations have an inferior degree of truth—in this, I say, he is like him; and he is also like him in being concerned with an inferior part of the soul; and therefore we shall be right in refusing to admit him into a well-ordered State, because he awakens and nourishes and strengthens the feelings and impairs the reason. As in a city when the evil are permitted to have authority and the good are put out of the way, so in the soul of man, as we maintain, the imitative poet implants an evil constitution, for he indulges the irrational nature which has no discernment of greater and less, but thinks the same thing at one time great and at another small—he is a manufacturer of images and is very far removed from the truth.

Exactly.

But we have not yet brought forward the heaviest count in our accusation:— the power which poetry has of harming even the good (and there are very few who are not harmed), is surely an awful thing?

Yes, certainly, if the effect is what you say.

Hear and judge: The best of us, as I conceive, when we listen to a passage of Homer, or one of the tragedians, in which he represents some pitiful hero who is drawling out his sorrows in a long oration, or weeping, and smiting his breast—the best of us, you know, delight in giving way to sympathy, and are in raptures at the excellence of the poet who stirs our feelings most.

Yes, of course I know.

But when any sorrow of our own happens to us, then you may observe that we pride ourselves on the opposite quality—we would fain be quiet and patient; this is the manly part, and the other which delighted us in the recitation is now deemed to be the part of a woman.

Very true, he said.

Now can we be right in praising and admiring another who is doing that which any one of us would abominate and be ashamed of in his own person?

No, he said, that is certainly not reasonable.

Nay, I said, quite reasonable from one point of view.

What point of view?

If you consider, I said, that when in misfortune we feel a natural hunger and desire to relieve our sorrow by weeping and lamentation, and that this feeling which is kept under control in our own calamities is satisfied and delighted by the poets;—the better nature in each of us, not having been sufficiently trained by reason or habit, allows the sympathetic element to break loose because the sorrow is another's; and the spectator fancies that there can be no disgrace to himself in praising and pitying any one who comes telling him what a good man he is, and making a fuss about his troubles; he thinks that the pleasure is a gain, and why should he be supercilious and lose this and the poem too? Few persons ever reflect, as I should imagine, that from the evil of other men something of evil is communicated to themselves. And so the feeling of sorrow which has gathered strength at the sight of the misfortunes of others is with difficulty repressed in our own.

How very true!

And does not the same hold also of the ridiculous? There are jests which you would be ashamed to make yourself, and yet on the comic stage, or indeed in private, when you hear them, you are greatly amused by them, and are not at all disgusted at their unseemliness;—the case of pity is repeated;—there is a principle in human nature which is disposed to raise a laugh, and this which you once restrained by reason, because you were afraid of being thought a buffoon, is now let out again; and having stimulated the risible faculty at the theatre, you are betrayed unconsciously to yourself into playing the comic poet at home.

Quite true, he said.

And the same may be said of lust and anger and all the other affections, of desire and pain and pleasure, which are held to be inseparable from every action—in all of them poetry feeds and waters the passions instead of drying them up; she lets them rule, although they ought to be controlled, if mankind are ever to increase in happiness and virtue.

I cannot deny it.

Therefore, Glaucon, I said, whenever you meet with any of the eulogists of Homer declaring that he has been the educator of Hellas, and that he is profitable for education and for the ordering of human things, and that you should take him up again and again and get to know him and regulate your whole life according to him, we may love and honor those who say these things—they are excellent people, as far as their lights extend; and we are ready to acknowledge that Homer is the greatest of poets and first of tragedy writers; but we must remain firm in our conviction that hymns to the gods and praises of famous men are the only poetry which ought to be admitted into our State. For if you go beyond this and allow the honeyed muse to enter, either in epic or lyric verse, not law and the reason of mankind, which by common consent have ever been deemed best, but pleasure and pain will be the rulers in our State.

That is most true, he said.

And now since we have reverted to the subject of poetry, let this our defense serve to show the reasonableness of our former judgment in sending away out of our State an art having the tendencies which we have described; for reason constrained us. But that she may impute to us any harshness or want of politeness, let us tell her that there is an ancient quarrel between philosophy and poetry; of which there are many proofs, such as the saying of 'the yelping hound howling at her lord,' or of one 'mighty in the vain talk of fools,' and 'the mob of sages circumventing Zeus,' and the 'subtle thinkers who are beggars after all'; and there are innumerable other signs of ancient enmity between them. Notwithstanding this, let us assure our sweet friend and the sister arts of imitation that if she will only prove her title to exist in a well-ordered State we shall be delighted to receive her—we are very conscious of her charms; but we may not on that account betray the truth. I dare say, Glaucon, that you are as much charmed by her as I am, especially when she appears in Homer?

Yes, indeed, I am greatly charmed.

Shall I propose, then, that she be allowed to return from exile, but upon this condition only—that she make a defense of herself in lyrical or some other meter?

Certainly.

And we may further grant to those of her defenders who are lovers of poetry and yet not poets the permission to speak in prose on her behalf: let them show not only that she is pleasant but also useful to States and to human life, and we will listen in a kindly spirit; for if this can be proved we shall surely be the gainers—I mean, if there is a use in poetry as well as a delight?

Certainly, he said, we shall be the gainers.

If her defense fails, then, my dear friend, like other persons who are enamored of something, but put a restraint upon themselves when they think their desires are opposed to their interests, so too must we after the manner of lovers give her up, though not without a struggle. We too are inspired by that love of poetry which the education of noble States has implanted in us, and therefore we would have her appear at her best and truest; but so long as she is unable to make good her defense, this argument of ours shall be a charm to us, which we will repeat to ourselves while we listen to her strains; that we may not fall away into the childish love of her which captivates the many. At all events we are well aware that poetry being such as we have described is not to be regarded seriously as attaining to the truth; and he who listens to her, fearing for the safety of the city which is within him, should be on his guard against her seductions and make our words his law.

Yes, he said, I quite agree with you.

Yes, I said, my dear Glaucon, for great is the issue at stake, greater than appears, whether a man is to be good or bad. And what will any one be profited if under the influence of honor or money or power, aye, or under the excitement of poetry, he neglect justice and virtue?

Yes, he said; I have been convinced by the argument, as I believe that any one else would have been.

2

ARISTOTLE (384–322 B.C.)

W. B. Yeats's "Among School Children," which has to do with schools and teachers, calls Aristotle "solider"—solider than Plato, that is: "Solider Aristotle played the taws / Upon the bottom of a king of kings," spanking a young pupil who would soon become Alexander the Great. Aristotle's philosophy is no respecter of persons, only of ideas, and only of ideas in their practical, technical, and more solid manifestations.

Aristotle spent twenty years as a student of Plato, and when Plato died in 347 B.C., Aristotle established himself as a teacher and writer in schools of his own in various places in Greece. Around four hundred writings have been attributed to him, including important works on natural science, metaphysics, logic, rhetoric, politics, ethics, and law.

T. S. Eliot's "The Perfect Critic" summed up Aristotle's achievement:

Aristotle is a person who has suffered from the adherence of persons who must be regarded less as his disciples than as his sectaries. One must be firmly distrustful of accepting Aristotle in a canonical spirit; this is to lose the whole living force of him. He was primarily a man of not only remarkable but universal intelligence; and universal intelligence means that he could apply his intelligence to anything. The ordinary intelligence is good only for certain classes of objects; a brilliant man of science, if he is interested in poetry at all, may conceive grotesque judgments: like one poet because he reminds him of himself, or another because he expresses emotions which he admires; he may use art, in fact, as the outlet for the egotism which is suppressed in his own speciality. But Aristotle had none of these impure desires to satisfy; in whatever sphere of interest, he looked solely and steadfastly at the object; in his short and broken treatise he provides an eternal example—not of laws, or even of method, for there is no method except to be very intelligent, but of intelligence itself swiftly operating the analysis of sensation to the point of principle and definition.

From "The Perfect Critic," in *The Sacred Wood:*
Essays on Poetry and Criticism (London: Methuen, 1920).

But Aristotle does have a method and even a system: he identifies poetry as an art that imitates, and what it imitates is the form of human actions. In reasoning about form, Aristotle arrives at enduring concepts of plot, character, thought and feeling, diction, sound, and spectacle; he applies these concepts to patterns that can be called tragic and comic. (Umberto Eco's *The Name of the Rose* has to do with a fanciful account of the last existing copy of Aristotle's treatise on comedy, which has in fact been lost for millennia.) What has remained useful for critics—especially for those at the University of Chicago in the mid-twentieth century, called Aristotelians or Neo-Aristotelians, led by R. P. McKeon and R. S. Crane—is a logic that systematically relates the parts of a work as cause and effect, end and means, form and matter.

POETICS (CA. 350 B.C.)

Adapted from S. H. Butcher, *Aristotle's Theory of Poetry and Fine Art* (New York: Macmillan, 1932). Unless otherwise marked, all bracketed insertions are Butcher's interpolations of missing or Greek text.

SECTION 1

PART I

I propose to treat of Poetry in itself and of its various kinds, noting the essential quality of each, to inquire into the structure of the plot as requisite to a good poem; into the number and nature of the parts of which a poem is composed; and similarly into whatever else falls within the same inquiry. Following, then, the order of nature, let us begin with the principles which come first.

Epic poetry and Tragedy, Comedy also and Dithyrambic poetry, and the music of the flute and of the lyre in most of their forms, are all in their general conception modes of imitation. They differ, however, from one another in three respects—the medium, the objects, the manner or mode of imitation, being in each case distinct.

For as there are persons who, by conscious art or mere habit, imitate and represent various objects through the medium of color and form, or again by the voice; so in the arts above mentioned, taken as a whole, the imitation is produced by rhythm, language, or "harmony," either singly or combined.

Thus in the music of the flute and of the lyre, "harmony" and rhythm alone are employed; also in other arts, such as that of the shepherd's pipe, which are essentially similar to these. In dancing, rhythm alone is used without "harmony"; for even dancing imitates character, emotion, and action, by rhythmical movement.

There is another art which imitates by means of language alone, and that either in prose or verse—which verse, again, may either combine different meters or consist of but one kind—but this has hitherto been without a name. For there is no common term we could apply to the mimes of Sophron and Xenarchus and the Socratic dialogues on the one hand; and, on the other, to poetic imitations in iambic, elegiac, or any similar meter. People do, indeed, add the word "maker" or "poet" to the name of the meter, and speak of elegiac poets, or epic (that is, hexameter) poets, as if it were not the imitation that makes the poet, but the verse that entitles them all to the name. Even when a treatise on medicine or natural science is brought out in verse, the name of poet is by custom given to the author; and yet Homer and Empedocles have nothing in common but the meter, so that it would be right to call the one poet, the other physicist rather than poet. On the same principle, even if a writer in his poetic imitation were to combine all meters, as Chaeremon did in his "Centaur," which is a medley composed of meters of all kinds, we should bring him too under the general term poet.

So much then for these distinctions.

There are, again, some arts which employ all the means above mentioned—namely, rhythm, tune, and meter. Such are Dithyrambic and Nomic poetry, and also Tragedy and Comedy; but between them originally the difference is, that in the first two cases these means are all employed in combination, in the latter, now one means is employed, now another.

Such, then, are the differences of the arts with respect to the medium of imitation.

PART II

Since the objects of imitation are men in action, and these men must be either of a higher or a lower type (for moral character mainly answers to these divisions, goodness and badness being the distinguishing marks of moral differences), it follows that we must represent men either as better than in real life, or as worse, or as they are. It is the same in painting. Polygnotus depicted men as nobler than they are, Pauson as less noble, Dionysius drew them true to life.

Now it is evident that each of the modes of imitation above mentioned will exhibit these differences, and become a distinct kind in imitating objects that are thus distinct. Such diversities may be found even in dancing, flute-playing, and lyre-playing. So again in language, whether prose or verse unaccompanied by music. Homer, for example, makes men better than they are; Cleophon as they are; Hegemon the Thasian, the inventor of parodies, and Nicochares, the author of the "Deiliad," worse than they are. The same thing holds good of Dithyrambs and Nomes; here too one may portray different types, as Timotheus and Philoxenus differed in representing their Cyclopes. The same distinction marks off Tragedy from Comedy; for Comedy aims at representing men as worse, Tragedy as better than in actual life.

PART III

There is still a third difference—the manner in which each of these objects may be imitated. For the medium being the same, and the objects the same, the poet may imitate by narration—in which case he can either take another personality as Homer does, or speak in his own person, unchanged—or he may present all his characters as living and moving before us.

These, then, as we said at the beginning, are the three differences which distinguish artistic imitation—the medium, the objects, and the manner. So that from one point of view, Sophocles is an imitator of the same kind as Homer—for both imitate higher types of character; from another point of view, of the same kind as Aristophanes—for both imitate persons acting and doing. Hence, some say, the name of "drama" is given to such poems, as representing action. For the same reason the Dorians claim the invention both of Tragedy and Comedy. The claim to Comedy is put forward by the Megarians—not only by those of Greece proper, who allege that it originated under their democracy, but also by the Megarians of Sicily, for the poet Epicharmus, who is much earlier than Chionides and Magnes, belonged to that country. Tragedy too is claimed by certain Dorians of the Peloponnese. In each case they appeal to the evidence of language. The outlying villages, they say, are by them called κῶμαι, by the Athenians δῆμοι: and they assume that comedians were so named not from κωμάζειν, "to revel," but because they wandered from village to village (κατὰ κώμας), being excluded contemptuously from the city. They add also that the Dorian word for "doing" is δρᾶν, and the Athenian, πράττειν.

This may suffice as to the number and nature of the various modes of imitation.

PART IV

Poetry in general seems to have sprung from two causes, each of them lying deep in our nature. First, the instinct of imitation is implanted in man from childhood, one difference between him and other animals being that he is the most imitative of living creatures, and through imitation learns his earliest lessons; and no less universal is the pleasure felt in things imitated. We have evidence of this in the facts of experience. Objects which in themselves we view with pain, we delight to contemplate when reproduced with minute fidelity: such as the forms of the most ignoble animals and of dead bodies. The cause of this again is, that to learn gives the liveliest pleasure, not only to philosophers but to men in general; whose capacity, however, of learning is more limited. Thus the reason why men enjoy seeing a likeness is, that in contemplating it they find themselves learning or inferring, and saying perhaps, "Ah, that is he." For if you happen not to have seen the original, the pleasure will be due not to the imitation as such, but to the execution, the coloring, or some such other cause.

Imitation, then, is one instinct of our nature. Next, there is the instinct for "harmony" and rhythm, meters being manifestly sections of rhythm. Persons, therefore, starting with this natural gift developed by degrees their special aptitudes, till their rude improvisations gave birth to Poetry.

Poetry now diverged in two directions, according to the individual character of the writers. The graver spirits imitated noble actions, and the actions of good men. The more trivial sort imitated the actions of meaner persons, at first composing satires, as the former did hymns to the gods and the praises of famous men. A poem of the satirical kind cannot indeed be put down to any author earlier than Homer; though many such writers probably there were. But from Homer onward, instances can be cited—his own "Margites," for example, and other similar compositions. The appropriate meter was also here introduced; hence the measure is still called the iambic or lampooning measure, being that in which people lampooned one another. Thus the older poets were distinguished as writers of heroic or of lampooning verse.

As, in the serious style, Homer is pre-eminent among poets, for he alone combined dramatic form with excellence of imitation so he too first laid down the main lines of comedy, by dramatizing the ludicrous instead of writing personal satire. His "Margites" bears the same relation to comedy that the *Iliad* and *Odyssey* do to tragedy. But when Tragedy and Comedy came to light, the two classes of poets still followed their natural bent: the lampooners became writers of Comedy, and the Epic poets were succeeded by Tragedians, since the drama was a larger and higher form of art.

Whether Tragedy has as yet perfected its proper types or not; and whether it is to be judged in itself, or in relation also to the audience—this raises another question. Be that as it may, Tragedy—as also Comedy—was at first mere improvisation. The one originated with the authors of the Dithyramb, the other with those of the phallic songs, which are still in use in many of our cities. Tragedy advanced by slow degrees; each new element that showed itself was in turn developed. Having passed through many changes, it found its natural form, and there it stopped.

Aeschylus first introduced a second actor; he diminished the importance of the Chorus, and assigned the leading part to the dialogue. Sophocles raised the number of actors to three, and added scene-painting. Moreover, it was not till late that the short plot was discarded for one of greater compass, and the grotesque diction of the earlier satyric form for the stately manner of Tragedy. The iambic measure then replaced the trochaic tetrameter, which was originally employed when the poetry was of the satyric order, and had greater affinities with dancing. Once dialogue had come in, Nature herself discovered the appropriate measure. For the iambic is, of all measures, the most colloquial: we see it in the fact that conversational speech runs into iambic lines more frequently than into any other kind of verse; rarely into hexameters, and only when we drop the colloquial intonation. The additions to the number of "episodes" or acts, and the other accessories of which tradition tells, must be taken as already described; for to discuss them in detail would, doubtless, be a large undertaking.

PART V

Comedy is, as we have said, an imitation of characters of a lower type—not, however, in the full sense of the word bad, the ludicrous being merely a subdivision of the ugly. It consists in some defect or ugliness which is not painful or destructive. To take an obvious example, the comic mask is ugly and distorted, but does not imply pain.

The successive changes through which Tragedy passed, and the authors of these changes, are well known, whereas Comedy has had no history, because it was not at first treated seriously. It was late before the Archon granted a comic chorus to a poet; the performers were till then voluntary. Comedy had already taken definite shape when comic poets, distinctively so called, are heard of. Who furnished it with masks, or prologues, or increased the number of actors— these and other similar details remain unknown. As for the plot, it came originally from Sicily; but of Athenian writers Crates was the first who abandoning the "iambic" or lampooning form, generalized his themes and plots.

Epic poetry agrees with Tragedy in so far as it is an imitation in verse of characters of a higher type. They differ in that Epic poetry admits but one kind of meter and is narrative in form. They differ, again, in their length: for Tragedy endeavors, as far as possible, to confine itself to a single revolution of the sun, or but slightly to exceed this limit, whereas the Epic action has no limits of time. This, then, is a second point of difference; though at first the same freedom was admitted in Tragedy as in Epic poetry.

Of their constituent parts some are common to both, some peculiar to Tragedy: whoever, therefore knows what is good or bad Tragedy, knows also about Epic poetry. All the elements of an Epic poem are found in Tragedy, but the elements of a Tragedy are not all found in the Epic poem.

PART VI

Of the poetry which imitates in hexameter verse, and of Comedy, we will speak hereafter. Let us now discuss Tragedy, resuming its formal definition, as resulting from what has been already said.

Tragedy, then, is an imitation of an action that is serious, complete, and of a certain magnitude; in language embellished with each kind of artistic ornament, the several kinds being found in separate parts of the play; in the form of action, not of narrative; through pity and fear effecting the proper purgation of these emotions. By "language embellished," I mean language into which rhythm, "harmony" and song enter. By "the several kinds in separate parts," I mean, that some parts are rendered through the medium of verse alone, others again with the aid of song.

Now as tragic imitation implies persons acting, it necessarily follows in the first place, that Spectacular equipment will be a part of Tragedy. Next, Song and Diction, for these are the media of imitation. By "Diction" I mean the mere metrical arrangement of the words: as for "Song," it is a term whose sense every one understands.

Again, Tragedy is the imitation of an action; and an action implies personal agents, who necessarily possess certain distinctive qualities both of character and thought; for it is by these that we qualify actions themselves, and these—thought and character—are the two natural causes from which actions spring, and on actions again all success or failure depends. Hence, the Plot is the imitation of the action—for by plot I here mean the arrangement of the incidents. By Character I mean that in virtue of which we ascribe certain qualities to the agents. Thought is required wherever a statement is proved, or, it may be, a general truth enunciated. Every Tragedy, therefore, must have six parts, which parts determine its quality—namely, Plot, Character, Diction, Thought, Spectacle, Song. Two of the parts constitute the medium of imitation, one the manner, and three the objects of imitation. And these complete the fist. These elements have been employed, we may say, by the poets to a man; in fact, every play contains Spectacular elements as well as Character, Plot, Diction, Song, and Thought.

But most important of all is the structure of the incidents. For Tragedy is an imitation, not of men, but of an action and of life, and life consists in action, and its end is a mode of action, not a quality. Now character determines men's qualities, but it is by their actions that they are happy or the reverse. Dramatic action, therefore, is not with a view to the representation of character: character comes in as subsidiary to the actions. Hence the incidents and the plot are the end of a tragedy; and the end is the chief thing of all. Again, without action there cannot be a tragedy; there may be without character. The tragedies of most of our modern poets fail in the rendering of character; and of poets in general this is often true. It is the same in painting; and here lies the difference between Zeuxis and Polygnotus. Polygnotus delineates character well; the style of Zeuxis is devoid of ethical quality. Again, if you string together a set of speeches expressive of character, and well finished in point of diction and thought, you will not produce the essential tragic effect nearly so well as with a play which, however deficient in these respects, yet has a plot and artistically constructed incidents. Besides which, the most powerful elements of emotional interest in Tragedy—Peripeteia or Reversal of the Situation, and Recognition scenes—are parts of the plot. A further proof is, that novices in the art attain to finish of diction and precision of portraiture before they can construct the plot. It is the same with almost all the early poets.

The plot, then, is the first principle, and, as it were, the soul of a tragedy; Character holds the second place. A similar fact is seen in painting. The most beautiful colors, laid on confusedly, will not give as much pleasure as the chalk outline of a portrait. Thus Tragedy is the imitation of an action, and of the agents mainly with a view to the action.

Third in order is Thought—that is, the faculty of saying what is possible and pertinent in given circumstances. In the case of oratory, this is the function of the political art and of the art of rhetoric: and so indeed the older poets make their characters speak the language of civic life; the poets of our time, the language of the rhetoricians. Character is that which reveals moral purpose, showing what kind of things a man chooses or avoids. Speeches, therefore, which do not make this manifest, or in which the speaker does not choose or avoid anything whatever, are not expressive of character. Thought, on the other hand, is found where something is proved to be or not to be, or a general maxim is enunciated.

Fourth among the elements enumerated comes Diction; by which I mean, as has been already said, the expression of the meaning in words; and its essence is the same both in verse and prose.

Of the remaining elements Song holds the chief place among the embellishments.

The Spectacle has, indeed, an emotional attraction of its own, but, of all the parts, it is the least artistic, and connected least with the art of poetry. For the power of Tragedy, we may be sure, is felt even apart from representation and actors. Besides, the production of spectacular effects depends more on the art of the stage machinist than on that of the poet.

PART VII

These principles being established, let us now discuss the proper structure of the Plot, since this is the first and most important thing in Tragedy.

Now, according to our definition Tragedy is an imitation of an action that is complete, and whole, and of a certain magnitude; for there may be a whole that is wanting in magnitude. A whole is that which has a beginning, a middle, and an end. A beginning is that which does not itself follow anything by causal necessity, but after which something naturally is or comes to be. An end, on the contrary, is that which itself naturally follows some other thing, either by necessity, or as a rule, but has nothing following it. A middle is that which follows something as some other thing follows it. A well constructed plot, therefore, must neither begin nor end at haphazard, but conform to these principles.

Again, a beautiful object, whether it be a living organism or any whole composed of parts, must not only have an orderly arrangement of parts, but must also be of a certain magnitude; for beauty depends on magnitude and order. Hence a very small animal organism cannot be beautiful; for the view of it is confused, the object being seen in an almost imperceptible moment of time. Nor, again, can one of vast size be beautiful; for as the eye cannot take it all in at once, the unity and sense of the whole is lost for the spectator; as for instance if there were one a thousand miles long. As, therefore, in the case of animate bodies and organisms a certain magnitude is necessary, and a magnitude which may be easily embraced in one view; so in the plot, a certain length is necessary, and a length which can be easily embraced by the memory. The limit of length in relation to dramatic competition and sensuous presentment is no part of artistic theory. For had it been the rule for a hundred tragedies to compete together, the performance would have been regulated by the water-clock—as indeed we are told was formerly done. But the limit as fixed by the nature of the drama itself is this: the greater the length, the more beautiful will the piece be by reason of its size, provided that the whole be perspicuous. And to define the matter roughly, we may say that the proper magnitude is comprised within such limits, that the sequence of events, according to the law of probability or necessity, will admit of a change from bad fortune to good, or from good fortune to bad.

PART VIII

Unity of plot does not, as some persons think, consist in the unity of the hero. For infinitely various are the incidents in one man's life which cannot be reduced to unity; and so, too, there are many actions of one man out of which we cannot make one action. Hence the error, as it appears, of all poets who have composed a Heracleid, a Theseid, or other poems of the kind. They imagine that as Heracles was one man, the story of Heracles must also be a unity. But Homer, as in all else he is of surpassing merit, here too—whether from art or natural genius—seems to have happily discerned the truth. In composing the *Odyssey* he did not include all the adventures of Odysseus—such as his wound on Parnassus, or his feigned madness at the mustering of the host—incidents between which there was no necessary or probable connection: but he made the Odyssey, and likewise the Iliad, to center round an action that in our sense of the word is one. As therefore, in the other imitative arts, the imitation is one when the object imitated is one, so the plot, being an imitation of an action, must imitate one action and that a whole, the structural union of the parts being such that, if any one of them is displaced or removed, the whole will be disjointed and disturbed. For a thing whose presence or absence makes no visible difference, is not an organic part of the whole.

PART IX

It is, moreover, evident from what has been said, that it is not the function of the poet to relate what has happened, but what may happen—what is possible according to the law of probability or necessity. The poet and the historian differ not by writing in verse or in prose. The work of Herodotus might be put into verse, and it would still be a species of history, with meter no less than without it. The true difference is that one relates what has happened, the other what may happen. Poetry, therefore, is a more philosophical and a higher thing than history: for poetry tends to express the universal, history the particular. By the universal I mean how a person of a certain type on occasion speak or act, according to the law of probability or necessity; and it is this universality at which poetry aims in the names she attaches to the personages. The particular is—for example—what Alcibiades did or suffered. In Comedy this is already apparent: for here the poet first constructs the plot on the lines of probability, and then inserts characteristic names—unlike the lampooners who write about particular individuals. But tragedians still keep to real names, the reason being that what is possible is credible: what has not happened we do not at once feel sure to be possible; but what has happened is manifestly possible: otherwise it would not have happened. Still there are even some tragedies in which there are only one or two well-known names, the rest being fictitious. In others, none are well known—as in Agathon's Antheus, where incidents and names alike are fictitious, and yet they give none the less pleasure. We must not, therefore, at all costs keep to the received legends, which are the usual subjects of Tragedy. Indeed, it would be absurd to attempt it; for even subjects that are known are known only to a few, and yet give pleasure to all. It clearly follows that the poet or "maker" should be the maker of plots rather than of verses; since he is a poet because he imitates, and what he imitates are actions. And even if he chances to take a historical subject, he is none the less a poet; for there is no reason why some events that have actually happened should not conform to the law of the probable and possible, and in virtue of that quality in them he is their poet or maker.

Of all plots and actions the episodic are the worst. I call a plot "episodic" in which the episodes or acts succeed one another without probable or necessary sequence. Bad poets compose such pieces by their own fault, good poets, to please the players; for, as they write show pieces for competition, they stretch the plot beyond its capacity, and are often forced to break the natural continuity.

But again, Tragedy is an imitation not only of a complete action, but of events inspiring fear or pity. Such an effect is best produced when the events come on us by surprise; and the effect is heightened when, at the same time, they follows as cause and effect. The tragic wonder will then be greater than if they happened of themselves or by accident; for even coincidences are most striking when they have an air of design. We may instance the statue of Mitys at Argos, which fell upon his murderer while he was a spectator at a festival, and killed him. Such events seem not to be due to mere chance. Plots, therefore, constructed on these principles are necessarily the best.

PART X

Plots are either Simple or Complex, for the actions in real life, of which the plots are an imitation, obviously show a similar distinction. An action which is one and continuous in the sense above defined, I call Simple, when the change of fortune takes place without Reversal of the Situation and without Recognition.

A Complex action is one in which the change is accompanied by such Reversal, or by Recognition, or by both. These last should arise from the internal structure of the plot, so that what follows should be the necessary or probable result of the preceding action. It makes all the difference whether any given event is a case of *propter hoc* [because of this—ed.] or *post hoc* [after this—ed.].

PART XI

Reversal of the Situation is a change by which the action veers round to its opposite, subject always to our rule of probability or necessity. Thus in the *Oedipus*, the messenger comes to cheer Oedipus and free him from his alarms about his mother, but by revealing who he is, he produces the opposite effect. Again in the "Lynceus," Lynceus is being led away to his death, and Danaus goes with him, meaning to slay him; but the outcome of the preceding incidents is that Danaus is killed and Lynceus saved.

Recognition, as the name indicates, is a change from ignorance to knowledge, producing love or hate between the persons destined by the poet for good or bad fortune. The best form of recognition is coincident with a Reversal of the Situation, as in the *Oedipus*. There are indeed other forms. Even inanimate things of the most trivial kind may in a sense be objects of recognition. Again, we may recognize or discover whether a person has done a thing or not. But the recognition which is most intimately connected with the plot and action is, as we have said, the recognition of persons. This recognition, combined with Reversal, will produce either pity or fear; and actions producing these effects are those which, by our definition, Tragedy represents. Moreover, it is upon such situations that the issues of good or bad fortune will depend. Recognition, then, being between persons, it may happen that one person only is recognized by the other—when the latter is already known—or it may be necessary that the recognition should be on both sides. Thus Iphigenia is revealed to Orestes by the sending of the letter; but another act of recognition is required to make Orestes known to Iphigenia.

Two parts, then, of the Plot—Reversal of the Situation and Recognition—turn upon surprises. A third part is the Scene of Suffering. The Scene of Suffering is a destructive or painful action, such as death on the stage, bodily agony, wounds, and the like.

SECTION 2

PART XII

The parts of Tragedy which must be treated as elements of the whole have been already mentioned. We now come to the quantitative parts—the separate parts into which Tragedy is divided—namely, Prologue, Episode, Exode, Choric song; this last being divided into Parode and Stasimon. These are common to all plays: peculiar to some are the songs of actors from the stage and the Commoi.

The Prologue is that entire part of a tragedy which precedes the Parode of the Chorus. The Episode is that entire part of a tragedy which is between complete choric songs. The Exode is that entire part of a tragedy which has no choric song after it. Of the Choric part the Parode is the first undivided utterance of the Chorus: the Stasimon is a Choric ode without anapaests or trochaic tetrameters: the Commos is a joint lamentation of Chorus and actors. The parts of Tragedy which must be treated as elements of the whole have been already mentioned. The quantitative parts—the separate parts into which it is divided—are here enumerated.

PART XIII

As the sequel to what has already been said, we must proceed to consider what the poet should aim at, and what he should avoid, in constructing his plots; and by what means the specific effect of Tragedy will be produced.

A perfect tragedy should, as we have seen, be arranged not on the simple but on the complex plan. It should, moreover, imitate actions which excite pity and fear, this being the distinctive mark of tragic imitation. It follows plainly, in the first place, that the change of fortune presented must not be the spectacle of a virtuous man brought from prosperity to adversity: for this moves neither pity nor fear; it merely shocks us. Nor, again, that of a bad man passing from adversity to prosperity: for nothing can be more alien to the spirit of Tragedy; it possesses no single tragic quality; it neither satisfies the moral sense nor calls forth pity or fear. Nor, again, should the downfall of the utter villain be exhibited. A plot of this kind would, doubtless, satisfy the moral sense, but it would inspire neither pity nor fear; for pity is aroused by unmerited misfortune, fear by the misfortune of a man like ourselves. Such an event, therefore, will be neither pitiful nor terrible. There remains, then, the character between these two extremes—that of a man who is not eminently good and just, yet whose misfortune is brought about not by vice or depravity, but by some error or frailty. He must be one who is highly renowned and prosperous—a personage like Oedipus, Thyestes, or other illustrious men of such families.

A well-constructed plot should, therefore, be single in its issue, rather than double as some maintain. The change of fortune should be not from bad to good, but, reversely, from good to bad. It should come about as the result not of vice, but of some great error or frailty, in a character either such as we have described, or better rather than worse. The practice of the stage bears out our view. At first the poets recounted any legend that came in their way. Now, the best tragedies are founded on the story of a few houses—on the fortunes of Alcmaeon, Oedipus, Orestes, Meleager, Thyestes, Telephus, and those others who have done or suffered something terrible. A tragedy, then, to be perfect according to the rules of art should be of this construction. Hence they are in error who censure Euripides just because he follows this principle in his plays, many of which end unhappily. It is, as we have said, the right ending. The best proof is that on the stage and in dramatic competition, such plays, if well worked out, are the most tragic in effect; and Euripides, faulty though he may be in the general management of his subject, yet is felt to be the most tragic of the poets.

In the second rank comes the kind of tragedy which some place first. Like the *Odyssey*, it has a double thread of plot, and also an opposite catastrophe for the good and for the bad. It is accounted the best because of the weakness of the spectators; for the poet is guided in what he writes by the wishes of his audience. The pleasure, however, thence derived is not the true tragic pleasure. It is proper rather to Comedy, where those who, in the piece, are the deadliest enemies—like Orestes and Aegisthus—quit the stage as friends at the close, and no one slays or is slain.

PART XIV

Fear and pity may be aroused by spectacular means; but they may also result from the inner structure of the piece, which is the better way, and indicates a superior poet. For the plot ought to be so constructed that, even without the aid of the eye, he who hears the tale told will thrill with horror and melt to pity at what takes place. This is the impression we should receive from hearing the story of the *Oedipus*. But to produce this effect by the mere spectacle is a less artistic method, and dependent on extraneous aids. Those who employ spectacular means to create a sense not of the terrible but only of the monstrous, are strangers to the purpose of Tragedy; for we must not demand of Tragedy any and every kind of pleasure, but only that which is proper to it. And since the pleasure which the poet should afford is that which comes from pity and fear through imitation, it is evident that this quality must be impressed upon the incidents.

Let us then determine what are the circumstances which strike us as terrible or pitiful.

Actions capable of this effect must happen between persons who are either friends or enemies or indifferent to one another. If an enemy kills an enemy, there is nothing to excite pity either in the act or the intention—except so far as the suffering in itself is pitiful. So again with indifferent persons. But when the tragic incident occurs between those who are near or dear to one another—if, for example, a brother kills, or intends to kill, a brother, a son his father, a mother her son, a son his mother, or any other deed of the kind is done—these are the situations to be looked for by the poet. He may not indeed destroy the framework of the received legends—the fact, for instance, that Clytemnestra was slain by Orestes and Eriphyle by Alcmaeon—but he ought to show of his own, and skilfully handle the traditional. material. Let us explain more clearly what is meant by skilful handling.

The action may be done consciously and with knowledge of the persons, in the manner of the older poets. It is thus too that Euripides makes Medea slay her children. Or, again, the deed of horror may be done, but done in ignorance, and the tie of kinship or friendship be discovered afterwards. The *Oedipus* of Sophocles is an example. Here, indeed, the incident is outside the drama proper; but cases occur where it falls within the action of the play: one may cite the "Alcmaeon" of Astydamas, or Telegonus in the "Wounded Odysseus." Again, there is a third case—[to be about to act with knowledge of the persons and then not to act. The fourth case] is when some one is about to do an irreparable deed through ignorance, and makes the discovery before it is done. These are the only possible ways. For the deed must either be done or not done—and that wittingly or unwittingly. But of all these ways, to be about to act knowing the persons, and then not to act, is the worst. It is shocking without being tragic, for no disaster follows It is, therefore, never, or very rarely, found in poetry. One instance, however, is in the *Antigone*, where Haemon threatens to kill Creon. The next and better way is that the deed should be perpetrated. Still better, that it should be perpetrated in ignorance, and the discovery made afterwards. There is then nothing to shock us, while the discovery produces a startling effect. The last case is the best, as when in the "Cresphontes" Merope is about to slay her son, but, recognizing who he is, spares his life. So in the *Iphigenia*, the sister recognizes the brother just in time. Again in the "Helle," the son recognizes the mother when on the point of giving her up. This, then, is why a few families only, as has been already observed, furnish the subjects of tragedy. It was not art, but happy chance, that led the poets in search of subjects to impress the tragic quality upon their plots. They are compelled, therefore, to have recourse to those houses whose history contains moving incidents like these.

Enough has now been said concerning the structure of the incidents, and the right kind of plot.

PART XV

In respect of Character there are four things to be aimed at. First, and most important, it must be good. Now any speech or action that manifests moral purpose of any kind will be expressive of character: the character will be good if the purpose is good. This rule is relative to each class. Even a woman may be good, and also a slave; though the woman may be said to be an inferior being, and the slave quite worthless. The second thing to aim at is propriety. There is a type of manly valor; but valor in a woman, or unscrupulous cleverness is inappropriate. Thirdly, character must be true to life: for this is a distinct thing from goodness and propriety, as here described. The fourth point is consistency: for though the subject of the imitation, who suggested the type, be inconsistent, still he must be consistently inconsistent. As an example of motiveless degradation of character, we have Menelaus in the *Orestes*, of character indecorous and inappropriate, the lament of Odysseus in the "Scylla"; and the speech of Melanippe; of inconsistency, the Iphigenia at Aulis—for Iphigenia the suppliant in no way resembles her later self.

As in the structure of the plot, so too in the portraiture of character, the poet should always aim either at the necessary or the probable. Thus a person of a given character should speak or act in a given way, by the rule either of necessity or of probability; just as this event should follow that by necessary or probable sequence. It is therefore evident that the unraveling of the plot, no less than the complication, must arise out of the plot itself, it must not be brought about by the *Deus ex Machina*—as in the *Medea*, or in the return of the Greeks in the Iliad.[1] The *Deus ex Machina* should be employed only for events external to the drama—for antecedent or subsequent events, which lie beyond the range of human knowledge, and which require to be reported or foretold; for to the gods we ascribe the power of seeing all things. Within the action there must be nothing irrational. If the irrational cannot be excluded, it should be outside the scope of the tragedy. Such is the irrational element the Oedipus of Sophocles.

Again, since Tragedy is an imitation of persons who are above the common level, the example of good portrait painters should be followed. They, while reproducing the distinctive form of the original, make a likeness which is true to life and yet more beautiful. So too the poet, in representing men who are irascible or indolent, or have other defects of character, should preserve the type and yet ennoble it. In this way Achilles is portrayed by Agathon and Homer.

These then are rules the poet should observe. Nor should he neglect those appeals to the senses, which, though not among the essentials, are the concomitants of poetry; for here too there is much room for error. But of this enough has been said in our published treatises.

PART XVI

What Recognition is has been already explained. We will now enumerate its kinds.

First, the least artistic form, which, from poverty of wit, is most commonly employed—recognition by signs. Of these some are congenital—such as "the spear which the earth-born race bear on their bodies," or the stars introduced by Carcinus in his "Thyestes." Others are acquired after birth; and of these some are bodily marks, as scars; some external tokens, as necklaces, or the little ark in the Tyro by which the discovery is effected. Even these admit of more or less skilful treatment. Thus in the recognition of Odysseus by his scar, the discovery is made in one way by the nurse, in another by the swineherds. The use of tokens for the express purpose of proof—and, indeed, any formal proof with or without tokens—is a less artistic mode of recognition. A better kind is that which comes about by a turn of incident, as in the Bath Scene in the *Odyssey*.

---

1. The *Deus ex Machina* was a god made to appear out of a mechanical device above the stage in Greek drama; any improbable or impossible recourse to get out of a jam.

Next come the recognitions invented at will by the poet, and on that account wanting in art. For example, Orestes in the *Iphigenia* reveals the fact that he is Orestes. She, indeed, makes herself known by the letter; but he, by speaking himself, and saying what the poet, not what the plot requires. This, therefore, is nearly allied to the fault above mentioned—for Orestes might as well have brought tokens with him. Another similar instance is the "voice of the shuttle" in the "Tereus" of Sophocles.

The third kind depends on memory when the sight of some object awakens a feeling: as in the Cyprians of Dicaeogenes, where the hero breaks into tears on seeing the picture; or again in the "Lay of Alcinous", where Odysseus, hearing the minstrel play the lyre, recalls the past and weeps; and hence the recognition.

The fourth kind is by process of reasoning. Thus in the *Choëphori*: "Some one resembling me has come: no one resembles me but Orestes: therefore Orestes has come." Such too is the discovery made by Iphigenia in the play of Polyidus the Sophist. It was a natural reflection for Orestes to make, "So I too must die at the altar like my sister." So, again, in the "Tydeus" of Theodectes, the father says, "I came to find my son, and I lose my own life." So too in the "Phineidae": the women, on seeing the place, inferred their fate—"Here we are doomed to die, for here we were cast forth." Again, there is a composite kind of recognition involving false inference on the part of one of the characters, as in the "Odysseus Disguised as a Messenger." A said [that no one else was able to bend the bow; . . . hence B (the disguised Odysseus) imagined that A would] recognize the bow which, in fact, he had not seen; and to bring about a recognition by this means—the expectation that A would recognize the bow— is false inference.

But, of all recognitions, the best is that which arises from the incidents themselves, where the startling discovery is made by natural means. Such is that in the *Oedipus* of Sophocles, and in the *Iphigenia*; for it was natural that Iphigenia should wish to dispatch a letter. These recognitions alone dispense with the artificial aid of tokens or amulets. Next come the recognitions by process of reasoning.

PART XVII

In constructing the plot and working it out with the proper diction, the poet should place the scene, as far as possible, before his eyes. In this way, seeing everything with the utmost vividness, as if he were a spectator of the action, he will discover what is in keeping with it, and be most unlikely to overlook inconsistencies. The need of such a rule is shown by the fault found in Carcinus. Amphiaraus was on his way from the temple. This fact escaped the observation of one who did not see the situation. On the stage, however, the Piece failed, the audience being offended at the oversight.

Again, the poet should work out his play, to the best of his power, with appropriate gestures; for those who feel emotion are most convincing through natural sympathy with the characters they represent; and one who is agitated storms, one who is angry rages, with the most lifelike reality. Hence poetry implies either a happy gift of nature or a strain of madness. In the one case a man can take the mould of any character; in the other, he is lifted out of his proper self.

As for the story, whether the poet takes it ready made or constructs it for himself, he should first sketch its general outline, and then fill in the episodes and amplify in detail. The general plan may be illustrated by the *Iphigenia*. A young girl is sacrificed; she disappears mysteriously from the eyes of those who sacrificed her; she is transported to another country, where the custom is to offer up an strangers to the goddess. To this ministry she is appointed. Some time later her own brother chances to arrive. The fact that the oracle for some reason ordered him to go there, is outside the general plan of the play. The purpose, again, of his coming is outside the action proper. However, he comes, he is seized, and, when on the point of being sacrificed, reveals who he is. The mode of recognition may be either that of Euripides or of Polyidus, in whose play he exclaims very naturally: "So it was not my sister only, but I too, who was doomed to be sacrificed"; and by that remark he is saved.

After this, the names being once given, it remains to fill in the episodes. We must see that they are relevant to the action. In the case of Orestes, for example, there is the madness which led to his capture, and his deliverance by means of the purificatory rite. In the drama, the episodes are short, but it is these that give extension to Epic poetry. Thus the story of the *Odyssey* can be stated briefly. A certain man is absent from home for many years; he is jealously watched by Poseidon, and left desolate. Meanwhile his home is in a wretched plight— suitors are wasting his substance and plotting against his son. At length, tempest-tost, he himself arrives; he makes certain persons acquainted with him; he attacks the suitors with his own hand, and is himself preserved while he destroys them. This is the essence of the plot; the rest is episode.

PART XVIII

Every tragedy falls into two parts—Complication and Unraveling or *Dénoue-ment*. Incidents extraneous to the action are frequently combined with a portion of the action proper, to form the Complication; the rest is the Unraveling. By the Complication I mean all that extends from the beginning of the action to the part which marks the turning-point to good or bad fortune. The Unraveling is that which extends from the beginning of the change to the end. Thus, in the "Lynceus" of Theodectes, the Complication consists of the incidents presupposed in the drama, the seizure of the child, and then again . . . [the Unraveling] extends from the accusation of murder to the end.

There are four kinds of Tragedy: the Complex, depending entirely on Reversal of the Situation and Recognition; the Pathetic (where the motive is passion)—such as the tragedies on Ajax and Ixion; the Ethical (where the motives are ethical)—such as the "Phthiotides" and the "Peleus." The fourth kind is the Simple. [We here exclude the purely spectacular element], exemplified by the "Phorcides," the "Prometheus," and scenes laid in Hades. The poet should endeavor, if possible, to combine all poetic elements; or failing that, the greatest number and those the most important; the more so, in face of the caviling criticism of the day. For whereas there have hitherto been good poets, each in his own branch, the critics now expect one man to surpass all others in their several lines of excellence.

In speaking of a tragedy as the same or different, the best test to take is the plot. Identity exists where the Complication and Unraveling are the same. Many poets tie the knot well, but unravel it ill. Both arts, however, should always be mastered.

Again, the poet should remember what has been often said, and not make an Epic structure into a tragedy—by an Epic structure I mean one with a multiplicity of plots—as if, for instance, you were to make a tragedy out of the entire story of the *Iliad*. In the Epic poem, owing to its length, each part assumes its proper magnitude. In the drama the result is far from answering to the poet's expectation. The proof is that the poets who have dramatized the whole story of the Fall of Troy, instead of selecting portions, like Euripides; or who have taken the whole tale of Niobe, and not a part of her story, like Aeschylus, either fail utterly or meet with poor success on the stage. Even Agathon has been known to fail from this one defect. In his Reversals of the Situation, however, he shows a marvelous skill in the effort to hit the popular taste—to produce a tragic effect that satisfies the moral sense. This effect is produced when the clever rogue, like Sisyphus, is outwitted, or the brave villain defeated. Such an event is probable in Agathon's sense of the word: "It is probable," he says, "that many things should happen contrary to probability."

The Chorus too should be regarded as one of the actors; it should be an integral part of the whole, and share in the action, in the manner not of Euripides but of Sophocles. As for the later poets, their choral songs pertain as little to the subject of the piece as to that of any other tragedy. They are, therefore, sung as mere interludes—a practice first begun by Agathon. Yet what difference is there between introducing such choral interludes, and transferring a speech, or even a whole act, from one play to another.

PART XIX

It remains to speak of Diction and Thought, the other parts of Tragedy having been already discussed. Concerning Thought, we may assume what is said in the *Rhetoric*, to which inquiry the subject more strictly belongs. Under Thought is included every effect which has to be produced by speech, the subdivisions being: proof and refutation; the excitation of the feelings, such as pity, fear, anger, and the like; the suggestion of importance or its opposite. Now, it is evident that the dramatic incidents must be treated from the same points of view as the dramatic speeches, when the object is to evoke the sense of pity, fear, importance, or probability. The only difference is that the incidents should speak for themselves without verbal exposition; while effects aimed at in speech should be produced by the speaker, and as a result of the speech. For what were the business of a speaker, if the Thought were revealed quite apart from what he says?

Next, as regards Diction. One branch of the inquiry treats of the Modes of Utterance. But this province of knowledge belongs to the art of Delivery and to the masters of that science. It includes, for instance—what is a command, a prayer, a statement, a threat, a question, an answer, and so forth. To know or not to know these things involves no serious censure upon the poet's art. For who can admit the fault imputed to Homer by Protagoras—that in the words, "Sing, goddess, of the wrath," he gives a command under the idea that he utters a prayer? For to tell some one to do a thing or not to do it is, he says, a command. We may, therefore, pass this over as an inquiry that belongs to another art, not to poetry.

PART XX

Language in general includes the following parts: Letter, Syllable, Connecting Word, Noun, Verb, Inflection or Case, Sentence or Phrase.

A Letter is an indivisible sound, yet not every such sound, but only one which can form part of a group of sounds. For even brutes utter indivisible sounds, none of which I call a letter. The sound I mean may be either a vowel, a semivowel, or a mute. A vowel is that which without impact of tongue or lip has an audible sound. A semivowel that which with such impact has an audible sound, as S and R. A mute, that which with such impact has by itself no sound, but joined to a vowel sound becomes audible, as G and D. These are distinguished according to the form assumed by the mouth and the place where they are produced; according as they are aspirated or smooth, long or short; as they are acute, grave, or of an intermediate tone; which inquiry belongs in detail to the writers on meter.

A Syllable is a non-significant sound, composed of a mute and a vowel: for GR without A is a syllable, as also with A—GRA. But the investigation of these differences belongs also to metrical science.

A Connecting Word is a non-significant sound, which neither causes nor hinders the union of many sounds into one significant sound; it may be placed at either end or in the middle of a sentence. Or, a non-significant sound, which out of several sounds, each of them significant, is capable of forming one significant sound—as ἀμφί, περί, and the like. Or, a non-significant sound, which marks the beginning, end, or division of a sentence; such, however, that it cannot correctly stand by itself at the beginning of a sentence—as μέυ, ἥτοι, δέ.

A Noun is a composite significant sound, not marking time, of which no part is in itself significant: for in double or compound words we do not employ the separate parts as if each were in itself significant. Thus in Theodorus, "god-given," the δῶρου or "gift" is not in itself significant.

A Verb is a composite significant sound, marking time, in which, as in the noun, no part is in itself significant. For "man" or "white" does not express the idea of "when"; but "he walks" or "he has walked" does connote time, present or past.

Inflection belongs both to the noun and verb, and expresses either the relation "of," "to," or the like; or that of number, whether one or many, as "man" or "men"; or the modes or tones in actual delivery, e.g., a question or a command. "Did he go?" and "go" are verbal inflections of this kind.

A Sentence or Phrase is a composite significant sound, some at least of whose parts are in themselves significant; for not every such group of words consists of verbs and nouns—"the definition of man," for example—but it may dispense even with the verb. Still it will always have some significant part, as "in walking," or "Cleon son of Cleon." A sentence or phrase may form a unity in two ways—either as signifying one thing, or as consisting of several parts linked together. Thus the *Iliad* is one by the linking together of parts, the definition of man by the unity of the thing signified.

SECTION 3

PART XXI

Words are of two kinds, simple and double. By simple I mean those composed of non-significant elements, such as γῆ "earth." By double or compound, those composed either of a significant and non-significant element (though within the whole word no element is significant), or of elements that are both significant. A word may likewise be triple, quadruple, or multiple in form, like so many Massilian expressions, e.g., "Hermo-caico-xanthus [who prayed to Father Zeus]."

Every word is either current, or strange, or metaphorical, or ornamental, or newly-coined, or lengthened, or contracted, or altered.

By a current or proper word I mean one which is in general use among a people; by a strange word, one which is in use in another country. Plainly, therefore, the same word may be at once strange and current, but not in relation to the same people. The word σίγυνον, "lance," is to the Cyprians a current term but to us a strange one.

Metaphor is the application of an alien name by transference either from genus to species, or from species to genus, or from species to species, or by analogy, that is, proportion. Thus from genus to species, as: "There lies my ship"; for lying at anchor is a species of lying. From species to genus, as: "Verily ten thousand noble deeds hath Odysseus wrought"; for ten thousand is a species of large number, and is here used for a large number generally. From species to species, as: "With blade of bronze drew away the life," and "Cleft the water with the vessel of unyielding bronze." Here ἀρύσαι, "to draw away" is used for ταμεῖν, "to cleave," and ταμεῖν, again for ἀρύσαι—each being a species of taking away. Analogy or proportion is when the second term is to the first as the fourth to the third. We may then use the fourth for the second, or the second for the fourth. Sometimes too we qualify the metaphor by adding the term to which the proper word is relative. Thus the cup is to Dionysus as the shield to Ares. The cup may, therefore, be called "the shield of Dionysus," and the shield "the cup of Ares." Or, again, as old age is to life, so is evening to day. Evening may therefore be called, "the old age of the day," and old age, "the evening of life," or, in the phrase of Empedocles, "life's setting sun." For some of the terms of the proportion there is at times no word in existence; still the metaphor may be used. For instance, to scatter seed is called sowing: but the action of the sun in scattering his rays is nameless. Still this process bears to the sun the same relation as sowing to the seed. Hence the expression of the poet "sowing the god-created light." There is another way in which this kind of metaphor may be employed. We may apply an alien term, and then deny of that term one of its proper attributes; as if we were to call the shield, not "the cup of Ares," but "the wineless cup."

A newly-coined word is one which has never been even in local use, but is adopted by the poet himself. Some such words there appear to be: as ἐρνύγες, "sprouters," for κέρατα, "horns"; and ἀρητήρ, "supplicator", for ἱερεύς, "priest."

A word is lengthened when its own vowel is exchanged for a longer one, or when a syllable is inserted. A word is contracted when some part of it is removed. Instances of lengthening are: πόληος for πόλεως, and Πηληιάδεω for Πηλείδου: of contraction,—κρῖ, δῶ, and ὄψ as in μία γίνεται ἀμφοτέρων ὄψ [the appearance of both is one].

An altered word is one in which part of the ordinary form is left unchanged, and part is recast: as in δεξιτερὸν κατὰ μαζόν [on the right breast], δεξιτερὸν is for δεξιόν.

Nouns in themselves are either masculine, feminine, or neuter. Masculine are such as end in ν, ρ, ς, or in some letter compounded with ς—these being two, ψ and ξ. Feminine, such as end in vowels that are always long, namely η and ω, and—among vowels that admit of lengthening—those in α. Thus the number of letters in which nouns masculine and feminine end is the same; for ψ and ξ are equivalent to endings in ς. No noun ends in a mute or a vowel short by nature. Three only end in ι—μέλι [honey], κόμμι [gum]. And πέπερι [pepper]; five end in υ. Neuter nouns end in these two latter vowels; also in ν and ς.

PART XXII

The perfection of style is to be clear without being mean. The clearest style is that which uses only current or proper words; at the same time it is mean—witness the poetry of Cleophon and of Sthenelus. That diction, on the other hand, is lofty and raised above the commonplace which employs unusual words. By unusual, I mean strange (or rare) words, metaphorical, lengthened—anything, in short, that differs from the normal idiom. Yet a style wholly composed of such words is either a riddle or a jargon; a riddle, if it consists of metaphors; a jargon, if it consists of strange (or rare) words. For the essence of a riddle is to express true facts under impossible combinations. Now this cannot be done by any arrangement of ordinary words, but by the use of metaphor it can. Such is the riddle: "A man I saw who on another man had glued the bronze by aid of fire," and others of the same kind. A diction that is made up of strange (or rare) terms is a jargon. A certain infusion, therefore, of these elements is necessary to style; for the strange (or rare) word, the metaphorical, the ornamental, and the other kinds above mentioned, will raise it above the commonplace and mean, while the use of proper words will make it perspicuous. But nothing contributes more to produce a cleanness of diction that is remote from commonness than the lengthening, contraction, and alteration of words. For by deviating in exceptional cases from the normal idiom, the language will gain distinction; while, at the same time, the partial conformity with usage will give perspicuity. The critics, therefore, are in error who censure these licenses of speech, and hold the author up to ridicule. Thus Eucleides, the elder, declared that it would be an easy matter to be a poet if you might lengthen syllables at will. He caricatured the practice in the very form of his diction, as in the verse:

> Ἐπιχάρην εἶδον Μαραθῶνάδε βαδίζοντα,
> [I saw Epichares walking to Marathon]

or,

οὐκ αν γ᾽ ἐράμενος τὸν ἐκείνου ἐλλέβορον.
[Not if you desire his hellebore].

To employ such license at all obtrusively is, no doubt, grotesque; but in any mode of poetic diction there must be moderation. Even metaphors, strange (or rare) words, or any similar forms of speech, would produce the like effect if used without propriety and with the express purpose of being ludicrous. How great a difference is made by the appropriate use of lengthening, may be seen in Epic poetry by the insertion of ordinary forms in the verse. So, again, if we take a strange (or rare) word, a metaphor, or any similar mode of expression, and replace it by the current or proper term, the truth of our observation will be manifest. For example, Aeschylus and Euripides each composed the same iambic line. But the alteration of a single word by Euripides, who employed the rarer term instead of the ordinary one, makes one verse appear beautiful and the other trivial. Aeschylus in his Philoctetes says:

φαγέδαινα <δ > ἥ μου σάρκας ἐσθίει ποδός.
[The tumor which is eating the flesh of my foot.]

Euripides substitutes θοινᾶται, "feasts on," for ἐσθίει, "feeds on." Again, in the line,

νῦν δέ μ᾽ ἐών ὀλίγος τε καὶ οὐτιδανὸς καὶ αειδής,
[Yet a small man, worthless and unseemly],

the difference will be felt if we substitute the common words,

νῦν δέ μ᾽ ἐών μικρός τε καὶ ασθεηικός καὶ αειδής.
[Yet a little fellow, weak and ugly].

Or, if for the line,

δίφρον αεικέλιον καταθεὶς ὀλίγην τε τράπεζαν,
[Setting an unseemly couch and a meager table],

we read,

δίφρον μοχθηρὸν καταθεὶς μικραν τε τράπεζαν,
[Setting a wretched couch and a puny table].

Or, for ἠιόνες βοόωσιν [the sea shores roar] ἠιόνες κράζουσιν [the sea shores screech].

Again, Ariphrades ridiculed the tragedians for using phrases which no one would employ in ordinary speech: for example, δωμάτων ἄπο [from the house away] instead of ἀπὸ δωμάτων [away from the house], σέθεν, ἐγὼ δέ νιν [to thee, and I to him], Ἀχιλλέως πέρι [Achilles about] instead of περὶ Ἀχιλλέως [about Achilles], and the like. It is precisely because such phrases are not part of the current idiom that they give distinction to the style. This, however, he failed to see.

It is a great matter to observe propriety in these several modes of expression, as also in compound words, strange (or rare) words, and so forth. But the greatest thing by far is to have a command of metaphor. This alone cannot be imparted by another; it is the mark of genius, for to make good metaphors implies an eye for resemblances.

Of the various kinds of words, the compound are best adapted to dithyrambs, rare words to heroic poetry, metaphors to iambic. In heroic poetry, indeed, all these varieties are serviceable. But in iambic verse, which reproduces, as far as may be, familiar speech, the most appropriate words are those which are found even in prose. These are the current or proper, the metaphorical, the ornamental.

Concerning Tragedy and imitation by means of action this may suffice.

PART XXIII

As to that poetic imitation which is narrative in form and employs a single meter, the plot manifestly ought, as in a tragedy, to be constructed on dramatic principles. It should have for its subject a single action, whole and complete, with a beginning, a middle, and an end. It will thus resemble a living organism in all its unity, and produce the pleasure proper to it. It will differ in structure from historical compositions, which of necessity present not a single action, but a single period, and all that happened within that period to one person or to many, little connected together as the events may be. For as the sea-fight at Salamis and the battle with the Carthaginians in Sicily took place at the same time, but did not tend to any one result, so in the sequence of events, one thing sometimes follows another, and yet no single result is thereby produced. Such is the practice, we may say, of most poets. Here again, then, as has been already observed, the transcendent excellence of Homer is manifest. He never attempts to make the whole war of Troy the subject of his poem, though that war had a beginning and an end. It would have been too vast a theme, and not easily embraced in a single view. If, again, he had kept it within moderate limits, it must have been over-complicated by the variety of the incidents. As it is, he detaches a single portion, and admits as episodes many events from the general story of the war—such as the Catalogue of the ships and others—thus diversifying the poem. All other poets take a single hero, a single period, or an action single indeed, but with a multiplicity of parts. Thus did the author of the "Cypria" and of the "Little Iliad." For this reason the *Iliad* and the *Odyssey* each furnish the subject of one tragedy, or, at most, of two; while the "Cypria" supplies materials for many, and the "Little Iliad" for eight—the "Award of the Arms," the *Philoctetes*, the "Neoptolemus," the "Eurypylus," the "Mendicant Odysseus," the "Laconian Women," the "Fall of Ilium," the "Departure of the Fleet."

PART XXIV

Again, Epic poetry must have as many kinds as Tragedy: it must be simple, or complex, or "ethical,"or "pathetic." The parts also, with the exception of song and spectacle, are the same; for it requires Reversals of the Situation, Recognitions, and Scenes of Suffering. Moreover, the thoughts and the diction must be artistic. In all these respects Homer is our earliest and sufficient model. Indeed each of his poems has a twofold character. The Iliad is at once simple and "pathetic," and the *Odyssey* complex (for Recognition scenes run through it), and at the same time "ethical." Moreover, in diction and thought they are supreme.

Epic poetry differs from Tragedy in the scale on which it is constructed, and in its meter. As regards scale or length, we have already laid down an adequate limit: the beginning and the end must be capable of being brought within a single view. This condition will be satisfied by poems on a smaller scale than the old epics, and answering in length to the group of tragedies presented at a single sitting.

Epic poetry has, however, a great—a special—capacity for enlarging its dimensions, and we can see the reason. In Tragedy we cannot imitate several lines of actions carried on at one and the same time; we must confine ourselves to the action on the stage and the part taken by the players. But in Epic poetry, owing to the narrative form, many events simultaneously transacted can be presented; and these, if relevant to the subject, add mass and dignity to the poem. The Epic has here an advantage, and one that conduces to grandeur of effect, to diverting the mind of the hearer, and relieving the story with varying episodes. For sameness of incident soon produces satiety, and makes tragedies fail on the stage.

As for the meter, the heroic measure has proved its fitness by test of experience. If a narrative poem in any other meter or in many meters were now composed, it would be found incongruous. For of all measures the heroic is the stateliest and the most massive; and hence it most readily admits rare words and metaphors, which is another point in which the narrative form of imitation stands alone. On the other hand, the iambic and the trochaic tetrameter are stirring measures, the latter being akin to dancing, the former expressive of action. Still more absurd would it be to mix together different meters, as was done by Chaeremon. Hence no one has ever composed a poem on a great scale in any other than heroic verse. Nature herself, as we have said, teaches the choice of the proper measure.

Homer, admirable in all respects, has the special merit of being the only poet who rightly appreciates the part he should take himself. The poet should speak as little as possible in his own person, for it is not this that makes him an imitator. Other poets appear themselves upon the scene throughout, and imitate but little and rarely. Homer, after a few prefatory words, at once brings in a man, or woman, or other personage; none of them wanting in characteristic qualities, but each with a character of his own.

The element of the wonderful is required in Tragedy. The irrational, on which the wonderful depends for its chief effects, has wider scope in Epic poetry, because there the person acting is not seen. Thus, the pursuit of Hector would be ludicrous if placed upon the stage—the Greeks standing still and not joining in the pursuit, and Achilles waving them back. But in the Epic poem the absurdity passes unnoticed. Now the wonderful is pleasing, as may be inferred from the fact that every one tells a story with some addition of his own knowing that his hearers like it. It is Homer who has chiefly taught other poets the art of telling lies skilfully. The secret of it lies in a fallacy. For, assuming that if one thing is or becomes, a second is or becomes, men imagine that, if the second is, the first likewise is or becomes. But this is a false inference. Hence, where the first thing is untrue, it is quite unnecessary, provided the second be true, to add that the first is or has become. For the mind, knowing the second to be true, falsely infers the truth of the first. There is an example of this in the Bath Scene of the *Odyssey*.

Accordingly, the poet should prefer probable impossibilities to improbable possibilities. The tragic plot must not be composed of irrational parts. Everything irrational should, if possible, be excluded; or, at all events, it should lie outside the action of the play (as, in the Oedipus, the hero's ignorance as to the manner of Laius's death); not within the drama—as in the Electra, the messenger's account of the Pythian games; or, as in the Mysians, the man who has come from Tegea to Mysia and is still speechless. The plea that otherwise the plot would have been ruined, is ridiculous; such a plot should not in the first instance be constructed. But once the irrational has been introduced and an air of likelihood imparted to it, we must accept it in spite of the absurdity. Take even the irrational incidents in the *Odyssey*, where Odysseus is left upon the shore of Ithaca. How intolerable even these might have been would be apparent if an inferior poet were to treat the subject. As it is, the absurdity is veiled by the poetic charm with which the poet invests it.

The diction should be elaborated in the pauses of the action, where there is no expression of character or thought. For, conversely, character and thought are merely obscured by a diction that is over-brilliant.

PART XXV

With respect to critical difficulties and their solutions, the number and nature of the sources from which they may be drawn may be thus exhibited.

The poet being an imitator, like a painter or any other artist, must of necessity imitate one of three objects—things as they were or are, things as they are said or thought to be, or things as they ought to be. The vehicle of expression is language—either current terms or, it may be, rare words or metaphors. There are also many modifications of language, which we concede to the poets. Add to this, that the standard of correctness is not the same in poetry and politics, any more than in poetry and any other art. Within the art of poetry itself there are two kinds of faults—those which touch its essence, and those which are accidental. If a poet has chosen to imitate something, [but has imitated it incorrectly] through want of capacity, the error is inherent in the poetry. But if the failure is due to a wrong choice—if he has represented a horse as throwing out both his off legs at once, or introduced technical inaccuracies in medicine, for example, or in any other art—the error is not essential to the poetry. These are the points of view from which we should consider and answer the objections raised by the critics.

First as to matters which concern the poet's own art. If he describes the impossible, he is guilty of an error; but the error may be justified, if the end of the art be thereby attained (the end being that already mentioned)—if, that is, the effect of this or any other part of the poem is thus rendered more striking. A case in point is the pursuit of Hector. If, however, the end might have been as well, or better, attained without violating the special rules of the poetic art, the error is not justified: for every kind of error should, if possible, be avoided.

Again, does the error touch the essentials of the poetic art, or some accident of it? For example, not to know that a hind has no horns is a less serious matter than to paint it inartistically.

Further, if it be objected that the description is not true to fact, the poet may perhaps reply, "But the objects are as they ought to be"; just as Sophocles said that he drew men as they ought to be; Euripides, as they are. In this way the objection may be met. If, however, the representation be of neither kind, the poet may answer, "This is how men say the thing is." This applies to tales about the gods. It may well be that these stories are not higher than fact nor yet true to fact: they are, very possibly, what Xenophanes says of them. But anyhow, "this is what is said." Again, a description may be no better than the fact: "Still, it was the fact"; as in the passage about the arms: "Upright upon their butt-ends stood the spears." This was the custom then, as it now is among the Illyrians.

Again, in examining whether what has been said or done by some one is poetically right or not, we must not look merely to the particular act or saying, and ask whether it is poetically good or bad. We must also consider by whom it is said or done, to whom, when, by what means, or for what end; whether, for instance, it be to secure a greater good, or avert a greater evil.

Other difficulties may be resolved by due regard to the usage of language. We may note a rare word, as in οὐρῆας μέν πρῶτον, "the mules first [he killed]," where the poet perhaps employs οὐρῆας not in the sense of mules, but of sentinels. So, again, of Dolon: "ill-favored indeed he was to look upon." It is not meant that his body was ill-shaped but that his face was ugly; for the Cretans use the word εὐειδές, "well-favored" to denote a fair face. Again, ζωρότερον δὲ κέραιε [mix the drink livelier], does not mean "mix it stronger" as for hard drinkers, but "mix it quicker."

Sometimes an expression is metaphorical, as "Now all gods and men were sleeping through the night," while at the same time the poet says: "Often indeed as he turned his gaze to the Trojan plain, he marveled at the sound of flutes and pipes." "All" is here used metaphorically for "many," all being a species of many. So in the verse, "alone she hath no part. . . ." οἴη [alone] is metaphorical; for the best known may be called the only one.

Again, the solution may depend upon accent or breathing. Thus Hippias of Thasos solved the difficulties in the lines, δίδομεν (διδόμεν) δέ οἱ and τό μὲν οὗ (οὐ) καταπύθεται ὄμβρῳ.

Or again, the question may be solved by punctuation, as in Empedocles: "Of a sudden things became mortal that before had learnt to be immortal, and things unmixed before mixed."

Or again, by ambiguity of meaning, as in παρῴχηκεν δὲ πλέω νύξ, where the word πλέω is ambiguous.

Or by the usage of language. Thus any mixed drink is called οἶνος, "wine." Hence Ganymede is said "to pour the wine to Zeus," though the gods do not drink wine. So too workers in iron are called χαλκέας, or "workers in bronze." This, however, may also be taken as a metaphor.

Again, when a word seems to involve some inconsistency of meaning, we should consider how many senses it may bear in the particular passage. For example: "there was stayed the spear of bronze"—we should ask in how many ways we may take "being checked there." The true mode of interpretation is the precise opposite of what Glaucon mentions. Critics, he says, jump at certain groundless conclusions; they pass adverse judgement and then proceed to reason on it; and, assuming that the poet has said whatever they happen to think, find fault if a thing is inconsistent with their own fancy.

The question about Icarius has been treated in this fashion. The critics imagine he was a Lacedaemonian. They think it strange, therefore, that Telemachus should not have met him when he went to Lacedaemon. But the Cephallenian story may perhaps be the true one. They allege that Odysseus took a wife from among themselves, and that her father was Icadius, not Icarius. It is merely a mistake, then, that gives plausibility to the objection.

In general, the impossible must be justified by reference to artistic requirements, or to the higher reality, or to received opinion. With respect to the requirements of art, a probable impossibility is to be preferred to a thing improbable and yet possible. Again, it may be impossible that there should be men such as Zeuxis painted. "Yes," we say, "but the impossible is the higher thing; for the ideal type must surpass the realty." To justify the irrational, we appeal to what is commonly said to be. In addition to which, we urge that the irrational sometimes does not violate reason; just as "it is probable that a thing may happen contrary to probability."

Things that sound contradictory should be examined by the same rules as in dialectical refutation—whether the same thing is meant, in the same relation, and in the same sense. We should therefore solve the question by reference to what the poet says himself, or to what is tacitly assumed by a person of intelligence.

The element of the irrational, and, similarly, depravity of character, are justly censured when there is no inner necessity for introducing them. Such is the irrational element in the introduction of Aegeus by Euripides and the badness of Menelaus in the *Orestes*.

Thus, there are five sources from which critical objections are drawn. Things are censured either as impossible, or irrational, or morally hurtful, or contradictory, or contrary to artistic correctness. The answers should be sought under the twelve heads above mentioned.

PART XXVI

The question may be raised whether the Epic or Tragic mode of imitation is the higher. If the more refined art is the higher, and the more refined in every case is that which appeals to the better sort of audience, the art which imitates anything and everything is manifestly most unrefined. The audience is supposed to be too dull to comprehend unless something of their own is thrown by the performers, who therefore indulge in restless movements. Bad flute-players twist and twirl, if they have to represent "the quoit-throw," or hustle the coryphaeus when they perform the Scylla. Tragedy, it is said, has this same defect. We may compare the opinion that the older actors entertained of their successors. Mynniscus used to call Callippides "ape" on account of the extravagance of his action, and the same view was held of Pindarus. Tragic art, then, as a whole, stands to Epic in the same relation as the younger to the elder actors. So we are told that Epic poetry is addressed to a cultivated audience, who do not need gesture; Tragedy, to an inferior public. Being then unrefined, it is evidently the lower of the two.

Now, in the first place, this censure attaches not to the poetic but to the histrionic art; for gesticulation may be equally overdone in epic recitation, as by Sosistratus, or in lyrical competition, as by Mnasitheus the Opuntian. Next, all action is not to be condemned—any more than all dancing—but only that of bad performers. Such was the fault found in Callippides, as also in others of our own day, who are censured for representing degraded women. Again, Tragedy like Epic poetry produces its effect even without action; it reveals its power by mere reading. If, then, in all other respects it is superior, this fault, we say, is not inherent in it.

And superior it is, because it has an the epic elements—it may even use the epic meter—with the music and spectacular effects as important accessories; and these produce the most vivid of pleasures. Further, it has vividness of impression in reading as well as in representation. Moreover, the art attains its end within narrower limits for the concentrated effect is more pleasurable than one which is spread over a long time and so diluted. What, for example, would be the effect of the Oedipus of Sophocles, if it were cast into a form as long as the *Iliad*? Once more, the Epic imitation has less unity; as is shown by this, that any Epic poem will furnish subjects for several tragedies. Thus if the story adopted by the poet has a strict unity, it must either be concisely told and appear truncated; or, if it conforms to the Epic canon of length, it must seem weak and watery. [Such length implies some loss of unity,] if, I mean, the poem is constructed out of several actions, like the *Iliad* and the *Odyssey*, which have many such parts, each with a certain magnitude of its own. Yet these poems are as perfect as possible in structure; each is, in the highest degree attainable, an imitation of a single action.

If, then, tragedy is superior to epic poetry in all these respects, and, moreover, fulfills its specific function better as an art—for each art ought to produce, not any chance pleasure, but the pleasure proper to it, as already stated—it plainly follows that tragedy is the higher art, as attaining its end more perfectly.

Thus much may suffice concerning Tragic and Epic poetry in general; their several kinds and parts, with the number of each and their differences; the causes that make a poem good or bad; the objections of the critics and the answers to these objections.

3

HORACE [QUINTUS HORATIUS FLACCUS] (65–8 B.C.)

Horace was educated at Rome and Athens and spent some years in his twenties in military and civil posts during and after the civil war between Caesar and Pompey. Eventually, he was recognized as a poet by Virgil, five years older, and given patronage by Maecenas. Horace is one of the greatest writers of satires, odes, and epistles, which were especially influential in England during the eighteenth century.

His most important work of criticism—called variously "Epistle to the Pisos," "Ars Poetica," "De Arte Poetica"—is the practical result of a lifetime of work. Horace is much less systematic than Aristotle, but he speaks with more authority, since he had written scores of poems before theorizing about the art of poetry. His emphasis is on consistency and decorum, which are social virtues as well as aesthetic values. As an exemplar, Horace has influenced English poets from the sixteenth century on—especially Ben Jonson, Alexander Pope, Lord Byron, and W. H. Auden. As a critic, both in precept and example, Horace meant much to Jonson and Byron, who attempted translations of Horace's text.

"ARS POETICA" (CA. 15 B.C.)

(EPISTLE TO THE PISOS)

Adapted from translations by C. Smart and by E. H. Blakeney (*Horace on the Art of Poetry*, [London: Scholartis Press, 1928]). Bracketed text is the translators' interpolations.

If a painter should wish to unite a horse's neck to a human head, and spread a variety of plumage over limbs [of different animals] taken from every part [of nature], so that what is a beautiful woman in the upper part terminates unsightly in an ugly fish below; could you, my friends, refrain from laughter, were you admitted to such a sight. Believe, ye Pisos, the book will be perfectly like such a picture, the ideas of which, like a sick man's dreams, are all vain and fictitious: so that neither head nor foot can correspond to any one form. "Poets and painters [you will say] have ever had equal authority for attempting any thing." We are conscious of this, and this privilege we demand and allow in turn: but not to such a degree, that the tame should associate with the savage; nor that serpents should be coupled with birds, lambs with tigers.

In pompous introductions, and such as promise a great deal, it generally happens that one or two verses of purple patch-work, that may make a great show, are tagged on; as when the grove and the altar of Diana and the meandering of a current hastening through pleasant fields, or the river Rhine, or the rainbow is described. But here there was no room for these [fine things]: perhaps, too, you know how to draw a cypress [used for funerals]: but what is that to the purpose, if he, who is painted for the given price, is [to be represented as] swimming hopeless out of a shipwreck? A large vase at first was designed: why, as the wheel revolves, turns out a little pitcher? In a word, be your subject what it will, let it be merely simple and uniform.

The great majority of us poets, father, and youths worthy such a father, are misled by the appearance of right. I labor to be concise, I become obscure: nerves and spirit fail him, that aims at the easy: one, that pretends to be sublime, proves bombastical: he who is too cautious and fearful of the storm, crawls along the ground: he who wants to vary his subject in a marvelous manner, paints the dolphin in the woods, the boar in the sea. The avoiding of an error leads to a fault, if it lack skill.

A statuary about the Aemilian school shall of himself, with singular skill, both express the nails, and imitate in brass the flexible hair; unhappy yet in the main, because he knows not how to finish a complete piece. I would no more choose to be such a one as this, had I a mind to compose any thing, than to live with a distorted nose, [though] remarkable for black eyes and jetty hair.

Ye who write, make choice of a subject suitable to your abilities; and revolve in your thoughts a considerable time what your strength declines, and what it is able to support. Neither elegance of style, nor a perspicuous disposition, shall desert the man, by whom the subject matter is chosen judiciously.

This, or I am mistaken, will constitute the merit and beauty of arrangement, that the poet just now say what ought just now to be said, put off most of his thoughts, and waive them for the present.

In the choice of his words, too, the author of the projected poem must be delicate and cautious, he must embrace one and reject another: you will express yourself eminently well, if a dexterous combination should give an air of novelty to a well-known word. If it happen to be necessary to explain some abstruse subjects by new invented terms; it will follow that you must frame words never heard of by the old-fashioned Cethegi: and the license will be granted, if modestly used: and new and lately-formed words will have authority, if they descend from a Greek source, with a slight deviation. But why should the Romans grant to Plutus and Caecilius a privilege denied to Virgil and Varius? Why should I be envied, if I have it in my power to acquire a few words, when the language of Cato and Ennius has enriched our native tongue, and produced new names of things. It has been, and ever will be, allowable to coin a word marked with the stamp in present request. As leaves in the woods are changed with the fleeting years; the earliest fall off first: in this manner words perish with old age, and those lately invented flourish and thrive, like men in the time of youth. We, and our works, are doomed to death: whether Neptune, admitted into the continent, defends our fleet from the north winds, a kingly work; or the lake, for a long time unfertile and fit for oars, now maintains its neighboring cities and feels the heavy plow; or the river, taught to run in a more convenient channel, has changed its course which was so destructive to the fruits. Mortal works must perish: much less can the honor and elegance of language be long-lived. Many words shall revive, which now have fallen off; and many which are now in esteem shall fall off, if it be the will of custom, in whose power is the decision and right and standard of language.

Homer has instructed us in what measure the achievements of kings, and chiefs, and direful war might be written.

Plaintive strains originally were appropriated to the unequal numbers [of the elegiac]: afterward [love and] successful desires were included. Yet what author first published humble [i.e., pentameter] elegies, the critics dispute, and the controversy still waits the determination of a judge.

Rage armed Archilochus with the iambic of his own invention. The sock[1] and the majestic buskin assumed this measure as adapted for dialogue, and to silence the noise of the populace, and calculated for action.

To celebrate gods, and the sons of gods, and the victorious wrestler, and the steed foremost in the race, and the inclination of youths, and the free joys of wine, the muse has allotted to the lyre.

If I am incapable and unskillful to observe the distinction described, and the complexions of works [of genius], why am I accosted by the name of "Poet?" Why, out of false modesty, do I prefer being ignorant to being learned?

A comic subject will not be handled in tragic verse: in like manner the banquet of Thyestes will not bear to be held in familiar verses, and such as almost suit the sock. Let each peculiar species [of writing] fill with decorum its proper place. Nevertheless sometimes even comedy exalts her voice, and passionate Chremes rails in a tumid strain: and a tragic writer generally expresses grief in a prosaic style. Telephus and Peleus, when they are both in poverty and exile, throw aside their rants and gigantic expressions if they have a mind to move the heart of the spectator with their complaint.

It is not enough that poems be beautiful; let them be tender and affecting, and bear away the soul of the auditor whithersoever they please. As the human countenance smiles on those that smile, so does it sympathize with those that weep. If you would have me weep you must first express the passion of grief yourself; then, Telephus or Peleus, your misfortunes hurt me: if you pronounce the parts assigned you ill, I shall either fall asleep or laugh.

Pathetic accents suit a melancholy countenance; words full of menace, an angry one; wanton expressions, a sportive look; and serious matter, an austere

---

1. Sock: According to the *OED*: "A light shoe worn by comic actors on the ancient Greek and Roman stage; hence used allusively to denote comedy or the comic muse."

one. For nature forms us first within to every modification of circumstances; she delights or impels us to anger, or depresses us to the earth and afflicts us with heavy sorrow: then expresses those emotions of the mind by the tongue, its interpreter. If the words be discordant to the station of the speaker, the Roman knights and plebeians will raise an immoderate laugh. It will make a wide difference, whether it be Davus that speaks, or a hero; a man well-stricken in years, or a hot young fellow in his bloom; and a matron of distinction, or an officious nurse; a roaming merchant, or the cultivator of a verdant little farm; a Colchian, or an Assyrian; one educated at Thebes, or one at Argos.

You, that write, either follow tradition, or invent such fables as are congruous to themselves. If as poet you have to represent the renowned Achilles; let him be indefatigable, wrathful, inexorable, courageous, let him deny that laws were made for him, let him arrogate every thing to force of arms. Let Medea be fierce and intractable, Ino an object of pity, Ixion perfidious, Io wandering, Orestes in distress.

If you offer to the stage any thing unattempted, and venture to form a new character; let it be preserved to the last such as it set out at the beginning, and be consistent with itself. It is difficult to write with propriety on subjects to which all writers have a common claim; and you with more prudence will reduce the *Iliad* into acts, than if you first introduce arguments unknown and never treated of before. A public story will become your own property, if you do not dwell upon the whole circle of events, which is paltry and open to every one; nor must you be so faithful a translator, as to take the pains of rendering [the original] word for word; nor by imitating throw yourself into straits, whence either shame or the rules of your work may forbid you to retreat. Nor must you make such an exordium, as the Cyclic writer of old: "I will sing the fate of Priam, and the noble war." What will this boaster produce worthy of all this gaping? The mountains are in labor, a ridiculous mouse will be brought forth. How much more to the purpose he, who attempts nothing improperly: "Sing for me, my muse, the man who, after the time of the destruction of Troy, surveyed the manners and cities of many men." He meditates not [to produce] smoke from a flash, but out of smoke to elicit fire, that he may thence bring forth his instances of the marvelous with beauty, [such as] Antiphates, Scylla, the Cyclops, and Charybdis. Nor does he date Diomede's return from Meleager's death, nor trace the rise of the Trojan war from [Leda's] eggs: he always hastens on to the event; and hurries away his reader in the midst of interesting circumstances, no otherwise than as if they were [already] known; and what he despairs of, as to receiving a polish from his touch, he omits; and in such a manner forms his fictions, so intermingles the false with the true, that the middle is not inconsistent with the beginning, nor the end with the middle. Do you attend to what I, and the public in my opinion, expect from you [as a dramatic writer]. If you are desirous of an applauding spectator, who will wait for [the falling of] the curtain, and till the chorus calls out "your plaudits"; the manners of every age must be marked by you, and a proper decorum assigned to men's varying dispositions and years. The boy, who is just able to pronounce his words, and prints the ground with a firm tread, delights to play with his fellows, and contracts and lays aside anger without reason, and is subject to change every hour. The beardless youth, his guardian being at length discharged, joys in horses, and dogs, and the verdure of the sunny Campus Martius; pliable as wax to the bent of vice, rough to advisers, a slow provider of useful things, prodigal of his money, high-spirited, and amorous, and hasty in deserting the objects of his passion. [After this,] our inclinations being changed, the age and spirit of manhood seeks after wealth, and [high] connections, is subservient to points of honor; and is cautious of committing any action, which he would subsequently be industrious to correct. Many inconveniences encompass a man in years; either because he seeks [eagerly] for gain, and abstains from what he has gotten, and is afraid to make use of it; or because he transacts every thing in a timorous and dispassionate manner, dilatory, slow in hope, remiss, and greedy of futurity. Peevish, querulous, a panegyrist of former times when he was a boy, a chastiser and censurer of his juniors. Our advancing years bring many advantages along with them. Many our declining ones take away. That the parts [therefore] belonging to age may not be given to youth, and those of a man to a boy, we must dwell upon those qualities which are joined and adapted to each person's age.

An action is either represented on the stage, or being done elsewhere is there related. The things which enter by the ear affect the mind more languidly, than such as are submitted to the faithful eyes, and what a spectator presents to himself. You must not, however, bring upon the stage things fit only to be acted behind the scenes: and you must take away from view many actions, which elegant description may soon after deliver in presence [of the spectators]. Let not Medea murder her sons before the people; nor the execrable Atreus openly dress human entrails: nor let Progne be metamorphosed into a bird, Cadmus into a serpent. Whatever you show to me in this manner, not able to give credit to, I detest.

Let a play which would be inquired after, and though seen, represented anew, be neither shorter nor longer than the fifth act. Neither let a god interfere, unless a difficulty worthy a god's unraveling should happen; nor let a fourth person be officious to speak.

Let the chorus sustain the part and manly character of an actor: nor let them sing any thing between the acts which is not conducive to, and fitly coherent with, the main design. Let them both patronize the good, and give them friendly advice, and regulate the passionate, and love to appease thou who swell [with rage]: let them praise the repast of a short meal, the salutary effects of justice, laws, and peace with her open gates; let them conceal what is told to them in confidence, and supplicate and implore the gods that prosperity may return to the wretched, and abandon the haughty.

The flute, (not as now, begirt with brass and emulous of the trumpet, but) slender and of simple form, with few stops, was of service to accompany and assist the chorus, and with its tone was sufficient to fill the rows that were not as yet too crowded, where an audience, easily numbered, as being small and sober, chaste and modest, met together. But when the victorious Romans began to extend their territories, and an ampler wall encompassed the city, and their genius was indulged on festivals by drinking wine in the day-time without censure; a greater freedom arose both to the numbers [of poetry], and the measure [of music]. For what taste could an unlettered clown and one just dismissed from labors have, when in company with the polite; the base, with the man of honor? Thus the musician added new movements and a luxuriance to the ancient art, and strutting backward and forward, drew a length of train over the stage; thus likewise new notes were added to the severity of the lyre, and precipitate eloquence produced an unusual language [in the theater]: and the sentiments [of the chorus, then] expert in teaching useful things and prescient of futurity, differ hardly from the oracular Delphi.

The poet, who first tried his skill in tragic verse for the paltry [prize of a] goat, soon after exposed to view wild satyrs naked, and attempted raillery with severity, still preserving the gravity [of tragedy]: because the spectator on festivals, when heated with wine and disorderly, was to be amused with captivating shows and agreeable novelty. But it will be expedient so to recommend the bantering, so the rallying satyrs, so to turn earnest into jest; that none who shall be exhibited as a god, none who is introduced as a hero lately conspicuous in regal purple and gold, may deviate into the low style of obscure, mechanical shops; or, [on the contrary,] while he avoids the ground, affect cloudy mist and empty jargon. Tragedy disdaining to prate forth trivial verses, like a matron commanded to dance on the festival days, will assume an air of modesty, even in the midst of wanton satyrs. As a writer of satire, ye Pisos, I shall never be fond of unornamented and reigning terms: nor shall I labor to differ so widely from the complexion of tragedy, as to make no distinction, whether Davus be the speaker. And the bold Pythias, who gained a talent by gulling Simo; or Silenus, the guardian and attendant of his pupil-god [Bacchus]. I would so execute a fiction taken from a well-known story, that any body might entertain hopes of doing the same thing; but, on trial, should sweat and labor in vain. Such power has a just arrangement and connection of the parts: such grace may be added to subjects merely common. In my judgment the Fauns, that are brought out of the woods, should not be too gamesome with their tender strains, as if they were educated in the city, and almost at the bar; nor, on the other hand, should blunder out their obscene and scandalous speeches. For [at such stuff] all are offended, who have a horse, a father, or an estate: nor will they receive with approbation, nor give the laurel crown, as the purchasers of parched peas and nuts are delighted with.

A long syllable put after a short one is termed an iambus, a lively measure, whence also it commanded the name of trimeters to be added to iambics, though it yielded six beats of time, being similar to itself from first to last. Not long ago, that it might come somewhat slower and with more majesty to the ear, it obligingly and contentedly admitted into its paternal heritage the steadfast spondees; agreeing however, by social league, that it was not to depart from the second and fourth place. But this [kind of measure] rarely makes its appearance in the notable trimeters of Accius, and brands the verse of Ennius brought upon the stage with a clumsy weight of spondees, with the imputation of being too precipitate and careless, or disgracefully accuses him of ignorance in his art.

It is not every judge that discerns inharmonious verses, and an undeserved indulgence is [in this case] granted to the Roman poets. But shall I on this account run riot and write licentiously? Or should not I rather suppose, that all the world are to see my faults; secure, and cautious [never to err] but with hope of being pardoned? Though, perhaps, I have merited no praise, I have escaped censure.

Ye [who are desirous to excel,] turn over the Grecian models by night, turn them by day. But our ancestors commended both the numbers of Plautus, and his strokes of pleasantry; too tamely, I will not say foolishly, admiring each of them; if you and I but know how to distinguish a coarse joke from a smart repartee, and understand the proper cadence, by [using] our fingers and ears.

Thespis is said to have invented a new kind of tragedy, and to have carried his pieces about in carts, which [certain strollers], who had their faces besmeared with lees of wine, sang and acted. After him Aeschylus, the inventor of the vizard mask and decent robe, laid the stage over with boards of a tolerable size, and taught to speak in lofty tone, and strut in the buskin. To these succeeded the old comedy, not without considerable praise: but its personal freedom degenerated into excess and violence, worthy to be regulated by law; a law was made accordingly, and the chorus, the right of abusing being taken away, disgracefully became silent.

Our poets have left no species [of the art] unattempted; nor have those of them merited the least honor, who dared to forsake the footsteps of the Greeks, and celebrate domestic facts; whether they have instructed us in tragedy, or comedy. Nor would Italy be raised higher by valor and feats of arms, than by its language, did not the fatigue and tediousness of using the file disgust every one of our poets. Do you, the descendants of Pompilius, reject that poem, which many days and many a blot have not ten times subdued to the most perfect accuracy. Because Democritus believes that genius is more successful than wretched art, and excludes from Helicon all poets who are in their senses, a great number do not care to part with their nails or beard, frequent places of solitude, shun the baths. For he will acquire, [he thinks,] the esteem and title of a poet, if he neither submits his head, which is not to be cured by even three Anticyras, to Licinius the barber. What an unlucky fellow am I, who am purged for the bile in spring-time! Else nobody would compose better poems; but the purchase is not worth the expense. Therefore I will serve instead of a whetstone, which though not able of itself to cut, can make steel sharp: so I, who can write no poetry myself, will teach the duty and business [of an author]; whence he may be stocked with rich materials; what nourishes and forms the poet; what gives grace, what not; what is the tendency of excellence, what that of error.

To have good sense, is the first principle and fountain of writing well. The Socratic papers will direct you in the choice of your subjects; and words will spontaneously accompany the subject, when it is well conceived. He who has learned what he owes to his country, and what to his friends; with what affection a parent, a brother, and a stranger, are to be loved; what is the duty of a senator, what of a judge; what the duties of a general sent out to war; he, [I say,] certainly knows how to give suitable attributes to every character. I should direct the learned imitator to have a regard to the mode of nature and manners, and thence draw his expressions to the life. Sometimes a play, that is showy with common-places, and where the manners are well marked, though of no elegance, without force or art, gives the people much higher delight and more effectually commands their attention, than verse void of matter, and tuneful trifles. To the Greeks, covetous of nothing but praise, the muse gave genius; to the Greeks the power of expressing themselves in round periods. The Roman youth learn by long computation to subdivide a pound into an hundred parts. Let the son of Albinus tell me, if from five ounces one be subtracted, what remains? He would have said the third of a pound. Bravely done! you will be able to take care of your own affairs. An ounce is added: what will that be? Half a pound.

When this sordid rust and hankering after wealth has once tainted their minds, can we expect that such verses should be made as are worthy of being anointed with the oil of cedar, and kept in the well-polished cypress?

Poets wish either to profit or to delight; or to deliver at once both the pleasures and the necessaries of life. Whatever precepts you give, be concise; that docile minds may soon comprehend what is said, and faithfully retain it. All superfluous instructions flow from the too full memory. Let whatever is imagined for the sake of entertainment, have as much likeness to truth as possible; let not your play demand belief for whatever [absurdities] it is inclinable [to exhibit]: nor take out of a witch's belly a living child that she had dined upon. The tribes of the seniors rail against every thing that is void of edification: the exalted knights disregard poems which are austere. He who joins the instructive with the agreeable, carries off every vote, by delighting and at the same time admonishing the reader. This book gains money for the Sosii; this crosses the sea, and continues to its renowned author a lasting duration.

Yet there are faults, which we should be ready to pardon: for neither does the string [always] form the sound which the hand and conception [of the performer] intends, but very often returns a sharp note when he demands a flat; nor will the bow always hit whatever mark it threatens. But when there is a great majority of beauties in a poem, I will not be offended with a few blemishes, which either inattention has dropped, or human nature has not sufficiently provided against. What therefore [is to be determined in this matter]? As a transcriber, if he still commits the same fault though he has been reproved, is without excuse; and the harper who always blunders on the same string, is sure to be laughed at; so he who is excessively deficient becomes another Choerilus; whom, when I find him tolerable in two or three places, I wonder at with laughter; and at the same time am I grieved whenever honest Homer grows drowsy But it is allowable, that sleep should steal upon [the progress of] a long work.

As is painting, so is poetry: some pieces will strike you more if you stand near, and some, if you are at a greater distance: one loves the dark; another, which is not afraid of the critic's subtle judgment, chooses to be seen in the light; the one has pleased once the other will give pleasure if ten times repeated. ye elder of the youths, though you are framed to a right judgment by your father's instructions, and are wise in yourself, yet take this truth along with you, [and] remember it; that in certain things a medium and tolerable degree of eminence may be admitted: a counselor and pleader at the bar of the middle rate is far removed from the merit of eloquent Messala, nor has so much knowledge of the law as Casselius Aulus, but yet he is in request; [but] a mediocrity in poets neither gods, nor men, nor [even] the booksellers' shops have endured. As at an agreeable entertainment discordant music, and muddy perfume, and poppies mixed with Sardinian honey give offense, because the supper might have passed without them; so poetry, created and invented for the delight of our souls, if it comes short ever so little of the summit, sinks to the bottom.

He who does not understand the game, abstains from the weapons of the Campus Martius: and the unskillful in the tennis-ball, the quoit, and the torques keeps himself quiet; lest the crowded ring should raise a laugh at his expense: notwithstanding this, he who knows nothing of verses presumes to compose. Why not! He is free-born, and of a good family; above all, he is registered at an equestrian sum of moneys, and clear from every vice. You, [I am persuaded,] will neither say nor do any thing in opposition to Minerva: such is your judgment, such your disposition. But if ever you shall write any thing, let it be submitted to the ears of Metius [Tarpa], who is a judge, and your father's, and mine; and let it be suppressed till the ninth year, your papers being laid up within your own custody. You will have it in your power to blot out what you have not made public: a word once sent abroad can never return.

Orpheus, the priest and interpreter of the gods, deterred the savage race of men from slaughters and inhuman diet; hence said to tame tigers and furious lions: Amphion too, the builder of the Theban wall, was said to give the stones motion with the sound of his lyre, and to lead them whithersoever he would, by engaging persuasion. This was deemed wisdom of yore, to distinguish the public from private weal; things sacred from things profane; to prohibit a promiscuous commerce between the sexes; to give laws to married people; to plan out cities; to engrave laws on [tables of] wood. Thus honor accrued to divine poets, and their songs. After these, excellent Homer and Tyrtaeus animated the manly mind to martial achievements with their verses. Oracles were delivered in poetry, and the economy of life pointed out, and the favor of sovereign princes was solicited by Pierian strains, games were instituted, and a [cheerful] period put to the tedious labors of the day; [this I remind you of,] lest haply you should be ashamed of the lyric muse, and Apollo the god of song.

It has been made a question, whether good poetry be derived from nature or from art. For my part, I can neither conceive what study can do without a rich [natural] vein, nor what rude genius can avail of itself: so much does the one require the assistance of the other, and so amicably do they conspire [to produce the same effect]. He who is industrious to reach the wished-for goal, has done and suffered much when a boy; he has sweated and shivered with cold; he has abstained from love and wine; he who sings the Pythian strains, was first a learner, and in awe of a master. But [in poetry] it is now enough for a man to say of himself:—"I make admirable verses: a murrain seize the hindmost: it is scandalous for me to be outstripped, and fairly to acknowledge that I am ignorant of that which I never learned."

As a crier who collects the crowd together to buy his goods, so a poet rich in land, rich in money put out at interest, invites flatterers to come [and praise his works] for a reward. But if he be one who is well able to set out an elegant table, and give security for a poor man, and relieve him when entangled in gloomy law-suits; I shall wonder if with his wealth he can distinguish a true friend from a false one. You, whether you have made, or intend to make, a present to any one, do not bring him full of joy directly to your finished verses: for then he will cry out, "Charming, excellent, judicious," he will turn pale; at some parts he will even distill the dew from his friendly eyes; he will jump about; he will beat the ground [with ecstasy]. As those who mourn at funerals for pay, do and say more than those that are afflicted from their hearts; so the sham admirer is more moved than he that praises with sincerity. Certain kings are said to ply with frequent bumpers, and by wine make trial of a man whom they are sedulous to know, whether he be worthy of their friendship or not. Thus, if you compose verses, let not the fox's concealed intentions impose upon you.

If you had recited any thing to Quintilius, he would say, "Alter, I pray, this and this." If you replied, you could do it no better, having made the experiment twice or thrice in vain; he would order you to blot out, and once more apply to the anvil your ill-formed verses: if you choose rather to defend than correct a fault, he spent not a word more nor fruitless labor, but you alone might be fond of yourself and your own works, without a rival. A good and sensible man will censure spiritless verses, he will condemn the rugged, on the incorrect he will draw across a black stroke with his pen; he will lop off ambitious [and redundant] ornaments; he will make him throw light on the parts that are not perspicuous; he will arraign what is expressed ambiguously; he will mark what should be altered; [in short,] he will be an Aristarchus: he will not say, "Why should I give my friend offense about mere trifles?" These trifles will lead into mischiefs of serious consequence, when once made an object of ridicule, and used in a sinister manner.

Like one whom an odious plague or jaundice, fanatic frenzy or lunacy, distresses; those who are wise avoid a mad poet, and are afraid to touch him; the boys jostle him, and the incautious pursue him. If, like a fowler intent upon his game, he should fall into a well or a ditch while he belches out his fustian verses and roams about, though he should cry out for a long time, "Come to my assistance, my countrymen," not one would give himself the trouble of taking him up. Were any one to take pains to give him aid, and let down a rope; "How do you know, but he threw himself in hither on purpose?" I shall say: and will relate the death of the Sicilian poet. Empedocles, while he was ambitious of being esteemed an immortal god, in cold blood leaped into burning Aetna. Let poets have the privilege and license to die [as they please]. He who saves a man against his will, does the same with him who kills him [against his will]. Neither is it the first time that he has behaved in this manner; nor, were he to be forced from his purposes, would he now become a man, and lay aside his desire of such a famous death. Neither does it appear sufficiently, why he makes verses: whether he has defiled his father's ashes, or sacrilegiously removed the sad enclosure of the vindictive thunder: it is evident that he is mad, and like a bear that has burst through the gates closing his den, this unmerciful rehearser chases the learned and unlearned. And whomsoever he seizes, he fastens on and assassinates with recitation: a leech that will not quit the skin, till satiated with blood.

4

PUBLIUS CORNELIUS TACITUS (A.D. ?55-?117)

Tacitus was one of the most distinguished of Roman historians. He served in various governmental positions: military tribune, quaestor, praetor, consul, and pro-consul. His speeches were celebrated for their eloquence. His *Germania*, written around A.D. 100, contains one of the earliest accounts of the poetry of Northern Europe. Tacitus clearly viewed the Germans as barbarians, but he was willing to concede that they cultivated at least some of the arts. For them, however, poetry was practical and instrumental, charged with civic, military, and religious significance.

His history resembles earlier works on foreign cultures, such as those in Greek by Herodotus and Pausanias. Typically, such studies mix fact with fiction and comment freely on curiosities of language and culture. Tacitus also gives the Germans credit for being a unified nation of related peoples ("german" and "germane" mean "having the same ancestors").

GERMANIA (CA. A.D. 100; excerpt)

Translation adapted from William Francis Allen, ed., *The Life of Agricola and the Germania* (Boston: Ginn, 1913).

The Germans, I am apt to believe, derive their original from no other people; and are nowise mixed with different nations arriving amongst them: since anciently those who went in search of new buildings, travelled not by land, but were carried in fleets; and into that mighty ocean so boundless, and, as I may call it, so repugnant and forbidding, ships from our world rarely enter. Moreover, besides the dangers from a sea tempestuous, horrid and unknown, who would relinquish Asia, or Africa, or Italy, to repair to Germany, a region hideous and rude, under a rigorous climate, dismal to behold or to manure unless the same were his native country? In their old ballads (which amongst them are the only sort of registers and history) they celebrate Tuisto, a God sprung from the earth, and Mannus his son, as the fathers and founders of the nation. To Mannus they assign three sons, after whose names so many people are called; the Ingævones, dwelling next the ocean; the Herminones, in the middle country; and all the rest, Instævones. Some, borrowing a warrant from the darkness of antiquity, maintain that the God had more sons, that thence came more denominations of people, the Marsians, Gambrians, Suevians, and Vandalians, and that these are the names truly genuine and original. For the rest, they affirm

Germany to be a recent word, lately bestowed: for that those who first passed the Rhine and expulsed the Gauls, and are now named Tungrians, were then called Germans: and thus by degrees the name of a tribe prevailed, not that of the nation; so that by an appellation at first occasioned by terror and conquest, they afterwards chose to be distinguished, and assuming a name lately invented were universally called Germans.

They have a tradition that Hercules also had been in their country, and him above all other heroes they extol in their songs when they advance to battle. Amongst them too are found that kind of verses by the recital of which (by them called Barding) they inspire bravery; nay, by such chanting itself they divine the success of the approaching fight. For, according to the different din of the battle, they urge furiously, or shrink timorously. Nor does what they utter, so much seem to be singing as the voice and exertion of valor. They chiefly study a tone fierce and harsh, with a broken and unequal murmur, and therefore apply their shields to their mouths, whence the voice may by rebounding swell with greater fulness and force. Besides there are some of opinion, that Ulysses, whilst he wandered about in his long and fabulous voyages, was carried into this ocean and entered Germany, and that by him Asciburgium was founded and named, a city at this day standing and inhabited upon the bank of the Rhine: nay, that in the same place was formerly found an altar dedicated to Ulysses, with the name of his father Laertes added to his own, and that upon the confines of Germany and Rhœtia are still extant certain monuments and tombs inscribed with Greek characters. Traditions these which I mean not either to confirm with arguments of my own or to refute. Let every one believe or deny the same according to his own bent.

5

LONGINUS (?)

THE AUTHOR OF "ON THE SUBLIME"

Nothing is known about the author or the exact date of the treatise that comes from antiquity as "Dionysius Longinus on the Sublime" or "Dionysius or Longinus on the Sublime." It is too early to be the work of Cassius Longinus (ca. A.D. 220–273), a Neo-Platonist who wrote a surviving treatise on rhetoric. "On the Sublime" is incomplete. "The Argument of Longinus' *On the Sublime*" by Elder Olson brilliantly reconstructs a likely outline for the whole (See *Critics and Criticism*, ed. R. S. Crane. [Chicago: University of Chicago Press, 1952]).

The treatise was admired by John Dryden, Joseph Addison, Alexander Pope, Oliver Goldsmith, and Edward Gibbon. The Romantic thinkers and writers of the eighteenth and nineteenth centuries, from Edmund Burke through Goethe and Coleridge to Matthew Arnold, were much affected by the general notion of sublimity, construed as the height of grandeur, nobility, and generosity, expressed as largeness and fineness of idea and feeling matched by largeness and fineness of expression.

"ON THE SUBLIME" (CA. A.D. 100; excerpt)

Adapted from *Longinus on the Sublime,* trans. W. Rhys Roberts (London: Cambridge University Press, 1899).

II

First of all, we must raise the question whether there is such a thing as an art of the sublime or lofty. Some hold that those are entirely in error who would bring such matters under the precepts of art. A lofty tone, says one, is innate, and does not come by teaching; nature is the only art that can compass it. Works of nature are, they think, made worse and altogether feebler when wizened by the rules of art. But I maintain that this will be found to be otherwise if it be observed that, while nature as a rule is free and independent in matters of passion and elevation, yet is she wont not to act at random and utterly without system. Further, nature is the original and vital underlying principle in all cases, but system can define limits and fitting seasons, and can also contribute the safest rules for use and practice. Moreover, the expression of the sublime is more exposed to danger when it goes its own way without the guidance of knowledge,—when it is suffered to be unstable and unballasted,—when it is left at the mercy of mere momentum and ignorant audacity. It is true that it often needs the spur, but it is also true that it often needs the curb. Demosthenes expresses the view, with regard to human life in general, that good fortune is the greatest of blessings, while good counsel, which occupies the second place, is hardly inferior in importance, since its absence contributes inevitably to the ruin of the former ("Against Aristocrates"). This we may apply to diction, nature occupying the position of good fortune, art that of good counsel. Most important of all, we must remember that the very fact that there are some elements of expression which are in the hands of nature alone, can be learnt from no other source than art. If, I say, the critic of those who desire to learn were to turn these matters over in his mind, he would no longer, it seems to me, regard the discussion of the subject as superfluous or useless . . . .

III

> Quell they the oven's far-flung splendor-glow!
> Ha, let me but one hearth-abider mark—
> One flame-wreath torrent-like I'll whirl on high;
> I'll burn the roof, to cinders shrivel it!—
> Nay, now my chant is not of noble strain.
>
> (Aeschylus, tr. A. S. Way)[1]

Such things are not tragic but pseudo-tragic—"flame-wreaths," and "belching to the sky," and Boreas represented as a "flute-player," and all the rest of it. They are turbid in expression and confused in imagery rather than the product of intensity, and each one of them, if examined in the light of day, sinks little by little from the terrible into the contemptible. But since even in tragedy, which is in its very nature stately and prone to bombast, tasteless tumidity is unpardonable, still less, I presume, will it harmonize with the narration of fact. And this is the ground on which the phrases of Gorgias of Leontini are ridiculed when he describes Xerxes as the "Zeus of the Persians" and vultures as "living tombs." So is it with some of the expressions of Callisthenes which are not sublime but high-flown, and still more with those of Cleitarchus, for the man is frivolous and blows, as Sophocles has it,

> On pigmy hautboys: mouthpiece have they none.
>
> (Sophocles, tr. A. S. Way)

---

1. In Roberts's translation of the treatise, translations of verse were by others, almost always Arthur S. Way (1847–1930), who later published his own *Aeschylus* (London: Macmillan, 1906–8) and *Sophocles in English Verse* (London: Macmillan, 1909–14).

Other examples will be found in Amphicrates and Hegesias and Matris, for often when these writers seem to themselves to be inspired they are in no true frenzy but are simply trifling. Altogether, tumidity seems particularly hard to avoid. The explanation is that all who aim at elevation are so anxious to escape the reproach of being weak and dry that they are carried, as by some strange law of nature, into the opposite extreme. They put their trust in the maxim that "failure in a great attempt is at least a noble error." But evil are the swellings, both in the body and in diction, which are inflated and unreal, and threaten us with the reverse of our aim; for nothing, say they, is drier than a man who has the dropsy. While tumidity desires to transcend the limits of the sublime, the defect which is termed puerility is the direct antithesis of elevation, for it is utterly low and mean and in real truth the most ignoble vice of style. What, then, is this puerility? Clearly, a pedant's thoughts, which begin in learned trifling and end in frigidity. Men slip into this kind of error because, while they aim at the uncommon and elaborate and most of all at the attractive, they drift unawares into the tawdry and affected. A third, and closely allied, kind of defect in matters of passion is that which Theodorus used to call *parenthyrsus*. By this is meant unseasonable and empty passion, where no passion is required, or immoderate, where moderation is needed. For men are often carried away, as if by intoxication, into displays of emotion which are not caused by the nature of the subject, but are purely personal and wearisome. In consequence they seem to hearers who are in no wise affected to act in an ungainly way. And no wonder; for they are beside themselves, while their hearers are not. But the question of the passions we reserve for separate treatment.

IV

Of the second fault of which we have spoken—frigidity—Timaeus supplies many examples. Timaeus was a writer of considerable general ability, who occasionally showed that he was not incapable of elevation of style. He was learned and ingenious, but very prone to criticize the faults of others while blind to his own. Through his passion for continually starting novel notions, he often fell into the merest childishness. I will set down one or two examples only of his manner, since the greater number have been already appropriated by Caecilius. In the course of a eulogy on Alexander the Great, he describes him as "the man who gained possession of the whole of Asia in fewer years than it took Isocrates to write his Panegyric urging war against the Persians." Strange indeed is the comparison of the man of Macedon with the rhetorician. How plain it is, Timaeus, that the Lacedaemonians, thus judged, were far inferior to Isocrates in prowess, for they spent thirty years in the conquest of Messene, whereas he composed his Panegyric in ten. Consider again the way in which he speaks of the Athenians who were captured in Sicily. "They were punished because they

had acted impiously towards Hermes and mutilated his images, and the inflic-
tion of punishment was chiefly due to Hermocrates the son of Hermon, who
was descended, in the paternal line, from the outraged god." I am surprised,
beloved Terentianus, that he does not write with regard to the despot Dionysius
that "Dion and Heracleides deprived him of his sovereignty because he had
acted impiously towards Zeus and Heracles." But why speak of Timaeus when
even those heroes of literature, Xenophon and Plato, though trained in the
school of Socrates, nevertheless sometimes forget themselves for the sake of
such paltry pleasantries? Xenophon writes in the *Policy of the Lacedaemonians*:
"You would find it harder to hear their voice than that of busts of marble, harder
to deflect their gaze than that of statues of bronze; you would deem them more
modest than the very maidens in their eyes" (*De Rep. Laced.* III. 5).

It was worthy of an Amphicrates and not of a Xenophon to call the pupils
of our eyes "modest maidens." Good heavens, how strange it is that the pupils
of the whole company should be believed to be modest notwithstanding the
common saying that the shamelessness of individuals is indicated by nothing
so much as the eyes! "Thou sot? that hast the eyes of a dog," as Homer has it
(*Iliad* 1.225. Way's translation). Timaeus, however, has not left even this piece
of frigidity to Xenophon, but clutches it as though it were hid treasure. At all
events, after saying of Agathocles that he abducted his cousin, who had been
given in marriage to another man, from the midst of the nuptial rites, he asks,
"Who could have done this had he not had wantons, in place of maidens, in
his eyes?" Yes, and Plato (usually so divine) when he means simply tablets says,
"They shall write and preserve cypress memorials in the temples" (*Laws* 5. 741c).

And again, "As touching walls, Megillus, I should hold with Sparta that they
be suffered to lie asleep in the earth and not summoned to arise" (*Laws* 778d).
The expression of Herodotus to the effect that beautiful women are "eye-smarts"
is not much better (*Histories* 5. 18). This, however, may be condoned in some
degree since those who use this particular phrase in his narrative are barbarians
and in their cups, but not even in the mouths of such characters is it well that
an author should suffer, in the judgment of posterity, from an unseemly exhibition of triviality.

V

All these ugly and parasitical growths arise in literature from a single cause, that
pursuit of novelty in the expression of ideas which may be regarded as the
fashionable craze of the day. Our defects usually spring, for the most part, from
the same sources as our good points. Hence, while beauties of expression and
touches of sublimity, and charming elegancies withal, are favorable to effective
composition, yet these very things are the elements and foundation, not only
of success, but also of the contrary. Something of the kind is true also of vari-

ations and hyperboles and the use of the plural number, and we shall show subsequently the dangers to which these seem severally to be exposed. It is necessary now to seek and to suggest means by which we may avoid the defects which attend the steps of the sublime.

VI

The best means would be, friend, to gain, first of all, clear knowledge and appreciation of the true sublime. The enterprise is, however, an arduous one. For the judgment of style is the last and crowning fruit of long experience. None the less, if I must speak in the way of precept, it is not impossible perhaps to acquire discrimination in these matters by attention to some such hints as those which follow.

VII

You must know, my dear friend, that it is with the sublime as in the common life of man. In life nothing can be considered great which it is held great to despise. For instance, riches, honors, distinctions, sovereignties, and all other things which possess in abundance the external trappings of the stage, will not seem, to a man of sense, to be supreme blessings, since the very contempt of them is reckoned good in no small degree, and in any case those who could have them, but are high-souled enough to disdain them, are more admired than those who have them. So also in the case of sublimity in poems and prose writings, we must consider whether some supposed examples have not simply the appearance of elevation with many idle accretions, so that when analyzed they are found to be mere vanity—objects which a noble nature will rather despise than admire. For, as if instinctively, our soul is uplifted by the true sublime; it takes a proud flight, and is filled with joy and vaunting, as though it had itself produced what it has heard.

When, therefore, a thing is heard repeatedly by a man of intelligence, who is well versed in literature, and its effect is not to dispose the soul to high thoughts, and it does not leave in the mind more food for reflection than the words seem to convey, but falls, if examined carefully through and through, into disesteem, it cannot rank as true sublimity because it does not survive a first hearing. For that is really great which bears a repeated examination, and which it is difficult or rather impossible to withstand, and the memory of which is strong and hard to efface. In general, consider those examples of sublimity, to be fine and genuine which please all and always. For when men of different pursuits, lives, ambitions, ages, languages, hold identical views on one and the same subject, then that verdict which results, so to speak, from a concert of discordant elements makes our faith in the object of admiration strong and unassailable.

VIII

There are, it may be said, five principal sources of elevated language. Beneath these five varieties there lies, as though it were a common foundation, the gift of discourse, which is indispensable. First and most important is the power of forming great conceptions, as we have elsewhere explained in our remarks on Xenophon. Secondly, there is vehement and inspired passion. These two components of the sublime are for the most part innate. Those which remain are partly the product of art. The due formation of figures deals with two sorts of figures, first those of thought and secondly those of expression. Next there is noble diction, which in turn comprises choice of words, and use of metaphors, and elaboration of language. The fifth cause of elevation—one which is the fitting conclusion of all that have preceded it—is dignified and elevated composition. Come now, let us consider what is involved in each of these varieties, with this one remark by way of preface, that Caecilius has omitted some of the five divisions, for example, that of passion. Surely he is quite mistaken if he does so on the ground that these two, sublimity and passion, are a unity, and if it seems to him that they are by nature one and inseparable. For some passions are found which are far removed from sublimity and are of a low order, such as pity, grief and fear; and on the other hand there are many examples of the sublime which are independent of passion, such as the daring words of Homer with regard to the Aloadae, to take one out of numberless instances,

> Yea, Ossa in fury they strove to upheave on Olympus on
> high,
> With forest-clad Pelion above, that thence they might step
> to the sky.
>
> (*Odyssey* 11. 315–16)

And so of the words which follow with still greater force:—

> Ay, and the deed had they done.
>
> (*Odyssey* 11. 317)

Among the orators, too, eulogies and ceremonial and occasional addresses contain on every side examples of dignity and elevation, but are for the most part void of passion. This is the reason why passionate speakers are the worst eulogists, and why, on the other hand, those who are apt in encomium are the least passionate. If, on the other hand, Caecilius thought that passion never contributes at all to sublimity, and if it was for this reason that he did not deem it worthy of mention, he is altogether deluded. I would affirm with confidence that there is no tone so lofty as that of genuine passion, in its right place, when it bursts out in a wild gust of mad enthusiasm and as it were fills the speaker's words with frenzy.

IX

Now the first of the conditions mentioned, namely elevation of mind, holds the foremost rank among them all. We must, therefore, in this case also, although we have to do rather with an endowment than with an acquirement, nurture our souls (as far as that is possible) to thoughts sublime, and make them always pregnant, so to say, with noble inspiration. In what way, you may ask, is this to be done? Elsewhere I have written as follows: "Sublimity is the echo of a great soul." Hence also a bare idea, by itself and without a spoken word, sometimes excites admiration just because of the greatness of soul implied. Thus the silence of Ajax in the Underworld is great and more sublime than words (*Odyssey* 11. 543 ff.). First, then, it is absolutely necessary to indicate the source of this elevation, namely, that the truly eloquent must be free from low and ignoble thoughts. For it is not possible that men with mean and servile ideas and aims prevailing throughout their lives should produce anything that is admirable and worthy of immortality. Great accents we expect to fall from the lips of those whose thoughts are deep and grave. Thus it is that stately speech comes naturally to the proudest spirits. [You will remember the answer of] Alexander to Parmenio when he said "For my part I had been well content" [quotation from Arrian—Roberts's note] . . .

. . . the distance [ellipses here indicate gap in text—ed.] from earth to heaven; and this might well be considered the measure of Homer no less than of Strife. How unlike to this the expression which is used of Sorrow by Hesiod, if indeed the *Shield* is to be attributed to Hesiod:

> Rheum from her nostrils was trickling.
> ("Shield of Heracles," 267, trans. A. S. Way)

The image he has suggested is not terrible but rather loathsome. Contrast the way in which Homer magnifies the higher powers:

> And far as a man with his eyes through the sea-line haze
>   may discern,
> On a cliff as he sitteth and gazeth away o'er the wine-dark
>   deep,

> So far at a bound do the loud-neighing steeds of the Death-
>   less leap.
>
> (*Iliad* 5. 770, trans. A. S. Way)

He makes the vastness of the world the measure of their leap. The sublimity is so overpowering as naturally to prompt the exclamation that if the divine steeds were to leap thus twice in succession they would pass beyond the confines of the world. How transcendent also are the images in the Battle of the Gods:—

> Far round wide heaven and Olympus echoed his clarion of
>   thunder;
>
> (*Iliad* 21. 388)

> And Hades, king of the realm of shadows, quaked thereunder.
> And he sprang from his throne, and he cried aloud in the
>   dread of his heart
> Lest o'er him earth-shaker Poseidon should cleave the
>   ground apart,
> And revealed to Immortals and mortals should stand those
>   awful abodes,
> Those mansions ghastly and grim, abhorred of the very Gods.
>
> (*Iliad* 20. 61–65)

You see, my friend, how the earth is torn from its foundations, Tartarus itself is laid bare, the whole world is upturned and parted asunder, and all things to-gether—heaven and hell, things mortal and things immortal—share in the con-flict and the perils of that battle!

But although these things are awe-inspiring, yet from another point of view, if they be not taken allegorically, they are altogether impious, and violate our sense of what is fitting. Homer seems to me, in his legends of wounds suffered by the gods, and of their feuds, reprisals, tears, bonds, and all their manifold passions, to have made, as far as lay within his power, gods of the men con-cerned in the Siege of Troy, and men of the gods. But whereas we mortals have death as the destined haven of our ills if our lot is miserable, he portrays the gods as immortal not only in nature but also in misfortune. Much superior to the passages respecting the Battle of the Gods are those which represent the divine nature as it really is—pure and great and undefiled; for example, what is said of Poseidon in a passage fully treated by many before ourselves:—

> Her far-stretching ridges, her forest-trees, quaked in dismay,
> And her peaks, and the Trojans' town, and the ships of
>   Achaia's array,

Beneath his immortal feet, as onward Poseidon strode.
Then over the surges he drave: leapt sporting before the
    God
Sea-beasts that uprose all round from the depths, for their
    king they knew,
And for rapture the sea was disparted, and onward the car-
    steeds flew.

(*Iliad* 13. 18)

Similarly, the legislator of the Jews, no ordinary man, having formed and expressed a worthy conception of the might of the Godhead, writes at the very beginning of his Laws, "God said"—what? "Let there be light, and there was light; let there be land, and there was land." Perhaps I shall not seem tedious, friend, if I bring forward one passage more from Homer—this time with regard to the concerns of men—in order to show that he is wont himself to enter into the sublime actions of his heroes. In his poem the battle of the Greeks is suddenly veiled by mist and baffling night. Then Ajax, at his wits' end, cries:

Zeus, Father, yet save thou Achaia's sons from beneath the
    gloom,
And make clear day, and vouchsafe unto us with our eyes
    to see!
So it be but in light, destroy us!

(*Iliad* 17. 645)

That is the true attitude of an Ajax. He does not pray for life, for such a petition would have ill beseemed a hero. But since in the hopeless darkness he can turn his valor to no noble end, he chafes at his slackness in the fray and craves the boon of immediate light, resolved to find a death worthy of his bravery, even though Zeus should fight in the ranks against him. In truth, Homer in these cases shares the full inspiration of the combat, and it is neither more nor less than true of the poet himself that

Mad rageth he as Arês the shaker of spears, or as mad
    flames leap
Wild-wasting from hill unto hill in the folds of a forest
    deep,
And the foam-froth fringeth his lips.

(*Iliad* 15. 605–7)

He shows, however, in the *Odyssey* (and this further observation deserves attention on many grounds) that, when a great genius is declining, the special token of old age is the love of marvelous tales.

It is clear from many indications that the *Odyssey* was his second subject. A special proof is the fact that he introduces in that poem remnants of the adventures before Ilium as episodes, so to say, of the Trojan War. And indeed, he there renders a tribute of mourning and lamentation to his heroes as though he were carrying out a long-cherished purpose. In fact, the *Odyssey* is simply an epilogue to the *Iliad*:—

> There lieth Ajax the warrior wight, Achilles is there,
> There is Patroclus, whose words had weight as a God he
>   were;
> There lieth mine own dear son.

(Odyssey 3. 109–11)

It is for the same reason, I suppose, that he has made the whole structure of the *Iliad*, which was written at the height of his inspiration, full of action and conflict, while the *Odyssey* for the most part consists of narrative, as is characteristic of old age. Accordingly, in the *Odyssey* Homer may be likened to a sinking sun, whose grandeur remains without its intensity. He does not in the *Odyssey* maintain so high a pitch as in those poems of Ilium. His sublimities are not evenly sustained and free from the liability to sink; there is not the same profusion of accumulated passions, nor the supple and oratorical style, packed with images drawn from real life. You seem to see henceforth the ebb and flow of greatness, and a fancy roving in the fabulous and incredible, as though the ocean were withdrawing into itself and was being laid bare within its own confines. In saying this I have not forgotten the tempests in the *Odyssey* and the story of the Cyclops and the like. If I speak of old age, it is nevertheless the old age of Homer. The fabulous element, however, prevails throughout this poem over the real. The object of this digression has been, as I said, to show how easily great natures in their decline are sometimes diverted into absurdity, as in the incident of the wine-skin and of the men who were fed like swine by Circe (whining porkers, as Zoilus called them), and of Zeus like a nestling nurtured by the doves, and of the hero who was without food for ten days upon the wreck, and of the incredible tale of the slaying of the suitors (*Odyssey* 9. 182; 10.17; 10.237; 12.62; 12.447; 22.79.) For what else can we term these things than veritable dreams of Zeus? These observations with regard to the *Odyssey* should be made for another reason—in order that you may know that the genius of great poets and prose-writers, as their passion declines, finds its final expression in the delineation of character. For such are the details which Homer gives, with an eye to characterization, of life in the home of Odysseus; they form as it were a comedy of manners.

X

Let us next consider whether we can point to anything further that contributes to sublimity of style. Now, there inhere in all things by nature certain constituents which are part and parcel of their substance. It must needs be, therefore, that we shall find one source of the sublime in the systematic selection of the most important elements, and the power of forming, by their mutual combination, what may be called one body. The former process attracts the hearer by the choice of the ideas, the latter by the aggregation of those chosen. For instance, Sappho everywhere chooses the emotions that attend delirious passion from its accompaniments in actual life. Wherein does she demonstrate her supreme excellence? In the skill with which she selects and binds together the most striking and vehement circumstances of passion: —

> Peer of Gods he seemeth to me, the blissful
> Man who sits and gazes at thee before him,
> Close beside thee sits, and in silence hears thee
> Silverly speaking,
>
> Laughing love's low laughter. Oh this, this only
> Stirs the troubled heart in my breast to tremble!
> For should I but see thee a little moment,
> Straight is my voice hushed;
>
> Yea, my tongue is broken, and through and through me
> 'Neath the flesh impalpable fire runs tingling;
> Nothing see mine eyes, and a noise of roaring
> Waves in my ear sounds;
>
> Sweat runs down in rivers, a tremor seizes
> All my limbs, and paler than grass in autumn,
> Caught by pains of menacing death, I falter,
> Lost in the love-trance.

Are you not amazed how at one instant she summons, as though they were all alien from herself and dispersed, soul, body, ears, tongue, eyes, color? Uniting contradictions, she is, at one and the same time, hot and cold, in her senses and out of her mind, for she is either terrified or at the point of death. The effect desired is that not one passion only should be seen in her, but a concourse of the passions. All such things occur in the case of lovers, but it is, as I said, the selection of the most striking of them and their combination into a single whole that has produced the singular excellence of the passage. In the same

way Homer, when describing tempests, picks out the most appalling circumstances. The author of the *Arimaspeia* thinks to inspire awe in the following way:

> A marvel exceeding great is this withal to my soul—
> Men dwell on the water afar from the land, where deep
>   seas roll.
> Wretches are they, for they reap but a harvest of travail and
>   pain,
> Their eyes on the stars ever dwell, while their hearts abide
>   in the main.
> Often, I ween, to the Gods are their hands upraised on
>   high,
> And with hearts in misery heavenward-lifted in prayer do
>   they cry.
>
> (Aristeas, trans. A. S. Way)

It is clear, I imagine, to everybody that there is more elegance than terror in
these words. But what says Homer ? Let one instance be quoted from among
many:—

> And he burst on them like as a wave swift-rushing beneath
>   black clouds,
> Heaved huge by the winds, bursts down on a ship, and the
>   wild foam shrouds
> From the stem to the stern her hull, and the storm-blast's
>   terrible breath
> Roars in the sail, and the heart of the shipmen shuddereth
> In fear, for that scantly upborne are they now from the
>   clutches of death.
>
> (*Iliad* 15. 624–28)

Aratus has attempted to convert this same expression to his own use:—

> And a slender plank averteth their death.

Only, he has made it trivial and neat instead of terrible. Furthermore, he has
put bounds to the danger by saying *A plank keeps off death*. After all, it does
keep it off. Homer, however, does not for one moment set a limit to the terror
of the scene, but draws a vivid picture of men continually in peril of their lives,
and often within an ace of perishing with each successive wave. Moreover, he
has in the words *hypek thanatoio*, forced into union, by a kind of unnatural
compulsion, prepositions not usually compounded. He has thus tortured his

line into the similitude of the impending calamity, and by the constriction of the verse has excellently figured the disaster and almost stamped upon the expression the very form and pressure of the danger, *hupek thanatoio pherontai.* This is true also of Archilochus in his account of the shipwreck and of Demosthenes in the passage which begins "It was evening," where he describes the bringing of the news ("On the Crown," 169). The salient points they winnowed, one might say, according to merit and massed them together, inserting in the midst nothing frivolous, mean, or trivial. For these faults mar the effect of the whole, just as though they introduced chinks or fissures into stately and co-ordered edifices, whose walls are compacted by their reciprocal adjustment.

XI

An allied excellence to those already set forth is that which is termed amplification. This figure is employed when the narrative or the course of a forensic argument admits, from section to section, of many starting-points and many pauses, and elevated expressions follow, one after the other, in an unbroken succession and in an ascending order. And this may be effected either by way of the rhetorical treatment of commonplaces, or by way of intensification (whether events or arguments are to be strongly presented), or by the orderly arrangement of facts or of passions; indeed, there are innumerable kinds of amplification. Only, the orator must in every case remember that none of these methods by itself, apart from sublimity, forms a complete whole, unless indeed where pity is to be excited or an opponent to be disparaged. In all other cases of amplification, if you take away the sublime, you will remove as it were the soul from the body. For the vigor of the amplification at once loses its intensity and its substance when not resting on a firm basis of the sublime. Clearness, however, demands that we should define concisely how our present precepts differ from the point under consideration a moment ago, namely the marking-out of the most striking conceptions and the unification of them; and wherein, generally, the sublime differs from amplification.

XII

Now the definition given by the writers on rhetoric does not satisfy me. Amplification is, say they, discourse which invests the subject with grandeur. This definition, however, would surely apply in equal measure to sublimity and passion and figurative language, since they too invest the discourse with a certain degree of grandeur. The point of distinction between them seems to me to be that sublimity consists in elevation, while amplification embraces a multitude of details. Consequently, sublimity is often comprised in a single thought, while amplification is universally associated with a certain magnitude and abundance. Amplification (to sum the matter up in a general way) is an aggregation of all the constituent parts and topics of a subject, lending strength to the argument by dwelling upon it, and differing herein from proof that, while the latter demonstrates the matter under investigation. . . .

XIII

To return from my digression. Although Plato thus flows on with noiseless stream, he is none the less elevated. You know this because you have read the *Republic* and are familiar with his manner. "Those," says he, "who are destitute of wisdom and goodness and are ever present at carousels and the like are carried on the downward path, it seems, and wander thus throughout their life. They never look upwards to the truth, nor do they lift their heads, nor enjoy any pure and lasting pleasure, but like cattle they have their eyes ever cast downwards and bent upon the ground and upon their feeding-places, and they graze and grow fat and breed, and through their insatiate desire of these delights they kick and butt with horns and hoofs of iron and kill one another in their greed" (*Republic* 9. 586a).

This writer shows us, if only we were willing to pay him heed, that another way (beyond anything we have mentioned) leads to the sublime. And what, and what manner of way, may that be? It is the imitation and emulation of previous great poets and writers. And let this, my dear friend, be an aim to which we steadfastly apply ourselves. For many men are carried away by the spirit of others as if inspired, just as it is related of the Pythian priestess when she approaches the tripod, where there is a rift in the ground which (they say) exhales divine vapor. By heavenly power thus communicated she is impregnated and straightway delivers oracles in virtue of the afflatus. Similarly from the great natures of the men of old there are borne in upon the souls of those who emulate them (as from sacred caves) what we may describe as effluences, so that even those who seem little likely to be possessed are thereby inspired and succumb to the spell of the others' greatness. Was Herodotus alone a devoted imitator of Homer? No, Stesichorus even before his time, and Archilochus, and above all Plato, who from the great Homeric source drew to himself innumerable tributary streams. And perhaps we should have found it necessary to prove this, point by point, had not Ammonius and his followers selected and recorded the particulars. This proceeding is not plagiarism; it is like taking an impression from beautiful forms or figures or other works of art. And it seems to me that there would not have been so fine a bloom of perfection on Plato's philosophical doctrines, and that he would not in many cases have found his way to poetical subject-matter and modes of expression, unless he had with all his heart and mind struggled with Homer for the primacy, entering the lists like a young champion matched against the man whom all admire, and showing perhaps too much love of contention and breaking a lance with him as it were, but deriving some profit from the contest none the less. For, as Hesiod says, "This strife is good for mortals" (*Works and Days*, 24). And in truth that struggle for the crown of glory is noble and best deserves the victory in which even to be worsted by one's predecessors brings no discredit.

XIV

Accordingly it is well that we ourselves also, when elaborating anything which requires lofty expression and elevated conception, should shape some idea in our minds as to how perchance Homer would have said this very thing, or how it would have been raised to the sublime by Plato or Demosthenes or by the historian Thucydides. For those personages, presenting themselves to us and inflaming our ardor and as it were illumining our path, will carry our minds in a mysterious way to the high standards of sublimity which are imaged within us. Still more effectual will it be to suggest this question to our thoughts, "What sort of hearing would Homer, had he been present, or Demosthenes have given to this or that when said by me, or how would they have been affected by the other?" For the ordeal is indeed a severe one, if we presuppose such a tribunal and theatre for our own utterances, and imagine that we are undergoing a scrutiny of our writings before these great heroes, acting as judges and witnesses. A greater incentive still will be supplied if you add the question, "In what spirit will each succeeding age listen to me who have written thus?" But if one shrinks from the very thought of uttering aught that may transcend the term of his own life and time, the conceptions of his mind must necessarily be incomplete, blind, and as it were untimely born, since they are by no means brought to the perfection needed to ensure a futurity of fame.

XV

Images, moreover, contribute greatly, my young friend, to dignity, elevation, and power as a pleader. In this sense some call them mental representations. In a general way the name of image or imagination is applied to every idea of the mind, in whatever form it presents itself, which gives birth to speech. But at the present day the word is predominantly used in cases where, carried away by enthusiasm and passion, you think you see what you describe, and you place it before the eyes of your hearers. Further, you will be aware of the fact that an image has one purpose with the orators and another with the poets, and that the design of the poetical image is enthrallment, of the rhetorical—vivid description. Both, however, seek to stir the passions and the emotions.

> Mother!—'beseech thee, hark not thou on me
> Yon maidens gory-eyed and snaky-haired!
> Lo there!—lo there!—they are nigh—they leap on me!
>> (Euripides, *Orestes*, 255, trans. A. S. Way)

And:

> Ah! she will slay me! whither can I fly?
>> (Euripides, *Iphigeneia in Taurus*, 291, trans. A. S. Way)

In these scenes the poet himself saw Furies, and the image in his mind he almost compelled his audience also to behold. Now, Euripides is most assiduous in giving the utmost tragic effect to these two emotions—fits of love and madness. Herein he succeeds more, perhaps, than in any other respect, although he is daring enough to invade all the other regions of the imagination. Notwithstanding that he is by nature anything but elevated, he forces his own genius, in many passages, to tragic heights, and everywhere in the matter of sublimity it is true of him (to adopt Homer's words) that

> The tail of him scourgeth his ribs and his flanks to left and
>> to right,
> And he lasheth himself into frenzy, and spurreth him on to
>> the fight.
>>> (*Iliad* 20.170, trans. A. S. Way)

When the Sun hands the reins to Phaethon, he says

> "Thou, driving, trespass not on Libya's sky,
> Whose heat, by dews untempered, else shall split
> Thy car asunder."

And after that,

> "Speed onward toward the Pleiads seven thy course."
> Thus far the boy heard; then he snatched the reins:
> He lashed the flanks of that wing-wafted team;
> Loosed rein; and they through folds of cloudland soared.
> Hard after on a fiery star his sire
> Rode, counseling his son—"Ho! thither drive!
> Hither thy car turn—hither!"

Would you not say that the soul of the writer enters the chariot at the same moment as Phaethon and shares in his dangers and in the rapid flight of his steeds? For it could never have conceived such a picture had it not been borne in no less swift career on that journey through the heavens. The same is true of the words which Euripides attributes to his Cassandra:—

> O chariot-loving Trojans.

Aeschylus, too, ventures on images of a most heroic stamp. An example will be found in his *Seven against Thebes*, where he says

> For seven heroes, squadron-captains fierce,
> Over a black-rimmed shield have slain a bull,
> And, dipping in the bull's blood each his hand,
> By Ares and Enyo, and by Panic
> Lover of blood, have sworn.
>
> *(Seven Against Thebes, 42, trans. A. S. Way)*

In mutual fealty they devoted themselves by that joint oath to a relentless doom. Sometimes, however, he introduces ideas that are rough-hewn and uncouth and harsh; and Euripides, when stirred by the spirit of emulation, comes perilously near the same fault, even in spite of his own natural bent. Thus in Aeschylus the palace of Lycurgus at the coming of Dionysus is strangely represented as possessed:—

> A frenzy thrills the hall; the roofs are bacchant
> With ecstasy:
>
> (Trans. A. S. Way)

an idea which Euripides has echoed, in other words, it is true, and with some abatement of its crudity, where he says:—

> The whole mount shared their bacchic ecstasy.
>
> *(Bacchae, 726, trans. A. S. Way)*

Magnificent are the images which Sophocles has conceived of the death of Oedipus, who makes ready his burial amid the portents of the sky (*Oedipus at Colonus*, 1586, trans. A. S. Way). Magnificent, too, is the passage where the Greeks are on the point of sailing away and Achilles appears above his tomb to those who are putting out to sea—a scene which I doubt whether anyone has depicted more vividly than Simonides. But it is impossible to cite all the examples that present themselves. It is no doubt true that those which are found in the poets contain, as I said, a tendency to exaggeration in the way of the fabulous and that they transcend in every way the credible, but in oratorical imagery the best feature is always its reality and truth. Whenever the form of a speech is poetical and fabulous and breaks into every kind of impossibility, such digressions have a strange and alien air. For example, the clever orators forsooth of our day, like the tragedians, see Furies, and—fine fellows that they are—cannot even understand that Orestes when he cries

> Unhand me!—of mine Haunting Fiends thou art—
> Dost grip my waist to hurl me into hell!
>
> (Euripides, Orestes, 264, trans. A. S. Way)

has these fancies because he is mad. What, then, can oratorical imagery effect? Well, it is able in many ways to infuse vehemence and passion into spoken words, while more particularly when it is combined with the argumentative passages it not only persuades the hearer but actually makes him its slave. Here is an example. "Why, if at this very moment," says Demosthenes, "a loud cry were to be heard in front of the courts, and we were told that the prison-house lies open and the prisoners are in full flight, no one, whether he be old or young, is so heedless as not to lend aid to the utmost of his power; aye, and if any one came forward and said that yonder stands the man who let them go, the offender would be promptly put to death without a hearing" (*Against Timocrates*, 208). In the same way, too, Hyperides on being accused, after he had proposed the liberation of the slaves subsequently to the great defeat, said, "This proposal was framed, not by the orator, but by the battle of Chaeroneia." The speaker has here at one and the same time followed a train of reasoning and indulged a flight of imagination. He has, therefore, passed the bounds of mere persuasion by the boldness of his conception. By a sort of natural law in all such matters we always attend to whatever possesses superior force; whence it is that we are drawn away from demonstration pure and simple to any startling image within whose dazzling brilliancy the argument lies concealed. And it is not unreasonable that we should be affected in this way, for when two things are brought together, the more powerful always attracts to itself the virtue of the weaker. It will be enough to have said thus much with regard to examples of the sublime in thought, when produced by greatness of soul, imitation, or imagery.

XVI

Here, however, in due order comes the place assigned to Figures; for they, if handled in the proper manner, will contribute, as I have said, in no mean degree to sublimity. But since to treat thoroughly of them all at the present moment would be a great, or rather an endless task, we will now, with the object of proving our proposition, run over a few only of those which produce elevation of diction. Demosthenes is bringing forward a reasoned vindication of his public policy. What was the natural way of treating the subject? It was this. "You were not wrong, you who engaged in the struggle for the freedom of Greece. You have domestic warrant for it. For the warriors of Marathon did no wrong, nor they of Salamis, nor they of Plataea." When, however, as though suddenly inspired by heaven and as it were frenzied by the God of Prophecy, he utters his famous oath by the champions of Greece ("assuredly ye did no wrong; I swear it by those who at Marathon stood in the forefront of the danger," ("On the Crown" 208)), in the public view by this one Figure of Adjuration, which I here term Apostrophe, he deifies his ancestors. He brings home the thought that we ought to swear by those who have thus nobly died as we swear by Gods, and he fills the mind of the judges with the high spirit of those who there bore the brunt of the danger, and he has transformed the natural course of the argument into transcendent sublimity and passion and that secure belief which rests upon strange and prodigious oaths. He instills into the minds of his hearers the conviction—which acts as a medicine and an antidote—that they should, uplifted by these eulogies, feel no less proud of the fight against Philip than of the triumph at Marathon and Salamis. By all these means he carries his hearers clean away with him through the employment of a single figure. It is said, indeed, that the germ of the oath is found in Eupolis:—

> For, by the fight I won at Marathon,
> No one shall vex my soul and rue it not.

But it is not sublime to swear by a person in any chance way; the sublimity depends upon the place and the manner and the circumstances and the motive. Now in the passage of Eupolis there is nothing but the mere oath, addressed to the Athenians when still prosperous and in no need of comfort. Furthermore, the poet in his oath has not made divinities of the men in order so to create in his hearers a worthy conception of their valor, but he has wandered away from those who stood in the forefront of the danger to an inanimate thing—the fight. In Demosthenes the oath is framed for vanquished men, with the intention that Chaeroneia should no longer appear a failure to the Athenians. He gives them at one and the same time, as I remarked, a demonstration that they have done no wrong, an example, the sure evidence of oaths, a eulogy, an exhortation. And since the orator was likely to be confronted with the objection, "You are speaking of the defeat which has attended your administration, and yet you swear by victories," in what follows he consequently measures even individual words, and chooses them unerringly, showing that even in the revels of the imagination sobriety is required. "Those," he says, "who stood in the forefront of the danger at Marathon, and those who fought by sea at Salamis and Artemisium, and those who stood in the ranks at Plataea." Nowhere does he use the word "conquered," but at every turn he has evaded any indication of the result, since it was fortunate and the opposite of what happened at Chaeroneia. So he at once rushes forward and carries his hearer off his feet. "All of whom," says he, "were accorded a public burial by the state, Aeschines, and not the successful only. . . ."

XVIII

But, what are we next to say of questions and interrogations? Is it not precisely by the visualizing qualities of these figures that Demosthenes strives to make his speeches far more effective and impressive? "Pray tell me,—tell me, you sir,—do you wish to go about and inquire of one another, Is there any news? Why, what greater news could there be than this, that a Macedonian is subduing Greece? Is Philip dead? No; but he is ill. Dead or ill, what difference to you? Should anything happen to him, you will speedily create another Philip" (*Philippic* 1, 10). Again he says, "Let us sail against Macedonia. Where shall we find a landing-place? someone asks. The war itself will discover the weak places in Philip's position" (*Philippic* 1, 44). All this, if stated plainly and directly, would have been altogether weaker. As it is, the excitement, and the rapid play of question and answer, and the plan of meeting his own objections as though they were urged by another, have by the help of the figure made the language used not only more elevated but also more convincing. For an exhibition of passion has a greater effect when it seems not to be studied by the speaker himself but to be inspired by the occasion; and questions asked and answered by oneself simulate a natural outburst of passion. For just as those who are interrogated by others experience a sudden excitement and answer the inquiry incisively and with the utmost candor, so the figure of question and answer leads the hearer to suppose that each deliberate thought is struck out and uttered on the spur of the moment, and so beguiles his reason. We may further quote that passage of Herodotus which is regarded as one of the most elevated: "if thus . . ."

XIX

The words issue forth without connecting links and are poured out as it were, almost outstripping the speaker himself. "Locking their shields," says Xenophon, "they thrust fought slew fell" (*Hellenica* IV. 3, 19). And so with the words of Eurylochus:—

> We passed, as thou badst, Odysseus, midst twilight of oak-
> trees round.

> There amidst of the forest-glens a beautiful palace we
>   found.

(Odyssey 10. 251–52, trans. A. S. Way)

For the lines detached from one another, but none the less hurried along, produce the impression of an agitation which interposes obstacles and at the same time adds impetuosity. This result Homer has produced by the omission of conjunctions.

XX

A powerful effect usually attends the union of figures for a common object, when two or three mingle together as it were in partnership, and contribute a fund of strength, persuasiveness, beauty. Thus, in the speech against Meidias, examples will be found of asyndeton, interwoven with instances of anaphora and diatyposis. "For the smiter can do many things (some of which the sufferer cannot even describe to another) by attitude, by look, by voice" (*Against Midias*, 72). Then, in order that the narrative may not, as it advances, continue in the same groove (for continuance betokens tranquillity, while passion—the transport and commotion of the soul—sets order at defiance), straightway he hurries off to other Asyndeta and Repetitions. "By attitude, by look, by voice, when he acts with insolence, when he acts like an enemy, when he smites with his fists, when he smites you like a slave." By these words the orator produces the same effect as the assailant—he strikes the mind of the judges by the swift succession of blow on blow. Starting from this point again, as suddenly as a gust of wind, he makes another attack. "When smitten with blows of fists," he says, "when smitten upon the cheek. These things stir the blood, these drive men beyond themselves, when unused to insult. No one can, in describing them, convey a notion of the indignity they imply." So he maintains throughout, though with continual variation, the essential character of the Repetitions and Asyndeta. In this way, with him, order is disorderly, and on the other hand disorder contains a certain element of order.

XXI

Come now, add, if you please, in these cases connecting particles after the fashion of the followers of Isocrates. "Furthermore, this fact too must not be overlooked that the smiter may do many things, first by attitude, then by look, then again by the mere voice." You will feel, if you transcribe the passage in this orderly fashion, that the rugged impetuosity of passion, once you make it smooth and equable by adding the copulatives, falls pointless and immediately loses all its fire. Just as the binding of the limbs of runners deprives them of their power of rapid motion, so also passion, when shackled by connecting links and other appendages, chafes at the restriction, for it loses the freedom of its advance and its rapid emission as though from an engine of war.

XXII

Hyperbata, or inversions, must be placed under the same category. They are departures in the order of expressions or ideas from the natural sequence; and they bear, it may be said, the very stamp and impress of vehement emotion. Just as those who are really moved by anger, or fear, or indignation, or jealousy, or any other emotion (for the passions are many and countless, and none can give their number), at times turn aside, and when they have taken one thing as their subject often leap to another, foisting in the midst some irrelevant matter, and then again wheel round to their original theme, and driven by their ve-hemence, as by a veering wind, now this way now that with rapid changes, transform their expressions, their thoughts, the order suggested by a natural sequence, into numberless variations of every kind; so also among the best writers it is by means of hyberbaton that imitation approaches the effects of nature. For art is perfect when it seems to be nature, and nature hits the mark when she contains art hidden within her. We may illustrate by the words of Dionysius of Phocaea in Herodotus. "Our fortunes lie on a razor's edge, men of Ionia; for freedom or for bondage, and that the bondage of runaway slaves. Now, therefore, if you choose to submit to hardships, you will have toil for the moment, but you will be able to overcome your foes" (*Histories*, 11). Here the natural order would have been: "Men of Ionia, now is the time for you to meet hardships; for our fortunes lie on a razor's edge." But the speaker postpones the words "Men of Ionia." He starts at once with the danger of the situation, as though in such imminent peril he had no time at all to address his hearers. Moreover, he inverts the order of ideas. For instead of saying that they ought to endure hardships, which is the real object of his exhortation, he first assigns the reason because of which they ought to endure hardships, in the words "our fortunes lie on a razor's edge." The result is that what he says seems not to be premeditated but to be prompted by the necessities of the moment. In a still higher degree Thucydides is most bold and skilful in disjoining from one an-other by means of transpositions things that are by nature intimately united and indivisible. Demosthenes is not so masterful as Thucydides, but of all writers he most abounds in this kind of figure, and through his use of hyperbata makes a great impression of vehemence, yes and of unpremeditated speech, and more-over draws his hearers with him into all the perils of his long inversions. For he will often leave in suspense the thought which he has begun to express, and meanwhile he will heap, into a position seemingly alien and unnatural, one thing upon another parenthetically and from any external source whatsoever, throwing his hearer into alarm lest the whole structure of his words should fall to pieces, and compelling him in anxious sympathy to share the peril of the speaker; and then unexpectedly, after a long interval, he adds the long-awaited conclusion at the right place, namely the end, and produces a far greater effect by this very use, so bold and hazardous, of hyperbaton. Examples may be spared because of their abundance.

XXIII

The figures, which are termed polyptota—accumulations, and variations, and climaxes—are excellent weapons of public oratory, as you are aware, and contribute to elegance and to every form of sublimity and passion. Again, how greatly do changes of cases, tenses, persons, numbers, genders, diversify and enliven exposition. Where the use of numbers is concerned, I would point out that style is not adorned only or chiefly by those words which are, as far as their forms go, in the singular but in meaning are, when examined, found to be plural: as in the lines

> A countless crowd forthright
> Far-ranged along the beaches were clamoring "Thunny
>   [tunny—ed.] in sight!"

The fact is more worthy of observation that in certain cases the use of the plural (for the singular) falls with still more imposing effect and impresses us by the very sense of multitude which the number conveys. Such are the words of Oedipus in Sophocles:

> O nuptials, nuptials,
> Ye gendered me, and, having gendered, brought
> To light the selfsame seed, and so revealed
> Sires, brothers, sons, in one—all kindred blood!—
> Brides, mothers, wives, in one!—yea, whatso deeds
> Most shameful among humankind are done.
> (Oedipus Tyrannus, 1403, trans. A. S. Way)

The whole enumeration can be summed up in a single proper name—on the one side Oedipus, on the other Jocasta. None the less, the expansion of the number into the plural helps to pluralize the misfortunes as well. There is a similar instance of multiplication in the line:—

> Forth Hectors and Sarpedons marching came,

and in that passage of Plato concerning the Athenians which we have quoted elsewhere. "For no Pelopes, nor Cadmi, nor Aegypti and Danai, nor the rest of the crowd of born foreigners dwell with us, but ours is the land of pure Greeks, free from foreign admixture," etc. (*Menexenus* 245d). For naturally a theme seems more imposing to the ear when proper names are thus added, one upon the other, in troops. But this must only be done in cases in which the subject admits of amplification or redundancy or exaggeration or passion—one or more of these—since we all know that a richly caparisoned style is extremely pretentious.

XXIV

Further (to take the converse case) particulars which are combined from the plural into the singular are sometimes most elevated in appearance. "Thereafter," says Demosthenes, "all Peloponnesus was at variance" ("On the Crown," 18). "And when Phrynichus had brought out a play entitled the *Capture of Miletus*, the whole theatre burst into tears (*Histories*, 21). For the compression of the number from multiplicity into unity gives more fully the feeling of a single body. In both cases the explanation of the elegance of expression is, I think, the same. Where the words are singular, to make them plural is the mark of unlooked-for passion; and where they are plural, the rounding of a number of things into a fine-sounding singular is surprising owing to the converse change.

XXV

If you introduce things which are past as present and now taking place, you will make your story no longer a narration but an actuality. Xenophon furnishes an illustration. "A man," says he, "has fallen under Cyrus' horse, and being trampled strikes the horse with his sword in the belly. He rears and unseats Cyrus, who falls" (Xenophon, *Cyropaideia* 7.1.37). This construction is specially characteristic of Thucydides.

XXVI

In like manner the interchange of persons produces a vivid impression, and often makes the hearer feel that he is moving in the midst of perils:—

> Thou hadst said that with toil unspent, and all unwasted of
> limb,

They closed in the grapple of war, so fiercely they rushed to
the fray;

(*Iliad* 15. 697)

and the line of Aratus:—

Never in that month launch thou forth amid lashing seas.

So also Herodotus: "From the city of Elephantine thou shalt sail upwards,
and then shalt come to a level plain; and after crossing this tract, thou shalt
embark upon another vessel and sail for two days, and then shalt thou come to
a great city whose name is Meroe" (Herodotus, *Histories*, 2. 29). Do you observe,
my friend, how he leads you in imagination through the region and makes you
see what you hear? All such cases of direct personal address place the hearer
on the very scene of action. So it is when you seem to be speaking, not to all
and sundry, but to a single individual:—

But Tydeides—thou wouldst not have known him, for
whom that hero fought.

(*Iliad* 5. 85)

You will make your hearer more excited and more attentive, and full of active
participation, if you keep him on the alert by words addressed to himself.

XXVII

There is further the case in which a writer, when relating something about a
person, suddenly breaks off and converts himself into that selfsame person. This
species of figure is a kind of outburst of passion:

Then with a far-ringing shout to the Trojans Hector cried,
Bidding them rush on the ships, bidding leave the spoils
blood-dyed—
And whomso I mark from the galleys aloof on the farther
side,
I will surely devise his death.

(*Iliad* 15. 346, trans. A. S. Way)

The poet assigns the task of narration, as is fit, to himself, but the abrupt
threat he suddenly, with no note of warning, attributes to the angered chief. He
would have been frigid had he inserted the words, "Hector said so and so." As
it is, the swift transition of the narrative has outstripped the swift transitions of

the narrator. Accordingly this figure should be used by preference when a sharp crisis does not suffer the writer to tarry, but constrains him to pass at once from one person to another. An example will be found in Hecataeus: "Ceyx treated the matter gravely, and straightway bade the descendants of Heracles depart; for I am not able to succor you. In order, therefore, that ye may not perish yourselves and injure me, get you gone to some other country." Demosthenes in dealing with Aristogeiton has, somewhat differently, employed this variation of person to betoken the quick play of emotion. "And will none of you," he asks, "be found to be stirred by loathing or even by anger at the violent deeds of this vile and shameless fellow, who—you whose license of speech, most abandoned of men, is not confined by barriers nor by doors, which might perchance be opened!" (*Against Aristogiton* 1, 27) With the sense thus incomplete, he suddenly breaks off and in his anger almost tears asunder a single expression into two persons,—"he who, O thou most abandoned!" Thus, although he has turned aside his address and seems to have left Aristogeiton, yet through passion he directs it upon him with far greater force. Similarly with the words of Penelope:—

> Herald, with what behest art thou come from the suitor-
>   band?
> To give to the maids of Odysseus the godlike their com-
>   mand
> To forsake their labors, and yonder for them the banquet to
>   lay?
> I would that of all their wooing this were the latest day,
> That this were the end of your banquets, your uttermost
>   reveling-hour,
> Ye that assemble together and all our substance devour,
> The wise Telemachus' store, as though ye never had heard,
> In the days overpast of your childhood, your fathers' prais-
>   ing word,
> How good Odysseus was.
>
> (*Odyssey* 4. 681–89, trans. A. S. Way)

XXVIII

As to whether or no Periphrasis contributes to the sublime, no one, I think, will hesitate. For just as in music the so-called accompaniments bring out the charm of the melody, so also periphrasis often harmonizes with the normal expression and adds greatly to its beauty, especially if it has a quality which is not inflated and dissonant but pleasantly tempered. Plato will furnish an instance in proof at the opening of his Funeral Oration. "In truth they have gained from us their rightful tribute, in the enjoyment of which they proceed along their destined path, escorted by their country publicly, and privately each by his kinsmen" (*Menexenus* 236d). Death he calls "their destined path," and the tribute of accustomed rites he calls "being escorted publicly by their fatherland." Is it in a slight degree only that he has magnified the conception by the use of these words? Has he not rather, starting with unadorned diction, made it musical, and shed over it like a harmony the melodious rhythm which comes from periphrasis? And Xenophon says, "You regard toil as the guide to a joyous life. You have garnered in your souls the goodliest of all possessions and the fittest for warriors. For you rejoice more in praise than in all else" (*Cyropaideia* 1.5.12). In using, instead of "you are willing to toil," the words "you deem toil the guide to a joyous life," and in expanding the rest of the sentence in like manner, he has annexed to his eulogy a lofty idea. And so with that inimitable phrase of Herodotus: "The goddess afflicted those Scythians who had pillaged the temple with an unsexing malady" (*Histories* 1. 105. 4).

XXIX

A hazardous business, however, eminently hazardous is periphrasis, unless it be handled with discrimination; otherwise it speedily falls flat, with its odor of empty talk and its swelling amplitude. This is the reason why Plato (who is always strong in figurative language, and at times unseasonably so) is taunted because in his Laws he says that "neither gold nor silver treasure should be allowed to establish itself and abide in the city" (*Laws* 801b). The critic says that, if he had been forbidding the possession of cattle, he would obviously have spoken of ovine and bovine treasure. But our parenthetical disquisition with regard to the use of figures as bearing upon the sublime has run to sufficient length, dear Terentianus; for all these things lend additional passion and animation to style, and passion is as intimately allied with sublimity as sketches of character with entertainment. . . .

6

SNORRI STURLUSON (1178–1241)

In 2002, a tourist could sign up for a "Snorri Sturlusson Saga Tour—History and Horses," described in seductive terms as "a mix of history and natural wonder on a ride through an area that is also important to the ancient arts of Icelandic writing." (His name appears variously as Snorri or Snorre, Sturluson, Sturlusson, or Sturlason.)

Snorri is the most valuable personage in Old Icelandic literature, and it is thanks to him that many texts were preserved. He was a conscientious historian and antiquarian. The *Prose Edda* includes the "Skáldskaparmál" (on poetic diction, especially as applied to divine beings) and the "Háttatal" (on meter). Medieval documents illuminate the practice and status of poets in all old Germanic cultures, since they all used the same devices and materials in their poetry. Old English poetry robustly participates in the medieval Germanic traditions represented by Snorri's writings. Iceland, remote and conservative, preserved many traits of medieval language and literature long after they had been outgrown or abandoned by Germanic peoples in Britain and on the continent. A kinship with Iceland persisted from the Middle Ages through the work of William Morris in the nineteenth century and W. H. Auden in the twentieth. An acquaintance with medieval Germanic poetry— with its runes, charms, riddles, and fabulous stories of heroes, monsters, and so forth—helps the modern reader to appreciate the roots of modern fictions by

J. R. R. Tolkien and J. K. Rowling, to say nothing of science fiction, much of which has looked into the future and found mostly medieval stories of saber-swinging knights and blood feuds. Another modern repository of recycled medieval lore is the group of musical dramas by Richard Wagner, many of which are based on legends from Iceland and elsewhere. Wagner's *Ring of the Nibelung* even employs an alliterative style that Snorri would probably have found congenial.

SKÁLDSKAPARMÁL (POETIC DICTION; CA. A.D. 1225)

Adapted from Snorri Sturluson, *The Prose Edda*, trans. Arthur Gilchrist Brodeur (New York: The American-Scandinavian Foundation, 1916).

ÆGIR PLAYS HOST TO THE ÆSIR

There was a man called Ægir or Hlér, who lived on the island now known as Hlésey [or Læsö]. He was very skilled in magic. He went on an expedition to Asgarð to visit the Æsir, who foresaw his journey and made him welcome, although they also worked a good many spells for him. When drinking-time in the evening came round, Óðin had swords brought into the hall and they were so bright that they illuminated it, and no other lights were used while the drinking went on.

Then the Æsir held festival, and twelve, that is those Æsir who had to be judges, sat down in their high seats. Their names are as follows: Thór, Njörð, Frey, Týr, Heimdall, Bragi, Víðar, Válí, Ull, Hœnir, Forseti, Loki; the goddesses who did likewise were Frigg, Freyja, Gefjon, Idunn, Gerð, Sigyn, Fulla, Nanna. Everything he saw there seemed splendidly lavish to Ægir. All the paneling was covered with fine shields. Moreover the mead was heady and a great deal of it was drunk. Bragi sat next Ægir and they occupied themselves in drinking and exchanging stories. Bragi told Ægir many tales about the doings of the gods.

THJAZI THE GIANT KIDNAPS IDUNN

He began relating how once three Æsir, Óðin, Loki and Hœnir, had left home and traveled over mountains and desert places without any provisions. Coming down into a valley they saw a herd of oxen and took one and set about cooking it. When they thought it was ready and scattered the fire, it was not done.

Some time later when they scattered the fire for a second time and it was [still] uncooked, they began to discuss amongst themselves what could be the cause. Then they heard a voice from an oak tree above them say that what was sitting up there was preventing their meat from being done. They looked up and saw an eagle sitting there, and it wasn't a small one.

The eagle said: "If you give me my fill of the ox, then your meat will get done."

They agreed to this. Then it sailed down from the tree and settling on the meat snatched up at once, without any hesitation, two of the thighs and both the shoulders of the ox.

At that Loki grew angry and catching up a great stick and thrusting with all his might he drove it into the eagle's body. The eagle recoiled from the blow and flew up into the air with one end of the stick stuck firmly in its back and Loki clinging to the other. The eagle was flying only just high enough for Loki's feet to be dragging along stones and scree and bushes, and he thought his arms would be pulled from their sockets. He called out imploring the eagle for mercy but it replied that it would not let Loki go unless he swore an oath to bring it Idunn and her apples out of Asgarð. Loki was willing so he was released and went back to his companions, and no more is told of their journey on this occasion until they came home.

At the time agreed on, Loki enticed Idunn out from Asgarð into a wood, telling her that he had found some apples she would prize greatly and asking her to bring her own with her for comparison. Then the giant Thjazi came there in the form of an eagle, and seizing Idunn flew away with her to his house in Thrymheim.

LOKI TRICKS IDUNN AND HELPS THJAZI

The Æsir, however, were much dismayed at Idunn's disappearance, and they soon grew old and gray-haired. They held an assembly and asked one another when Idunn had last been heard of, and realized that the last time she had been seen she was going out of Asgarð with Loki. Then Loki was captured and brought to the assembly and threatened with death or torture. He grew so frightened that he said he would go after Idunn into Giantland, if Freyja would lend him her falcon coat.

When he got the falcon coat, he flew north to Giantland. Loki arrived at the giant Thjazi's on a day when he had gone out rowing on the sea and Idunn was at home alone. Loki changed her into the form of a nut, and holding her in his claws flew off at top speed. When Thjazi came home, however, and saw that Idunn was missing, he assumed the shape of an eagle and flew after Loki, with a tremendous rush of air in his wake. The Æsir, seeing the falcon flying with the nut and the eagle in pursuit, went out under the walls of Asgarð carrying bundles of plane shavings. When the falcon reached the stronghold, he dropped plumb down at the fortress wall and then the Æsir set fire to the plane shavings. The eagle, however, was unable to check his course when he lost the falcon and his feathers caught fire and then he did stop. The Æsir were hard by then and they killed the giant Thjazi inside the gates, and that slaying is very famous.

Now giant Thjazi's daughter Skaði took helmet, coat-of-mail and a complete outfit of weapons and went to Asgarð to avenge her father. The Æsir, however, offered her compensation and damages, and first that she should choose a husband from amongst the Æsir and choose him by his feet without seeing any more of him.

Then she saw a very beautiful pair of feet and said: "I choose this one; there's not much that's ugly about Baldr!"

But that was Njörð of Nóatún.

A further condition was that the Æsir should make her laugh—which she thought would be impossible. When Loki, however, by his tricks succeeded in doing this their reconciliation was complete. . . .

We are told that (Óðin [further] compensated her by taking Thjazi's eyes and throwing them up into the sky, making of them two stars.

Then Ægir said: "It seems to me that Thjazi was very powerful. What family did he come from?"

Bragi replied: "His father was called Ölvaldi and you would find it interesting if I told you about him. He possessed a great deal of gold and when he died and his sons were going to divide the inheritance, they allotted the gold they were sharing between them in this way: each was to take the same-sized mouthfuls of it. Thjazi was one of them, Iði the second, and Gang the third. So now we have the expression by which we call gold the mouthful of these giants, and we conceal it in runes or poetry by calling it their speech or words or reckoning."

Ægir asked again: "Where did the accomplishment known as poetry come from?"

Bragi answered: "The beginning of it was that the gods were at war with the people known as the Vanir and they arranged for a peace-meeting between them and made a truce in this way: they both went up to a crock and spat into it. When they were going away, the gods took the truce token and would not allow it to be lost, and made of it a man. He was called Kvasir. He is so wise that nobody asks him any question he is unable to answer.

"He traveled far and wide over the world to teach men wisdom and came once to feast with some dwarfs, Fjalar and Galar. These called him aside for a word in private and killed him, letting his blood run into two crocks and one kettle. The kettle was called Óðrörir, but the crocks were known as Són and Boðn. They mixed his blood with honey, and it became the mead which makes whoever drinks of it a poet or scholar. The dwarfs told the Æsir that Kvasir had choked with learning, because there was no one sufficiently well informed to compete with him in knowledge.

"Then the dwarfs invited a giant called Gilling to their home with his wife, and they asked him to go out rowing on the sea with them. When they were far out, however, the dwarfs rowed on to a rock and upset the boat. Gilling could not swim and was drowned, but the dwarfs righted their craft and rowed ashore. They told his wife about this accident and she was very distressed and wept aloud. Fjalar asked her if she would be easier in her mind about it if she looked out to sea in the direction of where he had been drowned. She wanted to do this. Then he spoke with his brother Galar, telling him to climb up above the door when she was going out and let a millstone fall on to her head; he said he was tired of her wailing. Galar did so.

"When Gilling's son, Suttung, heard of this, he went to the dwarfs and seized them and took them out to sea and put them on to a skerry covered by the tide.[1] They begged Suttung to spare their lives offering him as compensation for his father the precious mead, and that brought about their reconciliation. Suttung took the mead home and hid it in a place called Hnitbjörg and he appointed his daughter Gunnlöð as its guardian. This is why we call poetry Kvasir's blood, or dwarfs' drink: or intoxication, or some sort of liquid of Óðrörir or Boðn or Són, or dwarfs' ship, because it was that mead which ransomed them from death on the skerry, or Suttung's mead or Hnitibjörg's sea."

Then Ægir spoke: "It seems to me that to call poetry by these names obscures things. How did the Æsir acquire Suttung's mead?"

HOW ODIN WON THE MEAD

Bragi answered: "The story goes that Óðin left home once and came across nine serfs mowing hay. He asked if they would like him to sharpen their scythes and they said they would. So he took a hone from his belt and put an edge on their tools and they all thought they cut much better and wanted to buy the hone. He stipulated that the would-be purchaser should pay for it by giving a

---

1. Skerry [a Scandinavian word surviving in parts of Scotland once under Scandinavian domination]: "A rugged insulated sea-rock or stretch of rocks, covered by the sea at high water or in stormy weather; a reef" (OED).

banquet. They replied they were all willing to do this and asked him to hand it over to them. He threw the hone up into the air, however, and as they all wanted to catch it, it ended with them all cutting one another's throats with their scythes.

"Óðin sought lodgings for the night with Suttung's brother, a giant called Baugi. Baugi said that his affairs were in a bad way; he told him that nine of his serfs had been killed and said that he had no hope of finding any other laborers. Óðin, giving his name as Bölverk, offered to do the work of nine men for Baugi, and asked as wages one drink of Suttung's mead. Baugi told him that he had nothing to do with the mead, adding that Suttung was anxious to keep it under his sole control, but he professed himself willing to go along with Bölverk to try to get hold of it.

"That summer Bölverk did the work of nine men for Baugi, and when winter came he asked Baugi for his wages. Then they both went to Suttung. Baugi told his brother Suttung of his bargain with Bölverk, but Suttung flatly refused them a single drop of mead. Then Bölverk said to Baugi that they must try to get hold of the mead by some kind of trick. Baugi said that that was a good idea. Bölverk then brought out the auger called Rati and said that if the auger would pierce it, Baugi was to bore a hole through the mountain. He did so. When Baugi said that the mountain had been pierced through, Bölverk blew into the hole left by the auger but chips flew up into his face. He realized then that Baugi wanted to cheat him, and told him to bore right through. Baugi bored again, and when Bölverk blew into the hole for the second time the chips were blown [all the way] through. Then Bölverk changed himself into a serpent and crawled into the auger-hole. Baugi stabbed at him with the auger but missed him.

"Bölverk came to where Gunrlöð was, and slept with her for three nights, and then she promised him three drinks of the mead. At his first drink he drank up all that was in Óðrörir, at his second, Boðn, and at his third, Són—and then he had finished all the mead. Then he changed himself into an eagle and flew away at top speed.

"When Suttung saw the eagle in flight, however, he also took on eagle shape and flew after him. Now when the Æsir saw where Óðin was flying, they put their crocks out in the courtyard, and when Óðin came inside Asgarð he spat the mead into the crocks. It was such a close shave that Suttung did not catch him, however, that he let some fall, but no one bothered about that. Anyone who wanted could have it; we call it the poetasters' share. Óðin gave Suttung's mead to the Æsir and those men who can compose poetry. So we call poetry Óðin's catch, Óðin's discovery, his drink and his gift, and the drink: of the Æsir."

7

SIR PHILIP SIDNEY (1554–1586)

Sidney was born at Penshurst Place, in Kent, which can still be visited today, 450 years after Sidney's birth. He attended Oxford briefly during his mid-teens and then traveled as a courtier, soldier, and diplomat. He belonged to a most distinguished family of public servants and was himself an up-and-coming member of Queen Elizabeth's court until a difference of religious opinion in 1580 resulted in his temporary banishment from the royal circle. In a brief but concentrated burst of creativity, he wrote dozens of poems as well as the first important critical text in English (it bore two titles in its posthumous editions: *The Defence of Poesie* and *An Apologie for Poetrie*; some adherents prefer to combine the titles into *The Defence of Poetry*). At about the same time, Sidney wrote a celebrated pastoral romance that mixes prose and poetry, the *Arcadia*.

He was engaged to Penelope Devereux, who became the model for Stella in the great sonnet sequence *Astrophil and Stella*. She married someone else in 1581, and in 1583 Sidney married Frances Walsingham. By this time he was back in royal favor, enough to be sent to the Continent as governor of Flushing in the Low Countries. He was wounded in battle and died of gangrene, at age thirty-two.

Sidney's work, written around 1583 but not published until 1595 (by two different publishers using two different titles: *The Defense of Poesie* and *An Apologie for Poetrie* with slightly different texts), stands head and shoulders above any such thing published in the sixteenth century and ranks with the greatest critical arguments in English. Others at the time were writing limited treatises, often in Latin, about rhetoric, prosody, diction, or language. Sidney produced, in clear robust English, a reasoned and sustained argument, rather like a defense speech in a court of law and not much like a feeble apology, unless that title can suggest ironic mock-humility. Sidney shows a breadth of learning and a depth of passion seldom matched by any critic in any language. He knew the classics, but he also knew the vernacular ballads of his own nation. Like Horace, he was himself a poet, but he mostly used his poetry for things other than criticism. (One of his sonnets does include the famous injunction from the Muse: "Look in thy heart and write.")

THE DEFENCE OF POESY (CA. 1583)

The text used here is from *An Apologie for Poetrie*, ed. Edward Arber (London, 1858), with additional material from *Sidney's Apologie for Poetrie*, ed. J. Churton Collins (Oxford, 1907) and *The Defense of Poesy*, ed. A. S. Cook (Boston, 1890).

When the right virtuous Edward Wotton and I were at the Emperor's [Maximilian II] court together, we gave ourselves to learn horsemanship of John Pietro Pugliano, one that with great commendation had the place of an esquire in his stable; and he, according to the fertileness of the Italian wit, did not only afford us the demonstration of his practice, but sought to enrich our minds with the contemplations therein which he thought most precious. But with none I remember mine ears were at any time more loaded, than when—either angered with slow payment, or moved with our learner-like admiration—he exercised his speech in the praise of his faculty. He said soldiers were the noblest estate of mankind, and horsemen the noblest of soldiers. He said they were the masters of war and ornaments of peace, speedy goers and strong abiders, triumphers both in camps and courts. Nay, to so unbelieved a point he proceeded, as that no earthly thing bred such wonder to a prince as to be a good horseman; skill of government was but a *pedanteria* [pedantry—ed.] in comparison. Then would he add certain praises, by telling what a peerless beast the horse was, the only serviceable courtier without flattery, the beast of most beauty, faithfulness, courage, and such more, that if I had not been a piece of a logician before I came to him, I think he would have persuaded me to have wished myself a horse. But thus much at least with his no few words he drove into me, that self-love is better than any gilding to make that seem gorgeous wherein ourselves be parties.

Wherein if Pugliano's strong affection and weak arguments will not satisfy you, I will give you a nearer example of myself, who, I know not by what mischance, in these my not old years and idlest times, having slipped into the title of a poet, am provoked to say something unto you in the defense of that my unelected vocation, which if I handle with more good will than good reasons, bear with me, since the scholar is to be pardoned that follows the steps of his master. And yet I must say that, as I have just cause to make a pitiful defense of poor poetry, which from almost the highest estimation of learning is fallen to be the laughing-stock of children, so have I need to bring some more available proofs, since the former is by no man barred of his deserved credit, the silly [weak—ed.] latter has had even the names of philosophers used to the defacing of it, with great danger of civil war among the Muses.

And first, truly, to all them that, professing learning, inveigh against poetry, may justly be objected that they go very near to ungratefulness, to seek to deface that which, in the noblest nations and languages that are known, has been the first light-giver to ignorance, and first nurse, whose milk by little and little enabled them to feed afterwards of tougher knowledges. And will they now play the hedgehog, that, being received into the den, drove out his host? Or rather the vipers, that with their birth kill their parents? Let learned Greece in any of her manifold sciences be able to show me one book before Musæus, Homer, and Hesiod, all three nothing else but poets. Nay, let any history be brought that can say any writers were there before them, if they were not men of the same skill, as Orpheus, Linus, and some other are named, who, having been the first of that country that made pens deliver of their knowledge to their posterity, may justly challenge to be called their fathers in learning. For not only in time they had this priority—although in itself antiquity be venerable—but went before them as causes, to draw with their charming sweetness the wild untamed wits to an admiration of knowledge. So as Amphion was said to move stones with his poetry to build Thebes, and Orpheus to be listened to by beasts,—indeed stony and beastly people. So among the Romans were Livius Andronicus and Ennius; so in the Italian language the first that made it aspire to be a treasure-house of science were the poets Dante, Boccace, and Petrarch; so in our English were Gower and Chaucer, after whom, encouraged and delighted with their excellent foregoing, others have followed to beautify our mother-tongue, as well in the same kind as in other arts.

This did so notably show itself, that the philosophers of Greece durst not a long time appear to the world but under the masks of poets. So Thales,

Empedocles, and Parmenides sang their natural philosophy in verses; so did Pythagoras and Phocylides their moral counsels; so did Tyrtæus in war matters, and Solon in matters of policy; or rather they, being poets, did exercise their delightful vein in those points of highest knowledge which before them lay hidden to the world. For that wise Solon was directly a poet it is manifest, having written in verse the notable fable of the Atlantic Island which was continued by Plato. And truly even Plato whosoever well considers, shall find that in the body of his work though the inside and strength were philosophy, the skin as it were and beauty depended most of poetry. For all stands upon dialogues; wherein he feigns many honest burgesses of Athens to speak of such matters that, if they had been set on the rack, they would never have confessed them; besides his poetical describing the circumstances of their meetings, as the well-ordering of a banquet, the delicacy of a walk, with interlacing mere tales, as Gyges' Ring and others, which who knows not to be flowers of poetry did never walk into Apollo's garden.

And even historiographers, although their lips sound of things done, and verity be written in their foreheads, have been glad to borrow both fashion and perchance weight of the poets. So Herodotus entitled [the various books of— ed.] his history by the name of the nine Muses; and both he and all the rest that followed him either stole or usurped of poetry their passionate describing of passions, the many particularities of battles which no man could affirm, or, if that be denied me, long orations put in the mouths of great kings and captains, which it is certain they never pronounced.

So that truly neither philosopher nor historiographer could at the first have entered into the gates of popular judgments, if they had not taken a great passport of poetry, which in all nations at this day, where learning flourishes not, is plain to be seen; in all which they have some feeling of poetry. In Turkey, besides their lawgiving divines they have no other writers but poets. In our neighbor country Ireland, where truly learning goes very bare, yet are their poets held in a devout reverence. Even among the most barbarous and simple Indians, where no writing is, yet have they their poets, who make and sing songs (which they call *areytos*), both of their ancestors' deeds and praises of their gods,—a sufficient probability that, if ever learning come among them, it must be by having their hard dull wits softened and sharpened with the sweet delights of poetry; for until they find a pleasure in the exercise of the mind, great promises of much knowledge will little persuade them that know not the fruits of knowledge. In Wales, the true remnant of the ancient Britons, as there are good authorities to show the long time they had poets which they called bards, so through all the conquests of Romans, Saxons, Danes, and Normans, some of whom did seek to ruin all memory of learning from among them, yet do their poets even to this day last; so as it is not more notable in soon beginning, than in long continuing.

But since the authors of most of our sciences were the Romans, and before them the Greeks, let us a little stand upon their authorities, but even [only— ed.] so far as to see what names they have given unto this now scorned skill. Among the Romans a poet was called *vates*, which is as much as a diviner, foreseer, or prophet, as by his conjoined words, *vaticinium* and *vaticinari*, is manifest; so heavenly a title did that excellent people bestow upon this heart-ravishing knowledge. And so far were they carried into the admiration thereof, that they thought in the chanceable hitting upon any such verses great fore-tokens of their following fortunes were placed; whereupon grew the word of *Sortes Virgilianæ*, when by sudden opening Virgil's book they lighted upon some verse of his making. Whereof the histories of the Emperors' lives are full: as of Albinus, the governor of our island, who in his childhood met with this verse,

> *Arma amens capio, nec sat rationis in armis,*
> [Angered, I take up arms, but reason does not lie in arms
>   —ed.]

and in his age performed it. Although it were a very vain and godless superstition, as also it was to think that spirits were commanded by such verses— whereupon this word charms, derived of *carmina*, comes—so yet serves it to show the great reverence those wits were held in, and altogether not [not alto-gether—ed.] without ground, since both the oracles of Delphos and Sibylla's prophecies were wholly delivered in verses; for that same exquisite observing of number and measure in words, and that high-flying liberty of conceit [concept, invention—ed.], proper to the poet, did seem to have some divine force in it.

And may not I presume a little further to show the reasonableness of this word *Vates*, and say that the holy David's Psalms are a divine poem? If I do, I shall not do it without the testimony of great learned men, both ancient and modern. But even the name of Psalms will speak for me, which, being inter-preted, is nothing but Songs; then, that it is fully written in metre, as all learned Hebricians agree, although the rules be not yet fully found; lastly and princi-pally, his handling his prophecy, which is merely poetical. For what else is the awaking his musical instruments, the often and free changing of persons, his notable prosopopoeias, when he makes you, as it were, see God coming in His majesty, his telling of the beasts' joyfulness and hills' leaping, but a heavenly poesy, wherein almost he shows himself a passionate lover of that unspeakable and everlasting beauty to be seen by the eyes of the mind, only cleared by faith? But truly now having named him, I fear I seem to profane that holy name, applying it to poetry, which is among us thrown down to so ridiculous an estimation. But they that with quiet judgments will look a little deeper into it, shall find the end and working of it such as, being rightly applied, deserves not to be scourged out of the church of God.

But now let us see how the Greeks named it and how they deemed of it. The Greeks called him "a poet," which name has, as the most excellent, gone through other languages. It comes of this word *poiein*, which is "to make"; wherein I know not whether by luck or wisdom we Englishmen have met with the Greeks in calling him "a maker." Which name how high and incomparable a title it is, I had rather were known by marking the scope of other sciences than by any partial allegation. There is no art delivered unto mankind that has not the works of nature for his principal object, without which they could not consist, and on which they so depend as they become actors and players, as it were, of what nature will have set forth. So doth the astronomer look upon the stars, and, by that he sees, set down what order nature has taken therein. So do the geometrician and arithmetician in their divers sorts of quantities. So doth the musician in times tell you which by nature agree, which not. The natural philosopher thereon has his name, and the moral philosopher stands upon the natural virtues, vices, and passions of man; and "follow nature," says he, "therein, and thou shalt not err." The lawyer says what men have determined, the historian what men have done. The grammarian speaks only of the rules of speech, and the rhetorician and logician, considering what in nature will soonest prove and persuade, thereon give artificial rules, which still are com- passed within the circle of a question, according to the proposed matter. The physician weighs the nature of man's body, and the nature of things helpful or hurtful unto it. And the metaphysic, though it be in the second and abstract notions, and therefore be counted supernatural, yet doth he, indeed, build upon the depth of nature.

Only the poet, disdaining to be tied to any such subjection, lifted up with the vigor of his own invention, doth grow, in effect, into another nature, in making things either better than nature brings forth, or, quite anew, forms such as never were in nature, as the heroes, demi-gods, cyclops, chimeras, furies, and such like; so as he goes hand in hand with nature, not enclosed within the narrow warrant of her gifts, but freely ranging within the zodiac of his own wit. Nature never set forth the earth in so rich tapestry as divers poets have done; neither with pleasant rivers, fruitful trees, sweet-smelling flowers, nor whatso- ever else may make the too-much-loved earth more lovely; her world is brazen, the poets only deliver a golden.

But let those things alone, and go to man—for whom as the other things are, so it seems in him her uttermost cunning is employed—and know whether she have brought forth so true a lover as Theagenes; so constant a friend as Pylades; so valiant a man as Orlando; so right a prince as Xenophon's Cyrus; so excellent a man every way as Virgil's Æneas? Neither let this be jestingly conceived, because the works of the one be essential, the other in imitation or fiction; for any understanding knows the skill of each artificer stands in that idea, or fore-conceit of the work, and not in the work itself. And that the poet has that idea is manifest, by delivering them forth in such excellency as he has imagined them. Which delivering forth, also, is not wholly imaginative, as we are wont to say by them that build castles in the air; but so far substantially it works, not only to make a Cyrus, which had been but a particular excellency, as nature might have done, but to bestow a Cyrus upon the world to make many Cyruses, if they will learn aright why and how that maker made him. Neither let it be deemed too saucy a comparison to balance the highest point of man's wit with the efficacy of nature; but rather give right honor to the Heavenly Maker of that maker, who, having made man to His own likeness, set him beyond and over all the works of that second nature. Which in nothing he shows so much as in poetry, when with the force of a divine breath he brings things forth far surpassing her doings, with no small argument to the incredulous of that first accursed fall of Adam,—since our erected wit makes us know what perfection is, and yet our infected will keeps us from reaching unto it. But these arguments will by few be understood, and by fewer granted; thus much I hope will be given me, that the Greeks with some probability of reason gave him the name above all names of learning.

Now let us go to a more ordinary opening of him, that the truth may be the more palpable; and so, I hope, though we get not so unmatched a praise as the etymology of his names will grant, yet his very description, which no man will deny, shall not justly be barred from a principal commendation.

Poesy, therefore, is an art of imitation, for so Aristotle terms it in his word *mimēsis*, that is to say, a representing, counterfeiting, or figuring forth; to speak metaphorically, a speaking picture, with this end,—to teach and delight.

Of this have been three general kinds. The chief, both in antiquity and excellency, were they that did imitate the inconceivable excellencies of God. Such were David in his Psalms; Solomon in his Song of Songs, in his Ecclesiastes and Proverbs; Moses and Deborah in their Hymns; and the writer of Job; which, beside other, the learned Emanuel Tremellius and Franciscus Junius do entitle the poetical part of the Scripture. Against these none will speak that has the Holy Ghost in due holy reverence. In this kind, though in a full wrong divinity, were Orpheus, Amphion, Homer in his Hymns, and many other, both Greeks and Romans. And this poesy must be used by whosoever will follow St. James' counsel in singing psalms when they are merry; and I know is used with the fruit of comfort by some, when, in sorrowful pangs of their death-bringing sins, they find the consolation of the never-leaving goodness.

The second kind is of them that deal with matters philosophical, either moral, as Tyrtæus, Phocylides, and Cato; or natural, as Lucretius and Virgil's Georgics; or astronomical, as Manilius and Pontanus; or historical, as Lucan;

which who mislike, the fault is in their judgment quite out of taste, and not in the sweet food of sweetly uttered knowledge.

But because this second sort is wrapped within the fold of the proposed subject, and takes not the free course of his own invention, whether they properly be poets or no, let grammarians dispute, and go to the third, indeed right poets, of whom chiefly this question arises. Betwixt whom and these second is such a kind of difference as betwixt the meaner sort of painters, who counterfeit only such faces as are set before them, and the more excellent, who having no law but wit, bestow that in colors upon you which is fittest for the eye to see, — as the constant though lamenting look of Lucretia, when she punished in herself another's fault; wherein he paints not Lucretia, whom he never saw, but paints the outward beauty of such a virtue. For these third be they which most properly do imitate to teach and delight; and to imitate borrow nothing of what is, has been, or shall be; but range, only reined with learned discretion, into the divine consideration of what may be and should be. These be they that, as the first and most noble sort may justly be termed vates, so these are waited on in the excellentest languages and best understandings with the fore-described name of poets. For these, indeed, do merely make to imitate, and imitate both to delight and teach, and delight to move men to take that goodness in hand, which without delight they would fly as from a stranger; and teach to make them know that goodness whereunto they are moved:—which being the noblest scope to which ever any learning was directed, yet want there not idle tongues to bark at them.

These be subdivided into sundry more special denominations. The most notable be the heroic, lyric, tragic, comic, satiric, iambic, elegiac, pastoral, and certain others, some of these being termed according to the matter they deal with, some by the sort of verse they liked best to write in,—for indeed the greatest part of poets have appareled their poetical inventions in that numberous kind of writing which is called verse. Indeed but appareled, verse being but an ornament and no cause to poetry, since there have been many most excellent poets that never versified, and now swarm many versifiers that need never answer to the name of poets. For Xenophon, who did imitate so excellently as to give us *effigiem justi imperii*—the portraiture of a just empire under the name of Cyrus (as Cicero says of him)—made therein an absolute heroical poem; so did Heliodorus in his sugared invention of that picture of love in Theagenes and Chariclea; and yet both these wrote in prose. Which I speak to show that it is not riming and versing that makes a poet—no more than a long gown makes an advocate, who, though he pleaded in armor, should be an advocate and no soldier—but it is that feigning notable images of virtues, vices, or what else, with that delightful teaching, which must be the right describing note to know a poet by. Although indeed the senate of poets has chosen verse as their fittest raiment, meaning, as in matter they passed all in all, so in manner to go beyond them; not speaking, table-talk fashion, or like men in a dream, words as they chanceably fall from the mouth, but peizing [weighing—ed.] each syllable of each word by just proportion, according to the dignity of the subject.

Now, therefore, it shall not be amiss, first to weigh this latter sort of poetry by his works, and then by his parts; and if in neither of these anatomies he be condemnable, I hope we shall obtain a more favorable sentence. This purifying of wit, this enriching of memory, enabling of judgment, and enlarging of conceit, which commonly we call learning, under what name soever it come forth or to what immediate end soever it be directed, the final end is to lead and draw us to as high a perfection as our degenerate souls, made worse by their clay lodgings, can be capable of. This, according to the inclination of man, bred many-formed impressions. For some that thought this felicity principally to be gotten by knowledge, and no knowledge to be so high or heavenly as acquaintance with the stars, gave themselves to astronomy; others, persuading themselves to be demi-gods if they knew the causes of things, became natural and supernatural philosophers. Some an admirable delight drew to music, and some the certainty of demonstration to the mathematics; but all, one and other, having this scope:—to know, and by knowledge to lift up the mind from the dungeon of the body to the enjoying his own divine essence. But when by the balance of experience it was found that the astronomer, looking to the stars, might fall into a ditch, that the inquiring philosopher might be blind in himself, and the mathematician might draw forth a straight line with a crooked heart; then lo! did proof, the overruler of opinions, make manifest, that all these are but serving sciences, which, as they have each a private end in themselves, so yet are they all directed to the highest end of the mistress knowledge, by the Greeks called *architektonikē*, which stands, as I think, in the knowledge of a man's self, in the ethic and politic consideration, with the end of well-doing, and not of well-knowing only:—even as the saddler's next end is to make a good saddle, but his further end to serve a nobler faculty, which is horsemanship; so the horseman's to soldiery; and the soldier not only to have the skill, but to perform the practice of a soldier. So that the ending end of all earthly learning being virtuous action, those skills that most serve to bring forth that have a most just title to be princes over all the rest; wherein, if we can show, the poet is worthy to have it before any other competitors.

Among whom as principal challengers step forth the moral philosophers; whom, me thinks, I see coming toward me with a sullen gravity, as though they could not abide vice by daylight; rudely clothed, for to witness outwardly their contempt of outward things; with books in their hands against glory, whereto they set their names; sophistically speaking against subtlety; and angry with any man in whom they see the foul fault of anger. These men, casting largess as they go of definitions, divisions, and distinctions, with a scornful interrogative do soberly ask whether it be possible to find any path so ready to lead a man to virtue, as that which teaches what virtue is, and teaches it not only by delivering forth his very being, his causes and effects, but also by making known his enemy, vice, which must be destroyed, and his cumbersome servant, passion, which must be mastered; by showing the generalities that contain it, and the specialities that are derived from it; lastly, by plain setting down how it extends itself out of the limits of a man's own little world, to the government of families, and maintaining of public societies?

The historian scarcely gives leisure to the moralist to say so much, but that he, loaded with old mouse-eaten records, authorizing himself for the most part upon other histories, whose greatest authorities are built upon the notable foundation of hearsay; having much ado to accord differing writers, and to pick truth out of partiality; better acquainted with a thousand years ago than with the present age, and yet better knowing how this world goes than how his own wit runs; curious for antiquities and inquisitive of novelties, a wonder to young folks and a tyrant in table-talk; denies, in a great chafe [agitation—ed.], that any man for teaching of virtue and virtuous actions is comparable to him. "I am *testis temporum, lux veritatis, vita memoriæ, magistra vitæ, nuntia vetustatis* [the witness of the times, the light of truth, the life of memory, the directress of life, the messenger of antiquity—ed.]. The philosopher," says he, "teaches a disputative virtue, but I do an active. His virtue is excellent in the dangerless Academy of Plato, but mine shows forth her honorable face in the battles of Marathon, Pharsalia, Poitiers, and Agincourt. He teaches virtue by certain abstract considerations, but I only bid you follow the footing of them that have gone before you. Old-aged experience goes beyond the fine-witted philosopher; but I give the experience of many ages. Lastly, if he make the songbook, I put the learner's hand to the lute; and if he be the guide, I am the light." Then would he allege you innumerable examples, confirming story by story, how much the wisest senators and princes have been directed by the credit of history, as Brutus, Alphonsus of Aragon—and who not, if need be? At length the long line of their disputation makes [comes to—ed.] a point in this,—that the one gives the precept, and the other the example.

Now whom shall we find, since the question stands for the highest form in the school of learning, to be moderator? Truly, as me seems, the poet; and if not a moderator, even the man that ought to carry the title from them both, and much more from all other serving sciences. Therefore compare we the poet with the historian and with the moral philosopher; and if he go beyond them both, no other human skill can match him. For as for the divine, with all reverence it is ever to be excepted, not only for having his scope as far beyond any of these as eternity exceeds a moment, but even for passing each of these in themselves. And for the lawyer, though *Jus* be the daughter of Justice, and Justice the chief of virtues, yet because he seeks to make men good rather *formidine poeœnæ* [fear of punishment] than *virtutis amore* [love of virtue—

ed.] or, to say righter, doth not endeavor to make men good, but that their evil hurt not others; having no care, so he be a good citizen, how bad a man he be; therefore, as our wickedness makes him necessary, and necessity makes him honorable, so is he not in the deepest truth to stand in rank with these, who all endeavor to take naughtiness away, and plant goodness even in the secretest cabinet of our souls. And these four are all that any way deal in that consideration of men's manners, which being the supreme knowledge, they that best breed it deserve the best commendation.

The philosopher therefore and the historian are they which would win the goal, the one by precept, the other by example; but both not having both, do both halt. For the philosopher, setting down with thorny arguments the bare rule, is so hard of utterance and so misty to be conceived, that one that has no other guide but him shall wade in him till he be old, before he shall find sufficient cause to be honest. For his knowledge stands so upon the abstract and general that happy is that man who may understand him, and more happy that can apply what he doth understand. On the other side, the historian, wanting the precept, is so tied, not to what should be but to what is, to the particular truth of things, and not to the general reason of things, that his example draws no necessary consequence, and therefore a less fruitful doctrine.

Now doth the peerless poet perform both; for whatsoever the philosopher says should be done, he gives a perfect picture of it in some one by whom he presupposes it was done, so as he couples the general notion with the particular example. A perfect picture, I say; for he yields to the powers of the mind an image of that whereof the philosopher bestows but a wordish description, which doth neither strike, pierce, nor possess the sight of the soul so much as that other doth. For as, in outward things, to a man that had never seen an elephant or a rhinoceros, who should tell him most exquisitely all their shapes, color, bigness, and particular marks; or of a gorgeous palace, an architector, with declaring the full beauties, might well make the hearer able to repeat, as it were by rote, all he had heard, yet should never satisfy his inward conceit with being witness to itself of a true lively [vital—ed.] knowledge; but the same man, as soon as he might see those beasts well painted, or that house well in model, should straightway grow, without need of any description, to a judicial comprehending of them; so no doubt the philosopher, with his learned definitions, be it of virtues or vices, matters of public policy or private government, replenishes the memory with many infallible grounds of wisdom, which notwithstanding lie dark before the imaginative and judging power, if they be not illuminated or figured forth by the speaking picture of poesy.

Tully takes much pains, and many times not without poetical helps, to make us know the force love of our country has in us. Let us but hear old Anchises speaking in the midst of Troy's flames, or see Ulysses, in the fullness of all

Calypso's delights, bewail his absence from barren and beggarly Ithaca. Anger, the Stoics said, was a short madness. Let but Sophocles bring you Ajax on a stage, killing and whipping sheep and oxen, thinking them the army of Greeks, with their chieftains Agamemnon and Menelaus, and tell me if you have not a more familiar insight into anger, than finding in the schoolmen his genus and difference. See whether wisdom and temperance in Ulysses and Diomedes, valor in Achilles, friendship in Nisus and Euryalus, even to an ignorant man carry not an apparent shining. And, contrarily, the remorse of conscience, in Oedipus; the soon-repenting pride of Agamemnon; the self-devouring cruelty in his father Atreus; the violence of ambition in the two Theban brothers; the sour sweetness of revenge in Medea; and, to fall lower, the Terentian Gnatho and our Chaucer's Pandar so expressed that we now use their names to signify their trades; and finally, all virtues, vices, and passions so in their own natural states laid to the view, that we seem not to hear of them, but clearly to see through them.

But even in the most excellent determination of goodness, what philosopher's counsel can so readily direct a prince, as the feigned Cyrus in Xenophon? Or a virtuous man in all fortunes, as Æneas in Virgil? Or a whole commonwealth, as the way of Sir Thomas More's Utopia? I say the way, because where Sir Thomas More erred, it was the fault of the man, and not of the poet; for that way of patterning a commonwealth was most absolute, though he, perchance, has not so absolutely performed it. For the question is, whether the feigned image of poesy, or the regular instruction of philosophy, has the more force in teaching. Wherein if the philosophers have more rightly showed themselves philosophers than the poets have attained to the high top of their profession,—as in truth,

> *Mediocribus esse poetis*
> *Non Dii, non homines, non concessere columnæ,—*
> [Not gods nor men nor booksellers allow poets to be medi-
> ocre—ed.]

it is, I say again, not the fault of the art, but that by few men that art can be accomplished.

Certainly, even our Savior Christ could as well have given the moral commonplaces of uncharitableness and humbleness as the divine narration of Dives and Lazarus; or of disobedience and mercy, as that heavenly discourse of the lost child and the gracious father; but that his thorough-searching wisdom knew the estate of Dives burning in hell, and of Lazarus in Abraham's bosom, would more constantly, as it were, inhabit both the memory and judgment. Truly, for myself, me seems I see before mine eyes the lost child's disdainful prodigality, turned to envy a swine's dinner; which by the learned divines are thought not historical acts, but instructing parables.

For conclusion, I say the philosopher teaches, but he teaches obscurely, so as the learned only can understand him; that is to say, he teaches them that are already taught. But the poet is the food for the tenderest stomachs; the poet is indeed the right popular philosopher. Whereof Æsop's tales give good proof; whose pretty allegories, stealing under the formal tales of beasts, make many, more beastly than beasts, begin to hear the sound of virtue from those dumb speakers.

But now it may be alleged that if this imagining of matters be so fit for the imagination, then must the historian needs surpass, who brings you images of true matters, such as indeed were done, and not such as fantastically [fanci-fully—ed.] or falsely may be suggested to have been done. Truly, Aristotle him-self, in his Discourse of Poesy, plainly determines this question, saying that poetry is *philosophōteron* and *spoudaioteron*, that is to say, it is more philosoph-ical and more studiously serious than history. His reason is, because poesy deals with *katholou*, that is to say with the universal consideration, and the history with *kathekaston*, the particular.

"Now," says he, "the universal weighs what is fit to be said or done, either in likelihood or necessity—which the poesy considers in his imposed names; and the particular only marks whether Alcibiades did, or suffered, this or that." Thus far Aristotle. Which reason of his, as all his, is most full of reason.

For, indeed, if the question were whether it were better to have a particular act truly or falsely set down, there is no doubt which is to be chosen, no more than whether you had rather have Vespasian's picture right as he was, or, at the painter's pleasure, nothing resembling. But if the question be for your own use and learning, whether it be better to have it set down as it should be or as it was, then certainly is more doctrinable [instructive—ed.] the feigned Cyrus in Xenophon than the true Cyrus in Justin; and the feigned Æneas in Virgil than the right Æneas in Dares Phrygius; as to a lady that desired to fashion her countenance to the best grace, a painter should more benefit her to portrait a most sweet face, writing Canidia upon it, than to paint Canidia as she was, who, Horace swears, was foul and ill-favored.

If the poet do his part aright, he will show you in Tantalus, Atreus, and such like, nothing that is not to be shunned; in Cyrus, Æneas, Ulysses, each thing to be followed. Where the historian, bound to tell things as things were, cannot be liberal—without he will be poetical—of a perfect pattern; but, as in Alex-ander, or Scipio himself, show doings, some to be liked, some to be misliked; and then how will you discern what to follow but by your own discretion, which you had without reading Quintus Curtius? And whereas a man may say, though in universal consideration of doctrine the poet prevails, yet that the history, in his saying such a thing was done, doth warrant a man more in that he shall follow,—the answer is manifest: that if he stand upon that *was*, as if he should argue, because it rained yesterday therefore it should rain to-day, then indeed it has some advantage to a gross conceit. But if he know an example only informs a conjectured likelihood, and so go by reason, the poet doth so far exceed him as he is to frame his example to that which is most reasonable, be it in warlike, politic, or private matters; where the historian in his bare *was* has many times that which we call fortune to overrule the best wisdom. Many times he must tell events whereof he can yield no cause; or if he do, it must be poetically.

For, that a feigned example has as much force to teach as a true example—for as for to move, it is clear, since the feigned may be tuned to the highest key of passion—let us take one example wherein a poet and a historian do concur. Herodotus and Justin do both testify that Zopyrus, king Darius' faithful servant, seeing his master long resisted by the rebellious Babylonians, feigned himself in extreme disgrace of his king; for verifying of which he caused his own nose and ears to be cut off, and so flying to the Babylonians, was received, and for his known valor so far credited, that he did find means to deliver them over to Darius. Muchlike matter doth Livy record of Tarquinius and his son. Xenophon excellently feigns such another stratagem, performed by Abradatas in Cyrus' behalf. Now would I fain know, if occasion be presented unto you to serve your prince by such an honest dissimulation, why do you not as well learn it of Xenophon's fiction as of the other's verity? and, truly, so much the better, as you shall save your nose by the bargain; for Abradatas did not counterfeit so far.

So, then, the best of the historian is subject to the poet; for whatsoever action or faction, whatsoever counsel, policy, or war-stratagem the historian is bound to recite, that may the poet, if he list, with his imitation make his own, beautifying it both for further teaching and more delighting, as it pleases him; having all, from Dante's Heaven to his Hell, under the authority of his pen. Which if I be asked what poets have done? so as I might well name some, yet say I, and say again, I speak of the art, and not of the artificer.

Now, to that which is commonly attributed to the praise of history, in respect of the notable learning is gotten by marking the success, as though therein a man should see virtue exalted and vice punished,—truly that commendation is peculiar to poetry and far off from history. For, indeed, poetry ever sets virtue so out in her best colors, making Fortune her well-waiting handmaid, that one must needs be enamored of her. Well may you see Ulysses in a storm, and in other hard plights; but they are but exercises of patience and magnanimity, to make them shine the more in the near following prosperity. And, of the contrary part, if evil men come to the stage, they ever go out—as the tragedy writer answered to one that misliked the show of such persons—so manacled as they little animate folks to follow them. But the historian, being captived to the truth of a foolish world, is many times a terror from well-doing, and an encouragement to unbridled wickedness. For see we not valiant Miltiades rot in his fetters? The just Phocion and the accomplished Socrates put to death like traitors? The cruel Severus live prosperously? The excellent Severus miserably murdered?

Sylla and Marius dying in their beds? Pompey and Cicero slain then, when they would have thought exile a happiness? See we not virtuous Cato driven to kill himself, and rebel Cæsar so advanced that his name yet, after sixteen hundred years, lasts in the highest honor? And mark but even Cæsar's own words of the forenamed Sylla—who in that only did honestly, to put down his dishonest tyranny—*literas nescivit*, [he was without learning—ed.] as if want of learning caused him to do well. He meant it not by poetry, which, not content with earthly plagues, devises new punishments in hell for tyrants; nor yet by philosophy, which teaches *occidendos esse* [that they are to be killed—ed.] but, no doubt, by skill in history, for that indeed can afford you Cypselus, Periander, Phalaris, Dionysius, and I know not how many more of the same kennel, that speed well enough in their abominable injustice or usurpation.

I conclude, therefore, that he excels history, not only in furnishing the mind with knowledge, but in setting it forward to that which deserves to be called and accounted good; which setting forward, and moving to well-doing, indeed sets the laurel crown upon the poet as victorious, not only of the historian, but over the philosopher, howsoever in teaching it may be questionable. For suppose it be granted—that which I suppose with great reason may be denied— that the philosopher, in respect of his methodical proceeding, teach more perfectly than the poet, yet do I think that no man is so much *Philophilosophos* [a friend to the philosopher—ed.] as to compare the philosopher in moving with the poet. And that moving is of a higher degree than teaching, it may by this appear, that it is well nigh both the cause and the effect of teaching; for who will be taught, if he be not moved with desire to be taught? And what so much good doth that teaching bring forth—I speak still of moral doctrine—as that it moves one to do that which it doth teach? For, as Aristotle says, it is not *Gnosis* [knowing] but *Praxis* [doing—ed.] must be the fruit; and how *Praxis* cannot be, without being moved to practice, it is no hard matter to consider. The philosopher shows you the way, he informs you of the particularities, as well of the tediousness of the way, as of the pleasant lodging you shall have when your journey is ended, as of the many by-turnings that may divert you from your way; but this is to no man but to him that will read him, and read him with attentive, studious painfulness; which constant desire whosoever has in him, has already passed half the hardness of the way, and therefore is beholding to the philosopher but for the other half. Nay, truly, learned men have learnedly thought, that where once reason has so much overmastered passion as that the mind has a free desire to do well, the inward light each mind has in itself is as good as a philosopher's book; since in nature we know it is well to do well, and what is well and what is evil, although not in the words of art which philosophers bestow upon us; for out of natural conceit the philosophers drew it. But to be moved to do that which we know, or to be moved with desire to know, *hoc opus, hic labor est* [this is the work, this is the labor—ed.].

Now therein of all sciences—I speak still of human, and according to the human conceit—is our poet the monarch. For he doth not only show the way, but gives so sweet a prospect into the way as will entice any man to enter into it. Nay, he doth, as if your journey should lie through a fair vineyard, at the very first give you a cluster of grapes, that full of that taste you may long to pass further. He begins not with obscure definitions, which must blur the margent [margin—ed.] with interpretations, and load the memory with doubtfulness. But he comes to you with words set in delightful proportion, either accompanied with, or prepared for, the well-enchanting skill of music; and with a tale, forsooth, he comes unto you, with a tale which holds children from play, and old men from the chimney-corner, and, pretending no more, doth intend the winning of the mind from wickedness to virtue; even as the child is often brought to take most wholesome things, by hiding them in such other as to have a pleasant taste,—which, if one should begin to tell them the nature of the aloes or rhubarb they should receive, would sooner take their physic at their ears than at their mouth. So is it in men, most of which are childish in the best things, till they be cradled in their graves,—glad they will be to hear the tales of Hercules, Achilles, Cyrus, Æneas; and, hearing them, must needs hear the right description of wisdom, valor, and justice; which, if they had been barely, that is to say philosophically, set out, they would swear they be brought to school again.

That imitation whereof poetry is, has the most conveniency to nature of all other; insomuch that, as Aristotle says, those things which in themselves are horrible, as cruel battles, unnatural monsters, are made in poetical imitation delightful. Truly, I have known men, that even with reading *Amadis de Gaule*, which, God knows, wants much of a perfect poesy, have found their hearts moved to the exercise of courtesy, liberality, and especially courage. Who reads Æneas carrying old Anchises on his back, that wishes not it were his fortune to perform so excellent an act? Whom do not those words of Turnus move, the tale of Turnus having planted his image in the imagination?

> *Fugientem haec terra videbit?*
> *Usque adeone mori miserum est?*
> [Shall this land see him in flight? Is it so wretched to die?
> —ed.]

Where the philosophers, as they scorn to delight, so must they be content little to move—saving wrangling whether virtue be the chief or the only good, whether the contemplative or the active life do excel—which Plato and Boethius well knew, and therefore made Mistress Philosophy very often borrow the masking raiment of Poesy. For even those hard-hearted evil men who think virtue a school-name, and know no other good but *indulgere genio* [indulge one's inclination—ed.], and therefore despise the austere admonitions of the philosopher, and feel not the inward reason they stand upon, yet will be content to be delighted, which is all the good-fellow poet seems to promise; and so steal to see the form of goodness—which seen, they cannot but love—ere themselves be aware, as if they took a medicine of cherries.

Infinite proofs of the strange effects of this poetical invention might be alleged; only two shall serve, which are so often remembered as I think all men know them. The one of Menenius Agrippa, who, when the whole people of Rome had resolutely divided themselves from the senate, with apparent show of utter ruin, though he were, for that time, an excellent orator, came not among them upon trust either of figurative speeches or cunning insinuations, and much less with far-fetched maxims of philosophy, which, especially if they were Platonic, they must have learned geometry before they could well have conceived; but, forsooth, he behaves himself like a homely and familiar poet. He tells them a tale, that there was a time when all parts of the body made a mutinous conspiracy against the belly, which they thought devoured the fruits of each other's labor; they concluded they would let so unprofitable a spender starve. In the end, to be short—for the tale is notorious, and as notorious that it was a tale—with punishing the belly they plagued themselves. This, applied by him, wrought such effect in the people, as I never read that ever words brought forth but then so sudden and so good an alteration; for upon reasonable conditions a perfect reconcilement ensued.

The other is of Nathan the prophet, who, when the holy David had so far forsaken God as to confirm adultery with murder, when he was to do the tenderest office of a friend, in laying his own shame before his eyes,—sent by God to call again so chosen a servant, how doth he it but by telling of a man whose beloved lamb was ungratefully taken from his bosom? The application most divinely true, but the discourse itself feigned; which made David (I speak of the second and instrumental cause) as in a glass to see his own filthiness, as that heavenly Psalm of Mercy well testifies.

By these, therefore, examples and reasons, I think it may be manifest that the poet, with that same hand of delight, doth draw the mind more effectually than any other art doth. And so a conclusion not unfitly ensues: that as virtue is the most excellent resting-place for all worldly learning to make his end of, so poetry, being the most familiar to teach it, and most princely to move towards it, in the most excellent work is the most excellent workman.

But I am content not only to decipher him by his works—although works in commendation or dispraise must ever hold a high authority—but more narrowly will examine his parts; so that, as in a man, though all together may carry a presence full of majesty and beauty, perchance in some one defectious piece we may find a blemish.

Now in his parts, kinds, or species, as you list to term them, it is to be noted that some poesies have coupled together two or three kinds,—as tragical and comical, whereupon is risen the tragi-comical; some, in the like manner, have mingled prose and verse, as Sannazzaro and Boethius; some have mingled matters heroical and pastoral; but that comes all to one in this question, for, if severed they be good, the conjunction cannot be hurtful. Therefore, perchance forgetting some, and leaving some as needless to be remembered, it shall not be amiss in a word to cite the special kinds, to see what faults may be found in the right use of them.

Is it then the pastoral poem which is misliked?—for perchance where the hedge is lowest they will soonest leap over. Is the poor pipe disdained, which sometimes out of Meliboeœus' mouth can show the misery of people under hard lords and ravening soldiers, and again, by Tityrus, what blessedness is derived to them that lie lowest from the goodness of them that sit highest? sometimes, under the pretty tales of wolves and sheep, can include the whole considerations of wrong-doing and patience; sometimes show that contention for trifles can get but a trifling victory; where perchance a man may see that even Alexander and Darius, when they strove who should be cock of this world's dunghill, the benefit they got was that the after-livers may say:

> *Hæc memini et victum frustra contendere Thyrsim;*
>   *Ex illo Corydon, Corydon est tempore nobis.*
> [I remember such things, and that the defeated Thyrsis
>   struggled vainly;
> From that time, with us Corydon is the Corydon—ed.]

Or is it the lamenting elegiac, which in a kind heart would move rather pity than blame; who bewails, with the great philosopher Heraclitus, the weakness of mankind and the wretchedness of the world; who surely is to be praised, either for compassionate accompanying just causes of lamentation, or for rightly painting out how weak be the passions of woefulness?

Is it the bitter and wholesome iambic, who rubs the galled mind, in making shame the trumpet of villainy with bold and open crying out against naughtiness?

Or the satiric? who

> *Omne vafer vitium ridenti tangit amico;*
> [The sly fellow touches every vice while making his friend
>   laugh—ed.]

who sportingly never leaves till he make a man laugh at folly, and at length ashamed to laugh at himself, which he cannot avoid without avoiding the folly; who, while *circum præcordia ludit* [he plays around his heartstrings], gives us to feel how many headaches a passionate life brings us to,—how, when all is done,

Est Ulubris, animus si nos non deficit æquus.
[If we do not lack the equable temperament, it is in Ulu-
      brae (noted for desolation) —ed.]

No, perchance it is the comic; whom naughty play-makers and stage-keepers have justly made odious. To the argument of abuse I will answer after. Only thus much now is to be said, that the comedy in an imitation of the common errors of our life, which he represents in the most ridiculous and scornful sort that may be, so as it is impossible that any beholder can be content to be such a one. Now, as in geometry the oblique must be known as well as the right, and in arithmetic the odd as well as the even; so in the actions of our life who sees not the filthiness of evil, wants a great foil to perceive the beauty of virtue. This doth the comedy handle so, in our private and domestic matters, as with hearing it we get, as it were, an experience what is to be looked for of a niggardly Demea, of a crafty Davus, of a flattering Gnatho, of a vain-glorious Thraso; and not only to know what effects are to be expected, but to know who be such, by the signifying badge given them by the comedian. And little reason has any man to say that men learn evil by seeing it so set out; since, as I said before, there is no man living, but by the force truth has in nature, no sooner sees these men play their parts, but wishes them *in pistrinum* [in the mill (place of punishment) —ed.], although perchance the sack of his own faults lie so behind his back, that he sees not himself to dance the same measure,—whereto yet nothing can more open his eyes than to find his own actions contemptibly set forth.

So that the right use of comedy will, I think, by nobody be blamed, and much less of the high and excellent tragedy, that opens the greatest wounds, and shows forth the ulcers that are covered with tissue; that makes kings fear to be tyrants, and tyrants manifest their tyrannical humors; that with stirring the effects of admiration and commiseration teaches the uncertainty of this world, and upon how weak foundations gilded roofs are builded; that makes us know:

Qui sceptra sævus duro imperio regit,
    Timet timentes, metus in auctorem redit.
[The savage king who wields the scepter with cruel sway
Fears those who fear him; dread comes back to the head of
    the originator—ed.]

But how much it can move, Plutarch yields a notable testimony of the abominable tyrant Alexander Pheræus; from whose eyes a tragedy, well made and represented, drew abundance of tears, who without all pity had murdered infinite numbers, and some of his own blood; so as he that was not ashamed to make matters for tragedies, yet could not resist the sweet violence of a tragedy. And if it wrought no further good in him, it was that he, in despite of himself, withdrew himself from hearkening to that which might mollify his hardened heart. But it is not the tragedy they do mislike, for it were too absurd to cast out so excellent a representation of whatsoever is most worthy to be learned.

Is it the lyric that most displeases, who with his tuned lyre and well accorded voice, gives praise, the reward of virtue, to virtuous acts; who gives moral precepts and natural problems; who sometimes raises up his voice to the height of the heavens, in singing the lauds of the immortal God? Certainly I must confess mine own barbarousness; I never heard the old song of Percy and Douglas that I found not my heart moved more than with a trumpet; and yet it is sung but by some blind crowder [a public entertainer, singing for a crowd—ed.], with no rougher voice than rude style; which being so evil appareled in the dust and cobwebs of that uncivil age, what would it work, trimmed in the gorgeous eloquence of Pindar? In Hungary I have seen it the manner of all feasts, and other such meetings, to have songs of their ancestors' valor, which that right soldierlike nation think the chiefest kindlers of brave courage. The incomparable Lacedæmonians did not only carry that kind of music ever with them to the field, but even at home, as such songs were made, so were they all content to be singers of them; when the lusty men were to tell what they did, the old men what they had done, and the young men what they would do. And where a man may say that Pindar many times praises highly victories of small moment, matters rather of sport than virtue; as it may be answered, it was the fault of the poet, and not of the poetry, so indeed the chief fault was in the time and custom of the Greeks, who set those toys at so high a price that Philip of Macedon reckoned a horserace won at Olympus among his three fearful felicities. But as the unimitable Pindar often did, so is that kind most capable and most fit to awake the thoughts from the sleep of idleness, to embrace honorable enterprises.

There rests the heroical, whose very name, I think, should daunt all backbiters. For by what conceit can a tongue be directed to speak evil of that which draws with it no less champions than Achilles, Cyrus, Æneas, Turnus Tydeus, Rinaldo? who doth not only teach and move to a truth, but teaches and moves to the most high and excellent truth; who makes magnanimity and justice shine through all misty fearfulness and foggy desires; who, if the saying of Plato and Tully be true, that who could see virtue would be wonderfully ravished with the love of her beauty, this man sets her out to make her more lovely, in her holiday apparel, to the eye of any that will deign not to disdain until they understand. But if anything be already said in the defense of sweet poetry, all concurs to the maintaining the heroical, which is not only a kind, but the best and most accomplished kind of poetry. For, as the image of each action stirs and instructs the mind, so the lofty image of such worthies most inflames the mind with desire to be worthy, and informs with counsel how to be worthy. Only let Æneas be worn in the tablet of your memory, how he governs himself in the ruin of his country; in the preserving his old father, and carrying away his religious ceremonies; in obeying the god's commandment to leave Dido, though not only all passionate kindness, but even the human consideration of virtuous gratefulness, would have craved other of him; how in storms, how in sports, how in war, how in peace, how a fugitive, how victorious, how besieged, how besieging, how to strangers, how to allies, how to enemies, how to his own; lastly, how in his inward self, and how in his outward government; and I think, in a mind most prejudiced with a prejudicating humor, he will be found in excellency fruitful,—yea, even as Horace says, *melius Chrysippo et Crantore* [better than Chrysippus and Crantor (famous philosophers) —ed.]. But truly I imagine it falls out with these poet-whippers as with some good women who often are sick, but in faith they cannot tell where. So the name of poetry is odious to them, but neither his cause nor effects, neither the sum that contains him nor the particularities descending from him, give any fast handle to their carping dispraise.

Since, then, poetry is of all human learnings the most ancient and of most fatherly antiquity, as from whence other learnings have taken their beginnings; since it is so universal that no learned nation doth despise it, nor barbarous nation is without it; since both Roman and Greek gave divine names unto it, the one of "prophesying," the other of "making," and that indeed that name of "making" is fit for him, considering that whereas other arts retain themselves within their subjects, and receive, as it were, their being from it, the poet only brings his own stuff, and doth not learn a conceit out of a matter, but makes matter for a conceit; since neither his description nor his end contains any evil, the thing described cannot be evil; since his effects be so good as to teach goodness, and delight the learners of it; since therein—namely in moral doctrine, the chief of all knowledges—he doth not only far pass the historian, but for instructing is well nigh comparable to the philosopher, and for moving leaves him behind him; since the Holy Scripture, wherein there is no uncleanness, has whole parts in it poetical, and that even our Savior Christ vouchsafed to use the flowers of it; since all his kinds are not only in their united forms, but in their several dissections fully commendable; I think, and think I think rightly, the laurel crown appointed for triumphant captains doth worthily, of all other learnings, honor the poet's triumph.

But because we have ears as well as tongues, and that the lightest reasons that may be will seem to weigh greatly, if nothing be put in the counter-balance, let us hear, and, as well as we can, ponder, what objections be made against this art, which may be worthy either of yielding or answering.

First, truly, I note not only in these *misomousoi*, poet-haters, but in all that kind of people who seek a praise by dispraising others, that they do prodigally spend a great many wandering words in quips and scoffs, carping and taunting at each thing which, by stirring the spleen, may stay the brain from a through-beholding the worthiness of the subject. Those kind of objections, as they are full of a very idle easiness—since there is nothing of so sacred a majesty but that an itching tongue may rub itself upon it—so deserve they no other answer, but, instead of laughing at the jest, to laugh at the jester. We know a playing wit can praise the discretion of an ass, the comfortableness of being in debt, and the jolly commodity of being sick of the plague. So of the contrary side, if we will turn Ovid's verse,

> *Ut lateat virtus proximitate mali,*

"that good lie hid in nearness of the evil," Agrippa will be as merry in showing the vanity of science, as Erasmus was in commending of folly; neither shall any man or matter escape some touch of these smiling railers. But for Erasmus and Agrippa, they had another foundation than the superficial part would promise. Marry, these other pleasant fault-finders, who will correct the verb before they understand the noun, and confute others' knowledge before they confirm their own, I would have them only remember that scoffing comes not of wisdom; so as the best title in true English they get with their merriments is to be called good fools,—for so have our grave forefathers ever termed that humorous kind of jesters.

But that which gives greatest scope to their scorning humor is riming and versing. It is already said, and as I think truly said, it is not riming and versing that makes poesy. One may be a poet without versing, and a versifier without poetry. But yet presuppose it were inseparable—as indeed it seems Scaliger judges—truly it were an inseparable commendation. For if *oratio* next to *ratio*, speech next to reason, be the greatest gift bestowed upon mortality, that cannot be praiseless which doth most polish that blessing of speech; which considers each word, not only as a man may say by his forcible quality, but by his best-measured quantity; carrying even in themselves a harmony,—without, per-chance, number, measure, order, proportion be in our time grown odious.

But lay aside the just praise it has by being the only fit speech for music—music, I say, the most divine striker of the senses—thus much is undoubtedly true, that if reading be foolish without remembering, memory being the only treasurer of knowledge, those words which are fittest for memory are likewise most convenient for knowledge. Now that verse far exceeds prose in the knitting up of the memory, the reason is manifest; the words, besides their delight, which has a great affinity to memory, being so set, as one cannot be lost but the whole work fails; which, accusing itself, calls the remembrance back to itself, and so most strongly confirms it. Besides, one word so, as it were, begetting another, as, be it in rime or measured verse, by the former a man shall have a near guess to the follower. Lastly, even they that have taught the art of memory have showed nothing so apt for it as a certain room divided into many places, well and thor-oughly known; now that has the verse in effect perfectly, every word having his natural seat, which seat must needs make the word remembered. But what needs more in a thing so known to all men? Who is it that ever was a scholar that doth not carry away some verses of Virgil, Horace, or Cato, which in his youth he learned, and even to his old age serve him for hourly lessons? as:

> *Percontatorem fugito, nam garrulus idem est*
> [Stay away from an inquisitive man: he is sure to be garru-
>   lous—ed.]
>   [and] *Dum sibi quisque placet, credula turba sumus.*
> [While each pleases himself, we are a credulous mob—ed.]

But the fitness it has for memory is notably proved by all delivery of arts, wherein, for the most part, from grammar to logic, mathematic, physic, and the rest, the rules chiefly necessary to be borne away are compiled in verses. So that verse being in itself sweet and orderly, and being best for memory, the only handle of knowledge, it must be in jest that any man can speak against it.

Now then go we to the most important imputations laid to the poor poets; for aught I can yet learn they are these.

First, that there being many other more fruitful knowledges, a man might better spend his time in them than in this.

Secondly, that it is the mother of lies.

Thirdly, that it is the nurse of abuse, infecting us with many pestilent desires, with a siren's sweetness drawing the mind to the serpent's tail of sinful fancies,— and herein especially comedies give the largest field to ear [plough—ed.] as Chaucer says; how, both in other nations and in ours, before poets did soften us, we were full of courage, given to martial exercises, the pillars of manlike liberty, and not lulled asleep in shady idleness with poets' pastimes.

And, lastly and chiefly, they cry out with an open mouth, as if they had overshot Robin Hood, that Plato banished them out of his Commonwealth. Truly this is much, if there be much truth in it.

First, to the first, that a man might better spend his time is a reason indeed; but it doth, as they say, but *petere principium* [to return or revert to the begin- ning—ed.]. For if it be, as I affirm, that no learning is so good as that which teaches and moves to virtue, and that none can both teach and move thereto so much as poesy, then is the conclusion manifest that ink and paper cannot be to a more profitable purpose employed. And certainly, though a man should grant their first assumption, it should follow, methinks, very unwillingly, that good is not good because better is better. But I still and utterly deny that there is sprung out of earth a more fruitful knowledge.

To the second, therefore, that they should be the principal liars, I answer paradoxically, but truly, I think truly, that of all writers under the sun the poet is the least liar; and though he would, as a poet can scarcely be a liar. The astronomer, with his cousin the geometrician, can hardly escape when they take upon them to measure the height of the stars. How often, think you, do the physicians lie, when they aver things good for sicknesses, which afterwards send Charon a great number of souls drowned in a potion before they come to his ferry? And no less of the rest which take upon them to affirm. Now for the poet, he nothing affirms, and therefore never lies. For, as I take it, to lie is to affirm that to be true which is false; so as the other artists, and especially the historian, affirming many things, can, in the cloudy knowledge of mankind, hardly escape from many lies. But the poet, as I said before, never affirms. The poet never makes any circles about your imagination, to conjure you to believe for true what he writes. He cites not authorities of other histories, but even for his entry calls the sweet Muses to inspire into him a good invention; in troth, not laboring to tell you what is or is not, but what should or should not be. And therefore though he recount things not true, yet because he tells them not for true he lies not; without we will say that Nathan lied in his speech, before alleged, to David; which, as a wicked man durst scarce say, so think I none so simple would say that Æsop lied in the tales of his beasts; for who thinks that Æsop wrote it for actually true, were well worthy to have his name chronicled among the beasts he writes of. What child is there that, coming to a play, and seeing Thebes written in great letters upon an old door, doth believe that it is Thebes? If then a man can arrive at that child's age, to know that the poet's persons and doings are but pictures what should be, and not stories what have been, they will never give the lie to things not affirmatively but allegorically and figuratively written. And therefore, as in history looking for truth, they may go away full-fraught with falsehood, so in poesy looking but for fiction, they shall use the narration but as an imaginative ground—plot of a profitable invention. But hereto is replied that the poets give names to men they write of, which argues a conceit of an actual truth, and so, not being true, proves a falsehood. And doth the lawyer lie then, when, under the names of John of the Stile, and John of the Nokes, he puts his case? But that is easily answered: their naming of men is but to make their picture the more lively, and not to build any history. Painting men, they cannot leave men nameless. We see we cannot play at chess but that we must give names to our chess-men; and yet, me thinks, he were a very partial champion of truth that would say we lied for giving a piece of wood the reverend title of a bishop. The poet names Cyrus and Æneas no other way than to show what men of their fames, fortunes, and estates should do.

Their third is, how much it abuses men's wit, training it to wanton sinfulness and lustful love. For indeed that is the principal, if not the only, abuse I can hear alleged. They say the comedies rather teach than reprehend amorous conceits. They say the lyric is larded with passionate sonnets, the elegiac weeps the want of his mistress, and that even to the heroical Cupid has ambitiously climbed. Alas! Love, I would thou couldst as well defend thyself as thou canst offend others! I would those on whom thou dost attend could either put thee away, or yield good reason why they keep thee! But grant love of beauty to be a beastly fault, although it be very hard, since only man, and no beast, has that gift to discern beauty; grant that lovely name of Love to deserve all hateful reproaches, although even some of my masters the philosophers spent a good deal of their lamp-oil in setting forth the excellency of it; grant, I say, whatsoever they will have granted that not only love, but lust, but vanity, but, if they list, scurrility possesses many leaves of the poets' books; yet think I when this is granted, they will find their sentence may with good manners put the last words foremost, and not say that poetry abuses man's wit, but that man's wit abuses poetry.

For I will not deny, but that man's wit may make poesy, which should be *eikastikē*, which some learned have defined "figuring forth good things," to be *phantastikē*, which doth contrariwise infect the fancy with unworthy objects; as the painter that should give to the eye either some excellent perspective, or some fine picture fit for building or fortification, or containing in it some notable example, as Abraham sacrificing his son Isaac, Judith killing Holofernes, David fighting with Goliath, may leave those, and please an ill pleased eye with wanton shows of better-hidden matters. But what! shall the abuse of a thing make the right use odious? Nay, truly, though I yield that poesy may not only be abused, but that being abused, by the reason of his sweet charming force, it can do more hurt than any other army of words, yet shall it be so far from concluding that the abuse should give reproach to the abused, that contrariwise it is a good reason, that whatsoever, being abused, doth most harm, being rightly used—and upon the right use each thing receives his title—doth most good. Do we not see the skill of physic, the best rampire [rampart—ed.] to our often-assaulted bodies, being abused, teach poison, the most violent destroyer? Doth not knowledge of law, whose end is to even and right all things, being abused, grow the crooked fosterer of horrible injuries? Doth not, to go in the highest, God's word abused breed heresy, and his name abused become blasphemy? Truly a needle cannot do much hurt, and as truly—with leave of ladies be it spoken—it cannot do much good. With a sword thou may kill thy father, and with a sword thou may defend thy prince and country. So that, as in their calling poets the fathers of lies they say nothing, so in this their argument of abuse they prove the commendation.

They allege herewith, that before poets began to be in price our nation has set their hearts' delight upon action, and not upon imagination; rather doing things worthy to be written, than writing things fit to be done. What that before-time was. I think scarcely Sphinx can tell; since no memory is so ancient that has the precedence of poetry. And certain it is that, in our plainest homeliness, yet never was the Albion nation without poetry. Marry, this argument, though

it be leveled against poetry, yet is it indeed a chainshot against all learning,—
or bookishness, as they commonly term it. Of such mind were certain Goths,
of whom it is written that, having in the spoil of a famous city taken a fair
library, one hangman—belike fit to execute the fruits of their wits—who had
murdered a great number of bodies, would have set fire in it. "No," said another
very gravely, "take heed what you do; for while they are busy about these toys,
we shall with more leisure conquer their countries." This, indeed, is the ordinary doctrine of ignorance, and many words sometimes I have heard spent in
it; but because this reason is generally against all learning, as well as poetry, or
rather all learning but poetry; because it were too large a digression to handle,
or at least too superfluous, since it is manifest that all government of action is
to be gotten by knowledge, and knowledge best by gathering many knowledges,
which is reading; I only, with Horace, to him that is of that opinion

> *Jubeo stultum esse libenter*
> [I gladly bid him to be a fool—ed.]

for as for poetry itself, it is the freest from this objection, for poetry is the
companion of the camps. I dare undertake, Orlando Furioso or honest King
Arthur will never displease a soldier; but the quiddity of *ens*, and *prima materia*,
will hardly agree with a corselet. And therefore, as I said in the beginning, even
Turks and Tartars are delighted with poets. Homer, a Greek, flourished before
Greece flourished; and if to a slight conjecture a conjecture may be opposed,
truly it may seem, that as by him their learned men took almost their first light
of knowledge, so their active men received their first motions of courage. Only
Alexander's example may serve, who by Plutarch is accounted of such virtue,
that Fortune was not his guide but his footstool; whose acts speak for him,
though Plutarch did not; indeed the phoenix of warlike princes. This Alexander
left his schoolmaster, living Aristotle, behind him, but took dead Homer with
him. He put the philosopher Callisthenes to death for his seeming philosophical, indeed mutinous, stubbornness; but the chief thing he was ever heard to
wish for was that Homer had been alive. He well found he received more
bravery of mind by the pattern of Achilles, than by hearing the definition of
fortitude. And therefore if Cato misliked Fulvius for carrying Ennius with him
to the field, it may be answered that if Cato misliked it, the noble Fulvius liked
it, or else he had not done it. For it was not the excellent Cato Uticensis, whose
authority I would much more have reverenced; but it was the former, in truth
a bitter punisher of faults, but else a man that had never sacrificed to the Graces.
He misliked and cried out upon all Greek learning; and yet, being fourscore
years old, began to learn it, belike fearing that Pluto understood not Latin.
Indeed, the Roman laws allowed no person to be carried to the wars but he
that was in the soldiers' roll. And therefore though Cato misliked his unmus-

tered person, he misliked not his work. And if he had, Scipio Nasica, judged by common consent the best Roman, loved him. Both the other Scipio brothers, who had by their virtues no less surnames than of Asia and Afric, so loved him that they caused his body to be buried in their sepulcher. So as Cato's authority being but against his person, and that answered with so far greater than himself, is herein of no validity.

But now, indeed, my burthen is great, that Plato's name is laid upon me, whom I must confess, of all philosophers I have ever esteemed most worthy of reverence; and with great reason, since of all philosophers he is the most poetical; yet if he will defile the fountain out of which his flowing streams have proceeded, let us boldly examine with what reasons he did it.

First, truly, a man might maliciously object that Plato, being a philosopher, was a natural enemy of poets. For, indeed, after the philosophers had picked out of the sweet mysteries of poetry the right discerning true points of knowledge, they forthwith, putting it in method, and making a school-art of that which the poets did only teach by a divine delightfulness, beginning to spurn at their guides, like ungrateful prentices were not content to set up shops for themselves, but sought by all means to discredit their masters; which by the force of delight being barred them, the less they could overthrow them the more they hated them. For, indeed, they found for Homer seven cities strove who should have him for their citizen; where many cities banished philosophers, as not fit members to live among them. For only repeating certain of Euripides' verses, many Athenians had their lives saved of the Syracusans, where the Athenians themselves thought many philosophers unworthy to live. Certain poets as Simonides and Pindar, had so prevailed with Heiro the First, that of a tyrant they made him a just king; where Plato could do so little with Dionysius, that he himself of a philosopher was made a slave. But who should do thus, I confess, should requite the objections made against poets with like cavillations against philosophers; as likewise one should do that should bid one read Phædrus or Symposium in Plato, or the Discourse of Love in Plutarch, and see whether any poet do authorize abominable filthiness, as they do.

Again, a man might ask out of what commonwealth Plato doth banish them. In sooth, thence where he himself allows community of women. So as belike this banishment grew not for effeminate wantonness, since little should poetical sonnets be hurtful when a man might have what woman he listed. But I honor philosophical instructions, and bless the wits which bred them, so as they be not abused, which is likewise stretched to poetry. Saint Paul himself, who yet, for the credit of poets, alleges twice two poets, and one of them by the name of a prophet, sets a watchword upon philosophy,—indeed upon the abuse. So doth Plato upon the abuse, not upon poetry. Plato found fault that the poets of his time filled the world with wrong opinions of the gods, making light tales of that unspotted essence, and therefore would not have the youth depraved with such opinions. Herein may much be said; let this suffice: the poets did not induce such opinions, but did imitate those opinions already induced. For all the Greek stories can well testify that the very religion of that time stood upon many and many-fashioned gods; not taught so by the poets, but followed according to their nature of imitation. Who list may read in Plutarch the discourses of Isis and Osiris, of the Cause why Oracles ceased, of the Divine Providence, and see whether the theology of that nation stood not upon such dreams,—which the poets indeed superstitiously observed; and truly, since they had not the light of Christ, did much better in it than the philosophers, who, shaking off superstition, brought in atheism.

Plato therefore, whose authority I had much rather justly construe than unjustly resist, meant not in general of poets, in those words of which Julius Scaliger says, *Qua authoritate barbari quidam atque hispidi, abuti velint ad poetas e republica exigendos* [which authority (Plato's) some barbarians want to abuse, in order to banish poets from the state—ed.] but only meant to drive out those wrong opinions of the Deity, whereof now, without further law, Christianity has taken away all the hurtful belief, perchance, as he thought, nourished by the then esteemed poets. And a man need go no further than to Plato himself to know his meaning; who, in his dialogue called *Ion*, gives high and rightly divine commendation unto poetry. So as Plato, banishing the abuse, not the thing, not banishing it, but giving due honor unto it, shall be our patron and not our adversary. For, indeed, I had much rather, since truly I may do it, show their mistaking of Plato, under whose lion's skin they would make an ass—like braying against poesy, than go about to overthrow his authority; whom, the wiser a man is, the more just cause he shall find to have in admiration; especially since he attributes unto poesy more than myself do, namely to be a very inspiring of a divine force, far above man's wit, as in the forenamed dialogue is apparent.

Of the other side, who would show the honors have been by the best sort of judgments granted them, a whole sea of examples would present themselves: Alexanders, Cæsars, Scipios, all favorers of poets; Lælius, called the Roman Socrates, himself a poet, so as part of *Heautontimoroumenos* in Terence was supposed to be made by him. And even the Greek Socrates, whom Apollo confirmed to be the only wise man, is said to have spent part of his old time in putting Æsop's Fables into verses; and therefore full evil should it become his scholar, Plato, to put such words in his master's mouth against poets. But what needs more? Aristotle writes the Art of Poesy; and why, if it should not be written? Plutarch teaches the use to be gathered of them; and how, if they should not be read? And who reads Plutarch's either history or philosophy, shall find he trims both their garments with guards [ornaments—ed.] of poesy. But I list not to defend poesy with the help of his underling historiography. Let it suffice that it is a fit soil for praise to dwell upon; and what dispraise may set upon it, is either easily overcome, or transformed into just commendation.

So that since the excellencies of it may be so easily and so justly confirmed, and the low-creeping objections so soon trodden down: it not being an art of lies, but of true doctrine; not of effeminateness, but of notable stirring of courage; not of abusing man's wit, but of strengthening man's wit; not banished, but honored by Plato; let us rather plant more laurels for to engarland our poets' heads—which honor of being laureate, as besides them only triumphant captains were, is a sufficient authority to show the price they ought to be held in—than suffer the ill-savored breath of such wrong speakers once to blow upon the clear springs of poesy.

But since I have run so long a career in this matter, methinks, before I give my pen a full stop, it shall be but a little more lost time to inquire why England, the mother of excellent minds, should be grown so hard a stepmother to poets; who certainly in wit ought to pass all others, since all only proceeds from their wit, being indeed makers of themselves, not takers of others. How can I but exclaim,

> Musa, mihi causas memora, quo numine læso?
> [O Muse, recall to me the causes by which her divine will
>   had been slighted—ed.]

Sweet poesy! that has anciently had kings, emperors, senators, great captains, such as, besides a thousand others, David, Adrian, Sophocles, Germanicus, not only to favor poets, but to be poets; and of our nearer times can present for her patrons a Robert, King of Sicily; the great King Francis of France; King James of Scotland; such cardinals as Bembus and Bibbiena; such famous preachers and teachers as Beza and Melancthon; so learned philosophers as Fracastorius and Scaliger; so great orators as Pontanus and Muretus; so piercing wits as George Buchanan; so grave counselors as—besides many, but before all—that Hospital of France, than whom, I think, that realm never brought forth a more accomplished judgment more firmly builded upon virtue; I say these, with numbers of others, not only to read others' poesies but to poetize for others' reading. That poesy, thus embraced in all other places, should only find in our time a hard welcome in England, I think the very earth laments it, and therefore decks our soil with fewer laurels than it was accustomed. For heretofore poets have in England also flourished; and, which is to be noted, even in those time when the trumpet of Mars did sound loudest. And now that an over-faint quietness should seem to strew the house for poets, they are almost in as good reputation as the mountebanks at Venice. Truly even that, as of the one side it gives great praise to poesy, which, like Venus—but to better purpose—has rather be troubled in the net with Mars, than enjoy the homely quiet of Vulcan; so serves it for a piece of a reason why they are less grateful to idle England, which now can scarce endure the pain of a pen. Upon this necessarily follows, that base men with servile wits undertake it, who think it enough if they can be rewarded of the printer. And so as Epaminondas is said, with the honor of his virtue to have made an office, by his exercising it, which before was contempt-ible, to become highly respected; so these men, no more but setting their names to it, by their own disgracefulness disgrace the most graceful poesy. For now, as if all the Muses were got with child to bring forth bastard poets, without any commission they do post over the banks of Helicon, till they make their readers more weary than posthorses; while, in the meantime, they,

> *Queis meliore luto finxit præcordia Titan,*
> [On hearts the Titan has formed better clay—ed.]

are better content to suppress the outflowings of their wit, than by publishing them to be accounted knights of the same order.

But I that, before ever I dust aspire unto the dignity, am admitted into the company of the paper-blurrers, do find the very true cause of our wanting estimation is want of desert, taking upon us to be poets in despite of Pallas [though lacking inspiration—ed.]. Now wherein we want desert were a thank-worthy labor to express; but if I knew, I should have mended myself. But as I never desired the title, so have I neglected the means to come by it; only, overmastered by some thoughts, I yielded an inky tribute unto them. Marry, they that delight in poesy itself should seek to know what they do and how they do; and especially look themselves in an unflattering glass of reason, if they be inclinable unto it. For poesy must not be drawn by the ears, it must be gently led, or rather it must lead; which was partly the cause that made the ancient learned affirm it was a divine gift, and no human skill, since all other knowl-edges lie ready for any that has strength of wit, a poet no industry can make if his own genius be not carried into it. And therefore is it an old proverb: *Orator fit, poeta nascitur* [the orator is made, the poet is born—ed.]. Yet confess I always that, as the fertilest ground must be manured [cultivated—ed.], so must the highest-flying wit have a Dædalus to guide him That Dædalus, they say, both in this and in other, has three wings to bear itself up into the air of due commen-dation: that is, art, imitation, and exercise. But these neither artificial rules nor imitative patterns, we much cumber ourselves withal. Exercise indeed we do, but that very fore-backwardly, for where we should exercise to know, we exercise as having known; and so is our brain delivered of much matter which never was begotten by knowledge. For there being two principal parts, matter to be expressed by words, and words to express the matter, in neither we use art or imitation rightly. Our matter is *quodlibet* indeed, though wrongly performing Ovid's verse,

> *Quicquid conabar dicere, versus erat;*
> [Whatever I tried to say was poetry—ed.]

never marshalling it into any assured rank, that almost the readers cannot tell where to find themselves.

Chaucer, undoubtedly, did excellently in his *Troilus and Cressida*; of whom, truly, I know not whether to marvel more, either that he in that misty time could see so clearly, or that we in this clear age walk so stumblingly after him. Yet had he great wants, fit to be forgiven in so revered antiquity. I account the *Mirror of Magistrates* meetly furnished of beautiful parts; and in the Earl of Surrey's lyrics many things tasting of a noble birth, and worthy of a noble mind. The *Shepherd's Calendar* has much poetry in his eclogues, indeed worthy the reading, if I be not deceived. That same framing of his style to an old rustic language I dare not allow, since neither Theocritus in Greek, Virgil in Latin, nor Sannazzaro in Italian did affect it. Besides these, I do not remember to have seen but few (to speak boldly) printed, that have poetical sinews in them. For proof whereof, let but most of the verses be put in prose, and then ask the meaning, and it will be found that one verse did but beget another, without ordering at the first what should be at the last; which becomes a confused mass of words, with a tinkling sound of rime, barely accompanied with reason.

Our tragedies and comedies not without cause cried out against, observing rules neither of honest civility nor of skilful poetry, excepting *Gorboduc*, — again I say of those that I have seen. Which notwithstanding as it is full of stately speeches and well-sounding phrases, climbing to the height of Seneca's style, and as full of notable morality, which it doth most delightfully teach, and so obtain the very end of poesy; yet in truth it is very defectious in the circumstances, which grieves me, because it might not remain as an exact model of all tragedies. For it is faulty both in place and time, the two necessary companions of all corporal actions. For where the stage should always represent but one place, and the uttermost time presupposed in it should be, both by Aristotle's precept and common reason, but one day; there is both many days and many places inartificially imagined.

But if it be so in *Gorboduc*, how much more in all the rest? where you shall have Asia of the one side, and Afric of the other, and so many other under-kingdoms, that the player, when he comes in, must ever begin with telling where he is, or else the tale will not be conceived. Now ye shall have three ladies walk to gather flowers, and then we must believe the stage to be a garden. By and by we hear news of shipwreck in the same place, and then we are to blame if we accept it not for a rock. Upon the back of that comes out a hideous monster with fire and smoke, and then the miserable beholders are bound to take it for a cave. While in the mean time two armies fly in, represented with four swords and bucklers, and then what hard heart will not receive it for a pitched field?

Now of time they are much more liberal. For ordinary it is that two young princes fall in love; after many traverses she is got with child, delivered of a fair boy, he is lost, grows a man, falls in love, and is ready to get another child, —

and all this in two hours' space; which how absurd it is in sense even sense may imagine, and art has taught, and all ancient examples justified, and at this day the ordinary players in Italy will not err in. Yet will some bring in an example of *Eunuchus* in Terence, that contains matter of two days, yet far short of twenty years. True it is, and so was it to be played in two days, and so fitted to the time it set forth. And though Plautus have in one place done amiss, let us hit with him, and not miss with him. But they will say, How then shall we set forth a story which contains both many places and many times? And do they not know that a tragedy is tied to the laws of poesy, and not of history; not bound to follow the story, but having liberty either to feign a quite new matter, or to frame the history to the most tragical convenience? Again, many things may be told which cannot be showed,—if they know the difference betwixt reporting and representing. As for example I may speak, though I am here, of Peru, and in speech digress from that to the description of Calicut; but in action I cannot represent it without Pacolet's horse. And so was the manner the ancients took, by some Nuntius [messenger—ed.] to recount things done in former time or other place.

Lastly, if they will represent a history, they must not, as Horace says, begin *ab ovo* [from the egg—ed.] but they must come to the principal point of that one action which they will represent. By example this will be best expressed. I have a story of young Polydorus, delivered for safety's sake, with great riches, by his father Priamus to Polymnestor, King of Thrace, in the Trojan war time. He, after some years, hearing the overthrow of Priamus, for to make the treasure his own murders the child; the body of the child is taken up by Hecuba; she, the same day, finds a sleight to be revenged most cruelly of the tyrant. Where now would one of our tragedy writers begin, but with the delivery of the child? Then should he sail over into Thrace, and so spend I know not how many years, and travel numbers of places. But where doth Euripides? Even with the finding of the body, leaving the rest to be told by the spirit of Polydorus. This needs no further to be enlarged; the dullest wit may conceive it.

But, besides these gross absurdities, how all their plays be neither right tragedies nor right comedies, mingling kings and clowns, not because the matter so carries it, but thrust in the clown by head and shoulders to play a part in majestical matters, with neither decency nor discretion; so as neither the admiration and commiseration, nor the right sportfulness, is by their mongrel tragi-comedy obtained. I know Apuleius did somewhat so, but that is a thing recounted with space of time, not represented in one moment; and I know the ancients have one or two examples of tragi-comedies, as Plautus has *Amphytrio*. But, if we mark them well, we shall find that they never, or very daintily, match hornpipes and funerals. So falls it out that, having indeed no right comedy in that comical part of our tragedy, we have nothing but scurrility, unworthy of any chaste ears, or some extreme show of doltishness, indeed fit to lift up a loud laughter, and nothing else; where the whole tract of a comedy should be full of delight, as the tragedy should be still maintained in a well-raised admiration.

But our comedians think there is no delight without laughter, which is very wrong; for though laughter may come with delight, yet comes it not of delight, as though delight should be the cause of laughter; but well may one thing breed both together. Nay, rather in themselves they have, as it were, a kind of contrariety. For delight we scarcely do, but in things that have a convenience to ourselves, or to the general nature; laughter almost ever comes of things most disproportioned to ourselves and nature. Delight has a joy in it either permanent or present; laughter has only a scornful tickling. For example, we are ravished with delight to see a fair woman, and yet are far from being moved to laughter. We laugh at deformed creatures, wherein certainly we cannot delight. We delight in good chances, we laugh at mischances. We delight to hear the happiness of our friends and country, at which he were worthy to be laughed at that would laugh. We shall, contrarily, laugh sometimes to find a matter quite mistaken and go down the hill against the bias, in the mouth of some such men, as for the respect of them one shall be heartily sorry he cannot choose but laugh, and so is rather pained than delighted with laughter. Yet deny I not but that they may go well together. For as in Alexander's picture well set out we delight without laughter, and in twenty mad antics we laugh without delight; so in Hercules, painted with his great beard and furious countenance, in woman's attire, spinning at Omphale's commandment, it breeds both delight and laughter; for the representing of so strange a power in love, procures delight, and the scornfulness of the action stirs laughter.

But I speak to this purpose, that all the end of the comical part be not upon such scornful matters as stir laughter only, but mixed with it that delightful teaching which is the end of poesy. And the great fault, even in that point of laughter, and forbidden plainly by Aristotle, is that they stir laughter in sinful things, which are rather execrable than ridiculous; or in miserable, which are rather to be pitied than scorned. For what is it to make folks gape at a wretched beggar or a beggarly clown, or, against law of hospitality, to jest at strangers because they speak not English so well as we do? what do we learn? since it is certain:

> Nil habet infelix paupertas durius in se,
> Quam quod ridiculos homines facit.
> [Unhappy poverty has nothing in it harder than this:
> It makes men ridiculous—ed.]

But rather a busy loving courtier; a heartless threatening Thraso; a self-wise-seeming schoolmaster; a wry transformed traveler: these if we saw walk in stage-names, which we play naturally, therein were delightful laughter and teaching delightfulness,—as in the other, the tragedies of Buchanan do justly bring forth a divine admiration.

But I have lavished out too many words of this playmatter. I do it, because as they are excelling parts of poesy, so is there none so much used in England, and none can be more pitifully abused; which, like an unmannerly daughter, showing a bad education, causes her mother Poesy's honesty to be called in question.

Other sorts of poetry almost have we none, but that lyrical kind of songs and sonnets, which, Lord if he gave us so good minds, how well it might be employed, and with how heavenly fruits both private and public, in singing the praises of the immortal beauty, the immortal goodness of that God who gives us hands to write, and wits to conceive!—of which we might well want words, but never matter; of which we could turn our eyes to nothing, but we should ever have new-budding occasions.

But truly, many of such writings as come under the banner of unresistible love, if I were a mistress would never persuade me they were in love; so coldly they apply fiery speeches, as men that had rather read lovers' writings, and so caught up certain swelling phrases—which hang together like a man which once told me the wind was at north-west and by south, because he would be sure to name winds enough—than that in truth they feel those passions, which easily, as I think, may be bewrayed by that same forcibleness, or *energia* (as the Greeks call it) of the writer. But let this be a sufficient, though short note, that we miss the right use of the material point of poesy.

Now for the outside of it, which is words, or (as I may term it) diction, it is even well worse, so is that honey-flowing matron eloquence appareled or rather disguised, in a courtesan-like painted affection: one time with so farfetched words, that many seem monsters—but must seem strangers—to any poor Englishman; another time with coursing of a letter [alliteration—ed.] as if they were bound to follow the method of a dictionary; another time with figures and flowers extremely winter-starved.

But I would this fault were only peculiar to versifiers, and had not as large possession among prose-printers, and, which is to be marveled, among many scholars, and, which is to be pitied, among some preachers. Truly I could wish—if at least I might be so bold to wish in a thing beyond the reach of my capacity—the diligent imitators of Tully and Demosthenes (most worthy to be imitated) did not so much keep Nizolian paper-books of their figures and phrases, as by attentive translation, as it were devour them whole, and make them wholly theirs. For now they cast sugar and spice upon every dish that is served to the table; like those Indians, not content to wear ear-rings at the fit and natural place of the ears, but they will thrust jewels through their nose and lips, because they will be sure to be fine. Tully, when he was to drive out Catiline as it were with a thunderbolt of eloquence, often used that figure of repetition, as *Vivit. Vivit? Immo vero etiam in senatum venit, etc.* [He lives. Does he live? In truth, he even comes to the Senate—ed.]. Indeed, inflamed with a well-grounded rage, he would have his words, as it were, double out of his mouth; and so do that artificially, which we see men in choler do naturally. And we, having noted the grace of those words, hale them in sometime to a familiar epistle, when it were too much choler to be choleric. How well store of *similiter* cadences [rhymes—ed.] doth sound with the gravity of the pulpit, I would but invoke Demosthenes' soul to tell, who with a rare daintiness uses them. Truly they have made me think of the sophister that with too much subtlety would prove two eggs three, and though he might be counted a sophister, had none for his labor. So these men bringing in such a kind of eloquence, well may they obtain an opinion of a seeming fineness, but persuade few,—which should be the end of their fineness.

Now for similitudes in certain printed discourses, I think all herbarists, all stories of beasts, fowls, and fishes are rifled up, that they may come in multitudes to wait upon any of our conceits, which certainly is as absurd a surfeit to the ears as is possible. For the force of a similitude not being to prove any thing to a contrary disputer, but only to explain to a willing hearer; when that is done, the rest is a most tedious prattling, rather overswaying the memory from the purpose whereto they were applied, then any whit informing the judgment, already either satisfied of by similitudes not to be satisfied.

For my part, I do not doubt, when Antonius and Crassus, the great forefathers of Cicero in eloquence, the one (as Cicero testifies of them) pretended not to know art, the other not to set by it, because [so that—ed.] with a plain sensibleness they might win credit of popular ears, which credit is the nearest step to persuasion, which persuasion is the chief mark of oratory,—I do not doubt, I say, but that they used these knacks, very sparingly; which who doth generally use any man may see doth dance to his own music, and so be noted by the audience more careful to speak curiously than truly. Undoubtedly (at least to my opinion undoubtedly) I have found in divers small-learned courtiers a more sound style than in some professors of learning; of which I can guess no other cause, but that the courtier following that which by practice he finds fittest to nature, therein, though he know it not, doth according to art—though not by art; where the other, using art to show art and not to hide art as in these cases he should do—flies from nature, and indeed abuses art.

But what! me thinks I deserve to be pounded for straying from poetry to oratory. But both have such an affinity in the wordish consideration, that I think this digression will make my meaning receive the fuller understanding:—which is not to take upon me to teach poets how they should do, but only, finding myself sick among the rest, to show some one or two spots of the common infection grown among the most part of writers; that, acknowledging ourselves somewhat awry, we may bend to the right use both of matter and manner:

whereto our language gives us great occasion, being, indeed, capable of any excellent exercising of it.

I know some will say it is a mingled language. And why not so much the better, taking the best of both the other? Another will say it wants grammar. Nay, truly, it has that praise that it wants not grammar. For grammar it might have, but it needs it not; being so easy in itself, and so void of those cumbersome differences of cases, genders, moods, and tenses, which, I think, was a piece of the Tower of Babylon's curse, that a man should be put to school to learn his mother-tongue. But for the uttering sweetly and properly the conceits of the mind, which is the end of speech, that has it equally with any other tongue in the world; and is particularly happy in compositions of two or three words together, near the Greek, far beyond the Latin,—which is one of the greatest beauties that can be in a language.

Now of versifying there are two sorts, the one ancient, the other modern. The ancient marked the quantity of each syllable, and according to that framed his verse; the modern observing only number, with some regard of the accent, the chief life of it stands in that like sounding of the words, which we call rime. Whether of these be the more excellent would bear many speeches; the ancient no doubt more fit for music, both words and tune observing quantity; and more fit lively to express divers passions, by the low or lofty sound of the well-weighed syllable. The latter likewise with his rime strikes a certain music to the ear; and, in fine, since it doth delight, though by another way, it obtains the same purpose; there being in either, sweetness, and wanting in neither, majesty. Truly the English, before any other vulgar language I know, is fit for both sorts. For, for the ancient, the Italian is so full of vowels that it must ever be cumbered with elisions; the Dutch so, of the other side, with consonants, that they cannot yield the sweet sliding fit for a verse. The French in his whole language has not one word that has his accent in the last syllable saving two, called antepenultima, and little more has the Spanish; and therefore very gracelessly may they use dactyls. The English is subject to none of these defects. Now for rime [rhythm—ed.], though we do not observe quantity, yet we observe the accent very precisely, which other languages either cannot do, or will not do so absolutely. That cæsura, or breathing-place in the midst of the verse, neither Italian nor Spanish have, the French and we never almost fail of.

Lastly, even the very rime itself the Italian cannot put in the last syllable, by the French named the masculine rime, but still in the next to the last, which the French call the female, or the next before that, which the Italians term *sdrucciola*. The example of the former is *buono: suono*; of the *sdrucciola* is *femina: semina*. The French, of the other side, has both the male, as *bon: son*, and the female, as *plaise: taise*; but the *sdrucciola* he has not. Where the English has all three, as *due: true, father: rather, motion: potion*; with much more which might be said, but that already I find the triflingness of this discourse is much too much enlarged.

So that since the ever praiseworthy poesy is full of virtue-breeding delightfulness, and void of no gift that ought to be in the noble name of learning; since the blames laid against it are either false or feeble; since the cause why it is not esteemed in England is the fault of poet-apes, not poets; since, lastly, our tongue is most fit to honor poesy, and to be honored by poesy; I conjure you all that have had the evil luck to read this ink-wasting toy of mine, even in the name of the Nine Muses, no more to scorn the sacred mysteries of poesy; no more to laugh at the name of poets, as though they were next inheritors to fools; no more to jest at the reverend title of "a rhymer"; but to believe, with Aristotle, that they were the ancient treasurers of the Grecians' divinity; to believe, with Bembus, that they were first bringers—in of all civility; to believe, with Scaliger, that no philosopher's precepts can sooner make you an honest man than the reading of Virgil; to believe, with Clauserus, the translator of Cornutus, that it pleased the Heavenly Deity by Hesiod and Homer, under the veil of fables, to give us all knowledge, logic, rhetoric, philosophy natural and moral, and *quid non?* to believe, with me, that there are many mysteries contained in poetry which of purpose were written darkly, lest by profane wits it should be abused; to believe, with Landino, that they are so beloved of the gods, that whatsoever they write proceeds of a divine fury; lastly, to believe themselves, when they tell you they will make you immortal by their verses.

Thus doing, your name shall flourish in the printers' shops. Thus doing, you shall be of kin to many a poetical preface. Thus doing, you shall be most fair, most rich, most wise, most all; you shall dwell upon superlatives. Thus doing, though you be *libertino patre natus* [the son of a freedman], you shall suddenly grow *Herculea proles* [Herculean offspring—ed.]:

> *Si quid mea carmina possunt.*
> [If my verses can do anything—ed.]

Thus doing, your soul shall be placed with Dante's Beatrice or Virgil's Anchises.

But if—fie of such a but!—you be born so near the dull-making cataract of Nilus, that you cannot hear the planet-like music of poetry; if you have so earth-creeping a mind that it cannot lift itself up to look to the sky of poetry, or rather, by a certain rustical disdain, will become such a mome [blockhead—ed.], as to be a Momus of poetry; then, though I will not wish unto you the ass' ears of Midas, nor to be driven by a poet's verses, as Bubonax was, to hang himself; nor to be rimed to death, as is said to be done in Ireland; yet thus much curse I must send you in the behalf of all poets:—that while you live in love, and never get favor for lacking skill of a sonnet; and when you die, your memory die from the earth for want of an epitaph.

8

JOHN MILTON (1608–1674)

Despite occasional attacks—notably by Samuel Johnson in the eighteenth century and by Ezra Pound and T. S. Eliot in the twentieth—Milton is securely in
place as the second-greatest poet in English, surpassed only by Shakespeare.
The son of a prosperous scrivener, Milton was born in London and educated
at Cambridge. After spending several years in seclusion, studying and preparing
himself for great things, he traveled on the Continent and met, among many
other notables, Galileo. Such meetings affected his concept of the solar system
and enlarged the scope of his references and metaphors. For about the middle
twenty years of his life, Milton took on some bureaucratic chores as Latin
Secretary to Oliver Cromwell's Council of State, and it was not until the Restoration in 1660 that he was free to return to poetry. His sight was failing during
his state service, and by the middle of the 1650s he was totally blind. His greatest
work, *Paradise Lost*, was published in 1667, and *Paradise Regained* and *Samson
Agonistes* followed four years later. He was a master of the epic style but could
also write tender personal sonnets. Around 1800 his influence reasserted itself,
and he become an important force in the work of William Blake, William
Wordsworth, Lord Byron, Percy Bysshe Shelley, and John Keats. It was at this
time that Robert Bridges wrote a brilliant study of Milton's prosody. Milton
served as an exemplar in more ways than one: he was a poet of noble elevation
and mythic scope; he was a polemicist of great vigor and eloquence; and, despite

limitations, he could be considered a patriotic Englishman. When Wordsworth expressed the sad condition of his country, he expressed it in a Miltonic sonnet beginning, "Milton! Thou shouldst be living at this hour. / England hath need of thee. . . ." The movie about English athletic patriotism, *Chariots of Fire*, takes its title from some lines by William Blake in a work called *Milton* (around 1802).

"OF EDUCATION" (1645; EXCERPT)

Originally published as a pamphlet-letter entitled "Of Education: To Master Samuel Hartlib" (1645), this text came to be known as "Tractate on Education," by which title it is known in *The Harvard Classics*, vol. 3 (New York: Collier, 1909–14).

For the studies, first they should begin with the chief and necessary rules of some good grammar, either that now used, or any better: and while this is doing, their speech is to be fashioned to a distinct and clear pronunciation, as near as may be to the Italian, especially in the vowels. For we Englishmen being far northerly, do not open our mouths in the cold air, wide enough to grace a southern tongue; but are observed by all other nations to speak exceeding close and inward: So that to smatter Latin with an English mouth, is as ill a hearing as Law-French. Next to make them expert in the usefulest points of grammar, and withal to season them, and win them early to the love of virtue and true labor, ere any flattering seducement, or vain principle seize them wandering, some easy and delightful book of education would be read to them; whereof the Greeks have store, as Cebes, Plutarch, and other Socratic discourses. But in Latin we have none of classic authority extant, except the two or three first books of Quintilian, and some select pieces elsewhere. But here the main skill and groundwork will be, to temper them such lectures and explanations upon every opportunity as may lead and draw them in willing obedience, inflamed with the study of learning, and the admiration of virtue; stirred up with high hopes of living to be brave men, and worthy patriots, dear to God, and famous to all ages. That they may despise and scorn all their childish, and ill-taught qualities, to delight in manly, and liberal exercises: which he who hath the art, and proper eloquence to catch them with, what with mild and effectual persuasions, and what with the intimation of some fear, if need be, but chiefly by his own example, might in a short space gain them to an incredible diligence and courage: infusing into their young breasts such an ingenuous and noble ardor, as would not fail to make many of them renowned and matchless men. . . .

And now lastly will be the time to read with them those organic [practical, instrumental—ed.] arts which enable men to discourse and write perspicuously, elegantly, and according to the fitted style of lofty, mean or lowly. Logic therefore so much as is useful, is to be referred to this due place with all her well couched heads and topics, until to be time to open her contracted palm into a graceful and ornate rhetoric taught out of the rule of Plato, Aristotle, Phalereus, Cicero, Hermogenes, Longinus. To which poetry would be made subsequent, or indeed rather precedent, as being less subtle and fine, but more simple, sensuous and passionate. I mean not here the prosody of a verse, which they could not have hit on before among the rudiments of grammar; but that sublime art which in Aristotle's *Poetics*, in Horace, and the Italian commentaries of Castelvetro, Tasso, Mazzoni, and others, teaches what the laws are of a true epic poem, what of a dramatic, what of a lyric, what decorum is, which is the grand masterpiece to observe. This would make them soon perceive what despicable creatures our common rimers and playwriters be, and show them, what religious, what glorious and magnificent use might be made of poetry both in divine and human things. From hence and not till now will be the right season of forming them to be able writers and composers in every excellent matter, when they shall be thus fraught with an universal insight into things. Or whether they be to speak in Parliament or council, honor and attention would be waiting on their lips. There would then also appear in pulpits other visages, other gestures, and stuff otherwise wrought than what we now sit under, ofttimes to as great a trial of our patience as any other that they preach to us. These are the studies wherein our noble and our gentle youth ought to bestow their time in a disciplinary way from twelve to one and twenty; unless they rely more upon their ancestors dead, than upon themselves living.

9

JOHN DRYDEN (1631–1700)

During the quarter-century between Milton's death in 1674 and his own death in 1700, Dryden was the most important and accomplished poet in England. (Samuel Johnson and others report that Milton regarded Dryden as "a good rhymist, but no poet.") A product of Westminster and Cambridge, Dryden was brilliant as a dramatist, a critic, a translator, and a satirist. Now and then he looked back to the work of Chaucer, Shakespeare, and Jonson, occasionally attempting modernizations of earlier writing, but he also looked ahead to the public poetry that dominated the first half of the eighteenth century in the forms of satire, translation, and ethical and aesthetic essays in prose and verse; he also looked ahead in the use of the heroic couplet and the heroic quatrain. These innovations are so striking that he is often counted as an eighteenth-century poet, even though he died in the seventeenth century.

"An Essay of Dramatic Poesy," published in 1668, takes the form of a dialogue on a boat on the River Thames in June of 1665, the time of a naval battle between the English and the Dutch. Dryden is represented by Neander ("New Man"). Other speakers have been identified as Charles Sackville ("Eugenius"), Sir Robert Howard ("Crites"), and Sir Charles Sedley ("Lisideius"). These people were influential thinkers and writers of the age. It remains a clever device (foreshadowed by Plato and later imitated by Oscar Wilde, T. S. Eliot, Elder

Olson, Hugh Kenner, and others)—to produce a dramatic dialogue on dramatic poetry. In the seventeenth century the "Essay" was strong evidence of England's claim to authority in literature and criticism; in the eighteenth century and afterwards the "Essay" continued as a model of orderly argument and patriotic ardor alike.

AN ESSAY OF DRAMATIC POESY (1668)

Text and notes, unless otherwise indicated, are adapted from *Essays of John Dryden*, ed. W. P. Ker (Oxford: Clarendon Press, 1926).

It was that memorable day, in the first Summer of the late War, when our Navy engaged the Dutch: a day wherein the two most mighty and best appointed Fleets which any age had ever seen, disputed the command of the greater half of the Globe, the commerce of Nations, and the riches of the Universe. While these vast floating bodies, on either side, moved against each other in parallel lines, and our Country men, under the happy conduct of his Royal Highness, went breaking, by little and little, into the line of the Enemies; the noise of the Cannon from both Navies reached our ears about the City: so that all men, being alarmed with it, and in a dreadful suspense of the event, which we knew was then deciding, every one went following the sound as his fancy led him; and leaving the Town almost empty, some took towards the Park, some cross the River, others down it; all seeking the noise in the depth of silence.

Amongst the rest, it was the fortune of Eugenius, Crites, Lisideius and Neander, to be in company together: three of them persons whom their wit and Quality have made known to all the Town: and whom I have chose to hide under these borrowed names, that they may not suffer by so ill a relation as I am going to make of their discourse.

Taking then a Barge which a servant of Lisideus had provided for them, they made haste to shoot the Bridge, and left behind them that great fall of waters which hindered them from hearing what they desired: after which, having disengaged themselves from many Vessels which rode at Anchor in the Thames, and almost blocked up the passage towards Greenwich, they ordered the Watermen to let fall their Oars more gently; and then every one favoring his own curiosity with a strict silence, it was not long ere they perceived the Air break about them like the noise of distant Thunder, or of Swallows in a Chimney: those little undulations of sound, though almost vanishing before they reached them, yet still seeming to retain somewhat of their first horror which they had betwixt the Fleets: after they had attentively listened till such time as the sound by little and little went from them; Eugenius lifting up his head, and taking notice of it, was the first who congratulated to the rest that happy Omen of our Nations Victory: adding, we had but this to desire in confirmation of it, that we might hear no more of that noise which was now leaving the English Coast. When the rest had concurred in the same opinion, Crites, a person of a sharp judgment, and somewhat too delicate a taste in wit, which the world have mistaken in him for ill nature, said, smiling to us, that if the concernment of this battle had not been so exceeding great, he could scarce have wished the Victory at the price he knew must pay for it, in being subject to the reading and hearing of so many ill verses as he was sure would be made upon it; adding, that no Argument could scape some of those eternal Rhymers, who watch a Battle with more diligence than the Ravens and birds of Prey; and the worst of them surest to be first in upon the quarry, while the better able, either out of modesty writ not at all, or set that due value upon their Poems, as to let them be often called for and long expected! "There are some of those impertinent people you speak of," answered Lisideius, "who to my knowledge, are already so provided, either way, that they can produce not only a Panegyric upon the Victory, but, if need be, a funeral elegy upon the Duke: and after they have crowned his valor with many Laurels, at last deplore the odds under which he fell, concluding that his courage deserved a better destiny." All the company smiled at the conceit of Lisideius, but Crites, more eager than before, began to make particular exceptions against some Writers, and said the public Magistrate ought to send betimes to forbid them; and that it concerned the peace and quiet of all honest people, that ill Poets should be as well silenced as seditious Preachers. "In my opinion," replied Eugenius, "you pursue your point too far; for as to my own particular, I am so great a lover of Poesy, that I could wish them all rewarded who attempt but to do well; at least I would not have them worse used than Sylla the Dictator did one of their brethren heretofore: *Quem in concione vidimus* (says Tully speaking of him) *cum ei libellum malus poeta de populo subjecisset, quod epigramma in eum fecisset tantummodo alternis versibus longiuculis, statim ex iis rebus quæ tunc vendebat jubere ei præmium tribui, sub ea conditione ne quid postea scriberet."* [We saw him once in an assembly, when out of the crowd a bad poet offered him an epigram in elegiac verse that he had just written as an attack on Sylla; he immediately ordered that the poet be given a reward out of the articles that he was selling, with the condition that he never again write anything. —ed.] "I could wish with all my heart," replied Crites, "that many whom we know were as bountifully thanked upon the same condition, that they would never trouble us again. For amongst others, I have a mortal apprehension of two Poets, whom this victory with the help of both her wings will never be able to escape." "'Tis easy to guess whom you intend," said Lisideius; "and without naming them, I ask you if one of them does not perpetually pay us with clenches upon words and a certain clownish kind of raillery? if now and then he does not offer at a Catachresis or Clevelandism, wresting and torturing a word into another meaning: In fine, if he be not one of those whom the French would call *un mauvais buffon*; one that is so much a well-willer to the Satire, that he spares no man; and though he cannot strike a blow to hurt any, yet ought to be punished for the malice of the action, as our Witches are justly hanged because they think themselves so; and suffer deservedly for believing they did mischief, because they meant it." "You have described him," said Crites, "so exactly, that I am afraid to come after you with my other extremity of Poetry: He is one of those who having had some advantage of education and converse, knows better than the other what a Poet should be, but puts it into practice more unluckily than any man; his stile and matter are every where alike; he is the most calm, peaceable Writer you ever read: he never disquiets your passions with the least concernment, but still leaves you in as even a temper as he found you; he is a very Leveller in Poetry , he creeps along with ten little words in every line, and helps out his Numbers with *For to*, and *Unto*, and all the pretty Expletives he can find, till he drags them to the end of another line; while the Sense is left tired half way behind it; he doubly starves all his Verses, first for want of thought, and then of expression; his Poetry neither has wit in it, nor seems to have it; like him in Martial: *Pauper videri Cinna vult, et est pauper* [Cinna wants to seem to be a pauper; and, sure enough, he is a pauper]: He affects plainness, to cover his want of imagination: when he writes the serious way, the highest flight of his fancy is some miserable Antithesis, or seeming contradiction; and in the Comic he is still reaching at some thin conceit, the ghost of a Jest, and that too flies before him, never to be caught; these Swallows which we see before us on the Thames, are just resemblance of his wit: you may observe how near the water they stoop, how many proffers they make to dip, and yet how seldom they touch it: and when they do, 'tis but the surface: they skim over it but to catch a gnat, and then mount into the air and leave it."

"Well Gentlemen," said Eugenius, "you may speak your pleasure of these Authors; but though I and some few more about the Town may give you a peaceable hearing, yet, assure yourselves, there are multitudes who would think you malicious and them injured: especially him who you first described; he is the very Withers of the City: they have bought more Editions of his Works than would serve to lay under all the Pies at the Lord Mayor's Christmas. When his famous Poem first came out in the year, I have seen them reading it in the midst of Change-time; many so vehement they were at it, that they lost their bargain by the Candles ends: but what will you say, if he has been received amongst the great Ones? I can assure you he is, this day, the envy of a great person, who is Lord in the Art of Quibbling; and who does not take it well, that any man should intrude so far into his Province." "All I would wish," replied Crites, "is, that they who love his Writings, may still admire him, and his fellow Poet: *Qui Bavium non odit, etc.* [who does not hate Bavius—ed.] is curse sufficient." "And farther," added Lisideius, "I believe there is no man who writes well, but would think himself very hardly dealt with, if their Admirers should praise any thing of his: *Nam quos contemnimus eorum quoque laudes contemnimus* [For we detest praise that comes from those we detest—ed.]." "There are so few who write well in this Age," said Crites, "that methinks any praises should be welcome; then neither rise to the dignity of the last Age, nor to any of the Ancients; and we may cry out of the Writers of this time, with more reason than Petronius of his, *Pace vestra liceat dixisse, primi omnium eloquentiam perdidistis* [If I may be permitted to say so, you were, of all, the first to lose the old eloquence]: you have debauched the true old Poetry so far, that Nature, which is the soul of it, is not in any of your Writings."

"If your quarrel," said Eugenius, "to those who now write, be grounded only upon your reverence to Antiquity, there is no man more ready to adore those great Greeks and Romans than I am: but on the other side, I cannot think so contemptibly of the Age I live in, or so dishonorably of my own Country, as not to judge we equal the Ancients in most kinds of Poesy, and in some surpass them; neither know I any reason why I may not be as zealous for the Reputation of our Age, as we find the Ancients themselves in reference to those who lived before them. For you hear your Horace saying,

> *Indignor quidquam reprehendi, non quia crassé*
> *Compositum, illepidève putetur, sed quia nuper*
> [I bristle when something is condemned, not because
> it is badly or obscurely written, but just because it is new
>   —ed.].

And after,

> *Si meliora dies, ut vina, poemata reddit,*
> *Scire velim pretium chartis quotus arroget annus?*

[If books, like wines, improve with age, tell me
in what year they achieve value?—ed.]

"But I see I am engaging in a wide dispute, where the arguments are not
like to reach close on either side; for Poesy is of so large extent, and so many
both of the Ancients and Moderns have done well in all kinds of it, that, in
citing one against the other, we shall take up more time this Evening, than
each man's occasions will allow him: therefore I would ask Crites to what part
of Poesy he would confine his Arguments, and whether he would defend the
general cause of the Ancients against the Moderns, or oppose any Age of the
Moderns against this of ours?"

Crites a little while considering upon this Demand, told Eugenius he ap-
proved his Propositions, and, if he pleased, he would limit their Dispute to
Dramatic Poesy; in which he thought it not difficult to prove, either that the
Ancients were superior to the Moderns, or the last Age to this of ours.

Eugenius was somewhat surprised, when he heard Crites make choice of that
Subject; "For ought I see," said he, "I have undertaken a harder Province than I
imagined; for though I never judged the Plays of the Greek or Roman Poets
comparable to ours; yet on the other side those we now see acted, come short of
many which were written in the last Age: but my comfort is if we are o'ercome,
it will be only by our own Countrymen: and if we yield to them in this one part
of Poesy, we more surpass them in all the other; for in the Epic or Lyric way it
will be hard for them to show us one such amongst them, as we have many now
living, or who lately were so. They can produce nothing so courtly writ, or which
expresses so much the Conversation of a Gentleman, as Sir John Suckling; nothing so even, sweet, and flowing as Mr. Waller; nothing so Majestic, so correct as
Sir John Denham; nothing so elevated, so copious, and full of spirit, as Mr.
Cowley; as for the Italian, French, and Spanish Plays, I can make it evident that
those who now write, surpass them; and that the Drama is wholly ours."

All of them were thus far of Eugenius's opinion, that the sweetness of English
Verse was never understood or practiced by our Fathers; even Crites himself did
not much oppose it: and every one was willing to acknowledge how much our
Poesy is improved, by the happiness of some Writers yet living; who first taught
us to mould our thoughts into easy and significant words; to retrench the super-
fluities of expression, and to make our Rime so properly a part of the Verse, that
it should never mislead the sense, but itself be led and governed by it.

Eugenius was going to continue this Discourse, when Lisideius told him it
was necessary, before they proceeded further, to take a standing measure of
their Controversy; for how was it possible to be decided who writ the best Plays,
before we know what a Play should be? but, this once agreed on by both Parties,
each might have recourse to it, either to prove his own advantages, or discover
the failings of his Adversary.

He had no sooner said this, but all desired the favor of him to give the definition of a Play; and they were the more importunate, because neither Aristotle, nor Horace, nor any other, who writ of that Subject, had ever done it.

Lisideius, after some modest denials, at last confessed he had a rude Notion of it; indeed rather a Description than a Definition: but which served to guide him in his private thoughts, when he was to make a judgment of what others writ: that he conceived a Play ought to be, *A just and lively Image of Humane Nature, representing its Passions and Humors, and the Changes of Fortune to which it is subject; for the Delight and Instruction of Mankind.*

This Definition, though Crites raised a Logical Objection against it; that it was only *a genere et fine* [that is, too broadly, according to category and purpose—as though one defined "shirt" as "a garment to keep one warm" —ed.], and so not altogether perfect; was yet well received by the rest: and after they had given order to the Water-men to turn their Barge, and row softly, that they might take the cool of the Evening in their return; Crites, being desired by the Company to begin, spoke on behalf of the Ancients, in this manner:

"If Confidence presage a Victory, Eugenius, in his own opinion, has already triumphed over the Ancients; nothing seems more easy to him, than to overcome those whom it is our greatest praise to have imitated well: for we do not only build upon their foundation; but by their models. Dramatic Poesy had time enough, reckoning from Thespis (who first invented it) to Aristophanes, to be born, to grow up, and to flourish in Maturity. It has been observed of Arts and Sciences, that in one and the same Century they have arrived to a great perfection; and no wonder, since every Age has a kind of Universal Genius, which inclines those that live in it to some particular Studies: the Work then being pushed on by many hands, must of necessity go forward.

"Is it not evident, in these last hundred years (when the Study of Philosophy has been the business of all the Virtuosi in Christendom) that almost a new Nature has been revealed to us? that more errors of the School have been detected, more useful Experiments in Philosophy have been made, more Noble Secrets in Optics, Medicine, Anatomy, Astronomy, discovered, than in all those credulous and doting Ages from Aristotle to us? so true it is that nothing spreads more fast than Science, when rightly and generally cultivated.

"Add to this the more than common emulation that was in those times of writing well; which though it be found in all Ages and all Persons that pretend to the same Reputation; yet Poesy being then in more esteem than now it is, had greater Honors decreed to the Professors of it; and consequently the Rivalship was more high between them; they had Judges ordained to decide their Merit, and Prizes to reward it: and Historians have been diligent to record of Aeschylus, Euripides, Sophocles, Lycophron, and the rest of them, both who they were that vanquished in these Wars of the Theater, and how often they were crowned: while the Asian Kings, and Grecian Commonwealths scarce afforded them a Nobler Subject than the unmanly Luxuries of a Debauched Court, or giddy Intrigues of a Factious City. *Alit æmulatio ingenia* (says Paterculus) *et nunc invidia, nunc admiratio incitationem accendit*: Emulation is the Spur of Wit, and sometimes Envy, sometimes Admiration quickens our Endeavors.

"But now since the Rewards of Honor are taken away, that Virtuous Emulation is turned into direct Malice; yet so slothful, that it contents itself to condemn and cry down others, without attempting to do better: 'Tis a Reputation too unprofitable, to take the necessary pains for it; yet wishing they had it, is incitement enough to hinder others from it. And this, in short, Eugenius, is the reason, why you have now so few good Poets; and so many severe Judges: Certainly, to imitate the Ancients well, much labor and long study is required: which pains, I have already shown, our Poets would want encouragement to take, if yet they had ability to go through with it. Those Ancients have been faithful Imitators and wise Observers of that Nature, which is so torn and ill represented in our Plays, they have handed down to us a perfect resemblance of her; which we, like ill Copiers, neglecting to look on, have rendered monstrous and disfigured. But, that you may know how much you are indebted to those your Masters, and be ashamed to have so ill requited them: I must remember you that all the Rules by which we practice the Drama at this day, either such as relate to the justness and symmetry of the Plot; or the Episodical Ornaments, such as Descriptions, Narrations, and other Beauties, which are not essential to the Play; were delivered to us from the Observations that Aristotle made, of those Poets, which either lived before him, or were his Contemporaries: we have added nothing of our own, except we have the confidence to say our wit is better; which none boast of in our Age, but such as understand not theirs. Of that Book which Aristotle has left us, *Peri tēs Poiēkēs*, Horace's *Art of Poetry* is an excellent Comment, and, I believe, restores to us that Second Book of his [Aristotle's—ed.] concerning Comedy, which is wanting [missing—ed.] in him.

"Out of these two has been extracted the Famous Rules which the French call, *Des Trois Unitez*, or, The Three Unities, which ought to be observed in every Regular Play; namely, of Time, Place, and Action.

"The unity of Time they comprehend in hours, the compass of a Natural Day; or as near it as can be contrived: and the reason of it is obvious to every one, that the time of the feigned action, or fable of the Play, should be proportioned as near as can be to the duration of that time in which it is represented; since therefore all Plays are acted on the Theater in a space of time much within the compass of hours, that Play is to be thought the nearest imitation of Nature, whose Plot or Action is confined within that time; and, by the same Rule which concludes this general proportion of time, it follows, that all the parts of it are to be equally subdivided; as namely, that one act take not up the supposed time of half a day; which is out of proportion to the rest: since the other four are then to be straitened within the compass of the remaining half; for it is unnatural that one Act, which being spoke or written, is not longer than the rest, should be supposed longer by the Audience; 'Tis therefore the poet's duty, to take care that no Act should be imagined to exceed the time in which it is represented on the Stage, and that the intervals and inequalities of time be supposed to fall out between the Acts.

"This Rule of Time how well it has been observed by the Ancients, most of their Plays will witness; you see them in their Tragedies (wherein to follow this Rule is certainly most difficult) from the very beginning of their Plays, falling close into that part of the Story which they intend for the action or principal object of it; leaving the former part to be delivered by Narration: so that they set the Audience, as it were, at the Post where the Race is to be concluded: and, saving them the tedious expectation of seeing the Poet set out and ride the beginning of the Course) you behold him not, till he is in sight of the Goal, and just upon you.

"For the Second Unity, which is that of place, the Ancients meant by it, That the Scene ought to be continued through the Play, in the same place where it was laid in the beginning: for the Stage, on which it is represented, being but one and the same place, it is unnatural to conceive it many; and those far distant from one another. I will not deny but by the variation of painted Scenes, the Fancy (which in these cases will contribute to its own deceit) may sometimes imagine it several places, with some appearance of probability; yet it still carries the greater likelihood of truth, if those places be supposed so near each other, as in the same Town or City; which may all be comprehended under the larger Denomination of one place: for a greater distance will bear no proportion to the shortness of time, which is allotted in the acting, to pass from one of them to another; for the Observation of this, next to the Ancients, the French are to be most commended. They tie themselves so strictly to the unity of place, that you never see in any of their Plays a Scene changed in the middle of the Act: if the Act begins in a Garden, a Street, or Chamber, 'tis ended in the same place; and that you may know it to be the same, the Stage is so supplied with persons that it is never empty all the time: he that enters the second has business with him who was on before; and before the second quits the Stage, a third appears who has business with him. This Corneille calls *La Liaison des Scenes*, the continuity or joining of the Scenes; and 'tis a good mark of a well contrived Play when all the Persons are known to each other, and every one of them has some affairs with all the rest.

"As for the third Unity which is that of Action, the Ancients meant no other by it than what the Logicians do by their Finis, the end or scope of an action: that which is the first in Intention, and last in Execution: now the Poet is to aim at one great and complete action, to the carrying on of which all things in his Play, even the very obstacles, are to be subservient; and the reason of this is as evident as any of the former.

"For two Actions equally labored and driven on by the Writer, would destroy the unity of the Poem; it would be no longer one Play, but two: not but that there may be many actions in a Play, as Ben Jonson has observed in his *Discoveries*; but they must be all subservient to the great one, which our language happily expresses in the name of under-plots: such as in Terence's *Eunuch* is the difference and reconcilement of Thais and Phædria, which is not the chief business of the Play, but promotes; the marriage of Chærea and Chreme's Sister, principally intended by the Poet. There ought to be one action, says Corneille, that is one complete action which leaves the mind of the Audience in a full repose: But this cannot be brought to pas but by many other imperfect ones which conduce to it, and hold the Audience in a delightful suspense of what will be.

"If by these Rules (to omit many other drawn from the Precepts and Practice of the Ancients) we should judge our modern Plays; 'Tis probable, that few of them would endure the trial: that which should be the business of a day, takes up in some of them an age; instead of one action they are the Epitomes of a man's life,; and for one spot of ground (which the Stage should represent) we are sometimes in more Countries than the Map can show us.

"But if we will allow the Ancients to have contrived well, we must acknowledge them to have writ better; questionless we are deprived of a great stock of wit in the loss of Meander among the Greek Poets, and of Caeilius, Affranius and Varius, among the Romans: we may guess of Menander's Excellency by the Plays of Terence, who translated some of his, and yet wanted so much of him that he was called by C. Cæsar the Half-Menander, and of Varius, by the Testimonies of Horace Martial, and Velleus Paterculus: 'Tis probable that these, could they be recovered, would decide the controversy; but so long as Aristophanes in the old Comedy, and Plautus in the new are extant; while the Tragedies of Euripides, Sophocles, and Seneca are to be had, I can never see one of those Plays which are now written, but it increases my admiration of the Ancients; and yet I must acknowledge further, that to admire them as we ought, we should understand them better than we do. Doubtless many things appear flat to us, whose wit depended upon some custom or story which never came to our knowledge, or perhaps upon some Criticism in their language, which being so long dead, and only remaining in their Books, 'tis not possible they should make us know it perfectly. To read Macrobius, explaining the propriety and elegancy of many words in Virgil, which I had before passed over without consideration, as common things, is enough to assure me that I ought to think the same of Terence; and that in the purity of his style (which Tully so much valued that he ever carried his works about him) there is yet left in him great room for admiration, if I knew but where to place it. In the mean time I must desire you to take notice, that the greatest man of the last age (Ben Jonson) was willing to give place to them in all things: He was not only a professed Imitator of Horace, but a learned Plagiary of all the others; you track him every where in their Snow: If Horace, Lucan, Petronius Arbiter, Seneca, and Juvenal, had their own from him, there are few serious thoughts which are new in him; you will pardon me therefore if I presume he loved their fashion when he wore their clothes. But since I have otherwise a great veneration for him, and you, Eugenius, prefer him above all other Poets, I will use no farther argument to you than his example: I will produce Father Ben to you, dressed in all the ornaments and colors of the Ancients, you will need no other guide to our Party if you follow him; and whether you consider the bad Plays of our Age, or regard the good ones of the last, both the best and worst of the Modern Poets will equally instruct you to esteem the Ancients."

Crites had no sooner left speaking, but Eugenius who waited with some impatience for it, thus began:

"I have observed in your Speech that the former part of it is convincing as to what the Moderns have profited by the rules of the Ancients, but in the latter you are careful to conceal how much they have excelled them: we own all the helps we have from them, and want neither veneration nor gratitude while we acknowledge that to overcome them we must make use of the advantages we have received from them; but to these assistances we have joined our own industry; for (had we sat down with a dull imitation of them) we might then have lost somewhat of the old perfection, but never acquired any that was new. We draw not therefore after their lines, but those of Nature; and having the life before us, besides the experience of all they knew, it is no wonder if we hit some airs and features which they have missed: I deny not what you urge of Arts and Sciences, that they have flourished in some ages more than others; but your instance in Philosophy makes for me: for if Natural Causes be more known now than in the time of Aristotle, because more studied, it follows that Poesy and other Arts may with the same pains arrive still nearer to perfection, and, that granted, it will rest for you to prove that they wrought more perfect images of human life than we; which, seeing in your Discourse you have avoided to make good, it shall now be my task to show you some part of their defects, and some few Excellencies of the Moderns; and I think there is none among us can imagine I do it enviously, or with purpose to detract from them; for what interest of Fame or Profit can the living lose by the reputation of the dead ? on the other side, it is a great truth which Velleius Paterculus affirms, *Audita visis libentius laudemus; et præsentia invidia, præterita admiratione prosequimur; et his nos obrui, illis instrui credimus* [we praise what we have heard more readily than what we have seen, and we regard the present with envy and the past with admiration; we feel weighed down by the former, lifted up by the latter]: That praise or censure is certainly the most sincere which unbribed posterity shall give us.

"Be pleased then in the first place to take notice, that the Greek Poesy, which Crites has affirmed to have arrived to perfection in the Reign of the old Comedy, was so far from it, that the distinction of it into Acts was not known to them; or if it were, it is yet so darkly delivered to us that we can not make it out.

"All we know of it is from the singing of their Chorus, and that too is so uncertain that in some of their Plays we have reason to conjecture they sung more than five times: Aristotle indeed divides the integral parts of a Play into four: First, The Protasis or entrance, which gives light only to the Characters of the persons, and proceeds very little into any part of the action: Secondly, The Epitasis, or working up of the Plot where the Play grows warmer: the design or action of it is drawing on, and you see something promising that it will come to pass: Thirdly, the Catastasis, or Counterturn, which destroys that expectation, embroils the action in new difficulties, and leaves you far distant from that hope in which it found you, as you may have observed in a violent stream resisted by a narrow passage; it runs round to an eddy, and carries back the waters with more swiftness than it brought them on: Lastly, the Catastrophe, which the Grecians called *lysis*, the French *le denouement*, and we the discovery or un-raveling of the Plot: there you see all things settling again upon their first foun-dations, and the obstacles which hindered the design or action of the Play once removed, it ends with that resemblance of truth and nature, that the audience are satisfied with the conduct of it. Thus this great man delivered to us the image of a Play, and I must confess it is so lively that from thence much light has been derived to the forming it more perfectly into Acts and Scenes; but what Poet first limited to five the number of the Acts I know not; only we see it so firmly established in the time of Horace, that he gives it for a rule in Comedy; *Neu brevior quinto, neu sit productior actu* [let it be neither shorter nor longer than five acts—ed.]: So that you see the Grecians cannot be said to have consummated this Art; writing rather by Entrances than by Acts, and having rather a general indigested notion of a Play, than knowing how and where to bestow the particular graces of it.

"But since the Spaniards at this day allow but three Acts, which they call *Jornadas*, to a Play; and the Italians in many of theirs follow them, when I condemn the Ancients, I declare it is not altogether because they have not five Acts to every Play, but because they have not confined themselves to one certain number; 'Tis building an House without a Model: and when the succeeded in such undertakings, they ought to have sacrificed to Fortune, not to the Muses.

Next, for the Plot, which Aristotle called *to mythos* and often *Tōn pragmatōn synthesis* [the ordering of the actions—ed.], and from him the Romans *Fabula*, it has already been judiciously observed by a late Writer, that in their Tragedies it was only some Tale derived from Thebes or Troy, or at least some thing that happened in those two Ages; which was worn so threadbare by the Pens of all the Epic Poets, and even by Tradition itself of the Talkative Greeklings (as Ben

Jonson calls them) that before it came upon the Stage, it was already known to all the Audience: and the people so soon as ever they heard the Name of Oedipus, knew as well as the Poet, that he had killed his Father by mistake, and committed Incest with his Mother, before the Play; that they were now to hear of a great Plague, an Oracle, and the Ghost of Laius: so that they sat with a yawning kind of expectation, till he was to come with his eyes pulled out, and speak a hundred or two of Verses in a Tragic tone, in complaint of his misfortunes. But one Oedipus, Hercules, or Medea, had been tolerable; poor people they scaped not so good cheap: they had still the *Chapon Bouillé* [boiled capon, a delicacy and a luxury—ed.] set before them, till their appetites were cloyed with the same dish, and the Novelty being gone, the pleasure vanished: so that one main end of Dramatic Poesy in its Definition, which was to cause Delight, as of consequence destroyed.

"In their Comedies, the Romans generally borrowed their Plots from the Greek Poets; and theirs was commonly a little Girl stolen or wandered from her Parents, brought back unknown to the same City, there got with child by some lewd young fellow; who, by the help of his servant, cheats his father, and when her time comes, to cry *Juno Lucina fer opem* [Juno, goddess of childbirth, bring help—ed.]; one or other sees a little Box or Cabinet which was carried away with her, and so discovers her to her friends, if some God do not prevent it, by coming down in a Machine, and take the thanks of it to himself.

"By the Plot you may guess much of the Characters of the Persons. An Old Father that would willingly before he dies see his Son well married; his Debauched Son, kind in his Nature to his Wench, but miserably in want of Money; a Servant or Slave, who has so much wit to strike in with him, and help to dupe his Father, a Braggadochio, Captain, a Parasite, and a Lady of Pleasure.

"As for the poor honest Maid, whom all the Story is built upon, and who ought to be one of the principal Actors in the Play, she is commonly a Mute in it: She has the breeding of the Old Elizabeth way, for Maids to be seen and not to be heard; and it is enough you know she is willing to be married, when the Fifth Act requires it.

"These are Plots built after the Italian Mode of Houses, you see through them all at once; the Characters are indeed the Imitations of Nature, but so narrow as if they had imitated only an Eye or an Hand, and did not dare to venture on the lines of a Face, or the Proportion of a Body.

"But in how straight a compass soever they have bounded their Plots and Characters, we will pass in by, if they have regularly pursued them, and perfectly observed those three Unities of Time, Place, and Action: the knowledge of which you say is derived to us from them. But in the first place give me leave to tell you, that the Unity of Place, how ever it might be practiced by them, was never any of their Rules: We neither find it in Aristotle, Horace, of any who have written of it, till in our age the French Poets first made it a Precept of the

Stage. The unity of time, even Terence himself (who was the best and the most regular of them) has neglected: His *Heautontimoroumenos* or *Self-Punisher* takes up visibly two days; therefore says Scaliger, the two first Acts concluding the first day, were acted over-night; the three last on the ensuing day: and Euripides, in trying himself to one day, has committed an absurdity never to be forgiven him: for in one of his Tragedies he has made Theseus go from Athens to Thebes, which was about forty English miles, under the walls of it to give battle, and appear victorious in the next Act; and yet from the time of his departure to the return of the Nuntius, who gives the relation of his Victory, Æthra and the Chorus have but Verses; that is not for every Mile a Verse.

"The like error is as evident in Terence's *Eunuch*, when Laches, the old man, enters in a mistake the house of Thais, where betwixt his Exit and the entrance of Pythias, who comes to give an ample relation of the Garboyles he has raised within, Parmeno who was left upon the Stage, has not above five lines to speak: *C'est bien employé un temps si court* [It is well to employ such a short time—Corneille, *Troisième Discours*—ed.], says the French Poet, who furnished me with one of the observations; And almost all their Tragedies will afford us examples of the like nature.

"'Tis true, they have kept the continuity, or as you called it *Liaison des Scenes* somewhat better: two do not perpetually come in together, talk, and go out together; and other two succeed them, and do the same throughout the Act, which the English call by the name of single Scenes; but the reason is, because they have seldom above two or three Scenes, properly so called, in every act; for it is to be accounted a new Scene, not every time the Stage is empty, but every person who enters, though to others, makes it so: because he introduces a new business: Now the Plots of their Plays being narrow, and the persons few, one of their Acts was written in a less compass than one of our well wrought Scenes, and yet they are often deficient even in this: To go no further than Terence, you find in the *Eunuch*, Antipho entering single in the midst of the third Act, after Chremes and Pythias were gone off: In the same Play you have likewise Dorias beginning the fourth Act alone; and after she has made a relation of what was done at the Soldier's entertainment (which by the way was very inartificial to do, because she was presumed to speak directly to the Audience, and to acquaint them with what was necessary to be known, but yet should have been so contrived by the Poet as to have been told by persons of the Drama to one another, and so by them to have come to the knowledge of the people) she quits the Stage, and Phœdria enters next, alone likewise: He also gives you an account of himself, and of his returning from the Country in Monologue, his *Adelphi* or *Brothers*, Syrus and Demea enter; after the Scene was broken by the departure of Sostrata, Geta and Cathara; and indeed you can scarce look into any of his Comedies, where you will not presently discover the same interruption.

"But as they have failed both in laying of their Plots, and managing of them, swerving from the Rules of their own Art, by misrepresenting Nature to us, in which they have ill satisfied one intention of a Play, which was delight, so in the instructive part they have erred worse: instead of punishing Vice and rewarding Virtue, they have often shown a Prosperous Wickedness, and Unhappy Piety: They have set before us a bloody image of revenge in Medea, and given her Dragons to convey her safe from punishment. A Priam and Astyanax murdered, and Cassandra ravished, and the lust and murder ending in the victory of him that acted them: In short, there is no indecorum in any of our modern Plays, which if I would excuse, I could not shadow with some Authority from the Ancients.

"And one farther note of them let me leave you: Tragedies and Comedies were not writ then as they are now, promiscuously, by the same person; but he who found his genius bending to the one, never attempted the other way. This is so plain, that I need not instance to you, that Aristophanes, Plautus, Terence, never any of them writ a Tragedy; Æschylus, Euripides, Sophocles and Seneca, never meddled with Comedy; the Sock and Buskin were not worn by the same Poet: having then so much care to excel in one kind, very little is to be pardoned them if they miscarried in it; and this would lead me to the consideration of their wit, had not Crites given me sufficient warning not to be too bold in my judgment of it; because the languages being dead, and many of the Customs and little accidents on which it depended, lost to us, we are not competent judges of it. But though I grant that here and there we may miss the application of a Proverb or a Custom, yet a thing well said will be wit in all Languages; and though it may lose something in the Translation, yet, to him who reads it in the Original, 'tis still the same; He has an Idea of its excellency, though it cannot pass from his mind into any other expression or words than those in which he finds it. When Phœdria, in the *Eunuch,* had a command from his Mistress to be absent two days; and encouraging himself to go through with it, said; *Tandem ego non illa caream, si opus sit, vel totum triduum?* [Shall I not do without her, if need be, even for three whole days? — ed.] Parmeno to mock the softness of his Master, lifting up his hands and eyes, cries out as it were in admiration; *Hui! universum triduum!* [Alas! all of three days! — ed.] the elegancy of which *universum,* though it cannot be rendered in our language, yet leaves an impression of the wit upon our souls: but this happens seldom in him, in Plautus oftener; who is infinitely too bold in his Metaphors and coining words; out of which many times his wit is nothing, which questionless was one reason why Horace falls upon him so severely in those Verses:

> *Sed Proavi nostri Plautinos et numeros, et*
> *Laudavere sales, nimium patienter utrumque,*
> *Ne dicam stolidè.*

[Our forebears praised both the versification
and the witticisms of Plautus—all too indulgently,
not to say stupidly—ed.]

For Horace himself was cautious to obtrude a new word upon his Readers, and
makes custom and common use the best measure of receiving it into our writings.

> *Multa renascentur quæ nunc cecidere, cadentque*
> *Quæ nunc sunt in honore vocabula, si volet usus,*
> *Quem penes, arbitrium est, et jus, et norma loquendi.*
> [Many words now fallen into disuse will be revived,
> Many now accepted will fall into disuse, according to the
>   demands
> Of practice, which governs the choice, the right, and the
>   norm of speech—ed.]

"The not observing this Rule is that which the world has blamed in our Satirist
Cleveland; to express a thing hard and unnaturally, is his new way of Elocution:
'Tis true, no Poet but may sometimes use a Catachresis; Virgil does it—

> *Mistaque ridenti Colocasia fundet Acantho*
> [And the colocasia will spread forth, mingled with the
>   laughing acanthus—ed.]

—in his Eclogue of *Pollio*, and in his 7th Æneid.

> *miratur et undæ,*
> *Miratur nemus, insuetum fulgentia longe,*
> *Scuta virum fluvio, pictasque innare carinas*
> [The woods and waters wonder at the gleam
> Of shields, and painted ships, that stem the stream (trans.
>   Dryden's)].

And Ovid once so modestly, that he asks leave to do it:

> *quem si verbo audacia detur,*
> *Haud metuam summi dixisse Palatia cœli*
> [if I may use such a bold figure,
> I should not hesitate to call it the palace of the sky—ed.]

—calling the Court of Jupiter by the name of Augustus's Palace, though in
another place he is more bold, where he says, *Et longas visent Capitolia pompas*

[And the capitol will see long processions—ed.]. But to do this always, and never be able to write a line without it, though it may be admired by some few Pedants, will not pass upon those who know that wit is best conveyed to us in the most easy language; and is most to be admired when a great thought comes dressed in words so commonly received that it is understood by the meanest apprehensions, as the best meat is the most easily digested: but we cannot read a verse of Cleveland's without making a face at it, as if every word were a Pill to swallow: he gives us many times a hard Nut to break our Teeth, without a Kernel for our pains. So that there is this difference betwixt his Satires and Doctor Donne's: That the one gives us deep thought in common language, though rough cadence; the other gives us common thoughts in abstruse words: 'Tis true, in some places his wit is independent of his words, as in that of the Rebel Scot:

> Had Cain been Scot God would have changed his doom;
> Not forced him wander, but confined him home.

"*Si sic, omnia dixisset!* [If only he had said everything thus—ed.] This is wit in all languages: 'Tis like Mercury, never to be lost or killed; and so that other—

> For Beauty like White-powder makes no noise,
> And yet the silent Hypocrite destroys.

You see the last line is highly Metaphorical, but it is so soft and gentle, that it does not shock us as we read it.

"But, to return from whence I have digressed, to the consideration of the Ancients' Writing and their Wit, (of which by this time you will grant us in some measure to be fit judges). Though I see many excellent thoughts in Seneca, yet he, of them who had a Genius most proper for the Stage, was Ovid; he had a way of writing so fit to stir up a pleasing admiration and concernment, which are the objects of a Tragedy, and to show the various movements of a Soul combating betwixt two different Passions, that, had he lived in our age, or in his own could have writ with our advantages, no man but must have yielded to him; and therefore I am confident the *Medea* is none of his: for, though I esteem it for the gravity and sententiousness of it, which he himself concludes to be suitable to a Tragedy, *Omne genus scripti gravitate Tragædia vincit* [Tragedy surpasses every kind of writing in gravity—ed.], yet it moves not my soul enough to judge that he, who in the Epic way wrote things so near the Drama, as the Story of Myrrha, of Caunus and Biblis, and the rest, should stir up no more concernment where he most endeavored it. The Master piece of Seneca I hold to be that Scene in the *Troades*, where Ulysses is seeking for Astyanax to kill him; There you see the tenderness of a Mother, so represented in Andromache, that it raises compassion to a high degree in the Reader, and bears the nearest resemblance of any thing in their Tragedies to the excellent Scenes of Passion in Shakespeare, or in Fletcher: for Love Scenes you will find few among them, their Tragic Poets dealt not with that soft passion, but with Lust, Cruelty, Revenge, Ambition, and those bloody actions they produced; which were more capable of raising horror than compassion in an audience: leaving love untouched, whose gentleness would have tempered them, which is the most frequent of all the passions, and which being the private concernment of every person, is soothed by viewing its own image in a public entertainment.

"Among their Comedies, we find a Scene or two of tenderness, and that where you would least expect it, in Plautus; but to speak generally, their Lovers say little, when they see each other, but *anima mea, vita mea* [my soul, my life—ed.], *zōē kai psychē* [my life, my soul—ed.], as the women in Juvenal's time used to cry out in the fury of their kindness: then indeed to speak sense were an offence. Any sudden gust of passion (as an ecstasy of love in an unexpected meeting) cannot better be expressed than in a word and a sigh, breaking one another. Nature is dumb on such occasions, and to make her speak, would be to represent her unlike her self. But there are a thousand other concernments of Lovers, as jealousies, complaints, contrivances and the like, where not to open their minds at large to each other, were to be wanting to their own love, and to the expectation of the Audience, who watch the movements of their minds, as much as the changes of their fortunes. For the imaging of the first is properly the work of a Poet, the latter he borrows of the Historian."

Eugenius was proceeding in that part of his Discourse, when Crites interrupted him. "I see," said he, "Eugenius and I are never like to have this Question decided betwixt us; for he maintains the Moderns have acquired a new perfection in writing, I can only grant they have altered the mode of it. Homer described his Heroes men of great appetites, lovers of beef broiled upon the coals, and good fellows; contrary to the practice of the French Romances, whose Heroes neither eat, nor drink, nor sleep, for love. Virgil makes Æneas a bold Avower of his own virtues,

> *Sum pius Æneas fama super athera notus*;
> [I am dutiful Aeneas of fame known above the heavens
>   —ed.]

which in the civility of our Poets is the Character of a fanfaron [braggart—ed.] or Hector: for with us the Knight takes occasion to walk out, or sleep, to avoid the vanity of telling his own Story, which the trusty Squire is ever to perform for him. So in their Love Scenes, of which Eugenius spoke last, the Ancients were more hearty; we more talkative: they writ love as it was then the mode to make it, and I will grant thus much to Eugenius, that perhaps one of their Poets, had he lived in our Age, *Si foret hoc nostrum fato delapsus in avum* [If he had been dropped by fate into our age—ed.] (as Horace says of Lucilius), he had altered many things; not that they were not as natural before, but that he might accommodate himself to the Age he lived in: yet in the mean time we are not to conclude any thing rashly against those great men; but preserve to them the dignity of Masters, and give that honor to their memories, (*Quos Libitina sacravit* [which Libitina has consecrated—ed.]) part of which we expect may be paid to us in future times."

This moderation of Crites, as it was pleasing to all the company, so it put an end to that dispute; which, Eugenius, who seemed to have the better of the Argument, would urge no farther: but Lisideius after he had acknowledged himself of Eugenius's opinion concerning the Ancients; yet told him he had forborne, till his Discourse were ended, to ask him why he preferred the English Plays above those of other Nations? and whether we ought not to submit our Stage to the exactness of our next Neighbors?

"Though," said Eugenius, "I am at all times ready to defend the honor of my Country against the French, and to maintain, we are as well able to vanquish them with our Pens as our Ancestors have been with their swords; yet, if you please," added he, looking upon Neander, "I will commit this cause to my friend's management; his opinion of our Plays is the same with mine: and besides, there is no reason, that Crites and I, who have now left the Stage, should re-enter so suddenly upon it; which is against the Laws of Comedy."

"If the Question had been stated," replied Lysideius, "who had writ best, the French or English, forty years ago, I should have been of your opinion, and adjudged the honor to our own Nation; but since that time," (said he, turning towards Neander) "we have been so long together bad Englishmen, that we had not leisure to be good Poets; Beaumont, Fletcher, and Jonson (who were only capable of bringing us to that degree of perfection which we have) were just then leaving the world; as if (in an Age of so much horror) wit and those milder studies of humanity, had no farther business among us. But the Muses, who ever follow Peace, went to plant in another Country; it was then that the great Cardinal of Richelieu began to take them into his protection; and that, by his encouragement, Corneille and some other Frenchmen reformed their Theatre, (which before was as much below ours as it now surpasses it and the rest of Europe). But because Crites, in his Discourse for the Ancients, has prevented me, by touching upon many Rules of the Stage, which the Moderns have borrowed from them; I shall only, in short, demand of you, whether you are not convinced that of all Nations the French have best observed them? In the unity of time you find them so scrupulous, that it yet remains a dispute among their Poets, whether the artificial day of twelve hours more or less, be not meant by Aristotle, rather than the natural one of twenty four; and consequently whether all Plays ought not to be reduced into that compass? This I can testify, that in all their Drama's writ within these last years and upwards, I have not observed any that have extended the time to thirty hours: in the unity of place they are full as scrupulous, for many of their Critics limit it to that very spot of ground where the Play is supposed to begin; none of them exceed the compass of the same Town or City. The unity of Action in all their Plays is yet more conspicuous, for they do not burden them with under-plots, as the English do; which is the reason why many Scenes of our Tragi-comedies carry on a design that is no thing of kin to the main Plot; and that we see two distinct webs in a Play; like those in ill wrought stuffs; and two actions, that is, two Plays carried on together, to the confounding of the Audience; who, before they are warm in their concernments for one part, are diverted to another; and by that means espouse the interest of neither. From hence likewise it arises that the one half of our Actors are not known to the other. They keep their distances as if they were Montagues and Capulets, and seldom begin an acquaintance till the last Scene of the Fifth Act, when they are all to meet upon the Stage. There is no Theatre in the world has any thing so absurd as the English Tragicomedy, 'tis a Drama of our own invention, and the fashion of it is enough to proclaim it so; here a course of mirth, there another of sadness and passion; a third of honor, and fourth a Duel: Thus in two hours and a half we run through all the fits of Bedlam. The French affords you as much variety on the same day, but they do it not so unseasonably, or *mal à propos* [inappropriately—ed.] as we: Our Poets present you the Play and the farce together; and our Stages still retain somewhat of the Original civility of the Red-Bull; *Atque ursum et pugiles media inter carmina poscunt* [they ask for a bear or boxers in the middle of plays. The end of Tragedies or serious Plays, says Aristotle, is to beget admiration, compassion, or concernment; but are not mirth and compassion things incompatible? and is it not evident that the Poet must of necessity destroy the former by intermingling of the latter? that is, he must ruin the sole end and object of his Tragedy to introduce somewhat that is forced in, and is not of the body of it: Would you not think that Physician mad, who having prescribed a Purge, should immediately order you to take restringents upon it?

"But to leave our Plays, and return to theirs, I have noted one great advantage they have had in the Plotting of their Tragedies; that is, they are always grounded upon some known History: according to that of Horace, *Ex noto fictum carmen sequar* [Out of a known story I should bring a poem—ed.]; and in that they have so imitated the Ancients that they have surpassed them. For the Ancients, as was observed before, took for the foundation of their Plays some Poetical Fiction, such as under that consideration could move but little concernment in the Audience, because they already knew the event of it. But the French goes farther;

> *Atque ita mentitur; sic veris falsæ remiscet,*
> *Primo ne medium, medio ne discrepet imum:*
> [He so lies and so mingles the false with the true

that the middle will not disagree with the first, nor the last
    with the middle—ed.]

He so interweaves Truth with probable Fiction, that he puts a pleasing Fallacy upon us; mends the intrigues of Fate, and dispenses with the severity of
History, to reward that virtue which has been rendered to us there unfortunate.
Sometimes the story has left the success so doubtful, that the Writer is free, by
the privilege of a Poet, to take that which of two or more relations will best suit
with his design: As for example, the death of Cyrus, whom Justin and some
others report to have perished in the Scythian war, but Xenophon affirms to
have died in his bed of extreme old age. Nay more, when the event is past
dispute, even then we are willing to be deceived, and the Poet, if he contrives
it with appearance of truth; has all the audience of his Party; at least during the
time his Play is acting: so naturally we are kind to virtue, when our own interest
is not in question, that we take it up as the general concernment of Mankind.
On the other side, if you consider the Historical Plays of Shakespeare, they are
rather so many Chronicles of Kings, or the business many times of thirty or
forty years, cramped into a representation of two hours and a half, which is not
to imitate or paint Nature, but rather to draw her in miniature, to take her in
little; to look upon her through the wrong end of a Perspective, and receive her
Images not only much less, but infinitely more imperfect than the life: this
instead of making a Play delightful, renders it ridiculous.

> *Quodcunque ostendis mihi sic, incredulus odi.*
> [Unbelieving, I hate whatever you show me in this man-
>   ner—ed.]

For the Spirit of man cannot be satisfied but with truth, or at least verisimility;
and a Poem is to contain, if not *ta etyma* [true things], yet *etymoisin homoia*
[things like the truth—ed.], as one of the Greek Poets has expressed it.
    "Another thing in which the French differ from us and from the Spaniards,
is, that they do not embarrass, or cumber themselves with too much Plot: they
only represent so much of a Story as will constitute one whole and great action
sufficient for a Play; we, who undertake more, do but multiply adventures; which,
not being produced from one another, as effects from causes, but barely following,
constitute many actions in the Drama, and consequently make it many Plays.
    "But by pursuing close one argument, which is not cloyed with many turns,
the French have gained more liberty for verse, in which they write: they have
leisure to dwell upon a subject which deserves it; and to represent the passions
(which we have acknowledged to be the Poet's work) without being hurried
from one thing to another, as we are in the Plays of Calderon, which we have
seen lately upon our Theaters, under the name of Spanish Plots. I have taken

notice but of one Tragedy of ours, whose Plot has that uniformity and unity of design in it which I have commended in the French; and that is *Rollo*, or rather, under the name of *Rollo*, the story of Bassianus and Geta in Herodian, there indeed the Plot is neither large nor intricate, but just enough to fill the minds of the Audience, not to cloy them. Besides, you see it founded upon the truth of History, only the time of the action is not reducible to the strictness of the Rules; and you see in some places a little farce mingled, which is below the dignity of the other parts; and in this all our Poets are extremely peccant, even Ben Jonson himself in *Sejanus* and *Catiline* has given us this Oleo [also Olio: a hodgepodge of many various ingredients—ed.] of a Play; this unnatural mixture of Comedy and Tragedy, which to me sounds just as ridiculously as the History of David with the merry humors of Golias. In *Sejanus* you may take notice of the Scene betwixt Livia and the Physician, which is a pleasant Satire upon the artificial helps of beauty: In *Catiline* you may see the Parliament of Women; the little envies of them to one another; and all that passes betwixt Curio and Fulvia: Scenes admirable in their kind, but of an ill mingle with the rest.

"But I return again to French Writers; who, as I have said, do not burden themselves too much with Plot, which has been reproached to them by an ingenious person of our Nation as a fault, for he says they commonly make but one person considerable in a Play; they dwell upon him, and his concernments, while the rest of the persons are only subservient to set him off. If he intends this by it, that there is one person in the Play who is of greater dignity than the rest, he must tax, not only theirs, but those of the Ancients, and which he would be loth to do, the best of ours; for 'tis impossible but that one person must be more conspicuous in it than any other, and consequently the greatest share in the action must devolve on him, We see it so in the management of all affairs; even in the most equal Aristocracy, the balance cannot be so justly poised, but some one will be superior to the rest; either in parts, fortune, interest, or the consideration of some glorious exploit; which will reduce the greatest part of business into his hands.

"But, if he would have us to imagine that in exalting of one character the rest of them are neglected, and that all of them have not some share or other in the action of the Play, I desire him to produce any of Corneille's Tragedies, wherein every person (like so many servants in a well governed Family) has not some employment, and who is not necessary to the carrying on of the Plot, or at least to your understanding it.

There are indeed some prosaic persons in the Ancients, whom they make use of in their Plays, either to hear, or give the Relation: but the French avoid this with great address, making their narrations only to, or by such who are some way interested in the main design. And now I am speaking of Relations, I cannot take a fitter opportunity to add this in favor of the French, that they often use them with better judgment and more *à propos* [to the purpose (the earliest recorded use in English)—ed.] than the English do. Not that I commend narrations in general, but there are two sorts of them; one of those things which are antecedent to the Play, and are related to make the conduct of it more clear to us, but, 'tis a fault to choose such subjects for the Stage which will enforce us upon that Rock; because we see they are seldom listened to by the Audience, and that is many times the ruin of the Play: for, being once let pass without attention, the Audience can never recover themselves to understand the Plot; and indeed it is somewhat unreasonable that they should be put to so much trouble, as, that to comprehend what passes in their sight, they must have recourse to what was done, perhaps, ten or twenty years ago.

"But there is another sort of Relations, that is, of things happening in the Action of the Play, and supposed to be done behind the Scenes: and this is many times both convenient and beautiful: for, by it, the French avoid the tumult, which we are subject to in England, by representing Duels, Battles, and the like; which renders our Stage too like the Theaters, where they fight Prizes. For what is more ridiculous than to represent an Army with a Drum and five men behind it; all which, the Hero of the other side is to drive in before him, or to see a Duel fought, and one slain with two or three thrusts of the foils, which we know are so blunted, that we might give a man an hour to kill another in good earnest with them.

"I have observed that in all our Tragedies, the Audience cannot forbear laughing when the Actors are to die; 'tis the most Comic part of the whole Play. All passions may be lively represented on the Stage, if to the well-writing of them the Actor supplies a good commanded voice, and limbs that move easily, and without stiffness; but there are many actions which can never be imitated to a just height: dying especially is a thing which none but a Roman Gladiator could naturally perform upon the Stage when he did not imitate or represent, but naturally do it; and therefore it is better to omit the representation of it.

"The words of a good Writer which describe it lively, will make a deeper impression of belief in us than all the Actor can persuade us to, when he seems to fall dead before us; as a Poet in the description of a beautiful Garden, or a Meadow, will please our imagination more than the place itself can please our sight. When we see death represented we are convinced it is but Fiction; but when we hear it related, our eyes (the strongest witnesses) are wanting, which might have undeceived us; and we are all willing to favor the sleight when the Poet does not too grossly impose upon us. They therefore who imagine these relations would make no concernment in the Audience, are deceived, by confounding them with the other, which are of things antecedent to the Play; those are made often in cold blood (as I may say) to the audience; but these are warmed with our concernments, which are before awakened in the Play. What the Philosophers say of motion, that when it is once begun it continues of it self, and will do so to Eternity without some stop put to it, is clearly true on this occasion; the soul being already moved with the Characters and Fortunes of those imaginary persons, continues going of its own accord, and we are no more weary to hear what becomes of them when they are not on the Stage, then we are to listen to the news of an absent Mistress. But it is objected, That if one part of the Play may be related, then why not all? I answer, Some parts of the action are more fit to be represented, some to be related. Corneille says judiciously, that the Poet is not obliged to expose to view all particular actions which conduce to the principal: he ought to select such of them to be seen which will appear with the greatest beauty; either by the magnificence of the show, or the vehemence of passions which they produce, or some other charm which they have in them, and let the rest arrive to the audience by narration. 'Tis a great mistake in us to believe the French present no part of the action upon the Stage: every alteration or crossing of a design, every new sprung passion, and turn of it, is a part of the action, and much the noblest, except we conceive nothing to be action till they come to blows; as if the painting of the Heroes mind were not more properly the Poets work than the strength of his body. Nor does this any thing contradict the opinion of Horace, where he tells us,

> Segnius irritant animos demissa per aurem
> Quam quæ sunt oculis subjecta fidelibus
> [Matters transmitted through the ear stir the spirit
> less forcibly than those set before the trustworthy eyes]

— For he says immediately after,

> Non tamen intus
> Digna geri promes in scenam, multaque tolles
> Ex oculis, quæ mox narret facundia præsens.
> [You shall not bring on the stage
> Things that should be accomplished offstage; you shall re-
>   move from my sight
> Things that resourceful eloquence will effectively narrate]

Among which many he recounts some.

> Nec pueros coram populo Medea trucidet,
> Aut in avem Progne mutetur, Cadmus in anguem, etc.
> [Medea should not butcher her children in public,
> Nor Procne be changed into a bird, Cadmus into a snake,
>   etc.]

That is, those actions which by reason of their cruelty will cause aversion in us, or by reason of their impossibility unbelief, ought either wholly to be avoided by a Poet, or only delivered by narration. To which, we may have leave to add such as to avoid tumult, (as was before hinted) or to reduce the Plot into a more reasonable compass of time, or for defect of Beauty in them, are rather to be related than presented to the eye. Examples of all these kinds are frequent, not only among all the Ancients, but in the best received of our English Poets. We find Ben Jonson using them in his *Magnetic Lady*, where one comes out from Dinner, and relates the quarrels and disorders of it to save the undecent appearing of them on the Stage, and to abbreviate the Story: and this in express imitation of Terence, who had done the same before him in his *Eunuch*, where Pythias makes the like relation of what had happened within at the Soldier's entertainment. The relations likewise of Sejanus's death, and the prodigies before it are remarkable, the one of which was hid from sight to avoid the horror and tumult of the representation; the other to shun the introducing of things impossible to be believed. In that excellent Play *The King and No King*, Fletcher goes yet farther; for the whole unraveling of the Plot is done by narration in the fifth Act, after the manner of the Ancients; and it moves great concernment in the Audience, though it be only a relation of what was done many years before the Play. I could multiply other instances, but these are sufficient to prove that there is no error in choosing a subject which requires this sort of narrations; in the ill managing of them, there may.

"But I find I have been too long in this discourse since the French have many other excellencies not common to use, as that you never see any of their Plays end with a conversion, or simple change of will, which is the ordinary way our Poets use to end theirs. It shows little art in the conclusion of a Dramatick Poem, when they who have hindered the felicity during the four Acts, desist from it in the fifth without some powerful cause to take them off; and though I deny not but such reasons may be found, yet it is a path that is cautiously to be trod, and the Poet is to be sure he convinces the Audience that the motive is strong enough. As for example, the conversion of the Usurer in *The Scornful Lady*, seems to me a little forced; for being an Usurer, which implies a lover of Money to the highest degree of covetousness, (and such the Poet has represented him) the account he gives for the sudden change is, that he has been duped by the wild young fellow, which in reason might render him more wary another time, and make him punish himself with harder fare and courser clothes to get it up again: but that he should look upon it as a judgment, and so repent, we may expect to hear of in a Sermon, but I should never endure it in a Play.

"I pass by this; neither will I insist upon the care they take, that no person after his first entrance shall ever appear, but the business which brings him upon the Stage shall be evident: which, if observed, must needs render all the events in the Play more natural; for there you see the probability of every accident, in the cause that produced it; and that which appears chance in the

Play, will seem so reasonable to you, that you will there find it almost necessary; so that in the exits of their Actors you have a clear account of their purpose and design in the next entrance: (though, if the Scene be well wrought, the event will commonly deceive you) for there is nothing so absurd, says Corneille, as for an Actor to leave the Stage, only because he has no more to say.

"I should now speak of the beauty of their Rhyme, and the just reason I have to prefer that way of writing in the Tragedies before ours in Blank verse; but because it is partly received by us, and therefore not altogether peculiar to them, I will say no more of it in relation to their Plays. For our own I doubt not but it will exceedingly beautify them, and I can see but one reason why it should not generally obtain, that is, because our Poets write so ill in it. This indeed may prove a more prevailing argument than all others which are used to destroy it, and therefore I am only troubled when great and judicious Poets, and those who acknowledged such, have writ or spoke against it; as for others they are to be answered by that one sentence of an ancient Author, *Sed ut primo ad consequendos eos quos priores ducimus accendimur, ita ubi autpræteriri, aut æquari eos posse desperavimus, studium cum spe senescit: quod, scilicet, assequi non potest, sequi desinit; præteritoque, eo in quo eminere no possumus, aliquid in quo nitamur conquirimus* [But as we are stimulated to follow those whom we consider foremost, so, when we despair of surpassing or even equaling them, our zeal wanes with our hope; indeed, because it cannot excel, it ceases to follow. When that in which we cannot excel is in the past, we look for something worthy of striving after—ed.]."

Lisideius concluded in this manner; and Neander after a little pause thus answered him.

"I shall grant Lisideius, without much dispute, a great part of what he has urged against us, for I acknowledge the French contrive their Plots more regularly, observe the Laws of Comedy, and decorum of the Stage (to speak generally) with more exactness than the English. Farther I deny not but he has taxed us justly in some irregularities of ours which he has mentioned; yet, after all, I am of opinion that neither our faults nor their virtues are considerable enough to place them above us.

"For the lively imitation of Nature being in the definition of a Play, those which best fulfill that law ought to be esteemed superior to the others. 'Tis true, those beauties of the French-poesy are such as will raise perfection higher where it is, but are not sufficient to give it where it is not: they are indeed the Beauties of a Statue, but not of a Man, because not animated with the Soul of Poesy, which is imitation of humor and passions: and this Lisideius himself, or any other, however biased to their Party, cannot but acknowledge, if he will either compare the humors of our Comedies, or the Characters of our serious Plays with theirs. He that will look upon theirs which have been written till these last ten years or thereabouts, will find it an hard matter to pick out two or three passable humors amongst them. Corneille himself, their Arch-Poet, what has he produced except *The Liar*, and you know how it was cried up in France; but when it came upon the English Stage, though well translated, and that part of Dorant acted to so much advantage by Mr. Hart, as I am confident it never received in its own Country, the most favourable to it would not put in competition with many of Fletcher's or Ben Jonson's. In the rest of Corneille's Comedies you have little humor; he tells you himself his way is first to show two Lovers in good intelligence with each other; in the working up of the Play to embroil them by some mistake, and in the latter end to clear it up.

"But of late years de Molière, the younger Corneille, Quinault, and some others, have been imitating of afar off the quick turns and graces of the English Stage. They have mixed their serious Plays with mirth, like our Tragicomedies since the death of Cardinal Richelieu, which Lisideius and many others not observing, have commended that in them for a virtue which they themselves no longer practice. Most of their new Plays are like some of ours, derived from the Spanish Novels. There is scarce one of them without a veil, and a trusty Diego, who drolls much after the rate of *The Adventures*. But their humors, if I may grace them with that name, are so thin sown that never above one of them come up in any Play: I dare take upon me to find more variety of them in some one Play of Ben Jonson's than in all theirs together: as he who has seen *The Alchemist*, *The Silent Woman*, or *Bartholomew Fair*, cannot but acknowledge with me.

"I grant the French have performed what was possible on the groundwork of the Spanish Plays; what was pleasant before they have made regular; but there is not above one good Play to be writ upon all those Plots; they are too much alike to please often, which we need not the experience of our own Stage to justify. As for their new way of mingling mirth with serious Plot I do not with Lysideius condemn the thing, though I cannot approve their manner of doing it: He tells us we cannot so speedily recollect our selves after a Scene of great passion and concernment as to pass to another of mirth and humor, and to enjoy it with any relish: but why should he imagine the soul of man more heavy than his Senses? Does not the eye pass from an unpleasant object to a pleasant in a much shorter time than is required to this? and does not the unpleasantness of the first commend the beauty of the latter? The old Rule of Logic might have convinced him, that contraries when placed near, set off each other. A continued gravity keeps the spirit too much bent; we must refresh it sometimes, as we bait upon a journey, that we may go on with greater ease. A Scene of mirth mixed with Tragedy has the same effect upon us which our music has betwixt the Acts, and that we find a relief to us from the best Plots and language of the Stage, if the discourses have been long. I must therefore have stronger arguments ere I am convinced, that compassion and mirth in the same subject destroy each other; and in the mean time cannot but conclude, to the honor of our Nation, that we have invented, increased and perfected a more pleasant way of writing for the Stage than was ever known to the Ancients or Moderns of any Nation, which is Tragicomedy.

"And this leads me to wonder why Lisideius and many others should cry up the barrenness of the French Plots above the variety and copiousness of the English. Their Plots are single, they carry on one design which is pushed forward by all the Actors, every Scene in the Play contributing and moving towards it: Ours, besides the main design, have under-plots or by-concernments, of less considerable Persons, and Intrigues, which are carried on with the motion of the main Plot: just as they say the Orb of the fixed Stars, and those of the Planets, though they have motions of their own, are whirled about by the motion of the *primum mobile* [prime mover—ed.], in which they are contained: that similitude expresses much of the English Stage: for if contrary motions may be found in Nature to agree; if a Planet can go East and West at the same time; one way by virtue of his own motion, the other by the force of the first mover; it will not be difficult to imagine how the under Plot, which is only different, not contrary to the great design, may naturally be conducted along with it.

"Eugenius has already shown us, from the confession of the French Poets, that the Unity of Action is sufficiently preserved if all the imperfect actions of the Play are conducing to the main design: but when those petty intrigues of a Play are so ill ordered that they have no coherence with the other, I must grant Lisideius has reason to tax that want of due connection; for Coordination in a Play is as dangerous and unnatural as in a State. In the mean time he must acknowledge our variety, if well ordered, will afford a greater pleasure to the audience.

"As for his other argument, that by pursuing one single Theme they gain an advantage to express and work up the passions, I wish any example he could bring from them would make it good: for I confess their verses are to me the coldest I have ever read: Neither indeed is it possible for them, in the way they take, so to express passion, as that the effects of it should appear in the concernment of an Audience: their Speeches being so many declamations, which tire us with length; so that instead of persuading us to grieve for their imaginary Heroes, we are concerned for our own trouble, as we are in the tedious visits of bad company; we are in pain till they are gone. When the French Stage came to be reformed by Cardinal Richelieu, those long Harangues were introduced, to comply with the gravity of a Churchman. Look upon the *Cinna* and the *Pompey*, they are not so properly to be called Plays, as long discourses of reason of State: and *Polieucte* in matters in Religion is as solemn as the long stops upon our Organs. Since that time it is grown into a custom, and their Actors speak by the Hour-glass, as our Parsons do; nay, they account it the grace of their parts: and think themselves disparaged by the Poet, if they may not twice or thrice in a Play entertain the Audience with a Speech of an hundred or two hundred lines. I deny not but this may suit well enough with the French; for as we, who are a more sullen people, come to be diverted at our Plays; they who are of an airy and gay temper come thither to make themselves more serious: And this I conceive to be one reason why Comedy is more pleasing to us, and Tragedies to them. But to speak generally, it cannot be denied that short Speeches and Replies are more apt to move the passions, and beget concernment in us than the other: for it is unnatural for any one in a gust of passion to speak long together, or for another in the same condition, to suffer him, without interruption. Grief and Passion are like floods raised in little Brooks by a sudden rain; they are quickly up, and if the concernment be poured unexpectedly in upon us, it overflows us: But a long sober shower gives them leisure to run out as they came in, without troubling the ordinary current. As for Comedy, Repartee is one of its chiefest graces; the greatest pleasure of the Audience is a chase of wit kept up on both sides, and swiftly managed. And this our forefathers, if not we, have had in Fletcher's Plays, to a much higher degree of perfection than the French Poets can arrive at.

"There is another part of Lisideius's Discourse, in which he has rather excused our neighbors than commended them; that is, for aiming only to make one person considerable in their Plays. 'Tis very true what he has urged, that one character in all Plays, even without the Poet's care, will have advantage of all the others; and that the design of the whole Drama will chiefly depend on it. But this hinders not that there may be more shining characters in the Play: many persons of a second magnitude, nay, some so very near, so almost equal to the first, that greatness may be opposed to greatness, and all the persons be made considerable, not only by their quality, but their action. 'Tis evident that the more the persons are, the greater will be the variety, of the Plot. If then the parts are managed so regularly that the beauty of the whole be kept entire, and that the variety become not a perplexed and confused mass of accidents, you will find it infinitely pleasing to be led in a labyrinth of design, where you see some of your way before you, yet discern not the end till you arrive at it. And that all this is practicable, I can produce for examples many of our English Plays: as *The Maid's Tragedy, The Alchemist, The Silent Woman*; I was going to have named *The Fox*, but that the unity of design seems not exactly observed in it; for there appears two actions in the Play; the first naturally ending with the fourth Act; the second forced from it in the fifth: which yet is the less to be condemned in him, because the disguise of Volpone, though it suited not with his character as a crafty or covetous person, agreed well enough with that of a voluptuary: and by it the Poet gained the end he aimed at, the punishment of Vice, and the reward of Virtue, which that disguise produced. So that to judge equally of it, it was an excellent fifth Act, but not so naturally proceeding from the former.

"But to leave this, and pass to the latter part of Lisideius's discourse, which concerns relations, I must acknowledge with him, that the French have reason when they hide that part of the action which would occasion too much tumult upon the Stage, and choose rather to have it made known by the narration to the Audience. Farther I think it very convenient, for the reasons he has given, that all incredible actions were removed; but, whither custom has so insinuated it self into our Country-men, or nature has so formed them to fierceness, I know not; but they will scarcely suffer combats and other objects of horror to be taken from them. And indeed, the indecency of tumults is all which can be objected against fighting: For why may not our imagination as well suffer itself to be deluded with the probability of it, as with any other thing in the Play? For my part, I can with as great ease persuade my self that the blows which are struck are given in good earnest, as I can, that they who strike them are Kings or Princes, or those persons which they represent. For objects of incredibility I would be satisfied from Lisideius, whether we have any so removed from all appearance of truth as are those of Corneille's *Andromede*? A Play which has been frequented the most of any he has writ? If the Perseus, or the Son of an Heathen God, the Pegasus and the Monster were not capable to choke a strong belief, let him blame any representation of ours hereafter. Those indeed were objects of delight; yet the reason is the same as to the probability: for he makes it not a Ballette or Masque, but a Play, which is to resemble truth. But for death, that it ought not to be represented, I have besides the Arguments alleged by Lisideius, the authority of Ben Jonson, who has forborne it in his Tragedies; for both the death of Sejanus and Catiline are related: though in the latter I cannot but observe one irregularity of that great Poet: he has removed the Scene in the same Act, from Rome to Catiline's Army, and from thence again to Rome; and besides has allowed a very inconsiderable time, after Catiline's Speech, for the striking of the battle, and the return of Petreius, who is to relate the event of it to the Senate: which I should not animadvert upon him, who was otherwise a painful observer of *to prepon*, or the decorum of the Stage, if he had not used extreme severity in his judgment upon the incomparable Shakespeare for the same fault. To conclude on this subject of Relations, if we are to be blamed for showing too much of the action, the French are as faulty for discovering too little of it: a mean betwixt both should be observed by every judicious Writer, so as the audience may neither be left unsatisfied by not seeing what is beautiful, or shocked by beholding what is either incredible or undecent.

"I hope I have already proved in this discourse, that though we are not altogether so punctual as the French, in observing the laws of Comedy; yet our errors are so few, and little, and those things wherein we excel them so considerable, that we ought of right to be preferred before them. But what will Lisideius say if they themselves acknowledge they are too strictly tied up by those laws, for breaking which he has blamed the English? I will allege Corneille's words, as I find them in the end of his Discourse of the three Unities; '*Il est facile aux spéculatifs d'estre sévères, &c.*' "'Tis easy for speculative persons to judge severely; but if they would produce to public view ten or twelve pieces of this nature, they would perhaps give more latitude to the Rules than I have done, when by experience they had known how much we are bound up and constrained by them, and how many beauties of the Stage they banished from it.' To illustrate a little what he has said, by their servile observations of the unities of time and place, and integrity of Scenes, they have brought upon themselves that dearth of Plot, and narrowness of Imagination, which may be observed in all their Plays. How many beautiful accidents might naturally happen in two or three days, which cannot arrive with any probability in the compass of hours? There is time to be allowed also for maturity of design, which amongst great and prudent persons, such as are often represented in Tragedy, cannot, with any likelihood of truth, be brought to pass at so short a warning. Farther, by tying themselves strictly to the unity of place, and unbroken Scenes, they are forced many times to omit some beauties which cannot be shown where the Act began; but might, if the Scene were interrupted, and the Stage cleared for the persons to enter in another place; and therefore the French Poets are often forced upon absurdities: for if the Act begins in a chamber all the persons in the Play must have some business or other to come thither, or else they are not to be shown that Act, and sometimes their characters are very unfitting to appear there; As, suppose it were the King's Bed-chamber, yet the meanest man in the Tragedy must come and dispatch his business rather than in the Lobby or Court-yard (which is fitter for him) for fear the Stage should be cleared, and the Scenes broken. Many times they fall by it into a greater inconvenience; for they keep their Scenes unbroken, and yet change the place; as in one of their newest Plays, where the Act begins in the Street. There a Gentleman is to meet his Friend; he sees him with his man, coming out from his Fathers house; they talk together, and the first goes out: the second, who is a Lover, has made an appointment with his Mistress; she appears at the window, and then we are to imagine the Scene lies under it. This Gentleman is called away, and leaves his servant with his Mistress: presently her Father is heard from within; the young Lady is afraid the Servingman should be discovered, and thrusts him in through a door which is supposed to be her Closet. After this, the Father enters to the Daughter, and now the Scene is in a House: for he is seeking from one room to another for this poor Philipin, or French Diego, who is heard from within, drolling [jesting—ed.] and breaking many a miserable conceit upon his sad condition. In this ridiculous manner the Play goes on, the Stage being never empty all the while: so that the Street, the Window, the two Houses, and the Closet, are made to walk about, and the Persons to stand still. Now what I beseech you is more easy than to write a regular French Play, or more difficult than to write an irregular English one, like those of Fletcher, or of Shakespeare.

"If they content themselves as Corneille did, with some flat design, which, like an ill Riddle, is found out ere it be half proposed; such Plots we can make every way regular as easily as they: but when e'er they endeavor to rise up to any quick turns and counterturns of Plot, as some of them have attempted, since Corneille's Plays have been less in vogue, you see they write as irregularly as we, though they cover it more speciously, Hence the reason is perspicuous, why no French Plays, when translated, have, or ever can succeed upon the English Stage. For, if you consider the Plots, our own are fuller of variety, if the writing ours are more quick and fuller of spirit: and therefore 'tis a strange mistake in those who decry the way of writing Plays in Verse, as if the English therein imitated the French. We have borrowed nothing from them; our Plots are weaved in English Looms: we endeavor therein to follow the variety and greatness of characters which are derived to us from Shakespeare and Fletcher: the copiousness and well-knitting of the intrigues we have from Jonson, and for the Verse if self we have English Presidents of elder date than any of Corneille's Plays: (not to name our old Comedies before Shakespeare, which were all writ in verse of six feet, or Alexandrines, such as the French now use) I can show in Shakespeare, many Scenes of rhyme together, and the like in Ben Jonson's Tragedies: In *Catiline* and *Sejanus* sometimes thirty or forty lines; I mean besides the Chorus, or the Monologues, which by the way, showed Ben no enemy to this way of writing, especially is you look upon his *Sad Shepherd* which goes sometimes upon rhyme, sometimes upon blank Verse, like an Horse who eases himself upon Trot and Amble. You find him likewise commending Fletcher's Pastoral of *The Faithful Shepherdess*; which is for the most part Rhyme, though not refined to that purity to which it hath since been brought: And these examples are enough to clear us from a servile imitation of the French.

"But to return from whence I have digressed, I dare boldly affirm these two things of the English Drama: First, That we have many Plays of ours as regular as any of theirs; and which, besides, have more variety of Plot and Characters: And secondly, that in most of the irregular Plays of Shakespeare or Fletcher (for Ben Jonson's are for the most part regular) there is a more masculine fancy and greater spirit in all the writing, than there is in any of the French. I could produce even in Shakespeare's and Fletcher's Works, some Plays which are almost exactly formed; as *The Merry Wives of Windsor*, and *The Scornful Lady*: but because (generally speaking) Shakespeare, who writ first, did not perfectly observe the Laws of Comedy, and Fletcher, who came nearer to perfection, yet through carelessness made many faults; I will take the pattern of a perfect Play from Ben Jonson, who was a careful and learned observer of the Dramatic Laws, and from all his Comedies I shall select *The Silent Woman*; of which I will make a short Examen, according to those Rules which the French observe."

As Neander was beginning to examine *The Silent Woman*, Eugenius, looking earnestly upon him; "I beseech you Neander," said he, "gratify the company and me in particular so far, as before you speak of the Play, to give us a Character of the Author; and tell us frankly your opinion, whether you do not think all Writers, both French and English, ought to give place to him?"

"I fear," replied Neander, "That in obeying your commands I shall draw a little envy upon my self. Besides, in performing them, it will be first necessary to speak somewhat of Shakespeare and Fletcher, his Rivals in Poesy; and one of them, in my opinion, at least his equal, perhaps his superior.

"To begin then with Shakespeare; he was the man who of all Modern, and perhaps Ancient Poets, had the largest and most comprehensive soul. All the Images of Nature were still present to him, and he drew them not laboriously, but luckily: when he describes any thing, you more than see it, you feel it too. Those who accuse him to have wanted learning, give him the greater commendation: he was naturally learned; he needed not the spectacles of Books to read Nature; he looked inwards, and found her there. I cannot say he is every where alike; were he so, I should do him injury to compare him with the greatest of Mankind. He is many times flat, insipid; his Comic wit degenerating into clenches [puns—ed.]; his serious swelling into Bombast. But he is always great, when some great occasion is presented to him: no man can say he ever had a fit subject for his wit, and did not then raise himself as high above the rest of the Poets,

> Quantum lenta solent, inter viburna cupressi.
> [As cypresses commonly do among bending shrubs—ed.]

The consideration of this made Mr. Hales of Eaton say, That there was no subject of which any Poet ever writ, but he would produce it much better treated of in Shakespeare; and however others are now generally preferred before him, yet the Age wherein he lived, which had contemporaries with him, Fletcher and Jonson never equaled them to him in their esteem: And in the last King's Court, when Ben's reputation was at highest, Sir John Suckling, and with him the greater part of the Courtiers, set our Shakespeare far above him.

"Beaumont and Fletcher of whom I am next to speak, had with the advantage of Shakespeare's wit, which was their precedent, great natural gifts, improved by study. Beaumont especially being so accurate a judge of Plays, that Ben Jonson while he lived, submitted all his Writings to his Censure, and 'tis thought, used his judgement in correcting, if not contriving all his Plots. What value he had for him, appears by the Verses he writ to him; and therefore I need speak no farther of it. The first Play which brought Fletcher and him in esteem was their *Philaster*: for before that, they had written two or three very unsuccessfully: as the like is reported of Ben Jonson, before he writ *Every Man in his Humor*. Their Plots were generally more regular than Shakespeare's, especially those which were made before Beaumont's death; and they understood and imitated the conversation of Gentlemen much better; whose wild debaucheries, and quickness of wit in repartees, no Poet can ever paint as they have done. This Humor of which Ben Jonson derived from particular persons, they made it not their business to describe: they represented all the passions very lively, but above all, Love. I am apt to believe the English Language in them arrived to its highest perfection; what words have since been taken in, are rather superfluous than necessary. Their Plays are now the most pleasant and frequent entertainments of the Stage; two of theirs being acted through the year for one of Shakespeare's or Jonson's: the reason is, because there is a certain gayety in their Comedies, and Pathos in their more serious Plays, which suits generally with all men's humors. Shakespeare's language is likewise a little obsolete, and Ben Jonson's wit comes short of theirs.

"As for Jonson, to whose Character I am now arrived, if we look upon him while he was himself, (for his last Plays were but his dotages) I think him the most learned and judicious Writer which any Theater ever had. He was a most severe Judge of himself as well as others. One cannot say he wanted wit, but rather that he was frugal of it. In his works you find little to retrench or alter. Wit and Language, and Humor also in some measure we had before him; but something of Art was wanting to the Drama till he came. He managed his strength to more advantage than any who preceded him. You seldom find him making Love in any of his Scenes, or endeavoring to move the Passions; his genius was too sullen and saturnine to do it gracefully, especially when he knew he came after those who had performed both to such an height. Humor was his proper Sphere, and in that he delighted most to represent Mechanic [laboring, vulgar—ed.] people. He was deeply conversant in the Ancients, both Greek and Latin, and he borrowed boldly from them: there is scarce a Poet or Historian among the Roman Authors of those times whom he has not translated in *Sejanus* and *Catiline*. But he has done his Robberies so openly, that one may see he fears not to be taxed by any Law. He invades Authors like a Monarch, and what would be theft in other Poets, is only victory in him. With the spoils of these Writers he so represents old Rome to us, in its Rites, Ceremonies and Customs, that if one of their Poets had written either of his Tragedies, we had seen less of it than in him. If there was any fault in his Language, 'twas that he weaved it too closely and laboriously in his serious Plays; perhaps too, he did a little too much Romanize our Tongue, leaving the words which he translated almost as much Latin as he found them: wherein though he learnedly followed the Idiom of their language, he did not enough comply with ours. If I would compare him with Shakespeare, I must acknowledge him the more correct Poet, but Shakespeare the greater wit. Shakespeare was the Homer, or Father of our Dramatick Poets; Jonson was the Virgil, the pattern of elaborate writing; I admire him, but I love Shakespeare. To conclude of him, as he has given us the most correct Plays, so in the precepts which he has laid down in his *Discoveries*, we have as many and profitable Rules for perfecting the Stage as any wherewith the French can furnish us.

"Having thus spoken of the Author, I proceed to the examination of his Comedy, *The Silent Woman*.

EXAMEN OF THE SILENT WOMAN.

"To begin first with the length of the Action, it is so far from exceeding the compass of a Natural day, that it takes not up an Artificial one. 'Tis all included in the limits of three hours and an half, which is not more than is required for the presentment on the Stage. A beauty perhaps not much observed; if it had, we should not have looked upon the Spanish Translation of five hours with so much wonder. The Scene of it is laid in London; the latitude of place is almost as little as you can imagine: for it lies all within the compass of two Houses, and after the first Act, in one. The continuity of Scenes is observed more than in any of our Plays, excepting his own *Fox* and *Alchemist*. They are not broken above twice or thrice at most in the whole Comedy, and in the two best of Corneille's Plays, the *Cid* and *Cinna*, they are interrupted once apiece. The action of the Play is entirely one; the end or aim of which is the settling of Morose's Estate on Dauphine. The Intrigue of it is the greatest and most noble of any pure unmixed Comedy in any Language: you see it in many persons of various characters and humors, and all delightful: As first, Morose, or an old Man, to whom all noise but his own talking is offensive. Some who would be thought Critics, say this humor of his is forced: but to remove that objection, we may consider him first to be naturally of a delicate hearing, as many are to whom all sharp sounds are unpleasant; and secondly, we may attribute much of it to the peevishness of his Age, or the wayward authority of an old man in his own house, where he may make himself obeyed; and this the Poet seems to allude to in his name Morose. Besides this, I am assured from diverse persons, that Ben Jonson was actually acquainted with such a man, one altogether as ridiculous as he is here represented. Others say it is not enough to find one man of such an humor; it must be common to more, and the more common the more natural. To prove this, they instance in the best of Comical Characters, Falstaff: There are many men resembling him; Old, Fat, Merry, Cowardly, Drunken, Amorous, Vain, and Lying: But to convince these people, I need but tell them, that humor is the ridiculous extravagance of conversation, wherein one man differs from all others. If then it be common, or communicated to many, how differs it from other men's? or what indeed causes it to be ridiculous so much as the singularity of it? As for Falstaff, he is not properly one humor, but a Miscellany of Humors or Images, drawn from so many several men; that wherein he is singular in his wit, or those things he says, *præter expectatum*

[beyond what is expected—ed.], unexpected by the Audience; his quick eva-
sions when you imagine him surprised, which as they are extremely diverting
of themselves, so receive a great addition from his person; for the very sight of
such an unwieldy old debauched fellow is a Comedy alone. And here having a
place so proper for it I cannot but enlarge somewhat upon this subject of humor
into which I am fallen. The Ancients had little of it in their Comedies; for the
to geloion [the laughable—ed.], of the Old Comedy, of which Aristophanes was
chief, was not so much to imitate a man, as to make the people laugh at some
odd conceit, which had commonly somewhat of unnatural or obscene in it.
Thus when you see Socrates brought upon the Stage, you are not to imagine
him made ridiculous by the imitation of his actions, but rather by making him
perform something very unlike himself: something so childish and absurd, as
by comparing it with the gravity of the true Socrates, makes a ridiculous object
for the Spectators. In their new Comedy which succeeded, the Poets fought
indeed to express the *ēthos* [moral character], as in their Tragedies the *pathos*
[emotion—ed.] of Mankind. But this *ēthos* contained only the general Characters of men and manners; as old men, Lovers, Servingmen, Courtesans, Par-
asites, and such other persons as we see in their Comedies; all which they made
alike: that is, one old man or Father; one Lover, one Courtesan so like another,
as if the first of them had begot the rest of every sort: *Ex homine hunc natum
dicas* [You would say that this man is born from that one—ed.]. The same
custom they observed likewise in their Tragedies. As for the French, though
they have the word *humeur* among them, yet they have small use of it in their
Comedies, or Farces; they being but ill imitations of the *ridiculum*, or that which
stirred up laughter in the old Comedy. But among the English 'tis otherwise:
where by humor is meant some extravagant habit, passion, or affection; particular (as I said before) to some one person: by the oddness of which, he is
immediately distinguished from the rest of men; which being lively and naturally represented, most frequently begets that malicious pleasure in the Audience which is testified by laughter: as all things which are deviations from
common customs are ever the aptest to produce it: though by the way this
laughter is only accidental, as the person represented is Fantastic or Bizarre;
but pleasure is essential to it, as the imitation of what is natural. The description
of these humors, drawn from the knowledge and observation of particular persons, was the peculiar genius and talent of Ben Jonson; To whose Play I now
return.

"Besides Morose, there are at least or different Characters and humors in
The Silent Woman, all which persons have several concernments of their own,
yet are all used by the Poet, to the conducting of the main design to perfection.
I shall not waste time in commending the writing of this Play, but I will give
you my opinion, that there is more wit and acuteness of Fancy in it than in any
of Ben Jonson's. Besides, that he has here described the conversation of Gen-

tlemen in the persons of True-Wit, and his Friends, with more gayety, air and freedom, than in the rest of his Comedies. For the contrivance of the Plot 'tis extreme elaborate, and yet withal easy; for the lusis, or untying of it, 'tis so admirable, that when it is done, no one of the Audience would think the Poet could have missed it; and yet it was concealed so much before the last Scene, that any other way would sooner have entered into your thoughts. But I dare not take upon me to commend the Fabric of it, because it is altogether so full of Art, that I must unravel every Scene in it to commend it as I ought. And this excellent contrivance is still the more to be admired, because 'tis Comedy where the persons are only of common rank, and their business private, not elevated by passions or high concernments as in serious Plays. Here every one is a proper Judge of all he sees; nothing is represented but that with which he daily converses: so that by consequence all faults lie open to discovery, and few are pardonable. 'Tis this which Horace has judiciously observed:

> Creditur ex medio quia res arcessit habere
> Sudoris minimum, sed habet Comedia tanto
> Plus oneris, quanto veniæ minus.
> [Comedy is thought to require the minimum of sweat,
> Because it takes its characters from ordinary life;
> But the less indulgence it encounters, the more work it
>   needs—ed.]

But our Poet, who was not ignorant of these difficulties, had prevailed himself of all advantages; as he who designs a large leap takes his rise from the highest ground. One of these advantages is that which Corneille has laid down as the greatest which can arrive to any Poem, and which he himself could never compass above thrice in all his Plays, viz. the making choice of some signal and long expected day, whereon the action of the Play is to depend. This day was that designed by Dauphine for the settling of his Uncle's Estate upon him; which to compass he contrives to marry him: that the marriage had been plotted by him long beforehand is made evident by what he tells True-Wit in the second Act, that in one moment he had destroy'd what he had been raising many months.

"There is another artifice of the Poet, which I cannot here omit, because by the frequent practice of it in his Comedies, he has left it to us almost as a Rule, that is, when he has any Character or humor wherein he would show a *Coup de Maistre*, or his highest skill; he recommends it to your observation by a pleasant description of it before the person first appears. Thus, in *Bartholomew Fair* he gives you the Pictures of Numps and Cokes, and in this those of Daw, Lafoole, Morose, and the Collegiate Ladies; all which you hear described before you see them. So that before they come upon the Stage you have a longing expectation of them, which prepares you to receive them favorably; and when they are there, even from their first appearance you are so far acquainted with them, that nothing of their humor is lost to you.

"I will observe yet one thing further of this admirable Plot; the business of it rises in every Act. The second is greater than the first; the third than the second, and so forward to the fifth. There too you see, till the very last Scene, new difficulties arising to obstruct the action of the Play; and when the Audience is brought into despair that the business can naturally be effected, then, and not before, the discovery is made. But that the Poet might entertain you with more variety all this while, he reserves some new Characters to show you, which he opens not till the second and third Act. In the second, Morose, Daw, the Barber and Otter; in the third the Collegiate Ladies: All which he moves afterwards in by-walks, or under-Plots, as diversions to the main design, lest it should grow tedious, though they are still naturally joined with it, and somewhere or other subservient to it. Thus, like a skilful Chess-player, by little and little he draws out his men, and makes his pawns of use to his greater persons.

"If this Comedy, and some others of his, were translated into French Prose (which would now be no wonder to them, since Molière has lately given them Plays out of Verse which have not displeased them) I believe the controversy would soon be decided betwixt the two Nations, even making them the Judges. But we need not call our heroes to our aid; Be it spoken to the honor of the English, our Nation can never want in any Age such who are able to dispute the Empire of Wit with any people in the Universe. And though the fury of a Civil War, and Power, for twenty years together, abandoned to a barbarous race of men, Enemies of all good Learning, had buried the Muses under the ruins of Monarchy; yet with the restoration of our happiness, we see revived Poesy lifting up its head, and already shaking off the rubbish which lay so heavy on it. We have seen since His Majesty's return, many Dramatick Poems which yield not to those of any foreign Nation, and which deserve all Laurels but the English. I will set aside Flattery and Envy: it cannot be denied but we have had some little blemish either in the Plot or writing of all those Plays which have been made within these seven years (and perhaps there is no Nation in the world so quick to discern them, or so difficult to pardon them, as ours): yet if we can persuade our selves to use the candor of that Poet, who (though the most severe of Critics) has left us this caution by which to moderate our censures—

> *ubi plura nitent in carmine non ego paucis*
> *Offendar maculis*
> [where many things shine in a poem, I am not offended
> by a few blemishes—ed.]

—if in consideration of their many and great beauties, we can wink at some slight, and little imperfections; if we, I say, can be thus equal to our selves, I ask no favor from the French. And if I do not venture upon any particular judgment of our late Plays, 'tis out of the consideration which an Ancient Writer gives me; *Vivorum, ut magna admiratio ita censura difficilis* [in proportion as admiration for the living is great, finding fault with them is difficult—ed.]: betwixt the extremes of admiration and malice, 'tis hard to judge uprightly of the living. Only I think it may be permitted me to say, that as it is no lessening to us to yield to some Plays, and those not many of our own Nation in the last Age, so can it be no addition to pronounce of our present Poets that they have far surpassed all the Ancients, and the Modern Writers of other Countries."

This, my Lord, was the substance of what was then spoke on that occasion; and Lisideius, I think was going to reply, when he was prevented thus by Crites: "I am confident," said he, "the most material things that can be said, have been already urged on either side; if they have not, I must beg of Lisideius that he will defer his answer till another time: for I confess I have a joint quarrel to you both, because you have concluded, without any reason given for it, that Rhyme is proper for the Stage. I will not dispute how ancient it hath been among us to write this way; perhaps our Ancestors knew no better till Shakespeare's time. I will grant it was not altogether left by him, and that Fletcher and Ben Jonson used it frequently in their Pastorals, and sometimes in other Plays. Farther, I will not argue whether we received it originally from our own Countrymen, or from the French; for that is an inquiry of as little benefit, as theirs who in the midst of the great Plague were not so solicitous to provide against it, as to know whether we had it from the malignity of our own air, or by transportation from Holland. I have therefore only to affirm, that it is not allowable in serious Plays; for Comedies I find you already concluding with me. To prove this, I might satisfy my self to tell you, how much in vain it is for you to strive against the stream of the peoples inclination; the greatest part of which are prepossessed so much with those excellent Plays of Shakespeare, Fletcher, and Ben Jonson, (which have been written out of Rhyme) that except you could bring them such as were written better in it, and those too by persons of equal reputation with them, it will be impossible for you to gain your cause with them, who will still be judges. This it is to which in fine all your reasons must submit. The unanimous consent of an Audience is so powerful, That even Julius Cæsar (as Macrobius reports of him) when he was perpetual Dictator, was not able to balance it on the other side. But when Laberius, a Roman Knight, at his request contended in the Mime with another Poet, he was forced to cry out, *Etiam favente me victus es Laberi* [Even with me favoring you, Laberius, you are beaten—ed.]. But I will not on this occasion, take the advantage of the greater number, but only urge such reasons against Rhyme, as I find in the Writings of those who have argued for the other way. First then I am of opinion, that Rhyme is unnatural in a Play, because Dialogue there is presented as the effect of sudden thought. For a Play is the imitation of Nature; and since no man, without premeditation speaks in Rhyme, neither ought he to do it on the Stage; this hinders not but the Fancy may be there elevated to a higher pitch of thought than it is in ordinary discourse: for there is a probability that men of excellent and quick parts may speak noble things *extempore*: but those thoughts are never fettered with the numbers or sound of Verse without study, and therefore it cannot be but unnatural to present the most free way of speaking, in that which is the most constrained. For this Reason, says Aristotle, 'tis best to write Tragedy in that kind of Verse which is the least such, or which is nearest Prose: and this amongst the Ancients was the Iambic, and with us is blank verse, or the measure of verse, kept exactly without rhyme. These numbers therefore are fittest for a Play; the others for a paper of Verses, or a Poem. Blank verse being as much below them as rhyme is improper for the Drama. And if it be objected that neither are blank verses made *extempore*, yet as nearest Nature, they are still to be preferred. But there are two particular exceptions which many besides my self have had to verse; by which it will appear yet more plainly, how improper it is in Plays. And the first of them is grounded upon that very reason for which some have commended Rhyme: they say the quickness of repartees in argumentative Scenes receives an ornament from verse. Now what is more unreasonable than to imagine that a man should not only light upon the Wit, but the Rhyme too upon the sudden? This nicking [striking—ed.] of him who spoke before both in sound and measure, is so great an happiness, that you must at least suppose the persons of your Play to be born Poets, *Arcades omnes et cantare pares et respondere parati* [in Virgil, *Arcades ambo* . . .; Dryden's translation: Both young Arcadians, both alike inspired / To sing, and answer as the song requir'd—ed.]: they must have arrived to the degree of *quicquid conabar dicere* [singing whatever they attempted—ed.]: to make Verses almost whether they will or no: if they are any thing below this, it will look rather like the design of two than the answer of one: it will appear that your Actors hold intelligence together, that they perform their tricks like Fortune-tellers, by confederacy. The hand of Art will be too visible in it against that maxim of all Professions; *Ars est celare artem*. That it is the greatest perfection of Art to keep it self undiscovered. Nor will it serve you to object, that however you manage it, 'tis still known to be a Play; and consequently the Dialogue of two persons understood to be the labor of one Poet. For a Play is still an imitation of Nature; we know we are to be deceived, and we desire to be so; but no man ever was deceived but with a probability of truth, for who will suffer a gross lie to be fastened on him? Thus we sufficiently understand that the Scenes which represent Cities and Countries to us, are not really such, but only painted on boards and Canvass: But shall that excuse the ill Painture or designment of them; Nay rather ought they not to be labored with so much the more diligence and exactness to help the imagination? since the mind of man does naturally tend to, and seek after Truth;

and therefore the nearer any thing comes to the imitation of it, the more it pleases.

"Thus, you see, your Rhyme is incapable of expressing the greatest thoughts naturally, and the lowest it cannot with any grace: for what is more unbefitting the Majesty of Verse, than to call a Servant, or bid a door be shut in Rhyme? And yet this miserable necessity you are forced upon. But Verse, you say, circumscribes a quick and luxuriant fancy, which would extend itself too far on every subject, did not the labor which is required to well turned and polished Rhyme, set bounds to it. Yet this Argument, if granted, would only prove that we may write better in Verse, but not more naturally. Neither is it able to evince that; for he who wants judgment to confine his fancy in blank Verse, may want it as much in Rhyme; and he who has it will avoid errors in both kinds. Latin verse was as great a confinement to the imagination of those Poets, as Rhyme to ours: and yet you find Ovid saying too much on every subject. *Nescivit* (says Seneca) *quod bene cessit relinquere* [He did not know how to leave off when it was proper to do so—ed.]: of which he gives you one famous instance in his Description of the Deluge:

> *Omnia pontus erat, deerant quoque Litora Ponto.*
> Now all was Sea, Nor had that Sea a shore. [trans.
>   Dryden's]

Thus Ovid's fancy was not limited by verse, and Virgil needed not verse to have bounded his.

"In our own language we see Ben Jonson confining himself to what ought to be said, even in the liberty of blank Verse; and yet Corneille, the most judicious of the French Poets, is still varying the same sense an hundred ways, and dwelling eternally upon the same subject, though confined by Rhyme. Some other exceptions I have to Verse, but being these I have named are for the most part already public; I conceive it reasonable they should first be answered."

"It concerns me less than any," said Neander, (seeing he had ended) "to reply to this Discourse; because when I should have proved that Verse may be natural in Plays, yet I should always be ready to confess, that those which I have written in this kind come short of that perfection which is required. Yet since you are pleased I should undertake this Province, I will do it, though with all imaginable respect and deference both to that person from whom you have borrowed your strongest Arguments, and to whose judgment when I have said all, I finally submit. But before I proceed to answer your objections, I must first remember [remind—ed.] you, that I exclude all Comedy from my defense; and next that I deny not but blank verse may be also used, and content my self only to assert, that in serious Plays where the subject and characters are great, and the Plot unmixed with mirth, which might allay or divert these concernments which are produced, Rhyme is there as natural, and more effectual than blank Verse.

"And now having laid down this as a foundation, to begin with Crites, I must crave leave to tell him, that some of his Arguments against rhyme reach no farther than from the faults or defects of ill rhyme, to conclude against the use of it in general. May not I conclude against blank verse by the same reason? If the words of some poets who write in it, are either ill chosen, or ill placed, which makes not only rhyme, but all kind of verse in any language unnatural, shall I, for their vicious affectation condemn those excellent lines of Fletcher, which are written in that kind? Is there anything in rhyme more constrained than this line in blank verse? "I Heav'n invoke, and strong resistance make," where you see both the clauses are placed unnaturally; that is, contrary to the common way of speaking, and that without the excuse of a rhyme to cause it: yet you would think me very ridiculous, if I should accuse the stubbornness of blank Verse for this, and not rather the stiffness of the Poet. Therefore, Crites, you must either prove that words, though well chosen, and duly placed, yet render not Rhyme natural in it self; or, that however natural and easy the rhyme may be, yet it is not proper for a Play. If you insist upon the former part, I would ask you what other conditions are required to make Rhyme natural in itself, besides an election of apt words, and a right disposing of them? For the due choice of your words expresses your sense naturally, and the due placing them adapts the rhyme to it. If you object that one verse may be made for the sake of another, though both the words and rhyme be apt; I answer it cannot possibly so fall out; for either there is a dependence of sense betwixt the first line and the second, or there is none: if there be that connection, then in the natural position of the words, the latter line must of necessity flow from the former: if there be no dependence, yet still the due ordering of words makes the last line as natural in itself as the other: so that the necessity of a rhyme never forces any but bad or lazy Writers to say what they would not otherwise. 'Tis true, there is both care and Art required to write in Verse; A good Poet never concludes upon the first line, till he has sought out such a rhyme as may fit the sense, already prepared to heighten the second: many times the close of the sense falls into the middle of the next verse, or farther of, and he may often prevail himself of the same advantages in English which Virgil had in Latin. He may break off in the Hemistich, and begin another line: indeed, the not observing these two last things, makes Plays which are writ in verse so tedious: for though, most commonly, the sense is to be confined to the Couplet, yet nothing that does *perpetuo tenore fluere*, run in the same channel, can please always. 'Tis like the murmuring of a stream, which not varying in the fall, causes at first attention, at last drowsiness. Variety of cadences is the best rule, the greatest help to the Actors, and refreshment to the Audience.

"If then Verse may be made natural in itself, how becomes it improper to a Play? You say the Stage is the representation of Nature, and no man in ordinary conversation speaks in rhyme. But you foresaw when you said this, that it might be answered; neither does any man speak in blank verse, or in measure without rhyme. Therefore you concluded, that which is nearest Nature is still to be preferred. But you took no notice that rhyme might be made as natural as blank verse, by the well placing of the words, etc. All the difference between them when they are both correct, is the sound in one, which the other wants; and if so, the sweetness of it, and all the advantage resulting from it, which are handled in the Preface to *The Rival Ladies*, will yet stand good. As for that place of Aristotle, where he says Plays should be writ in that kind of Verse which is nearest Prose; it makes little for you, blank verse being properly but measured Prose. Now measure alone in any modern Language, does not constitute verse; those of the Ancients in Greek and Latin, consisted in quantity of words, and a determinate number of feet. But when, by the inundation of the Goths and Vandals into Italy new Languages were brought in, and barbarously mingled with the Latin (of which the Italian, Spanish, French, and ours, [made out of them and the Teutonic] are Dialects): a new way of Poesy was practiced; new, I say in those Countries, for in all probability it was that of the Conquerors in their own Nations. This new way consisted in measure or number of feet and rhyme. The sweetness of Rhyme, and observation of Accent, supplying the place of quantity in words, which could neither exactly be observed by those Barbarians who knew not the Rules of it, neither was it suitable to their tongues as it had been to the Greek and Latin. No man is tied in modern Poesy to observe any farther rule in the feet of his verse, but that they be disyllables; whether Spondee, Trochee, or Iambic, it matters not; only he is obliged to rhyme: Neither do the Spanish, French, Italian or Germans acknowledge at all, or very rarely any such kind of Poesy as blank verse amongst them. Therefore at most 'tis but a Poetic Prose, a *Sermo pedestris* [prose discourse—ed.], and as such most fit for Comedies, where I acknowledge Rhyme to be improper. Farther, as to that quotation of Aristotle, our Couplet Verses may be rendered as near Prose as blank verse it self, by using those advantages I lately named, as breaks in a Hemistich, or running the sense into another line, thereby making Art and Order appear as loose and free as Nature: or not tying our selves to Couplets strictly, we may use the benefit of the Pindaric way, practiced in *The Siege of Rhodes*; where the numbers vary and the rhyme is disposed carelessly, and far from often chiming. Neither is that other advantage of the Ancients to be despised, of changing the kind of verse when they please with the change of the Scene, or some new entrance: for they confine not themselves always to Iambics, but extend their liberty to all Lyric numbers, and sometimes, even to Hexameter. But I need not go so far to prove that Rhyme, as it succeeds to all other offices of Greek and Latin Verse, so especially to this of Plays, since the custom of all

Nations at this day confirms it: All the French, Italian and Spanish Tragedies are generally writ in it, and sure the Universal consent of the most civilized parts of the world, ought in this, as it doth in other customs, include the rest.

"But perhaps you may tell me I have proposed such a way to make rhyme natural, and consequently proper to Plays, as is unpracticable, and that I shall scarce find six or eight lines together in any Play, where the words are so placed and chosen as is required to make it natural. I answer, no Poet need constrain himself at all times to it. It is enough he makes it his general Rule; for I deny not but sometimes there may be a greatness in placing the words otherwise; and sometimes they may sound better, sometimes also the variety itself is excuse enough. But if, for the most part, the words be placed as they are in the negligence of Prose, it is sufficient to denominate the way practicable; for we esteem that to be such, which in the Trial oftener succeeds than misses. And thus far you may find the practice made good in many Plays; where you do not, remember still, that if you cannot find six natural Rhymes together, it will be as hard for you to produce as many lines in blank Verse, even among the greatest of our Poets, against which I cannot make some reasonable exception.

"And this, Sir, calls to my remembrance the beginning of your discourse, where you told us we should never find the Audience favourable to this kind of writing, till we could produce as good Plays in Rhyme, as Ben Jonson, Fletcher, and Shakespeare, had writ out of it. But it is to raise envy to the living, to compare them with the dead. They are honored, and almost adored by us, as they deserve; neither do I know any so presumptuous of themselves as to contend with them. Yet give me leave to say thus much without injury to their Ashes, that not only we shall never equal them, but they could never equal themselves, were they to rise and write again. We acknowledge them our Fathers in wit, but they have ruined their Estates themselves before they came to their children's hands. There is scarce an Humor, a Character, or any kind of Plot, which they have not blown upon: all comes sullied or wasted to us: and were they to entertain this Age, they could not make so plenteous treatments out of such decayed Fortunes. This therefore will be a good Argument to us either not to write at all, or to attempt some other way. There is no bays to be expected in their Walks; *Tentanda via est quà me quoque possum tollere humo* [New ways I must attempt, my grov'ling name / To raise aloft—trans. Dryden's].

"This way of writing in verse they have only left free to us; our age is arrived to a perfection in it, which they never knew; and which (if we may guess by what of theirs we have seen in verse, as *The Faithful Shepherdess*, and *Sad Shepherd*) 'tis probable they never could have reached. For the Genius of every Age is different; and though ours excel in this, I deny not but that to imitate Nature in that perfection which they did in Prose, is a greater commendation than to write in verse exactly. As for what you have added, that the people are not generally inclined to like this way; if it were true, it would be no wonder, that betwixt the shaking off an old habit, and the introducing of a new, there should be difficulty. Do we not see them stick to Hopkins and Sternhold's Psalms, and forsake those of David, I mean Sandys's Translation of them? If by the people you understand the multitude, the *hoi polloi* [the multitude, the many; since *hoi* means "the," Dryden's "the" is superfluous, but the usage is general in English; this is the first recorded use of the phrase in English, with or without the superfluous article—ed.]. 'Tis no matter what they think; they are sometimes in the right, sometimes in the wrong; their judgment is a mere Lottery. *Est ubi plebs rectè putat, est ubi peccat* [There are times when the people think rightly and times when they err—ed.], Horace says it of the vulgar, judging Poesy. But if you mean the mixed audience of the populace, and the Noblesse, I dare confidently affirm that a great part of the latter sort are already favorable to verse; and that no serious Plays written since the King's return have been more kindly received by them, than *The Siege of Rhodes*, the *Mustapha*, *The Indian Queen*, and *Indian Emperor*.

"But I come now to the inference of your first Argument. You said the Dialogue of Plays is presented as the effect of sudden thought, but no man speaks suddenly, or *extempore* in Rhyme: And you inferred from thence, that Rhyme, which you acknowledge to be proper to Epic Poesy cannot equally be proper to Dramatick, unless we could suppose all men born so much more than Poets, that verses should be made in them, not by them.

"It has been formerly urged by you, and confessed by me, that since no man spoke any kind of verse *extempore*, that which was nearest Nature was to be preferred. I answer you therefore, by distinguishing betwixt what is nearest to the nature of Comedy, which is the imitation of common persons and ordinary speaking, and what is nearest the nature of a serious Play: this last is indeed the representation of Nature, but 'tis Nature wrought up to an higher pitch. The Plot, the Characters, the Wit, the Passions, the Descriptions, are all exalted above the level of common converse, as high as the imagination of the Poet can carry them, with proportion to verisimility. Tragedy we know is wont to image to us the minds and fortunes of noble persons, and to portray these exactly, Heroic Rhyme is nearest Nature, as being the noblest kind of modern verse.

> *Indignatur enim privatis, et prope socco.*
> *Dignis carminibus narrari cœna Thyestæ*
> [For the banquet of Thyestes should not
> Be narrated in casual verses, almost suitable for comedy
>   —ed.]

says Horace: And in another place,

Essutire leveis indigna tragœdia versus.
[Tragedy improper for the bubbling forth of light verses
    —ed.]

Blank Verse is acknowledged to be too low for a Poem, nay more, for a paper of verses; but if too low for an ordinary Sonnet, how much more for Tragedy, which is by Aristotle in the dispute betwixt the Epic Poesy and the Dramatick; for many reasons he there alleges ranked above it.

"But setting this defense aside, your Argument is almost as strong against the use of Rhyme in Poems as in Plays; for the Epic way is every where interlaced with Dialogue, or discoursive Scenes; and therefore you must either grant Rhyme to be improper there, which is contrary to your assertion, or admit it into Plays by the same title which you have given it to Poems. For though Tragedy be justly preferred above the other, yet there is a great affinity between them as may easily be discovered in that definition of a Play which Lisideius gave us. The Genus of them is the same, a just and lively Image of human nature, in its Actions, Passions, and traverses of Fortune: so is the end, namely for the delight and benefit of Mankind. The Characters and Persons are still the same, viz. the greatest of both sorts, only the manner of acquainting us with those Actions, Passions and Fortunes is different. Tragedy performs it *viva voce*, or by action, in Dialogue, wherein it excels the Epic Poem which does it chiefly by narration, and therefore is not so lively an Image of Humane Nature. However, the agreement betwixt them is such, that if Rhyme be proper for one, it must be for the other. Verse 'tis true is not the effect of sudden thought; but this hinders not that sudden thought may be represented in verse, since those thoughts are such as must be higher than Nature can raise them without premeditation, especially to a continuance of them even out of verse, and consequently you cannot imagine them to have been sudden either in the Poet, or the Actors. A Play, as I had said to be like Nature, is to be set above it; as Statues which are placed on high are made greater than the life, that they may descend to the sight in their just proportion.

"Perhaps I have insisted too long upon this objection; but the clearing of it will make my stay shorter on the rest. You tell us Crites, that rhyme appears most unnatural in repartees, or short replies: when he who answers, (it being presumed he knew not what the other would say, yet) makes up that part of the verse which was left incomplete, and supplies both the sound and measure of it. This you say looks rather like the confederacy of two, than the answer of one.

"This, I confess, is an objection which is in every ones mouth who loves not rhyme: but suppose, I beseech you, the repartee were made only in blank verse, might not part of the same argument be turned against you? for the measure is as often supplied there as it is in Rhyme. The latter half of the Hemistich as commonly made up, or a second line subjoined as a reply to the former; which any one leaf in Jonson's Plays will sufficiently clear to you. You will often find in the Greek Tragedians, and in Seneca, that when a Scene grows up in the warmth of repartees (which is the close sighting of it) the latter part of the Trimeter is supplied by him who answers; and yet it was never observed as a fault in them by any of the Ancient or Modern Critics. The case is the same in our verse as it was in theirs; Rhyme to us being in lieu of quantity to them. But if no latitude is to be allowed a Poet, you take from him not only his license of *quidlibet audendi* [daring what he wills—ed.], but you tie him up in a straighter compass than you would a Philosopher. This is indeed *Musas colere severiores* [to cultivate the muses intensely—ed.]: You would have him follow Nature, but he must follow her on foot: you have dismounted him from his Pegasus. But you tell us this supplying the last half of a verse, or adjoining a whole second to the former, looks more like the design of two than the answer of one. Suppose we acknowledge it: how comes this confederacy to be more displeasing to you than in a Dance which is well contrived? You see there the united design of many persons to make up one Figure: after they have separated themselves in many petty divisions, they rejoin one by one into a gross: the confederacy is plain amongst them; for chance could never produce any thing so beautiful, and yet there is nothing in it that shocks your sight. I acknowledge the hand of Art appears in repartee, as of necessity it must in all kind of verse. But there is also the quick and poignant brevity of it (which is an high imitation of Nature in those sudden gusts of passion) to mingle with it: and this joined with the cadency and sweetness of the Rhyme, leaves nothing in the soul of the hearer to desire. 'Tis an Art which appears; but it appears only like the shadowings of Painture, which being to cause the rounding of it, cannot be absent; but while that is considered they are lost: so while we attend to the other beauties of the matter, the care and labor of the Rhyme is carried from us, or at least drowned in its own sweetness, as Bees are sometimes buried in their Honey. When a Poet has found the repartee, the last perfection he can add to it, is to put it into verse. However good the thought may be; however apt the words in which 'tis couched, yet he finds himself at a little unrest while Rhyme is wanting: he cannot leave it till that comes naturally, and then is at ease, and sits down contented.

"From Replies, which are the most elevated thoughts of Verse, you pass to the most mean ones; those which are common with the lowest of household conversation. In these, you say, the Majesty of Verse suffers. You instance in the calling of a servant, or commanding a door to be shut in rhyme. This, Crites, is a good observation of yours, but no argument: for it proves no more but that such thoughts should be waved, as often as may be, by the address of the Poet. But suppose they are necessary in the places where he uses them, yet there is no need to put them into rhyme. He may place them in the beginning of a Verse, and break it off, as unfit, when so debased for any other use: or granting the worst, that they require more room than the Hemistich will allow; yet still there is a choice to be made of the best words, and least vulgar (provided they be apt) to express such thoughts. Many have blamed Rhyme in general, for this fault, when the Poet, with a little care, might have redressed it. But they do it with no more justice, than if English Poesy should be made ridiculous for the sake of the Water Poet's Rhymes. Our language is noble, full and significant; and I know not why he who is Master of it may not clothe ordinary things in it as decently as the Latin; if he use the same diligence in his choice of words. *Delectus verborum Origo est Eloquentiæ* [the picking of words is the source of eloquence—ed.]. It was the saying of Julius Cæsar, one so curious in his, that none of them can be changed but for a worse. One would think "Unlock the door" was a thing as vulgar as could be spoken; and yet Seneca could make it sound high and lofty in his Latin:

> *Reserate clusos Regii postes Laris*
> [Set wide the palace gates.—ed.]

"But I turn from this exception, both because it happens not above twice or thrice in any Play that those vulgar thoughts are used; and then too (were there no other Apology to be made, yet) the necessity of them (which is alike in all kind of writing) may excuse them. Besides that the great eagerness and precipitation with which they are spoken makes us rather mind the substance than the dress; that for which they are spoken, rather than what is spoke. For they are always the effect of some hasty concernment, and something of consequence depends upon them.

"Thus, Crites, I have endeavored to answer your objections; it remains only that I should vindicate an Argument for Verse, which you have gone about to overthrow. It had formerly been said, that the easiness of blank verse, renders the Poet too luxuriant; but that the labor of Rhyme bounds and circumscribes an over-fruitful fancy, The sense there being commonly confined to the couplet, and the words so ordered that the Rhyme naturally follows them, not they the Rhyme. To this you answered, that it was no Argument to the question in hand, for the dispute was not which way a man may write best: but which is most proper for the subject on which he writes.

"First, give me leave, Sir, to remember you that the Argument against which you raised this objection, was only secondary: it was built upon this Hypothesis, that to write in verse was proper for serious Plays. Which supposition being granted (as it was briefly made out in that discourse, by showing how verse might be made natural) it asserted, that this way of writing was an help to the Poet's judgment, by putting bounds to a wild overflowing Fancy. I think therefore it will not be hard for me to make good what it was to prove: But you add, that were this let pass, yet he who wants judgment in the liberty of his fancy, may as well show the defect of it when he is confined to verse: for he who has judgment will avoid errors, and he who has it not, will commit them in all kinds of writing.

"This Argument, as you have taken it from a most acute person, so I confess it carries much weight in it. But by using the word Judgment here indefinitely, you seem to have put a fallacy upon us: I grant he who has Judgment, that is, so profound, so strong, so infallible a judgment, that he needs no helps to keep it always poised and upright, will commit no faults either in rhyme or out of it. And on the other extreme, he who has a judgment so weak and crazed that no helps can correct or amend it, shall write scurvily out of Rhyme, and worse in it. But the first of these judgments is no where to be found, and the latter is not fit to write at all. To speak therefore of judgment as it is in the best Poets; they who have the greatest proportion of it, want other helps than from it within. As for example, you would be loth to say, that he who was endued with a sound judgment had no need of History, Geography, or Moral Philosophy, to write correctly. Judgment is indeed the Master-workman in a Play: but he requires many subordinate hands, many tools to his assistance. And Verse I affirm to be one of these: 'Tis a Rule and line by which he keeps his building compact and even, which otherwise lawless imagination would raise either irregularly or loosely. At least if the Poet commits errors with this help, he would make greater and more without it: 'Tis (in short) a slow and painful, but the surest kind of working. Ovid whom you accuse for luxuriancy in Verse, had perhaps been farther guilty of it had he writ in Prose. And for your instance of Ben Jonson, who you say, writ exactly without the help of Rhyme; you are to remember 'tis only an aid to a luxuriant Fancy, which his was not: As he did not want imagination, so none ever said he had much to spare. Neither was verse then refined so much to be an help to that Age as it is to ours. Thus then the second thoughts being usually the best, as receiving the maturest digestion from judgment, and the last and most mature product of those thoughts being artful and labored verse, it may well be inferred, that verse is a great help to a luxuriant Fancy, and this is what that Argument which you opposed was to evince."

Neander was pursuing this Discourse so eagerly, that Eugenius had called to him twice or thrice ere he took notice that the Barge stood still, and that they were at the foot of Somerset-Stairs, where they had appointed it to land. The company were all sorry to separate so soon, though a great part of the evening was already spent; and stood a while looking back upon the water, which the Moon-beams played upon, and made it appear like floating quick-silver: at last they went up through a crowd of French people who were merrily dancing in the open air, and nothing concerned for the noise of Guns which had alarmed the Town that afternoon. Walking thence together to the Piazze they parted there; Eugenius and Lysideius to some pleasant appointment they had made, and Crites and Neander to their several Lodgings.

FINIS.

10

ALEXANDER POPE (1688–1744)

Pope was the greatest English poet for a third of the eighteenth century, from about 1711, when he wrote his "Essay on Criticism," until his death thirty-three years later. He was most successful as a translator of Homer, but his reputation rests largely on his genius as a satirist, especially in the mock-epic mode displayed in "The Rape of the Lock" and *The Dunciad*. As the "Epistle to Dr. Arbuthnot" demonstrates, Pope was among the finest epistolary poets in English. Dr. John Arbuthnot (1667–1735) was the physician to Queen Anne. A friend of Swift and Pope, Arbuthnot was a gifted satirist; the figure of "John Bull" as the typical Englishman is Arbuthnot's invention. In the final months of his life, he cautioned Pope about making enemies through satire; this epistle is part of Pope's response.

Pope produced his effervescent "Essay on Criticism" at about age twenty. The period around 1710 was probably the last time anybody writing literary criticism in Europe could in effect limit his inquiry to poetry. Until the eighteenth century, serious creative literature was almost exclusively poetry. For some centuries, prose in drama was correlated with comedy, while poetry was associated with tragedy and other elevated forms. There were no important prose tragedies in English drama until 1731, when George Lillo's domestic tragedy *The London Merchant* was published. By this time, the novel was becoming established as a much more serious and substantial form than it had been earlier, and the scope of criticism was enlarging to match what writers were doing. But it would be a long time before any serious critics addressed themselves to writing in prose; novels, for the most part, were considered a form of light entertainment. Pope's main exemplars are Horace and Boileau, to whom he graciously acknowledges his debt. The poem is a verse essay on verse labors, which bears the double burden of needing to succeed as precept and example, but Pope manages it brilliantly.

AN ESSAY ON CRITICISM (1711)

'Tis hard to say, if greater Want of Skill
Appear in Writing or in Judging ill,
But, of the two, less dang'rous is th' Offence,
To tire our Patience, than mis-lead our Sense:
Some few in that, but Numbers err in this,
Ten Censure wrong for one who Writes amiss;
A Fool might once himself alone expose,
Now One in Verse makes many more in Prose.
'Tis with our Judgments as our Watches, none
Go just alike, yet each believes his own.
In Poets as true Genius is but rare,
True Taste as seldom is the Critick's Share;
Both must alike from Heav'n derive their Light,
These born to Judge, as well as those to Write.
Let such teach others who themselves excell,
And censure freely who have written well.
Authors are partial to their Wit, 'tis true,
But are not Criticks to their Judgment too?
Yet if we look more closely, we shall find
Most have the Seeds of Judgment in their Mind;

Nature affords at least a glimm'ring Light;
The Lines, tho' touch'd but faintly, are drawn right.
But as the slightest Sketch, if justly trac'd,
Is by ill Colouring but the more disgrac'd,
So by false Learning is good Sense defac'd.
Some are bewilder'd in the Maze of Schools,
And some made Coxcombs Nature meant but Fools.
In search of Wit these lose their common Sense,
And then turn Criticks in their own Defence.
Each burns alike, who can, or cannot write,
Or with a Rival's or an Eunuch's spite.
All Fools have still an Itching to deride,
And fain wou'd be upon the Laughing Side;
If Maevius Scribble in Apollo's spight,[1]
There are, who judge still worse than he can write
Some have at first for Wits, then Poets past,
Turn'd Criticks next, and prov'd plain Fools at last;
Some neither can for Wits nor Criticks pass,
As heavy Mules are neither Horse or Ass.
Those half-learn'd Witlings, num'rous in our Isle,
As half-form'd Insects on the Banks of Nile:
Unfinish'd Things, one knows now what to call,
Their Generation's so equivocal:[2]
To tell 'em, wou'd a hundred Tongues require,
Or one vain Wit's, that might a hundred tire.
But you who seek to give and merit Fame,
And justly bear a Critick's noble Name,
Be sure your self and your own Reach to know.
How far your Genius, Taste, and Learning go;
Launch not beyond your Depth, but be discreet,
And mark that Point where Sense and Dulness meet.
Nature to all things fix'd the Limits fit,
And wisely curb'd proud Man's pretending Wit:
As on the Land while here the Ocean gains,
In other Parts it leaves wide sandy Plains;
Thus in the Soul while Memory prevails,
The solid Pow'r of Understanding fails;

----

1. Maevius: a bad poet, often coupled with Bavius, another bad poet; ridiculed in Virgil's Third
Eclogue and Horace's Tenth Epode.
2. Their generation's so equivocal: thought to be born without parents.

Where Beams of warm Imagination play,
The Memory's soft Figures melt away.
One Science only will one Genius fit;
So vast is Art, so narrow Human Wit;[3]
Not only bounded to peculiar Arts,
But oft in those, confin'd to single Parts.
Like Kings we lose the Conquests gain'd before,
By vain Ambition still to make them more:
Each might his sev'ral Province well command,
Wou'd all but stoop to what they understand.
First follow NATURE, and your Judgment frame
By her just Standard, which is still the same:
Unerring Nature, still divinely bright,
One clear, unchang'd and Universal Light,
Life, Force, and Beauty, must to all impart,
At once the Source, and End, and Test of Art
Art from that Fund each just Supply provides,
Works without Show, and without Pomp presides:
In some fair Body thus th' informing Soul
With Spirits feeds, with Vigour fills the whole,
Each Motion guides, and ev'ry Nerve sustains;
It self unseen, but in th' Effects, remains.
Some, to whom Heav'n in Wit has been profuse.
Want as much more, to turn it to its use,
For Wit and Judgment often are at strife,
Tho' meant each other's Aid, like Man and Wife.
'Tis more to guide than spur the Muse's Steed;
Restrain his Fury, than provoke his Speed;
The winged Courser, like a gen'rous Horse,
Shows most true Mettle when you check his Course.
Those RULES of old discover'd, not devis'd,
Are Nature still, but Nature Methodiz'd;
Nature, like Liberty, is but restrain'd
By the same Laws which first herself ordain'd.
Hear how learn'd Greece her useful Rules indites,
When to repress, and when indulge our Flights:
High on Parnassus' Top her Sons she show'd,
And pointed out those arduous Paths they trod,
Held from afar, aloft, th' Immortal Prize,

---

3. So vast is Art: learning in general.

And urg'd the rest by equal Steps to rise;
Just Precepts thus from great Examples giv'n,
She drew from them what they deriv'd from Heav'n
The gen'rous Critick fann'd the Poet's Fire,
And taught the World, with Reason to Admire.
Then Criticism the Muse's Handmaid prov'd,
To dress her Charms, and make her more belov'd;
But following Wits from that Intention stray'd;
Who cou'd not win the Mistress, woo'd the Maid;
Against the Poets their own Arms they turn'd,
Sure to hate most the Men from whom they learn'd
So modern Pothecaries, taught the Art
By Doctor's Bills to play the Doctor's Part,
Bold in the Practice of mistaken Rules,
Prescribe, apply, and call their Masters Fools.
Some on the Leaves of ancient Authors prey,
Nor Time nor Moths e'er spoil'd so much as they:
Some dryly plain, without Invention's Aid,
Write dull Receits how Poems may be made:
These leave the Sense, their Learning to display,
And those explain the Meaning quite away
You then whose Judgment the right Course wou'd steer,
Know well each ANCIENT's proper Character,
His Fable, Subject, Scope in ev'ry Page,
Religion, Country, Genius of his Age:
Without all these at once before your Eyes,
Cavil you may, but never Criticize.
Be Homer's Works your Study, and Delight,
Read them by Day, and meditate by Night,
Thence form your Judgment, thence your Maxims bring,
And trace the Muses upward to their Spring;
Still with It self compar'd, his Text peruse;
And let your Comment be the Mantuan Muse.[4]
When first young Maro in his boundless Mind
A Work t' outlast Immortal Rome design'd,
Perhaps he seem'd above the Critick's Law,
And but from Nature's Fountains scorn'd to draw:
But when t'examine ev'ry Part he came,
Nature and Homer were, he found, the same:

---

4. Mantuan Muse: Virgil.

Convinc'd, amaz'd, he checks the bold Design,
And Rules as strict his labour'd Work confine,
As if the Stagyrite o'er looked each Line.[5]
Learn hence for Ancient Rules a just Esteem;
To copy Nature is to copy Them.
Some Beauties yet, no Precepts can declare,
For there's a Happiness as well as Care.
Musick resembles Poetry, in each
Are nameless Graces which no Methods teach,
And which a Master-Hand alone can reach.
If, where the Rules not far enough extend,
(Since Rules were made but to promote their End)
Some Lucky LICENCE answers to the full
Th' Intent propos'd, that Licence is a Rule.
Thus Pegasus, a nearer way to take,
May boldly deviate from the common Track.
Great Wits sometimes may gloriously offend,
And rise to Faults true Criticks dare not mend;
From vulgar Bounds with brave Disorder part,
And snatch a Grace beyond the Reach of Art,
Which, without passing thro' the Judgment, gains
The Heart, and all its End at once attains.
In Prospects, thus, some Objects please our Eyes,
Which out of Nature's common Order rise,
The shapeless Rock, or hanging Precipice.
But tho' the Ancients thus their Rules invade,
(As Kings dispense with Laws Themselves have made)
Moderns, beware! Or if you must offend
Against the Precept, ne'er transgress its End,
Let it be seldom, and compell'd by Need,
And have, at least, Their Precedent to plead.
The Critick else proceeds without Remorse,
Seizes your Fame, and puts his Laws in force.
I know there are, to whose presumptuous Thoughts
Those Freer Beauties, ev'n in Them, seem Faults:
Some Figures monstrous and mis-shap'd appear,
Consider'd singly, or beheld too near,
Which, but proportion'd to their Light, or Place,
Due Distance reconciles to Form and Grace.

---

5. Stagyrite: Aristotle.

A prudent Chief not always must display
His Pow'rs in equal Ranks, and fair Array,
But with th' Occasion and the Place comply,
Conceal his Force, nay seem sometimes to Fly.
Those oft are Stratagems which Errors seem,
Nor is it Homer Nods, but We that Dream.
Still green with Bays each ancient Altar stands,
Above the reach of Sacrilegious Hands,
Secure from Flames, from Envy's fiercer Rage,
Destructive War, and all-involving Age.
See, from each Clime the Learn'd their Incense bring;
Hear, in all Tongues consenting Paeans ring!
In Praise so just, let ev'ry Voice be join'd,
And fill the Gen'ral Chorus of Mankind!
Hail Bards Triumphant! born in happier Days;
Immortal Heirs of Universal Praise!
Whose Honours with Increase of Ages grow,
As streams roll down, enlarging as they flow!
Nations unborn your mighty Names shall sound,
And Worlds applaud that must not yet be found!
Oh may some Spark of your Coelestial Fire
The last, the meanest of your Sons inspire,
(That on weak Wings, from far, pursues your Flights;
Glows while he reads, but trembles as he writes)
To teach vain Wits a Science little known,
T' admire Superior Sense, and doubt their own!
Of all the Causes which conspire to blind
Man's erring Judgment, and misguide the Mind,
What the weak Head with strongest Byass rules,
Is Pride, the never-failing Vice of Fools.
Whatever Nature has in Worth deny'd,
She gives in large Recruits of needful Pride;
For as in Bodies, thus in Souls, we find
What wants in Blood and Spirits, swell'd with Wind;
Pride, where Wit fails, steps in to our Defence,
And fills up all the mighty Void of Sense!
If once right Reason drives that Cloud away,
Truth breaks upon us with resistless Day;
Trust not your self; but your Defects to know,
Make use of ev'ry Friend—and ev'ry Foe.
A little Learning is a dang'rous Thing;

Drink deep, or taste not the Pierian Spring:[6]
There shallow Draughts intoxicate the Brain,
And drinking largely sobers us again.
Fir'd at first Sight with what the Muse imparts,
In fearless Youth we tempt the Heights of Arts,
While from the bounded Level of our Mind,
Short Views we take, nor see the lengths behind,
But more advanc'd, behold with strange Surprize
New, distant Scenes of endless Science rise!
So pleas'd at first, the towring Alps we try,
Mount o'er the Vales, and seem to tread the Sky;
Th' Eternal Snows appear already past,
And the first Clouds and Mountains seem the last:
But those attain'd, we tremble to survey
The growing Labours of the lengthen'd Way,
Th' increasing Prospect tires our wandering Eyes,
Hills peep o'er Hills, and Alps on Alps arise!
A perfect Judge will read each Work of Wit
With the same Spirit that its Author writ,
Survey the Whole, nor seek slight Faults to find,
Where Nature moves, and Rapture warms the Mind;
Nor lose, for that malignant dull Delight,
The gen'rous Pleasure to be charm'd with Wit.
But in such Lays as neither ebb, nor flow,
Correctly cold, and regularly low,
That shunning Faults, one quiet Tenour keep;
We cannot blame indeed—but we may sleep.
In Wit, as Nature, what affects our Hearts
Is nor th' Exactness of peculiar Parts;
'Tis not a Lip, or Eye, we Beauty call,
But the joint Force and full Result of all.
Thus when we view some well-proportion'd Dome,
The World's just Wonder, and ev'n thine O Rome!)
No single Parts unequally surprize;
All comes united to th' admiring Eyes;
No monstrous Height, or Breadth, or Length appear;
The Whole at once is Bold, and Regular.
Whoever thinks a faultless Piece to see,

---

6. Pierian Spring: sacred to the Muses.

Thinks what ne'er was, nor is, nor e'er shall be.
In ev'ry Work regard the Writer's End,
Since none can compass more than they Intend;
And if the Means be just, the Conduct true,
Applause, in spite of trivial Faults, is due.
As Men of Breeding, sometimes Men of Wit,
T' avoid great Errors, must the less commit,
Neglect the Rules each Verbal Critick lays,
For not to know some Trifles, is a Praise.
Most Criticks, fond of some subservient Art,
Still make the Whole depend upon a Part,
They talk of Principles, but Notions prize,
And All to one lov'd Folly Sacrifice.
Once on a time, La Mancha's Knight, they say,[7]
A certain Bard encountring on the Way,
Discours'd in Terms as just, with Looks as Sage,
As e'er cou'd Dennis, of the Grecian Stage;
Concluding all were desp'rate Sots and Fools,
Who durst depart from Aristotle's Rules.
Our Author, happy in a Judge so nice,
Produc'd his Play, and beg'd the Knight's Advice,
Made him observe the Subject and the Plot,
The Manners, Passions, Unities, what not?
All which, exact to Rule were brought about,
Were but a Combate in the Lists left out.
What! Leave the Combate out? Exclaims the Knight;
Yes, or we must renounce the Stagyrite.
Not so by Heav'n (he answers in a Rage)
Knights, Squires, and Steeds, must enter on the Stage.
So vast a Throng the Stage can ne'er contain.
Then build a New, or act it in a Plain.
Thus Criticks, of less Judgment than Caprice,
Curious, not Knowing, not exact, but nice,
Form short Ideas; and offend in Arts
(As most in Manners) by a Love to Parts.
Some to Conceit alone their Taste confine,
And glitt'ring Thoughts struck out at ev'ry Line;
Pleas'd with a Work where nothing's just or fit;
One glaring Chaos and wild Heap of Wit;

---

7. La Mancha's Knight: in *Don Quixote*, bk. 3, ch. 10.

Poets like Painters, thus, unskill'd to trace
The naked Nature and the living Grace,
With Gold and Jewels cover ev'ry Part,
And hide with Ornaments their Want of Art.
True Wit is Nature to Advantage drest,
What oft was Thought, but ne'er so well Exprest,
Something, whose Truth convinc'd at Sight we find,
That gives us back the Image of our Mind:
As Shades more sweetly recommend the Light,
So modest Plainness sets off sprightly Wit:
For Works may have more Wit than does 'em good,
As Bodies perish through Excess of Blood.
Others for Language all their Care express,
And value Books, as Women Men, for Dress:
Their Praise is still—The Stile is excellent:
The Sense, they humbly take upon Content.
Words are like Leaves; and where they most abound,
Much Fruit of Sense beneath is rarely found.
False Eloquence, like the Prismatic Glass,
Its gawdy Colours spreads on ev'ry place;
The Face of Nature was no more Survey,
All glares alike, without Distinction gay:
But true Expression, like th' unchanging Sun,
Clears, and improves whate'er it shines upon,
It gilds all Objects, but it alters none.
Expression is the Dress of Thought, and still
Appears more decent as more suitable;
A vile Conceit in pompous Words exprest,
Is like a Clown in regal Purple drest;
For diff'rent Styles with diff'rent Subjects sort,
As several Garbs with Country, Town, and Court.
Some by Old Words to Fame have made Pretence;
Ancients in Phrase, meer Moderns in their Sense!
Such labour'd Nothings, in so strange a Style,
Amaze th'unlearn'd, and make the Learned Smile.
Unlucky, as Fungoso in the Play,[8]
These Sparks with aukward Vanity display
What the Fine Gentleman wore Yesterday!
And but so mimick ancient Wits at best,

---

8. Fungoso in the Play: Ben Jonson's *Every Man in His Humour.*

As Apes our Grandsires in their Doublets treat.
In Words, as Fashions, the same Rule will hold;
Alike Fantastick, if too New, or Old;
Be not the first by whom the New are try'd,
Nor yet the last to lay the Old aside.
But most by Numbers judge a Poet's Song,
And smooth or rough, with them, is right or wrong;
In the bright Muse tho' thousand Charms conspire,
Her Voice is all these tuneful Fools admire,
Who haunt Parnassus but to please their Ear,
Not mend their Minds; as some to Church repair,
Not for the Doctrine, but the Musick there.
These Equal Syllables alone require,
Tho' oft the Ear the open Vowels tire,
While Expletives their feeble Aid do join,
And ten low Words oft creep in one dull Line,
While they ring round the same unvary'd Chimes,
With sure Returns of still expected Rhymes.
Where-e'er you find the cooling Western Breeze,
In the next Line, it whispers thro' the Trees;
If Chrystal Streams with pleasing Murmurs creep,
The Reader's threaten'd (not in vain) with Sleep.
Then, at the last and only Couplet fraught
With some unmeaning Thing they call a Thought,
A needless Alexandrine ends the Song,
That like a wounded Snake, drags its slow length along.
Leave such to tune their own dull Rhimes, and know
What's roundly smooth, or languishingly slow;
And praise the Easie Vigor of a Line,
Where Denham's Strength, and Waller's Sweetness join.
True Ease in Writing comes from Art, not Chance,
As those move easiest who have learn'd to dance,
'Tis not enough no Harshness gives Offence,
The Sound must seem an Eccho to the Sense.
Soft is the Strain when Zephyr gently blows,
And the smooth Stream in smoother Numbers flows;
But when loud Surges lash the sounding Shore,
The hoarse, rough Verse shou'd like the Torrent roar.
When Ajax strives, some Rocks' vast Weight to throw,
The Line too labours, and the Words move slow;
Not so, when swift Camilla scours the Plain,
Flies o'er th'unbending Corn, and skims along the Main.

Hear how Timotheus' vary'd Lays surprize,
And bid Alternate Passions fall and rise!
While, at each Change, the Son of Lybian Jove
Now burns with Glory, and then melts with Love;
Now his fierce Eyes with sparkling Fury glow;
Now Sighs steal out, and Tears begin to flow:
Persians and Greeks like Turns of Nature found,
And the World's Victor stood subdu'd by Sound!
The Pow'rs of Musick all our Hearts allow;
And what Timotheus was, is Dryden now.
Avoid Extreams; and shun the Fault of such,
Who still are pleas'd too little, or too much.
At ev'ry Trifle scorn to take Offence,
That always shows Great Pride, or Little Sense;
Those Heads as Stomachs are not sure the best
Which nauseate all, and nothing can digest.
Yet let not each gay Turn thy Rapture move,
For Fools Admire, but Men of Sense Approve;
As things seem large which we thro' Mists descry,
Dulness is ever apt to Magnify.
Some foreign Writers, some our own despise;
The Ancients only, or the Moderns prize:
(Thus Wit, like Faith by each Man is apply'd
To one small Sect, and All are damn'd beside.)
Meanly they seek the Blessing to confine,
And force that Sun but on a Part to Shine;
Which not alone the Southern Wit sublimes,
But ripens Spirits in cold Northern Climes;
Which from the first has shone on Ages past,
Enlights the present, and shall warm the last:
(Tho' each may feel Increases and Decays,
And see now clearer and now darker Days)
Regard not then if Wit be Old or New,
But blame the False, and value still the True.
Some ne'er advance a Judgment of their own,
But catch the spreading Notion of the Town;
They reason and conclude by Precedent,
And own stale Nonsense which they ne'er invent.
Some judge of Authors' Names, not Works, and then
Nor praise nor blame the Writings, but the Men.
Of all this Servile Herd the worst is He
That in proud Dulness joins with Quality,

A constant Critick at the Great-man's Board,
To fetch and carry Nonsense for my Lord.
What woful stuff this Madrigal wou'd be,
To some starv'd Hackny Sonneteer, or me?
But let a Lord once own the happy Lines,
How the Wit brightens! How the Style refines!
Before his sacred Name flies ev'ry Fault,
And each exalted Stanza teems with Thought!
The Vulgar thus through Imitation err;
As oft the Learn'd by being Singular;
So much they scorn the Crowd, that if the Throng
By Chance go right, they purposely go wrong;
So Schismatics the plain Believers quit,
And are but damn'd for having too much Wit.
Some praise at Morning what they blame at Night;
But always think the last Opinion right.
A Muse by these is like a Mistress us'd,
This hour she's idoliz'd, the next abus'd,
While their weak Heads, like Towns unfortify'd,
'Twixt Sense and Nonsense daily change their Side.
Ask them the Cause; They're wiser still, they say;
And still to Morrow's wiser than to Day.
We think our Fathers Fools, so wise we grow;
Our wiser Sons, no doubt, will think us so.
Once School-Divines this zealous Isle o'erspread;
Who knew most Sentences was deepest read;
Faith, Gospel, All, seem'd made to be disputed,
And none had Sense enough to be Confuted.
Scotists and Thomists, now, in Peace remain,
Amidst their kindred Cobwebs in Duck-Lane.
If Faith it self has diff'rent Dresses worn,
What wonder Modes in Wit shou'd take their Turn?
Oft, leaving what is Natural and fit,
The current Folly proves the ready Wit,
And Authors think their Reputation safe,
Which lives as long as Fools are pleas'd to Laugh.
Some valuing those of their own, Side or Mind,
Still make themselves the measure of Mankind;
Fondly we think we honour Merit then,
When we but praise Our selves in Other Men.
Parties in Wit attend on those of State,

And publick Faction doubles private Hate.
Pride, Malice, Folly, against Dryden rose,
In various Shapes of Parsons, Criticks, Beaus;
But Sense surviv'd, when merry Jests were past;
For rising Merit will buoy up at last.
Might he return, and bless once more our Eyes,
New Blackmores and new Milbourns must arise;
Nay shou'd great Homer lift his awful Head,
Zoilus again would start up from the Dead.[9]
Envy will Merit as its Shade pursue,
But like a Shadow, proves the Substance true;
For envy'd Wit, like Sol Eclips'd, makes known
Th' opposing Body's Grossness, not its own.
When first that Sun too powerful Beams displays,
It draws up Vapours which obscure its Rays;
But ev'n those Clouds at last adorn its Way,
Reflect new Glories, and augment the Day.
Be thou the first true Merit to befriend;
His Praise is lost, who stays till All commend;
Short is the Date, alas, of Modern Rhymes;
And 'tis but just to let 'em live betimes.
No longer now that Golden Age appears,
When Patriarch-Wits surviv'd thousand Years;
Now Length of Fame (our second Life) is lost,
And bare Threescore is all ev'n That can boast:
Our Sons their Fathers' failing language see,
And such as Chaucer is, shall Dryden be.
So when the faithful Pencil has design'd
Some bright Idea of the Master's Mind,
Where a new World leaps out at his command,
And ready Nature waits upon his Hand;
When the ripe Colours soften and unite,
And sweetly melt into just Shade and Light,
When mellowing Years their full Perfection give,
And each Bold Figure just begins to Live;
The treach'rous Colours the fair Art betray,
And all the bright Creation fades away!

---

9. Zoilus: early Greek grammarian who castigated Homer.

Unhappy Wit, like most mistaken Things,
Attones not for that Envy which it brings.
In Youth alone its empty Praise we boast,
But soon the Short-liv'd Vanity is lost!
Like some fair Flow'r the early Spring supplies,
That gaily Blooms, but ev'n in blooming Dies.
What is this Wit which must our Cares employ?
The Owner's Wife, that other Men enjoy,
Then most our Trouble still when most admir'd,
And still the more we give, the more requir'd;
Whose Fame with Pains we guard, but lose with Ease,
Sure some to vex, but never all to please;
'Tis what the Vicious fear, the Virtuous shun;
By Fools 'tis hated, and by Knaves undone!
If Wit so much from Ign'rance undergo,
Ah let not Learning too commence its Foe!
Of old, those met Rewards who cou'd excel,
And such were Prais'd who but endeavour'd well:
Tho' Triumphs were to Gen'rals only due,
Crowns were reserv'd to grace the Soldiers too.
Now, they who reached Parnassus' lofty Crown,
Employ their Pains to spurn some others down;
And while Self-Love each jealous Writer rules,
Contending Wits becomes the Sport of Fools:
But still the Worst with most Regret commend,
For each Ill Author is as bad a Friend.
To what base Ends, and by what abject Ways,
Are Mortals urg'd thro' Sacred Lust of praise!
Ah ne'er so dire a Thirst of Glory boast,
Nor in the Critick let the Man be lost!
Good-Nature and Good-Sense must ever join;
To err is Humane; to Forgive, Divine.
But if in Noble Minds some Dregs remain,
Not yet purg'd off, of Spleen and sow'r Disdain,
Discharge that Rage on more Provoking Crimes,
Nor fear a Dearth in these Flagitious Times.
No Pardon vile Obscenity should find,
Tho' Wit and Art conspire to move your Mind;
But Dulness with Obscenity must prove
As Shameful sure as Importance in Love.
In the fat Age of Pleasure, Wealth, and Ease,
Sprung the rank Weed, and thriv'd with large Increase;

When Love was all an easie Monarch's Care;[10]
Seldom at Council, never in a War:
Jilts rul'd the State, and Statesmen Farces writ;
Nay Wits had Pensions, and young Lords had Wit:
The Fair sate panting at a Courtier's Play,
And not a Mask went un-improv'd away:
The modest Fan was liked up no more,
And Virgins smil'd at what they blush'd before—
The following Licence of a Foreign Reign
Did all the Dregs of bold Socinus drain;[11]
Then Unbelieving Priests reform'd the Nation,
And taught more Pleasant Methods of Salvation;
Where Heav'ns Free Subjects might their Rights dispute,
Lest God himself shou'd seem too Absolute.
Pulpits their Sacred Satire learn'd to spare,
And Vice admir'd to find a Flatt'rer there!
Encourag'd thus, Witt's Titans brav'd the Skies,
And the Press groan'd with Licenc'd Blasphemies—
These Monsters, Criticks! with your Darts engage,
Here point your Thunder, and exhaust your Rage!
Yet shun their Fault, who, Scandalously nice,
Will needs mistake an Author into Vice;
All seems Infected that th' Infected spy,
As all looks yellow to the Jaundic'd Eye.
LEARN then what MORALS Criticks ought to show,
For 'tis but half a Judge's Task, to Know.
'Tis not enough, Taste, Judgment, Learning, join;
In all you speak, let Truth and Candor shine:
That not alone what to your Sense is due,
All may allow; but seek your Friendship too.
Be silent always when you doubt your Sense;
And speak, tho' sure, with seeming Diffidence:
Some positive persisting Fops we know,
Who, if once wrong, will needs be always so;
But you, with Pleasure own your Errors past,
An make each Day a Critick on the last.
'Tis not enough your Counsel still be true,
Blunt Truths more Mischief than nice Falsehood do;

---

10. easie Monarch: King Charles II.
11. bold Socinus: Italian heretic (L. Sozzini, 1525–1562; he espoused a precursor of Unitarianism).

Men must be taught as if you taught them not;
And Things unknown propos'd as Things forgot:
Without Good Breeding, Truth is disapprov'd;
That only makes Superior Sense belov'd.
Be Niggards of Advice on no Pretence;
For the worst Avarice is that of Sense:
With mean Complacence ne'er betray your Trust,
Nor be so Civil as to prove Unjust;
Fear not the Anger of the Wise to raise;
Those best can bear Reproof, who merit Praise.
'Twere well, might Criticks still this Freedom take;
But Appius reddens at each Word you speak,
And stares, Tremendous! with a threatning Eye
Like some fierce Tyrant in Old Tapestry!
Fear most to tax an Honourable Fool,
Whose Right it is, uncensur'd to be dull;
Such without Wit are Poets when they please.
As without Learning they can take Degrees.
Leave dang'rous Truths to unsuccessful Satyrs,
And Flattery to fulsome Dedicators,
Whom, when they Praise, the World believes no more,
Than when they promise to give Scribling o'er.
'Tis best sometimes your Censure to restrain,
And charitably let the Dull be vain:
Your Silence there is better than your Spite,
For who can rail so long as they can write?
Still humming on, their drowzy Course they keep,
And lash'd so long, like Tops, are lash'd asleep.
False Steps but help them to renew the Race,
As after Stumbling, Jades will mend their Pace.
What Crouds of these, impenitently bold,
In Sounds and jingling Syllables grown old,
Still run on Poets in a raging Vein,
Ev'n to the Dregs and Squeezings of the Brain;
Strain out the last, dull droppings of their Sense,
And Rhyme with all the Rage of Impotence!
Such shameless Bards we have; and yet 'tis true,
There are as mad, abandon'd Criticks too.
The Bookful Blockhead, ignorantly read,
With Loads of Learned Lumber in his Head,
With his own Tongue still edifies his Ears,
And always List'ning to Himself appears.

All Books he reads, and all he reads assails,
From Dryden's Fables down to Durfey's Tales.
With him, most Authors steal their Works, or buy;
Garth did not write his own Dispensary.
Name a new Play, and he's the Poet's Friend,
Nay show'd his Faults—but when wou'd Poets mend?
No Place so Sacred from such Fops is barr'd,
Nor is Paul's Church more safe than Paul's Church-yard:
Nay, fly to Altars; there they'll talk you dead;
For Fools rush in where Angels fear to tread.
Distrustful Sense with modest Caution speaks;
It still looks home, and short Excursions makes;
But ratling Nonsense in full Vollies breaks;
And never shock'd, and never turn'd aside,
Bursts out, resistless, with a thundering Tyde!
But where's the Man, who Counsel can bestow,
Still pleas'd to teach, and not proud to know?
Unbiass'd, or by Favour or by Spite;
Not dully prepossest, nor blindly right;
Tho' Learn'd well-bred; and tho' well-bred, sincere;
Modestly bold, and Humanly severe?
Who to a Friend his Faults can freely show,
And gladly praise the Merit of a Foe?
Blest with a Taste exact, yet unconfin'd;
A Knowledge both of Books and Humankind;
Gen'rous Converse; a Sound exempt from Pride;
And Love to Praise, with Reason on his Side?
Such once were Criticks, such the Happy Few,
Athens and Rome in better Ages knew.
The mighty Stagyrite first left the Shore,
Spread all his Sails, and durst the Deeps explore;
He steer'd securely, and discover'd far,
Led by the Light of the Maeonian Star.[12]
Poets, a Race long unconfin'd and free,
Still fond and proud of Savage Liberty,
Receiv'd his Laws, and stood convinc'd 'twas fit
Who conquer'd Nature, shou'd preside o'er Wit.
Horace still charms with graceful Negligence,
And without Method talks us into Sense,

---

12. Maeonian star: Homer.

Will like a Friend familarly convey
The truest Notions in the easiest way.
He, who Supream in Judgment, as in Wit,
Might boldly censure, as he boldly writ,
Yet judg'd with Coolness tho' he sung with Fire;
His Precepts teach but what his Works inspire.
Our Criticks take a contrary Extream,
They judge with Fury, but they write with Fle'me:
Nor suffers Horace more in wrong Translations
By Wits, than Criticks in as wrong Quotations.
See Dionysius Homer's Thoughts refine,
And call new Beauties forth from ev'ry Line!
Fancy and Art in gay Petronius please,
The Scholar's Learning, with the Courtier's Ease.
In grave Quintilian's copious Work we find
The justest Rules, and clearest Method join'd;
Thus useful Arms in Magazines we place,
All rang'd in Order, and dispos'd with Grace,
But less to please the Eye, than arm the Hand,
Still fit for Use, and ready at Command.
Thee, bold Longinus! all the Nine inspire,
And bless their Critick with a Poet's Fire.
An ardent Judge, who Zealous in his Trust,
With Warmth gives Sentence, yet is always Just;
Whose own Example strengthens all his Laws,
And Is himself that great Sublime he draws.
Thus long succeeding Criticks justly reign'd,
Licence repress'd, and useful Laws ordain'd;
Learning and Rome alike in Empire grew,
And Arts still follow'd where her Eagles flew;
From the same Foes, at last, both felt their Doom,
And the same Age saw Learning fall, and Rome.
With Tyranny, then Superstition join'd,
As that the Body, this enslav'd the Mind;
Much was Believ'd, but little understood,
And to be dull was constru'd to be good;
A second Deluge Learning thus o'er-run,
And the Monks finish'd what the Goths begun.
At length, Erasmus, that great, injur'd Name,
(The Glory of the Priesthood, and the Shame!)
Stemm'd the wild Torrent of a barb'rous Age.
And drove those Holy Vandals off the Stage.

But see! each Muse, in Leo's Golden Days,
Starts from her Trance, and trims her wither'd Bays!
Rome's ancient Genius, o'er its Ruins spread,
Shakes off the Dust, and rears his rev'rend Head!
Then Sculpture and her Sister-Arts revive;
Stones leap'd to Form, and Rocks began to live;
With sweeter Notes each rising Temple rung;
A Raphael painted, and a Vida sung!
Immortal Vida! on whose honour'd Brow
The Poet's Bays and Critick's Ivy grow:
Cremona now shall ever boast thy Name,
As next in Place to Mantua, next in Fame!
But soon by Impious Arms from Latium chas'd,
Their ancient Bounds the banish'd Muses past:
Thence Arts o'er all the Northern World advance,
But Critic Learning flourish'd most in France.
The Rules, a Nation born to serve, obeys,
And Boileau still in Right of Horace sways.
But we, brave Britons, Foreign Laws despis'd,
And kept unconquer'd and unciviliz'd,
Fierce for the Liberties of Wit, and bold,
We still defy'd the Romans as of old.
Yet some there were, among the sounder Few
Of those who less presum'd, and better knew,
Who durst assert the juster Ancient Cause,
And here restor'd Wit's Fundamental Laws.
Such was the Muse, whose Rules and Practice tell,
Nature's chief Master-piece is writing well.
Such was Roscomon—not more learn'd than good,[13]
With Manners gen'rous as his Noble Blood;
To him the Wit of Greece and Rome was known,
And ev'ry Author's Merit, but his own.
Such late was Walsh,—the Muse's Judge and Friend,
Who justly knew to blame or to commend;
To Failings mild, but zealous for Desert;
The clearest Head, and the sincerest Heart.
This humble Praise, lamented Shade! receive,
This Praise at least a grateful Muse may give!
The Muse, whose early Voice you taught to Sing,

---

13. Roscomon: fourth earl of Roscommon, translator of Horace and early advocate of Milton.

Prescrib'd her Heights, and prun'd her tender Wing,
(Her Guide now lost) no more attempts to rise,
But in low Numbers short Excursions tries:
Content, if hence th' Unlearned their Wants may view,
The Learn'd reflect on what before they knew:
Careless of Censure, not too fond of Fame,
Still pleas'd to praise, yet not afraid to blame,
Averse alike to Flatter, or Offend,
Not free from Faults, nor yet too vain to mend.

EPISTLE TO DR. ARBUTHNOT (1735)

*Neque sermonibus vulgi dederis te, nec in præmiis spem
posueris rerum tuarum; suis te oportet illecebris ipsa virtus
trahat ad verum decus. Quid de te alii loquantur, ipsi
videant, sed loquentur tamen.*

["... you will not any longer attend to the vulgar mob's
gossip nor put your trust in human rewards for your deeds;
virtue, through her own charms, should lead you to true
glory. Let what others say about you be their concern;
whatever it is, they will say it anyway."]

Cicero, De Re Publica VI.

Shut, shut the door, good John! fatigu'd, I said,[1]
Tie up the knocker, say I'm sick, I'm dead.
The dog-star rages! nay 'tis past a doubt,[2]

---

1. good John: Pope's servant John Serle.
2. Dog-star: Sirius, associated with maddening heat.

All Bedlam, or Parnassus, is let out:[3]
Fire in each eye, and papers in each hand,
They rave, recite, and madden round the land.

What walls can guard me, or what shades can hide?
They pierce my thickets, through my grot they glide;
By land, by water, they renew the charge;
They stop the chariot, and they board the barge.
No place is sacred, not the church is free;
Ev'n Sunday shines no Sabbath-day to me:
Then from the Mint walks forth the man of rhyme,
Happy! to catch me just at dinner-time.

Is there a parson, much bemus'd in beer,
A maudlin poetess, a rhyming peer,
A clerk, foredoom'd his father's soul to cross,
Who pens a stanza, when he should engross?
Is there, who, lock'd from ink and paper, scrawls
With desp'rate charcoal round his darken'd walls?
All fly to Twit'nam, and in humble strain[4]
Apply to me, to keep them mad or vain.
Arthur, whose giddy son neglects the laws,
Imputes to me and my damn'd works the cause:
Poor Cornus sees his frantic wife elope,[5]
And curses wit, and poetry, and Pope.

Friend to my life! (which did not you prolong,
The world had wanted many an idle song)
What drop or nostrum can this plague remove?
Or which must end me, a fool's wrath or love?
A dire dilemma! either way I'm sped,
If foes, they write, if friends, they read me dead.
Seiz'd and tied down to judge, how wretched I!
Who can't be silent, and who will not lie;
To laugh, were want of goodness and of grace,
And to be grave, exceeds all pow'r of face.
I sit with sad civility, I read

---

3. Bedlam: an insane asylum in London. Parnassus: mountain sacred to the Muses and Apollo.
4. Twit'nam: Twickenham, where Pope lived.
5. Cornus: from Latin *cornu*, a horn, thus a cuckold.

With honest anguish, and an aching head;
And drop at last, but in unwilling ears,
This saving counsel, "Keep your piece nine years."

"Nine years!" cries he, who high in Drury-lane
Lull'd by soft zephyrs through the broken pane,
Rhymes ere he wakes, and prints before Term ends,[6]
Oblig'd by hunger, and request of friends:
"The piece, you think, is incorrect: why, take it,
I'm all submission, what you'd have it, make it."

Three things another's modest wishes bound,
My friendship, and a prologue, and ten pound.
Pitholeon sends to me: "You know his Grace,[7]
I want a patron; ask him for a place."

Pitholeon libell'd me—"but here's a letter
Informs you, sir, 'twas when he knew no better.
Dare you refuse him? Curll invites to dine,
He'll write a Journal, or he'll turn Divine."

Bless me! a packet—"'Tis a stranger sues,
A virgin tragedy, an orphan muse."
If I dislike it, "Furies, death and rage!"
If I approve, "Commend it to the stage."
There (thank my stars) my whole commission ends,
The play'rs and I are, luckily, no friends.
Fir'd that the house reject him, "'Sdeath I'll print it,
And shame the fools—your int'rest, sir, with Lintot!"
"Lintot, dull rogue! will think your price too much."
"Not, sir, if you revise it, and retouch."
All my demurs but double his attacks;
At last he whispers, "Do; and we go snacks."[8]
Glad of a quarrel, straight I clap the door,
"Sir, let me see your works and you no more."

---

6. before Term ends: the end of the summer law court terms; also the close of the publishing season.

7. Pitholeon: a foolish poet at Rhodes who pretended to Greek learning.

8. go snacks: "to divide profits" (*OED*).

'Tis sung, when Midas' ears began to spring,
(Midas, a sacred person and a king)
His very minister who spied them first,
(Some say his queen) was forc'd to speak, or burst.
And is not mine, my friend, a sorer case,
When ev'ry coxcomb perks them in my face?

"Good friend, forbear! you deal in dang'rous things.
I'd never name queens, ministers, or kings;
Keep close to ears, and those let asses prick;
'Tis nothing"—Nothing? if they bite and kick?
Out with it, Dunciad! let the secret pass,
That secret to each fool, that he's an ass:
The truth once told (and wherefore should we lie?)
The queen of Midas slept, and so may I.

You think this cruel? take it for a rule,
No creature smarts so little as a fool.
Let peals of laughter, Codrus! round thee break,[9]
Thou unconcern'd canst hear the mighty crack:
Pit, box, and gall'ry in convulsions hurl'd,
Thou stand'st unshook amidst a bursting world.
Who shames a scribbler? break one cobweb through,
He spins the slight, self-pleasing thread anew;
Destroy his fib or sophistry, in vain,
The creature's at his dirty work again;
Thron'd in the centre of his thin designs;
Proud of a vast extent of flimsy lines!
Whom have I hurt? has poet yet, or peer,
Lost the arch'd eye-brow, or Parnassian sneer?
And has not Colley still his lord, and whore?
His butchers Henley, his Free-masons Moore?
Does not one table Bavius still admit?[10]
Still to one bishop Philips seem a wit?[11]

---

9. Codrus: a traditional name for a bad poet, borrowed from Juvenal.
10. Bavius: a Roman poetaster who owed his immortality to the enmity which he held towards Horace and Virgil, and who was attacked by them. See Virgil, Eclogues, III.
11. Philips: Ambrose Philips (1675?–1749), a pastoral poet. He survives today in a nickname given by his enemies: Namby-Pamby.

Still Sappho—"Hold! for God-sake—you'll offend:[12]
No names!—be calm!—learn prudence of a friend!
I too could write, and I am twice as tall;
But foes like these!" One flatt'rer's worse than all.
Of all mad creatures, if the learn'd are right,
It is the slaver kills, and not the bite.
A fool quite angry is quite innocent;
Alas! 'tis ten times worse when they repent.

One dedicates in high heroic prose,
And ridicules beyond a hundred foes;
One from all Grub Street will my fame defend,[13]
And, more abusive, calls himself my friend.
This prints my Letters, that expects a bribe,
And others roar aloud, "Subscribe, subscribe."

There are, who to my person pay their court:
I cough like Horace, and, though lean, am short,
Ammon's great son one shoulder had too high,[14]
Such Ovid's nose, and "Sir! you have an eye"—
Go on, obliging creatures, make me see
All that disgrac'd my betters, met in me:
Say for my comfort, languishing in bed,
"Just so immortal Maro held his head:"[15]
And when I die, be sure you let me know
Great Homer died three thousand years ago.

Why did I write? what sin to me unknown
Dipp'd me in ink, my parents', or my own?
As yet a child, nor yet a fool to fame,
I lisp'd in numbers, for the numbers came.
I left no calling for this idle trade,
No duty broke, no father disobey'd.
The Muse but serv'd to ease some friend, not wife,

---

12. Sappho: Name of a great woman poet of the seventh century B.C., applied here to Lady Mary Wortley Montagu.
13. Grub Street: section of eighteenth-century London inhabited by hack writers.
14. Ammon's great son: Alexander the Great.
15. Maro: Virgil.

To help me through this long disease, my life,
To second, Arbuthnot! thy art and care,
And teach the being you preserv'd, to bear.

But why then publish? Granville the polite,
And knowing Walsh, would tell me I could write;
Well-natur'd Garth inflamed with early praise,
And Congreve lov'd, and Swift endur'd my lays;
The courtly Talbot, Somers, Sheffield read,
Ev'n mitred Rochester would nod the head,
And St. John's self (great Dryden's friends before)
With open arms receiv'd one poet more.
Happy my studies, when by these approv'd!
Happier their author, when by these belov'd!
From these the world will judge of men and books,
Not from the Burnets, Oldmixons, and Cookes.

Soft were my numbers; who could take offence,
While pure description held the place of sense?
Like gentle Fanny's was my flow'ry theme,
A painted mistress, or a purling stream.
Yet then did Gildon draw his venal quill;
I wish'd the man a dinner, and sat still.
Yet then did Dennis rave in furious fret;
I never answer'd, I was not in debt.
If want provok'd, or madness made them print,
I wag'd no war with Bedlam or the Mint.

Did some more sober critic come abroad?
If wrong, I smil'd; if right, I kiss'd the rod.
Pains, reading, study, are their just pretence,
And all they want is spirit, taste, and sense.
Commas and points they set exactly right,
And 'twere a sin to rob them of their mite.
Yet ne'er one sprig of laurel grac'd these ribalds,
From slashing Bentley down to pidling Tibbalds.
Each wight who reads not, and but scans and spells,
Each word-catcher that lives on syllables,
Ev'n such small critics some regard may claim,
Preserv'd in Milton's or in Shakespeare's name.
Pretty! in amber to observe the forms

Of hairs, or straws, or dirt, or grubs, or worms;
The things, we know, are neither rich nor rare,
But wonder how the devil they got there?

Were others angry? I excus'd them too;
Well might they rage; I gave them but their due.
A man's true merit 'tis not hard to find,
But each man's secret standard in his mind,
That casting weight pride adds to emptiness,
This, who can gratify? for who can guess?
The bard whom pilfer'd pastorals renown,
Who turns a Persian tale for half a crown,
Just writes to make his barrenness appear,
And strains, from hard-bound brains, eight lines a year:
He, who still wanting, though he lives on theft,
Steals much, spends little, yet has nothing left:
And he, who now to sense, now nonsense leaning,
Means not, but blunders round about a meaning:
And he, whose fustian's so sublimely bad,
It is not poetry, but prose run mad:
All these, my modest satire bade translate,
And own'd, that nine such poets made a Tate.
How did they fume, and stamp, and roar, and chafe?
And swear, not Addison himself was safe.

Peace to all such! but were there one whose fires
True genius kindles, and fair fame inspires,
Blest with each talent and each art to please,
And born to write, converse, and live with ease:
Should such a man, too fond to rule alone,
Bear, like the Turk, no brother near the throne,
View him with scornful, yet with jealous eyes,
And hate for arts that caus'd himself to rise;
Damn with faint praise, assent with civil leer,
And without sneering, teach the rest to sneer;
Willing to wound, and yet afraid to strike,
Just hint a fault, and hesitate dislike;
Alike reserv'd to blame, or to commend,
A tim'rous foe, and a suspicious friend;
Dreading ev'n fools, by flatterers besieg'd,
And so obliging, that he ne'er oblig'd;

Like Cato, give his little senate laws,[16]
And sit attentive to his own applause;
While wits and templars ev'ry sentence raise,[17]
And wonder with a foolish face of praise.
Who but must laugh, if such a man there be?
Who would not weep, if Atticus were he?[18]

What though my name stood rubric on the walls,
Or plaister'd posts, with claps, in capitals?[19]
Or smoking forth, a hundred hawkers' load,
On wings of winds came flying all abroad?
I sought no homage from the race that write;
I kept, like Asian monarchs, from their sight:
Poems I heeded (now berhym'd so long)
No more than thou, great George! a birthday song.
I ne'er with wits or witlings pass'd my days,
To spread about the itch of verse and praise;
Nor like a puppy, daggled through the town,
To fetch and carry sing-song up and down;
Nor at rehearsals sweat, and mouth'd, and cried,
With handkerchief and orange at my side;
But sick of fops, and poetry, and prate,
To Bufo left the whole Castalian state.[20]

Proud as Apollo on his forked hill,[21]
Sat full-blown Bufo, puff'd by every quill;
Fed with soft dedication all day long,
Horace and he went hand in hand in song.
His library (where busts of poets dead
And a true Pindar stood without a head,)
Receiv'd of wits an undistinguish'd race,
Who first his judgment ask'd, and then a place:
Much they extoll'd his pictures, much his seat,
And flatter'd ev'ry day, and some days eat:

---

16. Cato: Addison's tragedy *Cato*.
17. templars: lawyers, from those who had their chambers in the Inner or Middle Temple.
18. Atticus: Joseph Addison.
19. claps: posters.
20. Bufo: a composite portrait of a literary patron. Castalian state: Castalia is the name of a spring on Mount Parnassus; hence this refers to the poetic state.
21. forked hill: Parnassus, sacred to Apollo and the Muses.

Till grown more frugal in his riper days,
He paid some bards with port, and some with praise,
To some a dry rehearsal was assign'd,
And others (harder still) he paid in kind.
Dryden alone (what wonder?) came not nigh,
Dryden alone escap'd this judging eye:
But still the great have kindness in reserve,
He help'd to bury whom he help'd to starve.

May some choice patron bless each grey goose quill!
May ev'ry Bavius have his Bufo still!
So, when a statesman wants a day's defence,
Or envy holds a whole week's war with sense,
Or simple pride for flatt'ry makes demands,
May dunce by dunce be whistled off my hands!
Blest be the great! for those they take away,
And those they left me—for they left me Gay;
Left me to see neglected genius bloom,
Neglected die! and tell it on his tomb;
Of all thy blameless life the sole return
My verse, and Queensb'ry weeping o'er thy urn!

Oh let me live my own! and die so too!
("To live and die is all I have to do:")
Maintain a poet's dignity and ease,
And see what friends, and read what books I please.
Above a patron, though I condescend
Sometimes to call a minister my friend:
I was not born for courts or great affairs;
I pay my debts, believe, and say my pray'rs;
Can sleep without a poem in my head,
Nor know, if Dennis be alive or dead.

Why am I ask'd what next shall see the light?
Heav'ns! was I born for nothing but to write?
Has life no joys for me? or (to be grave)
Have I no friend to serve, no soul to save?
"I found him close with Swift"—"Indeed? no doubt,"
(Cries prating Balbus) "something will come out."
'Tis all in vain, deny it as I will.
"No, such a genius never can lie still,"
And then for mine obligingly mistakes

The first lampoon Sir Will. or Bubo makes.
Poor guiltless I! and can I choose but smile,
When ev'ry coxcomb knows me by my style?

Curs'd be the verse, how well soe'er it flow,
That tends to make one worthy man my foe,
Give virtue scandal, innocence a fear,
Or from the soft-ey'd virgin steal a tear!
But he, who hurts a harmless neighbour's peace,
Insults fall'n worth, or beauty in distress,
Who loves a lie, lame slander helps about,
Who writes a libel, or who copies out:
That fop, whose pride affects a patron's name,
Yet absent, wounds an author's honest fame;
Who can your merit selfishly approve,
And show the sense of it without the love;
Who has the vanity to call you friend,
Yet wants the honour, injur'd, to defend;
Who tells what'er you think, whate'er you say,
And, if he lie not, must at least betray:
Who to the Dean, and silver bell can swear,
And sees at Cannons what was never there;
Who reads, but with a lust to misapply,
Make satire a lampoon, and fiction, lie.
A lash like mine no honest man shall dread,
But all such babbling blockheads in his stead.

Let Sporus tremble—"What? that thing of silk,[22]
Sporus, that mere white curd of ass's milk?
Satire or sense, alas! can Sporus feel?
Who breaks a butterfly upon a wheel?"
Yet let me flap this bug with gilded wings,
This painted child of dirt that stinks and stings;
Whose buzz the witty and the fair annoys,
Yet wit ne'er tastes, and beauty ne'r enjoys,
So well-bred spaniels civilly delight
In mumbling of the game they dare not bite.
Eternal smiles his emptiness betray,

---

22. Sporus: a homosexual favourite of the Emperor Nero. Pope applies the name to Lord Hervey ("Fanny" earlier).

As shallow streams run dimpling all the way.
Whether in florid impotence he speaks,
And, as the prompter breathes, the puppet squeaks;
Or at the ear of Eve, familiar toad,
Half froth, half venom, spits himself abroad,
In puns, or politics, or tales, or lies,
Or spite, or smut, or rhymes, or blasphemies.
His wit all see-saw, between that and this,
Now high, now low, now Master up, now Miss,
And he himself one vile antithesis.
Amphibious thing! that acting either part,
The trifling head, or the corrupted heart,
Fop at the toilet, flatt'rer at the board,
Now trips a lady, and now struts a lord.
Eve's tempter thus the rabbins have express'd,
A cherub's face, a reptile all the rest;
Beauty that shocks you, parts that none will trust,
Wit that can creep, and pride that licks the dust.

Not fortune's worshipper, nor fashion's fool,
Not lucre's madman, nor ambition's tool,
Not proud, nor servile, be one poet's praise,
That, if he pleas'd, he pleas'd by manly ways;
That flatt'ry, even to kings, he held a shame,
And thought a lie in verse or prose the same:
That not in fancy's maze he wander'd long,
But stoop'd to truth, and moraliz'd his song:
That not for fame, but virtue's better end,
He stood the furious foe, the timid friend,
The damning critic, half-approving wit,
The coxcomb hit, or fearing to be hit;
Laugh'd at the loss of friends he never had,
The dull, the proud, the wicked, and the mad;
The distant threats of vengeance on his head,
The blow unfelt, the tear he never shed;
The tale reviv'd, the lie so oft o'erthrown;
Th' imputed trash, and dulness not his own;
The morals blacken'd when the writings 'scape;
The libell'd person, and the pictur'd shape;
Abuse, on all he lov'd, or lov'd him, spread,
A friend in exile, or a father, dead;
The whisper, that to greatness still too near,

Perhaps, yet vibrates on his sovereign's ear: —
Welcome for thee, fair Virtue! all the past:
For thee, fair Virtue! welcome ev'n the last!

"But why insult the poor? affront the great?"
A knave's a knave, to me, in ev'ry state:
Alike my scorn, if he succeed or fail,
Sporus at court, or Japhet in a jail,
A hireling scribbler, or a hireling peer,
Knight of the post corrupt, or of the shire;
If on a pillory, or near a throne,
He gain his prince's ear, or lose his own.

Yet soft by nature, more a dupe than wit,
Sappho can tell you how this man was bit:
This dreaded sat'rist Dennis will confess
Foe to his pride, but friend to his distress:
So humble, he has knock'd at Tibbald's door,
Has drunk with Cibber, nay, has rhym'd for Moore.
Full ten years slander'd, did he once reply?
Three thousand suns went down on Welsted's lie.
To please a mistress one aspers'd his life;
He lash'd him not, but let her be his wife.
Let Budgell charge low Grub Street on his quill,
And write whate'er he pleas'd, except his will;
Let the two Curlls of town and court, abuse
His father, mother, body, soul, and muse.
Yet why? that father held it for a rule,
It was a sin to call our neighbour fool:
That harmless mother thought no wife a whore, —
Hear this! and spare his family, James Moore!
Unspotted names! and memorable long,
If there be force in virtue, or in song.

Of gentle blood (part shed in honour's cause,
While yet in Britain honour had applause)
Each parent sprung—"What fortune, pray?"—Their own,
And better got, than Bestia's from the throne.[23]

---

23. Bestia: a Roman consul bribed into a dishonourable peace, possibly a reference to the Duke of Marlborough.

Born to no pride, inheriting no strife,
Nor marrying discord in a noble wife,
Stranger to civil and religious rage,
The good man walk'd innoxious through his age.
No courts he saw, no suits would ever try,
Nor dar'd an oath, nor hazarded a lie:
Un-learn'd, he knew no schoolman's subtle art,
No language, but the language of the heart.
By nature honest, by experience wise,
Healthy by temp'rance and by exercise;
His life, though long, to sickness past unknown;
His death was instant, and without a groan.
O grant me, thus to live, and thus to die!
Who sprung from kings shall know less joy than I.

O friend! may each domestic bliss be thine!
Be no unpleasing melancholy mine:
Me, let the tender office long engage
To rock the cradle of reposing age,
With lenient arts extend a mother's breath,
Make langour smile, and smooth the bed of death,
Explore the thought, explain the asking eye,
And keep a while one parent from the sky!
On cares like these if length of days attend,
May Heav'n, to bless those days, preserve my friend,
Preserve him social, cheerful, and serene,
And just as rich as when he serv'd a queen.
Whether that blessing be denied or giv'n,
Thus far was right, the rest belongs to Heav'n.

11

SAMUEL JOHNSON (1709–1784)

If Thomas Gray wants to conclude his "Ode on the Death of a Favorite Cat, Drowned in a Tub Of Gold Fishes" with an instructive moral—

> Not all that tempts your wand'ring eyes
> And heedless hearts, is lawful prize;
> Nor all, that glisters, gold—

then ninety-nine readers out of ninety-nine will applaud and go on. The poem is very famous, and at any hour of the day or night somewhere in the English-speaking world somebody is saying something like "all that glisters is not gold." And that is without doubt a true and useful piece of information. But wait: whoever says "ninety-nine readers out of ninety-nine" is forgetting one: Samuel Johnson, who, although scarcely ever bothering to quote Gray's title correctly, objected that the disconnect between glistering and gold was immaterial. The cat was not deceived by the gold appearance of the fish. Johnson notes that the poem "ends in a pointed sentence of no relation to the purpose; if what glistered had been gold, the cat would not have gone into the water; and, if she had, would not less have been drowned."

Poetry itself may be such a seduction, and we may need to be on guard against being deceived and misled. The same Samuel Johnson said that Shakespeare let himself be seduced by "quibbles" or puns ("A quibble poor and barren as it is, gave him such delight, that he was content to purchase it, by the sacrifice of reason, propriety and truth. A quibble was to him the fatal Cleopatra for which he lost the world, and was content to lose it" ["Preface to Shakespeare," 1765].), and he warns us that Milton should not let himself be derailed by fictions. In one of the greatest sentences ever pronounced on a poem, Johnson said of "Lycidas" that "where there is leisure for fiction there is little grief." And he seems to wait for someone in the club or coffee house to question his glib equation of fiction and leisure. Surely some fiction is the product of great grief. But Johnson did not traffic in last words or final verdicts: he became part of a great conversation, enjoying the exchange more than the material, the give and take itself more than what might be given and taken.

Johnson could be a traditional writer of poetry, drama, and romance, but he was more distinguished in certain modern occupations in which he was an innovator and a pioneer: periodical journalism (especially essays both formal and informal), travel writing, editing and practical criticism, biography, and lexicography. (Along the way he defined "lexicographer" as "a writer of dictionaries; a harmless drudge, that busies himself in tracing the original, and detailing the signification of words" [*Dictionary of the English Language*, 1755].) Johnson's *Dictionary of the English Language* is such a monument of the Enlightenment that it is the book that Becky Sharp throws out of a carriage window at the beginning of Thackeray's *Vanity Fair* in a complex gesture of homage and rejection.

It was also Johnson's miraculous good fortune to meet James Boswell, a younger man with a very different temperament but one perfectly suited to write what is probably the greatest biography in English and possibly the greatest in any language, *The Life of Samuel Johnson* (1791).

Johnson came from Lichfield, spent just over a year at Oxford, and by age thirty was working in London as a teacher, translator, and journalist. He published the poem "The Vanity of Human Wishes" in 1749, *Rasselas: Prince of Abyssinia* in 1759, an edition of Shakespeare in 1765, *A Journey to the Western Islands of Scotland* in 1775, and *The Lives of the English Poets* between 1779 and 1781. He was buried in Westminster Abbey.

"LIFE OF MILTON" (1779; EXCERPT)

He was at this time [1624, aged fifteen] eminently skilled in the Latin tongue; and he himself by annexing the dates to his first compositions, a boast of which the learned Politian [Angelo Poliziano (1454–94), poet and scholar—ed.] had given him an example, seems to commend the earliness of his own proficiency to the notice of posterity; but the products of his vernal fertility have been surpassed by many, and particularly by his contemporary Cowley. Of the powers of the mind it is difficult to form an estimate; many have excelled Milton in their first essays who never rose to works like *Paradise Lost.* . . .

His next production was "Lycidas," an elegy written in 1637 on the death of Mr. King, the son of Sir John King, secretary for Ireland in the time of Elizabeth, James, and Charles. King was much a favorite at Cambridge, and many of the wits joined to do honor to his memory. Milton's acquaintance with the Italian writers may be discovered by a mixture of longer and shorter verses, according to the rules of Tuscan poetry, and his malignity to the Church by some lines which are interpreted as threatening its extermination. . . .

For the subject of his epic poem, after much deliberation, "long choosing, and beginning late," he fixed upon *Paradise Lost*; a design so comprehensive that it could be justified only by success. He had once designed to celebrate King Arthur, as he hints in his verses to Mansus; but "Arthur was reserved," says Fenton, "to another destiny."

. . . Of the English poets he set most value upon Spenser, Shakespeare, and Cowley. Spenser was apparently his favorite; Shakespeare he may easily be supposed to like, with every other skilful reader, but I should not have expected that Cowley, whose ideas of excellence were different from his own, would have had much of his approbation. His character of Dryden, who sometimes visited him, was that he was a good rhymist, but no poet.

In the examination of Milton's poetical works I shall pay so much regard to time as to begin with his juvenile productions. For his earlier pieces he seems to have had a degree of fondness not very laudable: what he has once written he resolves to preserve, and gives to the public an unfinished poem, which he broke off because he was "nothing satisfied with what he had done," supposing his readers less nice than himself. These preludes to his future labours are in Italian, Latin, and English. Of the Italian I cannot pretend to speak as a critic, but I have heard them commended by a man well qualified to decide their merit. The Latin pieces are lusciously elegant; but the delight which they afford is rather by the exquisite imitation of the ancient writers, by the purity of the diction, and the harmony of the numbers, than by any power of invention or vigour of sentiment. They are not all of equal value; the elegies excel the odes, and some of the exercises on Gunpowder Treason [the foiled Gunpowder Plot to blow up the Houses of Parliament on November 5, 1605—ed.] might have been spared.

The English poems, though they make no promises of *Paradise Lost*, have this evidence of genius, that they have a cast original and unborrowed. But their peculiarity is not excellence: if they differ from verses of others, they differ for the worse; for they are too often distinguished by repulsive harshness; the combinations of words are new, but they are not pleasing; the rhymes and epithets seem to be laboriously sought and violently applied.

One of the poems on which much praise has been bestowed is "Lycidas"; of which the diction is harsh, the rhymes uncertain, and the numbers unpleasing. What beauty there is we must therefore seek in the sentiments and images. It is not to be considered as the effusion of real passion; for passion runs not after remote allusions and obscure opinions. Passion plucks no berries from the myrtle and ivy, nor calls upon Arethuse and Mincius, nor tells of "rough satyrs and fauns with cloven heel." Where there is leisure for fiction there is little grief.

In this poem there is no nature, for there is no truth; there is no art, for there is nothing new. Its form is that of a pastoral, easy, vulgar, and therefore disgusting: whatever images it can supply are long ago exhausted; and its inherent improbability always forces dissatisfaction on the mind. When Cowley tells of Hervey that they studied together, it is easy to suppose how much he must miss the companion of his labours and the partner of his discoveries; but what image of tenderness can be excited by these lines!

> We drove a field, and both together heard
> What time the grey fly winds her sultry horn,
> Battening our flocks with the fresh dews of night.

We know that they never drove a field, and that they had no flocks to batten; and though it be allowed that the representation may be allegorical, the true meaning is so uncertain and remote that it is never sought because it cannot be known when it is found.

Among the flocks and copses and flowers appear the heathen deities, Jove and Phoebus, Neptune and Æolus, with a long train of mythological imagery, such as a College easily supplies. Nothing can less display knowledge or less exercise invention than to tell how a shepherd has lost his companion and must now feed his flocks alone, without any judge of his skill in piping; and how one god asks another god what is become of Lycidas, and how neither god can tell. He who thus grieves will excite no sympathy; he who thus praises will confer no honor.

This poem has yet a grosser fault. With these trifling fictions are mingled the most awful and sacred truths, such as ought never to be polluted with such irreverent combinations. The shepherd likewise is now a feeder of sheep, and afterwards an ecclesiastical pastor, a superintendent of a Christian flock. Such equivocations are always unskillful; but here they are indecent, and at least approach to impiety, of which, however, I believe the writer not to have been conscious.

Such is the power of reputation justly acquired that its blaze drives away the eye from nice examination. Surely no man could have fancied that he read "Lycidas" with pleasure had he not known its author.

Of the two pieces, "L'Allegro" and "Il Penseroso," I believe opinion is uniform; every man that reads them, reads them with pleasure. The author's design is not, what Theobald has remarked, merely to show how objects derived their colors from the mind, by representing the operation of the same things upon the gay and the melancholy temper, or upon the same man as he is differently disposed; but rather how, among the successive variety of appearances, every disposition of mind takes hold on those by which it may be gratified.

The cheerful man hears the lark in the morning; the pensive man hears the nightingale in the evening. The cheerful man sees the cock strut, and hears the horn and hounds echo in the wood; then walks "not unseen" to observe the glory of the rising sun or listen to the singing milk-maid, and view the labours of the plowman and the mower; then casts his eyes about him over scenes of smiling plenty, and looks up to the distant tower, the residence of some fair inhabitant: thus he pursues rural gaiety through a day of labor or of play, and delights himself at night with the fanciful narratives of superstitious ignorance.

The pensive man at one time walks "unseen" to muse at midnight, and at another hears the sullen curfew. If the weather drives him home he sits in a room lighted only by "glowing embers"; or by a lonely lamp outwatches the North Star to discover the habitation of separate souls, and varies the shades of meditation by contemplating the magnificent or pathetic scenes of tragic and epic poetry. When the morning comes, a morning gloomy with rain and wind, he walks into the dark trackless woods, falls asleep by some murmuring water, and with melancholy enthusiasm expects some dream of prognostication or some music played by aerial performers.

Both Mirth and Melancholy are solitary, silent inhabitants of the breast that neither receive nor transmit communication; no mention is therefore made of a philosophical friend or a pleasant companion. The seriousness does not arise from any participation of calamity, nor the gaiety from the pleasures of the bottle.

The man of cheerfulness having exhausted the country tries what "towered cities" will afford, and mingles with scenes of splendor, gay assemblies, and nuptial festivities; but he mingles a mere spectator as, when the learned comedies of Jonson or the wild dramas of Shakespeare are exhibited, he attends the theatre.

The pensive man never loses himself in crowds, but walks the cloister or frequents the cathedral. Milton probably had not yet forsaken the Church.

Both his characters delight in music; but he seems to think that cheerful notes would have obtained from Pluto a complete dismission [liberation] of Eurydice, of whom solemn sounds only procured a conditional release.

For the old age of Cheerfulness he makes no provision; but Melancholy he conducts with great dignity to the close of life. His Cheerfulness is without levity, and his Pensiveness without asperity.

Through these two poems the images are properly selected and nicely distinguished, but the colors of the diction seem not sufficiently discriminated. I know not whether the characters are kept sufficiently apart. No mirth can, indeed, be found in his melancholy; but I am afraid that I always meet some melancholy in his mirth. They are two noble efforts of imagination.

The greatest of his juvenile performances is the Masque of *Comus*, in which may very plainly be discovered the dawn or twilight of *Paradise Lost*. Milton appears to have formed very early that system of diction and mode of verse which his maturer judgment approved, and from which he never endeavored nor desired to deviate.

Nor does *Comus* afford only a specimen of his language: it exhibits likewise his power of description and his vigour of sentiment, employed in the praise and defense of virtue. A work more truly poetical is rarely found; allusions, images, and descriptive epithets embellish almost every period with lavish decoration. As a series of lines, therefore, it may be considered as worthy of all the admiration with which the votaries have received it.

As a drama it is deficient. The action is not probable. A Masque, in those parts where supernatural intervention is admitted, must indeed be given up to all the freaks of imagination; but so far as the action is merely human it ought to be reasonable, which can hardly be said of the conduct of the two brothers, who, when their sister sinks with fatigue in a pathless wilderness, wander both away in search of berries too far to find their way back, and leave a helpless Lady to all the sadness and danger of solitude. This however is a defect over-balanced by its convenience.

What deserves more reprehension is that the prologue spoken in the wild wood by the attendant Spirit is addressed to the audience; a mode of communication so contrary to the nature of Dramatic representation that no precedents can support it.

The discourse of the Spirit is too long, an objection that may be made to almost all the following speeches; they have not the sprightliness of a dialogue animated by reciprocal contention, but seem rather declamations deliberately composed and formally repeated on a moral question. The auditor therefore listens as to a lecture, without passion, without anxiety.

The song of Comus has airiness and jollity; but, what may recommend Milton's morals as well as his poetry, the invitations to pleasure are so general that they excite no distinct images of corrupt enjoyment, and take no dangerous hold on the fancy.

The following soliloquies of Comus and the Lady are elegant, but tedious. The song must owe much to the voice, if it ever can delight. At last the Brothers enter, with too much tranquillity; and when they have feared lest their sister should be in danger, and hoped that she is not in danger, the Elder makes a speech in praise of chastity, and the Younger finds how fine it is to be a philosopher.

Then descends the Spirit in form of a shepherd; and the Brother, instead of being in haste to ask his help, praises his singing, and enquires his business in that place. It is remarkable that at this interview the Brother is taken with a short fit of rhyming. The Spirit relates that the Lady is in the power of Comus, the Brother moralizes again, and the Spirit makes a long narration, of no use because it is false, and therefore unsuitable to a good Being.

In all these parts the language is poetical and the sentiments are generous, but there is something wanting to allure attention.

The dispute between the Lady and Comus is the most animated and affecting scene of the drama, and wants nothing but a brisker reciprocation of objections and replies, to invite attention and detain it.

The songs are vigorous and full of imagery; but they are harsh in their diction, and not very musical in their numbers.

Throughout the whole the figures are too bold and the language too luxuriant for dialogue: it is a drama in the epic style, inelegantly splendid, and tediously instructive.

The Sonnets were written in different parts of Milton's life upon different occasions. They deserve not any particular criticism; for of the best it can only be said that they are not bad, and perhaps only the eighth ["When the Assault Was Intended to the City"] and the twenty-first ["Cyriack, whose grandsire on the royal bench"] are truly entitled to this slender commendation. The fabric of a sonnet, however adapted to the Italian language, has never succeeded in ours, which, having greater variety of termination, requires the rhymes to be often changed. . . .

Of *Paradise Regained* the general judgment seems now to be right, that it is in many parts elegant, and everywhere instructive. It was not to be supposed that the writer of *Paradise Lost* could ever write without great effusions of fancy and exalted precepts of wisdom. The basis of *Paradise Regained* is narrow; a dialogue without action can never please like an union of the narrative and Dramatic powers. Had this poem been written, not by Milton but by some imitator, it would have claimed and received universal praise.

If *Paradise Regained* has been too much depreciated, *Samson Agonistes* has in requital been too much admired. It could only be by long prejudice and the bigotry of learning that Milton could prefer the ancient tragedies with their encumbrance of a chorus to the exhibitions of the French and English stages; and it is only by a blind confidence in the reputation of Milton that a drama can be praised in which the intermediate parts have neither cause nor consequence, neither hasten nor retard the catastrophe.

In this tragedy are however many particular beauties, many just sentiments and striking lines; but it wants that power of attracting attention which a well-connected plan produces.

Milton would not have excelled in Dramatic writing; he knew human nature only in the gross, and had never studied the shades of character, nor the combinations of concurring or the perplexity of contending passions. He had read much and knew what books could teach; but had mingled little in the world, and was deficient in the knowledge which experience must confer.

Through all his greater works there prevails an uniform peculiarity of Diction, a mode and cast of expression which bears little resemblance to that of any former writer, and which is so far removed from common use that an unlearned reader when he first opens his book finds himself surprised by a new language.

This novelty has been, by those who can find nothing wrong in Milton, imputed to his laborious endeavors after words suitable to the grandeur of his ideas. "Our language," says Addison, "sunk under him." But the truth is, that both in prose and verse, he had formed his style by a perverse and pedantic principle. He was desirous to use English words with a foreign idiom. This in all his prose is discovered and condemned, for there judgment operates freely, neither softened by the beauty nor awed by the dignity of his thoughts; but such is the power of his poetry that his call is obeyed without resistance, the reader feels himself in captivity to a higher and a nobler mind, and criticism sinks in admiration.

Milton's style was not modified by his subject: what is shown with greater extent in *Paradise Lost* may be found in *Comus*. One source of his peculiarity was his familiarity with the Tuscan poets: the disposition of his words is, I think, frequently Italian; perhaps sometimes combined with other tongues. Of him, at last, may be said what Jonson says of Spenser, that "he wrote no language," but has formed what Butler calls "a Babylonish Dialect," in itself harsh and barbarous, but made by exalted genius and extensive learning the vehicle of so much instruction and so much pleasure that, like other lovers, we find grace in its deformity.

Whatever be the faults of his diction he cannot want the praise of copiousness and variety; he was master of his language in its full extent, and has selected the melodious words with such diligence that from his book alone the Art of English Poetry might be learned.

After his diction something must be said of his versification. "The measure," he says, "is the English heroic verse without rhyme." Of this mode he had many examples among the Italians, and some in his own country. The Earl of Surrey is said to have translated one of Virgil's books without rhyme, and besides our tragedies a few short poems had appeared in blank verse; particularly one tending to reconcile the nation to Raleigh's wild attempt upon Guiana, and probably written by Raleigh himself. These petty performances cannot be supposed to have much influenced Milton, who more probably took his hint from Trisino's *Italia Liberata*; and, finding blank verse easier than rhyme, was desirous of persuading himself that it is better.

"Rhyme," he says, and says truly, "is no necessary adjunct of true poetry." But perhaps of poetry as a mental operation metre or music is no necessary adjunct; it is however by the music of metre that poetry has been discriminated in all languages, and in languages melodiously constructed with a due proportion of long and short syllables metre is sufficient. But one language cannot communicate its rules to another; where metre is scanty and imperfect some help is necessary. The music of the English heroic line strikes the ear so faintly that it is easily lost, unless all the syllables of every line co-operate together; this co-operation can be only obtained by the preservation of every verse unmingled with another as a distinct system of sounds, and this distinctness is obtained and preserved by the artifice of rhyme. The variety of pauses, so much boasted by the lovers of blank verse, changes the measures of an English poet to the periods of a declaimer; and there are only a few skilful and happy readers of Milton who enable their audience to perceive where the lines end or begin. "Blank verse," said an ingenious critic, "seems to be verse only to the eye."

Poetry may subsist without rhyme, but English poetry will not often please; nor can rhyme ever be safely spared but where the subject is able to support itself. Blank verse makes some approach to that which is called the "lapidary style"; has neither the easiness of prose nor the melody of numbers, and therefore tires by long continuance. Of the Italian writers without rhyme, whom Milton alleges as precedents, not one is popular; what reason could urge in its defense has been confuted by the ear.

But whatever be the advantage of rhyme I cannot prevail on myself to wish that Milton had been a rhymer, for I cannot wish his work to be other than it is; yet like other heroes he is to be admired rather than imitated. He that thinks himself capable of astonishing may write blank verse, but those that hope only to please must condescend to rhyme.

The highest praise of genius is original invention. Milton cannot be said to have contrived the structure of an epic poem, and therefore owes reverence to that vigour and amplitude of mind to which all generations must be indebted for the art of poetical narration, for the texture of the fable, the variation of incidents, the interposition of dialogue, and all the stratagems that surprise and enchain attention. But of all the borrowers from Homer Milton is perhaps the least indebted. He was naturally a thinker for himself, confident of his own abilities and disdainful of help or hindrance; he did not refuse admission to the thoughts or images of his predecessors, but he did not seek them. From his contemporaries he neither courted nor received support; there is in his writings nothing by which the pride of other authors might be gratified or favor gained, no exchange of praise nor solicitation of support. His great works were performed under discountenance and in blindness, but difficulties vanished at his touch; he was born for whatever is arduous; and his work is not the greatest of heroic poems, only because it is not the first.

In the window of his mother's apartment lay Spenser's *Fairy Queen*; in which he very early took delight to read, till, by feeling the charms of verse, he became, as he relates, irrecoverably a Poet. Such are the accidents, which, sometimes remembered, and perhaps sometimes forgotten, produce that particular designation of mind, and propensity for some certain science or employment, which is commonly called Genius. The true Genius is a mind of large general powers, accidentally determined to some particular direction. The great painter of the present age had the first fondness for his art excited by the perusal of Richardson's treatise. . . .

Among the English poets, Cowley, Milton, and Pope might be said "to lisp in numbers;" and have given such early proofs, not only of powers of language, but of comprehension of things, as to more tardy minds seems scarcely credible. But of the learned puerilities of Cowley there is no doubt, since a volume of his poems was not only written but printed in his thirteenth year; containing, with other poetical compositions, "The Tragical History of Pyramus and Thisbe," written when he was ten years old; and "Constantia and Philetus," written two years after. . . .

This obligation to amorous ditties owes, I believe, its original to the fame of Petrarch, who, in an age rude and uncultivated, by his tuneful homage to his Laura, refined the manners of the lettered world, and filled Europe with love and poetry. But the basis of all excellence is truth: he that professes love ought to feel its power. Petrarch was a real lover, and Laura doubtless deserved his tenderness. Of Cowley, we are told by Barnes, who had means enough of information, that, whatever he may talk of his own inflammability, and the variety of characters by which his heart was divided, he in reality was in love but once, and then never had resolution to tell his passion.

Cowley, like other poets who have written with narrow views, and, instead of tracing intellectual pleasure to its natural sources in the mind of man, paid their court to temporary prejudices, has been at one time too much praised, and too much neglected at another.

Wit, like all other things subject by their nature to the choice of man, has its changes and fashions, and at different times takes different forms. About the beginning of the seventeenth century appeared a race of writers that may be termed the metaphysical poets; of whom, in a criticism on the works of Cowley, the last of the race, it is not improper to give some account.

The metaphysical poets were men of learning, and to show their learning was their whole endeavor; but, unluckily resolving to show it in rhyme, instead of writing poetry, they only wrote verses, and very often such verses as stood the trial of the finger better than of the ear; for the modulation was so imperfect, that they were only found to be verses by counting the syllables.

If the father of criticism has rightly denominated poetry, an imitative art, these writers will, without great wrong, lose their right to the name of poets for they cannot be said to have imitated any thing; they neither copied nature nor life; neither painted the forms of matter, nor represented the operations of intellect.

Those, however, who deny them to be poets, allow them to be wits. Dryden confesses of himself and his contemporaries, that they fall below Donne in wit, but maintains that they surpass him in poetry.

If Wit be well described by Pope, as being "that which has been often thought, but was never before so well expressed," they certainly never attained, nor ever sought it; for they endeavored to be singular in their thoughts, and were careless of their diction. But Pope's account of wit is undoubtedly erroneous: he depresses it below its natural dignity, and reduces it from strength of thought to happiness of language.

If by a more noble and more adequate conception that be considered as Wit, which is at once natural and new, that which, though not obvious, is, upon its first production, acknowledged to be just; if it be that, which he that never found it, wonders how he missed; to wit of this kind the metaphysical poets have seldom risen. Their thoughts are often new, but seldom natural; they are not obvious, but neither are they just; and the reader, far from wondering that he missed them, wonders more frequently by what perverseness of industry they were ever found.

But Wit, abstracted from its effects upon the hearer, may be more rigorously and philosophically considered as a kind of *discordia concors*; a combination of dissimilar images, or discovery of occult resemblances in things apparently unlike. Of wit thus defined, they have more than enough. The most heterogeneous ideas are yoked by violence together; nature and art are ransacked for illustrations, comparisons, and allusions; their learning instructs, and their subtlety surprises; but the reader commonly thinks his improvement dearly bought, and, though he sometimes admires, is seldom pleased. . . .

This kind of writing, which was, I believe, borrowed from Marino and his followers, had been recommended by the example of Donne, a man of very extensive and various knowledge; and by Jonson, whose manner resembled that of Donne more in the ruggedness of his lines than in the cast of his sentiments.

When their reputation was high, they had undoubtedly more imitators, than time has left behind. Their immediate successors, of whom any remembrance can be said to remain, were Suckling, Waller, Denham, Cowley, Cleveland, and Milton. Denham and Waller sought another way to fame, by improving the harmony of our numbers. Milton tried the metaphysic stile only in his lines upon Hobson the Carrier. Cowley adopted it, and excelled his predecessors, having as much sentiment, and more music. Suckling neither improved versification, nor abounded in conceits. The fashionable style remained chiefly with Cowley; Suckling could not reach it, and Milton disdained it. . . .

Cowley was, I believe, the first poet that mingled Alexandrines at pleasure with the common heroic ten syllables, and from him Dryden borrowed the practice, whether ornamental or licentious. He considered the verse of twelve syllables as elevated and majestic, and has therefore deviated into that measure when he supposes the voice heard of the Supreme Being.

Of his school performances has appeared only a poem on the death of Lord Hastings, composed with great ambition of such conceits as, notwithstanding the reformation begun by Waller and Denham, the example of Cowley still kept in reputation. Lord Hastings died of the small-pox, and his poet has made of the pustules first rosebuds, and then gems; at last exalts them into stars, and says,

> No comet need foretell his change drew on,
> Whose corps might seem a constellation.

At the university he does not appear to have been eager of poetical distinction, or to have lavished his early wit either on fictitious subjects or public occasions. He probably considered that he who purposed to be an author, ought first to be a student. He obtained, whatever was the reason, no fellowship in the College. Why he was excluded cannot now be known, and it is vain to guess; had he thought himself injured, he knew how to complain. In the "Life of Plutarch" he mentions his education in the College with gratitude; but in a prologue at Oxford, he has these lines:

> Oxford to him a dearer name shall be
> Than his own mother-university;

Thebes did his rude unknowing youth engage;
He chooses Athens in his riper age.

It was not till the death of Cromwell, in 1658, that he became a public candidate for fame, by publishing "Heroic Stanzas on the Late Lord Protector," which, compared with the verses of Sprat and Waller on the same occasion, were sufficient to raise great expectations of the rising poet.

When the king was restored Dryden, like the other panegyrists of usurpation, changed his opinion, or his profession, and published "Astrea Redux, A Poem on the Happy Restoration and Return of His Most Sacred Majesty King Charles the Second."

The reproach of inconstancy was, on this occasion, shared with such numbers that it produced neither hatred nor disgrace; if he changed, he changed with the nation. It was, however, not totally forgotten when his reputation raised him enemies. . . .

In 1667 he published "Annus Mirabilis, The Year of Wonders," which seems to be one of his most elaborate works.

It is addressed to Sir Robert Howard by a letter, which is not properly a dedication; and, writing to a poet, he has interspersed many critical observations, of which some are common, and some perhaps ventured without much consideration. He began, even now, to exercise the domination of conscious genius, by recommending his own performance: "I am satisfied that as the Prince and General [Rupert and Monk] are incomparably the best subjects I ever had, so what I have written on them is much better than what I have performed on any other. As I have endeavored to adorn my poem with noble thoughts, so much more to express those thoughts with elocution."

It is written in quatrains, or heroic stanzas of four lines; a measure which he had learned from the *Gondibert* of Davenant, and which he then thought the most majestic that the English language affords. Of this stanza he mentions the encumbrances, increased as they were by the exactness which the age required. It was, throughout his life, very much his custom to recommend his works by representation of the difficulties that he had encountered, without appearing to have sufficiently considered, that where there is no difficulty there is no praise. . . .

Dryden may be properly considered as the father of English criticism, as the writer who first taught us to determine upon principles the merit of composition. Of our former poets the greatest dramatist wrote without rules, conducted through life and nature by a genius that rarely misled, and rarely deserted him. Of the rest, those who knew the laws of propriety had neglected to teach them.

Two *Arts of English Poetry* were written in the days of Elizabeth by Webb and Puttenham, from which something might be learned, and a few hints had been given by Jonson and Cowley; but Dryden's *Essay on Dramatick Poetry* was the first regular and valuable treatise on the art of writing.

He who, having formed his opinions in the present age of English literature, turns back to peruse this dialogue, will not perhaps find much increase of knowledge or much novelty of instruction; but he is to remember that critical principles were then in the hands of a few, who had gathered them partly from the Ancients, and partly from the Italians and French. The structure of Dramatick poems was not then generally understood. Audiences applauded by instinct, and poets perhaps often pleased by chance.

A writer who obtains his full purpose loses himself in his own luster. Of an opinion which is no longer doubted, the evidence ceases to be examined. Of an art universally practiced, the first teacher is forgotten. Learning once made popular is no longer learning; it has the appearance of something which we have bestowed upon ourselves, as the dew appears to rise from the field which it refreshes.

To judge rightly of an author we must transport ourselves to his time, and examine what were the wants of his contemporaries, and what were his means of supplying them. That which is easy at one time was difficult at another. Dryden at least imported his science, and gave his country what it wanted before; or rather, he imported only the materials, and manufactured them by his own skill.

It may be doubted whether Waller and Denham could have over-borne the prejudices which had long prevailed, and which even then were sheltered by the protection of Cowley. The new versification, as it was called, may be considered as owing its establishment to Dryden; from whose time it is apparent that English poetry has had no tendency to relapse to its former savageness.

The affluence and comprehension of our language is very illustriously displayed in our poetical translations of Ancient Writers; a work which the French seem to relinquish in despair, and which we were long unable to perform with dexterity. Ben Jonson thought it necessary to copy Horace almost word by word; Feltham, his contemporary and adversary, considers it as indispensably requisite in a translation to give line for line. It is said that Sandys, whom Dryden calls the best versifier of the last age, has struggled hard to comprise every book of his English Metamorphoses in the same number of verses with the original. Holyday had nothing in view but to show that he understood his author, with so little regard to the grandeur of his diction, or the volubility of his numbers, that his meters can hardly be called verses; they cannot be read without reluctance, nor will the labor always be rewarded by understanding them. Cowley saw that such copiers were a servile race; he asserted his liberty, and spread his wings so boldly that he left his authors. It was reserved for Dryden to fix the limits of poetical liberty, and give us just rules and examples of translation.

When languages are formed upon different principles, it is impossible that the same modes of expression should always be elegant in both. While they run on together the closest translation may be considered as the best; but when they divaricate, each must take its natural course. Where correspondence cannot be obtained, it is necessary to be content with something equivalent. Translation therefore, says Dryden, is not so loose as paraphrase, nor so close as metaphrase.

All polished languages have different styles; the concise, the diffuse, the lofty, and the humble. In the proper choice of style consists the resemblance which Dryden principally exacts from the translator. He is to exhibit his author's thoughts in such a dress of diction as the author would have given them, had his language been English: rugged magnificence is not to be softened: hyperbolical ostentation is not to be repressed, nor sententious affectation to have its points blunted. A translator is to be like his author; it is not his business to excel him.

The reasonableness of these rules seems sufficient for their vindication; and the effects produced by observing them were so happy, that I know not whether they were ever opposed but by Sir Edward Sherburne, a man whose learning was greater than his powers of poetry; and who, being better qualified to give the meaning than the spirit of Seneca, has introduced his version of three tragedies by a defense of close translation. The authority of Horace, which the new translators cited in defense of their practice, he has, by a judicious explanation, taken fairly from them; but reason wants not Horace to support it.

It seldom happens that all the necessary causes concur to any great effect: will is wanting to power, or power to will, or both are impeded by external obstructions. The exigences in which Dryden was condemned to pass his life, are reasonably supposed to have blasted his genius, to have driven out his works in a state of immaturity, and to have intercepted the full-blown elegance which longer growth would have supplied. . . .

His prediction of the improvements which shall be made in the new city is elegant and poetical, and, with an event which Poets cannot always boast, has been happily verified. The poem concludes with a simile that might have better been omitted.

Dryden, when he wrote this poem, seems not yet fully to have formed his versification, or settled his system of propriety. In rhyme he continued to improve his diction and his numbers. According to the opinion of Harte, who had studied his works with great attention, he settled his principles of versification in 1676, when he produced the play of *Aureng Zebe*; and, according to his own account of the short time in which he wrote *Tyrannick Love* and *The State of Innocence*, he soon obtained the full effect of diligence, and added facility to exactness. . . .

Rhyme has been so long banished from the theatre that we know not its effect upon the passions of an audience; but it has this convenience, that sentences stand more independent on each other, and striking passages are therefore easily selected and retained. Thus the description of Night in *The Indian Emperor* and the rise and fall of empire in *The Conquest of Granada* are more frequently repeated than any lines in *All for Love* or *Don Sebastian*. . . .

"Absalom and Achitophel" is a work so well known that particular criticism is superfluous. If it be considered as a poem political and controversial it will be found to comprise all the excellences of which the subject is susceptible: acrimony of censure, elegance of praise, artful delineation of characters, variety and vigour of sentiment, happy turns of language, and pleasing harmony of numbers; and all these raised to such a height as can scarcely be found in any other English composition.

It is not however without faults; some lines are inelegant or improper, and too many are irreligiously licentious. The original structure of the poem was defective: allegories drawn to great length will always break; Charles could not run continually parallel with David.

The subject had likewise another inconvenience: it admitted little imagery or description, and a long poem of mere sentiments easily becomes tedious; though all the parts are forcible and every line kindles new rapture, the reader, if not relieved by the interposition of something that sooths the fancy, grows weary of admiration, and defers the rest.

As an approach to historical truth was necessary the action and catastrophe were not in the poet's power; there is therefore an unpleasing disproportion between the beginning and the end. We are alarmed by a faction formed out of many sects various in their principles, but agreeing in their purpose of mischief, formidable for their numbers, and strong by their supports, while the king's friends are few and weak. The chiefs on either part are set forth to view; but when expectation is at the height the king makes a speech, and

> Henceforth a series of new times began.

Who can forbear to think of an enchanted castle, with a wide moat and lofty battlements, walls of marble and gates of brass, which vanishes at once into air when the destined knight blows his horn before it? . . .

The alexandrine was, I believe, first used by Spenser, for the sake of closing his stanza with a fuller sound. We had a longer measure of fourteen syllables, into which the *Aeneid* was translated by Phaer, and other works of the ancients by other writers; of which Chapman's *Iliad* was, I believe, the last.

The two first lines of Phaer's third *Aeneid* will exemplify this measure:

> When Asia's state was overthrown, and Priam's kingdom
> stout,
> All guiltless, by the power of gods above was rooted out.

As these lines had their break or caesura always at the eighth syllable it was thought in time commodious to divide them; and quatrains of lines alternately consisting of eight and six syllables make the most soft and pleasing of our lyric measures, as

> Relentless Time, destroying power,
> Which stone and brass obey,
> Who giv'st to every flying hour
> To work some new decay.

In the alexandrine, when its power was once felt, some poems, as Drayton's *Polyolbion*, were wholly written; and sometimes the measures of twelve and fourteen syllables were interchanged with one another. Cowley was the first that inserted the alexandrine at pleasure among the heroic lines of ten syllables, and from him Dryden professes to have adopted it.

The triplet and alexandrine are not universally approved. Swift always censured them, and wrote some lines to ridicule them. In examining their propriety it is to be considered that the essence of verse is regularity, and its ornament is variety. To write verse is to dispose syllables and sounds harmonically by some known and settled rule—a rule however lax enough to substitute similitude for identity, to admit change without breach of order, and to relieve the ear without disappointing it. Thus a Latin hexameter is formed from dactyls and spondees differently combined; the English heroic admits of acute or grave syllables variously disposed. The Latin never deviates into seven feet, or exceeds the number of seventeen syllables; but the English alexandrine breaks the lawful bounds, and surprises the reader with two syllables more than he expected.

The effect of the triplet is the same: the ear has been accustomed to expect a new rhyme in every couplet; but is on a sudden surprised with three rhymes together, to which the reader could not accommodate his voice did he not obtain notice of the change from the braces of the margins. Surely there is something unskillful in the necessity of such mechanical direction.

Considering the metrical art simply as a science, and consequently excluding all casualty, we must allow that triplets and alexandrines inserted by caprice are interruptions of that constancy to which science aspires. And though the variety which they produce may very justly be desired, yet to make our poetry exact there ought to be some stated mode of admitting them.

But till some such regulation can be formed, I wish them still to be retained in their present state. They are sometimes grateful to the reader, and sometimes convenient to the poet. Fenton was of opinion that Dryden was too liberal and Pope too sparing in their use.

The rhymes of Dryden are commonly just, and he valued himself for his readiness in finding them; but he is sometimes open to objection.

It is the common practice of our poets to end the second line with a weak or grave syllable:

> Together o'er the Alps methinks we fly,
> Fill'd with ideas of fair Italy.

Dryden sometimes puts the weak rhyme in the first:

> Laugh all the powers that favor tyranny,
> And all the standing army of the sky.

Sometimes he concludes a period or paragraph with the first line of a couplet, which, though the French seem to do it without irregularity, always displeases in English poetry.

The alexandrine, though much his favorite, is not always very diligently fabricated by him. It invariably requires a break at the sixth syllable; a rule which the modern French poets never violate, but which Dryden sometimes neglected:

> And with paternal thunder vindicates his throne. . . .

In this year (1742) Gray seems to have applied himself seriously to poetry; for in this year were produced the "Ode to Spring," his "Prospect of Eton," and his "Ode to Adversity." He began likewise a Latin poem, *De Principiis Cogitandi*.

In . . . retirement he wrote (1747) an ode on "The Death of Mr. Walpole's Cat"; and the year afterwards attempted a poem of more importance, on "Government and Education," of which the fragments which remain have many excellent lines.

His next production (1750) was his far-famed "Elegy in the Church-yard," which, finding its way into a Magazine, first, I believe, made him known to the public. . . .

In 1757 be published "The Progress of Poetry" and "The Bard," two compositions at which the readers of poetry were at first content to gaze in mute amazement. Some that tried them confessed their inability to understand them, though Warburton said that they were understood as well as the works of Milton and Shakespeare, which it is the fashion to admire. Garrick wrote a few lines in their praise. Some hardy champions undertook to rescue them from neglect, and in a short time many were content to be showed beauties which they could not see.

Gray's reputation was now so high, that after the death of Cibber, he had the honor of refusing the laurel [the Poet Laureateship—ed.], which was then bestowed on Mr. Whitehead. . . .

As a writer he had this peculiarity, that he did not write his pieces first rudely, and then correct them, but labored every line as it arose in the train of composition; and he had a notion not very peculiar, that he could not write but at certain times, or at happy moments; a fantastic foppery; to which my kindness for a man of learning and of virtue wishes him to have been superior.

Gray's Poetry is now to be considered; and I hope not to be looked on as an enemy to his name, if I confess that I contemplate it with less pleasure than his life.

His "Ode on Spring" has something poetical, both in the language and the thought; but the language is too luxuriant, and the thoughts have nothing new. There has of late arisen a practice of giving to adjectives, derived from substantives, the termination of participles; such as the cultured plain, the daisied bank; but I was sorry to see, in the lines of a scholar like Gray, the honied Spring. The morality is natural, but too stale; the conclusion is pretty.

The poem "On the Cat" was doubtless by its author considered as a trifle, but it is not a happy trifle. In the first stanza "the azure flowers that blow," show resolutely a rhyme is sometimes made when it cannot easily be found. Selima, the Cat, is called a nymph, with some violence both to language and sense; but there is good use made of it when it is done; for of the two lines,

> What female heart can gold despise?
> What cat's averse to fish?

the first relates merely to the nymph, and the second only to the cat. The sixth stanza contains a melancholy truth, that "a favourite has no friend," but the last ends in a pointed sentence of no relation to the purpose; if what glistered had been gold, the cat would not have gone into the water; and, if she had, would not less have been drowned.

The "Prospect of Eton College" suggests nothing to Gray, which every beholder does not equally think and feel. His supplication to father Thames, to tell him who drives the hoop or tosses the ball, is useless and puerile. Father Thames has no better means of knowing than himself. His epithet "buxom health" is not elegant; he seems not to understand the word. Gray thought his language more poetical as it was more remote from common use: finding in Dryden "honey redolent of Spring," an expression that reaches the utmost limits of our language, Gray drove it a little more beyond apprehension, by making "gales" to be "redolent of joy and youth."

. . . My process has now brought me to the wonderful "wonder of wonders," the two sister odes; by which, though either vulgar ignorance or common sense at first universally rejected them, many have been since persuaded to think themselves delighted. I am one of those that are willing to be pleased, and therefore would gladly find the meaning of the first stanza of "The Progress of Poetry."

Gray seems in his rapture to confound the images of spreading sound and running water. A "stream of music" may be allowed; but where does music, however "smooth and strong," after having visited the "verdant vales, rowl down the steep amain," so as that "rocks and nodding groves rebellow to the roar?" If this be said of music, it is nonsense; if it be said of water, it is nothing to the purpose.

The second stanza, exhibiting Mars's car and Jove's eagle, is unworthy of further notice. Criticism disdains to chase a school-boy to his common-places.

To the third it may likewise be objected, that it is drawn from mythology, though such as may be more easily assimilated to real life. Idalia's "velvet green" has something of cant. An epithet or metaphor drawn from Nature ennobles Art; an epithet or metaphor drawn from Art degrades Nature. Gray is too fond of words arbitrarily compounded. "Many-twinkling" was formerly censured as not analogical; we may say "many-spotted" but scarcely "many-spotting." This stanza, however, has something pleasing.

Of the second ternary of stanzas, the first endeavors to tell something, and would have told it, had it not been crossed by Hyperion: the second describes well enough the universal prevalence of Poetry; but I am afraid that the conclusion will not rise from the premises. The caverns of the North and the plains of Chili are not the residences of "Glory and generous Shame." But that Poetry and Virtue go always together is an opinion so pleasing, that I can forgive him who resolves to think it true.

The third stanza sounds big with "Delphi," and "Egean," and "Illisus," and "Meander," and "hallowed fountains" and solemn sound; but in all Gray's odes there is a kind of cumbrous splendour which we wish away. His position is at last false: in the hue of Dante and Petrarch, from whom we derive our first school of poetry; Italy was overrun by "tyrant power" and "coward vice;" nor was our slate much better when we first borrowed the Italian arts.

Of the third ternary, the first gives a mythological birth of Shakespeare. What is said of that mighty genius is true; but it is not said happily: the real effects of this poetical power are put out of sight by the pomp of machinery. Where truth is sufficient to fill the mind, fiction is worse than useless; the counterfeit debases the genuine.

His account of Milton's blindness, if we suppose it caused by study in the formation of his poem, a supposition surely allowable, is poetically true, and happily imagined. But the car of Dryden, with his two coursers, has nothing in it peculiar; it is a car in which any other rider may be placed.

"The Bard" appears, at the first view, to be, as Algarotti and others have remarked, an imitation of the prophecy of Nereus. Algarotti thinks it superior to its original; and, if preference depends only on the imagery and animation of the two poems, his judgment is right. There is in "The Bard" more force, more thought, and more variety. But to copy is less than to invent, and the copy has been unhappily produced at a wrong time. The fiction of Horace was to the Romans credible; but its revival disgusts us with apparent and unconquerable falsehood. *Incredulus odi* [not believing it, I hate it—ed.].

To select a singular event, and swell it to a giant's bulk by fabulous appendages of specters and predictions, has little difficulty, for he that forsakes the probable may always find the marvelous. And it has little use; we are affected only as we believe; we are improved only as we find something to be imitated or declined. I do not see that "The Bard" promotes any truth, moral or political.

His stanzas are too long, especially his epodes; the ode is finished before the ear has learned its measures, and consequently before it can receive pleasure from their consonance and recurrence.

Of the first stanza the abrupt beginning has been celebrated; but technical beauties can give praise only to the inventor. It is in the power of any man to rush abruptly upon his subject, that has read the ballad of Johnny Armstrong,

Is there ever a man in all Scotland—

The initial resemblances, or alliterations, "ruin, ruthless, helm or hauberk," are below the grandeur of a poem that endeavors at sublimity.

In the second stanza the bard is well described; but in the third we have the puerilities of obsolete mythology. When we are told that "Cadwallo hush'd the stormy main," and that "Modred made huge Plinlimmon bow his cloud-top'd head," attention recoils from the repetition of a tale that, even when it was first heard, was heard with scorn.

The weaving of the winding sheet he borrowed, as he owns, from the northern bards; but their texture, however, was very properly the work of female powers, as the art of spinning the thread of life in another mythology. Theft is always dangerous; Gray has made weavers of slaughtered bards, by a fiction outrageous and incongruous. They are then called upon to "weave the warp, and weave the woof" perhaps with no great propriety; for it is by crossing the woof with the warp that men weave the web or piece; and the first line was dearly bought by the admission of its wretched correspondent, "Give ample room and verge enough." He has, however, no other line as bad.

The third stanza of the second ternary is commended, I think, beyond its merit. The personification is indistinct. Thirst and Hunger are not alike; and their features, to make the imagery perfect, should have been discriminated. We are told, in the same stanza, how "towers are fed." But I will no longer look for particular faults; yet let it be observed, that the ode might have been concluded with an action of better example; but suicide is always to be had, without expense of thought.

These odes are marked by glittering accumulations of ungraceful ornaments; they strike, rather than please; the images are magnified by affectation the language is labored into harshness. The mind of the writer seems to work with unnatural violence. "Double, double, toil and trouble." He has a kind of strutting dignity and is tall by walking on tiptoe. His art and his struggle are too visible, and there is too little appearance of ease and nature.

To say that he has no beauties, would be unjust: a man like him, of great learning and great industry, could not but produce something valuable. When he pleases least, it can only be said that a good design was ill directed. . . .

In the character of his Elegy I rejoice to concur with the common reader; for by the common sense of readers uncorrupted with literary prejudices, after all the refinements of subtlety and the dogmatism of learning, must be finally decided all claim to poetical honors. The Church-yard abounds with images which find a mirror in every mind, and with sentiments to which every bosom returns an echo. The four stanzas beginning "Yet even these bones," are to me original: I have never seen the notions in any other place; yet he that reads them here, persuades himself that he has always felt them. Had Gray written often thus, it had been vain to blame, and useless to praise him.

12

THOMAS GRAY (1716–1771)

Like John Milton, Thomas Gray was the son of a scrivener (someone involved in the legal and financial care of documents and investments). Gray was born in London and educated at Eton and Cambridge. Although he had a law degree, he never practiced, choosing instead to devote his life to the study of literature and antiquities. Toward the end of his life he was awarded the Professorship of Modern History at Cambridge.

Gray was a wonderfully versatile poet, and, though he may not rank among the topmost superstars, his "Elegy Written in a Country Churchyard" is probably better known than poems by more celebrated figures. Gray was a bridge, or at least a bridge-builder, between the neoclassical values of the Augustan age and the romantic values of the late eighteenth century, and also between the interest of scholarly learning and the fascination of great popularity. Archeological discoveries and careful scholarship throughout the eighteenth century contributed to a spirit of primitivism, especially as regards language and art. Gray, learned in the classical languages and also conversant with Old Celtic and Old Germanic texts, which were being rediscovered, could see the English poetry of his own age as part of a community of texts shared in space and as part of a continuum of endeavor extending from the earliest ages of the species. For Gray's contemporaries, the earliest times were understood as probably no longer ago than 6,000 years before, but the sentiment for the primitive shaped thinking about religion, philosophy, history, and the arts. "The Progress of Poesy," looking back at the legends and poems of ancient Greeks, Romans, and Hebrews, as well as Europeans of the middle ages, prepared the way for Robert Burns, William Blake, and their tribe of successors and imitators.

THE PROGRESS OF POESY (1758)

A PINDARIC ODE[1]

I . 1

Awake, Æolian lyre, awake,[2]
And give to rapture all thy trembling strings.
From Helicon's harmonious springs[3]
A thousand rills their mazy progress take:
The laughing flowers, that round them blow,
Drink life and fragrance as they flow.
Now the rich stream of music winds along
Deep, majestic, smooth, and strong,
Thro' verdant vales, and Ceres' golden reign:[4]

---

1. A Pindaric ode consists of subdivisions called strophe, antistrophe, and epode; the first two match, the third differs.
2. Awake: Gray's note refers to Psalm 57: "Awake, my glory: awake, lute and harp." Aeolian: Aeolis or Aeolia was a region on the coast of Asia Minor; Aeolus was god of the winds, and Aeolian harps, lyres, lutes, and so forth were played by the wind. According to Gray, "Pindar styles his own poetry, with its musical accompaniments, . . . Aeolian song, Aeolian strings, the breath of the Aeolian lute."
3. Helicon: a mountain sacred to the Muses. Its springs were Hippocrene and Aganippe.
4. Ceres: a goddess of agriculture, associated with grain (whence "cereal").

Now rolling down the steep amain,
Headlong, impetuous, see it pour:
The rocks and nodding groves rebellow to the roar.

1 . 2

Oh! Sovereign of the willing soul,
Parent of sweet and solemn-breathing airs,
Enchanting shell! the sullen Cares
And frantic Passions hear thy soft control.
On Thracia's hills the Lord of War,[5]
Has curb'd the fury of his car,
And dropp'd his thirsty lance at thy command.
Perching on the sceptred hand
Of Jove, thy magic lulls the feather'd king
With ruffled plumes and flagging wing:
Quench'd in dark clouds of slumber lie
The terror of his beak, and light'nings of his eye.

1 . 3

Thee the voice, the dance, obey,
Temper'd to thy warbled lay.
O'er Idalia's velvet-green[6]
The rosy-crowned Loves are seen
On Cytherea's day[7]
With antic Sports and blue-ey'd Pleasures,
Frisking light in frolic measures;
Now pursuing, now retreating,
Now in circling troops they meet:
To brisk notes in cadence beating
Glance their many-twinkling feet.
Slow melting strains their Queen's approach declare:
Where'er she turns the Graces homage pay.[8]
With arms sublime, that float upon the air,

---

5. Thracia: Thrace, in antiquity a region northeast of Macedonia, an area now comprising parts of Turkey, Bulgaria, and Greece; birthplace of Orpheus.
6. Idalia: town sacred to Aphrodite.
7. Cytherea: Aphrodite.
8. Graces: divine sisters (sometimes named Aglaia, Thalia, and Euphrosyne) who attend greater goddesses, in this instance Aphrodite.

In gliding state she wins her easy way:
O'er her warm cheek and rising bosom move
The bloom of young Desire and purple light of Love.

II.1

Man's feeble race what ills await,
Labour, and Penury, the racks of Pain,
Disease, and Sorrow's weeping train,
And Death, sad refuge from the storms of Fate!
The fond complaint, my song, disprove,
And justify the laws of Jove.
Say, has he giv'n in vain the heav'nly Muse?
Night, and all her sickly dews,
Her spectres wan, and birds of boding cry,
He gives to range the dreary sky:
Till down the eastern cliffs afar
Hyperion's march they spy, and glitt'ring shafts of war.[9]

II.2

In climes beyond the solar road,
Where shaggy forms o'er ice-built mountains roam,
The Muse has broke the twilight-gloom
To cheer the shiv'ring native's dull abode.
And oft, beneath the od'rous shade
Of Chile's boundless forests laid,
She deigns to hear the savage youth repeat
In loose numbers wildly sweet
Their feather-cinctur'd chiefs, and dusky loves.
Her track, where'er the goddess roves,
Glory pursue, and generous Shame,
Th' unconquerable Mind, and Freedom's holy flame.

II.3

Woods, that wave o'er Delphi's steep,[10]
Isles, that crown th' Ægean deep,

---

9. Hyperion: the sun.
10. Delphi: on Mount Parnassus, site of the Delphic Oracle, associated with Apollo.

Fields, that cool Ilissus laves,[11]
Or where Mæander's amber waves[12]
In ling'ring lab'rinths creep,
How do your tuneful echoes languish,
Mute, but to the voice of Anguish?
Where each old poetic mountain
Inspiration breath'd around:
Ev'ry shade and hallow'd Fountain
Murmur'd deep a solemn sound:
Till the sad Nine in Greece's evil hour
Left their Parnassus for the Latian plains.[13]
Alike they scorn the pomp of tyrant Power,
And coward Vice, that revels in her chains.
When Latium had her lofty spirit lost,
They sought, O Albion! next thy sea-encircled coast.[14]

III.1

Far from the sun and summer-gale,
In thy green lap was Nature's darling laid,[15]
What time, where lucid Avon stray'd,
To him the mighty Mother did unveil
Her awful face: the dauntless child
Stretch'd forth his little arms, and smiled.
This pencil take (she said) whose colours clear
Richly paint the vernal year:
Thine too these golden keys, immortal boy!
This can unlock the gates of Joy;
Of Horror that, and thrilling Fears,
Or ope the sacred source of sympathetic tears.

III.2

Nor second he, that rode sublime[16]
Upon the seraph-wings of Ecstasy,

---

11. Illisus: river near Athens.
12. Maeander: meandering river in Asia Minor.
13. Latian: Latin, Roman.
14. Albion: Britain.
15. Nature's Darling: according to Gray, Shakespeare.
16. He, that rode sublime: Milton.

The secrets of th' Abyss to spy.
He pass'd the flaming bounds of Place and Time:
The living throne, the sapphire-blaze,
Where angels tremble, while they gaze,
He saw; but blasted with excess of light,
Clos'd his eyes in endless night.
Behold, where Dryden's less presumptuous car,[17]
Wide o'er the fields of Glory bear
Two coursers of ethereal race,
With necks in thunder cloth'd, and long-resounding pace.

III.3

Hark, his hands thy lyre explore!
Bright-eyed Fancy hovering o'er
Scatters from her pictur'd urn
Thoughts that breathe, and words that burn.
But ah! 'tis heard no more—
O lyre divine, what daring spirit
Wakes thee now? tho' he inherit
Nor the pride, nor ample pinion,
That the Theban Eagle bear,
Sailing with supreme dominion
Thro' the azure deep of air:
Yet oft before his infant eyes would run
Such forms, as glitter in the Muse's ray
With orient hues, unborrow'd of the Sun:
Yet shall he mount, and keep his distant way[18]
Beyond the limits of a vulgar fate,
Beneath the good how far—but far above the great.[19]

---

17. car: chariot.
18. Yet shall he mount: Gray himself.
19. the great: the rich and powerful.

13

WILLIAM WORDSWORTH (1770–1850)

After being raised in Cumberland (in the Lake District of northwest England) and educated at Cambridge, Wordsworth spent some time in France at the height of the Revolution. There, also, he and Annette Vallon became the parents of a daughter, Caroline, but for complex reasons they did not marry. A succession of legacies, settlements, and sinecures permitted Wordsworth and his sister Dorothy to live simply without needing to work. They occupied dwellings in Dorset, then in Somerset, near Coleridge, at Grasmere back in the Lake District, and finally—in 1813, after he had married Mary Hutchinson—at Rydal Mount a few miles from Grasmere.

An on-again-off-again friendship with Coleridge was clearly the most important association of Wordsworth's literary life. The two collaborated on the volume called *Lyrical Ballads, with a Few Other Poems*, containing Coleridge's "The Rime of the Ancient Mariner" and a number of Wordsworth's poems, including the meditative masterpiece "Tintern Abbey."

Wordsworth's presence remains colossal, as both inspiration and irritation. After a radically revolutionary youth, he seemed to turn increasingly toward conservatism and solemnity. Byron repeatedly ribbed Wordsworth; there are notable caricatures and burlesques of Wordsworth in Byron's *English Bards and Scotch Reviewers* and in *Don Juan*. In 1816, Shelley addressed a sonnet of mild reprimand "To Wordsworth," and in 1845, after the elderly Wordsworth had accepted a government pension of £300 and the office of Poet Laureate, Robert Browning hotheadedly wrote "The Lost Leader" ("Just for a handful of silver he left us . . ."); in time Browning grew sorry for his attack. Later generations of literary revolutionaries, including T. S. Eliot, Ezra Pound, and Aldous Huxley, again attacked Wordsworth. Even so, now it is quite clear that, in his long and eventful life, Wordsworth had more to do with shaping the nature of English poetry than any other poet of the past two centuries.

It could be that the power of *Lyrical Ballads*, with or without Wordsworth's eventual Preface, was a function of the new-found dignity and force of poems in a form that had been associated with the popular and the primitive. As late as Samuel Johnson, "ballad" connoted a song in short stanzas that told a simple story. Before Wordsworth, the ballad stanza had enjoyed popularity as a setting for hymns (in which case the stanza is called Common Measure or Common Meter) as well as for folk ballads and art ballads, such as some familiar poems by Robert Burns. The title suggests a novel combination of two old concerns of poetry: expressing emotion ("lyrical") and telling a story ("ballad"). Many of the poems in the volume serve those ends; some, however, are of a very different sort. It is hard to make "ballad" fit such a meditative blank-verse poem as "Lines Composed a Few Miles Above Tintern Abbey" or any composition that deserves the title "Expostulation and Reply."

Or it could be that Wordsworth was such a great poet that anything he did would have influenced his contemporaries and successors. His Preface makes the case for certain choices of subject and diction—common or ordinary in both cases; these choices may represent something desirable rather than something actually accomplished in the volume. The effect, in any case, was to alter the course of English poetry for more than two centuries. Many readers at the turn of the nineteenth century, beset by the new anxieties of modern urban industrial life in a world torn apart by war and social injustice, felt little need for the rather dispassionate moral essays provided by Pope and others during the eighteenth century. Instead, they sought the various refuges promised by *Lyrical Ballads*.

Wordsworth took a risk in arguing for plain language and simple characters, and he suffered from attacks robustly delivered by Byron, Shelley, and several others. But Wordsworth survived and prevailed. Chapter 14 of Coleridge's *Biographia Literaria* aptly summarizes the situation: "Had Mr. Wordsworth's poems been the silly, the childish things, which they were for a long time described as being; had they been really distinguished from the compositions of other poets merely by meanness of language and inanity of thought; had they indeed contained nothing more than what is found in the parodies and pretended imitations of them; they must have sunk at once, a dead weight, into the slough of oblivion, and have dragged the preface along with them."

OBSERVATIONS PREFIXED TO

LYRICAL BALLADS (1800)

The first volume of these Poems has already been submitted to general perusal. It was published, as an experiment, which, I hoped, might be of some use to ascertain, how far, by fitting to metrical arrangement a selection of the real language of men in a state of vivid sensation, that sort of pleasure and that quantity of pleasure may be imparted, which a Poet may rationally endeavor to impart.

I had formed no very inaccurate estimate of the probable effect of those Poems: I flattered myself that they who should be pleased with them would read them with more than common pleasure: and, on the other hand, I was well aware, that by those who should dislike them, they would be read with more than common dislike. The result has differed from my expectation in this only, that a greater number have been pleased than I ventured to hope I should please.

Several of my Friends are anxious for the success of these Poems, from a belief, that, if the views with which they were composed were indeed realized, a class of Poetry would be produced, well adapted to interest mankind permanently, and not unimportant in the quality, and in the multiplicity of its moral relations: and on this account they have advised me to prefix a systematic defense of the theory upon which the Poems were written. But I was unwilling to undertake the task, knowing that on this occasion the Reader would look coldly upon my arguments, since I might be suspected of having been principally influenced by the selfish and foolish hope of reasoning him into an approbation of these particular Poems: and I was still more unwilling to undertake the task, because, adequately to display the opinions, and fully to enforce the arguments, would require a space wholly disproportionate to a preface. For, to treat the subject with the clearness and coherence of which it is susceptible, it would be necessary to give a full account of the present state of the public taste in this country, and to determine how far this taste is healthy or depraved; which, again, could not be determined, without pointing out in what manner language and the human mind act and re-act on each other, and without retracing the revolutions, not of literature alone, but likewise of society itself. I have therefore altogether declined to enter regularly upon this defense; yet I am sensible, that there would be something like impropriety in abruptly obtruding upon the Public, without a few words of introduction, Poems so materially different from those upon which general approbation is at present bestowed.

It is supposed, that by the act of writing in verse an Author makes a formal engagement that he will gratify certain known habits of association; that he not only thus apprises the Reader that certain classes of ideas and expressions will be found in his book, but that others will be carefully excluded. This exponent or symbol held forth by metrical language must in different eras of literature have excited very different expectations: for example, in the age of Catullus, Terence, and Lucretius, and that of Statius or Claudian; and in our own country, in the age of Shakespeare and Beaumont and Fletcher, and that of Donne and Cowley, or Dryden, or Pope. I will not take upon me to determine the exact import of the promise which, by the act of writing in verse, an Author in the present day makes to his reader: but it will undoubtedly appear to many persons that I have not fulfilled the terms of an engagement thus voluntarily contracted. They who have been accustomed to the gaudiness and inane phraseology of many modern writers, if they persist in reading this book to its conclusion, will, no doubt, frequently have to struggle with feelings of strangeness and awkwardness: they will look round for poetry, and will be induced to inquire by what species of courtesy these attempts can be permitted to assume that title. I hope therefore the reader will not censure me for attempting to state what I have proposed to myself to perform; and also (as far as the limits of a preface will permit) to explain some of the chief reasons which have determined me in the choice of my purpose: that at least he may be spared any unpleasant feeling of disappointment, and that I myself may be protected from one of the most dishonorable accusations which can be brought against an Author, namely, that of an indolence which prevents him from endeavoring to ascertain what is his duty, or, when his duty is ascertained, prevents him from performing it.

The principal object, then, proposed in these Poems was to choose incidents and situations from common life, and to relate or describe them, throughout, as far as was possible in a selection of language really used by men, and, at the same time, to throw over them a certain coloring of imagination, whereby ordinary things should be presented to the mind in an unusual aspect; and, further, and above all, to make these incidents and situations interesting by tracing in them, truly though not ostentatiously, the primary laws of our nature: chiefly, as far as regards the manner in which we associate ideas in a state of excitement. Humble and rustic life was generally chosen, because, in that condition, the essential passions of the heart find a better soil in which they can attain their maturity, are less under restraint, and speak a plainer and more emphatic language; because in that condition of life our elementary feelings coexist in a state of greater simplicity, and, consequently, may be more accurately contemplated, and more forcibly communicated; because the manners of rural life germinate from those elementary feelings, and, from the necessary character of rural occupations, are more easily comprehended, and are more durable; and, lastly, because in that condition the passions of men are incorporated with the beautiful and permanent forms of nature. The language, too, of these men has been adopted (purified indeed from what appear to be its real defects, from all lasting and rational causes of dislike or disgust) because such men hourly communicate with the best objects from which the best part of language is originally derived; and because, from their rank in society and the sameness and narrow circle of their intercourse, being less under the influence of social vanity, they convey their feelings and notions in simple and unelaborated expressions. Accordingly, such a language, arising out of repeated experience and regular feelings, is a more permanent, and a far more philosophical language, than that which is frequently substituted for it by Poets, who think that they are conferring honor upon themselves and their art, in proportion as they separate themselves from the sympathies of men, and indulge in arbitrary and capricious habits of expression, in order to furnish food for fickle tastes, and fickle appetites, of their own creation. [Wordsworth's Note: I here use the word 'Poetry' (though against my own judgment) as opposed to the word Prose, and synonymous with metrical composition. But much confusion has been introduced into criticism by this contradistinction of Poetry and Prose, instead of the more philosophical one of Poetry and Matter of Fact, or Science. The only strict antithesis to Prose is Metre; nor is this, in truth, a *strict* antithesis, because lines and passages of metre so naturally occur in writing prose, that it would be scarcely possible to avoid them, even were it desirable.]

I cannot, however, be insensible to the present outcry against the triviality and meanness, both of thought and language, which some of my contemporaries have occasionally introduced into their metrical compositions; and I acknowledge that this defect, where it exists, is more dishonorable to the Writer's own character than false refinement or arbitrary innovation, though I should contend at the same time, that it is far less pernicious in the sum of its consequences. From such verses the Poems in these volumes will be found distinguished at least by one mark of difference, that each of them has a worthy purpose. Not that I always began to write with a distinct purpose formerly conceived; but habits of meditation have, I trust, so prompted and regulated my feelings, that my descriptions of such objects as strongly excite those feelings, will be found to carry along with them a purpose. If this opinion be erroneous, I can have little right to the name of a Poet. For all good poetry is the spontaneous overflow of powerful feelings: and though this be true, Poems to which any value can be attached were never produced on any variety of subjects but by a man who, being possessed of more than usual organic sensibility, had also thought long and deeply. For our continued influxes of feeling are modified and directed by our thoughts, which are indeed the representatives of all our past feelings; and, as by contemplating the relation of these general representatives to each other, we discover what is really important to men, so, by the repetition and continuance of this act, our feelings will be connected with important subjects, till at length, if we be originally possessed of much sensibility, such habits of mind will be produced, that, by obeying blindly and mechanically the impulses of those habits, we shall describe objects, and utter sentiments, of such a nature, and in such connection with each other, that the understanding of the Reader must necessarily be in some degree enlightened, and his affections strengthened and purified.

It has been said that each of these poems has a purpose. Another circumstance must be mentioned which distinguishes these Poems from the popular Poetry of the day; it is this, that the feeling therein developed gives importance to the action and situation, and not the action and situation to the feeling.

A sense of false modesty shall not prevent me from asserting, that the Reader's attention is pointed to this mark of distinction, far less for the sake of these particular Poems than from the general importance of the subject. The subject is indeed important! For the human mind is capable of being excited without the application of gross and violent stimulants; and he must have a very faint perception of its beauty and dignity who does not know this, and who does not further know, that one being is elevated above another, in proportion as he possesses this capability. It has therefore appeared to me, that to endeavor to produce or enlarge this capability is one of the best services in which, at any period, a Writer can be engaged; but this service, excellent at all times, is especially so at the present day. For a multitude of causes, unknown to former times, are now acting with a combined force to blunt the discriminating powers of the mind, and, unfitting it for all voluntary exertion, to reduce it to a state of almost savage torpor. The most effective of these causes are the great national events which are daily taking place, and the increasing accumulation of men in cities, where the uniformity of their occupations produces a craving for extraordinary incident, which the rapid communication of intelligence hourly gratifies. To this tendency of life and manners the literature and theatrical exhibitions of the country have conformed themselves. The invaluable works of our elder writers, I had almost said the works of Shakespeare and Milton, are driven into neglect by frantic novels, sickly and stupid German Tragedies, and deluges of idle and extravagant stories in verse.—When I think upon this degrading thirst after outrageous stimulation, I am almost ashamed to have spoken of the feeble endeavor made in these volumes to counteract it; and, reflecting upon the magnitude of the general evil, I should be oppressed with no dishonorable melancholy, had I not a deep impression of certain inherent and indestructible qualities of the human mind, and likewise of certain powers in the great and permanent objects that act upon it, which are equally inherent and indestructible; and were there not added to this impression a belief, that the time is approaching when the evil will be systematically opposed, by men of greater powers, and with far more distinguished success.

Having dwelt thus long on the subjects and aim of these Poems, I shall request the Reader's permission to apprise him of a few circumstances relating to their style, in order, among other reasons, that he may not censure me for not having performed what I never attempted. The Reader will find that personifications of abstract ideas rarely occur in these volumes; and are utterly rejected, as an ordinary device to elevate the style, and raise it above prose. My purpose was to imitate, and, as far as possible, to adopt the very language of men; and assuredly such personifications do not make any natural or regular part of that language. They are, indeed, a figure of speech occasionally prompted by passion, and I have made use of them as such; but have endeavored utterly to reject them as a mechanical device of style, or as a family language which Writers in metre seem to lay claim to by prescription. I have wished to keep the Reader in the company of flesh and blood, persuaded that by so doing I shall interest him. Others who pursue a different track will interest him likewise; I do not interfere with their claim, but wish to prefer a claim of my own. There will also be found in these volumes little of what is usually called poetic diction; as much pains has been taken to avoid it as is ordinarily taken to produce it; this has been done for the reason already alleged, to bring my language near to the language of men; and further, because the pleasure which I have proposed to myself to impart, is of a kind very different from that which is supposed by many persons to be the proper object of poetry. Without being culpably particular, I do not know how to give my Reader a more exact notion of the style in which it was my wish and intention to write, than by informing him that I have at all times endeavored to look steadily at my subject; consequently, there is I hope in these Poems little falsehood of description, and my ideas are expressed in language fitted to their respective importance. Something must have been gained by this practice, as it is friendly to one property of all good poetry, namely, good sense: but it has necessarily cut me off from a large portion of phrases and figures of speech which from father to son have long been regarded as the common inheritance of Poets. I have also thought it expedient to restrict myself still further, having abstained from the use of many expressions, in themselves proper and beautiful, but which have been foolishly repeated by bad Poets, till such feelings of disgust are connected with them as it is scarcely possible by any art of association to overpower.

If in a poem there should be found a series of lines, or even a single line, in which the language, though naturally arranged, and according to the strict laws of metre, does not differ from that of prose, there is a numerous class of critics, who, when they stumble upon these prosaisms, as they call them, imagine that they have made a notable discovery, and exult over the Poet as over a man ignorant of his own profession. Now these men would establish a canon of criticism which the Reader will conclude he must utterly reject, if he wishes to be pleased with these volumes. and it would be a most easy task to prove to him, that not only the language of a large portion of every good poem, even of the most elevated character, must necessarily, except with reference to the metre, in no respect differ from that of good prose, but likewise that some of the most interesting parts of the best poems will be found to be strictly the language of prose when prose is well written. The truth of this assertion might be demonstrated by innumerable passages from almost all the poetical writings, even of Milton himself. To illustrate the subject in a general manner, I will here adduce a short composition of Gray, who was at the head of those who, by their reasonings, have attempted to widen the space of separation betwixt Prose and Metrical composition, and was more than any other man curiously elaborate in the structure of his own poetic diction.

> In vain to me the smiling mornings shine,
> And reddening Phœbus lifts his golden fire:
> The birds in vain their amorous descant join,
> Or cheerful fields resume their green attire.
> These ears, alas! for other notes repine;
> *A different object do these eyes require;*
> *My lonely anguish melts no heart but mine;*
> *And in my breast the imperfect joys expire;*
> Yet morning smiles the busy race to cheer,
> And new-born pleasure brings to happier men;
> The fields to all their wonted tribute bear;
> To warm their little loves the birds complain.
> *I fruitless mourn to him that cannot hear,*
> *And weep the more because I weep in vain.*

It will easily be perceived, that the only part of this Sonnet which is of any value is the lines printed in Italics; it is equally obvious, that, except in the rhyme, and in the use of the single word 'fruitless' for fruitlessly, which is so far a defect, the language of these lines does in no respect differ from that of prose.

By the foregoing quotation it has been shown that the language of Prose may yet be well adapted to Poetry; and it was previously asserted, that a large portion of the language of every good poem can in no respect differ from that of good Prose. We will go further. It may be safely affirmed, that there neither is, nor can be, any essential difference between the language of prose and metrical composition. We are fond of tracing the resemblance between Poetry and Painting, and, accordingly, we call them Sisters: but where shall we find bonds of connection sufficiently strict to typify the affinity betwixt metrical and prose composition? They both speak by and to the same organs; the bodies in which both of them are clothed may be said to be of the same substance, their affections are kindred, and almost identical, not necessarily differing even in degree; Poetry [Wordsworth's note: As sensibility to harmony of numbers, and the power of producing it, are invariably attendants upon the faculties above specified, nothing has been said upon those requisites.] sheds no tears 'such as Angels weep,' but natural and human tears; she can boast of no celestial choir that distinguishes her vital juices from those of prose; the same human blood circulates through the veins of them both.

If it be affirmed that rhyme and metrical arrangement of themselves constitute a distinction which overturns what has just been said on the strict affinity of metrical language with that of prose, and paves the way for other artificial distinctions which the mind voluntarily admits, I answer that the language of such Poetry as is here recommended is, as far as is possible, a selection of the language really spoken by men; that this selection, wherever it is made with true taste and feeling, will of itself form a distinction far greater than would at first be imagined, and will entirely separate the composition from the vulgarity and meanness of ordinary life; and, if metre be superadded thereto, I believe that a dissimilitude will be produced altogether sufficient for the gratification of a rational mind. What other distinction would we have? Whence is it to come? and where is it to exist? Not, surely, where the Poet speaks through the mouths of his characters: it cannot be necessary here, either for elevation of style, or any of its supposed ornaments: for, if the Poet's subject be judiciously chosen, it will naturally, and upon fit occasion, lead him to passions the language of which, if selected truly and judiciously, must necessarily be dignified and variegated, and alive with metaphors and figures. I forbear to speak of an incongruity which would shock the intelligent Reader, should the Poet interweave any foreign splendor of his own with that which the passion naturally suggests: it is sufficient to say that such addition is unnecessary. and, surely, it is more probable that those passages, which with propriety abound with metaphors and figures, will have their due effect, if, upon other occasions where the passions are of a milder character, the style also be subdued and temperate.

But, as the pleasure which I hope to give by the Poems now presented to the Reader must depend entirely on just notions upon this subject, and, as it is in itself of high importance to our taste and moral feelings, I cannot content myself with these detached remarks. and if, in what I am about to say, it shall appear to some that my labor is unnecessary, and that I am like a man fighting a battle without enemies, such persons may be reminded, that, whatever be the language outwardly holden by men, a practical faith in the opinions which I am wishing to establish is almost unknown. If my conclusions are admitted, and carried as far as they must be carried if admitted at all, our judgments concerning the works of the greatest Poets both ancient and modern will be far different from what they are at present, both when we praise, and when we censure: and our moral feelings influencing and influenced by these judgments will, I believe, be corrected and purified.

Taking up the subject, then, upon general grounds, let me ask, what is meant by the word Poet? What is a Poet? to whom does he address himself? and what language is to be expected from him?—He is a man speaking to men: a man, it is true, endowed with more lively sensibility, more enthusiasm and tenderness, who has a greater knowledge of human nature, and a more comprehensive soul, than are supposed to be common among mankind; a man pleased with his own passions and volitions, and who rejoices more than other men in the spirit of life that is in him; delighting to contemplate similar volitions and passions as manifested in the goings-on of the Universe, and habitually impelled to create them where he does not find them. to these qualities he has added a disposition to be affected more than other men by absent things as if they were present; an ability of conjuring up in himself passions, which are indeed far from being the same as those produced by real events, yet (especially in those parts of the general sympathy which are pleasing and delightful) do more nearly resemble the passions produced by real events, than anything which, from the motions of their own minds merely, other men are accustomed to feel in them-selves:—whence, and from practice, he has acquired a greater readiness and power in expressing what he thinks and feels, and especially those thoughts and feelings which, by his own choice, or from the structure of his own mind, arise in him without immediate external excitement.

But whatever portion of this faculty we may suppose even the greatest Poet to possess, there cannot be a doubt that the language which it will suggest to him, must often, in liveliness and truth, fall short of that which is uttered by men in real life, under the actual pressure of those passions, certain shadows of which the Poet thus produces, or feels to be produced, in himself.

However exalted a notion we would wish to cherish of the character of a Poet, it is obvious, that while he describes and imitates passions, his employment is in some degree mechanical, compared with the freedom and power of real and substantial action and suffering. So that it will be the wish of the Poet to bring his feelings near to those of the persons whose feelings he describes, nay, for short spaces of time, perhaps, to let himself slip into an entire delusion, and even confound and identify his own feelings with theirs; modifying only the language which is thus suggested to him by a consideration that he describes for a particular purpose, that of giving pleasure. Here, then, he will apply the principle of selection which has been already insisted upon. He will depend upon this for removing what would otherwise be painful or disgusting in the passion; he will feel that there is no necessity to trick out or to elevate nature: and, the more industriously he applies this principle, the deeper will be his faith that no words, which his fancy or imagination can suggest, will be to be compared with those which are the emanations of reality and truth.

But it may be said by those who do not object to the general spirit of these remarks, that, as it is impossible for the Poet to produce upon all occasions language as exquisitely fitted for the passion as that which the real passion itself suggests, it is proper that he should consider himself as in the situation of a translator, who does not scruple to substitute excellencies of another kind for those which are unattainable by him; and endeavors occasionally to surpass his original, in order to make some amends for the general inferiority to which he feels that he must submit. But this would be to encourage idleness and unmanly despair. Further, it is the language of men who speak of what they do not understand; who talk of Poetry as of a matter of amusement and idle pleasure; who will converse with us as gravely about a taste for Poetry, as they express it, as if it were a thing as indifferent as a taste for rope-dancing, or Frontiniac or Sherry. Aristotle, I have been told, has said, that Poetry is the most philosophic of all writing: it is so: its object is truth, not individual and local, but general, and operative; not standing upon external testimony, but carried alive into the heart by passion; truth which is its own testimony, which gives competence and confidence to the tribunal to which it appeals, and receives them from the same tribunal. Poetry is the image of man and nature. The obstacles which stand in the way of the fidelity of the Biographer and Historian, and of their consequent utility, are incalculably greater than those which are to be encountered by the Poet who comprehends the dignity of his art. The Poet writes under one restriction only, namely, the necessity of giving immediate pleasure to a human Being possessed of that information which may be expected from him, not as a lawyer, a physician, a mariner, an astronomer, or a natural philosopher, but as a Man. Except this one restriction, there is no object standing between the Poet and the image of things; between this, and the Biographer and Historian, there are a thousand.

Nor let this necessity of producing immediate pleasure be considered as a degradation of the Poet's art. It is far otherwise. It is an acknowledgement of the beauty of the universe, an acknowledgement the more sincere, because not formal, but indirect; it is a task light and easy to him who looks at the world in the spirit of love: further, it is a homage paid to the native and naked dignity of man, to the grand elementary principle of pleasure, by which he knows, and feels, and lives, and moves. We have no sympathy but what is propagated by pleasure: I would not be misunderstood; but wherever we sympathize with pain, it will be found that the sympathy is produced and carried on by subtle combinations with pleasure. We have no knowledge, that is, no general principles drawn from the contemplation of particular facts, but what has been built up by pleasure, and exists in us by pleasure alone. The Man of science, the Chemist and Mathematician, whatever difficulties and disgusts they may have had to struggle with, know and feel this. However painful may be the objects with which the Anatomist's knowledge is connected, he feels that his knowledge is pleasure; and where he has no pleasure he has no knowledge. What then does the Poet? He considers man and the objects that surround him as acting and re-acting upon each other, so as to produce an infinite complexity of pain and pleasure; he considers man in his own nature and in his ordinary life as contemplating this with a certain quantity of immediate knowledge, with certain convictions, intuitions, and deductions, which from habit acquire the quality of intuitions; he considers him as looking upon this complex scene of ideas and sensations, and finding everywhere objects that immediately excite in him sympathies which, from the necessities of his nature, are accompanied by an overbalance of enjoyment.

To this knowledge which all men carry about with them, and to these sympathies in which, without any other discipline than that of our daily life, we are fitted to take delight, the Poet principally directs his attention. He considers man and nature as essentially adapted to each other, and the mind of man as naturally the mirror of the fairest and most interesting properties of nature. and thus the Poet, prompted by this feeling of pleasure, which accompanies him through the whole course of his studies, converses with general nature, with affections akin to those, which, through labor and length of time, the Man of science has raised up in himself, by conversing with those particular parts of nature which are the objects of his studies. The knowledge both of the Poet and the Man of science is pleasure; but the knowledge of the one cleaves to us as a necessary part of our existence, our natural and unalienable inheritance; the other is a personal and individual acquisition, slow to come to us, and by no habitual and direct sympathy connecting us with our fellow-beings. The Man of science seeks truth as a remote and unknown benefactor; he cherishes and loves it in his solitude: the Poet, singing a song in which all human beings join with him, rejoices in the presence of truth as our visible friend and hourly companion. Poetry is the breath and finer spirit of all knowledge; it is the impassioned expression which is in the countenance of all Science. Emphatically may it be said of the Poet, as Shakespeare hath said of man, 'that he looks before and after.' He is the rock of defense for human nature; an upholder and preserver, carrying everywhere with him relationship and love. In spite of difference of soil and climate, of language and manners, of laws and customs: in spite of things silently gone out of mind, and things violently destroyed; the Poet binds together by passion and knowledge the vast empire of human society, as it is spread over the whole earth, and over all time. The objects of the Poet's thoughts are everywhere; though the eyes and senses of man are, it is true, his favorite guides, yet he will follow wheresoever he can find an atmosphere of sensation in which to move his wings. Poetry is the first and last of all knowledge—it is as immortal as the heart of man. If the labors of Men of science should ever create any material revolution, direct or indirect, in our condition, and in the impressions which we habitually receive, the Poet will sleep then no more than at present; he will be ready to follow the steps of the Man of science, not only in those general indirect effects, but he will be at his side, carrying sensation into the midst of the objects of the science itself. The remotest discoveries of the Chemist, the Botanist, or Mineralogist, will be as proper objects of the Poet's art as any upon which it can be employed, if the time should ever come when these things shall be familiar to us, and the relations under which they are contemplated by the followers of these respective sciences shall be manifestly and palpably material to us as enjoying and suffering beings. If the time should ever come when what is now called science, thus familiarized to men, shall be ready to put on, as it were, a form of flesh and blood, the Poet will lend his divine spirit to aid the transfiguration, and will welcome the Being thus produced, as a dear and genuine inmate of the household of man.—It is not, then, to be supposed that any one, who holds that sublime notion of Poetry which I have attempted to convey, will break in upon the sanctity and truth of his pictures by transitory and accidental ornaments, and endeavor to excite admiration of himself by arts, the necessity of which must manifestly depend upon the assumed meanness of his subject.

What has been thus far said applies to Poetry in general; but especially to those parts of composition where the Poet speaks through the mouths of his characters; and upon this point it appears to authorize the conclusion that there are few persons of good sense, who would not allow that the dramatic parts of composition are defective, in proportion as they deviate from the real language of nature, and are colored by a diction of the Poet's own, either peculiar to him as an individual Poet or belonging simply to Poets in general; to a body of men who, from the circumstance of their compositions being in metre, it is expected will employ a particular language.

It is not, then, in the dramatic parts of composition that we look for this distinction of language; but still it may be proper and necessary where the Poet speaks to us in his own person and character. To this I answer by referring the Reader to the description before given of a Poet. Among the qualities there enumerated as principally conducing to form a Poet, is implied nothing differing in kind from other men, but only in degree. The sum of what was said is, that the Poet is chiefly distinguished from other men by a greater promptness to think and feel without immediate external excitement, and a greater power in expressing such thoughts and feelings as are produced in him in that manner. But these passions and thoughts and feelings are the general passions and thoughts and feelings of men. And with what are they connected? Undoubtedly with our moral sentiments and animal sensations, and with the causes which excite these; with the operations of the elements, and the appearances of the visible universe; with storm and sunshine, with the revolutions of the seasons, with cold and heat, with loss of friends and kindred, with injuries and resentments, gratitude and hope, with fear and sorrow. These, and the like, are the sensations and objects which the Poet describes, as they are the sensations of other men, and the objects which interest them. The Poet thinks and feels in the spirit of human passions. How, then, can his language differ in any material degree from that of all other men who feel vividly and see clearly? It might be proved that it is impossible. But supposing that this were not the case, the Poet might then be allowed to use a peculiar language when expressing his feelings for his own gratification, or that of men like himself. But Poets do not write for Poets alone, but for men. Unless therefore we are advocates for that admiration which subsists upon ignorance, and that pleasure which arises from hearing what we do not understand, the Poet must descend from this supposed height; and, in order to excite rational sympathy, he must express himself as other men express themselves. to this it may be added, that while he is only selecting from the real language of men, or, which amounts to the same thing, composing accurately in the spirit of such selection, he is treading upon safe ground, and we know what we are to expect from him. Our feelings are the same with respect to metre; for, as it may be proper to remind the Reader, the distinction of metre is regular and uniform, and not, like that which is produced by what is usually called POETIC DICTION, arbitrary, and subject to infinite caprices upon which no calculation whatever can be made. In the one case, the Reader is utterly at the mercy of the Poet, respecting what imagery or diction he may choose to connect with the passion; whereas, in the other, the metre obeys certain laws, to which the Poet and Reader both willingly submit because they are certain, and because no interference is made by them with the passion, but such as the concurring testimony of ages has shown to heighten and improve the pleasure which co-exists with it.

It will now be proper to answer an obvious question, namely, Why, professing these opinions, have I written in verse? to this, in addition to such answer as is included in what has been already said, I reply, in the first place, because however I may have restricted myself, there is still left open to me what confessedly constitutes the most valuable object of all writing, whether in prose or verse; the great and universal passions of men, the most general and interesting of their occupations, and the entire world of nature before me—to supply end-less combinations of forms and imagery. Now, supposing for a moment that whatever is interesting in these objects may be as vividly described in prose, why should I be condemned for attempting to superadd to such description the charm which, by the consent of all nations, is acknowledged to exist in metrical language? To this, by such as are yet unconvinced, it may be answered that a very small part of the pleasure given by Poetry depends upon the metre, and that it is injudicious to write in metre, unless it be accompanied with the other artificial distinctions of style with which metre is usually accompanied, and that, by such deviation, more will be lost from the shock which will thereby be given to the Reader's associations than will be counterbalanced by any pleasure which he can derive from the general power of numbers. In answer to those who still contend for the necessity of accompanying metre with certain appro-priate colors of style in order to the accomplishment of its appropriate end, and who also, in my opinion, greatly underrate the power of metre in itself, it might, perhaps, as far as relates to these Volumes, have been almost sufficient to ob-serve, that poems are extant, written upon more humble subjects, and in a still more naked and simple style, which have continued to give pleasure from generation to generation. Now, if nakedness and simplicity be a defect, the fact here mentioned affords a strong presumption that poems somewhat less naked and simple are capable of affording pleasure at the present day; and, what I wish chiefly to attempt, at present, was to justify myself for having written under the impression of this belief.

But various causes might be pointed out why, when the style is manly, and the subject of some importance, words metrically arranged will long continue to impart such a pleasure to mankind as he who proves the extent of that pleasure will be desirous to impart. The end of Poetry is to produce excitement in co-existence with an overbalance of pleasure; but, by the supposition, ex-citement is an unusual and irregular state of the mind; ideas and feelings do not, in that state, succeed each other in accustomed order. If the words, how-ever, by which this excitement is produced be in themselves powerful, or the images and feelings have an undue proportion of pain connected with them, there is some danger that the excitement may be carried beyond its proper bounds. Now the co-presence of something regular, something to which the mind has been accustomed in various moods and in a less excited state, cannot but have great efficacy in tempering and restraining the passion by an intertex-ture of ordinary feeling, and of feeling not strictly and necessarily connected with the passion. This is unquestionably true; and hence, though the opinion will at first appear paradoxical, from the tendency of metre to divest language, in a certain degree, of its reality, and thus to throw a sort of half-consciousness of unsubstantial existence over the whole composition, there can be little doubt but that more pathetic situations and sentiments, that is, those which have a greater proportion of pain connected with them, may be endured in metrical composition, especially in rhyme, than in prose. The metre of the old ballads is very artless; yet they contain many passages which would illustrate this opinion; and, I hope, if the following Poems be attentively perused, similar instances will be found in them. This opinion may be further illustrated by appealing to the Reader's own experience of the reluctance with which he comes to the reperusal of the distressful parts of *Clarissa Harlowe*, or *The Gamester*; while Shakespeare's writings, in the most pathetic scenes, never act upon us, as pathetic, beyond the bounds of pleasure—an effect which, in a much greater degree than might at first be imagined, is to be ascribed to small, but continual and regular impulses of pleasurable surprise from the metrical arrangement.— On the other hand (what it must be allowed will much more frequently happen) if the Poet's words should be incommensurate with the passion, and inadequate to raise the Reader to a height of desirable excitement, then (unless the Poet's choice of his metre has been grossly injudicious), in the feelings of pleasure which the Reader has been accustomed to connect with metre in general, and in the feeling, whether cheerful or melancholy, which he has been accustomed to connect with that particular movement of metre, there will be found something which will greatly contribute to impart passion to the words, and to effect the complex end which the Poet proposes to himself.

If I had undertaken a SYSTEMATIC defense of the theory here maintained, it would have been my duty to develop the various causes upon which the pleasure received from metrical language depends. Among the chief of these causes is to be reckoned a principle which must be well known to those who have made any of the Arts the object of accurate reflection; namely, the pleasure which the mind derives from the perception of similitude in dissimilitude. This principle is the great spring of the activity of our minds, and their chief feeder. From this principle the direction of the sexual appetite, and all the passions connected with it, take their origin: it is the life of our ordinary conversation; and upon the accuracy with which similitude in dissimilitude, and dissimilitude in similitude are perceived, depend our taste and our moral feelings. It would not be a useless employment to apply this principle to the consideration of metre, and to show that metre is hence enabled to afford much pleasure, and to point out in what manner that pleasure is produced. But my limits will not permit me to enter upon this subject, and I must content myself with a general summary.

I have said that poetry is the spontaneous overflow of powerful feelings: it takes its origin from emotion recollected in tranquillity: the emotion is contemplated till, by a species of reaction, the tranquillity gradually disappears, and an emotion, kindred to that which was before the subject of contemplation, is gradually produced, and does itself actually exist in the mind. In this mood successful composition generally begins, and in a mood similar to this it is carried on; but the emotion, of whatever kind, and in whatever degree, from various causes, is qualified by various pleasures, so that in describing any passions whatsoever, which are voluntarily described, the mind will, upon the whole, be in a state of enjoyment. If Nature be thus cautious to preserve in a state of enjoyment a being so employed, the Poet ought to profit by the lesson held forth to him, and ought especially to take care, that, whatever passions he communicates to his Reader, those passions, if his Reader's mind be sound and vigorous, should always be accompanied with an overbalance of pleasure. Now the music of harmonious metrical language, the sense of difficulty overcome, and the blind association of pleasure which has been previously received from works of rhyme or metre of the same or similar construction, an indistinct perception perpetually renewed of language closely resembling that of real life, and yet, in the circumstance of metre, differing from it so widely—all these imperceptibly make up a complex feeling of delight, which is of the most important use in tempering the painful feeling always found intermingled with powerful descriptions of the deeper passions. This effect is always produced in pathetic and impassioned poetry; while, in lighter compositions, the ease and gracefulness with which the Poet manages his numbers are themselves confessedly a principal source of the gratification of the Reader. All that it is necessary to say, however, upon this subject, may be effected by affirming, what few persons will deny, that, of two descriptions, either of passions, manners, or characters, each of them equally well executed, the one in prose and the other in verse, the verse will be read a hundred times where the prose is read once.

Having thus explained a few of my reasons for writing in verse, and why I have chosen subjects from common life, and endeavored to bring my language near to the real language of men, if I have been too minute in pleading my own cause, I have at the same time been treating a subject of general interest; and for this reason a few words shall be added with reference solely to these particular poems, and to some defects which will probably be found in them. I am sensible that my associations must have sometimes been particular instead of general, and that, consequently, giving to things a false importance, I may have sometimes written upon unworthy subjects; but I am less apprehensive on this account, than that my language may frequently have suffered from those arbitrary connections of feelings and ideas with particular words and phrases, from which no man can altogether protect himself. Hence I have no doubt, that, in some instances, feelings, even of the ludicrous, may be given to my Readers by expressions which appeared to me tender and pathetic. Such faulty expressions, were I convinced they were faulty at present, and that they must necessarily continue to be so, I would willingly take all reasonable pains to correct. But it is dangerous to make these alterations on the simple authority of a few individuals, or even of certain classes of men; for where the understanding of an Author is not convinced, or his feelings altered, this cannot be done without great injury to himself: for his own feelings are his stay and support;

and, if he set them aside in one instance, he may be induced to repeat this act till his mind shall lose all confidence in itself, and become utterly debilitated. To this it may be added, that the critic ought never to forget that he is himself exposed to the same errors as the Poet, and, perhaps, in a much greater degree: for there can be no presumption in saying of most readers, that it is not probable they will be so well acquainted with the various stages of meaning through which words have passed, or with the fickleness or stability of the relations of particular ideas to each other; and, above all, since they are so much less interested in the subject, they may decide lightly and carelessly.

Long as the Reader has been detained, I hope he will permit me to caution him against a mode of false criticism which has been applied to Poetry, in which the language closely resembles that of life and nature. Such verses have been triumphed over in parodies, of which Dr. Johnson's stanza is a fair specimen:—

> I put my hat upon my head
> And walked into the Strand,
> And there I met another man
> Whose hat was in his hand.

Immediately under these lines let us place one of the most justly admired stanzas of the 'Babes in the Wood.'

> These pretty Babes with hand in hand
> Went wandering up and down;
> But never more they saw the Man
> Approaching from the town.

In both these stanzas the words, and the order of the words, in no respect differ from the most unimpassioned conversation. There are words in both, for example, 'the Strand,' and 'the town,' connected with none but the most familiar ideas; yet the one stanza we admit as admirable, and the other as a fair example of the superlatively contemptible. Whence arises this difference? Not from the metre, not from the language, not from the order of the words; but the matter expressed in Dr. Johnson's stanza is contemptible. The proper method of treating trivial and simple verses, to which Dr. Johnson's stanza would be a fair parallelism, is not to say, this is a bad kind of poetry, or, this is not poetry; but, this wants sense; it is neither interesting in itself nor can lead to anything interesting; the images neither originate in that sane state of feeling which arises out of thought, nor can excite thought or feeling in the Reader. This is the only sensible manner of dealing with such verses. Why trouble yourself about the species till you have previously decided upon the genus? Why take pains to prove that an ape is not a Newton, when it is self-evident that he is not a man?

One request I must make of my reader, which is, that in judging these Poems he would decide by his own feelings genuinely, and not by reflection upon what will probably be the judgment of others. How common is it to hear a person say, I myself do not object to this style of composition, or this or that expression, but, to such and such classes of people it will appear mean or ludicrous! This mode of criticism, so destructive of all sound unadulterated judgment, is almost universal: let the Reader then abide, independently, by his own feelings, and, if he finds himself affected, let him not suffer such conjectures to interfere with his pleasure.

If an Author, by any single composition, has impressed us with respect for his talents, it is useful to consider this as affording a presumption, that on other occasions where we have been displeased, he, nevertheless, may not have written ill or absurdly; and further, to give him so much credit for this one composition as may induce us to review what has displeased us, with more care than we should otherwise have bestowed upon it. This is not only an act of justice, but, in our decisions upon poetry especially, may conduce, in a high degree, to the improvement of our own taste; for an accurate taste in poetry, and in all the other arts, as Sir Joshua Reynolds has observed, is an acquired talent, which can only be produced by thought and a long continued intercourse with the best models of composition. This is mentioned, not with so ridiculous a purpose as to prevent the most inexperienced Reader from judging for himself (I have already said that I wish him to judge for himself), but merely to temper the rashness of decision, and to suggest, that, if Poetry be a subject on which much time has not been bestowed, the judgment may be erroneous; and that, in many cases, it necessarily will be so.

Nothing would, I know, have so effectually contributed to further the end which I have in view, as to have shown of what kind the pleasure is, and how that pleasure is produced, which is confessedly produced by metrical composition essentially different from that which I have here endeavored to recommend: for the Reader will say that he has been pleased by such composition; and what more can be done for him? The power of any art is limited; and he will suspect, that, if it be proposed to furnish him with new friends, that can be only upon condition of his abandoning his old friends. Besides, as I have said, the Reader is himself conscious of the pleasure which he has received from such composition, composition to which he has peculiarly attached the endearing name of Poetry; and all men feel an habitual gratitude, and something of an honorable bigotry, for the objects which have long continued to please them: we not only wish to be pleased, but to be pleased in that particular way in which we have been accustomed to be pleased. There is in these feelings enough to resist a host of arguments; and I should be the less able to combat them successfully, as I am willing to allow, that, in order entirely to enjoy the Poetry which I am recommending, it would be necessary to give up much of what is ordinarily enjoyed. But, would my limits have permitted me to point out how this pleasure is produced, many obstacles might have been removed, and the Reader assisted in perceiving that the powers of language are not so limited as he may suppose; and that it is possible for poetry to give other enjoyments, of a purer, more lasting, and more exquisite nature. This part of the subject has not been altogether neglected, but it has not been so much my present aim to prove, that the interest excited by some other kinds of poetry is less vivid, and less worthy of the nobler powers of the mind, as to offer reasons for presuming, that if my purpose were fulfilled, a species of poetry would be produced, which is genuine poetry; in its nature well adapted to interest mankind permanently, and likewise important in the multiplicity and quality of its moral relations.

From what has been said, and from a perusal of the Poems, the Reader will be able clearly to perceive the object which I had in view: he will determine how far it has been attained; and, what is a much more important question, whether it be worth attaining: and upon the decision of these two questions will rest my claim to the approbation of the Public.

14

SAMUEL TAYLOR COLERIDGE (1772–1834)

Coleridge belongs in the company of the great collaborators, the great poet-critics, and, paradoxically, the great popular poets. The paradox is that the most philosophical of philosophical critics, fit for the company of Plato and Bacon, should also be the least philosophical, fit for the company of the anonymous authors of "Sir Patrick Spens" and "Edward, Edward."

The son of a vicar, Coleridge received a sporadic but stimulating education and led a peculiarly vexed life, which included dependency on opium. He was in and out of school, and interrupted his stay at Cambridge to spend a short time in the military. That one so peculiar could believe for a minute that he ought to join the cavalry is one indication of just how peculiar he was. His ambitions forever outran his performance, and he started a dozen projects for every one that he even came close to finishing. He was married to a woman whom he scarcely loved, and he tended to fall in love with women he could not marry. Coleridge was supported for several years by the philanthropy of Josiah and Thomas Wedgwood of the Staffordshire family that is still famous for fine china.

Coleridge was, however, most fortunate in his associations; he was close to Charles Lamb, William Wordsworth, and Robert Southey. He and Southey hatched an elaborate scheme for an ideal community based on a concept called Pantisocracy. (The word means "equal rule by all"; the adherents contemplated a utopian community free of rank, class, and position.) They planned a model life to be pursued on the banks of the Susquehanna River in Pennsylvania.

Coleridge's most productive association was with Wordsworth, and a tourist can still visit many places that were the sites, two hundred years ago, of their dwellings. In Somerset, a "Coleridge Cottage" still exists in the village of Nether Stowey. Not far away is Alfoxden Park, a house (now a hotel) once occupied by Wordsworth when he and Coleridge were collaborating on some of their most important works.

His greatest sustained prose work, *Biographia Literaria,* which combines autobiography with criticism, remains a masterpiece of wisdom and insight into the subtlest of human arts. Coleridge's genius recognized and rejoiced that poetry is not one monotonously consistent thing but a complex of contradictory things with a power revealed "in the balance or reconciliation of opposite or discordant qualities: of sameness, with difference; of the general, with the concrete; the idea, with the image; the individual, with the representative; the sense of novelty and freshness, with old and familiar objects; a more than usual state of emotion, with more than usual order; judgment ever awake and steady self-possession, with enthusiasm and feeling profound or vehement."

BIOGRAPHIA LITERARIA (1817)

CHAPTER XIV

Occasion of the Lyrical Ballads, and the objects originally proposed—Preface to the second edition—The ensuing controversy, its causes and acrimony—Philosophic definitions of a poem and poetry with scholia. During the first year that Mr. Wordsworth and I were neighbors, our conversations turned frequently on the two cardinal points of poetry, the power of exciting the sympathy of the reader by a faithful adherence to the truth of nature, and the power of giving the interest of novelty by the modifying colors of imagination. The sudden charm, which accidents of light and shade, which moon-light or sun-set diffused over a known and familiar landscape, appeared to represent the practicability of combining both. These are the poetry of nature. The thought suggested itself (to which of us I do not recollect) that a series of poems might be composed of two sorts. In the one, the incidents and agents were to be, in part at least, supernatural; and the excellence aimed at was to consist in the interesting of the affections by the dramatic truth of such emotions as would naturally accompany such situations, supposing them real. And real in this sense they have been to every human being who, from whatever source of delusion, has at any time believed himself under supernatural agency. For the second class, subjects were to be chosen from ordinary life; the characters and incidents were to be such, as will be found in every village and its vicinity, where there is a meditative and feeling mind to seek after them, or to notice them, when they present themselves.

In this idea originated the plan of the "Lyrical Ballads"; in which it was agreed, that my endeavors should be directed to persons and characters supernatural, or at least romantic, yet so as to transfer from our inward nature a human interest and a semblance of truth sufficient to procure for these shadows of imagination that willing suspension of disbelief for the moment, which constitutes poetic faith. Mr. Wordsworth on the other hand was to propose to himself as his object, to give the charm of novelty to things of every day, and to excite a feeling analogous to the supernatural, by awakening the mind's attention from the lethargy of custom, and directing it to the loveliness and the wonders of the world before us; an inexhaustible treasure, but for which in consequence of the film of familiarity and selfish solicitude we have eyes, yet see not, ears that hear not, and hearts that neither feel nor understand.

With this view I wrote the "Ancient Mariner," and was preparing among other poems, the "Dark Ladie," and the "Christabel," in which I should have more nearly realized my ideal, than I had done in my first attempt. But Mr. Wordsworth's industry had proved so much more successful, and the number of his poems so much greater, that my compositions, instead of forming a balance, appeared rather an interpolation of heterogeneous matter. Mr. Wordsworth added two or three poems written in his own character, in the impassioned, lofty, and sustained diction, which is characteristic of his genius. In this form the "Lyrical Ballads" were published; and were presented by him as an *experiment*, whether subjects, which from their nature rejected the usual ornaments and extra-colloquial style of poems in general, might not be so managed in the language of ordinary life as to produce the pleasurable interest, which it is the peculiar business of poetry to impart. To the second edition he added a preface of considerable length; in which notwithstanding some passages of apparently a contrary import, he was understood to contend for the extension of this style to poetry of all kinds, and to reject as vicious and indefensible all phrases and forms of style that were not included in what he (unfortunately, I think, adopting an equivocal expression) called the language of *real* life. From this preface, prefixed to poems in which it was impossible to deny the presence of original genius, however mistaken its direction might be deemed, arose the whole long continued controversy. For from the conjunction of perceived power with supposed heresy I explain the inveteracy and in some instances, I grieve to say, the acrimonious passions, with which the controversy has been conducted by the assailants.

Had Mr. Wordsworth's poems been the silly, the childish things, which they were for a long time described as being; had they been really distinguished from the compositions of other poets merely by meanness of language and inanity of thought; had they indeed contained nothing more than what is found in the parodies and pretended imitations of them; they must have sunk at once, a dead weight, into the slough of oblivion, and have dragged the preface along with them. But year after year increased the number of Mr. Wordsworth's admirers. They were found too not in the lower classes of the reading public, but chiefly among young men of strong ability and meditative minds; and their admiration (inflamed perhaps in some degree by opposition) was distinguished by its intensity, I might almost say, by its *religious* fervor. These facts, and the intellectual energy of the author, which was more or less consciously felt, where it was outwardly and even boisterously denied, meeting with sentiments of aversion to his opinions, and of alarm at their consequences, produced an eddy of criticism, which would of itself have borne up the poems by the violence, with which it whirled them round and round. With many parts of this preface in the sense attributed to them and which the words undoubtedly seem to authorize, I never concurred; but on the contrary objected to them as erroneous in principle, and as contradictory (in appearance at least) both to other parts of the same preface, and to the author's own practice in the greater number of the poems themselves. Mr. Wordsworth in his recent collection has, I find, degraded this prefatory disquisition to the end of his second volume, to be read or not at the reader's choice. But he has not, as far as I can discover, announced any change in his poetic creed. At all events, considering it as the source of a controversy, in which I have been honored more than I deserve by the frequent conjunction of my name with his I think it expedient to declare once for all, in what points I coincide with his opinions, and in what points I altogether differ. But in order to render myself intelligible I must previously, in as few words as possible, explain my ideas, first, of a POEM; and secondly, of POETRY itself, in *kind*, and in *essence*.

The office of philosophical *disquisition* consists in just *distinction*; while it is the privilege of the philosopher to preserve himself constantly aware, that distinction is not division. In order to obtain adequate notions of any truth, we must intellectually separate its distinguishable parts; and this is the technical process of philosophy. But having so done, we must then restore them in our conceptions to the unity, in which they actually co-exist; and this is the *result* of philosophy. A poem contains the same elements as a prose composition; the difference therefore must consist in a different combination of them, in consequence of a different object proposed. According to the difference of the object will be the difference of the combination. It is possible, that the object may be merely to facilitate the recollection of any given facts or observations by artificial arrangement; and the composition will be a poem, merely because it is distinguished from composition in prose by metre, or by rhyme, or by both conjointly. In this, the lowest sense, a man might attribute the name of a poem to the well-known enumeration of the days in the several months;

Thirty days hath September,
April, June, and November, &c.

and others of the same class and purpose. And as a particular pleasure is found in anticipating the recurrence of sounds and quantities, all compositions that have this charm superadded, whatever be their contents, *may* be entitled poems.

So much for the superficial form. A difference of object and contents supplies an additional ground of distinction. The immediate purpose may be the communication of truths; either of truth absolute and demonstrable, as in works of science; or of facts experienced and recorded, as in history. Pleasure, and that of the highest and most permanent kind, may *result* from the *attainment* of the end; but it is not itself the immediate end. In other works the communication of pleasure may be the immediate purpose—and though truth either moral or intellectual, ought to be the ultimate end, yet this will distinguish the character of the author, not the class to which the work belongs. Blessed indeed is that state of society, in which the immediate purpose would be baffled by the perversion of the proper *ultimate* end; in which no charm of diction or imagery could exempt the Bathyllus even of an Anacreon, or the Alexis of Virgil, from disgust and aversion!

But the communication of pleasure may be the immediate object of a work not metrically composed; and that object may have been in a high degree attained, as in novels and romances. Would then the mere superaddition of metre, with or without rhyme, entitle *these* to the name of poems? The answer is, that nothing can permanently please, which does not contain in itself the reason why it is so, and not otherwise. If metre be superadded, all other parts must be made consonant with it. They must be such, as to justify the perpetual and distinct attention to each part, which an exact correspondent recurrence of accent and sound are calculated to excite. The final definition then so deduced, may be thus worded. A poem is that species of composition, which is opposed to works of science, by proposing for its *immediate* object pleasure, not truth; and from all other species (having *this* object in common with it) it is discriminated by proposing to itself such delight from the *whole*, as is compatible with a distinct ratification from each component *part*.

Controversy is not seldom excited in consequence of the disputants attaching each a different meaning to the same word; and in few instances has this been more striking, than in disputes concerning the present subject. If a man chooses to call every composition a poem, which is rhyme, or measure, or both, I must leave his opinion uncontroverted. The distinction is at least competent to characterize the writer's intention. If it were subjoined, that the whole is likewise entertaining or affecting, as a tale, or as a series of interesting reflections, I of course admit this as another fit ingredient of a poem, and an additional merit. But if the definition sought for be that of a legitimate poem, I answer, it must be one, the parts of which mutually support and explain each other; all in their proportion harmonizing with, and supporting the purpose and known influences of metrical arrangement. The philosophic critics of all ages coincide with the ultimate judgment of all countries, in equally denying the praises of a just poem, on the one hand, to a series of striking lines or distichs, each of which absorbing the whole attention of the reader to itself disjoins it from its context, and makes it a separate whole, instead of an harmonizing part; and on the other hand, to an unsustained composition, from which the reader collects rapidly the general result unattracted by the component parts. The reader should be carried forward, not merely or chiefly by the mechanical impulse of curiosity, or by a restless desire to arrive at the final solution; but by the pleasurable activity of mind excited by the attractions of the journey itself. Like the motion of a serpent, which the Egyptians made the emblem of intellectual power; or like the path of sound through the air; at every step he pauses and half recedes, and from the retrogressive movement collects the force which again carries him onward. *Precipitandus est liber spiritus* [the *free* spirit must be hurried onward— ed.], says Petronius Arbiter most happily. The epithet, *liber*, here balances the preceding verb; and it is not easy to conceive more meaning condensed in fewer words.

But if this should be admitted as a satisfactory character of a poem, we have still to seek for a definition of poetry. The writings of PLATO, and Bishop TAYLOR, and the Theoria Sacra of BURNET, furnish undeniable proofs that poetry of the highest kind may exist without metre and even without the contradistinguishing objects of a poem. The first chapter of Isaiah (indeed a very large proportion of the whole book) is poetry in the most emphatic sense, yet it would be not less irrational than strange to assert, that pleasure, and not truth, was the immediate object of the prophet. In short, whatever *specific* import we attach to the word, poetry, there, will be found involved in it, as a necessary consequence, that a poem of any length neither can be, or ought to be, all poetry. Yet if an harmonious whole is to be produced, the remaining parts must be preserved *in keeping* with the poetry; and this can be no otherwise effected than by such a studied selection and artificial arrangement, as will partake of one, though not a *peculiar*, property of poetry. And this again can be no other than the property of exciting a more continuous and equal attention, than the language of prose aims at, whether colloquial or written.

My own conclusions on the nature of poetry, in the strictest use of the word, have been in part anticipated in the preceding disquisition on the fancy and imagination. What is poetry? is so nearly the same question with, what is a poem? that the answer to the one is involved in the solution of the other. For it is a distinction resulting from the poetic genius itself, which sustains and modifies the images, thoughts, and emotions of the poet's own mind. A poet, described in *ideal* perfection, brings the whole soul of man into activity, with the subordination of its faculties to each other, according to their relative worth and dignity. He diffuses a tone, and spirit of unity, that blends, and (as it were) *fuses*, each into each, by that synthetic and magical power, to which we have exclusively appropriated the name of imagination. This power, first put in action by the will and understanding, and retained under their irremissive, though gentle and unnoticed, control (*laxis effertur habenis* [it is carried onwards with loose reins—ed.]) reveals itself in the balance or reconciliation of opposite or discordant qualities: of sameness, with difference; of the general, with the concrete; the idea, with the image; the individual, with the representative; the sense of novelty and freshness, with old and familiar objects; a more than usual state of emotion, with more than usual order; judgment ever awake and steady self-possession, with enthusiasm and feeling profound or vehement; and while it blends and harmonizes the natural and the artificial, still subordinates art to nature; the manner to the matter; and our admiration of the poet to our sympathy with the poetry. "Doubtless," as Sir John Davies observes of the soul (and his words may with slight alteration be applied, and even more appropriately to the poetic IMAGINATION)

> Doubtless this could not be, but that she turns
> Bodies to spirit by sublimation strange,
> As fire converts to fire the things it burns,
> As we our food into our nature change.
> From their gross matter she abstracts their forms,
> And draws a kind of quintessence from things,
> Which to her proper nature she transforms
> To bear them light, on her celestial wings.
> Thus does she, when from individual states
> She doth abstract the universal kinds;
> Which then re-clothed in divers names and fates
> Steal access through our senses to our minds.

Finally, GOOD SENSE is the BODY of poetic genius, FANCY its DRAPERY, MOTION its LIFE, and IMAGINATION the SOUL that is everywhere, and in each; and forms all into one graceful and intelligent whole.

15

FRANCIS JEFFREY (1773–1850)

Francis Jeffrey, a Scot, rose to become Lord Jeffrey, a judge and a member of Parliament. He is best known in literature as one of the founders and editors of *The Edinburgh Review*, which endured robustly from 1802 until 1929. In its early years, the magazine often published reactionary attacks against the Romantic poets. One of Jeffrey's colleagues, Henry Peter Brougham, wrote the article which caused Lord Byron to write his early satire, *English Bards and Scotch Reviewers*. Jeffrey himself is known for his disparagement of Wordsworth and others among the "Lake Poets." Jeffrey gained immortality by the opening sentence of his review of Wordsworth's *The Excursion*: "This will never do!"

A passage in *English Bards and Scotch Reviewers* connects Francis Jeffrey with the notorious seventeenth-century George Jeffreys (1648–1689), the original "Hanging Judge." (The so-called Bloody Assizes of 1685 were held at Dorchester, where today the Wessex Hotel operates the Judge Jeffreys Restaurant.) "Health to immortal Jeffrey!" Byron says, "once in name, / England could boast a judge almost the same."

Jeffrey was generally admired among people with Whig or liberal sympathies. Charles Dickens named his third son Francis Jeffrey Dickens (1844–1886).

The essay here, first published in 1828 in the *Edinburgh Review*, was the lead-in to a review of Edwin Atherstone's *The Fall of Nineveh: A Poem*. Jeffrey, near the end of his editing and reviewing career, was embarking on work in law and politics, at which he was to be very successful. He may have wanted to contribute a valedictory conspectus on his way out (he retired in 1829). Magazines, such as the *Edinburgh Review,* flourished throughout the nineteenth century and were the main outlets of political, literary, and even philosophical thought. They reached a huge audience; Jeffrey's articles were read by as many as 50,000 people. In time, Jeffrey came to be slighted for his extreme partisanship and relative shallowness. But he was eloquent and energetic, and his part in the creation and early development of periodical journalism will guarantee him a place in literary history.

THE STATE OF MODERN POETRY (1828, EXCERPT)

We have been rather in an odd state for some years, we think, both as to Poets and Poetry. Since the death of Lord Byron there has been no king in Israel; and none of his former competitors now seem inclined to push their pretensions to the vacant throne. Scott, and Moore, and Southey, appear to have nearly renounced verse, and finally taken service with the Muses of prose:—Crabbe, and Coleridge, and Wordsworth, we fear, are burnt out:—and Campbell and Rogers repose under their laurels, and, contented each with his own elegant little domain, seem but little disposed either to extend its boundaries, or to add new provinces to their rule. Yet we cannot say either that this indifference may be accounted for by the impoverished state of the kingdom whose sovereignty is thus in abeyance, or that the *interregnum* has as yet given rise to any notable disorders. On the contrary, we do not remember a time when it would have been a prouder distinction to be at the head of English poetry, or when the power which every man has to do what is good in his own eyes, seemed less in danger of being abused. Three poets of great promise have indeed been lost, "in the morn and liquid dew of their youth"—in Kirke White, in Keats, and in Pollok; and a powerful, though more uncertain genius extinguished, less prematurely, in Shelley. Yet there still survive writers of great talents and attraction. The elegance, the tenderness, the feminine sweetness of Felicia Hemans—the classical copiousness of Milman—the facility and graceful fancy of Hunt, though defrauded of half its praise by carelessness and presumption—and, besides many others, the glowing pencil and gorgeous profusion of the author more immediately before us.

There is no want, then, of poetry among us at the present day; nor even of very good and agreeable poetry. But there are no miracles of the art—nothing that marks its descent from "the highest heaven of invention"—nothing visibly destined to inherit immortality. Speaking very generally, we would say, that our poets never showed a better or less narrow taste, or a juster relish of what is truly excellent in the models that lie before them, and yet have seldom been more deficient in the powers of creative genius; or rather, perhaps, that with an unexampled command over the raw materials of poetry, and a true sense of their value, they have rarely been so much wanting in the skill to work them up to advantage—in the power of attaching human interests to sparkling fancies, making splendid descriptions subservient to intelligible purposes, or fixing the fine and fugitive spirit of poetry in some tangible texture of exalted reason or sympathetic emotion. The improvement in all departments is no doubt immense, since the days when Hoole and Hayley were thought great poets. But it is not quite clear to us, that the fervid and florid Romeos of the present day, may not be gathered, in no very long course of years, to the capacious tomb of these same ancient Capulets. They are but shadows, we fear, that have no independent or substantial existence—and though reflected from grand and beautiful originals, have but little chance to maintain their place in the eyes of the many generations by whom those originals will yet be worshipped—but who will probably prefer, each in their turn, shadows of their own creating.

The present age, we think, has an hundred times more poetry, and more true taste for poetry, than that which immediately preceded it,—and of which, reckoning its duration from the extinction of the last of Queen Anne's wits down to about thirty odd years ago, we take leave to say that it was, beyond all dispute, the most unpoetical age in the annals of this or any other considerable nation. Nothing, indeed, can be conceived more dreary and sterile than the aspect of our national poetry from the time of Pope and Thomson, down to that of Burns and Cowper. With the exception of a few cold and scattered lights—Gray, Goldsmith, Warton, Mason, and Johnson—men of sense and eloquence occasionally exercising themselves in poetry out of scholar-like ambition, but not poets in any genuine sense of the word—the whole horizon was dark, silent, and blank; or only presented objects upon which it is now impossible to look seriously without shame. These were the happy days of Pye and Whitehead—of Hoole and of Hayley—and then, throughout the admiring land, resounded the mighty names of Jerningham and Jage, of Edwards, of Murphy, of Moore, and of others whom we cannot but feel it is a baseness to remember.

The first man who broke "the numbing spell" was Cowper,—(for Burns was not generally known till long after,)—and, though less highly gifted than several who came after him, this great praise should always be remembered in his epitaph. He is entitled, in our estimation, to a still greater praise; and that is, to the praise of absolute and entire originality. Whatever he added to the resources of English poetry, was drawn directly from the fountains of his own genius, or the stores of his own observation. He was a copyist of no style—a restorer of no style; and did not, like the eminent men who succeeded him, merely recall the age to the treasures it had almost forgotten, open up anew a vein that had been long buried in rubbish, or revive a strain which had already delighted the ears of a more aspiring generation. That this, however, was the case with the poets who immediately followed, cannot, we think, be reasonably doubted; and the mere statement of the fact, seems to us sufficiently to explain the present state of our poetry—its strength and its weakness—its good taste and its deficient power—its resemblance to works that can never die—and its own obvious liability to the accidents of mortality.

It has advanced beyond the preceding age, simply by going back to one still older; and has put *its* poverty to shame only by unlocking the hoards of a remoter ancestor. It has reformed merely by restoring; and innovated by a systematic recurrence to the models of antiquity. Scott went back as far as to the Romances of Chivalry: and the poets of the lakes to the humbler and more pathetic simplicity of our early ballads; and both, and all who have since adventured in poetry, have drawn, without measure or disguise, from the living springs of Shakespeare and Spenser, and the other immortal writers who adorned the glorious era of Elizabeth and James.

It is impossible to value more highly than we do the benefits of this restoration. It is a great thing to have rendered the public once more familiar with these mighty geniuses—and, if we must be copyists, there is nothing certainly that deserves so well to be copied. The consequence, accordingly, has been, that, even in our least inspired writers, we can again reckon upon freedom and variety of style, some sparks of fancy, some traits of nature, and some echo, however feeble, of that sweet melody of rhythm and of diction, which must linger for ever in every ear which has once drank in the music of Shakespeare; while, in authors of greater vigour, we are sure to meet also with gorgeous descriptions and splendid imagery, tender sentiments expressed in simple words, and vehement passions pouring themselves out in fearless and eloquent declamation.

But with all this, it is but too true that we have still a feeling that we are glorying but in secondhand finery and counterfeit inspiration; and that the poets of the present day, though they have not only Taste enough to admire, but skill also to imitate, the great masters of an earlier generation, have not inherited the Genius that could have enabled them either to have written as they wrote, or even to have come up, without their example, to the level of their own imitations. The heroes of our modern poetry, indeed, are little better, as we take it, than the heroes of the modern theatres—attired, no doubt, in the exact costume of the persons they represent, and wielding their gorgeous antique arms with an exact imitation of heroic movements and deportment—nay, even evincing in their tones and gestures, a full sense of inward nobleness and dignity—and yet palpably unfit to engage in any feat of actual prowess, and incapable, in their own persons, even of conceiving what they have been so well taught to personate. We feel, in short, that our modern poetry is substantially derivative, and, as geologists say of our present earth, of secondary formation— made up of the *debris* of a former world, and composed, in its loftiest and most solid parts, of the fragments of things far more lofty and solid.

The consequence, accordingly, is, that we have abundance of admirable descriptions, ingenious similitudes, and elaborate imitations—but little invention, little direct or overwhelming passion, and little natural simplicity. On the contrary, every thing almost now resolves into description,—descriptions not only of actions and external objects, but of characters, and emotions, and the signs and accompaniments of emotion—and all given at full length, ostentatious, elaborate, and highly finished, even in their counterfeit carelessness and disorder. But no sudden unconscious bursts, either of nature or of passion—no casual flashes of fancy, no slight passing intimations of deep but latent emotions, no rash darings of untutored genius, soaring proudly up into the infinite unknown! The chief fault, however, is the want of subject and of matter—the absence of real persons, intelligible interests, and conceivable incidents, to which all this splendid apparatus of rhetoric and fancy may attach itself, and thus get a purpose and a meaning, which it never can possess without them. To satisfy a rational being, even in his most sensitive mood, we require not only a just representation of passion in the abstract, but also that it shall be embodied in some individual person whom we can understand and sympathize with— and cannot long be persuaded to admire splendid images and ingenious allusions which bear upon no comprehensible object, and seem to be introduced for no other purpose than to be admired.

Without going the full length of the mathematician, who could see no beauty in poetry because it *proved* nothing, we cannot think it quite unreasonable to insist on knowing a little what it is about; and must be permitted to hold it a good objection to the very finest composition, that it gives us no distinct conceptions, either of character, of action, of passion, or of the author's design in laying it before us. Now this, we think, is undeniably the prevailing fault of our modern poets. What they do best is description—in a story certainly they do not excel—their pathos is too often overstrained and rhetorical, and their reflections mystical and bombastic. The great want, however, as we have already said, is the want of solid subject, and of persons who can be supposed to have existed. There is plenty of splendid drapery and magnificent localities—but nobody to put on the one, or to inhabit and vivify the other. Instead of living persons, we have commonly little else than mere puppets or academy figures—and very frequently are obliged to be contented with scenes of still life altogether—with gorgeous dresses tossed into glittering heaps, or suspended in dazzling files—and enchanted solitudes, where we wait in vain for some beings like ourselves, to animate its beauties with their loves, or to aggravate its horrors by their contentions.

The consequence of all this is, that modern poems, with great beauty of diction, much excellent description, and very considerable displays of taste and imagination, are generally languid, obscure, and tiresome. Short pieces, however, it should be admitted, are frequently very delightful—elegant in composition, sweet and touching in sentiment, and just and felicitous in expressing the most delicate shades both of character and emotion. Where a single scene, thought, or person, is to be represented, the improved taste of the age, and its general familiarity with beautiful poetry, will generally ensure, from our better artists, not only a creditable, but a very excellent production. What used to be true of *female* poets only, is now true of all. We have not wings, it would seem, for a long flight—and the larger works of those who pleased us most with their small ones, scarcely ever fail of exhibiting the very defects from which we should have thought them most secure—and turn out insipid, verbose, and artificial, like their neighbours. In little poems, in short, which do not require any choice or management of subject, we succeed very well; but where a story is to be told, and an interest to be sustained, through a considerable train of incidents and variety of characters, our want of vigour and originality is but too apt to become apparent; and is only the more conspicuous from our skilful and familiar use of that inspired diction, and those poetical materials which we have derived from the mighty masters to whose vigour and originality they were subservient, and on whose genius they waited but as "servile ministers."

16

WILLIAM HAZLITT (1778–1830)

Hazlitt packed an extraordinary amount of work into his fifty-two years. He was accomplished enough as a painter to have his portrait of his father exhibited at the Royal Academy, and he later painted a portrait of Charles Lamb. Hazlitt was a gifted historian; he wrote a *Life of Napoleon* not long after Napoleon's death in 1821. He was conversant with all the subtleties of political and philosophical discourse at a time when such matters were dramatically in play all across Europe. He was a brilliant reader of books and watcher of plays, and he also made it his business to meet important writers, including Coleridge, Wordsworth, and Shelley, about whom he wrote with sympathy and verve.

Hazlitt summed up much of his own writing as "the thoughts of a metaphysician expressed by a painter"—which is to say, in effect, that he took advantage of the great fashion in periodical journalism that began in the eighteenth century and continued into the early twentieth century. In Hazlitt's day there were many more periodicals—daily, weekly, monthly, quarterly—than there are in the twenty-first century, and those periodicals had a more important function in the worlds of art and politics than any comparable publication today. Byron's adolescent *English Bards and Scotch Reviewers* was provoked by an unenthusiastic notice in *The Edinburgh Review*; when Shelley attributed Keats's death to the effects of a review, Byron mockingly supplied:

Who killed John Keats?
I, says the Quarterly
So savage & Tartarly
'Twas one of my feats . . . .

And Hazlitt was in the thick of it, producing essays, reviews, notes, biograph-
ical sketches, and features on any topic—he wrote about prizefighters and jug-
glers and dandies with equal fluency. Remembering his days as a painter,
Hazlitt was as subtle a critic of the graphic arts as of the literary. "Some artists
among ourselves," he wrote in 1816, "have carried the same principle [technical
difficulty] to a singular excess." He added a note on J. M. W. Turner (1775–
1851), who was only three years his senior and by no means widely recognized:
"We here allude particularly to Turner, the ablest landscape painter now living,
whose pictures are, however, too much abstractions of aerial perspective, and
representations not so properly of the objects of nature as of the medium
through which they are seen. They are the triumph of the knowledge of the
artist, and of the power of the pencil over the barrenness of the subject. They
are pictures of the elements of air, earth, and water. The artist delights to go
back to the first chaos of the world, or to that state of things when the waters
were separated from the dry land, and light from darkness, but as yet no living
thing nor tree bearing fruit was seen upon the face of the earth. All is 'without
form and void.' Some one said of his landscapes that they were *pictures of
nothing, and very like.*"

That account is as profound as it is humorous. And it came before Turner's
greatest period, which would have obliged Hazlitt to add Fire among the elements; it came before Ruskin was even born.

Poetry, then, is an imitation of nature, but the imagination and the passions are a part of man's nature. We shape things according to our wishes and fancies, without poetry; but poetry is the most emphatical language that can be found for those creations of the mind "which ecstasy is very cunning in." Neither a mere description of natural objects, nor a mere delineation of natural feelings, however distinct or forcible, constitutes the ultimate end and aim of poetry, without the heightenings of the imagination. The light of poetry is not only a direct but also a reflected light, that, while it shows us the object, throws a sparkling radiance on all around it: the flame of the passions, communicated to the imagination, reveals to us, as with a flash of lightning, the inmost recesses of thought, and penetrates our whole being. Poetry represents forms chiefly as they suggest other forms; feelings, as they suggest forms or other feelings. Poetry puts a spirit of life and motion into the universe. It describes the flowing, not the fixed. It does not define the limits of sense, or analyze the distinctions of the understanding, but signifies the excess of the imagination beyond the actual or ordinary impression of any object or feeling. The poetical impression of any object is that uneasy, exquisite sense of beauty or power that cannot be contained within itself; that is impatient of all limit; that (as flame bends to flame) strives to link itself to some other image of kindred beauty or grandeur; to enshrine itself, as it were, in the highest forms of fancy, and to relieve the aching sense of pleasure by expressing it in the boldest manner, and by the most striking examples of the same quality in other instances. Poetry, according to Lord Bacon, for this reason, "has something divine in it, because it raises the mind and hurries it into sublimity, by conforming the shows of things to the desires of the soul, instead of subjecting the soul to external things, as reason and history do." It is strictly the language of the imagination; and the imagination is that faculty which represents objects, not as they are in themselves, but as they are moulded by other thoughts and feelings, into an infinite variety of shapes and combinations of power. This language is not the less true to nature, because it is false in point of fact; but so much the more true and natural, if it conveys the impression which the object under the influence of passion makes on the mind. Let an object, for instance, be presented to the senses in a state of agitation or fear—and the imagination will distort or magnify the object, and convert it into the likeness of whatever is most proper to encourage the fear. "Our eyes are made the fools" of our other faculties. This is the universal law of the imagination,

> That if it would but apprehend some joy,
> It comprehends some bringer of that joy;
> Or in the night, imagining some fear,
> How easy is a bush suppos'd a bear!

When Iachimo says of Imogen,

> The flame o' th' taper
> Bows toward her, and would under-peep her lids
> To see the enclosed lights,

this passionate interpretation of the motion of the flame to accord with the speaker's own feelings, is true poetry. The lover, equally with the poet, speaks of the auburn tresses of his mistress as locks of shining gold. We compare a man of gigantic stature to a tower: not that he is anything like so large, but because the excess of his size beyond what we are accustomed to expect, or the usual size of things of the same class, produces by contrast a greater feeling of magnitude and ponderous strength than another object of ten times the same dimensions. The intensity of the feeling makes up for the disproportion of the objects. Things are equal, to the imagination, which have the power of affecting the mind with an equal degree of terror, admiration, delight, or love. When Lear calls upon the heavens to avenge his cause, "for they are old like him," there is nothing extravagant or impious in this sublime identification of his age with theirs; for there is no other image which could do justice to the agonizing sense of his wrongs and his despair!

17

THOMAS LOVE PEACOCK (1785–1866)

Peacock, a brilliant wit, revived a classical model of criticism in several works wherein a typical group of people gather to eat and talk (along the lines of Plato's *Symposium*). *Headlong Hall* (1816) presents an optimist, a pessimist, a glutton, and so forth. *Melincourt* (1817) makes fun of literary personages: Southey (Mr. Feathernest), Coleridge (Mr. Mystic), Wordsworth (Mr. Paperstamp), and others. The fun continues in *Nightmare Abbey* (1818), with a caricature of Coleridge again (Mr. Flosky), Byron (Mr. Cypress), and Shelley (Scythrop Glowry). *Crotchet Castle* (1831) travesties Coleridge one more time (Mr. Skionar) along with a medievalist named Chainmail. Peacock continued to write such satires for many more years; *Gryll Grange* appeared in 1861. Peacock's chief descendant in such satires was Aldous Huxley, notably in *Crome Yellow* (1921).

Peacock's essay "The Four Ages of Poetry" (1820) provoked Shelley (who was a friend) to write his "Defense of Poetry."

THE FOUR AGES OF POETRY (1820, EXCERPT)

Adapted from Peacock's *Four Ages of Poetry, Shelley's Defence of Poetry, Browning's Essay on Shelley*, ed. H. F. B. Brett-Smith, 2nd ed. (Oxford: Basil Blackwell, 1923).

> *Qui inter hæc nutriuntur non magis sapere possunt, quam*
> *bene olere qui in culinâ habitant.*
>
> [Those so trained (in schools of rhetoric) can no more
> acquire good taste those who live in a kitchen can smell
> good—ed.]
>
> Petronius

Poetry, like the world, may be said to have four ages, but in a different order: the first age of poetry being the age of iron; the second, of gold; the third, of silver; and the fourth, of brass.

The first, or iron age of poetry, is that in which rude bards celebrate in rough numbers the exploits of ruder chiefs, in days when every man is a warrior, and when the great practical maxim of every form of society, "to keep what we have and to catch what we can," is not yet disguised under names of justice and forms of law, but is the naked motto of the naked sword, which is the only judge and jury in every question of *meum* and *tuum* ["mine" and "yours"—ed.]. In these days, the only three trades flourishing (besides that of priest which flourishes always) are those of king, thief, and beggar: the beggar being for the most part a king deject, and the thief a king expectant. The first question asked of a stranger is, whether he is a beggar or a thief [See the *Odyssey*, passim: and Thucydides, I. 5—ed.]: the stranger, in reply, usually assumes the first, and awaits a convenient opportunity to prove his claim to the second appellation.

The natural desire of every man to engross to himself as much power and property as he can acquire by any of the means which might makes right, is accompanied by the no less natural desire of making known to as many people as possible the extent to which he has been a winner in this universal game. The successful warrior becomes a chief; the successful chief becomes a king: his next want is an organ to disseminate the fame of his achievements and the extent of his possessions; and this organ he finds in a bard, who is always ready to celebrate the strength of his arm, being first duly inspired by that of his liquor. This is the origin of poetry, which, like all other trades, takes its rise in the demand for the commodity, and flourishes in proportion to the extent of the market.

Poetry is thus in its origin panegyrical. The first rude songs of all nations appear to be a sort of brief historical notices, in a strain of tumid hyperbole, of the exploits and possessions of a few pre-eminent individuals. They tell us how many battles such an one has fought, how many helmets he has cleft, how many breastplates he has pierced, how many widows he has made, how much land he has appropriated, how many houses he has demolished for other people, what a large one he has built for himself, how much gold he has stowed away in it, and how liberally and plentifully he pays, feeds, and intoxicates the divine and immortal bards, the sons of Jupiter, but for whose everlasting songs the names of heroes would perish.

This is the first stage of poetry before the invention of written letters. The numerical modulation is at once useful as a help to memory, and pleasant to the ears of uncultured men, who are easily caught by sound: and from the exceeding flexibility of the yet unformed language, the poet does no violence to his ideas in subjecting them to the fetters of number. The savage indeed lisps in numbers, and all rude and uncivilized people express themselves in the manner which we call poetical.

The scenery by which he is surrounded, and the superstitions which are the creed of his age, form the poet's mind. Rocks, mountains, seas, unsubdued forests, unnavigable rivers, surround him with forms of power and mystery, which ignorance and fear have peopled with spirits, under multifarious names of gods, goddesses, nymphs, genii, and dæmons. Of all these personages marvellous tales are in existence: the nymphs are not indifferent to handsome young men, and the gentlemen-genii are much troubled and very troublesome with a propensity to be rude to pretty maidens: the bard therefore finds no difficulty in tracing the genealogy of his chief to any of the deities in his neighbourhood with whom the said chief may be most desirous of claiming relationship.

In this pursuit, as in all others, some of course will attain a very marked pre-eminence; and these will be held in high honour, like Demodocus in the *Odyssey*, and will be consequently inflated with boundless vanity, like Thamyris in the *Iliad*. Poets are as yet the only historians and chroniclers of their time, and the sole depositories of all the knowledge of their age; and though this knowledge is rather a crude congeries of traditional phantasies than a collection of useful truths, yet, such as it is, they have it to themselves. They are observing and thinking, while others are robbing and fighting: and though their object be nothing more than to secure a share of the spoil, yet they accomplish this end by intellectual, not by physical, power: their success excites emulation to the attainment of intellectual eminence: thus they sharpen their own wits and awaken those of others, at the same time that they gratify vanity and amuse curiosity. A skilful display of the little knowledge they have gains them credit for the possession of much more which they have not. Their familiarity with the secret history of gods and genii obtains for them, without much difficulty, the reputation of inspiration; thus they are not only historians but theologians, moralists, and legislators: delivering their oracles *ex cathedrâ*, and being indeed often themselves (as Orpheus and Amphion) regarded as portions and emana-tions of divinity: building cities with a song, and leading brutes with a sym-phony; which are only metaphors for the faculty of leading multitudes by the nose.

The golden age of poetry finds its materials in the age of iron. This age begins when poetry begins to be retrospective; when something like a more extended system of civil polity is established; when personal strength and cour-age avail less to the aggrandizing of their possessor and to the making and marring of kings and kingdoms, and are checked by organized bodies, social institutions, and hereditary successions. Men also live more in the light of truth and within the interchange of observation; and thus perceive that the agency of gods and genii is not so frequent among themselves as, to judge from the songs and legends of the past time, it was among their ancestors. From these two circumstances, really diminished personal power, and apparently dimin-ished familiarity with gods and genii, they very easily and naturally deduce two conclusions: 1st, That men are degenerated, and 2nd, That they are less in favour with the gods. The people of the petty states and colonies, which have now acquired stability and form, which owed their origin and first prosperity to the talents and courage of a single chief, magnify their founder through the mists of distance and tradition, and perceive him achieving wonders with a god or goddess always at his elbow. They find his name and his exploits thus mag-nified and accompanied in their traditionary songs, which are their only memorials. All that is said of him is in this character. There is nothing to contradict it. The man and his exploits and his tutelary deities are mixed and blended in one invariable association. The marvellous too is very much like a snowball: it grows as it rolls downward, till the little nucleus of truth which began its descent from the summit is hidden in the accumulation of superinduced hyperbole.

When tradition, thus adorned and exaggerated, has surrounded the founders of families and states with so much adventitious power and magnificence, there is no praise which a living poet can, without fear of being kicked for clumsy flattery, address to a living chief, that will not still leave the impression that the latter is not so great a man as his ancestors. The man must in this case be praised through his ancestors. Their greatness must be established, and he must be shown to be their worthy descendant. All the people of a state are interested in the founder of their state. All states that have harmonized into a common form of society, are interested in their respective founders. All men are interested in their ancestors. All men love to look back into the days that are past. In these circumstances traditional national poetry is reconstructed and brought like chaos into order and form. The interest is more universal: understanding is enlarged: passion still has scope and play: character is still various and strong: nature is still unsubdued and existing in all her beauty and magnificence, and men are not yet excluded from her observation by the magnitude of cities or the daily confinement of civic life: poetry is more an art: it requires greater skill in numbers, greater command of language, more extensive and various knowledge, and greater comprehensiveness of mind. It still exists without rivals in any other department of literature; and even the arts, painting and sculpture certainly, and music probably, are comparatively rude and imperfect. The whole field of intellect is its own. It has no rivals in history, nor in philosophy, nor in science. It is cultivated by the greatest intellects of the age, and listened to by all the rest. This is the age of Homer, the golden age of poetry. Poetry has now attained its perfection: it has attained the point which it cannot pass: genius therefore seeks new forms for the treatment of the same subjects: hence the lyric poetry of Pindar and Alcæus, and the tragic poetry of Æschylus and Sophocles. The favour of kings, the honour of the Olympic crown, the applause of present multitudes, all that can feed vanity and stimulate rivalry, await the successful cultivator of this art, till its forms become exhausted, and new rivals arise around it in new fields of literature, which gradually acquire more influence as, with the progress of reason and civilization, facts become more interesting than fiction: indeed the maturity of poetry may be considered the infancy of history. The transition from Homer to Herodotus is scarcely more remarkable than that from Herodotus to Thucydides: in the gradual dereliction of fabulous incident and ornamented language, Herodotus is as much a poet in relation to Thucydides as Homer is in relation to Herodotus. The history of Herodotus is half a poem: it was written while the whole field of literature yet belonged to the Muses, and the nine books of which it was composed were therefore of right, as well as of courtesy, superinscribed with their nine names.

Speculations, too, and disputes, on the nature of man and of mind; on moral duties and on good and evil; on the animate and inanimate components of the visible world; begin to share attention with the eggs of Leda and the horns of Io, and to draw off from poetry a portion of its once undivided audience.

Then comes the silver age, or the poetry of civilized life. This poetry is of two kinds, imitative and original. The imitative consists in recasting, and giving an exquisite polish to, the poetry of the age of gold: of this Virgil is the most obvious and striking example. The original is chiefly comic, didactic, or satiric: as in Menander, Aristophanes, Horace, and Juvenal. The poetry of this age is characterized by an exquisite and fastidious selection of words, and a laboured and somewhat monotonous harmony of expression: but its monotony consists in this, that experience having exhausted all the varieties of modulation, the civilized poetry selects the most beautiful, and prefers the repetition of these to ranging through the variety of all. But the best expression being that into which the idea naturally falls, it requires the utmost labour and care so to reconcile the inflexibility of civilized language and the laboured polish of versification with the idea intended to be expressed, that sense may not appear to be sacrificed to sound. Hence numerous efforts and rare success.

This state of poetry is however a step towards its extinction. Feeling and passion are best painted in, and roused by, ornamental and figurative language; but the reason and the understanding are best addressed in the simplest and most unvarnished phrase. Pure reason and dispassionate truth would be perfectly ridiculous in verse, as we may judge by versifying one of Euclid's demonstrations. This will be found true of all dispassionate reasoning whatever, and all reasoning that requires comprehensive views and enlarged combinations. It is only the more tangible points of morality, those which command assent at once, those which have a mirror in every mind, and in which the severity of reason is warmed and rendered palatable by being mixed up with feeling and imagination, that are applicable even to what is called moral poetry: and as the sciences of morals and of mind advance towards perfection, as they become more enlarged and comprehensive in their views, as reason gains the ascendancy in them over imagination and feeling, poetry can no longer accompany them in their progress, but drops into the back ground, and leaves them to advance alone.

Thus the empire of thought is withdrawn from poetry, as the empire of facts had been before. In respect of the latter, the poet of the age of iron celebrates the achievements of his contemporaries; the poet of the age of gold celebrates the heroes of the age of iron; the poet of the age of silver re-casts the poems of the age of gold: we may here see how very slight a ray of historical truth is sufficient to dissipate all the illusions of poetry. We know no more of the men than of the gods of the Iliad; no more of Achilles than we do of Thetis; no more of Hector and Andromache than we do of Vulcan and Venus: these belong altogether to poetry; history has no share in them: but Virgil knew better than to write an epic about Cæsar; he left him to Livy; and travelled out of the confines of truth and history into the old regions of poetry and fiction.

Good sense and elegant learning, conveyed in polished and somewhat monotonous verse, are the perfection of the original and imitative poetry of civilized life. Its range is limited, and when exhausted, nothing remains but the *crambe repetita* [warmed-over cabbage—from Juvenal's *Satires*, VII—ed.] of common-place, which at length becomes thoroughly wearisome, even to the most indefatigable readers of the newest new nothings.

It is now evident that poetry must either cease to be cultivated, or strike into a new path. The poets of the age of gold have been imitated and repeated till no new imitation will attract notice: the limited range of ethical and didactic poetry is exhausted: the associations of daily life in an advanced state of society are of very dry, methodical, unpoetical matters-of-fact: but there is always a multitude of listless idlers, yawning for amusement, and gaping for novelty: and the poet makes it his glory to be foremost among their purveyors.

Then comes the age of brass, which, by rejecting the polish and the learning of the age of silver, and taking a retrograde stride to the barbarisms and crude traditions of the age of iron, professes to return to nature and revive the age of gold. This is the second childhood of poetry. To the comprehensive energy of the Homeric Muse, which, by giving at once the grand outline of things, presented to the mind a vivid picture in one or two verses, inimitable alike in simplicity and magnificence, is substituted a verbose and minutely-detailed description of thoughts, passions, actions, persons, and things, in that loose rambling style of verse, which any one may write, *stans pede in uno* [while standing on one foot—from Horace's *Satires*, I, 4—ed.], at the rate of two hundred lines in an hour. To this age may be referred all the poets who flourished in the decline of the Roman Empire. The best specimen of it, though not the most generally known, is the Dionysiaca of Nonnus, which contains many passages of exceeding beauty in the midst of masses of amplification and repetition.

The iron age of classical poetry may be called the bardic; the golden, the Homeric; the silver, the Virgilian; and the brass, the Nonnic.

Modern poetry has also its four ages: but "it wears its rue with a difference."

To the age of brass in the ancient world succeeded the dark ages, in which the light of the Gospel began to spread over Europe, and in which, by a mysterious and inscrutable dispensation, the darkness thickened with the progress of the light. The tribes that overran the Roman Empire brought back the days of barbarism, but with this difference, that there were many books in the world, many places in which they were preserved, and occasionally some one by whom they were read, who indeed (if he escaped being burned *pour l'amour de Dieu* [for the love of God—ed.]) generally lived an object of mysterious fear, with the reputation of magician, alchymist, and astrologer. The emerging of the nations of Europe from this superinduced barbarism, and their settling into new forms of polity, was accompanied, as the first ages of Greece had been, with a wild spirit of adventure, which, co-operating with new manners and new superstitions, raised up a fresh crop of chimæras, not less fruitful, though far less beautiful, than those of Greece. The semi- deification of women by the maxims of the age of chivalry, combining with these new fables, produced the romance of the middle ages. The founders of the new line of heroes took the place of the demi-gods of Grecian poetry. Charlemagne and his Paladins, Arthur and his knights of the round table, the heroes of the iron age of chivalrous poetry, were seen through the same magnifying mist of distance, and their exploits were celebrated with even more extravagant hyperbole. These legends, combined with the exaggerated love that pervades the songs of the troubadours, the reputation of magic that attached to learned men, the infant wonders of natural philosophy, the crazy fanaticism of the crusades, the power and privileges of the great feudal chiefs, and the holy mysteries of monks and nuns, formed a state of society in which no two laymen could meet without fighting, and in which the three staple ingredients of lover, prize-fighter, and fanatic, that composed the basis of the character of every true man, were mixed up and diversified, in different individuals and classes, with so many distinctive excellencies, and under such an infinite motley variety of costume, as gave the range of a most extensive and picturesque field to the two great constituents of poetry, love and battle.

From these ingredients of the iron age of modern poetry, dispersed in the rhymes of minstrels and the songs of the troubadours, arose the golden age, in which the scattered materials were harmonized and blended about the time of the revival of learning; but with this peculiar difference, that Greek and Roman literature pervaded all the poetry of the golden age of modern poetry, and hence resulted a heterogeneous compound of all ages and nations in one picture; an infinite licence, which gave to the poet the free range of the whole field of imagination and memory. This was carried very far by Ariosto, but farthest of all by Shakespeare and his contemporaries, who used time and locality merely because they could not do without them, because every action must have its when and where: but they made no scruple of deposing a Roman Emperor by an Italian Count, and sending him off in the disguise of a French pilgrim to be shot with a blunderbuss by an English archer. This makes the old English drama very picturesque, at any rate, in the variety of costume, and very diversified in action and character; though it is a picture of nothing that ever was seen on earth except a Venetian carnival.

The greatest of English poets, Milton, may be said to stand alone between the ages of gold and silver, combining the excellencies of both; for with all the energy, and power, and freshness of the first, he united all the studied and elaborate magnificence of the second.

The silver age succeeded; beginning with Dryden, coming to perfection with Pope, and ending with Goldsmith, Collins, and Gray.

Cowper divested verse of its exquisite polish; he thought in metre, but paid more attention to his thoughts than his verse. It would be difficult to draw the boundary of prose and blank verse between his letters and his poetry.

The silver age was the reign of authority; but authority now began to be shaken, not only in poetry but in the whole sphere of its dominion. The contemporaries of Gray and Cowper were deep and elaborate thinkers. The subtle scepticism of Hume, the solemn irony of Gibbon, the daring paradoxes of Rousseau, and the biting ridicule of Voltaire, directed the energies of four extraordinary minds to shake every portion of the reign of authority. Enquiry was roused, the activity of intellect was excited, and poetry came in for its share of the general result. The changes had been rung on lovely maid and sylvan shade, summer heat and green retreat, waving trees and sighing breeze, gentle swains and amorous pains, by versifiers who took them on trust, as meaning something very soft and tender, without much caring what: but with this general activity of intellect came a necessity for even poets to appear to know something of what they professed to talk of. Thomson and Cowper looked at the trees and hills which so many ingenious gentlemen had rhymed about so long without looking at them at all, and the effect of the operation on poetry was like the discovery of a new world. Painting shared the influence, and the principles of picturesque beauty were explored by adventurous essayists with indefatigable pertinacity. The success which attended these experiments, and the pleasure which resulted from them, had the usual effect of all new enthusiasms, that of turning the heads of a few unfortunate persons, the patriarchs of the age of brass, who, mistaking the prominent novelty for the all-important totality, seem to have ratiocinated much in the following manner: "Poetical genius is the finest of all things, and we feel that we have more of it than any one ever had. The way to bring it to perfection is to cultivate poetical impressions exclusively. Poetical impressions can be received only among natural scenes: for all that is artificial is anti-poetical. Society is artificial, therefore we will live out of society. The mountains are natural, therefore we will live in the mountains. There we shall be shining models of purity and virtue, passing the whole day in the innocent and amiable occupation of going up and down hill, receiving poetical impressions, and communicating them in immortal verse to admiring generations." To some such perversion of intellect we owe that egregious confraternity of rhymesters, known by the name of the Lake Poets; who certainly did receive and communicate to the world some of the most extraordinary poetical impressions that ever were heard of, and ripened into models of public virtue, too splendid to need illustration. They wrote verses on a new principle; saw rocks and rivers in a new light; and remaining studiously ignorant of history, society, and human nature, cultivated the phantasy only at the expence of the memory and the reason; and contrived, though they had retreated from the world for the express purpose of seeing nature as she was, to see her only as she was not, converting the land they lived in into a sort of fairy-land, which they peopled with mysticisms and chimæras. This gave what is called a new tone to poetry, and conjured up a herd of desperate imitators, who have brought the age of brass prematurely to its dotage.

The descriptive poetry of the present day has been called by its cultivators a return to nature. Nothing is more impertinent than this pretension. Poetry cannot travel out of the regions of its birth, the uncultivated lands of semi-civilized men. Mr. Wordsworth, the great leader of the returners to nature, cannot describe a scene under his own eyes without putting into it the shadow of a Danish boy or the living ghost of Lucy Gray, or some similar phantastical parturition of the moods of his own mind.

In the origin and perfection of poetry, all the associations of life were composed of poetical materials. With us it is decidedly the reverse. We know too that there are no Dryads in Hyde-park nor Naiads in the Regent's-canal. But barbaric manners and supernatural interventions are essential to poetry. Either in the scene, or in the time, or in both, it must be remote from our ordinary perceptions. While the historian and the philosopher are advancing in, and accelerating, the progress of knowledge, the poet is wallowing in the rubbish of departed ignorance, and raking up the ashes of dead savages to find gewgaws and rattles for the grown babies of the age. Mr. Scott digs up the poachers and cattle-stealers of the ancient border. Lord Byron cruises for thieves and pirates on the shores of the Morea and among the Greek Islands. Mr. Southey wades through ponderous volumes of travels and old chronicles, from which he carefully selects all that is false, useless, and absurd, as being essentially poetical; and when he has a commonplace book full of monstrosities, strings them into an epic. Mr. Wordsworth picks up village legends from old women and sextons; and Mr. Coleridge, to the valuable information acquired from similar sources, superadds the dreams of crazy theologians and the mysticisms of German metaphysics, and favours the world with visions in verse, in which the quadruple elements of sexton, old woman, Jeremy Taylor, and Emanuel Kant, are harmonized into a delicious poetical compound. Mr. Moore presents us with a Persian, and Mr. Campbell with a Pennsylvanian tale, both formed on the same principle as Mr. Southey's epics, by extracting from a perfunctory and desultory perusal of a collection of voyages and travels, all that useful investigation would not seek for and that common sense would reject.

These disjointed relics of tradition and fragments of second-hand observation, being woven into a tissue of verse, constructed on what Mr. Coleridge calls a new principle (that is, no principle at all), compose a modern-antique compound of frippery and barbarism, in which the puling sentimentality of the present time is grafted on the misrepresented ruggedness of the past into a heterogeneous congeries of unamalgamating manners, sufficient to impose on the common readers of poetry, over whose understandings the poet of this class possesses that commanding advantage, which, in all circumstances and conditions of life, a man who knows something, however little, always possesses over one who knows nothing.

A poet in our times is a semi-barbarian in a civilized community. He lives in the days that are past. His ideas, thoughts, feelings, associations, are all with barbarous manners, obsolete customs, and exploded superstitions. The march of his intellect is like that of a crab, backward. The brighter the light diffused around him by the progress of reason, the thicker is the darkness of antiquated barbarism, in which he buries himself like a mole, to throw up the barren hillocks of his Cimmerian labours. The philosophic mental tranquillity which looks round with an equal eye on all external things, collects a store of ideas, discriminates their relative value, assigns to all their proper place, and from the materials of useful knowledge thus collected, appreciated, and arranged, forms new combinations that impress the stamp of their power and utility on the real business of life, is diametrically the reverse of that frame of mind which poetry inspires, or from which poetry can emanate. The highest inspirations of poetry are resolvable into three ingredients: the rant of unregulated passion, the whining of exaggerated feeling, and the cant of factitious sentiment: and can therefore serve only to ripen a splendid lunatic like Alexander, a puling driveller like Werter, or a morbid dreamer like Wordsworth. It can never make a philosopher, nor a statesman, nor in any class of life an useful or rational man. It cannot claim the slightest share in any one of the comforts and utilities of life of which we have witnessed so many and so rapid advances. But though not useful, it may be said it is highly ornamental, and deserves to be cultivated for the pleasure it yields. Even if this be granted, it does not follow that a writer of poetry in the present state of society is not a waster of his own time, and a robber of that of others. Poetry is not one of those arts which, like painting, require repetition and multiplication, in order to be diffused among society. There are more good poems already existing than are sufficient to employ that portion of life which any mere reader and recipient of poetical impressions should devote to them, and these having been produced in poetical times, are far superior in all the characteristics of poetry to the artificial reconstructions of a few morbid ascetics in unpoetical times. To read the promiscuous rubbish of the present time to the exclusion of the select treasures of the past, is to substitute the worse for the better variety of the same mode of enjoyment.

But in whatever degree poetry is cultivated, it must necessarily be to the neglect of some branch of useful study: and it is a lamentable spectacle to see minds, capable of better things, running to seed in the specious indolence of these empty aimless mockeries of intellectual exertion. Poetry was the mental rattle that awakened the attention of intellect in the infancy of civil society: but for the maturity of mind to make a serious business of the playthings of its childhood, is as absurd as for a full-grown man to rub his gums with coral, and cry to be charmed to sleep by the jingle of silver bells.

As to that small portion of our contemporary poetry, which is neither descriptive, nor narrative, nor dramatic, and which, for want of a better name, may be called ethical, the most distinguished portion of it, consisting merely of querulous, egotistical rhapsodies, to express the writer's high dissatisfaction with the world and every thing in it, serves only to confirm what has been said of the semibarbarous character of poets, who from singing dithyrambics and "Io Triumphe," while society was savage, grow rabid, and out of their element, as it becomes polished and enlightened.

Now when we consider that it is not the thinking and studious, and scientific and philosophical part of the community, not to those whose minds are bent on the pursuit and promotion of permanently useful ends and aims, that poets must address their minstrelsy, but to that much larger portion of the reading public, whose minds are not awakened to the desire of valuable knowledge, and who are indifferent to any thing beyond being charmed, moved, excited, affected, and exalted: charmed by harmony, moved by sentiment, excited by passion, affected by pathos, and exalted by sublimity: harmony, which is language on the rack of Procrustes; sentiment, which is canting egotism in the mask of refined feeling; passion, which is the commotion of a weak and selfish mind; pathos, which is the whining of an unmanly spirit; and sublimity, which is the inflation of an empty head: when we consider that the great and permanent interests of human society become more and more the main spring of intellectual pursuit; that in proportion as they become so, the subordinacy of the ornamental to the useful will be more and more seen and acknowledged; and that therefore the progress of useful art and science, and of moral and political knowledge, will continue more and more to withdraw attention from frivolous and unconducive, to solid and conducive studies: that therefore the poetical audience will not only continually diminish in the proportion of its number to that of the rest of the reading public, but will also sink lower and lower in the comparison of intellectual acquirement: when we consider that the poet must still please his audience, and must therefore continue to sink to their level, while the rest of the community is rising above it: we may easily conceive that the day is not distant, when the degraded state of every species of poetry will be as generally recognized as that of dramatic poetry has long been: and this not from any decrease either of intellectual power, or intellectual acquisition, but because intellectual power and intellectual acquisition have turned themselves into other and better channels, and have abandoned the cultivation and the fate of poetry to the degenerate fry of modern rhymesters, and their olympic judges, the magazine critics, who continue to debate and promulgate oracles about poetry, as if it were still what it was in the Homeric age, the all-in-all of intellectual progression, and as if there were no such things in existence as mathematicians, astronomers, chemists, moralists, metaphysicians, historians, politicians, and political economists, who have built into the upper air of intelligence a pyramid, from the summit of which they see the modern Parnassus far beneath them, and, knowing how small a place it occupies in the comprehensiveness of their prospect, smile at the little ambition and the circumscribed perceptions with which the drivellers and mountebanks upon it are contending for the poetical palm and the critical chair.

18

GEORGE GORDON, LORD BYRON (1788–1824)

Lord Byron still shines among the great Romantic writers who flourished during the first quarter of the nineteenth century—maybe more for his personality than for his poetry, although he is widely regarded as a very great writer indeed, especially as a wit and a satirist. Byron was not only a genius; he was also a millionaire, a hero, a nobleman, a sinner, and a beauty. The world is still learning how to catch up with him.

He was born into a tormented and tempestuous family; his father, who died when Byron was three, was nicknamed "Mad Jack." Byron was a peer for all of his teens and his adult life, inheriting the family title at age ten. He began publishing poetry while still an adolescent and by 1812 was among the most famous poets in England. He married most unhappily in 1815, and in the next year—hounded by accusations of insanity and incest—he exiled himself from England, never to come home. He spent some time in Switzerland but devoted most of his remaining life to working in Italy, often in the company of Percy Bysshe Shelley and his wife Mary.

Byron fits into the same category as Horace, Dryden, and Pope: poet-critics who excel in satire and ridicule. When his early *Hours of Idleness* (1807) was disparaged in the pages of *The Edinburgh Review*, Byron reacted with *English Bards and Scotch Reviewers* (1809). It was published as a thin octavo volume in 1809 and went through four editions, with some corrections and revisions, by

1811. At the time, the adjective "Scotch" had not acquired some of the negative connotations that subsequently caused many natives or adherents of Scotland to prefer "Scottish" or "Scots," except in reference to whisky. In the late eighteenth century, Robert Burns and Sir Walter Scott usually said "Scotch," although "Scottish" already bore a note of formality. Two years later Byron continued his dispute with the publication of the poem's sequel, *Hints from Horace*, an adaptation of Horace's *Ars Poetica*.

ENGLISH BARDS AND SCOTCH REVIEWERS

(EXCERPT, 1809)

A SATIRE

"I had rather be a kitten, and cry mew!
Than one of these same metre ballad-mongers"

Shakespeare

"Such shameless bards we have; and yet 'tis true,
There are as mad, abandon'd critics too,"

Pope

O nature's noblest gift—my grey goose-quill!
Slave of my thoughts, obedient to my will,
Torn from thy parent bird to form a pen,—
That mighty instrument of little men!
The pen! foredoom'd to aid the mental throes
Of brains that labour, big with verse or prose,
Though nymphs forsake, and critics may deride,
The lover's solace, and the author's pride.
What wits, what poets dost thou daily raise!
How frequent is thy use, how small thy praise!

Condemn'd at length to be forgotten quite,
With all the pages which 'twas thine to write.
But thou, at least, mine own especial pen!
Once laid aside, but now assumed again,
Our task complete, like Hamet's shall be free;[1]
Though spurn'd by others, yet beloved by me:
Then let us soar to-day, no common theme,
No eastern vision, no distemper'd dream
Inspires—our path, though full of thorns, is plain;
Smooth be the verse, and easy be the strain.
When Vice triumphant holds her sov'reign sway,
Obey'd by all who nought beside obey;
When Folly, frequent harbinger of crime,
Bedecks her cap with bells of every clime;
When knaves and fools combined o'er all prevail,
And weigh their justice in a golden scale;
E'en then the boldest start from public sneers,
Afraid of shame, unknown to other fears,
More darkly sin, by satire kept in awe,
And shrink from ridicule, though not from law.

Such is the force of wit! but not belong
To me the arrows of satiric song;
The royal vices of our age demand
A keener weapon, and a mightier hand.
Still there are follies, e'en for me to chase,
And yield at least amusement in the race:
Laugh when I laugh, I seek no other fame;
The cry is up, and scribblers are my game.
Speed, Pegasus!—ye strains of great and small,
Ode, epic, elegy, have at you all!
I too can scrawl, and once upon a time
I pour'd along the town a flood of rhyme,
A schoolboy freak, unworthy praise or blame;
I printed—older children do the same.
'Tis pleasant, sure, to see one's name in print;
A book's a book, although there's nothing in't.
Not that a title's sounding charm can save
Or scrawl or scribbler from an equal grave:

---

1. Hamet: Cid Hamet Benengali, at the end of *Don Quixote*.

This Lambe must own, since his patrician name[2]
Fail'd to preserve the spurious farce from shame.
No matter, George continues still to write,
Though now the name is veil'd from public sight.
Moved by the great example, I pursue
The self-same road, but make my own review:
Not seek great Jeffrey's, yet, like him, will be[3]
Self-constituted judge of poesy.

A man must serve his time to every trade
Save censure—critics all are ready made.
Take hackney'd jokes from Miller, got by rote,[4]
With just enough of learning to misquote;
A mind well skill'd to find or forge a fault;
A turn for punning, call it Attic salt;
To Jeffrey go, be silent and discreet,
His pay is just ten sterling pounds per sheet:
Fear not to lie, 'twill seem a sharper hit;
Shrink not from blasphemy, 'twill pass for wit;
Care not for feeling—pass you proper jest,
And stand a critic, hated yet carress'd.

And shall we own such judgment? no—as soon
Seek roses in December—ice in June;
Hope constancy in wind, or corn in chaff;
Believe a woman or an epitaph,
Or any other thing that's false, before
You trust in critics, who themselves are sore;
Or yield one single thought to be misled
By Jeffrey's heart, or Lambe's Boeotian head.[5]
To these young tyrants, by themselves misplaced,
Combined usurpers on the throne of taste;
To these, when authors bend in humble awe,

---

2. Lambe: William and George Lambe (or Lamb), first cousins of Lady Byron; George wrote for the *Edinburgh Review*.

3. Jeffrey: Francis Jeffrey (1773–1850), one of the founders of the *Edinburgh Review*. Byron repeatedly associates him with George Jeffreys (1644–1689), one of the first of the Hanging Judges. Francis Jeffrey himself became a judge after Byron's death.

4. Miller: the legendary Joe Miller, to whom a collection of jokes was attributed in the eighteenth century.

5. Boeotian: stupid.

And hail their voice as truth, their word as law—
While these are censors, 'twould be sin to spare;
While such are critics, why should I forebear?
But yet, so near all modern worthies run,
'Tis doubtful whom to seek, or whom to shun:
Nor know we when to spare, or where to strike,
Our bards and censors are so much alike.

Then should you ask me, why I venture o'er
The path which Pope and Gifford trod before;[6]
If not yet sicken'd, you can still proceed;
Go on; my rhyme will tell you as you read.
"But hold!" exclaims a friend, "here's come neglect:
This—that—and t'other line seem incorrect."
What then? the self-same blunder Pope has got,
And careless Dryden—"Ay, but Pye has not:"—[7]
Indeed!—'tis granted, faith!—but what care I?
Better to err with Pope, than shine with Pye.

Time was, ere yet in these degenerate days
Ignoble themes obtain'd mistaken praise,
When sense and wit with poesy allied,
No fabl'd graces, flourish'd side by side;
From the same fount their inspiration drew,
And, rear'd by taste, bloom'd fairer as they grew.
Then, in this happy isle, a Pope's pure strain
Sought the rapt soul to charm, nor sought in vain;
A polish'd nation's praise aspir'd to claim,
And rais'd the people's, as the poet's fame.
Like him great Dryden pour'd the tide of song,
In stream less smooth, indeed, yet doubly strong.
Then Congreve's scenes could cheer, or Otway's melt—[8]
For nature then an English audience felt.
But why these names, or greater still, retrace,
When all to feebler bards resign their place?
Yet to such times our lingering looks are cast,

---

6. Gifford: William Gifford (1756–1826), brilliant scholar, translator, and satirist.
7. Pye: Henry James Pye (1745–1813), Poet Laureate from 1790 until his death; succeeded by Southey.
8. Otway: Thomas Otway (1652–1685), playwright.

When taste and reason with those times are past.
Now look around, and turn each trifling page,
Survey the precious works that please the age;
This truth at least let satire's self allow,
No dearth of bards can be complain'd of now.
The loaded press beneath her labour groans,
And printers' devils shake their weary bones;
While Southey's epics cram the creaking shelves,
And Little's lyrics shine in hot-press'd twelves.[9]
Thus saith the Preacher: "Nought beneath the sun
Is new"; yet still from change to change we run:
What varied wonders tempt us as they pass!
The cow-pox, tractors, galvanism and gas,[10]
In turns appear, to make the vulgar stare,
Till the swoln bubble bursts—and all is air!
Nor less new schools of Poetry arise,
Where dull pretenders grapple for the prize:
O'er taste awhile these pseudo-bards prevail;
Each country book-club bows the knee to Baal,
And, hurling lawful genius from the throne,
Erects a shrine and idol of its own;
Some leaden calf—but whom it matters not,
From soaring Southey down to grovelling Stott.[11]

Behold! in various throngs the scribbling crew,
For notice eager, pass in long review:
Each spurs his jaded Pegasus apace,
And rhyme and blank maintain an equal race;
Sonnets on sonnets crowd, and ode on ode;
And tales of terror jostle on the road;[12]
Immeasurable measures move along;
For simpering folly loves a varied song,

---

9. Little's lyrics shine in hot-press'd twelves: Byron's friend, the Irish poet and satirist Thomas Moore, used the name Thomas Little for his early works. "Twelves" is a reference to the book size called "duodecimo," which is about 5 × 8 inches. Hot-pressing made the pages smooth.
10. Tractors: rods of two different metals rubbed over the skin as a cure for many maladies. They were called "tractors" because they were thought to draw or pull out the affliction. Marketed by an American physician named Elisha Perkins who died in 1799.
11. Stott: Robert Stott published poems in the *Morning Press*, or the *Morning Post*, under the pen-name Hafiz.
12. tales of terror: A book by Matthew Gregory Lewis ("Monk" Lewis) was called *Tales of Terror*.

To strange mysterious dulness still the friend,
Admires the strain she cannot comprehend.
Thus Lays of Minstrels—may they be the last!—[13]
On half-strung harps whine mournful to the blast.
While mountain spirits prate to river sprites,
That dames may listen to the sound at nights;
And goblin brats, of Gilpin Horner's brood,[14]
Decoy young border-nobles through the wood,
And skip at every step, Lord knows how high,
And frighten foolish babes, the Lord knows why;
While high-born ladies in their magic cell,
Forbidding knights to read who cannot spell,
Despatch a courier to a wizard's grave,
And fight with honest men to shield a knave.

Next view in state, proud prancing on his roan,
The golden-crested haughty Marmion,[15]
Now forging scrolls, now foremost in the fight,
Not quite a felon, yet but half a knight,
The gibbet or the field prepar'd to grace;
A mighty mixture of the great and base.
And think'st thou, Scott! by vain conceit perchance,
On public taste to foist thy stale romance,
Though Murray with his Miller may combine
To yield thy muse just half-a-crown per line?
No! when the sons of song descend to trade,
Their bays are sear, their former laurels fade.
Let such forego the poet's sacred name,
Who rack their brains for lucre, not for fame:
Still for stern Mammon may they toil in vain!
And sadly gaze on gold they cannot gain!
Such be their meed, such still the just reward
Of prostituted muse and hireling bard!
For this we spurn Apollo's venal son,
And bid a long "good night to Marmion."

---

13. Lays of Minstrels: Sir Walter Scott published a poem called *The Lay of the Last Minstrel.*
14. Gilpin Horner: the legendary Scottish character whose story was the germ of *The Lay of the Last Minstrel.*
15. Marmion: *Marmion,* another of Scott's poems.

These are the themes that claim our plaudits now;
These are the bards to whom the muse must bow;
While Milton, Dryden, Pope, alike forgot,
Resign their hallow'd bays to Walter Scott.

The time has been, when yet the muse was young,
When Homer swept the lyre, and Maro sung,[16]
An epic scarce ten centuries could claim,
While awe-struck nations hail'd the magic name;
The work of each immortal bard appears
The single wonder of a thousand years.
Empires have moulder'd from the face of earth,
Tongues have expir'd with those who gave them birth,
Without the glory such a strain can give,
As even in ruin bids the language live.
Not so with us, though minor bards, content
On one great work a life of labour spent:
With eagle pinion soaring to the skies,
Behold the ballad-monger Southey rise!
To him let Camoëns, Milton, Tasso yield,[17]
Whose annual strains, like armies, take the field.
First in the ranks see Joan of Arc advance,
The scourge of England and the boast of France!
Though burnt by wicked Bedford for a witch,
Behold her statue plac'd in glory's niche;
Her fetters burst, and just releas'd from prison,
A virgin phoenix from her ashes risen.
Next see tremendous Thalaba come on,[18]
Arabia's monstrous, wild and wondrous son:
Domdaniel's dread destroyer, who o'erthrew[19]
More mad magicians than the world e'er knew.
Immortal hero! all thy foes o'ercome,
For ever reign—the rival of Tom Thumb![20]
Since startled metre fled before thy face,

---

16. Maro: Virgil.
17. Camoëns, Milton, Tasso: great epic poets of Portugal, England, and Italy.
18. Thalaba: *Thalaba*, poem by Southey.
19. Domdaniel: in Southey's *Thalaba*, "a seminary for evil magicians, under the roots of the sea."
20. Tom Thumb: Henry Fielding's mock-heroic of 1730: *The Tragedy of Tragedies, or the Life and Death of Tom Thumb the Great.*

Well wert thou doom'd the last of all thy race!
Well might triumphant genii bear thee hence,
Illustrious conqueror of common sense!
Now, last and greatest, Madoc spreads his sails,[21]
Cacique in Mexico, and prince in Wales;
Tells us strange tales, as other travellers do,
More old than Mandeville's, and not so true.[22]
Oh Southey! Southey! cease thy varied song!
A bard may chant too often and too long:
As thou art strong in verse, in mercy, spare!
A fourth, alas! were more than we could bear.
But if, in spite of all the world can say,
Thou still wilt verseward plod thy weary way;
If still in Berkley ballads most uncivil,[23]
Thou wilt devote old women to the devil,
The babe unborn thy dread intent may rue:
"God help thee," Southey, and thy readers too.

Next comes the dull disciple of thy school,
That mild apostate from poetic rule,
The simple Wordsworth, framer of a lay
As soft as evening in his favourite May,
Who warns his friend "to shake off toil and trouble,
And quit his books, for fear of growing double";[24]
Who, both by precept and example, shows
That prose is verse, and verse is merely prose;
Convincing all, by demonstration plain,
Poetic souls delight in prose insane;
And Christmas stories tortur'd into rhyme
Contain the essence of the true sublime.
Thus, when he tells the tale of Betty Foy,
The idiot mother of "an idiot boy";[25]
A moon-struck, silly lad, who lost his way,
And, like his bard, confounded night with day;

---

21. Madoc: *Madoc*, a poem by Southey.
22. Mandeville: "Sir John Mandeville," supposed author of a fourteenth-century travel book that combines geography with fantasy.
23. Berkley ballads: refers to Southey's *The Old Woman of Berkeley*.
24. growing double: in Wordsworth's "The Tables Turned."
25. an idiot boy: Wordsworth's "The Idiot Boy."

So close on each pathetic part he dwells,
And each adventure so sublimely tells,
That all who view the "idiot in his glory"
Conceive the bard the hero of the story.

Shall gentle Coleridge pass unnotic'd here,
To turgid ode and tumid stanza dear?
Though themes of innocence amuse him best,
Yet still obscurity's a welcome guest.
If Inspiration should her aid refuse
To him who takes a pixy for a muse,[26]
Yet none in lofty numbers can surpass
The bard who soars to elegize an ass.
So well the subject suits his noble mind,
He brays the laureat of the long-ear'd kind . . . .

Health to immortal Jeffrey! once, in name,
England could boast a judge almost the same;
In soul so like, so merciful, yet just,
Some think that Satan has resign'd his trust,
And given the spirit to the world again,
To sentence letters, as he sentenced men.
With hand less mighty, but with heart as black,
With voice as willing to decree the rack;
Bred in the courts betimes, though all that law
As yet hath taught him is to find a flaw;
Since well instructed in the patriot school
To rail at party, though a party tool,
Who knows, if chance his patrons should restore
Back to the sway they forfeited before,
His scribbling toils some recompense may meet,
And raise this Daniel to the judgment-seat?
Let Jeffreys' shade indulge the pious hope,
And greeting thus, present him with a rope:
"Heir to my virtues! man of equal mind!
Skill'd to condemn as to traduce mankind,
This cord receive, for thee reserved with care,
To wield in judgment, and at length to wear."

---

26. Pixy: Coleridge wrote a poem called "Songs of the Pixies."

. . . Then prosper, Jeffrey! pertest of the train
Whom Scotland pampers with her fiery grain!
Whatever blessing waits a genuine Scot,
In double portion swells thy glorious lot;
For thee Edina culls her evening sweets,[27]
And showers their odours on thy candid sheets,
Whose hue and fragrance to thy work adhere—
This scents its pages, and that gilds its rear.[28]
Lo! blushing Itch, coy nymph, enamour'd grown,
Forsakes the rest, and cleaves to thee alone;
And, too unjust to other Pictish men,
Enjoys thy person, and inspires thy pen! . . .

Such are we now. Ah! wherefore should we turn
To what our fathers were, unless to mourn?
Degenerate Britons! are ye dead to shame,
Or, kind to dulness, do you fear to blame?
Well may the nobles of our present race
Watch each distortion of a Naldi's face;
Well may they smile on Italy's buffoons,
And worship Catalani's pantaloons,[29]
Since their own drama yields no fairer trace
Of wit than puns, of humour than grimace . . . .

To the famed throng now paid the tribute due,
Neglected genius! let me turn to you,
Come forth, oh Campbell give thy talents scope;
Who dares aspire if thou must cease to hope?
And thou, melodious Rogers! rise at last,[30]
Recall the pleasing memory of the past;
Arise! let blest remembrance still inspire,
And strike to wonted tones thy hallow'd lyre;
Restore Apollo to his vacant throne,
Assert thy country's honour and thine own.

---

27. Edina: the ancient and poetic name for Edinburgh, Scotland, as in Burns's "Address To Edinburgh": "Edina! Scotia's darling seat!"
28. gilds its rear: the back cover of the magazine was gilt.
29. Naldi's face . . . Catalani's pantaloons: Giuseppe Naldi and Angelica Catalani, celebrated musical performers.
30. Campbell . . . Rogers: Thomas Campbell (1777–1844) and Samuel Rogers (1763–1855) were among Byron's most accomplished and respected contemporaries.

What! must deserted Poesy still weep
Where her last hopes with pious Cowper sleep?[31]
Unless, perchance, from his cold bier she turns,
To deck the turf that wraps her mistral, Burns!
No! though contempt hath mark'd the spurious brood,
The race who rhyme from folly, or for food,
Yet still some genuine sons 'tis hers to boast,
Who, least affecting, still affect the most:
Feel as they write, and write but as they feel—
Bear witness Gifford, Sotheby, Macneil.[32]

. . . There be who say, in these enlighten'd days,
That splendid lies are all the poet's praise;
That strain'd invention, ever on the wing,
Alone impels the modern bard to sing:
'Tis true, that all who rhyme—nay, all who write,
Shrink from that fatal word to genius—trite;
Yet Truth sometimes will lend her noblest fires,
And decorate the verse herself inspires:
This fact in Virtue's name let Crabbe attest;[33]
Though nature's sternest painter, yet the best.

. . . Let these, or such as these with just applause,
Restore the muse's violated laws;
But not in flimsy Darwin's pompous chime,[34]
That mighty master of unmeaning rhyme,
Whose gilded cymbals, more adorn'd than clear,
The eye delighted, but fatigued the ear;
In show the simple lyre could once surpass,
But now, worn down, appear in native brass;
While all his train of hovering sylphs around
Evaporate in similes and sound:
Him let them shun, with him let tinsel die:

---

31. Cowper: William Cowper (1731–1800), poet much admired by Wordsworth and others; known for piety and patriotism and also for his abiding melancholy.
32. Sotheby: William Sotheby (1757–1833), translator and playwright. Macneil: Hector Macneil (1746–1818), minor Scottish poet, known for songs and pastorals; his poetical works were published in two volumes in 1801.
33. Crabbe: George Crabbe (1754–1832), poet admired by Byron and by many others, including Edwin Arlington Robinson and Ezra Pound.
34. Darwin: Erasmus Darwin (1731–1802), grandfather of the biologist.

False glare attracts, but more offends the eye.
Yet let them not to vulgar Wordsworth stoop,
The meanest object of the lowly group,
Whose verse, of all but childish prattle void,
Seems blessed harmony to Lamb and Lloyd:[35]
Let them—but hold, my muse, nor dare to teach
A strain far, far beyond thy humble reach:
The native genius with their being given
Will point the path, and peal their notes to heaven.
And thou, too, Scott! resign to minstrels rude
The wilder slogan of a border feud:
Let others spin their meagre lines for hire;
Enough for genius, if itself inspire!
Let Southey sing, although his teeming muse,
Prolific every spring, be too profuse;
Let simple Wordsworth chime his childish verse,
And brother Coleridge lull the babe at nurse;
Let spectre-mongering Lewis aim, at most,
To rouse the galleries, or to raise a ghost;
Let Moore still sigh; let Strangford steal from Moore,[36]
And swear that Camoëns sang such notes of yore;
Let Hayley hobble on, Montgomery rave,[37]
And godly Grahame chant a stupid stave:[38]
Let sonneteering Bowles his strains refine,[39]
And whine and whimper to the fourteenth line;
Let Stott, Carlisle, Matilda, and the rest[40]
Of Grub Street, and of Grosvenor Place the best,
Scrawl on, till death release us from the strain,
Or Common Sense assert her rights again.
But thou, with powers that mock the aid of praise,
Shouldst leave to humbler bards ignoble lays:
Thy country's voice, the voice of all the nine,
Demand a hallow'd harp—that harp is thine.

---

35. Lloyd: Charles Lloyd (1775–1839), journalist and poet.
36. Strangford: Viscount Strangford, translator of Camoëns.
37. Let Hayley hobble on: William Hayley, author of a biography of Milton. Montgomery: James Montgomery, minor poet.
38. Grahame: James Grahame, author of religious poems.
39. Bowles: Rev. W. Lisle Bowles, known for sonnets and for longer poems as well.
40. Carlisle: Frederick Howard, fifth earl of Carlisle (1748–1825), politician. Matilda: "Rosa Matilda" and "Anna Matilda" were pseudonyms used by poets.

Say! will not Caledonia's annals yield
The glorious record of some nobler field,
Than the wild foray of a plundering clan,
Whose proudest deeds disgrace the name of man?
Or Marmion's acts of darkness, fitter food
For Sherwood's outlaw tales of Robin Hood?
Scotland! still proudly claim thy native bard,
And be thy praise his first, his best reward!
Yet not with thee alone his name should live,
But own the vast renown a world can give:
Be known, perchance, when Albion is no more,
And tell the tale of what she was before;
To future times her faded fame recall,
And save her glory, though his country fall.

. . . Shall hoary Granta call her sable sons,[41]
Expert in science, more expert at puns?
Shall these approach the muse? ah, no! she flies,
Even from the tempting ore of Seaton's prize:[42]
Though printers condescend the press to soil
With rhyme by Hoare, the epic blank by Hoyle:[43]
Not him whose page, if still upheld by whist,
Requires no sacred theme to bid us list.
Ye! who in Granta's honours would surpass,
Must mount her Pegasus, a full-grown ass;
A foal well worthy of her ancient dam,
Whose Helicon is duller than her Cam.[44]

. . . Then, hapless Britain! be thy rulers blest,
The senate's oracles, the people's jest!
Still hear thy motley orators dispense
The flowers of rhetoric, though not of sense,

---

41. Granta: Small stream running into the Cam. Byron wrote a "medley" called "Granta."

42. Seaton: Thomas Seaton (1684–1741), the founder of the Seatonian prize, awarded for religious poetry at Cambridge.

43. Hoare: Charles James Hoare (1781–1865), clergyman and minor poet. Hoyle: Charles Hoyle, minor poet. Byron connects him with Edmund Hoyle (1672–1769), still honored in card-playing contexts. He invented the modern game of whist.

44. Helicon: Byron admitted that he made a mistake. Helicon is a mountain; Byron meant Hippocrene, one of the fountains of poetic inspiration on Helicon. Cam: the river that flows through Cambridge.

While Canning's colleagues hate him for his wit,[45]
And old dame Portland fills the place of Pitt.[46]

Yet, once again, adieu! ere this the sail
That wafts me hence is shivering in the gale;
And Afric's coast and Calpe's adverse height,
And Stamboul's minarets must greet my sight:
Thence shall I stray through beauty's native clime,
Where Kaff is clad in rocks, and crown'd with snows
    sublime.
But should I back return, no tempting press
Shall drag my journal from the desk's recess;
Let coxcombs, printing as they come from far,
Snatch his own wreath of ridicule from Carr;
Let Aberdeen and Elgin still pursue[47]
The shade of fame through regions of virtù;
Waste useless thousands on their Phidian freaks,
Misshapen monuments and maim'd antiques;
And make their grand saloons a general mart
For all the mutilated blocks of art;
Of Dardan tours let dilettanti tell,
I leave topography to rapid Gell;[48]
And, quite content, no more shall interpose
To stun the public ear—at least with prose.

Thus far I've held my undistrub'd career,
Prepared for rancour, steel'd 'gainst selfish fear;
This thing of rhyme I ne'er disdain'd to own—
Though not obtrusive, yet not quite unknown:
My voice was heard again, though not so loud,

---

45. Canning: George Canning (1770–1827), politician and author.
46. Pitt: William Pitt the Younger (1759–1806), politician.
47. Aberdeen: Earl of Aberdeen (1784–1869); while touring Europe at the beginning of the nineteenth century, he excavated an amphitheatre in Athens and sent the reliefs to Britain (along with the Elgin Marbles). He founded the Athenian Society and wrote for the *Edinburgh Review*. Byron, who was Aberdeen's cousin, castigated him for taking antiquities from Greece. Elgin: Lord Elgin (1766–1841); the "Elgin Marbles," about which Keats wrote a poem, were parts of the Parthenon that Elgin collected and sold to the British government, who placed them in the British Museum. Byron also attacked Elgin in "The Curse of Minerva" and *Childe Harold's Pilgrimage* (II, 11).
48. Gell: Sir William Gell (1777–1836), archaeologist. He wrote and illustrated *Topography of Troy* (1804).

My page, though nameless, never disavow'd;
And now at once I tear the veil away: —
Cheer on the pack! the quarry stands at bay,
Unscared by all the din of Melbourne House,
By Lambe's resentment, or by Holland's spouse,[49]
By Jeffrey's harmless pistol, Hallam's rage,[50]
Edina's brawny sons and brimstone page.
Our men in buckram shall have blows enough,
And feel they too are "penetrable stuff":
And though I hope not hence unscathed to go,
Who conquers me shall find a stubborn foe.
The time hath been, when no harsh sound would fall
From lips that now may seem imbued with gall;
Nor fools nor follies tempt me to despise
The meanest thing that crawl'd beneath my eyes;
But now, so callous grown, so changed since youth,
I've learn'd to think, and sternly speak the truth;
Learn'd to deride the critic's starch decree,
And break him on the wheel he meant for me;
To spurn the rod a scribbler bids me kiss,
Nor care if courts and crowds applaud or hiss:
Nay more, though all my rival rhymesters frown,
I too can hunt a poetaster down;
And, arm'd in proof, the gauntlet cast at once
To Scotch marauder, and to southern dunce.
Thus much I've dared; if my incondite lay
Hath wrong'd these righteous times, let others say;
This, let the world, which knows not how to spare,
Yet rarely blames unjustly, now declare.

---

49. Holland: Lord Holland (1773–1840); one of the very few Whigs in the House of Lords, Holland was a patron of the *Edinburgh Review*. The critics returned the favor by giving positive reviews to his essays and translations. He married a woman who had been scandalously divorced from a baronet (she had borne Holland's child earlier) — a rare phenomenon at the time.
50. Hallam: Henry Hallam (1777–1859), distinguished historian; father of Tennyson's friend Arthur Henry Hallam.

19

PERCY BYSSHE SHELLEY (1792–1822)

Born into a substantial Sussex family, Shelley was educated at Eton and Oxford. During his first year at Oxford he was expelled for authoring a pamphlet favoring atheism. His life was complex and turbulent, with an early marriage to the sixteen-year-old Harriet Westbrook, whom he subsequently abandoned to take up with Mary, the daughter of the radical thinker William Godwin and his first wife, Mary Wollstonecraft. When Harriet committed suicide in 1816, Shelley and Mary were married. (In 1818 she published *Frankenstein, or the Modern Prometheus.*) Shelley fathered two children by Harriet and three by Mary.

Shelley resembles William Blake in his originality and his dedication to radical causes; he resembles Coleridge in his high-minded intellect and critical faculty; he resembles his close friend Byron in his love of liberty and his affection for the south of Europe, especially Italy; and he resembles Keats (on whose death he wrote the noble elegy "Adonais") in the range and depth of his lyrics. Shelley was a resourceful translator as well as a great lyric and dramatic poet. He drowned when his yacht *Ariel* foundered in a storm off the Italian coast near Leghorn.

Later during the nineteenth century, Shelley attracted some enthusiastic adherents, including Robert Browning and Thomas Hardy. Others, including Matthew Arnold, were less enthusiastic. Arnold wrote, "It always seems to me that the right sphere for Shelley's genius was the sphere of music, not of poetry;

the medium of sounds he can master, but to master the more difficult medium of words he has neither intellectual force nor sanity enough." Later, Arnold summed up Shelley as a "beautiful and ineffectual angel, beating in the void his luminous wings in vain." Later critics, such as D. H. Lawrence and T. S. Eliot, were even more skeptical, but, after about 1970, Shelley's stock has been rising again, especially with more tolerant critics such as Harold Bloom.

In 1821, the year before his death, Shelley was at the height of his powers; he wrote *Adonais* and *Epipsychidion*, two of his greatest poems, as well as *A Defence of Poetry*, inspired by Shelley's reading of "The Four Ages of Poetry," a witty magazine piece by his friend Thomas Love Peacock. For complex reasons, Shelley ignored the witty elements of Peacock's treatise, which suggested that the best poetry belongs to the most primitive age. Peacock teased the extravagances of Coleridge, Wordsworth, Scott, Southey, Thomas Moore, Thomas Campbell, and Byron. "In the origin and perfection of poetry," Peacock argued, "all the associations of life were composed of poetical materials. With us it is decidedly the reverse." Shelley's *Defence* is more than just a reply to Peacock. It is most serious and sustained argument that began under the impetus of what might have been an elaborate joke to Peacock but soon transcended its trivial origins to become a lofty argument for the continuing primacy of poetry among human activities.

According to one mode of regarding those two classes of mental action, which are called reason and imagination, the former may be considered as mind contemplating the relations borne by one thought to another, however produced, and the latter, as mind acting upon those thoughts so as to color them with its own light, and composing from them, as from elements, other thoughts, each containing within itself the principle of its own integrity. The one is the τὸ ποιεῖν, or the principle of synthesis, and has for its objects those forms which are common to universal nature and existence itself; the other is the τὸ λογίζειν, or principle of analysis, and its action regards the relations of things simply as relations; considering thoughts, not in their integral unity, but as the algebraical representations which conduct to certain general results. Reason is the enumeration of qualities already known; imagination is the perception of the value of those qualities, both separately and as a whole. Reason respects the differences, and imagination the similitudes of things. Reason is to imagination as the instrument to the agent, as the body to the spirit, as the shadow to the substance.

Poetry, in a general sense, may be defined to be "the expression of the imagination": and poetry is connate with the origin of man. Man is an instrument over which a series of external and internal impressions are driven, like the alternations of an ever-changing wind over an Æolian lyre, which move it by their motion to ever-changing melody. But there is a principle within the human being, and perhaps within all sentient beings, which acts otherwise than in the lyre, and produces not melody alone, but harmony, by an internal adjustment of the sounds or motions thus excited to the impressions which excite them. It is as if the lyre could accommodate its chords to the motions of that which strikes them, in a determined proportion of sound; even as the musician can accommodate his voice to the sound of the lyre. A child at play by itself will express its delight by its voice and motions; and every inflexion of tone and every gesture will bear exact relation to a corresponding antitype in the pleasurable impressions which awakened it; it will be the reflected image of that impression; and as the lyre trembles and sounds after the wind has died away, so the child seeks, by prolonging in its voice and motions the duration of the effect, to prolong also a consciousness of the cause. In relation to the objects which delight a child these expressions are what poetry is to higher objects. The savage (for the savage is to ages what the child is to years) expresses the emotions produced in him by surrounding objects in a similar manner; and language and gesture, together with plastic or pictorial imitation, become the image of the combined effect of those objects, and of his apprehension of them. Man in society, with all his passions and his pleasures, next becomes the object of the passions and pleasures of man; an additional class of emotions produces an augmented treasure of expressions; and language, gesture, and the imitative arts, become at once the representation and the medium, the pencil and the picture, the chisel and the statue, the chord and the harmony. The social sympathies, or those laws from which, as from its elements, society results, begin to develop themselves from the moment that two human beings coexist; the future is contained within the present, as the plant within the seed; and equality, diversity, unity, contrast, mutual dependence, become the principles alone capable of affording the motives according to which the will of a social being is determined to action, inasmuch as he is social; and constitute pleasure in sensation, virtue in sentiment, beauty in art, truth in reasoning, and love in the intercourse of kind. Hence men, even in the infancy of society, observe a certain order in their words and actions, distinct from that of the objects and the impressions represented by them, all expression being subject to the laws of that from which it proceeds. But let us dismiss those more general considerations which might involve an inquiry into the principles of society itself, and restrict our view to the manner in which the imagination is expressed upon its forms.

In the youth of the world, men dance and sing and imitate natural objects, observing in these actions, as in all others, a certain rhythm or order. And, although all men observe a similar, they observe not the same order, in the motions of the dance, in the melody of the song, in the combinations of language, in the series of their imitations of natural objects. For there is a certain order or rhythm belonging to each of these classes of mimetic representation, from which the hearer and the spectator receive an intenser and purer pleasure than from any other: the sense of an approximation to this order has been called taste by modern writers. Every man in the infancy of art observes an order which approximates more or less closely to that from which this highest delight results: but the diversity is not sufficiently marked, as that its gradations should be sensible, except in those instances where the predominance of this faculty of approximation to the beautiful (for so we may be permitted to name the relation between this highest pleasure and its cause) is very great. Those in whom it exists in excess are poets, in the most universal sense of the word; and the pleasure resulting from the manner in which they express the influence of society or nature upon their own minds, communicates itself to others, and gathers a sort of reduplication from that community. Their language is vitally metaphorical; that is, it marks the before unapprehended relations of things and perpetuates their apprehension, until the words which represent them, become, through time, signs for portions or classes of thoughts instead of pictures of integral thoughts; and then if no new poets should arise to create afresh the associations which have been thus disorganized, language will be dead to all the nobler purposes of human intercourse. These similitudes or relations are finely said by Lord Bacon to be "the same footsteps of nature impressed upon the various subjects of the world" ["De Augment. Scient.," cap. 1, lib. iii—Shelley]—and he considers the faculty which perceives them as the storehouse of axioms common to all knowledge. In the infancy of society every author is necessarily a poet, because language itself is poetry; and to be a poet is to apprehend the true and the beautiful, in a word, the good which exists in the relation, subsisting, first between existence and perception, and secondly between perception and expression. Every original language near to its source is in itself the chaos of a cyclic poem: the copiousness of lexicography and the distinctions of grammar are the works of a later age, and are merely the catalogue and the form of the creations of poetry.

But poets, or those who imagine and express this indestructible order, are not only the authors of language and of music, of the dance, and architecture, and statuary, and painting: they are the institutors of laws, and the founders of civil society, and the inventors of the arts of life, and the teachers, who draw into a certain propinquity with the beautiful and the true that partial apprehension of the agencies of the invisible world which is called religion. Hence all original religions are allegorical, or susceptible of allegory, and, like Janus, have a double face of false and true. Poets, according to the circumstances of the age and nation in which they appeared, were called, in the earlier epochs of the world, legislators, or prophets: a poet essentially comprises and unites both these characters. For he not only beholds intensely the present as it is, and discovers those laws according to which present things ought to be ordered, but he beholds the future in the present, and his thoughts are the germs of the flower and the fruit of latest time. Not that I assert poets to be prophets in the gross sense of the word, or that they can foretell the form as surely as they foreknow the spirit of events: such is the pretence of superstition, which would make poetry an attribute of prophecy, rather than prophecy an attribute of poetry. A poet participates in the eternal, the infinite, and the one; as far as relates to his conceptions, time and place and number are not. The grammatical forms which express the moods of time, and the difference of persons, and the distinction of place, are convertible with respect to the highest poetry without injuring it as poetry; and the choruses of Æschylus, and the book of Job, and Dante's "Paradise" would afford, more than any other writings, examples of this fact, if the limits of this essay did not forbid citation. The creations of sculpture, painting, and music are illustrations still more decisive.

Language, color, form, and religious and civil habits of action, are all the instruments and materials of poetry; they may be called poetry by that figure of speech which considers the effect as a synonym of the cause. But poetry in a more restricted sense expresses those arrangements of language, and especially metrical language, which are created by that imperial faculty, whose throne is curtained within the invisible nature of man. And this springs from the nature itself of language, which is a more direct representation of the actions and passions of our internal being, and is susceptible of more various and delicate combinations, than color, form, or motion, and is more plastic and obedient to the control of that faculty of which it is the creation. For language is arbitrarily produced by the imagination, and has relation to thoughts alone; but all other materials, instruments, and conditions of art have relations among each other, which limit and interpose between conception and expression. The former is as a mirror which reflects, the latter as a cloud which enfeebles, the light of which both are mediums of communication. Hence the fame of sculptors, painters, and musicians, although the intrinsic powers of the great masters of these arts may yield in no degree to that of those who have employed language as the hieroglyphic of their thoughts, has never equalled that of poets in the restricted sense of the term; as two performers of equal skill will produce un-equal effects from a guitar and a harp. The fame of legislators and founders of religions, so long as their institutions last, alone seems to exceed that of poets in the restricted sense; but it can scarcely be a question, whether, if we deduct the celebrity which their flattery of the gross opinions of the vulgar usually conciliates, together with that which belonged to them in their higher character of poets, any excess will remain.

We have thus circumscribed the word poetry within the limits of that art which is the most familiar and the most perfect expression of the faculty itself. It is necessary, however, to make the circle still narrower, and to determine the distinction between measured and unmeasured language; for the popular di-vision into prose and verse is inadmissible in accurate philosophy.

Sounds as well as thoughts have relation both between each other and to-wards that which they represent, and a perception of the order of those relations has always been found connected with a perception of the order of the relations of thoughts. Hence the language of poets has ever affected a certain uniform and harmonious recurrence of sound, without which it were not poetry, and which is scarcely less indispensable to the communication of its influence, than the words themselves, without reference to that peculiar order. Hence the vanity of translation; it were as wise to cast a violet into a crucible that you might discover the formal principle of its color and odor, as seek to transfuse from one language into another the creations of a poet. The plant must spring again from its seed, or it will bear no flower—and this is the burden of the curse of Babel.

An observation of the regular mode of the recurrence of harmony in the language of poetical minds, together with its relation to music, produced metre, or a certain system of traditional forms of harmony and language. Yet it is by no means essential that a poet should accommodate his language to this tra-ditional form, so that the harmony, which is its spirit, be observed. The practice is indeed convenient and popular, and to be preferred, especially in such com-position as includes much action: but every great poet must inevitably innovate upon the example of his predecessors in the exact structure of his peculiar versification. The distinction between poets and prose writers is a vulgar error. The distinction between philosophers and poets has been anticipated. Plato was essentially a poet—the truth and splendor of his imagery, and the melody of his language, are the most intense that it is possible to conceive. He rejected the measure of the epic, dramatic, and lyrical forms, because he sought to kindle a harmony in thoughts divested of shape and action, and he forebore to invent any regular plan of rhythm which would include, under determinate forms, the varied pauses of his style. Cicero sought to imitate the cadence of his periods, but with little success. Lord Bacon was a poet. [See the "Filum Labyrinthi," and the "Essay on Death" particularly.—Shelley] His language has a sweet and majestic rhythm, which satisfies the sense, no less than the almost superhuman wisdom of his philosophy satisfies the intellect; it is a strain which distends, and then bursts the circumference of the reader's mind, and pours itself forth together with it into the universal element with which it has perpet-ual sympathy. All the authors of revolutions in opinion are not only necessarily poets as they are inventors, nor even as their words unveil the permanent anal-ogy of things by images which participate in the life of truth; but as their periods are harmonious and rhythmical, and contain in themselves the elements of verse; being the echo of the eternal music. Nor are those supreme poets, who have employed traditional forms of rhythm on account of the form and action of their subjects, less capable of perceiving and teaching the truth of things, than those who have omitted that form. Shakespeare, Dante, and Milton (to confine ourselves to modern writers) are philosophers of the very loftiest power.

A poem is the very image of life expressed in its eternal truth. There is this difference between a story and a poem, that a story is a catalogue of detached facts, which have no other connection than time, place, circumstance, cause and effect; the other is the creation of actions according to the unchangeable forms of human nature, as existing in the mind of the Creator, which is itself the image of all other minds. The one is partial, and applies only to a definite period of time, and a certain combination of events which can never again recur; the other is universal, and contains within itself the germ of a relation to whatever motives or actions have place in the possible varieties of human nature. Time, which destroys the beauty and the use of the story of particular facts, stripped of the poetry which should invest them, augments that of poetry, and forever develops new and wonderful applications of the eternal truth which it contains. Hence epitomes have been called the moths of just history; they eat out the poetry of it. A story of particular facts is as a mirror which obscures and distorts that which should be beautiful; poetry is a mirror which makes beautiful that which is distorted.

The parts of a composition may be poetical, without the composition as a whole being a poem. A single sentence may be considered as a whole, though it may be found in the midst of a series of unassimilated portions; a single word even may be a spark of inextinguishable thought. And thus all the great historians, Herodotus, Plutarch, Livy, were poets; and although the plan of these writers, especially that of Livy, restrained them from developing this faculty in its highest degree, they made copious and ample amends for their subjection, by filling all the interstices of their subjects with living images.

Having determined what is poetry, and who are poets, let us proceed to estimate its effects upon society.

Poetry is ever accompanied with pleasure: all spirits on which it falls open themselves to receive the wisdom which is mingled with its delight. In the infancy of the world, neither poets themselves nor their auditors are fully aware of the excellence of poetry: for it acts in a divine and unapprehended manner, beyond and above consciousness; and it is reserved for future generations to contemplate and measure the mighty cause and effect in all the strength and splendor of their union. Even in modern times, no living poet ever arrived at the fulness of his fame; the jury which sits in judgment upon a poet, belonging as he does to all time, must be composed of his peers: it must be impanelled by Time from the selectest of the wise of many generations. A poet is a nightingale, who sits in darkness and sings to cheer its own solitude with sweet sounds; his auditors are as men entranced by the melody of an unseen musician, who feel that they are moved and softened, yet know not whence or why. The poems of Homer and his contemporaries were the delight of infant Greece; they were the elements of that social system which is the column upon which all succeeding civilization has reposed. Homer embodied the ideal perfection of his age in human character; nor can we doubt that those who read his verses were awakened to an ambition of becoming like to Achilles, Hector, and Ulysses: the truth and beauty of friendship, patriotism, and persevering devotion to an object, were unveiled to the depths in these immortal creations: the sentiments of the auditors must have been refined and enlarged by a sympathy with such great and lovely impersonations, until from admiring they imitated, and from imitation they identified themselves with the objects of their admiration. Nor let it be objected that these characters are remote from moral perfection, and that they can by no means be considered as edifying patterns for general imitation. Every epoch, under names more or less specious, has deified its peculiar errors; Revenge is the naked idol of the worship of a semi-barbarous age: and Self-deceit is the veiled image of unknown evil, before which luxury and satiety lie prostrate. But a poet considers the vices of his contemporaries as the temporary dress in which his creations must be arrayed, and which cover without concealing the eternal proportions of their beauty. An epic or dramatic personage is understood to wear them around his soul, as he may the ancient armor or the modern uniform around his body; whilst it is easy to conceive a dress more graceful than either. The beauty of the internal nature cannot be so far concealed by its accidental vesture, but that the spirit of its form shall communicate itself to the very disguise, and indicate the shape it hides from the manner in which it is worn. A majestic form and graceful motions will express themselves through the most barbarous and tasteless costume. Few poets of the highest class have chosen to exhibit the beauty of their conceptions in its naked truth and splendor; and it is doubtful whether the alloy of costume, habit, etc., be not necessary to temper this planetary music for mortal ears.

The whole objection, however, of the immorality of poetry rests upon a misconception of the manner in which poetry acts to produce the moral improvement of man. Ethical science arranges the elements which poetry has created, and propounds schemes and proposes examples of civil and domestic life: nor is it for want of admirable doctrines that men hate, and despise, and censure, and deceive, and subjugate one another. But poetry acts in another and diviner manner. It awakens and enlarges the mind itself by rendering it the receptacle of a thousand unapprehended combinations of thought. Poetry lifts the veil from the hidden beauty of the world, and makes familiar objects be as if they were not familiar; it reproduces all that it represents, and the impersonations clothed in its Elysian light stand thenceforward in the minds of those who have once contemplated them, as memorials of that gentle and exalted content which extends itself over all thoughts and actions with which it coexists. The great secret of morals is love; or a going out of our nature, and an identification of ourselves with the beautiful which exists in thought, action, or person, not our own. A man, to be greatly good, must imagine intensely and comprehensively; he must put himself in the place of another and of many others; the pains and pleasure of his species must become his own. The great instrument of moral good is the imagination; and poetry administers to the effect by acting upon the cause. Poetry enlarges the circumference of the imagination by replenishing it with thoughts of ever new delight, which have the power of attracting and assimilating to their own nature all other thoughts, and which form new intervals and interstices whose void forever craves fresh food. Poetry strengthens the faculty which is the organ of the moral nature of man, in the same manner as exercise strengthens a limb. A poet therefore would do ill to embody his own conceptions of right and wrong, which are usually those of his place and time, in his poetical creations, which participate in neither. By this assumption of the inferior office of interpreting the effect, in which perhaps after all he might acquit himself but imperfectly, he would resign a glory in a participation in the cause. There was little danger that Homer, or any of the eternal poets, should have so far misunderstood themselves as to have abdicated this throne of their widest dominion. Those in whom the poetical faculty, though great, is less intense, as Euripides, Lucan, Tasso, Spenser, have frequently affected a moral aim, and the effect of their poetry is diminished in exact proportion to the degree in which they compel us to advert to this purpose.

Homer and the cyclic poets were followed at a certain interval by the dramatic and lyrical poets of Athens, who flourished contemporaneously with all that is most perfect in the kindred expressions of the poetical faculty; architecture, painting, music, the dance, sculpture, philosophy, and, we may add, the forms of civil life. For although the scheme of Athenian society was deformed by many imperfections which the poetry existing in chivalry and Christianity has erased from the habits and institutions of modern Europe; yet never at any other period has so much energy, beauty, and virtue been developed; never was blind strength and stubborn form so disciplined and rendered subject to the will of man, or that will less repugnant to the dictates of the beautiful and the true, as during the century which preceded the death of Socrates. Of no other epoch in the history of our species have we records and fragments stamped so visibly with the image of the divinity in man. But it is poetry alone, in form, in action, or in language, which has rendered this epoch memorable above all others, and the store-house of examples to everlasting time. For written poetry existed at that epoch simultaneously with the other arts, and it is an idle inquiry to demand which gave and which received the light, which all, as from a common focus, have scattered over the darkest periods of succeeding time. We know no more of cause and effect than a constant conjunction of events: poetry is ever found to coexist with whatever other arts contribute to the happiness and perfection of man. I appeal to what has already been established to distinguish between the cause and the effect.

It was at the period here adverted to that the drama had its birth; and however a succeeding writer may have equalled or surpassed those few great specimens of the Athenian drama which have been preserved to us, it is indisputable that the art itself never was understood or practised according to the true philosophy of it, as at Athens. For the Athenians employed language, action, music, painting, the dance, and religious institutions, to produce a common effect in the representation of the highest idealism of passion and of power; each division in the art was made perfect in its kind of artists of the most consummate skill, and was disciplined into a beautiful proportion and unity one towards the other. On the modern stage a few only of the elements capable of expressing the image of the poet's conception are employed at once. We have tragedy without music and dancing; and music and dancing without the highest impersonations of which they are the fit accompaniment, and both without religion and solemnity. Religious institution has indeed been usually banished from the stage. Our system of divesting the actor's face of a mask, on which the many expressions appropriated to his dramatic character might be moulded into one permanent and unchanging expression, is favorable only to a partial and inharmonious effect; it is fit for nothing but a monologue, where all the attention may be directed to some great master of ideal mimicry. The modern practice of blending comedy with tragedy, though liable to great abuse in point of practice, is undoubtedly an extension of the dramatic circle; but the comedy should be as in "King Lear," universal, ideal, and sublime. It is perhaps the intervention of this principle which determines the balance in favor of "King Lear" against the "Oedipus Tyrannus" or the "Agamemnon," or, if you will, the trilogies with which they are connected; unless the intense power of the choral poetry, especially that of the latter, should be considered as restoring the equilibrium. *King Lear*, if it can sustain this comparison, may be judged to be the most perfect specimen of the dramatic art existing in the world; in spite of the narrow conditions to which the poet was subjected by the ignorance of the philosophy of the drama which has prevailed in modern Europe. Calderon, in his religious autos, has attempted to fulfil some of the high conditions of dramatic representation neglected by Shakespeare; such as the establishing a relation between the drama and religion, and the accommodating them to music and dancing; but he omits the observation of conditions still more important, and more is lost than gained by the substitution of the rigidly defined and ever-repeated idealisms of a distorted superstition for the living impersonations of the truth of human passion.

But I digress. The connection of scenic exhibitions with the improvement or corruption of the manners of men has been universally recognized; in other words, the presence or absence of poetry in its most perfect and universal form has been found to be connected with good and evil in conduct or habit. The corruption which has been imputed to the drama as an effect, begins, when the poetry employed in its constitution ends: I appeal to the history of manners whether the periods of the growth of the one and the decline of the other have not corresponded with an exactness equal to any example of moral cause and effect.

The drama at Athens, or wheresoever else it may have approached to its perfection, ever coexisted with the moral and intellectual greatness of the age. The tragedies of the Athenian poets are as mirrors in which the spectator beholds himself, under a thin disguise of circumstance, stripped of all but that ideal perfection and energy which everyone feels to be the internal type of all that he loves, admires, and would become. The imagination is enlarged by a sympathy with pains and passions so mighty, that they distend in their conception the capacity of that by which they are conceived; the good affections are strengthened by pity, indignation, terror, and sorrow; and an exalted calm is prolonged from the satiety of this high exercise of them into the tumult of familiar life: even crime is disarmed of half its horror and all its contagion by being represented as the fatal consequence of the unfathomable agencies of nature; error is thus divested of its wilfulness; men can no longer cherish it as the creation of their choice. In a drama of the highest order there is little food for censure or hatred; it teaches rather self-knowledge and self-respect. Neither the eye nor the mind can see itself, unless reflected upon that which it resembles. The drama, so long as it continues to express poetry, is as a prismatic and many-sided mirror, which collects the brightest rays of human nature and divides and reproduces them from the simplicity of these elementary forms, and touches them with majesty and beauty, and multiplies all that it reflects, and endows it with the power of propagating its like wherever it may fall.

But in periods of the decay of social life, the drama sympathizes with that decay. Tragedy becomes a cold imitation of the form of the great masterpieces of antiquity, divested of all harmonious accompaniment of the kindred arts; and often the very form misunderstood, or a weak attempt to teach certain doctrines, which the writer considers as moral truths; and which are usually no more than specious flatteries of some gross vice or weakness, with which the author, in common with his auditors, are infected. Hence what has been called the classical and domestic drama. Addison's "Cato" is a specimen of the one; and would it were not superfluous to cite examples of the other! To such purposes poetry cannot be made subservient. Poetry is a sword of lightning, ever unsheathed, which consumes the scabbard that would contain it. And thus we observe that all dramatic writings of this nature are unimaginative in a singular degree; they affect sentiment and passion, which, divested of imagination, are other names for caprice and appetite. The period in our own history of the grossest degradation of the drama is the reign of Charles II, when all forms in which poetry had been accustomed to be expressed became hymns to the triumph of kingly power over liberty and virtue. Milton stood alone illuminating an age unworthy of him. At such periods the calculating principle pervades all the forms of dramatic exhibition, and poetry ceases to be expressed upon them. Comedy loses its ideal universality: wit succeeds to humor; we laugh from self-complacency and triumph, instead of pleasure; malignity, sarcasm, and contempt succeed to sympathetic merriment; we hardly laugh, but we smile. Obscenity, which is ever blasphemy against the divine beauty in life, becomes, from the very veil which it assumes, more active if less disgusting: it is a monster for which the corruption of society forever brings forth new food, which it devours in secret.

The drama being that form under which a greater number of modes of expression of poetry are susceptible of being combined than any other, the connection of poetry and social good is more observable in the drama than in whatever other form. And it is indisputable that the highest perfection of human society has ever corresponded with the highest dramatic excellence; and that the corruption or the extinction of the drama in a nation where it has once flourished is a mark of a corruption of manners, and an extinction of the energies which sustain the soul of social life. But, as Machiavelli says of political institutions, that life may be preserved and renewed, if men should arise capable of bringing back the drama to its principles. And this is true with respect to poetry in its most extended sense: all language, institution, and form require not only to be produced but to be sustained: the office and character of a poet participate in the divine nature as regards providence, no less than as regards creation.

Civil war, the spoils of Asia, and the fatal predominance first of the Macedonian, and then of the Roman arms, were so many symbols of the extinction or suspension of the creative faculty in Greece. The bucolic writers, who found patronage under the lettered tyrants of Sicily and Egypt, were the latest representatives of its most glorious reign. Their poetry is intensely melodious; like the odor of the tuberose, it overcomes and sickens the spirit with excess of sweetness; whilst the poetry of the preceding age was as a meadow-gale of June, which mingles the fragrance of all the flowers of the field, and adds a quickening and harmonizing spirit of its own which endows the sense with a power of sustaining its extreme delight. The bucolic and erotic delicacy in written poetry is correlative with that softness in statuary, music, and the kindred arts, and even in manners and institutions, which distinguished the epoch to which I now refer. Nor is it the poetical faculty itself, or any misapplication of it, to which this want of harmony is to be imputed. An equal sensibility to the influence of the senses and the affections is to be found in the writings of Homer and Sophocles: the former, especially, has clothed sensual and pathetic images with irresistible attractions. Their superiority over these succeeding writers consists in the presence of those thoughts which belong to the inner faculties of our nature, not in the absence of those which are connected with the external; their incomparable perfection consists in a harmony of the union of all. It is not what the erotic poets have, but what they have not, in which their imperfection consists. It is not inasmuch as they were poets, but inasmuch as they were not poets, that they can be considered with any plausibility as connected with the corruption of their age. Had that corruption availed so as to extinguish in them the sensibility to pleasure, passion, and natural scenery, which is imputed to them as an imperfection, the last triumph of evil would have been achieved. For the end of social corruption is to destroy all sensibility to pleasure; and, therefore, it is corruption. It begins at the imagination and the intellect as at the core, and distributes itself thence as a paralyzing venom, through the affections into the very appetites, until all become a torpid mass in which hardly sense survives. At the approach of such a period, poetry ever addresses itself to those faculties which are the last to be destroyed, and its voice is heard, like the footsteps of Astræa, departing from the world. Poetry ever communicates all the pleasure which men are capable of receiving: it is ever still the light of life; the source of whatever of beautiful or generous or true can have place in an evil time. It will readily be confessed that those among the luxurious citizens of Syracuse and Alexandria, who were delighted with the poems of Theocritus, were less cold, cruel, and sensual than the remnant of their tribe. But corruption must utterly have destroyed the fabric of human society before poetry can ever cease. The sacred links of that chain have never been entirely disjoined, which descending through the minds of many men is attached to those great minds, whence as from a magnet the invisible effluence is sent forth, which at once connects, animates, and sustains the life of all. It is the faculty which contains within itself the seeds at once of its own and of social renovation. And let us not circumscribe the effects of the bucolic and erotic poetry within the limits of the sensibility of those to whom it was addressed. They may have perceived the beauty of those immortal compositions, simply as fragments and isolated portions: those who are more finely organized, or born in a happier age, may recognize them as episodes to that great poem, which all poets, like the co-operating thoughts of one great mind, have built up since the beginning of the world.

The same revolutions within a narrower sphere had place in ancient Rome; but the actions and forms of its social life never seem to have been perfectly saturated with the poetical element. The Romans appear to have considered the Greeks as the selectest treasuries of the selectest forms of manners and of nature, and to have abstained from creating in measured language, sculpture, music, or architecture, anything which might bear a particular relation to their own condition, whilst it should bear a general one to the universal constitution of the world. But we judge from partial evidence, and we judge perhaps partially. Ennius, Varro, Pacuvius, and Accius, all great poets, have been lost. Lucretius is in the highest, and Virgil in a very high sense, a creator. The chosen delicacy of expressions of the latter are as a mist of light which conceal from us the intense and exceeding truth of his conceptions of nature. Livy is instinct with poetry. Yet Horace, Catullus, Ovid, and generally the other great writers of the Vergilian age, saw man and nature in the mirror of Greece. The institutions also, and the religion of Rome, were less poetical than those of Greece, as the shadow is less vivid than the substance. Hence poetry in Rome seemed to follow, rather than accompany, the perfection of political and domestic society. The true poetry of Rome lived in its institutions; for whatever of beautiful, true, and majestic, they contained, could have sprung only from the faculty which creates the order in which they consist. The life of Camillus, the death of Regulus; the expectation of the senators, in their godlike state, of the victorious Gauls; the refusal of the republic to make peace with Hannibal, after the battle of Cannæ, were not the consequences of a refined calculation of the probable personal advantage to result from such a rhythm and order in the shows of life, to those who were at once the poets and the actors of these immortal dramas. The imagination beholding the beauty of this order, created it out of itself according to its own idea; the consequence was empire, and the reward ever-living fame. These things are not the less poetry, *quia carent vate sacro* [because they lack the sacred prophet (or divine poet)—ed.]. They are the episodes of that cyclic poem written by Time upon the memories of men. The Past, like an inspired rhapsodist, fills the theatre of everlasting generations with their harmony.

At length the ancient system of religion and manners had fulfilled the circle of its revolutions. And the world would have fallen into utter anarchy and darkness, but that there were found poets among the authors of the Christian and chivalric systems of manners and religion, who created forms of opinion and action never before conceived; which, copied into the imaginations of men, became as generals to the bewildered armies of their thoughts. It is foreign to the present purpose to touch upon the evil produced by these systems: except that we protest, on the ground of the principles already established, that no portion of it can be attributed to the poetry they contain.

It is probable that the poetry of Moses, Job, David, Solomon, and Isaiah had produced a great effect upon the mind of Jesus and his disciples. The scattered fragments preserved to us by the biographers of this extraordinary person are all instinct with the most vivid poetry. But his doctrines seem to have been quickly distorted. At a certain period after the prevalence of a system of opinions founded upon those promulgated by him, the three forms into which Plato had distributed the faculties of mind underwent a sort of apotheosis, and became the object of the worship of the civilized world. Here it is to be confessed that "Light seems to thicken," and

> The crow makes wing to the rooky wood,
> Good things of day begin to droop and drowse,
> And night's black agents to their preys do rouse.

But mark how beautiful an order has sprung from the dust and blood of this fierce chaos! how the world, as from a resurrection, balancing itself on the golden wings of Knowledge and of Hope, has reassumed its yet unwearied flight into the heaven of time. Listen to the music, unheard by outward ears, which is as a ceaseless and invisible wind, nourishing its everlasting course with strength and swiftness.

The poetry in the doctrines of Jesus Christ, and the mythology and institutions of the Celtic conquerors of the Roman Empire, outlived the darkness and the convulsions connected with their growth and victory, and blended themselves in a new fabric of manners and opinion. It is an error to impute the ignorance of the dark ages to the Christian doctrines or the predominance of the Celtic nations. Whatever of evil their agencies may have contained sprang from the extinction of the poetical principle, connected with the progress of despotism and superstition. Men, from causes too intricate to be here discussed, had become insensible and selfish: their own will had become feeble, and yet they were its slaves, and thence the slaves of the will of others: lust, fear, avarice, cruelty, and fraud, characterized a race amongst whom no one was to be found capable of creating in form, language, or institution. The moral anomalies of such a state of society are not justly to be charged upon any class of events immediately connected with them, and those events are most entitled to our approbation which could dissolve it most expeditiously. It is unfortunate for those who cannot distinguish words from thoughts, that many of these anomalies have been incorporated into our popular religion.

It was not until the eleventh century that the effects of the poetry of the Christian and chivalric systems began to manifest themselves. The principle of equality had been discovered and applied by Plato in his *Republic* as the theoretical rule of the mode in which the materials of pleasure and of power produced by the common skill and labor of human beings ought to be distributed among them. The limitations of this rule were asserted by him to be determined only by the sensibility of each, or the utility to result to all. Plato, following the doctrines of Timæus and Pythagoras, taught also a moral and intellectual system of doctrine, comprehending at once the past, the present, and the future condition of man. Jesus Christ divulged the sacred and eternal truths contained in these views to mankind, and Christianity, in its abstract purity, became the exoteric expression of the esoteric doctrines of the poetry and wisdom of antiquity. The incorporation of the Celtic nations with the exhausted population of the south impressed upon it the figure of the poetry existing in their mythology and institutions. The result was a sum of the action and reaction of all the causes included in it; for it may be assumed as a maxim that no nation or religion can supersede any other without incorporating into itself a portion of that which it supersedes. The abolition of personal and domestic slavery, and the emancipation of women from a great part of the degrading restraints of antiquity, were among the consequences of these events.

The abolition of personal slavery is the basis of the highest political hope that it can enter into the mind of man to conceive. The freedom of women produced the poetry of sexual love. Love became a religion, the idols of whose worship were ever present. It was as if the statues of Apollo and the Muses had been endowed with life and motion, and had walked forth among their worshippers; so that earth became peopled with the inhabitants of a diviner world. The familiar appearance and proceedings of life became wonderful and heavenly, and a paradise was created as out of the wrecks of Eden. And as this creation itself is poetry, so its creators were poets; and language was the instrument of their art: "Galeotto fù il libro, e chi lo scrisse" ["Galeotto was the book and the one who wrote it"—ed.]. The Provençal Trouveurs, or inventors, preceded Petrarch, whose verses are as spells, which unseal the inmost enchanted fountains of the delight which is in the grief of love. It is impossible to feel them without becoming a portion of that beauty which we contemplate: it were superfluous to explain how the gentleness and the elevation of mind connected with these sacred emotions can render men more amiable, more generous and wise, and lift them out of the dull vapors of the little world of self. Dante understood the secret things of love even more than Petrarch. His *Vita Nuova* is an inexhaustible fountain of purity of sentiment and language: it is the idealized history of that period, and those intervals of his life which were dedicated to love. His apotheosis of Beatrice in Paradise, and the gradations of his own love and her loveliness, by which as by steps he feigns himself to have ascended to the throne of the Supreme Cause, is the most glorious imagination of modern poetry. The acutest critics have justly reversed the judgment of the vulgar, and the order of the great acts of the "Divine Drama," in the measure of the admiration which they accord to the Hell, Purgatory, and Paradise. The latter is a perpetual hymn of everlasting love. Love, which found a worthy poet in Plato alone of all the ancients, has been celebrated by a chorus of the greatest writers of the renovated world; and the music has penetrated the caverns of society, and its echoes still drown the dissonance of arms and superstition. At successive intervals, Ariosto, Tasso, Shakespeare, Spenser, Calderon, Rousseau, and the great writers of our own age, have celebrated the dominion of love, planting as it were trophies in the human mind of that sublimest victory over sensuality and force. The true relation borne to each other by the sexes into which humankind is distributed has become less misunderstood; and if the error which confounded diversity with inequality of the powers of the two sexes has been partially recognised in the opinions and institutions of modern Europe, we owe this great benefit to the worship of which chivalry was the law, and poets the prophets.

The poetry of Dante may be considered as the bridge thrown over the stream of time, which unites the modern and ancient world. The distorted notions of invisible things which Dante and his rival Milton have idealized, are merely the mask and the mantle in which these great poets walk through eternity enveloped and disguised. It is a difficult question to determine how far they were conscious of the distinction which must have subsisted in their minds between their own creeds and that of the people. Dante at least appears to wish to mark the full extent of it by placing Rhipæus, whom Vergil calls *justissimus unus* [the one most just—ed.], in Paradise, and observing a most heretical caprice in his distribution of rewards and punishments. And Milton's poem contains within itself a philosophical refutation of that system, of which, by a strange and natural antithesis, it has been a chief popular support. Nothing can exceed the energy and magnificence of the character of Satan as expressed in *Paradise Lost*. It is a mistake to suppose that he could ever have been intended for the popular personification of evil. Implacable hate, patient cunning, and a sleepless refinement of device to inflict the extremist anguish on an enemy, these things are evil; and, although venial in a slave, are not to be forgiven in a tyrant; although redeemed by much that ennobles his defeat in one subdued, are marked by all that dishonors his conquest in the victor. Milton's Devil as a moral being is as far superior to his God, as one who perseveres in some purpose which he has conceived to be excellent in spite of adversity and torture, is to one who in the cold security of undoubted triumph inflicts the most horrible revenge upon his enemy, not from any mistaken notion of inducing him to repent of a perseverance in enmity, but with the alleged design of exasperating him to deserve new torments. Milton has so far violated the popular creed (if this shall be judged to be a violation) as to have alleged no superiority of moral virtue to his God over his Devil. And this bold neglect of a direct moral purpose is the most decisive proof of the supremacy of Milton's genius. He mingled as it were the elements of human nature as colors upon a single pallet, and arranged them in the composition of his great picture according to the laws of epic truth; that is, according to the laws of that principle by which a series of actions of the external universe and of intelligent and ethical beings is calculated to excite the sympathy of succeeding generations of mankind. The "Divina Commedia" and "Paradise Lost" have conferred upon modern mythology a systematic form; and when change and time shall have added one more superstition to the mass of those which have arisen and decayed upon the earth, commentators will be learnedly employed in elucidating the religion of ancestral Europe, only not utterly forgotten because it will have been stamped with the eternity of genius.

Homer was the first and Dante the second epic poet: that is, the second poet, the series of whose creations bore a defined and intelligible relation to the knowledge and sentiment and religion of the age in which he lived, and of the ages which followed it, developing itself in correspondence with their de-velopment. For Lucretius had limed the wings of his swift spirit in the dregs of the sensible world; and Vergil, with a modesty that ill became his genius, had affected the fame of an imitator, even whilst he created anew all that he copied; and none among the flock of mock-birds, though their notes were sweet, Apollonius Rhodius, Quintus Calaber, Nonnus, Lucan, Statius, or Claudian, have sought even to fulfil a single condition of epic truth. Milton was the third epic poet. For if the title of epic in its highest sense be refused to the "Æneid," still less can it be conceded to the "Orlando Furioso," the "Gerusalemme Lib-erata," the "Lusiad," or the "Faerie Queene."

Dante and Milton were both deeply penetrated with the ancient religion of the civilized world; and its spirit exists in their poetry probably in the same proportion as its forms survived in the unreformed worship of modern Europe. The one preceded and the other followed the Reformation at almost equal intervals. Dante was the first religious reformer, and Luther surpassed him rather in the rudeness and acrimony than in the boldness of his censures of papal usurpation. Dante was the first awakener of entranced Europe; he created a language, in itself music and persuasion, out of a chaos of inharmonious barbarians. He was the congregator of those great spirits who presided over the resurrection of learning; the Lucifer of that starry flock which in the thirteenth century shone forth from republican Italy, as from a heaven, into the darkness of the benighted world. His very words are instinct with spirit; each is as a spark, a burning atom of inextinguishable thought; and many yet lie covered in the ashes of their birth, and pregnant with the lightning which has yet found no conductor. All high poetry is infinite; it is as the first acorn, which contained all oaks potentially. Veil after veil may be undrawn, and the inmost naked beauty of the meaning never exposed. A great poem is a fountain forever overflowing with the waters of wisdom and delight; and after one person and one age has exhausted all its divine effluence which their peculiar relations enable them to share, another and yet another succeeds, and new relations are ever developed, the source of an unforeseen and an unconceived delight.

The age immediately succeeding to that of Dante, Petrarch, and Boccaccio was characterized by a revival of painting, sculpture, and architecture. Chaucer caught the sacred inspiration, and the superstructure of English literature is based upon the materials of Italian invention.

But let us not be betrayed from a defence into a critical history of poetry and its influence on society. Be it enough to have pointed out the effects of poets, in the large and true sense of the word, upon their own and all succeeding times.

But poets have been challenged to resign the civic crown to reasoners and mechanists, on another plea. It is admitted that the exercise of the imagination is most delightful, but it is alleged that that of reason is more useful. Let us examine as the grounds of this distinction what is here meant by utility. Pleasure or good, in a general sense, is that which the consciousness of a sensitive and intelligent being seeks, and in which, when found, it acquiesces. There are two kinds of pleasure, one durable, universal, and permanent; the other transitory and particular. Utility may either express the means of producing the former or the latter. In the former sense, whatever strengthens and purifies the affections, enlarges the imagination, and adds spirit to sense, is useful. But a narrower meaning may be assigned to the word utility, confining it to express that which banishes the importunity of the wants of our animal nature, the surrounding men with security of life, the dispersing the grosser delusions of superstitions, and the conciliating such a degree of mutual forbearance among men as may consist with the motives of personal advantage.

Undoubtedly the promoters of utility, in this limited sense, have their appointed office in society. They follow the footsteps of poets, and copy the sketches of their creations into the book of common life. They make space, and give time. Their exertions are of the highest value, so long as they confine their administration of the concerns of the inferior powers of our nature within the limits due to the superior ones. But whilst the sceptic destroys gross superstitions, let him spare to deface, as some of the French writers have defaced, the eternal truths charactered upon the imaginations of men. Whilst the mechanist abridges, and the political economist combines labor, let them beware that their speculations, for want of correspondence with those first principles which belong to the imagination, do not tend, as they have in modern England, to exasperate at once the extremes of luxury and want. They have exemplified the saying, "To him that hath, more shall be given; and from him that hath not, the little that he hath shall be taken away." The rich have become richer, and the poor have become poorer; and the vessel of the State is driven between the Scylla and Charybdis of anarchy and despotism. Such are the effects which must ever flow from an unmitigated exercise of the calculating faculty.

It is difficult to define pleasure in its highest sense; the definition involving a number of apparent paradoxes. For, from an inexplicable defect of harmony in the constitution of human nature, the pain of the inferior is frequently connected with the pleasures of the superior portions of our being. Sorrow, terror, anguish, despair itself, are often the chosen expressions of an approximation to the highest good. Our sympathy in tragic fiction depends on this principle; tragedy delights by affording a shadow of the pleasure which exists in pain. This is the source also of the melancholy which is inseparable from the sweetest melody. The pleasure that is in sorrow is sweeter than the pleasure of pleasure itself. And hence the saying, "It is better to go to the house of mourning than to the house of mirth." Not that this highest species of pleasure is necessarily linked with pain. The delight of love and friendship, the ecstasy of the admiration of nature, the joy of the perception and still more of the creation of poetry, is often wholly unalloyed.

The production and assurance of pleasure in this highest sense is true utility. Those who produce and preserve this pleasure are poets or poetical philosophers.

The exertions of Locke, Hume, Gibbon, Voltaire, Rousseau [although Rousseau has been thus classed, he was essentially a poet. The others, even Voltaire, were mere reasoners.—Shelley's note], and their disciples, in favor of oppressed and deluded humanity, are entitled to the gratitude of mankind. Yet it is easy to calculate the degree of moral and intellectual improvement which the world would have exhibited, had they never lived. A little more nonsense would have been talked for a century or two; and perhaps a few more men, women, and children burnt as heretics. We might not at this moment have been congratulating each other on the abolition of the Inquisition in Spain. But it exceeds all imagination to conceive what would have been the moral condition of the world if neither Dante, Petrarch, Boccaccio, Chaucer, Shakespeare, Calderon, Lord Bacon, nor Milton, had ever existed; if Raphael and Michael Angelo had never been born; if the Hebrew poetry had never been translated; if a revival of the study of Greek literature had never taken place; if no monuments of ancient sculpture had been handed down to us; and if the poetry of the religion of the ancient world had been extinguished together with its belief. The human mind could never, except by the intervention of these excitements, have been awakened to the invention of the grosser sciences, and that application of analytical reasoning to the aberrations of society, which it is now attempted to exalt over the direct expression of the inventive and creative faculty itself.

We have more moral, political, and historical wisdom than we know how to reduce into practice; we have more scientific and economical knowledge than can be accommodated to the just distribution of the produce which it multiplies. The poetry in these systems of thought is concealed by the accumulation of facts and calculating processes. There is no want of knowledge respecting what is wisest and best in morals, government, and political economy, or at least, what is wiser and better than what men now practise and endure. But we let I dare not wait upon I would, like the poor cat in the adage. We want the creative faculty to imagine that which we know; we want the generous impulse to act that which we imagine; we want the poetry of life; our calculations have outrun conception; we have eaten more than we can digest. The cultivation of those sciences which have enlarged the limits of the empire of man over the external world, has, for want of the poetical faculty, proportionally circumscribed those of the internal world; and man, having enslaved the elements, remains himself a slave. To what but a cultivation of the mechanical arts in a degree disproportioned to the presence of the creative faculty, which is the basis of all knowledge, is to be attributed the abuse of all invention for abridging and combining labor, to the exasperation of the inequality of mankind? From what other cause has it arisen that the discoveries which should have lightened, have added a weight to the curse imposed on Adam? Poetry, and the principle of Self, of which money is the visible incarnation, are the God and Mammon of the world.

The functions of the poetical faculty are twofold: by one it creates new materials of knowledge, and power, and pleasure; by the other it engenders in the mind a desire to reproduce and arrange them according to a certain rhythm and order which may be called the beautiful and the good. The cultivation of poetry is never more to be desired than at periods when, from an excess of the selfish and calculating principle, the accumulation of the materials of external life exceed the quantity of the power of assimilating them to the internal laws of human nature. The body has then become too unwieldy for that which animates it.

Poetry is indeed something divine. It is at once the centre and circumference of knowledge; it is that which comprehends all science, and that to which all science must be referred. It is at the same time the root and blossom of all other systems of thought; it is that from which all spring, and that which adorns all; and that which, if blighted, denies the fruit and the seed, and withholds from the barren world the nourishment and the succession of the scions of the tree of life. It is the perfect and consummate surface and bloom of all things; it is as the odor and the color of the rose to the texture of the elements which compose it, as the form and splendor of unfaded beauty to the secrets of anatomy and corruption. What were virtue, love, patriotism, friendship—what were the scenery of this beautiful universe which we inhabit; what were our consolations on this side of the grave—and what were our aspirations beyond it, if poetry did not ascend to bring light and fire from those eternal regions where the owl-winged faculty of calculation dare not ever soar? Poetry is not like reasoning, a power to be exerted according to the determination of the will. A man cannot say, "I will compose poetry." The greatest poet even cannot say it; for the mind in creation is as a fading coal, which some invisible influence, like an inconstant wind, awakens to transitory brightness; this power arises from within, like the color of a flower which fades and changes as it is developed, and the conscious portions of our natures are unprophetic either of its approach or its departure. Could this influence be durable in its original purity and force, it is impossible to predict the greatness of the results; but when composition begins, inspiration is already on the decline, and the most glorious poetry that has ever been communicated to the world is probably a feeble shadow of the original conceptions of the poet. I appeal to the greatest poets of the present day, whether it is not an error to assert that the finest passages of poetry are produced by labor and study. The toil and the delay recommended by critics can be justly interpreted to mean no more than a careful observation of the inspired moments, and an artificial connection of the spaces between their suggestions by the intertexture of conventional expressions; a necessity only imposed by the limitedness of the poetical faculty itself; for Milton conceived the "Paradise Lost" as a whole before he executed it in portions. We have his own authority also for the Muse having "dictated" to him the "unpremeditated song." And let this be an answer to those who would allege the fifty-six various readings of the first line of the "Orlando Furioso." Compositions so produced are to poetry what mosaic is to painting. This instinct and intuition of the poetical faculty are still more observable in the plastic and pictorial arts; a great statue or picture grows under the power of the artist as a child in a mother's womb; and the very mind which directs the hands in formation is incapable of accounting to itself for the origin, the gradations, or the media of the process.

Poetry is the record of the best and happiest moments of the happiest and best minds. We are aware of evanescent visitations of thought and feeling some-times associated with place or person, sometimes regarding our own mind alone, and always arising unforeseen and departing unbidden, but elevating and delightful beyond all expression: so that even in the desire and the regret they leave, there cannot but be pleasure, participating as it does in the nature of its object. It is as it were the interpretation of a diviner nature through our own; but its footsteps are like those of a wind over the sea, which the coming calm erases, and whose traces remain only as on the wrinkled sand which paves it. These and corresponding conditions of being are experienced principally by those of the most delicate sensibility and the most enlarged imagination; and the state of mind produced by them is at war with every base desire. The enthusiasm of virtue, love, patriotism, and friendship is essentially linked with such emotions; and whilst they last, self appears as what it is, an atom to a universe. Poets are not only subject to these experiences as spirits of the most refined organization, but they can color all that they combine with the evanes-cent hues of this ethereal world; a word, a trait in the representation of a scene or a passion will touch the enchanted chord, and reanimate, in those who have ever experienced these emotions, the sleeping, the cold, the buried image of the past. Poetry thus makes immortal all that is best and most beautiful in the world; it arrests the vanishing apparitions which haunt the interlunations of life, and veiling them, or in language or in form, sends them forth among mankind, bearing sweet news of kindred joy to those with whom their sisters abide— abide, because there is no portal of expression from the caverns of the spirit which they inhabit into the universe of things. Poetry redeems from decay the visitations of the divinity in man.

Poetry turns all things to loveliness; it exalts the beauty of that which is most beautiful, and it adds beauty to that which is most deformed; it marries exul-tation and horror, grief and pleasure, eternity and change; it subdues to union under its light yoke all irreconcilable things. It transmutes all that it touches, and every form moving within the radiance of its presence is changed by wondrous sympathy to an incarnation of the spirit which it breathes: its secret alchemy turns to potable gold the poisonous waters which flow from death through life; it strips the veil of familiarity from the world, and lays bare the naked and sleeping beauty, which is the spirit of its forms.

All things exist as they are perceived: at least in relation to the percipient. "The mind is its own place, and of itself can make a heaven of hell, a hell of heaven." But poetry defeats the curse which binds us to be subjected to the accident of surrounding impressions. And whether it spreads its own figured curtain, or withdraws life's dark veil from before the scene of things, it equally creates for us a being within our being. It makes us the inhabitants of a world to which the familiar world is a chaos. It reproduces the common universe of which we are portions and percipients, and it purges from our inward sight the film of familiarity which obscures from us the wonder of our being. It compels us to feel that which we perceive, and to imagine that which we know. It creates anew the universe, after it has been annihilated in our minds by the recurrence of impressions blunted by reiteration. It justifies the bold and true words of Tasso—"Non merita nome di creatore, se non Iddio ed il Poeta" [none but God and the poet deserve the name of Creator—ed.].

A poet, as he is the author to others of the highest wisdom, pleasure, virtue, and glory, so he ought personally to be the happiest, the best, the wisest, and the most illustrious of men. As to his glory, let time be challenged to declare whether the fame of any other institutor of human life be comparable to that of a poet. That he is the wisest, the happiest, and the best, inasmuch as he is a poet, is equally incontrovertible: the greatest poets have been men of the most spotless virtue, of the most consummate prudence, and, if we would look into the interior of their lives, the most fortunate of men: and the exceptions, as they regard those who possessed the poetic faculty in a high yet inferior degree, will be found on consideration to confine rather than destroy the rule. Let us for a moment stoop to the arbitration of popular breath, and usurping and uniting in our own persons the incompatible characters of accuser, witness, judge, and executioner, let us decide without trial, testimony, or form, that certain motives of those who are "there sitting where we dare not soar," are reprehensible. Let us assume that Homer was a drunkard, that Vergil was a flatterer, that Horace was a coward, that Tasso was a madman, that Lord Bacon was a peculator, that Raphael was a libertine, that Spenser was a poet laureate. It is inconsistent with this division of our subject to cite living poets, but posterity has done ample justice to the great names now referred to. Their errors have been weighed and found to have been dust in the balance; if their sins "were as scarlet, they are now white as snow"; they have been washed in the blood of the mediator and redeemer, Time. Observe in what a ludicrous chaos the imputations of real or fictitious crime have been confused in the contemporary calumnies against poetry and poets; consider how little is as it appears—or appears as it is; look to your own motives, and judge not, lest ye be judged.

Poetry, as has been said, differs in this respect from logic, that it is not subject to the control of the active powers of the mind, and that its birth and recurrence have no necessary connection with the consciousness or will. It is presumptuous to determine that these are the necessary conditions of all mental causation, when mental effects are experienced unsusceptible of being referred to them. The frequent recurrence of the poetical power, it is obvious to suppose, may produce in the mind a habit of order and harmony correlative with its own nature and with its effects upon other minds. But in the intervals of inspiration, and they may be frequent without being durable, a poet becomes a man, and is abandoned to the sudden reflux of the influences under which others habitually live. But as he is more delicately organized than other men, and sensible to pain and pleasure, both his own and that of others, in a degree unknown to them, he will avoid the one and pursue the other with an ardor proportioned to this difference. And he renders himself obnoxious to calumny, when he neglects to observe the circumstances under which these objects of universal pursuit and flight have disguised themselves in one another's garments.

But there is nothing necessarily evil in this error, and thus cruelty, envy, revenge, avarice, and the passions purely evil have never formed any portion of the popular imputations on the lives of poets.

I have thought it most favorable to the cause of truth to set down these remarks according to the order in which they were suggested to my mind, by a consideration of the subject itself, instead of observing the formality of a polemical reply; but if the view which they contain be just, they will be found to involve a refutation of the arguers against poetry, so far at least as regards the first division of the subject. I can readily conjecture what should have moved the gall of some learned and intelligent writers who quarrel with certain versifiers; I confess myself, like them, unwilling to be stunned by the Theseids of the hoarse Codri of the day. Bavius and Mævius undoubtedly are, as they ever were, insufferable persons. But it belongs to a philosophical critic to distinguish rather than confound.

The first part of these remarks has related to poetry in its elements and principles; and it has been shown, as well as the narrow limits assigned them would permit, that what is called poetry, in a restricted sense, has a common source with all other forms of order and of beauty, according to which the materials of human life are susceptible of being arranged, and which is poetry in an universal sense.

The second part will have for its object an application of these principles to the present state of the cultivation of poetry, and a defence of the attempt to idealize the modern forms of manners and opinions, and compel them into a subordination to the imaginative and creative faculty. For the literature of England, an energetic development of which has ever preceded or accompanied a great and free development of the national will, has arisen as it were from a new birth. In spite of the low-thoughted envy which would undervalue contemporary merit, our own will be a memorable age in intellectual achievements, and we live among such philosophers and poets as surpass beyond comparison any who have appeared since the last national struggle for civil and religious liberty. The most unfailing herald, companion, and follower of the awakening of a great people to work a beneficial change in opinion or institution, is poetry. At such periods there is an accumulation of the power of communicating and receiving intense and impassioned conceptions respecting man and nature. The person in whom this power resides, may often, as far as regards many portions of their nature, have little apparent correspondence with that spirit of good of which they are the ministers. But even whilst they deny and abjure, they are yet compelled to serve, that power which is seated on the throne of their own soul. It is impossible to read the compositions of the most celebrated writers of the present day without being startled with the electric life which burns within their words. They measure the circumference and sound the depths of human nature with a comprehensive and all-penetrating spirit, and they are themselves perhaps the most sincerely astonished at its manifestations; for it is less their spirit than the spirit of the age. Poets are the hierophants of an unapprehended inspiration; the mirrors of the gigantic shadows which futurity casts upon the present; the words which express what they understand not; the trumpets which sing to battle, and feel not what they inspire; the influence which is moved not, but moves. Poets are the unacknowledged legislators of the world.

20

WILLIAM CULLEN BRYANT (1794–1878)

Bryant established himself as a poet while still in his teens and was generally regarded as the leading American poet from about 1825 until his death more than fifty years later. During the same period, he was an editor of the New York *Evening Post*. His most admired poem has always been "Thanatopsis," which he published in 1817 but began much earlier. He was trained as a lawyer and employed as a journalist. Originally a Democrat, he later became one of the founders of the Republican Party. Late in life he published translations of Homer's epics: the *Iliad* (1870) and the *Odyssey*(1871–1872).

Published in 1863, "The Poet" comes relatively late in Bryant's career, so that it may be read as a summing up, the advice that an old poet may give to someone aspiring to excel in the art. Bryant's diction recalls Wordsworth's famous claim, "All good poetry is the spontaneous overflow of powerful feelings: it takes its origin from emotion recollected in tranquillity." In some senses, Bryant is participating in an old debate about the springs of poetry. For most novices, it ought to be enough to express one's feelings honestly and spontaneously, without anxiety that some cruel critic is going to count off for spelling. Most who get beyond their novitiate know—as Bryant suggests—that the feeling, while necessary, is not sufficient. Feeling is just the beginning. The strongest advocate of the opposing party had been Edgar Allan Poe, who was born fifteen years after Bryant and who died thirty-eight years before him (he did say some words in praise of the older poet). Poe argued that the work of literature is conscious and intelligent calculation of psychological effects. In 1888, not so very long after Bryant's death, Oscar Wilde remarked that "All bad poetry springs from genuine feeling" (*The Critic as Artist*). Does that mean that all poetry that springs from genuine feeling is bad? Not necessarily. It is possible that all poetry, the bad as well as the good, springs from genuine feeling. But genuine feeling is not enough. The argument continues.

THE POET (1863)

Thou, who wouldst wear the name
    Of poet mid thy brethren of mankind,
And clothe in words of flame
    Thoughts that shall live within the general mind!
Deem not the framing of a deathless lay
The pastime of a drowsy summer day.

But gather all thy powers,
    And wreak them on the verse that thou dost weave,
And in thy lonely hours,
    At silent morning or at wakeful eve,
While the warm current tingles through thy veins,
Set forth the burning words in fluent strains.

No smooth array of phrase,
    Artfully sought and ordered though it be,
Which the cold rhymer lays
    Upon his page with languid industry,
Can wake the listless pulse to livelier speed,
Or fill with sudden tears the eyes that read.

The secret wouldst thou know
    To touch the heart or fire the blood at will?
Let thine own eyes o'erflow;
    Let thy lips quiver with the passionate thrill;
Seize the great thought, ere yet its power be past,
And bind, in words, the fleet emotion fast.

Then should thy verse appear
    Halting and harsh, and all unaptly wrought,
Touch the crude line with fear,
    Save in the moment of impassioned thought;
Then summon back the original glow, and mend
The strain with rapture that with fire was penned.

Yet let no empty gust
    Of passion find an utterance in thy lay,
A blast that whirls the dust
    Along the howling street and dies away;
But feelings of calm power and mighty sweep,
Like currents journeying through the windless deep.

Seek'st thou, in living lays,
    To limn the beauty of the earth and sky?
Before thine inner gaze
    Let all that beauty in clear vision lie;
Look on it with exceeding love, and write
The words inspired by wonder and delight.

Of tempests wouldst thou sing,
    Or tell of battles—make thyself a part
Of the great tumult; cling
    To the tossed wreck with terror in thy heart;
Scale, with the assaulting host, the rampart's height,
And strike and struggle in the thickest fight.

So shalt thou frame a lay
    That haply may endure from age to age,
And they who read shall say:
    "What witchery hangs upon this poet's page!
What art is his the written spells to find
That sway from mood to mood the willing mind!"

21

JOHN KEATS (1795–1821)

It is probable that John Keats produced more great poetry at an earlier age than any other major poet in English. Readers can play a game that asks, "What would Shakespeare's (or Milton's, or anyone else's) reputation be if he or she had died, like Keats, at twenty-five?" In almost every case the answer is "Zilch."

Keats's father, who kept a livery stable, died in a mishap in 1804; his mother died of consumption a few years later, when Keats was fourteen. As a teenager Keats was apprenticed to a surgeon and was qualified as a "dresser" and subsequently as a surgeon, in accordance with the medical regulations of the day.

Keats's first poems were written under the influence of Edmund Spenser, and all of Keats's work shows something of a Spenserian blend of sensuousness and intellectual depth, along with a love for the past, especially classical antiquity and the Middle Ages. Keats renders the sights and sounds that we are accustomed to in poetry, but, more than any other, he also attends to tastes, odors, and textures.

Friendship with the poet and editor Leigh Hunt was most helpful to Keats in his brief career as a poet. Thanks to Hunt, Keats's poetry was published in the *Examiner* and Keats got to meet Wordsworth and Shelley. When his poetry was viciously attacked in conservative magazines (such things were much rougher two centuries ago than is the rule today), Keats retreated somewhat into himself, at the same time having to take care of younger siblings (two brothers and a sister) who depended on him for friendship and support.

Toward the end of his life Keats lived in Hampstead next door to the house occupied by the family of his fiancée, Fanny Brawne. By 1819 Keats was ill with tuberculosis, possibly contracted from his brother Tom. Later, in search of a better climate, he went to Italy, but he died in Rome in early 1821, having asked that his epitaph read, "Here lies one whose name was writ in water."

Keats was never a formal critic of the sort who writes essays, reviews, and dissertations, but his marvelous letters display one of the finest critical minds ever in England. Some of his poems that delight in the pleasures and powers of poetry itself have become important critical documents. Keats was writing just when universal free public education was catching on in Europe and America, with a newly literate public eager to read and learn. To serve these new readers, literary periodicals proliferated in great numbers, and writers capable of furnishing the journals with writings of all sorts also proliferated. Keats was the most sensuous of poets, and one of those most devoted to sound and feeling. But he was also a reader, for whom the experience of specifically sitting down to read was profoundly emotional and intellectual. His poetry reports some of the experience of sitting down to read; he also records the experience of being a poet in England, with a living community of companions and a virtually living continuity of tradition going back far in time but not far at all in space.

POEMS

ON FIRST LOOKING INTO CHAPMAN'S HOMER
 (1817)

Much have I travell'd in the realms of gold,
  And many goodly states and kingdoms seen;
  Round many western islands have I been
Which bards in fealty to Apollo hold.
Oft of one wide expanse had I been told
  That deep-brow'd Homer ruled as his demesne;
  Yet did I never breathe its pure serene
Till I heard Chapman speak out loud and bold:
Then felt I like some watcher of the skies
  When a new planet swims into his ken;
Or like stout Cortez when with eagle eyes
  He star'd at the Pacific—and all his men
Look'd at each other with a wild surmise—
  Silent, upon a peak in Darien.

ON SITTING DOWN TO READ KING LEAR ONCE AGAIN (1818)

O golden-tongued Romance with serene lute!
   Fair plumed Syren! Queen of far away!
   Leave melodizing on this wintry day,
Shut up thine olden pages, and be mute:
Adieu! for once again the fierce dispute,
   Betwixt damnation and impassion'd clay
   Must I burn through; once more humbly assay
The bitter-sweet of this Shakespearian fruit.
Chief Poet! and ye clouds of Albion,
   Begetters of our deep eternal theme,
When through the old oak forest I am gone,
   Let me not wander in a barren dream,
But when I am consumed in the fire,
Give me new Phoenix wings to fly at my desire.

THE MERMAID TAVERN (1820)

Souls of poets dead and gone,
What Elysium have ye known—
Happy field or mossy cavern,
Choicer than the Mermaid Tavern?[1]
Have ye tippled drink more fine
Than mine host's Canary wine?[2]
Or are fruits of Paradise
Sweeter than those dainty pies
Of venison? O generous food!
Drest as though bold Robin Hood
Would, with his Maid Marian,
Sup and bowse from horn and can.[3]
I have heard that on a day
Mine host's signboard flew away,

---

1. Mermaid Tavern: Dating back to the sixteenth century, this tavern stood in London, to the east of St. Paul's Cathedral, with one entrance on Friday Street. There was a Friday Street Club, which is said to have included Shakespeare, Raleigh, Donne, and Jonson.
2. Canary wine: light sweet wine from the Canary Islands; mentioned more than once by Shakespeare.
3. bowse: booze.

Nobody knew whither, till
An astrologer's old quill
To a sheepskin gave the story,
Said he saw you in your glory
Underneath a new-old sign
Sipping beverage divine,
And pledging with contented smack
The Mermaid in the Zodiac.
Souls of poets dead and gone,
What Elysium have ye known—
Happy field or mossy cavern,
Choicer than the Mermaid Tavern?

22

RALPH WALDO EMERSON (1803–1882)

Known chiefly as a thinker and writer, Emerson began as a clergyman, ordained as a Unitarian minister and established as a popular preacher. In 1832,
after a crisis of conscience involving the sacrament of the Eucharist, he re-
signed his position at the Second Church of Boston. He studied classical
philosophy, particularly Plato, Platonists, and Neo-Platonists, along with Eastern religions, empirical philosophers such as Berkeley, Hume, and Locke,
and mystics such as Swedenborg. He was also deeply conversant with history,
language, and literature. In 1832 and 1833 he toured Europe and managed to
establish a lasting and mutually influential friendship with Thomas Carlyle;
he also met Wordsworth and Coleridge.

Returning from his travels with a new sense of purpose, he became a lecturer
and writer on an impressive range of topics. After 1835 he settled in Concord
(near Boston, Massachusetts) and cultivated the friendship of Henry David
Thoreau, Henry Wadsworth Longfellow, Nathaniel Hawthorne, Margaret
Fuller, and leaders of the Transcendentalist movement. During the 1850s he
was among the first to salute the genius of Walt Whitman. Much of Emerson's
poetry is inventive and profound, but now, two centuries after his birth, he may
be best known for the "Concord Hymn" ("Sung at the completion of the Battle
Monument, July 4, 1837") and its famous lines, "Here once the embattled farmers stood / And fired the shot heard round the world."

One of Emerson's best-known epigrams—"A foolish consistency is the hobgoblin of little minds, adored by little statesmen and philosophers and divines"—comes from "Self-Reliance," one of his best-known prose works. But he was capable of showing a wise consistency when he had to. The apparent inconsistency of his thought results in part from his habitual returning to primitive roots and his habitual expression in epigrams. The unit of his expression seems to be the phrase, with clauses, sentences, and paragraphs progressively giving up consistency and design. That may be a radically American approach. Like Whitman, Emerson acted as though he was one of the first thinkers and first poets, and the two of them habitually allied themselves with legendary personages from biblical and classical antiquity. Their practice is also radically democratic in its view of language, literature, and culture. Emerson's prose is raw and unfinished, like a home-made tool. Like Shelley, Emerson endowed poetry with the most solemn responsibilities of human life, so that he had little use for prettiness and jingles. But, it must be remembered, he was not foolishly consistent in his thinking or writing.

THE POET (1844, EXCERPT)

A moody child and wildly wise
Pursued the game with joyful eyes,
Which chose, like meteors, their way,
And rived the dark with private ray:
They overleapt the horizon's edge,
Searched with Apollo's privilege;
Through man, and woman, and sea, and star,
Saw the dance of nature forward far;
Through worlds, and races, and terms, and times,
Saw musical order, and pairing rhymes.[1]

Olympian bards who sung
Divine ideas below,
Which always find us young,
And always keep us so.[2]

---

1. Part of an uncompleted poem published posthumously as "The Poet."
2. From Emerson's "Ode to Beauty."

Those who are esteemed umpires of taste, are often persons who have acquired some knowledge of admired pictures or sculptures, and have an inclination for whatever is elegant; but if you inquire whether they are beautiful souls, and whether their own acts are like fair pictures, you learn that they are selfish and sensual. Their cultivation is local, as if you should rub a log of dry wood in one spot to produce fire, all the rest remaining cold. Their knowledge of the fine arts is some study of rules and particulars, or some limited judgment of color or form, which is exercised for amusement or for show. It is a proof of the shallowness of the doctrine of beauty, as it lies in the minds of our amateurs, that men seem to have lost the perception of the instant dependence of form upon soul. There is no doctrine of forms in our philosophy. We were put into our bodies, as fire is put into a pan, to be carried about; but there is no accurate adjustment between the spirit and the organ, much less is the latter the germination of the former. So in regard to other forms, the intellectual men do not believe in any essential dependence of the material world on thought and volition. Theologians think it a pretty air-castle to talk of the spiritual meaning of a ship or a cloud, of a city or a contract, but they prefer to come again to the solid ground of historical evidence; and even the poets are contented with a civil and conformed manner of living, and to write poems from the fancy, at a safe distance from their own experience. But the highest minds of the world have never ceased to explore the double meaning, or, shall I say, the quadruple, or the centuple, or much more manifold meaning, of every sensuous fact: Orpheus, Empedocles, Heraclitus, Plato, Plutarch, Dante, Swedenborg, and the masters of sculpture, picture, and poetry. For we are not pans and barrows, nor even porters of the fire and torch-bearers, but children of the fire, made of it, and only the same divinity transmuted, and at two or three removes, when we know least about it. And this hidden truth, that the fountains whence all this river of Time, and its creatures, floweth, are intrinsically ideal and beautiful, draws us to the consideration of the nature and functions of the Poet, or the man of Beauty, to the means and materials he uses, and to the general aspect of the art in the present time.

The breadth of the problem is great, for the poet is representative. He stands among partial men for the complete man, and apprises us not of his wealth, but of the commonwealth. The young man reveres men of genius, because, to speak truly, they are more himself than he is. They receive of the soul as he also receives, but they more. Nature enhances her beauty, to the eye of loving men, from their belief that the poet is beholding her shows at the same time. He is isolated among his contemporaries, by truth and by his art, but with this consolation in his pursuits, that they will draw all men sooner or later. For all men live by truth, and stand in need of expression. In love, in art, in avarice, in politics, in labor, in games, we study to utter our painful secret. The man is only half himself, the other half is his expression.

Notwithstanding this necessity to be published, adequate expression is rare. I know not how it is that we need an interpreter: but the great majority of men seem to be minors, who have not yet come into possession of their own, or mutes, who cannot report the conversation they have had with nature. There is no man who does not anticipate a supersensual utility in the sun, and stars, earth, and water. These stand and wait to render him a peculiar service. But there is some obstruction, or some excess of phlegm in our constitution, which does not suffer them to yield the due effect. Too feeble fall the impressions of nature on us to make us artists. Every touch should thrill. Every man should be so much an artist, that he could report in conversation what had befallen him. Yet, in our experience, the rays or appulses have sufficient force to arrive at the senses, but not enough to reach the quick, and compel the reproduction of themselves in speech. The poet is the person in whom these powers are in balance, the man without impediment, who sees and handles that which others dream of, traverses the whole scale of experience, and its representative of man, in virtue of being the largest power to receive and to impart.

For the Universe has three children, born at one time, which reappear, under different names, in every system of thought, whether they be called cause, operation, and effect; or, more poetically, Jove, Pluto, Neptune; or, theologically, the Father, the Spirit, and the Son; but which we will call here, the Knower, the Doer, and the Sayer. These stand respectively for the love of truth, for the love of good, and for the love of beauty. These three are equal. Each is that which he is essentially, so that he cannot be surmounted or analyzed, and each of these three has the power of the others latent in him, and his own patent.

The poet is the sayer, the namer, and represents beauty. He is a sovereign, and stands on the centre. For the world is not painted, or adorned, but is from the beginning beautiful; and God has not made some beautiful things, but Beauty is the creator of the universe. Therefore the poet is not any permissive potentate, but is emperor in his own right. Criticism is infested with a cant of materialism, which assumes that manual skill and activity is the first merit of all men, and disparages such as say and do not, overlooking the fact, that some men, namely, poets, are natural sayers, sent into the world to the end of expression, and confounds them with those whose province is action, but who quit it to imitate the sayers. But Homer's words are as costly and admirable to Homer, as Agamemnon's victories are to Agamemnon. The poet does not wait for the hero or the sage, but, as they act and think primarily, so he writes primarily what will and must be spoken, reckoning the others, though primaries also, yet, in respect to him, secondaries and servants; as sitters or models in the studio of a painter, or as assistants who bring building materials to an architect.

For poetry was all written before time was, and whenever we are so finely organized that we can penetrate into that region where the air is music, we hear those primal warblings, and attempt to write them down, but we lose ever and anon a word, or a verse, and substitute something of our own, and thus miswrite the poem. The men of more delicate ear write down these cadences more faithfully, and these transcripts, though imperfect, become the songs of the nations. For nature is as truly beautiful as it is good, or as it is reasonable, and must as much appear, as it must be done, or be known. Words and deeds are quite indifferent modes of the divine energy. Words are also actions, and actions are a kind of words.

The sign and credentials of the poet are, that he announces that which no man foretold. He is the true and only doctor; he knows and tells; he is the only teller of news, for he was present and privy to the appearance which he describes. He is a beholder of ideas, and an utterer of the necessary and causal. For we do not speak now of men of poetical talents, or of industry and skill in metre, but of the true poet. I took part in a conversation the other day, concerning a recent writer of lyrics, a man of subtle mind, whose head appeared to be a music-box of delicate tunes and rhythms, and whose skill, and command of language, we could not sufficiently praise. But when the question arose, whether he was not only a lyrist, but a poet, we were obliged to confess that he is plainly a contemporary, not an eternal man. He does not stand out of our low limitations, like a Chimborazo under the line, running up from the torrid base through all the climates of the globe, with belts of the herbage of every latitude on its high and mottled sides; but this genius is the landscape garden of a modern house, adorned with fountains and statues, with well-bred men and women standing and sitting in the walks and terraces. We hear, through all the varied music, the ground-tone of conventional life. Our poets are men of talents who sing, and not the children of music. The argument is secondary, the finish of the verses is primary.

For it is not metres, but a metre-making argument, that makes a poem,—a thought so passionate and alive, that, like the spirit of a plant or an animal, it has an architecture of its own, and adorns nature with a new thing. The thought and the form are equal in the order of time, but in the order of genesis the thought is prior to the form. The poet has a new thought: he has a whole new experience to unfold; he will tell us how it was with him, and all men will be the richer in his fortune. For, the experience of each new age requires a new confession, and the world seems always waiting for its poet, I remember, when I was young, how much I was moved one morning by tidings that genius had appeared in a youth who sat near me at table. He had left his work, and gone rambling none knew whither, and had written hundreds of lines, but could not tell whether that which was in him was therein told: he could tell nothing but that all was changed,—man, beast, heaven, earth, and sea. How gladly we listened! how credulous! Society seemed to be compromised. We sat in the aurora of a sunrise which was to put out all the stars. Boston seemed to be at twice the distance it had the night before, or was much farther than that.

Rome,—what was Rome? Plutarch and Shakspeare were in the yellow leaf, and Homer no more should be heard of. It is much to know that poetry has been written this very day, under this very roof by your side. What! that wonderful spirit has not expired! these stony moments are still sparkling and animated! I had fancied that the oracles were all silent, and nature had spent her fires, and behold! all night, from every pore, these fine auroras have been streaming. Every one has some interest in the advent of the poet, and no one knows how much it may concern him. We know that the secret of the world is profound, but who or what shall be our interpreter, we know not. A mountain ramble, a new style of face, a new person, may put the key into our hands. Of course, the value of genius to us is in the veracity of its report. Talent may frolic and juggle; genius realizes and adds. Mankind, in good earnest, have availed so far in understanding themselves and their work, that the foremost watchman on the peak announces his news. It is the truest word ever spoken, and the phrase will be the fittest, most musical, and the unerring voice of the world for that time.

All that we call sacred history attests that the birth of a poet is the principal event in chronology. Man, never so often deceived, still watches for the arrival of a brother who can hold him steady to a truth, until he has made it his own. With what joy I begin to read a poem, which I confide in as an inspiration. And now my chains are to be broken; I shall mount above these clouds and opaque airs in which I live,—opaque, though they seem transparent,—and from the heaven of truth I shall see and comprehend my relations. That will reconcile me to life, and renovate nature, to see trifles animated by a tendency, and to know what I am doing. Life will no more be a noise; now I shall see men and women, and know the signs by which they may be discerned from fools and satans. This day shall be better than my birthday: then I became an animal: now I am invited into the science of the real. Such is the hope, but the fruition is postponed. Oftener it falls, that this winged man, who will carry me into the heaven, whirls me into the clouds, then leaps and frisks about with me from cloud to cloud, still affirming that he is bound heavenward; and I, being myself a novice, and slow in perceiving that he does not know the way into the heavens, and is merely bent that I should admire his skill to rise, like a fowl or a flying fish, a little way from the ground or the water; but the all-piercing, all-feeding, and ocular air of heaven, that man shall never inhabit. I tumble down again soon into my old nooks, and lead the life of exaggerations as before, and have lost my faith in the possibility of any guide who can lead me thither where I would be.

But leaving these victims of vanity, let us, with new hope, observe how nature, by worthier impulses, has ensured the poet's fidelity to his office of announcement and affirming, namely, by the beauty of things, which becomes a new, and higher beauty, when expressed. Nature offers all her creatures to him as a picture-language. Being used as a type, a second wonderful value appears in the object, far better than its old value, as the carpenter's stretched cord, if you hold your ear close enough, is musical in the breeze.

"Things more excellent than every image," says Jamblichus, "are expressed through images." Things admit of being used as symbols, because nature is a symbol, in the whole, and in every part. Every line we can draw in the sand, has expression; and there is no body without its spirit of genius. All form is an effect of character; all condition, of the quality of life; all harmony, of health; (and for this reason, a perception of beauty should be sympathetic, or proper only to the good). The beautiful rests on the foundations of the necessary. The soul makes the body, as the wise Spenser teaches:—So every spirit, as it is most pure,

> And hath in it the more of heavenly light,
> So it the fairer body doth procure
> To habit in, and it more fairly dight,
> With cheerful grace and amiable sight.
> For, of the soul, the body form doth take,
> For soul is form, and doth the body make.

Here we find ourselves, suddenly, not in a critical speculation, but in a holy place, and should go very warily and reverently. We stand before the secret of the world, there where Being passes into Appearance, and Unity into Variety.

The Universe is the externization of the soul. Wherever the life is, *that* bursts into appearance around it. Our science is sensual, and therefore superficial. The earth, and the heavenly bodies, physics, and chemistry, we sensually treat, as if they were self-existent; but these are the retinue of that Being we have. "The mighty heaven," said Proclus, "exhibits, in its transfigurations, clear images of the splendor of intellectual perceptions; being moved in conjunction with the unapparent periods of intellectual natures." Therefore, science always goes abreast with the just elevation of the man, keeping step with religion and metaphysics; or, the state of science is an index of our self-knowledge. Since every thing in nature answers to a moral power, if any phenomenon remains brute and dark, it is that the corresponding faculty in the observer is not yet active.

No wonder, then, if these waters be so deep, that we hover over them with a religious regard. The beauty of the fable proves the importance of the sense; to the poet, and to all others; or if you please, every man is so far a poet as to be susceptible of these enchantments of nature: for all men have the thoughts whereof the universe is the celebration. I find that the fascination resides in the symbol. Who loves nature? Who does not? Is it only poets, and men of leisure and cultivation, who live with her? No; but also hunters, farmers, grooms, and butchers, though they express their affection in their choice of life, and not in their choice of words. The writer wonders what the coachman or the hunter values in riding, in horses, and dogs. It is not superficial qualities. When you talk with him, he holds these at as slight a rate as you. His worship is sympathetic; he has no definitions, but he is commanded in nature, by the living power which he feels to be there present. No imitation, or playing of these things, would content him; he loves the earnest of the northwind, of rain, of stone, and wood, and iron. A beauty not explicable, is dearer than a beauty which we can see to the end of. It is nature the symbol, nature certifying the supernatural, body overflowed by life, which he worships, with coarse, but sincere rites.

The inwardness and mystery of this attachment, drives men of every class to the use of emblems. The schools of poets, and philosophers, are not more intoxicated with their symbols, than the populace with theirs. In our political parties, compute the power of badges and emblems. See the great ball which they roll from Baltimore to Bunker Hill! In the political processions, Lowell goes in a loom, and Lynn in a shoe, and Salem in a ship. Witness the cider-barrel, the log cabin, the hickory-stick, the palmetto, and all the cognizances of party. See the power of national emblems. Some stars, lilies, leopards, a crescent, a lion, an eagle, or other figure, which came into credit God knows how, on an old rag of bunting, blowing in the wind, on a fort, at the ends of the earth, shall make the blood tingle under the rudest, or the most conventional exterior. The people fancy they hate poetry, and they are all poets and mystics!

Beyond this universality of the symbolic language, we are apprised of the divineness of this superior use of things, whereby the world is a temple, whose walls are covered with emblems, pictures, and commandments of the Deity, in this, that there is no fact in nature which does not carry the whole sense of nature; and the distinctions which we make in events, and in affairs, of low and high, honest and base, disappear when nature is used as a symbol. Thought makes every thing fit for use. The vocabulary of an omniscient man would embrace words and images excluded from polite conversation. What would be base, or even obscene, to the obscene, becomes illustrious, spoken in a new connection of thought. The piety of the Hebrew prophets purges their grossness. The circumcision is an example of the power of poetry to raise the low and offensive. Small and mean things serve as well as great symbols. The meaner the type by which a law is expressed, the more pungent it is, and the more lasting in the memories of men: just as we choose the smallest box, or case, in which any needful utensil can be carried. Bare lists of words are found suggestive, to an imaginative and excited mind; as it is related of Lord Chatham, that he was accustomed to read in Bailey's Dictionary, when he was preparing to speak in Parliament. The poorest experience is rich enough for all the purposes of expressing thought. Why covet a knowledge of new facts? Day and night, house and garden, a few books, a few actions, serve us as well as would all trades and all spectacles. We are far from having exhausted the significance of the few symbols we use. We can come to use them yet with a terrible simplicity. It does not need that a poem should be long. Every word was once a poem. Every new relation is a new word. Also, we use defects and deformities to a sacred purpose, so expressing our sense that the evils of the world are such only to the evil eye. In the old mythology, mythologists observe, defects are ascribed to divine natures, as lameness to Vulcan, blindness to Cupid, and the like, to signify exuberances.

For, as it is dislocation and detachment from the life of God, that makes things ugly, the poet, who re-attaches things to nature and the Whole,—re-attaching even artificial things and violations of nature, to nature, by a deeper insight—disposes very easily of the most disagreeable facts. Readers of poetry see the factory-village, and the railway, and fancy that the poetry of the landscape is broken up by these; for these works of art are not yet consecrated in their readings; but the poet sees them fall within the great Order not less than the bee-hive, or the spider's geometrical web. Nature adopts them very fast into her vital circles, and the gliding train of cars she loves like her own. Besides, in a centred mind, it signifies nothing how many mechanical inventions you exhibit. Though you add millions, and never so surprising, the fact of mechanics has not gained a grain's weight. The spiritual fact remains unalterable, by many or by few particulars; as no mountain is of any appreciable height to break the curve of the sphere. As shrewd country-boy goes to the city for the first time, and the complacent citizen is not satisfied with his little wonder. It is not that he does not see all the fine houses, and know that he never saw such before, but he disposes of them as easily as the poet finds place for the railway. The chief value of the new fact, is to enhance the great and constant fact of Life, which can dwarf any and every circumstance, and to which the belt of wampum, and the commerce of America, are alike.

The world being thus put under the mind for verb and noun, the poet is he who can articulate it. For, though life is great, and fascinates, and absorbs, and though all men are intelligent of the symbols through which it is named, yet they cannot originally use them. We are symbols, and inhabit symbols; workman, work, and tools, words and things, birth and death, all are emblems; but we sympathize with the symbols, and, being infatuated with the economical uses of things, we do not know that they are thoughts. The poet, by an ulterior intellectual perception, gives them a power which makes their old use forgotten, and puts eyes, and a tongue into every dumb and inanimate object. He perceives the independence of the thought on the symbol, the stability of the thought, the accidency and fugacity of the symbol. As the eyes of Lyncaeus were said to see through the earth, so the poet turns the world to glass, and shows us all things in their right series and procession. For, through that better perception, he stands one step nearer to things, and sees the flowing or meta-morphosis; perceives that thought is multiform; that within the form of every creature is a force impelling it to ascend into a higher form; and, following with his eyes the life, uses the forms which express that life, and so his speech flows with the flowing of nature. All the facts of the animal economy, sex, nutriment, gestation, birth, growth, are symbols of the passage of the world into the soul of man, to suffer there a change, and reappear a new and higher fact. He uses forms according to the life, and not according to the form. This is true science. The poet alone knows astronomy, chemistry, vegetation, and animation, for he does not stop at these facts, but employs them as signs. He knows why the plain, or meadow of space, was strown with these flowers we call suns, and moons, and stars; why the great deep is adorned with animals, with men, and gods; for, in every word he speaks he rides on them as the horses of thought.

By virtue of this science the poet is the Namer, or Language-maker, naming things sometimes after their appearance, sometimes after their essence, and giving to every one its own name and not another's, thereby rejoicing the in-tellect, which delights in detachment or boundary. The poets made all the words, and therefore language is the archives of history, and, if we must say it, a sort of tomb of the muses. For, though the origin of most of our words is forgotten, each word was at first a stroke of genius, and obtained currency, because for the moment it symbolized the world to the first speaker and to the hearer. The etymologist finds the deadest word to have been once a brilliant picture. Language is fossil poetry. As the limestone of the continent consists of infinite masses of the shells of animalcules, so language is made up of images, or tropes, which now, in their secondary use, have long ceased to remind us of their poetic origin. But the poet names the thing because he sees it, or comes one step nearer to it than any other. This expression or naming, is not art, but a second nature, grown out of the first, as a leaf out of a tree. What we call nature, is a certain self-regulated motion, or change; and nature does all things by her own hands, and does not leave another to baptize her, but baptizes herself; and this through the metamorphosis again. I remember that a certain poet described it to me thus:

Genius is the activity which repairs the decays of things, whether wholly or partly of a material and finite kind. Nature through all her kingdoms, insures herself. Nobody cares for planting the poor fungus: so she shakes down from the gills of one agaric countless spores, any one of which, being preserved, transmits new billions of spores to-morrow or next day. The new agaric of this hour has a chance which the old one had not. This atom of seed is thrown into a new place, not subject to the accidents which destroyed its parent two rods off. She makes a man; and having brought him to ripe age, she will no longer run the risk of losing this wonder at a blow, but she detaches from him a new self, that the kind may be safe from accidents to which the individual is exposed. So when the soul of the poet has come to ripeness of thought she detaches and sends away from it its poems or songs,—a fearless, sleepless, deathless progeny, which is not exposed to the accidents of the weary kingdom of time: a fearless, vivacious offspring, clad with wings (such was the virtue of the soul out of which they came), which carry them fast and far, and infix them irrecoverably into the hearts of men. These wings are the beauty of the poet's soul. The songs, thus flying immortal from their mortal parent, are pursued by clamorous flights of censures, which swarm in far greater numbers, and threaten to devour them; but these last are not winged. At the end of a very short leap they fall plump down, and rot, having received from the souls out of which they came no beautiful wings. But the melodies of the poet ascend, and leap, and pierce into the deeps of infinite time.

So far the bard taught me, using his freer speech. But nature has a higher end, in the production of new individuals, than security, namely, ascension, or the passage of the soul into higher forms. I knew, in my younger days, the sculptor who made the statue of the youth which stands in the public garden. He was, as I remember, unable to tell directly, what made him happy, or un-happy, but by wonderful indirections he could tell. He rose one day, according to his habit, before the dawn, and saw the morning break, grand as the eternity out of which it came, and, for many days after, he strove to express this tran-quillity, and lo! his chisel had fashioned out of marble the form of a beautiful youth, Phosphorus, whose aspect is such, that, it is said, all persons who look on it become silent. The poet also resigns himself to his mood, and that thought which agitated him is expressed, but alter idem in a manner totally new. The expression is organic, or, the new type which things themselves take when liberated. As, in the sun, objects paint their images on the retina of the eye, so they, sharing the aspiration of the whole universe, tend to paint a far more delicate copy of their essence in his mind. Like the metamorphosis of things into higher organic forms, is their change into melodies. Over every thing stands its daemon, or soul, and, as the form of the thing is reflected by the eye, so the soul of the thing is reflected by a melody. The sea, the mountain-ridge, Niagara, and every flower-bed, pre-exist, or super-exist, in pre-cantations, which sail like odors in the air, and when any man goes by with an ear sufficiently fine, he overhears them, and endeavors to write down the notes, without diluting or depraving them. And herein is the legitimation of criticism, in the mind's faith, that the poems are a corrupt version of some text in nature, with which they ought to be made to tally. A rhyme in one of our sonnets should not be less pleasing than the iterated nodes of a sea-shell, or the resembling difference of a group of flowers. The pairing of the birds is an idyl, not tedious as our idyls are; a tempest is a rough ode, without falsehood or rant: a summer, with its harvest sown, reaped, and stored, is an epic song, subordinating how many admirably executed parts. Why should not the symmetry and truth that modulate these, glide into our spirits, and we participate the invention of nature?

This insight, which expresses itself by what is called Imagination, is a very high sort of seeing, which does not come by study, but by the intellect being where and what it sees, by sharing the path, or circuit of things through forms, and making them translucid to others. The path of things is silent. Will they suffer a speaker to go with them? A spy they will not suffer; a lover, a poet, is the transcendency of their own nature,—him they will suffer. The condition of true naming, on the poet's part, is his resigning himself to the divine aura which breathes through forms, and accompanying that.

It is a secret which every intellectual man quickly learns, that, beyond the energy of his possessed and conscious intellect, he is capable of a new energy (as of an intellect doubled on itself), by abandonment to the nature of things; that, beside his privacy of power as an individual man, there is a great public power, on which he can draw, by unlocking, at all risks, his human doors, and suffering the ethereal tides to roll and circulate through him: then he is caught up into the life of the Universe, his speech is thunder, his thought is law, and his words are universally intelligible as the plants and animals. The poet knows that he speaks adequately, then, only when he speaks somewhat wildly, or, "with the flower of the mind"; not with the intellect, used as an organ, but with the intellect released from all service, and suffered to take its direction from its celestial life; or, as the ancients were wont to express themselves, not with intellect alone, but with the intellect inebriated by nectar. As the traveller who has lost his way, throws his reins on his horse's neck, and trusts to the instinct of the animal to find his road, so must we do with the divine animal who carries us through this world. For if in any manner we can stimulate this instinct, new passages are opened for us into nature, the mind flows into and through things hardest and highest, and the metamorphosis is possible.

This is the reason why bards love wine, mead, narcotics, coffee, tea, opium, the fumes of sandalwood and tobacco, or whatever other species of animal exhilaration. All men avail themselves of such means as they can, to add this extraordinary power to their normal powers; and to this end they prize conversation, music, pictures, sculpture, dancing, theatres, travelling, war, mobs, fires, gaming, politics, or love, or science, or animal intoxication, which are several coarser or finer quasi-mechanical substitutes for the true nectar, which is the ravishment of the intellect by coming nearer to the fact. These are auxiliaries to the centrifugal tendency of a man, to his passage out into free space, and they help him to escape the custody of that body in which he is pent up, and of that jail-yard of individual relations in which he is enclosed. Hence a great number of such as were professionally expressors of Beauty, as painters, poets, musicians, and actors, have been more than others wont to lead a life of pleasure and indulgence; all but the few who received the true nectar; and, as it was a spurious mode of obtaining freedom, an emancipation not into the heavens, but into the freedom of baser places, they were punished for that advantage they won, by a dissipation and deterioration. But never can any advantage be taken of nature by a trick. The spirit of the world, the great calm presence of the creator, comes not forth to the sorceries of opium or of wine. The sublime vision comes to the pure and simple soul in a clean and chaste body. That is not an inspiration which we owe to narcotics, but some counterfeit excitement and fury. Milton says, that the lyric poet may drink wine and live generously, but the epic poet, he who shall sing of the gods, and their descent unto men, must drink water out of a wooden bowl.

For poetry is not "Devil's wine," but God's wine. It is with this as it is with toys. We fill the hands and nurseries of our children with all manner of dolls, drums, and horses, withdrawing their eyes from the plain face and sufficing object of nature, the sun, and moon, the animals, the water, and stones, which should be their toys. So the poet's habit of living should be set on a key so low and plain, that the common influences should delight him. His cheerfulness should be the gift of the sunlight; the air should suffice for his inspiration, and he should be tipsy with water. That spirit which suffices quiet hearts, which seems to come forth to such from every dry knoll of sere grass, from every pine-stump, and half-imbedded stone, on which the dull March sun shines, comes forth to the poor and hungry, and such as are of simple taste. If thou fill thy brain with Boston and New York, with fashion and covetousness, and wilt stimulate thy jaded senses with wine and French coffee, thou shalt find no radiance of wisdom in the lonely waste of the pinewoods.

If the imagination intoxicates the poet, it is not inactive in other men. The metamorphosis excites in the beholder an emotion of joy.

The use of symbols has a certain power of emancipation and exhilaration for all men. We seem to be touched by a wand, which makes us dance and run about happily, like children. We are like persons who come out of a cave or cellar into the open air. This is the effect on us of tropes, fables, oracles, and all poetic forms. Poets are thus liberating gods. Men have really got a new sense, and found within their world, another world or nest of worlds; for the metamorphosis once seen, we divine that it does not stop. I will not now consider how much this makes the charm of algebra and the mathematics, which also have their tropes, but it is felt in every definition; as, when Aristotle defines space to be an immovable vessel, in which things are contained;—or, when Plato defines a line to be a flowing point; or, figure to be a bound of solid; and many the like. What a joyful sense of freedom we have, when Vitruvius announces the old opinion of artists, that no architect can build any house well,

who does not know something of anatomy. When Socrates, in "Charmides",
tells us that the soul is cured of its maladies by certain incantations, and that
these incantations are beautiful reasons, from which temperance is generated
in souls; when Plato calls the world an animal; and Timaeus affirms that the
plants also are animals; or affirms a man to be a heavenly tree, growing with
his root, which is his head, upward; and, as George Chapman, following him,
writes,—

> So in our tree of man, whose nervie root
> Springs in his top;

when Orpheus speaks of hoariness as "that white flower which marks extreme
old age;" when Proclus calls the universe the statue of the intellect; when
Chaucer, in his praise of "Gentilesse," compares good blood in mean condition
to fire, which, though carried to the darkest house betwixt this and the mount
of Caucasus, will yet hold its natural office, and burn as bright as if twenty
thousand men did it behold; when John saw, in the apocalypse, the ruin of the
world through evil, and the stars fall from heaven, as the figtree casteth her
untimely fruit; when Æsop reports the whole catalogue of common daily relations through the masquerade of birds and beasts;—we take the cheerful hint
of the immortality of our essence, and its versatile habit and escapes, as when
the gypsies say, "it is vain to hang them, they cannot die."

The poets are thus liberating gods. The ancient British bards had for the
title of their order, "Those who are free throughout the world." They are free,
and they make free. An imaginative book renders us much more service at first,
by stimulating us through its tropes, than afterward, when we arrive at the
precise sense of the author. I think nothing is of any value in books, excepting
the transcendental and extraordinary. If a man is inflamed and carried away by
his thought, to that degree that he forgets the authors and the public, and heeds
only this one dream, which holds him like an insanity, let me read his paper,
and you may have all the arguments and histories and criticism. All the value
which attaches to Pythagoras, Paracelsus, Cornelius Agrippa, Cardan, Kepler,
Swedenborg, Schelling, Oken, or any other who introduces questionable facts
into his cosmogony, as angels, devils, magic, astrology, palmistry, mesmerism,
and so on, is the certificate we have of departure from routine, and that here
is a new witness. That also is the best success in conversation, the magic of
liberty, which puts the world like a ball, in our hands. How cheap even the
liberty then seems; how mean to study, when an emotion communicates to the
intellect the power to sap and upheave nature: how great the perspective! nations, times, systems, enter and disappear like threads in tapestry of large figure
and many colors; dream delivers us to dream, and, while the drunkenness lasts,
we will sell our bed, our philosophy, our religion, in our opulence.

There is good reason why we should prize this liberation. The fate of the poor shepherd, who, blinded and lost in the snow-storm, perishes in a drift within a few feet of his cottage door, is an emblem of the state of man. On the brink of the waters of life and truth, we are miserably dying. The inaccessibleness of every thought but that we are in, is wonderful. What if you come near to it,—you are as remote, when you are nearest, as when you are farthest. Every thought is also a prison; every heaven is also a prison. Therefore we love the poet, the inventor, who in any form, whether in an ode, or in an action, or in looks and behavior, has yielded us a new thought. He unlocks our chains, and admits us to a new scene.

This emancipation is dear to all men, and the power to impart it, as it must come from greater depth and scope of thought, is a measure of intellect. Therefore all books of the imagination endure, all which ascend to that truth, that the writer sees nature beneath him, and uses it as his exponent. Every verse or sentence, possessing this virtue, will take care of its own immortality. The religions of the world are the ejaculations of a few imaginative men.

But the quality of the imagination is to flow, and not to freeze. The poet did not stop at the color, or the form, but read their meaning; neither may he rest in this meaning; but he makes the same objects exponents of his new thought. Here is the difference betwixt the poet and the mystic, that the last nails a symbol to one sense, which was a true sense for a moment, but soon becomes old and false. For all symbols are fluxional; all language is vehicular and transitive, and is good, as ferries and horses are, for conveyance, not as farms and houses are, for homestead. Mysticism consists in the mistake of an accidental and individual symbol for an universal one. The morning-redness happens to be the favorite meteor to the eyes of Jacob Behman, and comes to stand to him for truth and faith; and he believes should stand for the same realities to every reader. But the first reader prefers as naturally the symbol of a mother and child, or a gardener and his bulb, or a jeweller polishing a gem. Either of these, or of a myriad more, are equally good to the person to whom they are significant. Only they must be held lightly, and be very willingly translated into the equivalent term which others use. And the mystic must be steadily told,—All that you say is just as true without the tedious use of that symbol as with it. Let us have a little algebra, instead of this trite rhetoric,—universal signs, instead of these village symbols,—and we shall both be gainers. The history of hierarchies seems to show, that all religious error consisted in making the symbol too stark and solid, and, at last, nothing but an excess of the organ of language.

Swedenborg, of all men in the recent ages, stands eminently for the translator of nature into thought. I do not know the man in history to whom things stood so uniformly for words. Before him the metamorphosis continually plays. Every thing on which his eye rests, obeys the impulses of moral nature. The figs become grapes whilst he eats them. When some of his angels affirmed a truth, the laurel twig which they held blossomed in their hands. The noise which, at a distance, appeared like gnashing and thumping, on coming nearer was found to be the voice of disputants. The men, in one of his visions, seen in heavenly light, appeared like dragons, and seemed in darkness: but, to each other, they appeared as men, and, when the light from heaven shone into their cabin, they complained of the darkness, and were compelled to shut the window that they might see.

There was this perception in him, which makes the poet or seer, an object of awe and terror, namely, that the same man, or society of men, may wear one aspect to themselves and their companions, and a different aspect to higher intelligences. Certain priests, whom he describes as conversing very learnedly together, appeared to the children, who were at some distance, like dead horses: and many the like misappearances. And instantly the mind inquires, whether these fishes under the bridge, yonder oxen in the pasture, those dogs in the yard, are immutably fishes, oxen, and dogs, or only so appear to me, and perchance to themselves appear upright men; and whether I appear as a man to all eyes. The Brahmins and Pythagoras propounded the same question, and if any poet has witnessed the transformation, he doubtless found it in harmony with various experiences. We have all seen changes as considerable in wheat and caterpillars. He is the poet, and shall draw us with love and terror, who sees, through the flowing vest, the firm nature, and can declare it.

I look in vain for the poet whom I describe. We do not, with sufficient plainness, or sufficient profoundness, address ourselves to life, nor dare we chant our own times and social circumstance. If we filled the day with bravery, we should not shrink from celebrating it. Time and nature yield us many gifts, but not yet the timely man, the new religion, the reconciler, whom all things await. Dante's praise is, that he dared to write his autobiography in colossal cipher, or into universality. We have yet had no genius in America, with tyrannous eye, which knew the value of our incomparable materials, and saw, in the barbarism and materialism of the times, another carnival of the same gods whose picture he so much admires in Homer; then in the middle age; then in Calvinism. Banks and tariffs the newspaper and caucus, methodism and unitarianism, are flat and dull to dull people, but rest on the same foundations of wonder as the town of Troy, and the temple of Delphos, and are as swiftly passing away. Our logrolling, our stumps and their politics, our fisheries, our Negroes, and Indians, our boats, and our repudiations, the wrath of rogues, and the pusillanimity of honest men, the northern trade, the southern planting, the western clearing, Oregon, and Texas, are yet unsung. Yet America is a poem in our eyes; its ample geography dazzles the imagination, and it will not wait long for metres. If I have not found that excellent combination of gifts in my countrymen which I seek, neither could I aid myself to fix the idea of the poet by reading now and then in Chalmers' collection of five centuries of English poets. These are wits, more than poets, though there have been poets among them. But when we adhere to the ideal of the poet, we have our difficulties even with Milton and Homer. Milton is too literary, and Homer too literal and historical.

But I am not wise enough for a national criticism, and must see the old largeness a little longer, to discharge my errand from the muse to the poet concerning his art.

Art is the path of the creator to his work. The paths, or methods, are ideal and eternal, though few men ever see them, not the artist himself for years, or for a lifetime, unless he come into the conditions. The painter, the sculptor, the composer, the epic rhapsodist, the orator, all partake one desire, namely, to express themselves symmetrically and abundantly, not dwarfishly and fragmentarily. They found or put themselves in certain conditions, as, the painter and sculptor before some impressive human figures; the orator, into the assembly of the people; and the others, in such scenes as each has found exciting to his intellect; and each presently feels the new desire. He hears a voice, he sees a beckoning. Then he is apprised, with wonder, what herds of daemons hem him in. He can no more rest; he says, with the old painter, "By God, it is in me, and must go forth of me." He pursues a beauty, half seen, which flies before him. The poet pours out verses in every solitude. Most of the things he says are conventional, no doubt; but by and by he says something which is original and beautiful. That charms him. He would say nothing else but such things. In our way of talking, we say, "That is yours, this is mine;" but the poet knows well that it is not his; that it is as strange and beautiful to him as to you; he would fain hear the like eloquence at length. Once having tasted this immortal ichor, he cannot have enough of it, and, as an admirable creative power exists in these intellections, it is of the last importance that these things get spoken. What a little of all we know is said! What drops of all the sea of our science are baled up! and by what accident it is that these are exposed, when so many secrets sleep in nature! Hence the necessity of speech and song; hence these throbs and heart-beatings in the orator, at the door of the assembly, to the end, namely, that thought may be ejaculated as Logos, or Word.

Doubt not, O poet, but persist. Say, "It is in me, and shall out." Stand there, balked and dumb, stuttering and stammering, hissed and hooted, stand and strive, until, at last, rage draw out of thee that dream-power which every night shows thee is thine own; a power transcending all limit and privacy, and by virtue of which a man is the conductor of the whole river of electricity. Nothing walks, or creeps, or grows, or exists, which must not in turn arise and walk before him as exponent of his meaning. Comes he to that power, his genius is no longer exhaustible. All the creatures, by pairs and by tribes, pour into his mind as into a Noah's ark, to come forth again to people a new world. This is like the stock of air for our respiration, or for the combustion of our fireplace, not a measure of gallons, but the entire atmosphere if wanted. And therefore the rich poets, as Homer, Chaucer, Shakespeare, and Raphael, have obviously no limits to their works, except the limits of their lifetime, and resemble a mirror carried through the street, ready to render an image of every created thing.

O poet! a new nobility is conferred in groves and pastures, and not in castles, or by the sword-blade, any longer. The conditions are hard, but equal. Thou shalt leave the world, and know the muse only. Thou shalt not know any longer the times, customs, graces, politics, or opinions of men, but shalt take all from the muse. For the time of towns is tolled from the world by funeral chimes, but in nature the universal hours are counted by succeeding tribes of animals and plants, and by growth of joy on joy. God wills also that thou abdicate a manifold and duplex life, and that thou be content that others speak for thee. Others shall be thy gentlemen, and shall represent all courtesy and worldly life for thee; others shall do the great and resounding actions also. Thou shalt lie close hid with nature, and canst not be afforded to the Capitol or the Exchange. The world is full of renunciations and apprenticeships, and this is thine: thou must pass for a fool and a churl for a long season. This is the screen and sheath in which Pan has protected his well-beloved flower, and thou shalt be known only to thine own, and they shall console thee with tenderest love. And thou shalt not be able to rehearse the names of thy friends in thy verse, for an old shame before the holy ideal. And this is the reward: that the ideal shall be real to thee, and the impressions of the actual world shall fall like summer rain, copious, but not troublesome, to thy invulnerable essence. Thou shalt have the whole land for thy park and manor, the sea for thy bath and navigation, without tax and without envy; the woods and the rivers thou shalt own; and thou shalt possess that wherein others are only tenants and boarders. Thou true land-lord! sea-lord! air-lord! Wherever snow falls, or water flows, or birds fly, wherever day and night meet in twilight, wherever the blue heaven is hung by clouds, or sown with stars, wherever are forms with transparent boundaries, wherever are outlets into celestial space, wherever is danger, and awe, and love, there is Beauty, plenteous as rain, shed for thee, and though thou shouldest walk the world over, thou shalt not be able to find a condition inopportune or ignoble.

23

ELIZABETH BARRETT BROWNING (1806–1861)

Elizabeth Barrett Browning and her husband Robert are the only married couple among English writers who have any claim to genuine distinction as poets. One can speculate about what that unique fact means for poetry and for matrimony, but it says something about the great distinction and durability of both Brownings as poets. Elizabeth was some years older than Robert, and, when they first met, she was the more famous poet. Her first book, *Essay on Mind, with Other Poems*, was published in 1826, when she was barely twenty and he was still in his teens. She died twenty-eight years before he did, and he spent the last quarter of his life as a lonely widower.

Their story still reads like a soap opera with many melodramatic features, including bodily illness, paternal opposition, romantic art, and a secret wedding. Elizabeth developed a lingering affliction in 1838 and was an invalid for several years thereafter. Robert wrote to her in 1845, praising her work, and they soon met and began corresponding. In September of 1846 they were wed in secrecy and fled to Italy, where they lived for most of the rest of her relatively short life.

She is most celebrated for one or two lyrics from the collection called *Sonnets from the Portuguese*, but she wrote much more than short romantic lyrics. *The Seraphim and Other Poems* (1838) and *Poems* (1844) show an impressive variety of subjects and styles. *Aurora Leigh* (1857) is a novel in verse (11,000 lines) about a woman writer—one of the boldest and most audacious experiments in English poetry. The "novel in verse" combines the subject matter of fiction (and in this case autobiography) and the manner of narrative or dramatic poetry in blank verse. The only notable precursor is Alexander Pushkin's *Eugene Onegin* (1823–1831), which uses a rhymed fourteen-lined stanza. (Byron's *English Bards and Scotch Reviewers* had teased Wordsworth, whose example "shows / That prose is verse, and verse is merely prose.") Elizabeth Barrett Browning reserved her rhymed verse for lyrics and meditations; for a more sustained examination of character and thought, the scope of the novel was more appropriate, although without the subdued interest of prose. A reader pleased with the results in *Aurora Leigh* may experience the best of both worlds.

AURORA LEIGH, FIFTH BOOK (EXCERPT)

Aurora Leigh, be humble. Shall I hope
To speak my poems in mysterious tune
With man and nature,—with the lava-lymph
That trickles from successive galaxies
Still drop by drop adown the finger of God,
In still new worlds?—with summer-days in this,
That scarce dare breathe, they are so beautiful?—
With spring's delicious trouble in the ground
Tormented by the quickened blood of roots.
And softly pricked by golden crocus-sheaves
In token of the harvest-time of flowers?—
With winters and with autumns,—and beyond,
With the human heart's large seasons,—when it hopes
And fears, joys, grieves, and loves?—with all that strain
Of sexual passion, which devours the flesh
In a sacrament of souls? with mother's breasts,
Which, round the new made creatures hanging there,
Throb luminous and harmonious like pure spheres?—
With multitudinous life, and finally
With the great out-goings of ecstatic souls,

408 ELIZABETH BARRETT BROWNING

Who, in a rush of too long prisoned flame,
Their radiant faces upward, burn away
This dark of the body, issuing on a world
Beyond our mortal?—can I speak my verse
So plainly in tune to these things and the rest,
That men shall feel it catch them on the quick,
As having the same warrant over them
To hold and move them, if they will or no,
Alike imperious as the primal rhythm
Of that theurgic nature? I must fail,[1]
Who fail at the beginning to hold and move
One man,—and he my cousin, and he my friend,
And he born tender, made intelligent,
Inclined to ponder the precipitous sides
Of difficult questions; yet, obtuse to me,—
Of me, incurious! likes me very well,
And wishes me a paradise of good,
Good looks, good means, and good digestion!—ay,
But otherwise evades me, puts me off
With kindness, with a tolerant gentleness,—
Too light a book for a grave man's reading! Go,
Aurora Leigh: be humble.

                                        There it is;
We women are too apt to look to one,
Which proves a certain impotence in art.
We strain our natures at doing something great,
Far less because it's something great to do,
Than, haply, that we, so, commend ourselves
As being not small, and more appreciable
To some one friend. We must have mediators
Betwixt our highest conscience and the judge;
Some sweet saint's blood must quicken in our palms.
Or all the life in heaven seems slow and cold:
Good only, being perceived as the end of good,
And God alone pleased,—that's too poor, we think,
And not enough for us, by any means.
Ay—Romney, I remember, told me once
We miss the abstract, when we comprehend!
We miss it most when we aspire, . . . and fail.

---

1. theurgic: relating to sorcery or divine working.

Yet, so, I will not.—This vile woman's way
Of trailing garments, shall not trip me up.
I'll have no traffic with the personal thought
In art's pure temple. Must I work in vain,
Without the approbation of a man?
It cannot be; it shall not. Fame itself,
That approbation of the general race,
Presents a poor end, (though the arrow speed,
Shot straight with vigorous finger to the white,)
And the highest fame was never reached except
By what was aimed above it. Art for art,
And good for God Himself, the essential Good!
We'll keep our aims sublime, our eyes erect,
Although our woman-hands should shake and fail;
And if we fail . . . . But must we?—
                                        Shall I fail?

The Greeks said grandly in their tragic phrase,
"Let no one be called happy till his death."
To which I add,—Let no one till his death
Be called unhappy. Measure not the work
Until the day's out and the labour done;
Then bring your gauges. If the day's work's scant,
Why, call it scant; affect no compromise;
And, in that we have nobly striven at least,
Deal with us nobly, women though we be,
And honour us with truth, if not with praise.

My ballads prospered; but the ballad's race
Is rapid for a poet who bears weights
Of thought and golden image. He can stand
Like Atlas, in the sonnet,—and support
His own heavens pregnant with dynastic stars;
But then he must stand still, nor take a step.

In that descriptive poem called "The Hills,"
The prospects were too far and indistinct.
'Tis true my critics said, "A fine view, that!"
The public scarcely cared to climb the book
For even the finest; and the public's right,
A tree's mere firewood, unless humanised;
Which well the Greeks knew, when they stirred the bark
With close-pressed bosoms of subsiding nymphs,

And made the forest-rivers garrulous
With babble of gods. For us, we are called to mark
A still more intimate humanity
In this inferior nature,—or, ourselves,
Must fall like dead leaves trodden underfoot
By veritabler artists. Earth shut up
By Adam, like a fakir in a box
Left too long buried, remained stiff and dry,
A mere dumb corpse, till Christ the Lord came down,
Unlocked the doors, forced open the blank eyes,
And used his kingly chrisms to straighten out
The leathery tongue turned back into the throat:
Since when, she lives, remembers, palpitates
In every lip, aspires in every breath,
Embraces infinite relations. Now,
We want no half-gods, Panomphæan Joves,[2]
Fauns, Naiads, Tritons, Oreads, and the rest,
To take possession of a senseless world
To unnatural vampire-uses. See the earth,
The body of our body, the green earth,
Indubitably human, like this flesh
And these articulated veins through which
Our heart drives blood! There's not a flower of spring,
That dies ere June, but vaunts itself allied
By issue and symbol, by significance
And correspondence, to that spirit-world
Outside the limits of our space and time,
Whereto we are bound. Let poets give it voice
With human meanings; else they miss the thought,
And henceforth step down lower, stand confessed
Instructed poorly for interpreters,—
Thrown out by an easy cowslip in the text.

Even so my pastoral failed: it was a book
Of surface-pictures—pretty, cold, and false
With literal transcript,—the worse done, I think,
For being not ill-done. Let me set my mark
Against such doings, and do otherwise.
This strikes me. If the public whom we know,

---

2. Panomphæan: of or pertaining to Zeus, as sender of all ominous voices. (*OED*)

Could catch me at such admissions, I should pass
For being right modest. Yet how proud we are,
In daring to look down upon ourselves!

The critics say that epics have died out
With Agamemnon and the goat-nursed gods—
I'll not believe it. I could never dream
As Payne Knight did, (the mythic mountaineer
Who travelled higher than he was born to live,
And showed sometimes the goitre in his throat
Discoursing of an image seen through fog,)
That Homer's heroes measured twelve feet high.
They were but men!—his Helen's hair turned grey
Like any plain Miss Smith's, who wears a front:
And Hector's infant blubbered at a plume
As yours last Friday at a turkey-cock.
All men are possible heroes: every age,
Heroic in proportions, double-faced,
Looks backward and before, expects a morn
And claims an epos.
                                        Ay, but every age
Appears to souls who live in it, (ask Carlyle)
Most unheroic. Ours, for instance, ours!
The thinkers scout it, and the poets abound
Who scorn to touch it with a finger-tip:
A pewter age,—mixed metal, silver-washed;
An age of scum, spooned off the richer past;
An age of patches for old gabardines;
An age of mere transition, meaning nought,
Except that what succeeds must shame it quite,
If God please. That's wrong thinking, to my mind,
And wrong thoughts make poor poems.
                                        Every age,
Through being beheld too close, is ill-discerned
By those who have not lived past it. We'll suppose
Mount Athos carved, as Persian Xerxes schemed,
To some colossal statue of a man:
The peasants, gathering brushwood in his ear,
Had guessed as little of any human form
Up there, as would a flock of browsing goats.
They'd have, in fact, to travel ten miles off
Or ere the giant image broke on them,

Full human profile, nose and chin distinct,
Mouth, muttering rhythms of silence up the sky,
And fed at evening with the blood of suns;
Grand torso,—hand, that flung perpetually
The largesse of a silver river down
To all the country pastures. 'Tis even thus
With times we live in,—evermore too great
To be apprehended near.

                                        But poets should

Exert a double vision; should have eyes
To see near things as comprehensibly
As if afar they took their point of sight,
And distant things, as intimately deep,
As if they touched them. Let us strive for this.
I do distrust the poet who discerns
No character or glory in his times,
And trundles back his soul five hundred years,
Past moat and drawbridge, into a castle-court,
Oh not to sing of lizards or of toads
Alive i' the ditch there!—'twere excusable;
But of some black chief, half knight, half sheep-lifter,
Some beauteous dame, half chattel and half queen,
As dead as must be, for the greater part,
The poems made on their chivalric bones.
And that's no wonder: death inherits death.

Nay, if there's room for poets in the world
A little overgrown, (I think there is)
Their sole work is to represent the age,
Their age, not Charlemagne's,—this live, throbbing age,
That brawls, cheats, maddens, calculates, aspires,
And spends more passion, more heroic heat,
Betwixt the mirrors of its drawing-rooms,
Than Roland with his knights, at Roncesvalles.
To flinch from modern varnish, coat or flounce,
Cry out for togas and the picturesque,
Is fatal,—foolish too. King Arthur's self
Was commonplace to Lady Guenever;
And Camelot to minstrels seemed as flat,
As Regent street to poets.

                                        Never flinch,

But still, unscrupulously epic, catch

Upon a burning lava of a song,
The full-veined, heaving, double-breasted Age:
That, when the next shall come, the men of that
May touch the impress with reverent hand, and say
"Behold,—behold the paps we all have sucked!
That bosom seems to beat still, or at least
It sets ours beating. This is living art,
Which thus presents, and thus records true life."

What form is best for poems ? Let me think
Of forms less, and the external. Trust the spirit,
As sovran nature does, to make the form;
For otherwise we only imprison spirit,
And not embody. Inward evermore
To outward,—so in life, and so in art,
Which still is life.
                          Five acts to make a play.
And why not fifteen? Why not ten? or seven?
What matter for the number of the leaves,
Supposing the tree lives and grows? exact
The literal unities of time and place,
When 'tis the essence of passion to ignore
Both time and place? Absurd. Keep up the fire
And leave the generous flames to shape themselves.

'Tis true the stage requires obsequiousness
To this or that convention; "exit" here
And "enter" there; the points for clapping, fixed,
Like Jacob's white-peeled rods before the rams;
And all the close-curled imagery clipped
In manner of their fleece at shearing time.
Forget to prick the galleries to the heart
Precisely at the fourth act,—culminate
Our five pyramidal acts with one act more,—
We're lost so! Shakspeare's ghost could scarcely plead
Against our just damnation. Stand aside;
We'll muse for comfort that, last century,
On this same tragic stage on which we have failed,
A wigless Hamlet would have failed the same.

And whosoever writes good poetry,
Looks just to art. He does not write for you

Or me,—for London or for Edinburgh;
He will not suffer the best critic known
To step into his sunshine of free thought
And self-absorbed conception, and exact
An inch-long swerving of the holy lines.
If virtue done for popularity
Defiles like vice, can art for praise or hire
Still keep its splendour, and remain pure art?
Eschew such serfdom. What the poet writes,
He writes: mankind accepts it, if it suits,
And that's success: if not, the poem's passed
From hand to hand, and yet from hand to hand,
Until the unborn snatch it, crying out
In pity on their fathers' being so dull,
And that's success too.

                              I will write no plays.
Because the drama, less sublime in this,
Makes lower appeals, defends more menially,
Adopts the standard of the public taste
To chalk its height on, wears a dog chain round
Its regal neck, and learns to carry and fetch
The fashions of the day to please the day;
Fawns close on pit and boxes, who clap hands,
Commending chiefly its docility
And humour in stage-tricks; or else indeed
Gets hissed at, howled at, stamped at like a dog,
Or worse, we'll say. For dogs, unjustly kicked,
Yell, bite at need; but if your dramatist
(Being wronged by some five hundred nobodies
Because their grosser brains most naturally
Misjudge the fineness of his subtle wit)
Shows teeth an almond's breath, protests the length
Of a modest phrase,—"My gentle countrymen,
There's something in it, haply of your fault,"—
Why then, besides five hundred nobodies,
He'll have five thousand, and five thousand more,
Against him,—the whole public,—all the hoofs
Of King Saul's father's asses, in full drove,—
And obviously deserve it. He appealed
To these,—and why say more if they condemn,
Than if they praised him?—Weep, my Æschylus,
But low and far, upon Sicilian shores!

For since 'twas Athens (so I read the myth)
Who gave commission to that fatal weight,
The tortoise, cold and hard, to drop on thee
And crush thee,—better cover thy bald head;
She'll hear the softest hum of Hyblan bee[3]
Before thy loud'st protesting.—For the rest,
The risk's still worse upon the modern stage;
I could not, in so little, accept success,
Nor would I risk so much, in ease and calm,
For manifester gains; let those who prize,
Pursue them: I stand off.

                           And yet, forbid,
That any irreverent fancy or conceit
Should litter in the Drama's throne-room, where
The rulers of our art, in whose full veins
Dynastic glories mingle, sit in strength
And do their kingly work,—conceive, command,
And, from the imagination's crucial heat,
Catch up their men and women all a-flame
For action all alive, and forced to prove
Their life by living out heart, brain, and nerve,
Until mankind makes witness, "These be men
As we are," and vouchsafes the kiss that's due
To Imogen and Juliet—sweetest kin
On art's side.

                     'Tis that, honouring to its worth
The drama, I would fear to keep it down
To the level of the footlights. Dies no more
The sacrificial goat, for Bacchus slain,—
His filmed eyes fluttered by the whirling white
Of choral vestures,—troubled in his blood
While tragic voices that clanged keen as swords,
Leapt high together with the altar-flame,
And made the blue air wink. The waxen mask,
Which set the grand still front of Themis' son
Upon the puckered visage of a player;—
The buskin, which he rose upon and moved,
As some tall ship, first conscious of the wind,
Sweeps slowly past the piers;—the mouthpiece, where

---

3. Hyblan: usually Hyblaean; pertaining to Hybla in Sicily, famous for honey.

The mere man's voice with all its breaths and breaks
Went sheathed in brass, and clashed on even heights
Its phrasèd thunders;—these things are no more,
Which once were. And concluding, which is clear,
The growing drama has outgrown such toys
Of simulated stature, faces and speech,
It also, peradventure, may outgrow
The simulation of the painted scene,
Boards, actors, prompters, gaslight, and costume;
And take for a worthier stage the soul itself,
Its shifting fancies and celestial lights,
With all its grand orchestral silences
To keep the pauses of the rhythmic sounds.

Alas, I still see something to be done,
And what I do falls short of what I see,
Though I waste myself on doing. Long green days,
Worn bare of grass and sunshine,—long calm nights,
From which the silken sleeps were fretted out,—
Be witness for me, with no amateur's
Irreverent haste and busy idleness
I've set myself to art! What then? what's done?
What's done, at last?
                                        Behold, at last, a book.
If life-blood's necessary,—which it is,
(By that blue vein athrob on Mahomet's brow,
Each prophet-poet's book must show man's blood!)
If life-blood's fertilising, I wrung mine
On every leaf of this,—unless the drops
Slid heavily on one side and left it dry.
That chances often: many a fervid man
Writes books as cold and flat as grave-yard stones
From which the lichen's scraped; and if St. Preux
Had written his own letters, as he might,
We had never wept to think of the little mole
'Neath Julie's drooping eyelid. Passion is
But something suffered, after all.
                                        While art
Sets action on the top of suffering:
The artist's part is both to be and do,
Transfixing with a special, central power
The flat experience of the common man,

And turning outward, with a sudden wrench,
Half agony, half ecstasy, the thing
He feels the inmost: never felt the less
Because he sings it. Does a torch less burn
For burning next reflectors of blue steel,
That he should be the colder for his place
'Twixt two incessant fires,—his personal life's,
And that intense refraction which burns back
Perpetually against him from the round
Of crystal conscience he was born into
If artist born? O sorrowful great gift
Conferred on poets, of a twofold life,
When one life has been found enough for pain!
We staggering 'neath our burden as mere men,
Being called to stand up straight as demi-gods,
Support the intolerable strain and stress
Of the universal, and send clearly up
With voices broken by the human sob,
Our poems to find rhymes among the stars!
But soft!—a "poet" is a word soon said;
A book's a thing soon written. Nay, indeed,
The more the poet shall be questionable,
The more unquestionably comes his book!
And this of mine,—well, granting to myself
Some passion in it, furrowing up the flats,
Mere passion will not prove a volume worth
Its gall and rags even. Bubbles round a keel
Mean nought, excepting that the vessel moves.
There's more than passion goes to make a man,
Or book, which is a man too.

                                        I am sad:

I wonder if Pygmalion had these doubts,
And, feeling the hard marble first relent,
Grow supple to the straining of his arms,
And tingle through its cold to his burning lip,
Supposed his senses mocked, and that the toil
Of stretching past the known and seen, to reach
The archetypal Beauty out of sight,
Had made his heart beat fast enough for two,
And with his own life dazed and blinded him!
Not so; Pygmalion loved,—and whoso loves
Believes the impossible.

                                                  And I am sad:
I cannot thoroughly love a work of mine,
Since none seems worthy of my thought and hope
More highly mated. He has shot them down,
My Phoebus Apollo, soul within my soul,
Who judges by the attempted, what's attained,
And with the silver arrow from his height,
Has struck down all my works before my face,
While I say nothing. Is there aught to say?
I called the artist but a greatened man:
He may be childless also, like a man.

I laboured on alone. The wind and dust
And sun of the world beat blistering in my face;
And hope, now for me, now against me, dragged
My spirits onward,—as some fallen balloon,
Which, whether caught by blossoming tree or bare,
Is torn alike. I sometimes touched my aim,
Or seemed,—and generous souls cried out, "Be strong,
Take courage; now you're on our level,—now!
The next step saves you!" I was flushed with praise,
But, pausing just a moment to draw breath,
I could not choose but murmur to myself
"Is this all? all that's done? and all that's gained?
If this then be success, 'tis dismaller
Than any failure."
                                     O my God, my God,
O supreme Artist, who as sole return
For all the cosmic wonder of Thy work,
Demandest of us just a word . . . a name,
"My Father!"—thou hast knowledge, only thou,
How dreary 'tis for women to sit still
On winter nights by solitary fires,
And hear the nations praising them far off;
Too far! ay, praising our quick sense of love,
Our very heart of passionate womanhood,
Which could not beat so in the verse without
Being present also in the unkissed lips,
And eyes undried because there's none to ask
The reason they grew moist.
                                          To sit alone,
And think, for comfort, how, that very night,

Affianced lovers, leaning face to face
With sweet half-listenings for each other's breath,
Are reading haply from some page of ours,
To pause with a thrill, as if their cheeks had touched,
When such a stanza, level to their mood,
Seems floating their own thoughts out—"So I feel
For thee," "And I, for thee: this poet knows
What everlasting love is!"—how, that night,
A father, issuing from the misty roads
Upon the luminous round of lamp and hearth
And happy children, having caught up first
The youngest there until it shrunk and shrieked
To feel the cold chin prick its dimple through
With winter from the hills, may throw i' the lap
Of the eldest, (who has learnt to drop her lids
To hide some sweetness newer than last year's)
Our book and cry, . . . "Ah you, you care for rhymes;
So here be rhymes to pore on under trees,
When April comes to let you! I've been told
They are not idle as so many are,
But set hearts beating pure as well as fast:
It's yours, the book: I'll write your name in it,—
That so you may not lose, however lost
In poet's lore and charming reverie,
The thought of how your father thought of you
In riding from the town."

                                  To have our books
Appraised by love, associated with love,
While we sit loveless! is it hard, you think?
At least 'tis mournful. Fame, indeed, 'twas said,
Means simply love. It was a man said that.
And then there's love and love: the love of all
(To risk, in turn, a woman's paradox,)
Is but a small thing to the love of one.
You bid a hungry child be satisfied
With a heritage of many corn-fields: nay,
He says he's hungry,—he would rather have
That little barley-cake you keep from him
While reckoning up his harvests. So with us;
(Here, Romney, too, we fail to generalise!)
We're hungry.

                            Hungry! but it's pitiful

To wail like unweaned babes and suck our thumbs
Because we're hungry. Who, in all this world,
(Wherein we are haply set to pray and fast,
And learn what good is by its opposite)
Has never hungered? Woe to him who has found
The meal enough: if Ugolino's full,
His teeth have crunched some foul unnatural thing:
For here satiety proves penury
More utterly irremediable. And since
We needs must hunger,—better, for man's love,
Than God's truth! better, for companions sweet,
Than great convictions! let us bear our weights,
Preferring dreary hearths to desert souls.

Well, well, they say we're envious, we who rhyme;
But I, because I am a woman, perhaps,
And so rhyme ill, am ill at envying.
I never envied Graham his breadth of style,
Which gives you, with a random smutch or two,
(Near-sighted critics analyse to smutch)
Such delicate perspectives of full life;
Nor Belmore, for the unity of aim
To which he cuts his cedarn poems, fine
As sketchers do their pencils; not Mark Gage,
For that caressing colour and trancing tone
Whereby you're swept away and melted in
The sensual element, which, with a back wave,
Restores you to the level of pure souls
And leaves you with Plotinus. None of these,
For native gifts or popular applause,
I've envied; but for this,—that when, by chance,
Says some one,—"There goes Belmore, a great man!
He leaves clean work behind him, and requires
No sweeper up of the chips," . . . a girl I know,
Who answers nothing, save with her brown eyes,
Smiles unawares, as if a guardian saint
Smiled in her:—for this, too,—that Gage comes home
And lays his last book's prodigal review
Upon his mother's knees, where, years ago,
He had laid his childish spelling-book and learned
To chirp and peck the letters from her mouth,
As young birds must. "Well done," she murmured then,

She will not say it now more wonderingly;
And yet the last "Well done" will touch him more,
As catching up to-day and yesterday
In a perfect chord of love; and so, Mark Gage,
I envy you your mother!—and you, Graham,
Because you have a wife who loves you so,
She half forgets, at moments, to be proud
Of being Graham's wife, until a friend observes,
"The boy here, has his father's massive brow,
Done small in wax . . . if we push back the curls."

Who loves me? Dearest father,—mother sweet,—
I speak the names out sometimes by myself,
And make the silence shiver: they sound strange,
As Hindostanee to an Ind-born man
Accustomed many years to English speech;
Or lovely poet-words grown obsolete,
Which will not leave off singing. Up in heaven
I have my father,—with my mother's face
Beside him in a blotch of heavenly light;
No more for earth's familiar household use,
No more! The best verse written by this hand,
Can never reach them where they sit, to seem
Well-done to them. Death quite unfellows us,
Sets dreadful odds betwixt the live and dead,
And makes us part as those at Babel did,
Through sudden ignorance of a common tongue.

24

HENRY WADSWORTH LONGFELLOW (1807–1882)

Longfellow was a great teacher in two senses: he was an innovator in the teaching of modern languages at Harvard and elsewhere, and he graciously subjected his art to what he perceived to be the duty of poetry: to deliver academic and moral lessons. He was probably the most distinguished and most effective didactic poet ever to write in the United States; people who know almost no other poems will know "Listen, my children, and you shall hear. . . ." Longfellow is also notable as an innovator in developing a long unrhymed measure that was *not* blank verse; he wrote two fine long poems in unrhymed dactylic hexameter (*Evangeline* and *The Courtship of Miles Standish*) and an unforgettable epic is unrhymed trochaic tetrameter (*The Song of Hiawatha*). Some of his sonnets capture the spirit of his most notable precursors among the English poets.

POEMS

CHAUCER

An old man in a lodge within a park;
    The chamber walls depicted all around
    With portraitures of huntsman, hawk, and hound,
    And the hurt deer. He listeneth to the lark,
Whose song comes with the sunshine through the dark
    Of painted glass in leaden lattice bound;
    He listeneth and he laugheth at the sound,
    Then writeth in a book like any clerk.
He is the poet of the dawn, who wrote
    The Canterbury Tales, and his old age
    Made beautiful with song; and as I read
I hear the crowing cock, I hear the note
    Of lark and linnet, and from every page
    Rise odors of ploughed field or flowery mead.

SHAKESPEARE

A vision as of crowded city streets,
 With human life in endless overflow;
 Thunder of thoroughfares; trumpets that blow
 To battle; clamor, in obscure retreats,
Of sailors landed from their anchored fleets;
 Tolling of bells in turrets, and below
 Voices of children, and bright flowers that throw
 O'er garden-walls their intermingled sweets!
This vision comes to me when I unfold
 The volume of the Poet paramount,
 Whom all the Muses loved, not one alone;—
Into his hands they put the lyre of gold,
 And, crowned with sacred laurel at their fount,
 Placed him as Musagetes on their throne.

MILTON

I pace the sounding sea-beach and behold
 How the voluminous billows roll and run,
 Upheaving and subsiding, while the sun
 Shines through their sheeted emerald far unrolled,
And the ninth wave, slow gathering fold by fold
 All its loose-flowing garments into one,
 Plunges upon the shore, and floods the dun
 Pale reach of sands, and changes them to gold.
So in majestic cadence rise and fall
 The mighty undulations of thy song,
 O sightless bard, England's Mæonides!
And ever and anon, high over all
 Uplifted, a ninth wave superb and strong,
 Floods all the soul with its melodious seas.

KEATS

The young Endymion sleeps Endymion's sleep;
 The shepherd-boy whose tale was left half told!
 The solemn grove uplifts its shield of gold

To the red rising moon, and loud and deep
The nightingale is singing from the steep;
    It is midsummer, but the air is cold;
    Can it be death? Alas, beside the fold
    A shepherd's pipe lies shattered near his sheep.
Lo! in the moonlight gleams a marble white,
    On which I read: "Here lieth one whose name
    Was writ in water." And was this the meed
Of his sweet singing? Rather let me write:
    "The smoking flax before it burst to flame
    Was quenched by death, and broken the bruised reed."

THE POETS

O ye dead Poets, who are living still
    Immortal in your verse, though life be fled,
    And ye, O living Poets, who are dead
    Though ye are living, if neglect can kill,
Tell me if in the darkest hours of ill,
    With drops of anguish falling fast and red
    From the sharp crown of thorns upon your head,
    Ye were not glad your errand to fulfil?
Yes; for the gift and ministry of Song
    Have something in them so divinely sweet,
    It can assuage the bitterness of wrong;
Not in the clamor of the crowded street,
    Not in the shouts and plaudits of the throng,
    But in ourselves, are triumph and defeat.

THE BROKEN OAR

Once upon Iceland's solitary strand
    A poet wandered with his book and pen,
    Seeking some final word, some sweet Amen,
    Wherewith to close the volume in his hand.
The billows rolled and plunged upon the sand,
    The circling sea-gulls swept beyond his ken,
    And from the parting cloud-rack now and then
    Flashed the red sunset over sea and land.
Then by the billows at his feet was tossed

A broken oar; and carved thereon he read,
　"Oft was I weary, when I toiled at thee;"
And like a man, who findeth what was lost,
　He wrote the words, then lifted up his head,
　And flung his useless pen into the sea.

25

EDGAR ALLAN POE (1809–1849)

Poe's life was short; he was evidently an undiagnosed diabetic, on whom alcohol had a terrible effect (although, as one sympathetic student of his life has remarked, the sad thing is less a matter of Poe's drinking too much as of eating too little). He was born in Boston but, having been orphaned at an early age, raised in Virginia. Between 1811 and 1815 he lived in Richmond, then he went with his adoptive family to England until 1820. He spent a short period at the University of Virginia, then left to join the Army, eventually attending the United States Military Academy at West Point for a year.

From about the age of fourteen, he had been writing poetry, and after his dismissal from West Point in 1831, he lived hand-to-mouth in various literary and journalistic jobs all over the eastern seaboard: in New York, Baltimore, Richmond, Philadelphia. In 1835 he received a license to marry his cousin, Virginia Clemm, who was thirteen at the time. They married in 1836 and seem to have lived together happily until her death from tuberculosis in 1845. Poe himself died in Baltimore in 1849 under suspicious circumstances. A century and a half after Poe's death, a dispassionate diagnostician reviewing the facts in the case concluded that Poe probably died of rabies.

Poe spent most of his adult life as a literary editor and journalist. In a pitifully abbreviated career, he managed to make himself famous as a fabulous inventor—a veritable American Daedalus—so that one can argue that Poe, just about single-handedly, invented the short story, science fiction, detective fiction, the symbolist poem, and New Criticism. He also exposed hoaxes and deflated reputations—not always justly but usually with wit and vigor.

For various reasons. some of which remain mysterious, Poe has enjoyed, all along, a higher standing in France than in America or England. True, Poe's diction can be lurid and his verbal effects may seem vulgar, but it seems unfair to say—as both Walter Pater and T. S. Eliot suggested—that the full appreciation of Poe can come only to those whose knowledge of English is imperfect. Since Poe was a great inventor and explorer in one of the oldest American traditions, William Carlos Williams called him "a new DeSoto."

As his two-hundredth birthday approaches, it is certain that Poe remains the American writer with the farthest-reaching influence: he understood our deepest fears and desires, and his shadow stretches over many literary provinces, from Jules Verne to Vladimir Nabokov to the films of Stanley Kubrick (a cipher key in *Doctor Strangelove* is "P.O.E."), to say nothing of the name and nickname of the highest award given by the Mystery Writers of America—the Edgar—as well as the name of Baltimore's team in the American Football Conference—the Ravens.

THE PHILOSOPHY OF COMPOSITION

Charles Dickens, in a note now lying before me, alluding to an examination I once made of the mechanism of "Barnaby Rudge," says — "By the way, are you aware that Godwin wrote his 'Caleb Williams' backwards? He first involved his hero in a web of difficulties, forming the second volume, and then, for the first, cast about him for some mode of accounting for what had been done."

I cannot think this the precise mode of procedure on the part of Godwin — and indeed what he himself acknowledges, is not altogether in accordance with Mr. Dickens' idea — but the author of "Caleb Williams" was too good an artist not to perceive the advantage derivable from at least a somewhat similar process. Nothing is more clear than that every plot, worth the name, must be elaborated to its denouement before anything be attempted with the pen. It is only with the denouement constantly in view that we can give a plot its indispensable air of consequence, or causation, by making the incidents, and especially the tone at all points, tend to the development of the intention.

There is a radical error, I think, in the usual mode of constructing a story. Either history affords a thesis — or one is suggested by an incident of the day — or, at best, the author sets himself to work in the combination of striking events to form merely the basis of his narrative — designing, generally, to fill in with description, dialogue, or autorial comment, whatever crevices of fact, or action, may, from page to page, render themselves apparent.

I prefer commencing with the consideration of an effect. Keeping originality always in view—for he is false to himself who ventures to dispense with so obvious and so easily attainable a source of interest—I say to myself, in the first place, "Of the innumerable effects, or impressions, of which the heart, the intellect, or (more generally) the soul is susceptible, what one shall I, on the present occasion, select?" Having chosen a novel, first, and secondly a vivid effect, I consider whether it can be best wrought by incident or tone—whether by ordinary incidents and peculiar tone, or the converse, or by peculiarity both of incident and tone—afterward looking about me (or rather within) for such combinations of event, or tone, as shall best aid me in the construction of the effect.

I have often thought how interesting a magazine paper might be written by any author who would—that is to say, who could—detail, step by step, the processes by which any one of his compositions attained its ultimate point of completion. Why such a paper has never been given to the world, I am much at a loss to say—but, perhaps, the autorial vanity has had more to do with the omission than any one other cause. Most writers—poets in especial—prefer having it understood that they compose by a species of fine frenzy—an ecstatic intuition—and would positively shudder at letting the public take a peep behind the scenes, at the elaborate and vacillating crudities of thought—at the true purposes seized only at the last moment—at the innumerable glimpses of idea that arrived not at the maturity of full view—at the fully-matured fancies discarded in despair as unmanageable—at the cautious selections and rejections—at the painful erasures and interpolations—in a word, at the wheels and pinions—the tackle for scene-shifting—the step-ladders, and demon-traps—the cock's feathers, the red paint and the black patches, which, in ninety-nine cases out of a hundred, constitute the properties of the literary histrio.

I am aware, on the other hand, that the case is by no means common, in which an author is at all in condition to retrace the steps by which his conclusions have been attained. In general, suggestions, having arisen pell-mell are pursued and forgotten in a similar manner.

For my own part, I have neither sympathy with the repugnance alluded to, nor, at any time, the least difficulty in recalling to mind the progressive steps of any of my compositions, and, since the interest of an analysis or reconstruction, such as I have considered a desideratum, is quite independent of any real or fancied interest in the thing analysed, it will not be regarded as a breach of decorum on my part to show the modus operandi by which some one of my own works was put together. I select "The Raven" as most generally known. It is my design to render it manifest that no one point in its composition is referable either to accident or intuition—that the work proceeded step by step, to its completion, with the precision and rigid consequence of a mathematical problem.

Let us dismiss, as irrelevant to the poem, per se, the circumstance—or say the necessity—which, in the first place, gave rise to the intention of composing a poem that should suit at once the popular and the critical taste.

We commence, then, with this intention.

The initial consideration was that of extent. If any literary work is too long to be read at one sitting, we must be content to dispense with the immensely important effect derivable from unity of impression—for, if two sittings be required, the affairs of the world interfere, and everything like totality is at once destroyed. But since, *ceteris paribus*, no poet can afford to dispense with anything that may advance his design, it but remains to be seen whether there is, in extent, any advantage to counterbalance the loss of unity which attends it. Here I say no, at once. What we term a long poem is, in fact, merely a succession of brief ones—that is to say, of brief poetical effects. It is needless to demonstrate that a poem is such only inasmuch as it intensely excites, by elevating the soul; and all intense excitements are, through a psychal necessity, brief. For this reason, at least, one-half of the "Paradise Lost" is essentially prose—a succession of poetical excitements interspersed, inevitably, with corresponding depressions—the whole being deprived, through the extremeness of its length, of the vastly important artistic element, totality, or unity of effect.

It appears evident, then, that there is a distinct limit, as regards length, to all works of literary art—the limit of a single sitting—and that, although in certain classes of prose composition, such as "Robinson Crusoe" (demanding no unity), this limit may be advantageously overpassed, it can never properly be overpassed in a poem. Within this limit, the extent of a poem may be made to bear mathematical relation to its merit—in other words, to the excitement or elevation—again, in other words, to the degree of the true poetical effect which it is capable of inducing; for it is clear that the brevity must be in direct ratio of the intensity of the intended effect—this, with one proviso—that a certain degree of duration is absolutely requisite for the production of any effect at all.

Holding in view these considerations, as well as that degree of excitement which I deemed not above the popular, while not below the critical taste, I reached at once what I conceived the proper length for my intended poem— a length of about one hundred lines. It is, in fact, a hundred and eight.

My next thought concerned the choice of an impression, or effect, to be conveyed: and here I may as well observe that throughout the construction, I kept steadily in view the design of rendering the work universally appreciable. I should be carried too far out of my immediate topic were I to demonstrate a point upon which I have repeatedly insisted, and which, with the poetical, stands not in the slightest need of demonstration—the point, I mean, that Beauty is the sole legitimate province of the poem. A few words, however, in elucidation of my real meaning, which some of my friends have evinced a disposition to misrepresent. That pleasure which is at once the most intense, the most elevating, and the most pure is, I believe, found in the contemplation of the beautiful. When, indeed, men speak of Beauty, they mean, precisely, not a quality, as is supposed, but an effect—they refer, in short, just to that intense and pure elevation of soul—not of intellect, or of heart—upon which I have commented, and which is experienced in consequence of contemplating the "beautiful." Now I designate Beauty as the province of the poem, merely because it is an obvious rule of Art that effects should be made to spring from direct causes—that objects should be attained through means best adapted for their attainment—no one as yet having been weak enough to deny that the peculiar elevation alluded to is most readily attained in the poem. Now the object Truth, or the satisfaction of the intellect, and the object Passion, or the excitement of the heart, are, although attainable to a certain extent in poetry, far more readily attainable in prose. Truth, in fact, demands a precision, and Passion, a homeliness (the truly passionate will comprehend me), which are absolutely antagonistic to that Beauty which, I maintain, is the excitement or pleasurable elevation of the soul. It by no means follows, from anything here said, that passion, or even truth, may not be introduced, and even profitably introduced, into a poem for they may serve in elucidation, or aid the general effect, as do discords in music, by contrast—but the true artist will always contrive, first, to tone them into proper subservience to the predominant aim, and, secondly, to enveil them, as far as possible, in that Beauty which is the atmosphere and the essence of the poem.

Regarding, then, Beauty as my province, my next question referred to the tone of its highest manifestation—and all experience has shown that this tone is one of sadness. Beauty of whatever kind in its supreme development invariably excites the sensitive soul to tears. Melancholy is thus the most legitimate of all the poetical tones.

The length, the province, and the tone, being thus determined, I betook myself to ordinary induction, with the view of obtaining some artistic piquancy which might serve me as a key-note in the construction of the poem—some pivot upon which the whole structure might turn. In carefully thinking over all the usual artistic effects—or more properly points, in the theatrical sense—I did not fail to perceive immediately that no one had been so universally employed as that of the refrain. The universality of its employment sufficed to assure me of its intrinsic value, and spared me the necessity of submitting it to analysis. I considered it, however, with regard to its susceptibility of improvement, and soon saw it to be in a primitive condition. As commonly used, the refrain, or burden, not only is limited to lyric verse, but depends for its impression upon the force of monotone—both in sound and thought. The pleasure is deduced solely from the sense of identity—of repetition. I resolved to diversify, and so heighten the effect, by adhering in general to the monotone of sound, while I continually varied that of thought: that is to say, I determined to produce continuously novel effects, by the variation of the application of the refrain—the refrain itself remaining for the most part, unvaried.

These points being settled, I next bethought me of the nature of my refrain. Since its application was to be repeatedly varied it was clear that the refrain itself must be brief, for there would have been an insurmountable difficulty in frequent variations of application in any sentence of length. In proportion to the brevity of the sentence would, of course, be the facility of the variation. This led me at once to a single word as the best refrain.

The question now arose as to the character of the word. Having made up my mind to a refrain, the division of the poem into stanzas was of course a corollary, the refrain forming the close to each stanza. That such a close, to have force, must be sonorous and susceptible of protracted emphasis, admitted no doubt, and these considerations inevitably led me to the long *o* as the most sonorous vowel in connection with *r* as the most producible consonant.

The sound of the refrain being thus determined, it became necessary to select a word embodying this sound, and at the same time in the fullest possible keeping with that melancholy which I had pre-determined as the tone of the poem. In such a search it would have been absolutely impossible to overlook the word "Nevermore." In fact it was the very first which presented itself.

The next desideratum was a pretext for the continuous use of the one word "nevermore." In observing the difficulty which I had at once found in inventing a sufficiently plausible reason for its continuous repetition, I did not fail to perceive that this difficulty arose solely from the preassumption that the word was to be so continuously or monotonously spoken by a human being—I did not fail to perceive, in short, that the difficulty lay in the reconciliation of this monotony with the exercise of reason on the part of the creature repeating the word. Here, then, immediately arose the idea of a non-reasoning creature capable of speech, and very naturally, a parrot, in the first instance, suggested itself, but was superseded forthwith by a Raven as equally capable of speech, and infinitely more in keeping with the intended tone.

I had now gone so far as the conception of a Raven, the bird of ill-omen, monotonously repeating the one word "Nevermore" at the conclusion of each stanza in a poem of melancholy tone, and in length about one hundred lines. Now, never losing sight of the object—supremeness or perfection at all points, I asked myself—"Of all melancholy topics what, according to the universal understanding of mankind, is the most melancholy?" Death, was the obvious reply. "And when," I said, "is this most melancholy of topics most poetical?" From what I have already explained at some length the answer here also is obvious—"When it most closely allies itself to Beauty: the death then of a beautiful woman is unquestionably the most poetical topic in the world, and equally is it beyond doubt that the lips best suited for such topic are those of a bereaved lover."

I had now to combine the two ideas of a lover lamenting his deceased mistress and a Raven continuously repeating the word "Nevermore." I had to combine these, bearing in mind my design of varying at every turn the application of the word repeated, but the only intelligible mode of such combination is that of imagining the Raven employing the word in answer to the queries of the lover. And here it was that I saw at once the opportunity afforded for the effect on which I had been depending, that is to say, the effect of the variation of application. I saw that I could make the first query propounded by the lover—the first query to which the Raven should reply "Nevermore"—that I could make this first query a commonplace one, the second less so, the third still less, and so on, until at length the lover, startled from his original nonchalance by the melancholy character of the word itself, by its frequent repetition, and by a consideration of the ominous reputation of the fowl that uttered it, is at length excited to superstition, and wildly propounds queries of a far different character—queries whose solution he has passionately at heart—propounds them half in superstition and half in that species of despair which delights in self-torture—propounds them not altogether because he believes in the prophetic or demoniac character of the bird (which reason assures him is merely repeating a lesson learned by rote), but because he experiences a frenzied pleasure in so modelling his questions as to receive from the expected "Nevermore" the most delicious because the most intolerable of sorrows. Perceiving the opportunity thus afforded me, or, more strictly, thus forced upon me in the progress of the construction, I first established in my mind the climax or concluding query—that query to which "Nevermore" should be in the last place an answer—that query in reply to which this word "Nevermore" should involve the utmost conceivable amount of sorrow and despair.

Here then the poem may be said to have had its beginning—at the end where all works of art should begin—for it was here at this point of my preconsiderations that I first put pen to paper in the composition of the stanza:

> "Prophet!" said I, "thing of evil! prophet still if bird or
>   devil!
> By that Heaven that bends above us—by that God we both
>   adore,
> Tell this soul with sorrow laden, if, within the distant Aidenn,
> It shall clasp a sainted maiden whom the angels name Le-
>   nore—
> Clasp a rare and radiant maiden whom the angels name
>   Lenore."
> Quoth the Raven—"Nevermore."

I composed this stanza, at this point, first that, by establishing the climax, I might the better vary and graduate, as regards seriousness and importance, the preceding queries of the lover, and secondly, that I might definitely settle the rhythm, the metre, and the length and general arrangement of the stanza, as well as graduate the stanzas which were to precede, so that none of them might surpass this in rhythmical effect. Had I been able in the subsequent composition to construct more vigorous stanzas I should without scruple have purposely enfeebled them so as not to interfere with the climacteric effect.

And here I may as well say a few words of the versification. My first object (as usual) was originality. The extent to which this has been neglected in versification is one of the most unaccountable things in the world. Admitting that there is little possibility of variety in mere rhythm, it is still clear that the possible varieties of metre and stanza are absolutely infinite, and yet, for centuries, no man, in verse, has ever done, or ever seemed to think of doing, an original thing. The fact is that originality (unless in minds of very unusual force) is by no means a matter, as some suppose, of impulse or intuition. In general, to be found, it must be elaborately sought, and although a positive merit of the highest class, demands in its attainment less of invention than negation.

Of course I pretend to no originality in either the rhythm or metre of the "Raven." The former is trochaic—the latter is octametre acatalectic, alternating with heptametre catalectic repeated in the refrain of the fifth verse, and terminating with tetrametre catalectic. Less pedantically the feet employed throughout (trochees) consist of a long syllable followed by a short, the first line of the stanza consists of eight of these feet, the second of seven and a half (in effect two-thirds), the third of eight, the fourth of seven and a half, the fifth the same, the sixth three and a half. Now, each of these lines taken individually has been employed before, and what originality the "Raven" has, is in their combination into stanza; nothing even remotely approaching this has ever been attempted. The effect of this originality of combination is aided by other unusual and some altogether novel effects, arising from an extension of the application of the principles of rhyme and alliteration.

The next point to be considered was the mode of bringing together the lover and the Raven—and the first branch of this consideration was the locale. For this the most natural suggestion might seem to be a forest, or the fields—but it has always appeared to me that a close circumscription of space is absolutely necessary to the effect of insulated incident—it has the force of a frame to a picture. It has an indisputable moral power in keeping concentrated the attention, and, of course, must not be confounded with mere unity of place.

I determined, then, to place the lover in his chamber—in a chamber rendered sacred to him by memories of her who had frequented it. The room is represented as richly furnished—this in mere pursuance of the ideas I have already explained on the subject of Beauty, as the sole true poetical thesis.

The locale being thus determined, I had now to introduce the bird—and the thought of introducing him through the window was inevitable. The idea of making the lover suppose, in the first instance, that the flapping of the wings of the bird against the shutter, is a "tapping" at the door, originated in a wish to increase, by prolonging, the reader's curiosity, and in a desire to admit the incidental effect arising from the lover's throwing open the door, finding all dark, and thence adopting the half-fancy that it was the spirit of his mistress that knocked.

I made the night tempestuous, first to account for the Raven's seeking admission, and secondly, for the effect of contrast with the (physical) serenity within the chamber.

I made the bird alight on the bust of Pallas, also for the effect of contrast between the marble and the plumage—it being understood that the bust was absolutely suggested by the bird—the bust of Pallas being chosen, first, as most in keeping with the scholarship of the lover, and secondly, for the sonorousness of the word, Pallas, itself.

About the middle of the poem, also, I have availed myself of the force of contrast, with a view of deepening the ultimate impression. For example, an air of the fantastic—approaching as nearly to the ludicrous as was admissible—is given to the Raven's entrance. He comes in "with many a flirt and flutter."

> Not the least obeisance made he—not a moment stopped
>   or stayed he,
> But with mien of lord or lady, perched above my chamber
>   door.

In the two stanzas which follow, the design is more obviously carried out:—

> Then this ebony bird, beguiling my sad fancy into smiling
> By the grave and stern decorum of the countenance it
>   wore,
> "Though thy crest be shorn and shaven, thou," I said, "art
>   sure no craven,
> Ghastly grim and ancient Raven wandering from the
>   Nightly shore—
> Tell me what thy lordly name is on the Night's Plutonian
>   shore?"
> Quoth the Raven—"Nevermore."
>
> Much I marvelled this ungainly fowl to hear discourse so
>   plainly,
> Though its answer little meaning—little relevancy bore;

> For we cannot help agreeing that no living human being
> Ever yet was blessed with seeing bird above his chamber
>   door—
> Bird or beast upon the sculptured bust above his chamber
>   door,
> With such name as "Nevermore."

The effect of the denouement being thus provided for, I immediately drop the fantastic for a tone of the most profound seriousness—this tone commencing in the stanza directly following the one last quoted, with the line,

> But the Raven, sitting lonely on that placid bust, spoke
>   only, etc.

From this epoch the lover no longer jests—no longer sees anything even of the fantastic in the Raven's demeanour. He speaks of him as a "grim, ungainly, ghastly, gaunt, and ominous bird of yore," and feels the "fiery eyes" burning into his "bosom's core." This revolution of thought, or fancy, on the lover's part, is intended to induce a similar one on the part of the reader—to bring the mind into a proper frame for the denouement—which is now brought about as rapidly and as directly as possible.

With the denouement proper—with the Raven's reply, "Nevermore," to the lover's final demand if he shall meet his mistress in another world—the poem, in its obvious phase, that of a simple narrative, may be said to have its completion. So far, everything is within the limits of the accountable—of the real. A raven, having learned by rote the single word "Nevermore," and having escaped from the custody of its owner, is driven at midnight, through the violence of a storm, to seek admission at a window from which a light still gleams—the chamber-window of a student, occupied half in poring over a volume, half in dreaming of a beloved mistress deceased. The casement being thrown open at the fluttering of the bird's wings, the bird itself perches on the most convenient seat out of the immediate reach of the student, who amused by the incident and the oddity of the visitor's demeanour, demands of it, in jest and without looking for a reply, its name. The raven addressed, answers with its customary word, "Nevermore"—a word which finds immediate echo in the melancholy heart of the student, who, giving utterance aloud to certain thoughts suggested by the occasion, is again startled by the fowl's repetition of "Nevermore." The student now guesses the state of the case, but is impelled, as I have before explained, by the human thirst for self-torture, and in part by superstition, to propound such queries to the bird as will bring him, the lover, the most of the luxury of sorrow, through the anticipated answer, "Nevermore." With the indulgence, to the extreme, of this self-torture, the narration, in what I have termed its first or obvious phase, has a natural termination, and so far there has been no overstepping of the limits of the real.

But in subjects so handled, however skillfully, or with however vivid an array of incident, there is always a certain hardness or nakedness which repels the artistical eye. Two things are invariably required—first, some amount of complexity, or more properly, adaptation; and, secondly, some amount of suggestiveness—some under-current, however indefinite, of meaning. It is this latter, in especial, which imparts to a work of art so much of that richness (to borrow from colloquy a forcible term), which we are too fond of confounding with the ideal. It is the excess of the suggested meaning—it is the rendering this the upper instead of the under-current of the theme—which turns into prose (and that of the very flattest kind), the so-called poetry of the so-called transcendentalists.

Holding these opinions, I added the two concluding stanzas of the poem— their suggestiveness being thus made to pervade all the narrative which has preceded them. The under-current of meaning is rendered first apparent in the line—

> "Take thy beak from out my heart, and take thy form from
>   off my door!"
> Quoth the Raven "Nevermore!"

It will be observed that the words, "from out my heart," involve the first meta-phorical expression in the poem. They, with the answer, "Nevermore," dispose the mind to seek a moral in all that has been previously narrated. The reader begins now to regard the Raven as emblematical—but it is not until the very last line of the very last stanza that the intention of making him emblematical of Mournful and never ending Remembrance is permitted distinctly to be seen:

> And the Raven, never flitting, still is sitting, still is sitting,
> On the pallid bust of Pallas just above my chamber door;
> And his eyes have all the seeming of a demon that is
>   dreaming,
> And the lamplight o'er him streaming throws his shadow on
>   the floor;
> And my soul from out that shadow that lies floating on the
>   floor
> Shall be lifted—nevermore.

26

WALT WHITMAN (1819–1892)

Whitman wrote a lot about himself—or about a self called "Walt Whitman"—so that most readers are familiar with the outlines of his history: born on Long Island, worked as a printer and journalist, especially for Democrat organs, traveled to New Orleans, served as a wound-dresser during the Civil War, stayed on in Washington for some years thereafter, moving finally to Camden, New Jersey, where he spent the last nineteen years of his life. Whitman was extraordinarily susceptible to influences of every sort. In creating his prodigiously capacious idiom for American poetry, he used slang, opera, phrenology, all religions and philosophies, the oratorical manners of preachers and platform lecturers, free association, the cut-and-paste assemblage of newspapers—in short, anything. He was always a democrat (although during the Civil War he changed his party allegiance from Democrat to Republican). He was hailed by Ralph Waldo Emerson on the first appearance of *Leaves of Grass* in 1855; praise also came from W. M. Rossetti and Algernon Charles Swinburne.

Whitman was like Shelley and Emerson in viewing the poet's calling as among the highest and most ancient. He especially embraced the ancient epic as a national work by a legendary prophet, but he did the American thing by modernizing and personalizing the epic, singing, instead of the worn-out materials suggested by the Muses, himself, by name and even by nickname. Emerson had already equated the country with the poem, saying in 1844, "Our logrolling, our stumps and their politics, our fisheries, our Negroes, and Indians, our boasts, and our repudiations, the wrath of rogues, and the pusillanimity of honest men, the northern trade, the southern planting, the western clearing, Oregon, and Texas, are yet unsung. Yet America is a poem in our eyes; its ample geography dazzles the imagination, and it will not wait long for metres." If the country is a poem, Whitman argued further that the poem is the poet ("Camerado, this is no book, / Who touches this touches a man . . ."). It is unlikely that anyone but Whitman—with his very peculiar genius and his very peculiar kind of limitation—could have done it with such grandeur.

PREFACE TO *LEAVES OF GRASS*, FIRST EDITION
(EXCERPT; 1855)

America does not repel the past or what it has produced under its forms or amid other politics or the idea of castes or the old religions . . . accepts the lesson with calmness . . . is not so impatient as has been supposed that the slough still sticks to opinions and manners and literature while the life which served its requirements has passed into the new life of the new forms . . . perceives that the corpse is slowly borne from the eating and sleeping rooms of the house . . . perceives that it waits a little while in the door . . . that it was fittest for its days . . . that its action has descended to the stalwart and wellshaped heir who approaches . . . and that he shall be fittest for his days.

The Americans of all nations at any time upon the earth have probably the fullest poetical nature. The United States themselves are essentially the greatest poem. In the history of the earth hitherto the largest and most stirring appear tame and orderly to their ampler largeness and stir. Here at last is something in the doings of man that corresponds with the broadcast doings of the day and night. Here is not merely a nation but a teeming nation of nations. Here is action untied from strings necessarily blind to particulars and details magnificently moving in vast masses. Here is the hospitality which forever indicates heroes. . . . Here are the roughs and beards and space and ruggedness and nonchalance that the soul loves. Here the performance disdaining the trivial unapproached in the tremendous audacity of its crowds and groupings and the push of its perspective spreads with crampless and flowing breadth and showers its prolific and splendid extravagance. One sees it must indeed own the riches of the summer and winter, and need never be bankrupt while corn grows from the ground or the orchards drop apples or the bays contain fish or men beget children upon women.

Other states indicate themselves in their deputies . . . but the genius of the United States is not best or most in its executives or legislatures, nor in its ambassadors or authors or colleges or churches or parlors, nor even in its newspapers or inventors . . . but always most in the common people. Their manners speech dress friendships—the freshness and candor of their physiognomy— the picturesque looseness of their carriage . . . their deathless attachment to freedom—their aversion to anything indecorous or soft or mean—the practical acknowledgment of the citizens of one state by the citizens of all other states— the fierceness of their roused resentment—their Curiosity and welcome of novelty—their self-esteem and wonderful sympathy—their susceptibility to a slight—the air they have of persons who never knew how it felt to stand in the presence of superiors—the fluency of their speech their delight in music, the sure symptom of manly tenderness and native elegance of soul . . . their good temper and openhandedness—the terrible significance of their elections—the President's taking off his hat to them not they to him—these too are unrhymed poetry. It awaits the gigantic and generous treatment worthy of it.

The largeness of nature or the nation were monstrous without a corresponding largeness and generosity of the spirit of the citizen. Not nature nor swarming states nor streets and steamships nor prosperous business nor farms nor capital nor learning may suffice for the ideal of man . . . nor suffice the poet. No reminiscences may suffice either. A live nation can always cut a deep mark and can have the best authority the cheapest . . . namely from its own soul. This is the sum of the profitable uses of individuals or states and of present action and grandeur and of the subjects of poets.—As if it were necessary to trot back generation after generation to the eastern records! As if the beauty and sacredness of the demonstrable must fall behind that of the mythical! As if men do not make their mark out of any times! As if the opening of the western continent by discovery and what has transpired since in North and South America were less than the small theatre of the antique or the aimless sleepwalking of the middle ages! The pride of the United States leaves the wealth and finesse of the cities and all returns of commerce and agriculture and all the magnitude of geography or shows of exterior victory to enjoy the breed of full-sized men or one full-sized man unconquerable and simple.

The American poets are to enclose old and new for America is the race of races. Of them a bard is to be commensurate with a people. To him the other continents arrive as contributions . . . he gives them reception for their sake and his own sake. His spirit responds to his country's spirit. . . . he incarnates its geography and natural life and rivers and lakes. Mississippi with annual freshets and changing chutes, Missouri and Columbia and Ohio and Saint Lawrence with the falls and beautiful masculine Hudson, do not embouchure where they spend themselves more than they embouchure into him. The blue breadth over the inland sea of Virginia and Maryland and the sea off Massachusetts and Maine and over Manhattan bay and over Champlain and Erie and over Ontario and Huron and Michigan and Superior, and over the Texan and Mexican and Floridian and Cuban seas and over the seas off California and Oregon, is not tallied by the blue breadth of the waters below more than the breadth of above and below is tallied by him. When the long Atlantic coast stretches longer and the Pacific coast stretches longer he easily stretches with them north or south. He spans between them also from east to west and reflects what is between them. On him rise solid growths that offset the growths of pine and cedar and hemlock and liveoak and locust and chestnut and cypress and hickory and limetree and cottonwood and tuliptree and cactus and wildvine and tamarind and persimmon . . . and tangles as tangled as any canebrake or swamp . . . and forests coated with transparent ice and icicles hanging from the boughs and crackling in the wind . . . and sides and peaks of mountains . . . and pasturage sweet and free as savannah or upland or prairie . . . with flights and songs and screams that answer those of the wildpigeon and highhold and orchard-oriole and coot and surf-duck and redshouldered-hawk and fish-hawk and white-ibis and indian-hen and cat-owl and water-pheasant and qua-bird and pied-sheldrake and blackbird and mockingbird and buzzard and condor and night-heron and eagle. To him the hereditary countenance descends both mother's and father's. To him enter the essences of the real things and past and present events—of the enormous diversity of temperature and agriculture and mines—the tribes of red aborigines—the weather-beaten vessels entering new ports or making landings on rocky coasts—the first settlements north or south— the rapid stature and muscle—the haughty defiance of '76, and the war and peace and formation of the constitution. . . . the union always surrounded by blatherers and always calm and impregnable—the perpetual coming of immigrants—the wharfhem'd cities and superior marine—the unsurveyed interior— the loghouses and clearings and wild animals and hunters and trappers. . . . the free commerce—the fisheries and whaling and gold-digging—the endless gestation of new states—the convening of Congress every December, the members duly coming up from all climates and the uttermost parts . . . the noble character of the young mechanics and of all free American workmen and workwomen . . . the general ardor and friendliness and enterprise—the perfect equality of the female with the male. . . . the large amativeness—the fluid movement of the population—the factories and mercantile life and laborsaving machinery—the Yankee swap—the New-York firemen and the target excursion—the southern plantation life—the character of the northeast and of the northwest and south-west—slavery and the tremulous spreading of hands to protect it, and the stern opposition to it which shall never cease till it ceases or the speaking of tongues and the moving of lips cease. For such the expression of the American poet is to be transcendant and new. It is to be indirect and not direct or descriptive or epic. Its quality goes through these to much more. Let the age and wars of other nations be chanted and their eras and characters be illustrated and that finish the verse. Not so the great psalm of the republic. Here the theme is creative and has vista. Here comes one among the wellbeloved stonecutters and plans with decision and science and sees the solid and beautiful forms of the future where there are now no solid forms.

Of all nations the United States with veins full of poetical stuff most need poets and will doubtless have the greatest and use them the greatest. Their Presidents shall not be their common referee so much as their poets shall. Of all mankind the great poet is the equable man. Not in him but off from him things are grotesque or eccentric or fail of their sanity. Nothing out of its place is good and nothing in its place is bad. He bestows on every object or quality its fit proportions neither more nor less. He is the arbiter of the diverse and he is the key. He is the equalizer of his age and land. . . . he supplies what wants supplying and checks what wants checking. If peace is the routine out of him speaks the spirit of peace, large, rich, thrifty, building vast and populous cities, encouraging agriculture and the arts and commerce—lighting the study of man, the soul, immortality—federal, state or municipal government, marriage, health, freetrade, intertravel by land and sea. . . . nothing too close, nothing too far off . . . the stars not too far off. In war he is the most deadly force of the war. Who recruits him recruits horse and foot . . . he fetches parks of artillery the best that engineer ever knew. If the time becomes slothful and heavy he knows how to arouse it . . . he can make every word he speaks draw blood. Whatever stagnates in the flat of custom or obedience or legislation he never stagnates. Obedience does not master him, he masters it. High up out of reach he stands turning a concentrated light . . . he turns the pivot with his finger . . . he baffles the swiftest runners as he stands and easily overtakes and envelops them. The time straying toward infidelity and confections and persiflage he withholds by his steady faith . . . he spreads out his dishes . . . he offers the sweet firmfibred meat that grows men and women. His brain is the ultimate brain. He is no arguer . . . he is judgment. He judges not as the judge judges but as the sun falling around a helpless thing. As he sees the farthest he has the most faith. His thoughts are the hymns of the praise of things. In the talk on the soul and eternity and God off of his equal plane he is silent. He sees eternity less like a play with a prologue and denouement. . . . he sees eternity in men and women. . . . he does not see men and women as dreams or dots. Faith is the antiseptic of the soul . . . it pervades the common people and preserves them . . . they never give up believing and expecting and trusting. There is that indescribable freshness and unconsciousness about an illiterate person that humbles and mocks the power of the noblest expressive genius. The poet sees for a certainty how one not a great artist may be just as sacred and perfect as the greatest artist. . . . The power to destroy or remould is freely used by him but never the power of attack. What is past is past. If he does not expose superior models and prove himself by every step he takes he is not what is wanted. The presence of the greatest poet conquers . . . not parleying or struggling or any prepared attempts. Now he has passed that way see after him! there is not left any vestige of despair or misanthropy or cunning or exclusiveness or the ignominy of a nativity of color or delusion of hell or the necessity of hell and no man thenceforward shall be degraded for ignorance or weakness or sin.

The greatest poet hardly knows pettiness or triviality. If he breathes into any thing that was before thought small it dilates with the grandeur and life of the universe. He is a seer. . . . he is individual . . . he is complete in himself. . . . the others are as good as he, only he sees it and they do not. He is not one of the chorus. . . . he does not stop for any regulation . . . he is the president of regulation. What the eyesight does to the rest he does to the rest. Who knows the curious mystery of the eyesight? The other senses corroborate themselves, but this is removed from any proof but its own and foreruns the identities of the spiritual world. A single glance of it mocks all the investigations of man and all the instruments and books of the earth and all reasoning. What is marvellous? what is unlikely? what is impossible or baseless or vague? after you have once just opened the space of a peachpit and given audience to far and near and to the sunset and had all things enter with electric swiftness softly and duly without confusion or jostling or jam.

The land and sea, the animals, fishes and birds, the sky of heaven and the orbs, the forests mountains and rivers, are not small themes . . . but folk expect of the poet to indicate more than the beauty and dignity which always attach to dumb real objects. . . . they expect him to indicate the path between reality and their souls. Men and women perceive the beauty well enough . . . probably as well as he. The passionate tenacity of hunters, woodmen, early risers, cultivators of gardens and orchards and fields, the love of healthy women for the manly form, seafaring persons, drivers of horses, the passion for light and the open air, all is an old varied sign of the unfailing perception of beauty and of a residence of the poetic in outdoor people. They can never be assisted by poets to perceive. . . . some may but they never can. The poetic quality is not marshalled in rhyme or uniformity or abstract addresses to things nor in melancholy complaints or good precepts, but is the life of these and much else and is in the soul. The profit of rhyme is that it drops seeds of a sweeter and more luxuriant rhyme, and of uniformity that it conveys itself into its own roots in the ground out of sight. The rhyme and uniformity of perfect poems show the free growth of metrical laws and bud from them as unerringly and loosely as lilacs or roses on a bush, and take shapes as compact as the shapes of chestnuts and oranges and melons and pears, and shed the perfume impalpable to form. The fluency and ornaments of the finest poems or music or orations or recitations are not independent but dependent. All beauty comes from beautiful blood and a beautiful brain. If the greatnesses are in conjunction in a man or woman it is enough. . . . the fact will prevail through the universe . . . but the gaggery and gilt of a million years will not prevail. Who troubles himself about his ornaments or fluency is lost. This is what you shall do: Love the earth and sun and the animals, despise riches, give alms to every one that asks, stand up for the stupid and crazy, devote your income and labor to others, hate tyrants, argue not concerning God, have patience and indulgence toward the people, take off your hat to nothing known or unknown or to any man or number of men, go freely with powerful uneducated persons and with the young and with the mothers of families, read these leaves in the open air every season of every year of your life, re-examine all you have been told at school or church or in any book, dismiss whatever insults your own soul, and your very flesh shall be a great poem and have the richest fluency not only in its words but in the silent lines of its lips and face and between the lashes of your eyes and in every motion and joint of your body. . . . The poet shall not spend his time in unneeded work. He shall know that the ground is always ready ploughed and manured. . . . others may not know it but he shall. He shall go directly to the creation. His trust shall master the trust of everything he touches . . . and shall master all attachment.

The known universe has one complete lover and that is the greatest poet. He consumes an eternal passion and is indifferent which chance happens and which possible contingency of fortune or misfortune and persuades daily and hourly his delicious pay. What balks or breaks others is fuel for his burning progress to contact and amorous joy. Other proportions of the reception of pleasure dwindle to nothing to his proportions. All expected from heaven or from the highest he is rapport with in the sight of the daybreak or a scene of the winter woods or the presence of children playing or with his arm round the neck of a man or woman. His love above all love has leisure and expanse. . . . he leaves room ahead of himself. He is no irresolute or suspicious lover . . . he is sure . . . he scorns intervals. His experience and the showers and thrills are not for nothing. Nothing can jar him . . . suffering and darkness cannot—death and fear cannot. To him complaint and jealousy and envy are corpses buried and rotten in the earth. . . . he saw them buried. The sea is not surer of the shore or the shore of the sea than he is of the fruition of his love and of all perfection and beauty.

The fruition of beauty is no chance of hit or miss . . . it is inevitable as life. . . . it is exact and plumb as gravitation. From the eyesight proceeds another eyesight and from the hearing proceeds another hearing and from the voice proceeds another voice eternally curious of the harmony of things with man. To these respond perfections not only in the committees that were supposed to stand for the rest but in the rest themselves just the same. These understand the law of perfection in masses and floods . . . that its finish is to each for itself and onward from itself . . . that it is profuse and impartial . . . that there is not a minute of the light or dark nor an acre of the earth or sea without it—nor any direction of the sky nor any trade or employment nor any turn of events. This is the reason that about the proper expression of beauty there is precision and balance. . . . one part does not need to be thrust above the other. The best singer is not the one who has the most lithe and powerful organ . . . the pleasure of poems is not in them that take the handsomest measure and similes and sound.

Without effort and without exposing in the least how it is done the greatest poet brings the spirit of any or all events and passions and scenes and persons some more and some less to bear on your individual character as you hear or read. To do this well is to compete with the laws that pursue and follow time. What is the purpose must surely be there and the clue of it must be there . . . and the faintest indication is the indication of the best and then becomes the clearest indication. Past and present and future are not disjoined but joined. The greatest poet forms the consistence of what is to be from what has been and is. He drags the dead out of their coffins and stands them again on their feet. . . . he says to the past, Rise and walk before me that I may realize you. He learns the lesson. . . . he places himself where the future becomes present. The greatest poet does not only dazzle his rays over character and scenes and passions . . . he finally ascends and finishes all. . . . he exhibits the pinnacles that no man can tell what they are for or what is beyond. . . . he glows a moment on the extremest verge. He is most wonderful in his last half-hidden smile or frown . . . by that flash of the moment of parting the one that sees it shall be encouraged or terrified afterward for many years. The greatest poet does not moralize or make applications of morals . . . he knows the soul. The soul has that measureless pride which consists in never acknowledging any lessons but its own. But it has sympathy as measureless as its pride and the one balances the other and neither can stretch too far while it stretches in company with the other. The inmost secrets of art sleep with the twain. The greatest poet has lain close betwixt both and they are vital in his style and thoughts.

The art of art, the glory of expression and the sunshine of the light of letters is simplicity. Nothing is better than simplicity. . . . nothing can make up for excess or for the lack of definiteness. To carry on the heave of impulse and pierce intellectual depths and give all subjects their articulations are powers neither common nor very uncommon. But to speak in literature with the perfect rectitude and insouciance of the movements of animals and the unimpeach-ableness of the sentiment of trees in the woods and grass by the roadside is the flawless triumph of art. If you have looked on him who has achieved it you have looked on one of the masters of the artists of all nations and times. You shall not contemplate the flight of the graygull over the bay or the mettlesome action of the blood horse or the tall leaning of sunflowers on their stalk or the appearance of the sun journeying through heaven or the appearance of the moon afterward with any more satisfaction than you shall contemplate him. The greatest poet has less a marked style and is more the channel of thoughts and things without increase or diminution, and is the free channel of himself. He swears to his art, I will not be meddlesome, I will not have in my writing any elegance or effect or originality to hang in the way between me and the rest like curtains. I will have nothing hang in the way, not the richest curtains. What I tell I tell precisely for what it is. Let who may exalt or startle or fascinate or sooth I will have purposes as health or heat or snow has and be as regardless of observation. What I experience or portray shall go from my composition without a shred of my composition. You shall stand by my side and look in the mirror with me.

The old red blood and stainless gentility of great poets will be proved by their unconstraint. A heroic person walks at his ease through and out of that custom or precedent or authority that suits him not. Of the traits of the brotherhood of writers savans musicians inventors and artists nothing is finer than silent defiance advancing from new free forms. In the need of poems philosophy politics mechanism science behaviour, the craft of art, an appropriate native grand-opera, shipcraft, or any craft, he is greatest forever and forever who contributes the greatest original practical example. The cleanest expression is that which finds no sphere worthy of itself and makes one.

The messages of great poets to each man and woman are, Come to us on equal terms, only then can you understand us, We are no better than you, What we enclose you enclose, What we enjoy you may enjoy. Did you suppose there could be only one Supreme? We affirm there can be unnumbered Supremes, and that one does not countervail another any more than one eyesight countervails another . . . and that men can be good or grand only of the consciousness of their supremacy within them. What do you think is the grandeur of storms and dismemberments and the deadliest battles and wrecks and the wildest fury of the elements and the power of the sea and the motion of nature and of the throes of human desires and dignity and hate and love? It is that something in the soul which says, Rage on, Whirl on, I tread master here and everywhere, Master of the spasms of the sky and of the shatter of the sea, Master of nature and passion and death, And of all terror and all pain.

The American bards shall be marked for generosity and affection and for encouraging competitors. . . . They shall be kosmos . . . without monopoly or secresy . . . glad to pass any thing to any one . . . hungry for equal night and day. They shall not be careful of riches and privilege. . . . they shall be riches and privilege. . . . they shall perceive who the most affluent man is. The most affluent man is he that confronts all the shows he sees by equivalents out of the stronger wealth of himself. The American bard shall delineate no class of persons nor one or two out of the strata of interests nor love most nor truth most nor the soul most nor the body most . . . and not be for the eastern states more than the western or the northern states more than the southern.

Exact science and its practical movements are no checks on the greatest poets but always his encouragement and support. The outself and remembrance are there. . . . there the arms that lifted him first and brace him best. . . . there he returns after all his goings and comings. The sailor and traveler . . . the anatomist, chemist, astronomer, geologist, phrenologist, spiritualist, mathematician, historian and lexicographer are not poets, but they are the lawgivers of poets and their construction underlies the structure of every perfect poem. No matter what rises or is uttered they sent the seed of the conception of it . . . of them and by them stand the visible proofs of souls . . . always of their fatherstuff must be begotten the sinewy races of bards. If there shall be love and content between the father and the son and if the greatness of the son is the exuding of the greatness of the father there shall be love between the poet and the man of demonstrable science. In the beauty of poems are the tuft and final applause of science.

Great is the faith of the flush of knowledge and of the investigation of the depth of qualities and things. Cleaving and circling here swells the soul of the poet yet is president of itself always. The depths are fathomless and therefore calm. The innocence and nakedness are resumed . . . they are neither modest nor immodest. The whole theory of the special and supernatural and all that was twined with it or educed out of it departs as a dream. What has ever happened. . . . what happens and whatever may or shall happen, the vital laws enclose all. . . . they are sufficient for any case and for all cases . . . none to be hurried or retarded. . . . any miracle of affairs or persons inadmissible in the vast clear scheme where every motion and every spear of grass and the frames and spirits of men and women and all that concerns them are unspeakably perfect miracles all referring to all and each distinct and in its place. It is also not consistent with the reality of the soul to admit that there is anything in the known universe more divine than men and women.

Men and women and the earth and all upon it are simply to be taken as they are, and the investigation of their past and present and future shall be unintermitted and shall be done with perfect candor. Upon this basis philosophy speculates ever looking toward the poet, ever regarding the eternal tendencies of all toward happiness never inconsistent with what is clear to the senses and to the soul. For the eternal tendencies of all toward happiness make the only point of sane philosophy. Whatever comprehends less than that . . . whatever is less than the laws of light and of astronomical motion . . . or less than the laws that follow the thief the liar the glutton and the drunkard through this life and doubtless afterward . . . or less than vast stretches of time or the slow formation of density or the patient upheaving of strata — is of no account. Whatever would put God in a poem or system of philosophy as contending against some being or influence is also of no account. Sanity and ensemble characterize the great master . . . spoilt in one principle all is spoilt. The great master has nothing to do with miracles. He sees health for himself in being one of the mass. . . . he sees the hiatus in singular eminence. To the perfect shape comes common ground. To be under the general law is great for that is to correspond with it. The master knows that he is unspeakably great and that all are unspeakably great . . . that nothing for instance is greater than to conceive children and bring them up well . . . that to be is just as great as to perceive or tell.

In the make of the great masters the idea of political liberty is indispensible. Liberty takes the adherence of heroes wherever men and women exist. . . . but never takes any adherence or welcome from the rest more than from poets. They are the voice and exposition of liberty. They out of ages are worthy the grand idea. . . . to them it is confided and they must sustain it. Nothing has precedence of it and nothing can warp or degrade it. The attitude of great poets is to cheer up slaves and horrify despots. The turn of their necks, the sound of their feet, the motions of their wrists, are full of hazard to the one and hope to the other. Come nigh them awhile and though they neither speak or advise you shall learn the faithful American lesson. Liberty is poorly served by men whose good intent is quelled from one failure or two failures or any number of failures, or from the casual indifference or ingratitude of the people, or from the sharp show of the tushes of power, or the bringing to bear soldiers and cannon or any penal statutes. Liberty relies upon itself, invites no one, promises nothing, sits in calmness and light, is positive and composed, and knows no discouragement. The battle rages with many a loud alarm and frequent advance and retreat. . . . the enemy triumphs. . . . the prison, the handcuffs, the iron necklace and anklet, the scaffold, garrote and leadballs do their work. . . . the cause is asleep. . . . the strong throats are choked with their own blood. . . . the young men drop their eyelashes toward the ground when they pass each other. . . . and is liberty gone out of that place? No never. When liberty goes it is not the first to go nor the second or third to go. . . . it waits for all the rest to go. . . . it is the last. . . . When the memories of the old martyrs are faded utterly away . . . when the large names of patriots are laughed at in the public halls from the lips of the orators . . . when the boys are no more christened after the same but christened after tyrants and traitors instead . . . when the laws of the free are grudgingly permitted and laws for informers and bloodmoney are sweet to the taste of the people . . . when I and you walk abroad upon the earth stung with compassion at the sight of numberless brothers answering our equal friendship and caffing no man master — and when we are elated with noble joy at the sight of slaves . . . when the soul retires in the cool communion of the night and surveys its experience and has much extasy over the word and deed that put back a helpless innocent person into the gripe of the gripers or into any cruel inferiority . . . when those in all parts of these states who could easier realize the true American character but do not yet—when the swarms of cringers, suckers, doughfaces, lice of politics, planners of sly involutions for their own preferment to city offices or state legislatures or the judiciary or congress or the presidency, obtain a response of love and natural deference from the people whether they get the offices or no . . . when it is better to be a bound booby and rogue in office at a high salary than the poorest free mechanic or farmer with his hat unmoved from his head and firm eyes and a candid and generous heart . . . and when servility by town or state or the federal government or any oppression on a large scale or small scale can be tried on without its own punishment following duly after in exact proportion against the smallest chance of escape . . . or rather when all life and all the souls of men and women are discharged from any part of the earth—then only shall the instinct of liberty be discharged from that part of the earth.

As the attributes of the poets of the kosmos concentre in the real body and soul and in the pleasure of things they possess the superiority of genuineness over all fiction and romance. As they emit themselves facts are showered over with light. . . . the daylight is lit with more volatile light. . . . also the deep between the setting and rising sun goes deeper many fold. Each precise object or condition or combination or process exhibits a beauty. . . . the multiplication table its—old age its—the carpenter's trade its—the grand-opera its. . . . the hugehulled cleanshaped New-York clipper at sea under steam or full sail gleams with unmatched beauty. . . . the American circles and large harmonies of government gleam with theirs. . . . and the commonest definite intentions and actions with theirs. The poets of the kosmos advance through all interpositions and coverings and turmoils and stratagems to first principles. They are of use. . . . they dissolve poverty from its need and riches from its conceit. You large proprietor they say shall not realize or perceive more than any one else. The owner of the library is not he who holds a legal title to it having bought and paid for it. Any one and every one is owner of the library who can read the same through all the varieties of tongues and subjects and styles, and in whom they enter with ease and take residence and force toward paternity and maternity, and make supple and powerful and rich and large. . . .

These American states strong and healthy and accomplished shall receive no pleasure from violations of natural models and must not permit them. In paintings or mouldings or carvings in mineral or wood, or in the illustrations of books or newspapers, or in any comic or tragic prints, or in the patterns of woven stuffs or any thing to beautify rooms or furniture or costumes, or to put upon cornices or monuments or on the prows or sterns of ships, or to put anywhere before the human eye indoors or out, that which distorts honest shapes or which creates unearthly beings or places or contingencies is a nuisance and revolt. Of the human form especially it is so great it must never be made ridiculous. Of ornaments to a work nothing outre can be allowed . . . but those ornaments can be allowed that conform to the perfect facts of the open air and that flow out of the nature of the work and come irrepressibly from it and are necessary to the completion of the work. Most works are most beautiful without ornament. . . . Exaggerations will be revenged in human physiology. Clean and vigorous children are jetted and conceived only in those communities where the models of natural forms are public every day. . . . Great genius and the people of these states must never be demeaned to romances. As soon as histories are properly told there is no more need of romances.

The great poets are also to be known by the absence in them of tricks and by the justification of perfect personal candor. Then folks echo a new cheap joy and a divine voice leaping from their brains: How beautiful is candor! All faults may be forgiven of him who has perfect candor. Henceforth let no man of us lie, for we have seen that openness wins the inner and outer world and that there is no single exception, and that never since our earth gathered itself in a mass have deceit or subterfuge or prevarication attracted its smallest particle or the faintest tinge of a shade—and that through the enveloping wealth and rank of a state or the whole republic of states a sneak or sly person shall be discovered and despised. . . . and that the soul has never been once fooled and never can be fooled. . . . and thrift without the loving nod of the soul is only a foetid puff. . . . and there never grew up in any of the continents of the globe nor upon any planet or satellite or star, nor upon the asteroids, nor in any part of ethereal space, nor in the midst of density, nor under the fluid wet of the sea, nor in that condition which precedes the birth of babes, nor at any time during the changes of life, nor in that condition that follows what we term death, nor in any stretch of abeyance or action afterward of vitality, nor in any process of formation or reformation anywhere, a being whose instinct hated the truth.

Extreme caution or prudence, the soundest organic health, large hope and comparison and fondness for women and children, large alimentiveness and destructiveness and causality, with a perfect sense of the oneness of nature and the propriety of the same spirit applied to human affairs . . . these are called up of the float of the brain of the world to be parts of the greatest poet from his birth out of his mother's womb and from her birth out of her mother's. Caution seldom goes far enough. It has been thought that the prudent citizen was the citizen who applied himself to solid gains and did well for himself and his family and completed a lawful life without debt or crime. The greatest poet sees and admits these economies as he sees the economies of food and sleep, but has higher notions of prudence than to think he gives much when he gives a few slight attentions at the latch of the gate. The premises of the prudence of life are not the hospitality of it or the ripeness and harvest of it. Beyond the independence of a little sum laid aside for burial-money, and of a few clap-boards around and shingles overhead on a lot of American soil owned, and the easy dollars that supply the year's plain clothing and meals, the melancholy prudence of the abandonment of such a great being as a man is to the toss and pallor of years of moneymaking with all their scorching days and icy nights and all their stifling deceits and underhanded dodgings, or infinitesimals of parlors, or shameless stuffing while others starve. . . . and all the loss of the bloom and odor of the earth and of the flowers and atmosphere and of the sea and of the true taste of the women and men you pass or have to do with in youth or middle age, and the issuing sickness and desperate revolt at the close of a life without elevation of naiveté, and the ghastly chatter of a death without serenity or maj-esty, is the great fraud upon modern civilization and forethought, blotching the surface and system which civilization undeniably drafts, and moistening with tears the immense features it spreads and spreads with such velocity before the reached kisses of the soul. . . . Still the right explanation remains to be made about prudence. The prudence of the mere wealth and respectability of the most esteemed life appears too faint for the eye to observe at all when little and large alike drop quietly aside at the thought of the prudence suitable for im-mortality. What is wisdom that fills the thinness of a year or seventy or eighty years to wisdom spaced out by ages and coming back at a certain time with strong reinforcements and rich presents and the clear faces of wedding-guests as far as you can look in every direction running gaily toward you? Only the soul is of itself. . . . all else has reference to what ensues. All that a person does or thinks is of consequence. Not a move can a man or woman make that affects him or her in a day or a month or any part of the direct lifetime or the hour of death but the same affects him or her onward afterward through the indirect lifetime. The indirect is always as great and real as the direct. The spirit receives from the body just as much as it gives to the body. Not one name of word or deed . . . not of venereal sores or discolorations . . . not the privacy of the onanist . . . not of the putrid veins of gluttons or rumdrinkers . . . not peculation or cunning or betrayal or murder . . . no serpentine poison of those that seduce women . . . not the foolish yielding of women . . . not prostitution . . . not of any depravity of young men . . . not of the attainment of gain by discreditable means . . . not any nastiness of appetite not any harshness of officers to men or judges to prisoners or fathers to sons or sons to fathers or of husbands to wives or bosses to their boys . . . not of greedy looks or malignant wishes . . . nor any of the wiles practised by people upon themselves . . . ever is or ever can be stamped on the programme but it is duly realized and returned, and that re-turned in further performances . . . and they returned again. Nor can the push of charity or personal force ever be anything else than the profoundest reason, whether it bring arguments to hand or no. No specification is necessary . . . to add or subtract or divide is in vain. Little or big, learned or unlearned, white or black, legal or illegal, sick or well, from the first inspiration down the wind-pipe to the last expiration out of it, all that a male or female does that is vigorous and benevolent and clean is so much sure profit to him or her in the unshakable order of the universe and through the whole scope of it forever. If the savage or felon is wise it is well . . . if the greatest poet or savan is wise it is simply the same . . . if the President or chief justice is wise it is the same . . . if the young mechanic or farmer is wise it is no more or less . . . if the prostitute is wise it is no more or less. The interest will come round . . . all will come round. All the best actions of war and peace . . . all help given to relatives and strangers and the poor and old and sorrowful and young children and widows and the sick, and to all shunned persons . . . all furtherance of fugitives and of the escape of slaves . . . all the self-denial that stood ready and aloof on wrecks and saw others take the seats of the boats . . . all offering of substance or life for the good old cause, or for a friend's sake or opinion's sake . . . all pains of enthusiasts scoffed at by their neighbors . . . all the vast sweet love and precious suffering of mothers . . . all honest men baffled in strifes recorded or unrecorded . . . all the grandeur and good of the few ancient nations whose fragments of animals we inherit . . . and all the good of the hundreds of far mightier and more ancient nations unknown to us by name or date or location . . . all that was ever manfully begun, whether it succeeded or no . . . all that has at any time been well suggested out of the divine heart of man or by the divinity of his mouth or by the shaping of his great hands . . . and all that is well thought or done this day on any part of the surface of the globe . . . or on any of the wandering stars or fixed stars by those there as we are here . . . or that is henceforth to be well thought or done by you whoever you are, or by any one— these singly and wholly inured at their time and inure now and will inure always to the identities from which they sprung or shall spring. . . . Did you guess any of them lived only its moment? The world does not so exist . . . no parts palpable or impalpable so exist . . . no result exists now without being from its long antecedent result, and that from its antecedent, and so backward without the farthest mentionable spot coming a bit nearer the beginning than any other spot. . . . Whatever satisfies the soul is truth. The prudence of the greatest poet answers at last the craving and glut of the soul, is not contemptuous of less ways of prudence if they conform to its ways, puts off nothing, permits no let-up for its own case or any case, has no particular sabbath or judgment-day, divides not the living from the dead or the righteous from the unrighteous, is satisfied with the present, matches every thought or act by its correlative, knows no possible forgiveness or deputed atonement . . . knows that the young man who com-posedly periled his life and lost it has done exceeding well for himself, while the man who has not periled his life and retains it to old age in riches and ease has perhaps achieved nothing for himself worth mentioning . . . and that only that person has no great prudence to learn who has learnt to prefer real longlived things, and favors body and soul the same, and perceives the indirect assuredly following the direct, and what evil or good he does leaping onward and waiting to meet him again—and who in his spirit in any emergency whatever neither hurries or avoids death.

The direct trial of him who would be the greatest poet is today. If he does not flood himself with the immediate age as with vast oceanic tides . . . and if he does not attract his own land body and soul to himself and hang on its neck with incomparable love and plunge his semitic muscle into its merits and de-merits . . . and if he be not himself the age transfigured . . . and if to him is not opened the eternity which gives similitude to all periods and locations and processes and animate and inanimate forms, and which is the bond of time, and rises up from its inconceivable vagueness and infiniteness in the swimming shape of today, and is held by the ductile anchors of life, and makes the present spot the passage from what was to what shall be, and commits itself to the representation of this wave of an hour and this one of the sixty beautiful children of the wave—let him merge in the general run and wait his development. . . . Still the final test of poems or any character or work remains. . . .

The prescient poet projects himself centuries ahead and judges performer or performance after the changes of time. Does it live through them? Does it still hold on untired? Will the same style and the direction of genius to similar points be satisfactory now? Has no new discovery in science or arrival at superior planes of thought and judgment and behaviour fixed him or his so that either can be looked down upon? Have the marches of tens and hundreds and thou-sands of years made willing detours to the right hand and the left hand for his sake? Is he beloved long and long after he is buried? Does the young man think often of him? and the young woman think often of him? and do the middle-aged and the old think of him?

A great poem is for ages and ages in common and for all degrees and com-plexions and all departments and sects and for a woman as much as a man and a man as much as a woman. A great poem is no finish to a man or woman but rather a beginning. Has any one fancied he could sit at last under some due authority and rest satisfied with explanations and realize and be content and full? To no such terminus does the greatest poet bring . . . he brings neither cessation or sheltered fatness and ease. The touch of him tells in action. Whom he takes he takes with firm sure grasp into live regions previously unattained thenceforward is no rest . . . they see the space and ineffable sheen that turn the old spots and lights into dead vacuums. The companion of him beholds the birth and progress of stars and learns one of the meanings. Now there shall be a man cohered out of tumult and chaos . . . the elder encourages the younger and shows him how . . . they two shall launch off fearlessly together till the new world fits an orbit for itself and looks unabashed on the lesser orbits of the stars and sweeps through the ceaseless rings and shall never be quiet again.

There will soon be no more priests. Their work is done. They may wait awhile . . . perhaps a generation or two . . . dropping off by degrees. A superior breed shall take their place . . . the gangs of kosmos and prophets en masse shall take their place. A new order shall arise and they shall be the priests of man, and every man shall be his own priest. The churches built under their umbrage shall be the churches of men and women. Through the divinity of themselves shall the kosmos and the new breed of poets be interpreters of men and women and of all events and things. They shall find their inspiration in real objects today, symptoms of the past and future. . . . They shall not deign to defend immortality or God or the perfection of things or liberty or the exquisite beauty and reality of the soul. They shall arise in America and be responded to from the remainder of the earth.

The English language befriends the grand American expression. . . . it is brawny enough and limber and full enough. On the tough stock of a race who through all change of circumstance was never without the idea of political liberty, which is the animus of all liberty, it has attracted the terms of daintier and gayer and subtler and more elegant tongues. It is the powerful language of resistance . . . it is the dialect of common sense. It is the speech of the proud and melancholy races and of all who aspire. It is the chosen tongue to express growth faith self-esteem freedom justice equality friendliness amplitude prudence decision and courage. It is the medium that shall well nigh express the inexpressible.

No great literature nor any like style of behaviour or oratory or social intercourse or household arrangements or public institutions or the treatment by bosses of employed people, nor executive detail or detail of the army or navy, nor spirit of legislation or courts or police or tuition or architecture or songs or amusements or the costumes of young men, can long elude the jealous and passionate instinct of American standards. Whether or no the sign appears from the mouths of the people, it throbs a live interrogation in every freeman's and freewoman's heart after that which passes by or this built to remain. Is it uniform with my country? Are its disposals without ignominious distinctions? Is it for the evergrowing communes of brothers and lovers, large, well-united, proud beyond the old models, generous beyond all models? Is it something grown fresh out of the fields or drawn from the sea for use to me today here? I know that what answers for me an American must answer for any individual or nation that serves for a part of my materials. Does this answer? or is it without reference to universal needs? or sprung of the needs of the less developed society of special ranks? or old needs of pleasure overlaid by modern science and forms? Does this acknowledge liberty with audible and absolute acknowledgement, and set slavery at nought for life and death? Will it help breed one goodshaped and wellhung man, and a woman to be his perfect and independent mate? Does it improve manners? Is it for the nursing of the young of the republic? Does it solve readily with the sweet milk of the nipples of the breasts of the mother of many children? Has it too the old ever-fresh forbearance and impartiality? Does it look with the same love on the last born and on those hardening toward stature, and on the errant, and on those who disdain all strength of assault outside of their own?

The poems distilled from other poems will probably pass away. The coward will surely pass away. The expectation of the vital and great can only be satisfied by the demeanor of the vital and great. The swarms of the polished deprecating and reflectors and the polite float off and leave no remembrance. America prepares with composure and goodwill for the visitors that have sent word. It is not intellect that is to be their warrant and welcome. The talented, the artist, the ingenious, the editor, the statesman, the erudite . . . they are not unappreciated . . . they fall in their place and do their work. The soul of the nation also does its work. No disguise can pass on it . . . no disguise can conceal from it. It rejects none, it permits all. Only toward as good as itself and toward the like of itself will it advance half-way. An individual is as superb as a nation when he has the qualities which make a superb nation. The soul of the largest and wealthiest and proudest nation may well go half-way to meet that of its poets. The signs are effectual. There is no fear of mistake. If the one is true the other is true. The proof of a poet is that his country absorbs him as affectionately as he has absorbed it.

27

MATTHEW ARNOLD (1822–1888)

Matthew Arnold was one son of the famous Dr. Thomas Arnold, headmaster of Rugby and later professor of modern history at Oxford. (Another son, called Thomas Arnold the Younger [1823–1900], was also an eminent scholar and writer.) The Arnolds collectively exerted a potent influence over intellectual life in England for much of the nineteenth century.

Matthew Arnold formed a lasting friendship with Arthur Hugh Clough while both were at Oxford and wrote a memorable elegy, "Thyrsis," when Clough died. In 1851 Arnold was appointed an inspector of schools and for the next thirty-five years, on and off, traveled throughout England on official visits. Exposure to the daily life in schools of many sorts made Arnold think deeply about the problems of education, culture, and society. Free universal public education had existed only since 1800, and the problems in Arnold's day were as complex and pervasive as those in the twenty-first century—and in some cases were the same problems. Between 1857 and 1867, Arnold held the Chair of Poetry at Oxford; during this period he produced his first books of literary criticism. He also wrote a substantial amount of important social and cultural criticism.

In essays, books, and public lectures—some delivered in America during the 1880s—Arnold urged society to guide itself by constant reference to "the best that is thought and known in the world," a high standard best stated in the great texts of literature, philosophy, and religion. Walt Whitman, who heard Arnold lecture, dismissed him as a "literary dude," and some later writers have ridiculed Arnold as a moral teacher. One of T. S. Eliot's early poems groups Arnold with Emerson as "Matthew and Waldo, guardians of the faith." Robert Frost's long poem "New Hampshire" presents a prudent character who "stood on the safe side of the line talking; / Which is sheer Matthew Arnoldism." Despite such genial mockery, however, Arnold was an important and benevolent influence on both Eliot and Frost, and Eliot's "The Love Song of J. Alfred Prufrock" can be read as an extension of Arnold's greatest poem, "Dover Beach," into the modern world.

THE STUDY OF POETRY

The essay was originally published as the introduction to T. H. Ward's anthology, *The English Poets* (1880). It appeared later in *Essays in Criticism, Second Series*.

"The future of poetry is immense, because in poetry, where it is worthy of its high destinies, our race, as time goes on, will find an ever surer and surer stay. There is not a creed which is not shaken, not an accredited dogma which is not shown to be questionable, not a received tradition which does not threaten to dissolve. Our religion has materialised itself in the fact, in the supposed fact; it has attached its emotion to the fact, and now the fact is failing it. But for poetry the idea is everything; the rest is a world of illusion, of divine illusion. Poetry attaches its emotion to the idea; the idea is the fact. The strongest part of our religion to-day is its unconscious poetry."

Let me be permitted to quote these words of my own [from *The Hundred Greatest Men*—ed.], *as uttering the thought which should, in my opinion, go with us and govern us in all our study of poetry. In the present work [The English Poets*—ed.] it is the course of one great contributory stream to the world-river of poetry that we are invited to follow. We are here invited to trace the stream of English poetry. But whether we set ourselves, as here, to follow only one of the several streams that make the mighty river of poetry, or whether we seek to know them all, our governing thought should be the same. We should conceive of poetry worthily, and more highly than it has been the custom to conceive of it. We should conceive of it as capable of higher uses, and called to higher destinies, than those which in general men have assigned to it hitherto. More and more mankind will discover that we have to turn to poetry to interpret life for us, to console us, to sustain us. Without poetry, our science will appear incomplete; and most of what now passes with us for religion and philosophy will be replaced by poetry. Science, I say, will appear incomplete without it. For finely and truly does Wordsworth call poetry "the impassioned expression which is in the countenance of all science"; and what is a countenance without its expression? Again, Wordsworth finely and truly calls poetry "the breath and finer spirit of all knowledge"; our religion, parading evidences such as those on which the popular mind relies now; our philosophy, pluming itself on its reasonings about causation and finite and infinite being; what are they but the shadows and dreams and false shows of knowledge? The day will come when we shall wonder at ourselves for having trusted to them, for having taken them seriously; and the more we perceive their hollowness, the more we shall prize "the breath and finer spirit of knowledge" offered to us by poetry.

But if we conceive thus highly of the destinies of poetry, we must also set our standard for poetry high, since poetry, to be capable of fulfilling such high destinies, must be poetry of a high order of excellence. We must accustom ourselves to a high standard and to a strict judgment. Sainte-Beuve relates that Napoleon one day said, when somebody was spoken of in his presence as a charlatan: "Charlatan as much as you please; but where is there not charlatanism?"—"Yes" answers Sainte-Beuve, "in politics, in the art of governing mankind, that is perhaps true. But in the order of thought, in art, the glory, the eternal honour is that charlatanism shall find no entrance; herein lies the inviolableness of that noble portion of man's being" [*Les Cahiers*—ed.]. It is admirably said, and let us hold fast to it. In poetry, which is thought and art in one, it is the glory, the eternal honour, that charlatanism shall find no entrance; that this noble sphere be kept inviolate and inviolable. Charlatanism is for confusing or obliterating the distinctions between excellent and inferior, sound and unsound or only half-sound, true and untrue or only half-true. It is charlatanism, conscious or unconscious, whenever we confuse or obliterate these. And in poetry, more than anywhere else, it is unpermissible to confuse or obliterate them. For in poetry the distinction between excellent and inferior, sound and unsound or only half-sound, true and untrue or only half-true, is of paramount importance. It is of paramount importance because of the high destinies of poetry. In poetry, as in criticism of life under the conditions fixed for such a criticism by the laws of poetic truth and poetic beauty, the spirit of our race will find, we have said, as time goes on and as other helps fail, its consolation and stay. But the consolation and stay will be of power in proportion to the power of the criticism of life. And the criticism of life will be of power in proportion as the poetry conveying it is excellent rather than inferior, sound rather than unsound or half-sound, true rather than untrue on half-true.

The best poetry is what we want; the best poetry will be found to have a power of forming, sustaining, and delighting us, as nothing else can. A clearer, deeper sense of the best in poetry, and of the strength and joy to be drawn from it, is the most precious benefit which we can gather from a poetical collection such as the present. And yet in the very nature and conduct of such a collection there is inevitably something which tends to obscure in us the consciousness of what our benefit should be, and to distract us from the pursuit of it. We should therefore steadily set it before our minds at the outset, and should compel ourselves to revert constantly to the thought of it as we proceed.

Yes; constantly in reading poetry, a sense for the best, the really excellent, and of the strength and joy to be drawn from it, should be present in our minds and should govern our estimate of what we read. But this real estimate, the only true one, is liable to be superseded, if we are not watchful, by two other kinds of estimate, the historic estimate and the personal estimate, both of which are fallacious. A poet or a poem may count to us historically, they may count to us on grounds personal to ourselves, and they may count to us really. They may count to us historically. The course of development of a nation's language, thought, and poetry, is profoundly interesting; and by regarding a poet's work as a stage in this course of development we may easily bring ourselves to make it of more importance as poetry than in itself it really is, we may come to use a language of quite exaggerated praise in criticising it; in short, to overrate it. So arises in our poetic judgments the fallacy caused by the estimate which we may call historic. Then, again, a poet or poem may count to us on grounds personal to ourselves. Our personal affinities, likings and circumstances, have great power to sway our estimate of this or that poet's work, and to make us attach more importance to it as poetry than in itself it really possesses, because to us it is, or has been, of high importance. Here also we overrate the object of our interest, and apply to it a language of praise which is quite exaggerated. And thus we get the source of a second fallacy in our poetic judgments—the fallacy caused by an estimate which we may call personal.

Both fallacies are natural. It is evident how naturally the study of the history and development of poetry may incline a man to pause over reputations and works once conspicuous but now obscure, and to quarrel with a careless public for skipping, in obedience to mere tradition and habit, from one famous name or work in its national poetry to another, ignorant of what it misses, and of the reason for keeping what it keeps, and of the whole process of growth in its poetry. The French have become diligent students of their own early poetry, which they long neglected; the study makes many of them dissatisfied with their so-called classical poetry, the court-tragedy of the seventeenth century, a poetry which Pellisson long ago reproached with its want of the true poetic stamp, with its *politesse stérile et rampante* [sterile and bombastic politeness—ed.], but which nevertheless has reigned in France as absolutely as if it had been the perfection of classical poetry indeed. The dissatisfaction is natural; yet a lively and accomplished critic, M. Charles d'Héricault, the editor of Clément Marot, goes too far when he says that "the cloud of glory playing round a classic is a mist as dangerous to the future of a literature as it is intolerable for the purposes of history." "It hinders," he goes on, "it hinders us from seeing more than one single point, the culminating and exceptional point; the summary, fictitious and arbitrary, of a thought and of a work. It substitutes a halo for a physiognomy, it puts a statue where there was once a man, and hiding from us all trace of the labour, the attempts, the weaknesses, the failures, it claims not study but veneration; it does not show us how the thing is done, it imposes upon us a model. Above all, for the historian this creation of classic personages is inadmissible; for it withdraws the poet from his time, from his proper life, it breaks historical relationships, it blinds criticism by conventional admiration, and renders the investigation of literary origins unacceptable. It gives us a human personage no longer but a God seated immovable amidst His perfect work, like Jupiter on Olympus; and hardly will it be possible for the young student to whom such work is exhibited at such a distance from him, to believe that it did not issue ready—made from that divine head."

All this is brilliantly and tellingly said, but we must plead for a distinction. Everything depends on the reality of a poet's classic character. If he is a dubious classic, let us sift him; if he is a false classic, let us explode him. But if he is a real classic, if his work belongs to the class of the very best (for this is the true and right meaning of the word classic, classical), then the great thing for us is to feel and enjoy his work as deeply as ever we can, and to appreciate the wide difference between it and all work which has not the same high character. This is what is salutary, this is what is formative; this is the great benefit to be got from the study of poetry. Everything which interferes with it, which hinders it, is injurious. True, we must read our classic with open eyes, and not with eyes blinded with superstition; we must perceive when his work comes short, when it drops out of the class of the very best, and we must rate it, in such cases, at its proper value. But the use of this negative criticism is not in itself, it is entirely in its enabling us to have a clearer sense and a deeper enjoyment of what is truly excellent. To trace the labour, the attempts, the weaknesses, the failures of a genuine classic, to acquaint oneself with his time and his life and his historical relationships, is mere literary dilettantism unless it has that clear sense and deeper enjoyment for its end. It may be said that the more we know about a classic the better we shall enjoy him; and, if we lived as long as Methuselah and had all of us heads of perfect clearness and wills of perfect steadfastness, this might be true in fact as it is plausible in theory. But the case here is much the same as the case with the Greek and Latin studies of our schoolboys. The elaborate philological groundwork which we require them to lay is in theory an admirable preparation for appreciating the Greek and Latin authors worthily. The more thoroughly we lay the groundwork, the better we shall be able, it may be said, to enjoy the authors. True, if time were not so short, and schoolboys' wits not so soon tired and their power of attention exhausted; only, as it is, the elaborate philological preparation goes on, but the authors are little known and less enjoyed. So with the investigator of "historic origins" in poetry. He ought to enjoy the true classic all the better for his investigations; he often is distracted from the enjoyment of the best, and with the less good he overbusies himself, and is prone to over-rate it in proportion to the trouble which it has cost him.

The idea of tracing historic origins and historical relationships cannot be absent from a compilation like the present. And naturally the poets to be exhibited in it will be assigned to those persons for exhibition who are known to prize them highly, rather than to those who have no special inclination towards them. Moreover, the very occupation with an author, and the business of exhibiting him, disposes us to affirm and amplify his importance. In the present work, therefore, we are sure of frequent temptation to adopt the historic estimate, or the personal estimate, and to forget the real estimate; which latter, nevertheless, we must employ if we are to make poetry yield us its full benefit. So high is that benefit, the benefit of clearly feeling and of deeply enjoying the really excellent, the truly classic in poetry, that we do well, I say, to set it fixedly before our minds as our object in studying poets and poetry, and to make the desire of attaining it the one principle to which, as the *Imitation* says, whatever we may read or come to know, we always return. *Cum multa legeris et cognoveris, ad unum semper oportet redire principium* ["When you have read and learned many things, you should always return to the one principle." Thomas à Kempis, *The Imitation of Christ*—ed.].

The historic estimate is likely in especial to affect our judgment and our language when we are dealing with ancient poets; the personal estimate when we are dealing with poets our contemporaries, or at any rate modern. The exaggerations due to the historic estimate are not in themselves, perhaps, of very much gravity. Their report hardly enters the general ear; probably they do not always impose even on the literary men who adopt them. But they lead to a dangerous abuse of language. So we hear Cædmon, amongst our own poets, compared to Milton. I have already noticed the enthusiasm of one accomplished French critic for "historic origins." Another eminent French critic, M. Vitet, comments upon that famous document of the early poetry of his nation, the Chanson de Roland. It is indeed a most interesting document. The joculator or jongleur Taillefer, who was with William the Conqueror's army at Hastings, marched before the Norman troops, so said the tradition, singing "of Charlemagne and of Roland and of Oliver, and of the vassals who died at Roncevaux"; and it is suggested that in the Chanson de Roland by one

Turoldus or Théroulde, a poem preserved in a manuscript of the twelfth century in the Bodleian Library at Oxford, we have certainly the matter, perhaps even some of the words, of the chant which Taillefer sang. The poem has vigour and freshness; it is not without pathos. But M. Vitet is not satisfied with seeing in it a document of some poetic value, and of very high historic and linguistic value; he sees in it a grand and beautiful work, a monument of epic genius. In its general design he finds the grandiose conception, in its details he finds the constant union of simplicity with greatness, which are the marks, he truly says, of the genuine epic, and distinguish it from the artificial epic of literary ages. One thinks of Homer; this is the sort of praise which is given to Homer, and justly given. Higher praise there cannot well be, and it is the praise due to epic poetry of the highest order only, and to no other. Let us try, then, the Chanson de Roland at its best. Roland, mortally wounded, lay himself down under a pine-tree, with his face turned towards Spain and the enemy—

> De plusurs choses à remembrer li prist,
> De tantes teres cume li bers cunquist,
> De dulce France, des humes de sun lign,
> De Carlemagne sun seignor ki l'nurrit."

["Then began he to call many things to remembrance,—all the lands which his valour conquered, and pleasant France, and the men of his lineage, and Charlemagne, his liege lord who nourished him"—*Chanson de Roland*, iii, 939–42. Arnold's note.]

That is primitive work, I repeat, with an undeniable poetic quality of its own. It deserves such praise, and such praise is sufficient for it. But now turn to Homer—

> *Hōs phato tous d'ēidē katechen physizoos aia*
> *en Lakedaimoni auphi philēi en patridi gaiēi*

["So said she; they long since in Earth's soft arms were reposing, / There, in their own dear land, their fatherland, Lacedaemon"—*Iliad*, iii, 243, 244 (translated by Dr. Hawtry). Arnold's note.]

We are here in another world, another order of poetry altogether; here is rightly due such supreme praise as that which M. Vitet gives to the *Chanson de Roland*. If our words are to have any meaning, if our judgments are to have any solidity, we must not heap that supreme praise upon poetry of an order immeasurably inferior.

Indeed there can be no more useful help for discovering what poetry belongs to the class of the truly excellent, and can therefore do us most good, than to have always in one's mind lines and expressions of the great masters, and to apply them as a touchstone to other poetry. Of course we are not to require this other poetry to resemble them; it may be very dissimilar. But if we have any tact we shall find them, when we have lodged them well in our minds, infallible touchstone for detecting the presence or absence of high poetic quality, and also the degree of this quality, in all other poetry which we may place beside them. Short passages, even single lines, will serve our turn quite sufficiently. Take the two lines which I have just quoted from Homer, the poet's comment on Helen's mention of her brothers;—or take his

> A *deilō, ti sphōi domen Pēlēi anakti*
> *Thnēta; hymeis d' eston agērō t' athanatō te.*
> *ēi hina dystēnoisi met' andrasin alge' echēton*

["Ah, unhappy pair, why gave we you to King Peleus, to a mortal? but ye are without old age, and immortal. Was it that with men born to misery ye might have sorrow?"—*Iliad*, xvii. 443–45]

the address of Zeus to the horses of Peleus;—or take finally his

> *Kai se, geron, to prin men akouomen olbion einai*

["Nay, and thou too, old man, in former days wast, as we hear, happy."— *Iliad*, xxiv. 543]

the words of Achilles to Priam, a suppliant before him. Take that incomparable line and a half of Dante, Ugolino's tremendous words—

> Io no piangeva; sì dentro impietrai.
> Piangevan elli . . .

["I wailed not, so of stone grew I within; / they wailed.—*Inferno*, xxxiii. 39–40]

take the lovely words of Beatrice to Virgil—

> Io son fatta da Dio, sua mercè, tale,
> Che la vostra miseria non mi tange,
> Nè fiamma d'esto incendio non m'assale . . .

["Of such sort hath God, thanked be His mercy, made me, / That your misery toucheth me not, / Neither doth the flame of this fire strike me." — *Inferno*, ii. 91–93]

take the simple, but perfect, single line —

> In la sua volontade è nostra pace

["In His will is our peace." — *Paradiso*, iii. 85.]

Take of Shakespeare a line or two of Henry the Fourth's expostulation with sleep —

> Wilt thou upon the high and giddy mast
> Seal up the ship-boy's eyes, and rock his brains
> In cradle of the rude imperious surge . . .

and take, as well, Hamlet's dying request to Horatio —

> If thou didst ever hold me in thy heart,
> Absent thee from felicity awhile,
> And in this harsh world draw thy breath in pain
> To tell my story . . .

Take of Milton that Miltonic passage —

> Darken'd so, yet shone
> Above them all the archangel; but his face
> Deep scars of thunder had intrench'd, and care
> Sat on his faded cheek . . .

add two such lines as —

> And courage never to submit or yield
> And what is else not to be overcome . . .

and finish with the exquisite close to the loss of Proserpine, the loss

> . . . which cost Ceres all that pain
> To seek her through the world."

These few lines, if we have tact and can use them, are enough even of themselves to keep clear and sound our judgments about poetry, to save us from fallacious estimates of it, to conduct us to a real estimate.

The specimens I have quoted differ widely from one another, but they have in common this: the possession of the very highest poetical quality. If we are thoroughly penetrated by their power, we shall find that we have acquired a sense enabling us, whatever poetry may be laid before us, to feel the degree in which a high poetical quality is present or wanting there. Critics give themselves great labour to draw out what in the abstract constitutes the characters of a high quality of poetry. It is much better simply to have recourse to concrete examples;—to take specimens of poetry of the high, the very highest quality, and to say: The characters of a high quality of poetry are what is expressed there. They are far better recognised by being felt in the verse of the master, than by being perused in the prose of the critic. Nevertheless if we are urgently pressed to give some critical account of them, we may safely, perhaps, venture on laying down, not indeed how and why the characters arise, but where and in what they arise. They are in the matter and substance of the poetry, and they are in its manner and style. Both of these, the substance and matter on the one hand, the style and manner on the other, have a mark, an accent, of high beauty, worth, and power. But if we are asked to define this mark and accent in the abstract, our answer must be: No, for we should thereby be darkening the question, not clearing it. The mark and accent are as given by the substance and matter of that poetry, by the style and manner of that poetry, and of all other poetry which is akin to it in quality.

Only one thing we may add as to the substance and matter of poetry, guiding ourselves by Aristotle's profound observation that the superiority of poetry over history consists in its possessing a higher truth and a higher seriousness (*philosophōteron kai spoudaioteron* [*Poetics*, ix—ed.]). Let us add, therefore, to what we have said, this: that the substances and matter of the best poetry acquire their special character from possessing, in an eminent degree, truth and seriousness. We may add yet further, what is in itself evident, that to the style and manner of the best poetry their special character, their accent, is given by their diction, and, even yet more, by their movement. And though we distinguish between the two characters, the two accents, of superiority, yet they are nevertheless vitally connected one with the other. The superior character of truth and seriousness, in the matter and substance of the best poetry, is inseparable from the superiority of diction and movement marking its style and manner. The two superiorities are closely related, and are in steadfast proportion one to the other. So far as high poetic truth and seriousness are wanting to a poet's matter and substance, so far also, we may be sure, will a high poetic stamp of diction and movement be wanting to his style and manner. In proportion as this high stamp of diction and movement, again, is absent from a poet's style and manner, we shall find, also, that high poetic truth and seriousness are absent from his substance and matter.

So stated, these are but dry generalities; their whole force lies in their application. And I could wish every student of poetry to make the application of them for himself. Made by himself, the application would impress itself upon his mind far more deeply than made by me. Neither will my limits allow me to make any full application of the generalities above propounded; but in the hope of bringing out, at any rate, some significance in them, and of establishing an important principle more firmly by their means, I will, in the space which remains to me, follow rapidly from the commencement the course of our English poetry with them in my view.

Once more I return to the early poetry of France, with which our own poetry, in its origins, is indissolubly connected. In the twelfth and thirteenth centuries, that seedtime of all modern language and literature, the poetry of France had a clear predominance in Europe. Of the two divisions of that poetry, its productions in the *langue d'oil* and its productions in the *langue d'oc*, the poetry of the *langue d'oc*, of southern France, of the troubadours, is of importance because of its effect on Italian literature;—the first literature of modern Europe to strike the true and grand note, and to bring forth, as in Dante and Petrarch it brought forth, classics. But the predominance of French poetry in Europe, during the twelfth and thirteenth centuries, is due to its poetry of the *langue d'oil*, the poetry of northern France and of the tongue which is now the French language. In the twelfth century the bloom of this romance-poetry was earlier and stronger in England, at the court of our Anglo-Norman kings, than in France itself. But it was a bloom of French poetry; and as our native poetry formed itself, it formed itself out of this. The romance-poems which took possession of the heart and imagination of Europe in the twelfth and thirteenth centuries are French; "they are," as Southey justly says, "the pride of French literature, nor have we anything which can be placed in competition with them." Themes were supplied from all quarters; but the romance-setting which was common to them all, and which gained the ear of Europe, was French. This constituted for the French poetry, literature, and language, at the height of the Middle Age, an unchallenged predominance. The Italian Brunetto Latini, the master of Dante, wrote his *Treasure* in French because, he says, "*la parleure en est plus delitable et plus commune a toutes gens*" [the language is more agreeable and more widely known—ed.]. In the same century, the thirteenth, the French romance-writer, Christian of Troyes, formulates the claims, in chivalry and letters, of France, his native country, as follows:—

> Or vous ert par ce livre apris,
> Que Gresse ot de chevalerie

Le premier los et de clergie;
Puis vint chevalerie à Rome,
Et de la clergie la some,
Qui ore est en France venue.
Diex doinst qu'ele i soit retenue,
Et que li lius li abelisse
Tant que de France n'isse
L'onor qui s'i est arestée!

"Now by this book you will learn that first Greece had the renown for chivalry and letters: then chivalry and the primacy in letters passed to Rome, and now it is come to France. God grant it may be kept there; and that the place may please it so well, that the honour which has come to make stay in France may never depart thence!"

Yet it is now all gone, this French romance-poetry of which the weight of substance and the power of style are not unfairly represented by this extract from Christian of Troyes. Only by means of the historic estimate can we persuade ourselves not to think that any of it is of poetical importance.

But in the fourteenth century there comes an Englishman nourished on this poetry, taught his trade by this poetry, getting words, rhyme, metre from this poetry; for even of that stanza which the Italians used, and which Chaucer derived immediately from the Italians, the basis and suggestion was probably given in France. Chaucer (I have already named him) fascinated his contemporaries, but so too did Christian of Troyes and Wolfram of Eschenbach. Chaucer's power of fascination, however, is enduring; his poetical importance does not need the assistance of the historic estimate; it is real. He is a genuine source of joy and strength, which is flowing still for us and will flow always. He will be read, as time goes on, far more generally than he is read now. His language is a cause of difficulty for us; but so also, and I think in quite as great a degree, is the language of Burns. In Chaucer's case, as in that of Burns, it is a difficulty to be unhesitatingly accepted and overcome.

If we ask ourselves wherein consists the immense superiority of Chaucer's poetry over the romance-poetry—why it is that in passing from this to Chaucer we suddenly feel ourselves to be in another world, we shall find that his superiority is both in the substance of his poetry and in the style of his poetry. His superiority in substance is given by his large, free, simple, clear yet kindly view of human life,—so unlike the total want, in the romance-poets, of all intelligent command of it. Chaucer has not their helplessness; he has gained the power to survey the world from a central, a truly human point of view. We have only to call to mind the Prologue to *The Canterbury Tales*. The right comment upon it is Dryden's: "It is sufficient to say, according to the proverb, that here is God's plenty." And again: "He is a perpetual fountain of good sense." It is by a large, free, sound representation of things, that poetry, this high criticism of life, has truth of substance; and Chaucer's poetry has truth of substance.

Of his style and manner, if we think first of the romance-poetry and then of Chaucer's divine liquidness of diction, his divine fluidity of movement, it is difficult to speak temperately. They are irresistible, and justify all the rapture with which his successors speak of his "gold dew-drops of speech." Johnson misses the point entirely when he finds fault with Dryden for ascribing to Chaucer the first refinement of our numbers, and says that Gower also can show smooth numbers and easy rhymes. The refinement of our numbers means something far more than this. A nation may have versifiers with smooth numbers and easy rhymes, and yet may have no real poetry at all. Chaucer is the father of our splendid English poetry; he is our "well of English undefiled," because by the lovely charm of his diction, the lovely charm of his movement, he makes an epoch and founds a tradition. In Spenser, Shakespeare, Milton, Keats, we can follow the tradition of the liquid diction, the fluid movement of Chaucer; at one time it is his liquid diction of which in these poets we feel the virtue, and at another time it is his fluid movement. And the virtue is irresistible.

Bounded as is my space, I must yet find room for an example of Chaucer's virtue, as I have given examples to show the virtue of the great classics. I feel disposed to say that a single line is enough to show the charm of Chaucer's verse; that merely one line like this—

O martyr souded in virginitee!

["The French soudé; soldered, fixed fast." Arnold's note.]

has a virtue of manner and movement such as we shall not find in all the verse of romance—poetry;—but this is saying nothing. The virtue is such as we shall not find, perhaps, in all English poetry, outside the poets whom I have named as the special inheritors of Chaucer's tradition. A single line, however, is too little if we have not the strain of Chaucer's verse well in our memory; let us take a stanza. It is from The Prioress' Tale, the story of the Christian child murdered in a Jewry—

My throte is cut unto my nekke-bone
Saidè this child, and as by way of kinde
I should have deyd, yea, longè time agone;
But Jesus Christ, as ye in bookès finde,
Will that his glory last and be in minde,
And for the worship of his mother dere
Yet may I sing O Alma loud and clere."

Wordsworth has modernised this Tale, and to feel how delicate and evanescent is the charm of verse, we have only to read Wordsworth's first three lines of this stanza after Chaucer's—

> My throat is cut unto the bone, I trow,
> Said this young child, and by the law of kind
> I should have died, yea, many hours ago.

The charm is departed. It is often said that the power of liquidness and fluidity in Chaucer's verse was dependent upon a free, a licentious dealing with language, such as is now impossible; upon a liberty, such as Burns too enjoyed, of making words like neck, bird, into a disyllable by adding to them, and words like cause, rhyme, into a disyllable by sounding the e mute. It is true that Chaucer's fluidity is conjoined with this liberty, and is admirably served by it; but we ought not to say that it was dependent upon it. It was dependent upon his talent. Other poets with a like liberty do not attain to the fluidity of Chaucer; Burns himself does not attain to it. Poets, again, who have a talent akin to Chaucer's, such as Shakespeare or Keats, have known how to attain his fluidity without the like liberty.

And yet Chaucer is not one of the great classics. His poetry transcends and effaces, easily and without effort, all the romance-poetry of Catholic Christendom; it transcends and effaces all the English poetry contemporary with it, it transcends and effaces all the English poetry subsequent to it down to the age of Elizabeth. Of such avail is poetic truth of substance, in its natural and necessary union with poetic truth of style. And yet, I say, Chaucer is not one of the great classics. He has not their accent. What is wanting to him is suggested by the mere mention of the name of the first great classic of Christendom, the immortal poet who died eighty years before Chaucer,—Dante. The accent of such verse as

> In la sua volontade è nostra pace . . .

is altogether beyond Chaucer's reach; we praise him, but we feel that this accent is out of the question for him. It may be said that it was necessarily out of the reach of any poet in the England of that stage of growth. Possibly; but we are to adopt a real, not a historic, estimate of poetry. However we may account for its absence, something is wanting, then, to the poetry of Chaucer, which poetry must have before it can be placed in the glorious class of the best. And there is no doubt what that something is. It is the *spoudaiotēs*, the high and excellent seriousness, which Aristotle assigns as one of the grand virtues of poetry. The substance of Chaucer's poetry, his view of things and his criticism of life, has largeness, freedom, shrewdness, benignity; but it has not this high seriousness.

Homer's criticism of life has it, Dante's has it, Shakespeare's has it. It is this chiefly which gives to our spirits what they can rest upon; and with the increasing demands of our modern ages upon poetry, this virtue of giving us what we can rest upon will be more and more highly esteemed. A voice from the slums of Paris, fifty or sixty years after Chaucer, the voice of poor Villon out of his life of riot and crime, has at its happy moments (as, for instance, in the last stanza of *La Belle Heaulmière*) ["The name Heaulmière is said to be derived from a head-dress (helm) worn as a mark by courtesans. In Villon's ballad, a poor old creature of this class laments her days of youth and beauty. . . ." — Arnold's note.] more of this important poetic virtue of seriousness than all the productions of Chaucer. But its apparition in Villon, and in men like Villon, is fitful; the greatness of the great poets, the power of their criticism of life, is that their virtue is sustained.

To our praise, therefore, of Chaucer as a poet there must be this limitation; he lacks the high seriousness of the great classics, and therewith an important part of their virtue. Still, the main fact for us to bear in mind about Chaucer is his sterling value according to that real estimate which we firmly adopt for all poets. He has poetic truth of substance, though he has not high poetic seriousness, and corresponding to his truth of substance he has an exquisite virtue of style and manner. With him is born our real poetry.

For my present purpose I need not dwell on our Elizabethan poetry, or on the continuation and close of this poetry in Milton. We all of us profess to be agreed in the estimate of this poetry; we all of us recognise it as great poetry, our greatest, and Shakespeare and Milton as our poetical classics. The real estimate, here, has universal currency. With the next age of our poetry divergency and difficulty begin. An historic estimate of that poetry has established itself; and the question is, whether it will be found to coincide with the real estimate.

The age of Dryden, together with our whole eighteenth century which followed it, sincerely believed itself to have produced poetical classics of its own, and even to have made advance, in poetry, beyond all its predecessors. Dryden regards as not seriously disputable the opinion "that the sweetness of English verse was never understood or practised by our fathers." Cowley could see nothing at all in Chaucer's poetry. Dryden heartily admired it, and, as we have seen, praised its matter admirably; but of its exquisite manner and movement all he can find to say is that "there is the rude sweetness of a Scotch tune in it, which is natural and pleasing, though not perfect." Addison, wishing to praise Chaucer's numbers, compares them with Dryden's own. And all through the eighteenth century, and down even into our own times, the stereotyped phrase of approbation for good verse found in our early poetry has been, that it even approached the verse of Dryden, Addison, Pope, and Johnson.

Are Dryden and Pope poetical classics? Is the historic estimate, which represents them as such, and which has been so long established that it cannot easily give way, the real estimate? Wordsworth and Coleridge, as is well known, denied it; but the authority of Wordsworth and Coleridge does not weigh much with the young generation, and there are many signs to show that the eighteenth century and its judgments are coming into favour again. Are the favourite poets of the eighteenth century classics?

It is impossible within my present limits to discuss the question fully. And what man of letters would not shrink from seeming to dispose dictatorially of the claims of two men who are, at any rate, such masters in letters as Dryden and Pope; two men of such admirable talent, both of them, and one of them, Dryden, a man, on all sides, of such energetic and genial power? And yet, if we are to gain the full benefit from poetry, we must have the real estimate of it. I cast about for some mode of arriving, in the present case, at such an estimate without offence. And perhaps the best way is to begin, as it is easy to begin, with cordial praise.

When we find Chapman, the Elizabethan translator of Homer, expressing himself in this preface thus: "Though truth in her very nakedness sits in so deep a pit, that from Gades to Aurora and Ganges few eyes can sound her, I hope yet those few here will so discover and confirm that, the date being out of her darkness in this morning of our poet, he shall now gird his temples with the sun," —we pronounce that such a prose is intolerable. When we find Milton writing: "And long it was not after, when I was confirmed in this opinion, that he, who would not be frustrate of his hope to write well hereafter in laudable things, ought himself to be a true poem," —we pronounce that such a prose has its own grandeur, but that it is obsolete and inconvenient. But when we find Dryden telling us: "What Virgil wrote in the vigour of his age, in plenty and at ease, I have undertaken to translate in my declining years; struggling with wants, oppressed with sickness, curbed in my genius, liable to be misconstrued in all I write," —then we exclaim that here at last we have the true English prose, a prose such as we would all gladly use if we only knew how. Yet Dryden was Milton's contemporary.

But after the Restoration the time had come when our nation felt the imperious need of a fit prose. So, too, the time had likewise come when our nation felt the imperious need of freeing itself from the absorbing preoccupation which religion in the Puritan age had exercised. It was impossible that this freedom should be brought about without some negative excess, without some neglect and impairment of the religious life of the soul; and the spiritual history of the eighteenth century shows us that the freedom was not achieved without them. Still, the freedom was achieved; the preoccupation, an undoubtedly baneful and retarding one if it had continued, was got rid of. And as with religion amongst us at that period, so it was also with letters. A fit prose was a necessity; but it was impossible that a fit prose should establish itself amongst us without some touch of frost to the imaginative life of the soul. The needful qualities for a fit prose are regularity, uniformity, precision, balance. The men of letters, whose destiny it may be to bring their nation to the attainment of a fit prose, must of necessity, whether they work in prose or in verse, give a predominating, an almost exclusive attention to the qualities of regularity, uniformity, precision, balance. But an almost exclusive attention to these qualities involves some repression and silencing of poetry.

We are to regard Dryden as the puissant and glorious founder, Pope as the splendid high priest, of our age of prose and reason, of our excellent and indispensable eighteenth century. For the purposes of their mission and destiny their poetry, like their prose, is admirable. Do you ask me whether Dryden's verse, take it almost where you will, is not good?

> A milk-white Hind, immortal and unchanged,
> Fed on the lawns and in the forest ranged.

I answer: Admirable for the purposes of the inaugurator of an age of prose and reason. Do you ask me whether Pope's verse, take it almost where you will, is not good?

> To Hounslow Heath I point, and Banstead Down
> Thence comes your mutton, and these chicks my own.

I answer: Admirable for the purposes of the high priest of an age of prose and reason. But do you ask me whether such verse proceeds from men with an adequate poetic criticism of life, from men whose criticism of life has a high seriousness, or even, without that high seriousness, has poetic largeness, freedom, insight, benignity? Do you ask me whether the application of ideas to life in the verse of these men, often a powerful application, no doubt, is a powerful poetic application? Do you ask me whether the poetry of these men has either the matter or the inseparable manner of such an adequate poetic criticism; whether it has the accent of

> Absent thee from felicity awhile . . .

or of

> And what is else not to be overcome . . .

or of

> O martyr souded in virginitee!

I answer: It has not and cannot have them; it is the poetry of the builders of an age of prose and reason. Though they may write in verse, though they may in a certain sense be masters of the art of versification, Dryden and Pope are not classics of our poetry, they are classics of our prose.

Gray is our poetical classic of that literature and age; the position of Gray is singular, and demands a word of notice here. He has not the volume or the power of poets who, coming in times more favourable, have attained to an independent criticism of life. But he lived with the great poets, he lived, above all, with the Greeks, through perpetually studying and enjoying them; and he caught their poetic point of view for regarding life, caught their poetic manner. The point of view and the manner are not self-sprung in him, he caught them of others; and he had not the free and abundant use of them. But, whereas Addison and Pope never had the use of them, Gray had the use of them at times. He is the scantiest and frailest of classics in our poetry, but he is a classic.

And now, after Gray, we are met, as we draw towards the end of the eighteenth century, we are met by the great name of Burns. We enter now on times where the personal estimate of poets begins to be rife, and where the real estimate of them is not reached without difficulty. But in spite of the disturbing pressures of personal partiality, of national partiality, let us try to reach a real estimate of the poetry of Burns.

By his English poetry Burns in general belongs to the eighteenth century, and has little importance for us.

> Mark ruffian Violence, distain'd with crimes,
> Rousing elate in these degenerate times;
> View unsuspecting Innocence a prey,
> As guileful Fraud points out the erring way;
> While subtle Litigation's pliant tongue
> The life-blood equal sucks of Right and Wrong!

Evidently this is not the real Burns, or his name and fame would have disappeared long ago. Nor is Clarinda's love-poet, Sylvander, the real Burns either. But he tells us himself: "These English songs gravel me to death. I have not the command of the language that I have of my native tongue. In fact, I think that my ideas are more barren in English than in Scotch. I have been at Duncan Gray to dress it in English, but all I can do is desperately stupid." We English turn naturally, in Burns, to the poems in our own language, because we can read them easily; but in those poems we have not the real Burns.

The real Burns is of course in this Scotch poems. Let us boldly say that of much of this poetry, a poetry dealing perpetually with Scotch drink, Scotch religion, and Scotch manners, a Scotchman's estimate is apt to be personal. A Scotchman is used to this world of Scotch drink, Scotch religion, and Scotch manners; he has a tenderness for it; he meets its poet halfway. In this tender mood he reads pieces like the *Holy Fair* or *Halloween*. But this world of Scotch drink, Scotch religion, and Scotch manners is against a poet, not for him, when it is not a partial countryman who reads him; for in itself it is not a beautiful world, and no one can deny that it is of advantage to a poet to deal with a beautiful world. Burns' world of Scotch drink, Scotch religion, and Scotch manners, is often a harsh, a sordid, a repulsive world: even the world of his *Cotter's Saturday Night* is not a beautiful world. No doubt a poet's criticism of life may have such truth and power that it triumphs over its world and delights us. Burns may triumph over his world, often he does triumph over his world, but let us observe how and where. Burns is the first case we have had where the bias of the personal estimate tends to mislead; let us look at him closely, he can bear it.

Many of his admirers will tell us that we have Burns, convivial, genuine, delightful, here—

> Leeze me on drink! it gies us mair
> Than either school or college;
> It kindles wit, it waukens lair,
> It pangs us fou o' knowledge.
> Be't whisky gill or penny wheep
> Or only stronger potion,
> It never fails, on drinking deep,
> To kittle up our notion
> By night or day.

There is a great deal of that sort of thing in Burns, and it is unsatisfactory, not because it is bacchanalian poetry, but because it has not that accent of sincerity which bacchanalian poetry, to do it justice, very often has. There is something in it of bravado, something which makes us feel that we have not the man speaking to us with his real voice; something, therefore, poetically unsound.

With still more confidence will his admirers tell us that we have the genuine Burns, the great poet, when his strain asserts the independence, equality, dignity, of men, as in the famous song "For A' That, and A' That"—

> A prince can mak' a belted knight,
> A marquis, duke, and a' that;
> But an honest man's aboon his might,
> Guid faith he mauna fa' that!
> For a' that, and a' that,
> Their dignities, and a' that,

> The pith o' sense, a pride o' worth,
> Are higher rank than a' that.

Here they find his grand, genuine touches; and still more, when this puissant genius, who so often set morality at defiance, falls moralising—

> The sacred lowe o' weel-placed love
> Luxuriantly indulge it;
> But never tempt th' illicit rove,
> Tho' naething should divulge it.
> I waive the quantum o' the sin,
> The hazard o' concealing,
> But och! it hardens a' within,
> And petrifies the feeling.

Or in a higher strain—

> Who made the heart, 'tis He alone
> Decidedly can try us;
> He knows each chord, its various tone;
> Each spring, its various bias.
> Then at the balance let's be mute,
> We never can adjust it;
> What's done we partly may compute,
> But know not what's resisted.

Or in a better strain yet, a strain, his admirers will say, unsurpassable—

> To make a happy fireside clime
> To weans and wife,
> That's the true pathos and sublime
> Of human life.

There is criticism of life for you, the admirers of Burns will say to us; there is the application of ideas to life! There is, undoubtedly. The doctrine of the last-quoted lines coincides almost exactly with what was the aim and end, Xenophon tells us, of all the teaching of Socrates. And the application is a powerful one; made by a man of vigorous understanding, and (need I say?) a master of language.

But for supreme poetical success more is required than the powerful application of ideas to life; it must be an application under the conditions fixed by the laws of poetic truth and poetic beauty. Those laws fix as an essential condition, in the poet's treatment of such matters as are here in question, high seriousness;— the high seriousness which comes from absolute sincerity. The accent of high seriousness, born of absolute sincerity, is what gives to such verse as

> In la sua volontade e nostra pace . . .

to such criticism of life as Dante's, its power. Is this accent felt in the passages which I have been quoting from Burns? Surely not; surely, if our sense is quick, we must perceive that we have not in those passages a voice from the very inmost soul of the genuine Burns; he is not speaking to us from these depths, he is more or less preaching. And the compensation for admiring such passages less, from missing the perfect poetic accent in them, will be that we shall admire more the poetry where that accent is found.

No; Burns, like Chaucer, comes short of the high seriousness of the great classics, and the virtue of matter and manner which goes with that high seriousness is wanting to his work. At moments he touches it in a profound and passionate melancholy, as in those four immortal lines taken by Byron as a motto for *The Bride of Abydos*, but which have in them a depth of poetic quality such as resides in no verse of Byron's own—

> Had we never loved sae kindly,
> Had we never loved sae blindly,
> Never met, or never parted,
> We had ne'er been broken-hearted.

But a whole poem of that quality Burns cannot make; the rest, in the *Farewell to Nancy*, is verbiage.

We arrive best at the real estimate of Burns, I think, by conceiving his work as having truth of matter and truth of manner, but not the accent or the poetic virtue of the highest masters. His genuine criticism of life, when the sheer poet in him speaks, is ironic; it is not—

> Thou Power Supreme, whose mighty scheme
> These woes of mine fulfil,
> Here firm I rest, they must be best
> Because they are Thy will!

It is far rather: *Whistle owre the lave o't!* Yet we may say of him as of Chaucer, that of life and the world, as they come before him, his view is large, free, shrewd, benignant,—truly poetic therefore; and his manner of rendering what he sees is to match. But we must note, at the same time, his great difference from Chaucer. The freedom of Chaucer is heightened, in Burns, by a fiery, reckless energy; the benignity of Chaucer deepens, in Burns, into an over-whelming sense of the pathos of things;—of the pathos of human nature, the pathos, also, of non-human nature. Instead of the fluidity of Chaucer's manner, the manner of Burns has spring, boundless swiftness. Burns is by far the greater force, though he has perhaps less charm. The world of Chaucer is fairer, richer, more significant than that of Burns; but when the largeness and freedom of Burns get full sweep, as in *Tam o' Shanter*, or still more in that puissant and splendid production, *The Jolly Beggars*, his world may be what it will, his poetic genius triumphs over it. In the world of *The Jolly Beggars* there is more than hideousness and squalor, there is bestiality; yet the piece is a superb poetic success. It has a breadth, truth, and power which make the famous scene in Auerbach's Cellar, of Goethe's *Faust*, seem artificial and tame beside it, and which are only matched by Shakespeare and Aristophanes.

Here, where his largeness and freedom serve him so admirably, and also in those poems and songs where to shrewdness he adds infinite archness and wit, and to benignity infinite pathos, where his manner is flawless, and a perfect poetic whole is the result,—in things like the address to the mouse whose home he had ruined, in things like "Duncan Gray," "Tam Glen," "Whistle and I'll Come To You, My Lad," "Auld Lang Syne" (this list might be made much longer),—here we have the genuine Burns, of whom the real estimate must be high indeed. Not a classic, nor with the excellent *spoudaiotēs* [high serious-ness—ed.] of the great classics, nor with a verse rising to a criticism of life and a virtue like theirs; but a poet with thorough truth of substance and an answering truth of style, giving us a poetry sound to the core. We all of us have a leaning towards the pathetic, and may be inclined perhaps to prize Burns most for his touches of piercing, sometimes almost intolerable, pathos; for verse like—

> We twa hae paidl't i' the burn
> From mornin' sun till dine;
> But seas between us braid hae roar'd
> Sin auld lang syne . . .

where he is as lovely as he is sound. But perhaps it is by the perfection of soundness of his lighter and archer masterpieces that he is poetically most wholesome for us. For the votary misled by a personal estimate of Shelley, as so many of us have been, are, and will be,—of that beautiful spirit building his many-coloured haze of words and images

> Pinnacled dim in the intense inane—

no contact can be wholesomer than the contact with Burns at his archest and soundest. Side by side with the

On the brink of the night and the morning
My coursers are wont to respire,
But the Earth has just whispered a warning
That their flight must be swifter than fire . . .

of *Prometheus Unbound,* how salutary, how very salutary, to place this from *Tam Glen*—

My minnie does constantly deave me
And bids me beware o' young men;
They flatter, she says, to deceive me;
But wha can think sae o' Tam Glen?

But we enter on burning ground as we approach the poetry of times so near to us—poetry like that of Byron, Shelley, and Wordsworth—of which the estimates are so often not only personal, but personal with passion. For my purpose, it is enough to have taken the single case of Burns, the first poet we come to of whose work the estimate formed is evidently apt to be personal, and to have suggested how we may proceed, using the poetry of the great classics as a sort of touchstone, to correct this estimate, as we had previously corrected by the same means the historic estimate where we met with it. A collection like the present, with its succession of celebrated names and celebrated poems, offers a good opportunity to us for resolutely endeavouring to make our estimates of poetry real. I have sought to point out a method which will help us in making them so, and to exhibit it in use so far as to put any one who likes in a way of applying it for himself.

At any rate the end to which the method and the estimate are designed to lead, and from leading to which, if they do lead to it, they get their whole value,—the benefit of being able clearly to feel and deeply to enjoy the best, the truly classic, in poetry,—is an end, let me say it once more at parting, of supreme importance. We are often told that an era is opening in which we are to see multitudes of a common sort of readers, and masses of a common sort of literature; that such readers do not want and could not relish anything better than such literature, and that to provide it is becoming a vast and profitable industry. Even if good literature entirely lost currency with the world, it would still be abundantly worth while to continue to enjoy it by oneself. But it never will lose currency with the world, in spite of monetary appearances; it never will lose supremacy. Currency and supremacy are insured to it, not indeed by the world's deliberate and conscious choice, but by something far deeper,—by the instinct of self-preservation in humanity.

28

EMILY DICKINSON (1830–1886)

We know so little about Emily Dickinson that the recent discovery of what may be a photograph of her has been front-page news. Although she wrote almost 1,800 poems (they are usually published with numbers for titles and sometimes referred to by their first lines), very few were published in her lifetime, and the only reliable information we have about her outward life is that she was reclusive and eccentric. About her inward life, however, we know a good deal, since her poems deal obsessively with the interior world of a brilliant, passionate, extravagant, absolutely honest and original poet. She was so much a poet that the poetry spills over into the prose of her letters, but she was also so much of a poet that it is impossible to imagine her writing a reasoned critical essay on poetry.

Some of her marvelous letters contain revelations about her reading, writing, and thinking; these come from letters to Thomas Wentworth Higginson, a mentor:

> Are you too deeply occupied to say if my verse is alive? The mind is so near itself it cannot see distinctly, and I have none to ask. Should you think it breathed, and had you the leisure to tell me, I should feel quick gratitude. . . .
>
> While my thought is undressed, I can make the distinction; but when I put them in the gown, they look alike and numb. You asked how old I

was? I made no verse, but one or two, until this winter [1862], sir. I had a terror since September, I could tell to none; and so I sing, as the boy does of the burying ground, because I am afraid. You inquire my books. For poets, I have Keats, and Mr. and Mrs. Browning. For prose, Mr. Ruskin, Sir Thomas Browne, and the Revelations. I went to school, but in your manner of the phrase had no education. When a little girl, I had a friend who taught me Immortality; but venturing too near, himself, he never returned. Soon after my tutor died, and for several years my lexicon was my only companion. Then I found one more, but he was not contented I be his scholar, so he left the land. You ask of my companions. Hills, sir, and the sundown, and a dog large as myself, that my father bought me. They are better than beings because they know, but do not tell; and the noise in the pool at noon excels my piano. . . .

Could you tell me how to grow, or is it unconveyed, like melody or witchcraft? You speak of Mr. Whitman. I never read his book, but was told that it was disgraceful. I read Miss Prescott's "Circumstance," but it followed me in the dark, so I avoided her. Two editors of journals came to my father's house this winter, and asked me for my mind, and when I asked them "why" they said I was penurious, and they would use it for the world. I could not weigh myself, myself. My size felt small to me. . . .

My dying tutor told me that he would like to live till I had been a poet, but Death was much of mob as I could master, then. And when, far afterward, a sudden light on orchards, or a new fashion in the wind troubled my attention, I felt a palsy, here, the verses just relieve. . . .

My business is circumference. An ignorance, not of customs, but if caught with the dawn, or the sunset see me, myself the only kangaroo among the beauty, sir, if you please, it afflicts me, and I thought that instruction would take it away. . . .

'Twas noting some such scene made Vaughan humbly say, "My days that are at best but dim and hoary." I think it was Vaughan. . . .

If I read a book and it makes my whole body so cold no fire can ever warm me, I know that is poetry. If I feel physically as if the top of my head were taken off, I know that is poetry. These are the only ways I know it. Is there any other way?

POEMS

Besides the Autumn poets sing,
A few prosaic days
A little this side of the snow
And that side of the Haze—
A few incisive Mornings—
A few Ascetic Eves—
Gone—Mr. Bryant's "Golden Rod"—
And Mr. Thomson's "sheaves."
Still, is the bustle in the Brook—
Sealed are the spicy valves—
Mesmeric fingers softly touch
The Eyes of many Elves—
Perhaps a squirrel may remain—
My sentiments to share—
Grant me, O Lord, a sunny mind—
Thy windy will to bear!

POEM 312

[Written after the death of Elizabeth Barrett Browning in 1861.]

Her—"last Poems"—
Poets—ended—
Silver—perished—with her Tongue—
Not on Record—bubbled other,
Flute—or Woman—
So divine—
Not unto its Summer—Morning
Robin—uttered Half the Tune—
Gushed too free for the Adoring—
From the Anglo-Florentine—
Late—the praise—
'Tis dull—conferring
On a Head too High to Crown—
Diadem—or Ducal Showing—
Be its Grave—sufficient sign—
Nought—that We—No Poet's Kinsman—
Suffocate—with easy woe—
What, and if, Ourself a Bridegroom—
Put Her down—in Italy?

POEM 441

This is my letter to the World
That never wrote to Me—
The simple News that Nature told—
With tender Majesty
Her Message is committed
To Hands I cannot see—
For love of Her—Sweet—countrymen—
Judge tenderly—of Me

POEM 448

This was a Poet—It is That
Distills amazing sense

From ordinary Meanings—
And Attar so immense
From the familiar species
That perished by the Door—
We wonder it was not Ourselves
Arrested it—before—
Of Pictures, the Discloser—
The Poet—it is He—
Entitles Us—by Contrast—
To ceaseless Poverty—
Of portion—so unconscious—
The Robbing—could not harm—
Himself—to Him—a Fortune—
Exterior—to Time—

POEM 544

The Martyr Poets—did not tell—
But wrought their Pang in syllable—
That when their mortal name be numb—
Their mortal fate—encourage Some—
The Martyr Painters—never spoke—
Bequeathing—rather—to their Work—
That when their conscious fingers cease—
Some seek in Art—the Art of Peace—

POEM 613

They shut me up in Prose—
As when a little Girl
They put me in the Closet—
Because they like me "still"—
Still! Could themself have peeped—
And seen my Brain—go round—
They might as wise have lodged a Bird
For Treason—in the Pound—
Himself has but to will
And easy as a Star
Look down upon Captivity—
And laugh—No more have I—

POEM 657

I dwell in Possibility—
A fairer House than Prose—
More numerous of Windows—
Superior—for Doors—
Of Chambers as the Cedars—
Impregnable of Eye—
And for an Everlasting Roof
The Gambrels of the Sky—
Of Visitors—the fairest—
For Occupation—This—
The spreading wide my narrow Hands
To gather Paradise—

POEM 1126

Shall I take thee, the Poet said
To the propounded word?
Be stationed with the Candidates
Till I have finer tried—
The Poet searched Philology
And when about to ring
For the suspended Candidate
There came unsummoned in—
That portion of the Vision
The Word applied to fill
Not unto nomination
The Cherubim reveal—

POEM 1212

A word is dead
When it is said,
Some say.
I say it just
Begins to live
That day.

POEM 1247

To pile like Thunder to its close
Then crumble grand away
While Everything created hid
This—would be Poetry—
Or Love—the two coeval come—
We both and neither prove—
Experience either and consume—
For None see God and live

POEM 1263

There is no Frigate like a Book
To take us Lands away,
Nor any Coursers like a Page
Of prancing Poetry—
This Traverse may the poorest take
Without oppress of Toll—
How frugal is the Chariot
That bears a Human soul!

POEM 1409

Could mortal lip divine
The undeveloped Freight
Of a delivered syllable,
'Twould crumble with the weight.

POEM 1472

To see the Summer Sky
Is Poetry, though never in a Book it lie—
True Poems flee—

29

RUDYARD KIPLING (1865–1936)

Rudyard Kipling, who was born in India, emerged very early as a prodigiously versatile and extremely popular journalist, novelist, poet, and children's writer. His popular appeal is still attested by the sales of his books, and over the years many excellent movies have been made from his poems and tales (including *Gunga Din, Captains Courageous, Kim, The Jungle Book,* and *The Man Who Would Be King*). In 1907 Kipling became the first British writer to be awarded the Nobel Prize for Literature.

Kipling also endures as an important figure in the development of Scouting. Kipling wrote "The Scout's Patrol Song." The ranks of wolf, bear, and lion, as well as "Law of the Pack," "Akela," "Wolf Cub," " Grand Howl," "den," and "pack" all come from Kipling's *The Jungle Book.*

The title "'Proofs of Holy Writ'" plays on a passage from Shakespeare's *Othello*: "Trifles light as air / Are to the jealous confirmations strong / As proofs of holy writ." In Kipling's story, however, the "proofs" are proof-copies of what was to become the Authorized (or King James) Version of the Bible in 1611. The story, usually counted as Kipling's last, dates from 1934. It has been said to result from a discussion between Kipling and another popular writer, John Buchan (author of *The Thirty-Nine Steps*), about how such a distinguished translation of the Bible could have been produced by a committee of forty-seven theological scholars. Is it possible that some of the best writing of the Jacobean Age was secretly produced by some of the best writers?

The Bible in use at the beginning of the sixteenth century, when England was still a Catholic country, was in Latin. The earliest translation into English is associated with John Wyclif and his followers (fourteenth century). William Tyndale prepared a translation of the New Testament and parts of the Old Testament early in the sixteenth century, and Miles Coverdale produced a complete English Bible in 1535. Coverdale also supervised the production of the Great Bible (or "Cranmer's Bible") in 1539. The Geneva Bible, with marginal glosses, appeared in 1560. The Authorized Version appeared in 1611, produced by a committee that had been at work since 1604. Much of their version is essentially Tyndale's text.

Adherents have long suspected that Shakespeare must have had a hand in what was the most important literary work during his lifetime. There has even been detective work based on the fact that in Psalm 46 the forty-sixth word from the beginning is "shake" and the forty-sixth from the end "spear"—along with the possibility that this version of Psalm 46 was composed in 1610, when Shakespeare turned forty-six.

It is more interesting, however, to consider that Kipling's story is unique in a couple of respects: it is an historical fiction that also earns a place in a collection of criticism. Furthermore, it is one of the very few places that offer a detailed discussion by a poet (or by a poet writing about other poets) of what actually goes on in the syllable-by-syllable production of literature.

"PROOFS OF HOLY WRIT"

ARISE, shine: for thy light is come, and the glory of the
Lord is risen upon thee.

2. For, behold, the darkness shall cover the earth, and
gross darkness the people: but the Lord shall arise upon thee,
and his glory shall be seen upon thee.

3. And the Gentiles shall come to thy light, and kings to
the brightness of thy rising. . . .

19. The sun shall be no more thy light by day; neither for
brightness shall the moon give light unto thee: but the Lord
shall be unto thee an everlasting light, and thy God thy
glory.

20. Thy sun shall no more go down; neither shall thy
moon withdraw itself: for the Lord shall be thine everlasting
light, and the days of thy mourning shall be ended.

Isaiah 60 (Authorized Version, 1611)

They seated themselves in the heavy chairs on the pebbled floor beneath the
eaves of the summer-house by the orchard. A table between them carried wine
and glasses, and a packet of papers, with pen and ink. The larger man of the

two, his doublet unbuttoned, his broad face blotched and scarred, puffed a little as he came to rest. The other picked an apple from the grass, bit it, and went on with the thread of the talk that they must have carried out of doors with them.

"But why waste time fighting atomies who do not come up to your belly-button, Ben?" he asked.

"It breathes me — it breathes me, between bouts! You'd be better for a tussle or two."

"But not to spend mind and verse on 'em. What was Dekker to you? Ye knew he'd strike back — and hard."

"He and Marston had been baiting me like dogs . . . about my trade as they called it, though it was only my cursed stepfather's. 'Bricks and mortar,' Dekker said, and 'hod-man.'

And he mocked my face. 'Twas clean as curds in my youth. This humour has come on me since."

"Ah! 'Every man and his humour'? But why did ye not have at Dekker in peace — over the sack, as you do at me?"

"Because I'd have drawn on him — and he's no more worth a hanging than Gabriel. Setting aside what he wrote of me, too, the hireling dog has merit, of a sort. His Shoe-maker's Holiday. Hey ? Though my Bartlemy Fair, when 'tis presented, will furnish out three of it and — "

"Ride all the easier. I have suffered two readings of it already. It creaks like an overloaded hay-wain," the other cut in. "You give too much."

Ben smiled loftily, and went on. "But I'm glad I lashed him in my Poetaster, for all I've worked with him since. How comes it that I've never fought with thee, Will?"

"First, Behemoth," the other drawled, "it needs two to engender any sort of iniquity. Second, the betterment of this present age — and the next, maybe — lies, in chief, on our four shoulders. If the Pillars of the Temple fall out, Nature, Art, and Learning come to a stand. Last, I am not yet ass enough to hawk up my private spites before the groundlings. What do the Court, citizens, or 'prentices give for thy fallings-out or fallings-in with Dekker — or the Grand Devil?"

"They should be taught, then — taught."

"Always that? What's your commission to enlighten us?"

"My own learning which I have heaped up, lifelong, at my own pains. My assured knowledge, also, of my craft and art. I'll suffer no man's mock or malice on it."

"The one sure road to mockery."

"I deny nothing of my brain-store to my lines. I — I build up my own works throughout."

"Yet when Dekker cries 'hodman' y'are not content."

Ben half heaved in his chair. "I'll owe you a beating for that when I'm thinner. Meantime here's on account. I say I build upon my own foundations;

devising and perfecting my own plots; adorning 'em justly as fits time, place, and action. In all of which you sin damnably. I set no landward principalities on sea-beaches."

"They pay their penny for pleasure—not learning," Will answered above the apple-core.

"Penny or tester, you owe 'em justice. In the facture of plays—nay, listen, Will — at all points they must be dressed historically—*teres atque rotundus*— in ornament and temper. As my Sejanus, of which the mob was unworthy."

Here Will made a doleful face, and echoed, "Unworthy! I was—what did I play, Ben, in that long weariness? Some most grievous ass."

"The part of Caius Silius," said Ben stiffly.

Will laughed aloud. "True. 'Indeed that place was not my sphere.' "

It must have been a quotation, for Ben winced a little, ere he recovered himself and went on: "Also my Alchemist which the world in part apprehends. The main of its learning is necessarily yet hid from 'em. To come to your works, Will—"

"I am a sinner on all sides. The drink's at your elbow."

"Confession shall not save ye—nor bribery." Ben filled his glass. "Sooner than labour the right cold heat to devise your own plots you filch, botch, and clap 'em together out o' ballads, broadsheets, old wives' tales, chap-books—"

Will nodded with complete satisfaction. "Say on," quoth he.

"'Tis so with nigh all yours. I've known honester jack-daws. And whom among the learned do ye deceive? Reckoning up those—forty, is it?—your plays you've misbegot, there's not six which have not plots common as Moorditch."

"Ye're out, Ben. There's not one. My Love's Labour (how I came to write it, I know not) is nearest to lawful issue. My Tempest (how I came to write that, I know) is, in some part my own stuff. Of the rest, I stand guilty. Bastards all !"

"And no shame?"

"None! Our business must be fitted with parts hot and hot—and the boys are more trouble than the men. Give me the bones of any stuff, I'll cover 'em as quickly as any. But to hatch new plots is to waste God's unreturning time like a—" he chuckled—"like a hen."

"Yet see what ye miss! Invention next to Knowledge, whence it proceeds, being the chief glory of Art—"

"Miss, say you? Dick Burbage—in my Hamlet that I botched for him when he had staled of our Kings? (Nobly he played it.) Was he a miss?"

Ere Ben could speak Will overbore him.

"And when poor Dick was at odds with the world in general and womankind in special, I clapped him up my Lear for a vomit."

"An hotchpotch of passion, outrunning reason," was the verdict.

"Not altogether. Cast in a mould too large for any boards to bear. (My fault!) Yet Dick evened it. And when he'd come out of his whoremongering aftermaths of repentance, I served him my Macbeth to toughen him. Was that a miss ?"

"I grant your Macbeth as nearest in spirit to my Sejanus; showing for example: 'How fortune plies her sports when she begins To practise 'em.' We'll see which of the two lives longest."

"Amen! I'll bear no malice among the worms."

A liveried man, booted and spurred, led a saddle-horse through a gate into the orchard. At a sign from Will he tethered the beast to a tree, lurched aside, and stretched on the grass. Ben, curious as a lizard, for all his bulk, wanted to know what it meant.

"There's a nosing Justice of the Peace lost in thee," Will returned. "Yon's a business I've neglected all this day for thy fat sake—and he by so much the drunker. . . . Patience! It's all set out on the table. Have a care with the ink!"

Ben reached unsteadily for the packet of papers and read the superscription: "To William Shakespeare, Gentleman, at his house of New Place in the town of Stratford, these—with diligence from M.S." Why does the fellow withhold his name? Or is it one of your women? I'll look."

Muzzy as he was, he opened and unfolded a mass of printed papers expertly enough.

"From the most learned divine, Miles Smith of Brazen Nose College," Will explained. "You know this business as well as I. The King has set all the scholars of England to make one Bible, which the Church shall be bound to, out of all the Bibles that men use."

"I knew." Ben could not lift his eyes from the printed page. "I'm more about Court than you think. The learning of Oxford and Cambridge—'most noble and most equal,' as I have said—and Westminster, to sit upon a clutch of Bibles. Those 'ud be Geneva (my mother read to me out of it at her knee), Douai, Rheims, Coverdale, Matthew's, the Bishops', the Great, and so forth."

"They are all set down on the page there—text against text. And you call me a botcher of old clothes?"

"Justly. But what's your concern with this botchery? To keep peace among the Divines? There's fifty of 'em at it as I've heard."

"I deal with but one. He came to know me when we played at Oxford—when the plague was too hot in London."

"I remember this Miles Smith now. Son of a butcher? Hey?" Ben grunted.

"Is it so?" was the quiet answer. "He was moved, he said, with some lines of mine in Dick's part. He said they were, to his godly apprehension, a parable, as it might be, of his reverend self, going down darkling to his tomb 'twixt cliffs of ice and iron."

"What lines? I know none of thine of that power. But in my Sejanus—"

"These were in my Macbeth. They lost nothing at Dick's mouth:—

'To-morrow, and tomorrow, and to-morrow
Creeps in this petty pace from day to day
To the last syllable of recorded time,
And all our yesterdays have lighted fools
The way to dusty death —'

or something in that sort. Condell writes 'em out fair for him, and tells him I am Justice of the Peace (wherein he lied) and armiger, which brings me within the pale of God's creatures and the Church. Little and little, then, this very reverend Miles Smith opens his mind to me. He and a half-score others, his cloth, are cast to furbish up the Prophets—Isaiah to Malachi. In his opinion by what he'd heard, I had some skill in words, and he'd condescend—"

"How?" Ben barked. "Condescend?"

"Why not? He'd condescend to inquire o' me privily, when direct illumination lacked, for a tricking-out of his words or the turn of some figure. For example"—Will pointed to the papers—"here be the first three verses of the Sixtieth of Isaiah, and the nineteenth and twentieth of that same. Miles has been at a stand over 'em a week or more."

"They never called on me." Ben caressed lovingly the hand-pressed proofs on their lavish linen paper. "Here's the Latin atop and"—his thick forefinger ran down the slip—"some three — four—Englishings out of the other Bibles. They spare 'emselves nothing. Let's to it together. Will you have the Latin first?"

"Could I choke ye from that, Holofernes?"

Ben rolled forth, richly: "'Surge, illumare, Jerusalem, quia venit lumen tuum, et gloria Domini super te orta est. Quia ecce tenebrae aperient terram et caligo populos. Super te autem orietur Dominus, et gloria ejus in te videbitur. Et ambulabunt gentes in lumine tuo, et reges in splendore ortus tui.' Er—hum? Think you to better that?"

"How have Smith's crew gone about it?"

"Thus." Ben read from the paper. "'Get thee up, O Jerusalem, and be bright, for thy light is at hand. and the glory of God has risen up upon thee.'"

"Up-pup-up!" Will stuttered profanely.

Ben held on. "'See how darkness is upon the earth and the peoples thereof.'"

"That's no great stuff to put into Isaiah's mouth. And further, Ben?"

"'But on thee God shall shew light and on—' or 'in,' is it?" (Ben held the proof closer to the deep furrow at the bridge of his nose) "'on thee shall His glory be manifest. So that all peoples shall walk in thy light and the Kings in the glory of thy morning.'"

"It may be mended. Read me the Coverdale of it now. 'Tis on the same sheet—to the right, Ben."

"Umm-umm! Coverdale saith, 'And therefore get thee up betimes, for thy light cometh, and the glory of the Lord shall rise up upon thee. For lo! while the darkness and cloud covereth the earth and the people, the Lord shall shew thee light, and His glory shall be seen in thee. The Gentiles shall come to thy light, and kings to the brightness that springeth forth upon thee.' But 'gentes' is for the most part, 'peoples.' " Ben concluded.

"Eh?" said Will indifferently. "Art sure?"

This loosed an avalanche of instances from Ovid, Quintilian, Terence, Columella, Seneca, and others. Will took no heed till the rush ceased. but stared into the orchard through the September haze. "Now give me the Douai and Geneva for this 'Get thee up, O Jerusalem,' " said he at last.

"They'll be all there." Ben referred to the proofs. "'Tis 'arise' in both," said he. " 'Arise and be bright' in Geneva. In the Douai 'tis 'Arise and be illuminated.'"

"So? Give me the paper now." Will took it from his companion, rose, and paced towards a tree in the orchard, turning again, when he had reached it, by a well-worn track through the grass. Ben leaned forward in his chair. The other's free hand went up warningly.

"Quiet, man!" said he. "I wait on my Demon!" He fell into the stage-stride of his art at that time, speaking to the air.

"How shall this open? 'Arise?' No! 'Rise!' Yes. And we'll no weak coupling. 'Tis a call to a City! 'Rise—shine.' . . . Nor yet any schoolmaster's 'because'— because Isaiah is not Holofernes. 'Rise—shine; for thy light is come, and—!'" He refreshed himself from the apple and the proofs as he strode. "'And—and the glory of God!'—No 'God's' over short. We need the long roll here. 'And the glory of the Lord is risen on thee.' (Isaiah speaks the part. We'll have it from his own lips.) What's next in Smith's stuff? . . . 'See how?' Oh, vile—vile! . . . And Geneva hath 'Lo'? (Still, Ben! Still!) 'Lo' is better by all odds: but to match the long roll of 'the Lord' we'll have it 'Behold." How goes it now? For, behold, darkness clokes the earth and—and—' What's the colour and use of this cursed caligo, Ben?—'Et caligo populos.'"

" 'Mistiness' or, as in Pliny, 'blindness.' And further—"

"No-o. . . . Maybe, though, caligo will piece out tenebrae. 'Quia ecce tenebrae operient terram et caligo populos.' Nay! 'Shadow' and 'mist' are not men enough for this work. . . . Blindness, did ye say, Ben? . . . The blackness of blindness atop of mere darkness? . . . By God, I've used it in my own stuff many times! 'Gross' searches it to the hilts! 'Darkness covers'—no—'clokes' (short always). 'Darkness clokes the earth, and gross—gross darkness the people!' (But Isaiah's prophesying, with the storm behind him. Can ye not feel it, Ben? It must be 'shall')—'Shall cloke the earth.' . . . The rest comes clearer. . . . 'But on thee God Shall arise.' . . . (Nay, that's sacrificing the Creator to the Creature!) 'But the Lord shall arise on thee,' and—yes, we sound that 'thee' again—'and on thee shall'—No! . . . 'And His glory shall be seen on thee.' Good!" He walked his beat a little in silence, mumbling the two verses before he mouthed them.

"I have it! Heark, Ben! 'Rise—shine; for thy light is come, and the glory of the Lord is risen on thee. For, behold, darkness shall cloke the earth, and gross darkness the people. But the Lord shall arise on thee, and His glory shall be seen upon thee.' "

"There's something not all amiss there," Ben conceded.

"My Demon never betrayed me yet, while I trusted him. Now for the verse that runs to the blast of rams'-horns. 'Et ambulabunt gentes in lumine tuo, et reges in splendore ortus tui.' How goes that in the Smithy? 'The Gentiles shall come to thy light, and kings to the brightness that springs forth upon thee?' The same in Coverdale and the Bishops'—eh? We'll keep 'Gentiles,' Ben, for the sake of the indraught of the last syllable. But it might be 'And the Gentiles shall draw.' No! The plainer the better! 'The Gentiles shall come to thy light, and kings to the splendour of—' (Smith's out here! We'll need something that shall lift the trumpet anew.) 'Kings shall—shall—Kings to—' (Listen, Ben, but on your life speak not!) 'Gentiles shall come to thy light, and kings to thy brightness'—No! 'Kings to the brightness that springeth—' Serves not! . . . One trumpet must answer another. And the blast of a trumpet is always ai-ai. 'The brightness of'—'Ortus' signifies 'rising,' Ben—or what?"

"Ay, or 'birth,' or the East in general."

"Ass! 'Tis the one word that answers to 'light.' 'Kings to the brightness of thy rising.' Look! The thing shines now within and without. God! That so much should lie on a word." He repeated the verse—" 'And the Gentiles shall come to thy light, and kings to the brightness of thy rising.' "

He walked to the table and wrote rapidly on the proof margin all three verses as he had spoken them. "If they hold by this," said he, raising his head, "they'll not go far astray. Now for the nineteenth and twentieth verses. On the other sheet, Ben. What? What? Smith says he has held back his rendering till he hath seen mine? Then we'll botch 'em as they stand. Read me first the Latin; next the Coverdale, and last the Bishops'. There's a contagion of sleep in the air." He handed back the proofs, yawned, and took up his walk.

Obedient, Ben began: " 'Non erit tibi amplius Sol ad lucendum per diem, nec splendor Lunae illuminabit te.' Which Coverdale rendereth, 'The Sun shall never be thy day light, and the light of the Moon shall never shine unto thee.' The Bishops read: 'Thy sun shall never be thy daylight and the light of the moon shall never shine on thee.' "

"Coverdale is the better," said Will, and, wrinkling his nose a little, "The Bishops put out their lights clumsily. Have at it, Ben."

Ben pursed his lips and knit his brow. "The two verses are in the same mode, changing a hand's-breadth in the second. By so much, therefore, the more difficult."

"Ye see that, then?" said the other, staring past him, and muttering as he paced, concerning suns and moons. Presently he took back the proof, chose him another apple, and grunted. "Umm-umm! 'Thy Sun shall never be'—No! Flat as a split viol. 'Non erit tibi amplius Sol—' That amplius must give tongue. Ah! . . . 'Thy Sun shall not—shall not—shall no more be thy light by day.' A fair entry. 'Nor?'— No! Not on the heels of 'day.' 'Neither' it must be—'Neither the Moon'—but here's splendor and the rams'-horns again. (Therefore—ai-ai!) 'Neither for brightness shall the Moon—' (Pest! It is the Lord who is taking the Moon's place over Israel. It must be 'thy Moon.') 'Neither for brightness shall thy Moon light—give—make—give light unto thee.' Ah! . . . Listen here! . . . 'The Sun shall no more be thy light by day: neither for brightness shall thy Moon give light unto thee.' That serves, and more, for the first entry. What next, Ben?"

Ben nodded magisterially as Will neared him, reached out his hand for the proofs, and read: "'Sed erit tibi Dominus in lucem sempiternam et Deus tuus in gloriam tuam.' Here is a jewel of Coverdale's that the Bishops have wisely stolen whole. Hear! 'But the Lord Himself shall be thy everlasting light, and thy God shall be thy glory.'" Ben paused. "There's a hand's-breadth of splendour for a simple man to gather!"

"Both hands rather. He's swept the strings as divinely as David before Saul," Will assented. "We'll convey it whole, too. . . . What's amiss now, Holofernes?"

For Ben was regarding him with a scholar's cold pity. "Both hands! Will, hast thou ever troubled to master any shape or sort of prosody—the mere names of the measures and pulses of strung words?"

"I beget some such stuff and send it to you to christen. What's your wisdom-hood in labour of?"

"Naught. Naught. But not to know the names of the tools of his trade!" Ben half muttered and pronounced some Greek word or other which conveyed nothing to the listener, who replied: "Pardon, then, for whatever sin it was. I do but know words for my need of 'em, Ben. Hold still awhile!"

He went back to his pacings and mutterings. "'For the Lord Himself shall be thy—or thine?—everlasting light.' Yes. We'll convey that." He repeated it twice. "Nay! Can be bettered. Hark ye, Ben. Here is the Sun going up to over-run and possess all Heaven for evermore. Therefore (Still, man!) we'll harness the horses of the dawn. Hear their hooves? 'The Lord Himself shall be unto thee thy everlasting light, and—' Hold again! After that climbing thunder must be some smooth check—like great wings gliding. Therefore we'll not have 'shall be thy glory,' but 'And thy God thy glory!' Ay—even as an eagle alighteth! Good—good! Now again, the sun and moon of that twentieth verse, Ben."

Ben read: "'Non occidet ultra Sol tuus et Luna tua non minuetur: quia erit tibi Dominus in lucem sempiternam et complebuntur dies luctus tui.'"

Will snatched the paper and read aloud from the Coverdale version. "'Thy

Sun shall never go down, and thy Moon shall not be taken away.' . . . What a plague's Coverdale doing with his blocking ets and urs, Ben? What's minuetur? . . . I'll have it all anon."

"Minish—make less—appease—abate, as in—"

"So?" Will threw the proofs back. "Then 'wane' should serve. 'Neither shall thy moon wane.' . . . 'Wane' is good, but over-weak for place next to 'moon'. . . ." He swore softly. "Isaiah hath abolished both earthly sun and moon. Exeunt ambo. Aha! I begin to see ! . . . Sol, the man, goes down—down stairs or trap—as needs be. Therefore 'Go down' shall stand. 'Set' would have been better—as a sword sent home in the scabbard—but it jars—it jars. Now Luna must retire herself in some simple fashion. . . . Which? Ass that I be! 'Tis common talk in all the plays . . . 'Withdrawn' . . . 'Favour withdrawn' . . . 'Countenance withdrawn.' 'The Queen withdraws herself' . . . 'Withdraw,' it shall be! 'Neither shall thy moon withdraw herself.' (Hear her silver train rasp the boards, Ben?) 'Thy sun shall no more go down—neither shall thy moon withdraw herself. For the Lord . . . '—ay, the Lord, simple of Himself—'shall be thine'—yes, 'thine' here—'everlasting light, and. . . . ' How goes the ending, Ben?"

" 'Et complebuntur dies luctus tui.' " Ben read. " 'And thy sorrowful days shall be rewarded thee,' says Coverdale."

"And the Bishops?"

" 'And thy sorrowful days shall be ended.' "

"By no means. And Douai?"

" 'Thy sorrow shall be ended.' "

"And Geneva?"

" 'And the days of thy mourning shall be ended.' "

"The Switzers have it! Lay the tail of Geneva to the head of Coverdale and the last is without flaw.

He began to thump Ben on the shoulder. "We have it! I have it all, Boanerges! Blessed be my Demon! Hear!

" 'The sun shall no more be thy light by day, neither for brightness the moon by night. But the Lord Himself shall be unto thee thy everlasting light, and thy God thy glory.' "

He drew a deep breath and went on.

" 'Thy sun shall no more go down; neither shall thy moon withdraw herself, for the Lord shall be thine everlasting light, and the days of thy mourning shall be ended.' "

The rain of triumphant blows began again. "If those other seven devils in London let it stand on this sort, it serves. But God knows what they can not turn upsee-dejee!"

Ben wriggled. "Let be!" he protested. "Ye are more moved by this jugglery than if the Globe were burned."

"Thatch—old thatch! And full of fleas! . . . But, Ben, ye should have heard my Ezekiel making mock of fallen Tyrus in his twenty-seventh chapter. Miles sent me the whole, for, he said, some small touches. I took it to the Bank—four o'clock of a summer morn; stretched out in one of our wherries—and watched London, Port and Town, up and down the river, waking all arrayed to heap more upon evident excess. Ay! 'A merchant for the peoples of many isles. . . . ' The ships of Tarshish 'did sing of thee in thy markets'? Yes! I saw all Tyre before me neighing her pride against lifted heaven. . . . But what will they let stand of all mine at long last? Which? I'll never know."

He had set himself neatly and quickly to refolding and cording the packet while he talked. "That's secret enough," he said at the finish.

"He'll lose it by the way." Ben pointed to the sleeper beneath the tree. "He's owl-drunk."

"But not his horse," said Will. He crossed the orchard, roused the man; slid the packet into an holster which he carefully rebuckled; saw him out of the gate, and returned to his chair.

"Who will know we had part in it?" Ben asked.

"God, maybe—if He ever lay ear to earth. I've gained and lost enough—lost enough." He lay back and sighed. There was long silence till he spoke half aloud. "And Kit that was my master in the beginning, he died when all the world was young."

"Knifed on a tavern reckoning—not even for a wench!" Ben nodded.

"Ay. But if he'd lived he'd have breathed me! 'Fore God, he'd have breathed me!"

"Was Marlowe, or any man, ever thy master, Will?"

"He alone. Very he. I envied Kit. Ye do not know that envy, Ben?"

"Not as touching my own works. When the mob is led to prefer a baser Muse, I have felt the hurt, and paid home. Ye know that—as ye know my doctrine of play-writing."

"Nay—not wholly—tell it at large," said Will, relaxing in his seat, for virtue had gone out of him. He put a few drowsy questions. In three minutes Ben had launched full-flood on the decayed state of the drama, which he was born to correct; on cabals and intrigues against him which he had fought without cease; and on the inveterate muddle-headedness of the mob unless duly scourged into approbation by his magisterial hand.

It was very still in the orchard now that the horse had gone. The heat of the day held though the sun sloped and the wine had done its work. Presently, Ben's discourse was broken by a snort from the other chair.

"I was listening, Ben! Missed not a word—missed not a word." Will sat up and rubbed his eyes. "Ye held me throughout." His head dropped again before he had done speaking.

Ben looked at him with a chuckle and quoted from one of his own plays: —

> " 'Mine earnest vehement botcher
> And deacon also, Will, I cannot dispute with you.' "

He drew out flint, steel and tinder, pipe and tobacco-bag from somewhere round his waist, lit and puffed against the midges till he, too, dozed.

30

EZRA POUND (1885–1972)

The cosmopolitan Pound, born in Idaho, raised and educated in the American northeast, spent most of his adult years in Europe, with the exception of a twelve-year hiatus (1945–1957) when he was confined to the prison wing of a federal mental hospital in Washington, D.C. (A zealous adherent of Mussolini, he had made such provocative radio broadcasts before and during World War II that he was accused of treason in wartime; judged too insane to stand trial and too dangerous to release, he was detained until he had grown so old that he was freed on the condition that he leave the country.)

Pound was an active poet for most of the twentieth century and an influential critical and personal presence who provided material and intellectual assistance to dozens of important writers: W. B. Yeats, Ford Madox Ford, Robert Frost, James Joyce, William Carlos Williams, Wyndham Lewis, D. H. Laawrence, Hilda Doolittle, T. S. Eliot, Marianne Moore, Ernest Hemingway, Louis Zukofsky, Robert Lowell, and many others. He at least provided material support, and for many he was the source of critical ideas that shaped modern writing in poetry and prose. After his death, his written criticism continued to supply inspiration and clarification to generations of poets around the world.

A RETROSPECT

From *Pavannes and Divagations* (1918)

There has been so much scribbling about a new fashion in poetry, that I may perhaps be pardoned this brief recapitulation and retrospect.

In the spring or early summer of 1912, "H. D.," Richard Aldington and myself decided that we were agreed upon the three principles following:

1. Direct treatment of the "thing" whether subjective or objective.
2. To use absolutely no word that does not contribute to the presentation.
3. As regarding rhythm: to compose in the sequence of the musical phrase, not in sequence of a metronome.

Upon many points of taste and of predilection we differed, but agreeing upon these three positions we thought we had as much right to a group name, at least as much right, as a number of French "schools" proclaimed by Mr. Flint in the August number of Harold Monro's magazine for 1911.

This school has since been "joined" or "followed" by numerous people who, whatever their merits, do not show any signs of agreeing with the second specification. Indeed vers libre has become as prolix and as verbose as any of the flaccid varieties that preceded it. It has brought faults of its own. The actual language and phrasing is often as bad as that of our elders without even the excuse that the words are shovelled in to fill a metric pattern or to complete the noise of a rhyme-sound. Whether or no the phrases followed by the followers are musical must be left to the reader's decision. At times I can find a marked metre in "vers libres," as stale and hackneyed as any pseudo-Swinburnian, at times the writers seem to follow no musical structure whatever. But it is, on the whole, good that the field should be ploughed. Perhaps a few good poems have come from the new method, and if so it is justified.

Criticism is not a circumscription or a set of prohibitions. It provides fixed points of departure. It may startle a dull reader into alertness. That little of it which is good is mostly in stray phrases; or if it be an older artist helping a younger it is in great measure but rules of thumb, cautions gained by experience.

I set together a few phrases on practical working about the time the first remarks on imagisme were published. The first use of the word "Imagiste" was in my note to T. E. Hulme's five poems, printed at the end of my "Ripostes" in the autumn of 1912. I reprint my cautions from *Poetry* for March, 1913.

A FEW DON'TS

An "Image" is that which presents an intellectual and emotional complex in an instant of time. I use the term "complex" rather in the technical sense employed by the newer psychologists, such as Hart, though we may not agree absolutely in our application.

It is the presentation of such a "complex" instantaneously which gives that sense of sudden liberation; that sense of freedom from time limits and space limits; that sense of sudden growth, which we experience in the presence of the greatest works of art.

It is better to present one Image in a lifetime than to produce voluminous works.

All this, however, some may consider open to debate. The immediate necessity is to tabulate A LIST OF DON'TS for those beginning to write verses. I can not put all of them into Mosaic negative.

To begin with, consider the three propositions (demanding direct treatment, economy of words, and the sequence of the musical phrase), not as dogma—never consider anything as dogma—but as the result of long contemplation, which, even if it is some one else's contemplation, may be worth consideration.

Pay no attention to the criticism of men who have never themselves written a notable work. Consider the discrepancies between the actual writing of the

Greek poets and dramatists, and the theories of the Graeco-Roman grammarians, concocted to explain their metres.

LANGUAGE

Use no superfluous word, no adjective which does not reveal something.

Don't use such an expression as "dim lands of peace." It dulls the image. It mixes an abstraction with the concrete. It comes from the writer's not realizing that the natural object is always the adequate symbol.

Go in fear of abstractions. Do not retell in mediocre verse what has already been done in good prose. Don't think any intelligent person is going to be deceived when you try to shirk all the difficulties of the unspeakably difficult art of good prose by chopping your composition into line lengths.

What the expert is tired of today the public will be tired of tomorrow.

Don't imagine that the art of poetry is any simpler than the art of music, or that you can please the expert before you have spent at least as much effort on the art of verse as an average piano teacher spends on the art of music.

Be influenced by as many great artists as you can, but have the decency either to acknowledge the debt outright, or to try to conceal it.

Don't allow "influence" to mean merely that you mop up the particular decorative vocabulary of some one or two poets whom you happen to admire. A Turkish war correspondent was recently caught red-handed babbling in his despatches of "dove-grey" hills, or else it was "pearl-pale," I can not remember.

Use either no ornament or good ornament.

RHYTHM AND RHYME

Let the candidate fill his mind with the finest cadences he can discover, preferably in a foreign language [This is for rhythm, his vocabulary must of course be found in his native tongue], so that the meaning of the words may be less likely to divert his attention from the movement; e.g. Saxon charms, Hebridean Folk Songs, the verse of Dante, and the lyrics of Shakespeare — if he can dissociate the vocabulary from the cadence. Let him dissect the lyrics of Goethe coldly into their component sound values, syllables long and short, stressed and unstressed, into vowels and consonants.

It is not necessary that a poem should rely on its music, but if it does rely on its music that music must be such as will delight the expert.

Let the neophyte know assonance and alliteration, rhyme immediate and delayed, simple and polyphonic, as a musician would expect to know harmony and counterpoint and all the minutiae of his craft. No time is too great to give to these matters or to any one of them, even if the artist seldom have need of them.

Don't imagine that a thing will "go" in verse just because it's too dull to go in prose.

Don't be "viewy"—leave that to the writers of pretty little philosophic essays. Don't be descriptive; remember that the painter can describe a landscape much better than you can, and that he has to know a deal more about it.

When Shakespeare talks of the "Dawn in russet mantle clad" he presents something which the painter does not present. There is in this line of his nothing that one can call description; he presents.

Consider the way of the scientists rather than the way of an advertising agent for a new soap.

The scientist does not expect to be acclaimed as a great scientist until he has discovered something. He begins by learning what has been discovered already. He goes from that point onward. He does not bank on being a charming fellow personally. He does not expect his friends to applaud the results of his freshman class work. Freshmen in poetry are unfortunately not confined to a definite and recognizable class room. They are "all over the shop." Is it any wonder "the public is indifferent to poetry?"

Don't chop your stuff into separate iambs. Don't make each line stop dead at the end and then begin every next line with a heave.

Let the beginning of the next line catch the rise of the rhythm wave, unless you want a definite longish pause.

In short, behave as a musician, a good musician, when dealing with that phase of your art which has exact parallels in music. The same laws govern, and you are bound by no others.

Naturally, your rhythmic structure should not destroy the shape of your words, or their natural sound, or their meaning. It is improbable that, at the start, you will he able to get a rhythm-structure strong enough to affect them very much, though you may fall a victim to all sorts of false stopping due to line ends, and caesurae.

The Musician can rely on pitch and the volume of the orchestra. You can not. The term harmony is misapplied in poetry; it refers to simultaneous sounds of different pitch. There is, however, in the best verse a sort of residue of sound which remains in the ear of the hearer and acts more or less as an organ-base.

A rhyme must have in it some slight element of surprise if it is to give pleasure, it need not be bizarre or curious, but it must be well used if used at all.

Vide further Vildrac and Duhamel's notes on rhyme in "Technique Poétique."

That part of your poetry which strikes upon the imaginative eye of the reader will lose nothing by translation into a foreign tongue; that which appeals to the ear can reach only those who take it in the original.

Consider the definiteness of Dante's presentation, as compared with Milton's rhetoric. Read as much of Wordsworth as does not seem too unutterably dull.

If you want the gist of the matter go to Sappho, Catullus, Villon, Heine when he is in the vein, Gautier when he is not too frigid; or, if you have not the tongues, seek out the leisurely Chaucer. Good prose will do you no harm, and there is good discipline to be had by trying to write it.

Translation is likewise good training, if you find that your original matter "wobbles" when you try to rewrite it. The meaning of the poem to be translated can not "wobble."

If you are using a symmetrical form, don't put in what you want to say and then fill up the remaining vacuums with slush.

Don't mess up the perception of one sense by trying to define it in terms of another. This is usually only the result of being too lazy to find the exact word. To this clause there are possibly exceptions.

The first three simple prescriptions will throw out nine-tenths of all the bad poetry now accepted as standard and classic; and will prevent you from many a crime of production.

". . . Mais d'abord il faut être un poète," as MM. Duhamel and Vildrac have said at the end of their little book, "Notes sur la Technique Poétique."

Since March 1913, Ford Madox Hueffer has pointed out that Wordsworth was so intent on the ordinary or plain word that he never thought of hunting for le mot juste.

John Butler Yeats has handled or man-handled Wordsworth and the Victorians, and his criticism, contained in letters to his son, is now printed and available.

I do not like writing about art, my first, at least I think it was my first essay on the subject, was a protest against it.

PROLEGOMENA

[*Poetry and Drama* (then the *Poetry Review*, edited by Harold Monro), Feb. 1912.]
Time was when the poet lay in a green field with his head against a tree and played his diversion on a ha'penny whistle, and, Caesar's predecessors conquered the earth, and the predecessors of golden Crassus embezzled, and fashions had their say, and let him alone. And presumably he was fairly content in this circumstance, for I have small doubt that the occasional passerby, being attracted by curiosity to know why any one should lie under a tree and blow diversion on a ha'penny whistle, came and conversed, with him, and that among these passers-by there was on occasion a person of charm or a young lady who had not read *Man and Superman*; and looking back upon this naïve state of affairs we call it the age of gold.

Metastasio, and he should know if any one, assures us that this age endures — even though the modern poet is expected to holloa his verses down a speaking tube to the editors of cheap magazines — S. S. McClure, or some one of that sort—even though hordes of authors meet in dreariness and drink healths to the "Copyright Bill"; even though these things be, the age of gold pertains. Imperceivably, if you like, but pertains. You meet unkempt Amyclas in a Soho restaurant and chant together of dead and forgotten things—it is a manner of speech among poets to chant of dead, half-forgotten things, there seems no special harm in it, it has always been done—and it's rather better to be a clerk in the Post Office than to look after a lot of stinking, verminous sheep—and at another hour of the day one substitutes the drawing-room for the restaurant and tea is probably more palatable than mead and mare's milk, and little cakes than honey. And in this fashion one survives the resignation of Mr. Balfour, and the iniquities of the American customs-house, e quel bufera infernal, the periodical press. And then in the middle of it, there being apparently no other person at once capable and available one is stopped and asked to explain oneself.

I begin on the chord thus querulous, for I would much rather lie on what is left of Catullus' parlour floor and speculate the azure beneath it and the hills off to Salo and Riva with their forgotten gods moving unhindered amongst them, than discuss any processes and theories of art whatsoever. I would rather play tennis. I shall not argue.

CREDO

Rhythm.—I believe in an "absolute rhythm," a rhythm, that is, in poetry which corresponds exactly to the emotion or shade of emotion to be expressed. A man's rhythm must be interpretative, it will be, therefore, in the end, his own, un-counterfeiting, uncounterfeitable.

Symbols.—I believe that the proper and perfect symbol is the natural object, that if a man use "symbols" he must so use them that their symbolic function does not obtrude; so that a sense, and the poetic quality of the passage, is not lost to those who do not understand the symbol as such, to whom, for instance, a hawk is a hawk.

Technique.—I believe in technique as the test of a man's sincerity; in law when it is ascertainable; in the trampling down of every convention that impedes or obscures the determination of the law, or the precise rendering of the impulse.

Form.—I think there is a "fluid" as well as a "solid" content, that some poems may have form as a tree has form, some as water poured into a vase. That most symmetrical forms have certain uses. That a vast number of subjects cannot be precisely, and therefore not properly rendered in symmetrical forms.

"Thinking that alone worthy wherein the whole art is employed" [Dante, *De Volgari Eloquio*]. I think the artist should master all known forms and systems of metric, and I have with some persistence set about doing this, searching particularly into those periods wherein the systems came to birth or attained their maturity. It has been complained, with some justice, that I dump my note-books on the public. I think that only after a long struggle will poetry attain such a degree of development, or, if you will, modernity, that it will vitally concern people who are accustomed, in prose, to Henry James and Anatole France, in music to Debussy. I am constantly contending that it took two centuries of Provence and one of Tuscany to develop the media of Dante's masterwork, that it took the latinists of the Renaissance, Pleiade, and his own age of painted speech to prepare Shakespeare his tools. It is tremendously important that great poetry be written, it makes no jot of difference who writes it. The experimental demonstrations of one man may save the time of many—hence my furore over Arnaut Daniel—if a man's experiments try out one new rime, or dispense conclusively with one iota of currently accepted nonsense, he is merely playing fair with his colleagues when he chalks up his result.

No man ever writes very much poetry that "matters." In bulk, that is, no one produces much that is final, and when a man is not doing this highest thing, this saying the thing once for all and perfectly. . . . [H]e had much better be making the sorts of experiment which may be of use to him in his later work, to his successors.

"The lyf so short, the craft so long to lerne." It is a foolish thing for a man to begin his work on a too narrow foundation, it is a disgraceful thing for a man's work not to show steady growth and increasing fineness from first to last.

As for "adaptations"; one finds that all the old masters of painting recommend to their pupils that they begin by copying masterwork, and proceed to their own composition.

As for "Every man his own poet," the more every man knows about poetry the better. I believe in every one writing poetry who wants to; most do. I believe in every man knowing enough of music to play "God bless our home" on the harmonium, but I do not believe in every man giving concerts and printing his sin.

The mastery of any art is the work of a lifetime. I should not discriminate between the "amateur" and the "professional." Or rather I should discriminate quite often in favour of the amateur, but I should discriminate between the amateur and the expert. It is certain that the present chaos will endure until the Art of poetry has been preached down the amateur gullet, until there is such a general understanding of the fact that poetry is an art and not a pastime; such a knowledge of technique, of technique of surface and technique of content, that the amateurs will cease to try to drown out the masters.

If a certain thing was said once for all in Atlantis or Arcadia, in 450 Before Christ or in 1290 after, it is not for us moderns to go saying it over, or to go obscuring the memory of the dead by saying the same thing with less skill and less conviction.

My pawing over the ancients and semi-ancients has been one struggle to find out what has been done, once for all, better than it can ever be done again, and to find out what remains for us to do, and plenty does remain, for if we still feel the same emotions as those which launched the thousand ships, it is quite certain that we come on these feelings differently, through different nuances, by different intellectual gradations. Each age has its own abounding gifts yet only some ages transmute them into matter of duration. No good poetry is ever written in a manner twenty years old, for to write in such a manner shows conclusively that the writer thinks from books, convention and cliché, and not from life, yet a man feeling the divorce of life and his art may naturally try to resurrect a forgotten mode if he finds in that mode some leaven, or if he think he sees in it some element lacking in contemporary art which might unite that art again to its sustenance, life.

In the art of Daniel and Cavalcanti, I have seen that precision which I miss in the Victorians, that explicit rendering, be it of external nature, or of emotion. Their testimony is of the eyewitness, their symptoms are first hand.

As for the nineteenth century, with all respect to its achievements, I think we shall look back upon it as a rather blurry, messy sort of a period, a rather sentimentalistic, mannerish sort of a period. I say this without any self-righteousness, with no self-satisfaction.

As for there being a "movement" or my being of it, the conception of poetry as a "pure art" in the sense in which I use the term, revived with Swinburne. From the puritanical revolt to Swinburne, poetry had been merely the vehicle — yes, definitely, Arthur Symons's scruples and feelings about the word not withholding — the ox-cart and post-chaise for transmitting thoughts poetic or otherwise. And perhaps the "great Victorians," though it is doubtful, and assuredly the "nineties" continued the development of the art, confining their improvements, however, chiefly to sound and to refinements of manner.

Mr. Yeats has once and for all stripped English poetry of its perdamnable rhetoric. He has boiled away all that is not poetic — and a good deal that is. He has become a classic in his own lifetime and nel mezzo del cammin. He has made our poetic idiom a thing pliable, a speech without inversions.

Robert Bridges, Maurice Hewlett and Frederic Manning are [Dec. 1911] in their different ways seriously concerned with overhauling the metric, in testing the language and its adaptability to certain modes. Ford Hueffer is making some sort of experiments in modernity. The Provost of Oriel continues his translation of the Divina Commedia.

As to Twentieth century poetry, and the poetry which I expect to see written during the next decade or so, it will, I think, move against poppy-cock, it will be harder and saner, it will be what Mr Hewlett calls "nearer the bone." It will be as much like granite as it can be, its force will lie in its truth, its interpretative power (of course, poetic force does always rest there); I mean it will not try to seem forcible by rhetorical din, and luxurious riot. We will have fewer painted adjectives impeding the shock and stroke of it. At least for myself, I want it so, austere, direct, free from emotional slither.

What is there now, in 1917, to be added?

RE VERS LIBRE

I think the desire for vers libre is due to the sense of quantity reasserting itself after years of starvation. But I doubt if we can take over, for English, the rules of quantity laid down for Greek and Latin, mostly by Latin grammarians.

I think one should write vers libre only when one "must," that is to say, only when the "thing" builds up a rhythm more beautiful than that of set metres, or more real, more a part of the emotion of the "thing," more germane, intimate, interpretative than the measure of regular accentual verse; a rhythm which discontents one with set iambic or set anapaestic.

Eliot has said the thing very well when he said, "No vers is libre for the man who wants to do a good job."

As a matter of detail, there is vers libre with accent heavily marked as a drum-beat (as par example my "Dance Figure"), and on the other hand I think I have gone as far as can profitably be gone in the other direction (and perhaps too far). I mean I do not think one can use to any advantage rhythms much more tenuous and imperceptible than some I have used. I think progress lies rather in an attempt to approximate classical quantitative metres (NOT to copy them) than in a carelessness regarding such things. [Let me date this statement 20 Aug. 1917.]

I agree with John Yeats on the relation of beauty to certitude. I prefer satire, which is due to emotion, to any sham of emotion.

I have had to write, or at least I have written a good deal about art, sculpture, painting and poetry. I have seen what seemed to me the best of contemporary work reviled and obstructed. Can any one write prose of permanent or durable interest when he is merely saying for one year what nearly every one will say at the end of three or four years? I have been battistrada for a sculptor, a painter, a novelist, several poets. I wrote also of certain French writers in The New Age in nineteen twelve or eleven.

I would much rather that people would look at Brzeska's sculpture and Lewis's drawings, and that they would read Joyce, Jules Romains, Eliot, than that they should read what I have said of these men, or that I should be asked to republish argumentative essays and reviews.

All that the critic can do for the reader or audience or spectator is to focus his gaze or audition. Rightly or wrongly I think my blasts and essays have done their work, and that more people are now likely to go to the sources than are likely to read this book.

Jammes's "Existences" in "La Triomphe de la Vie" is available. So are his early poems. I think we need a convenient anthology rather than descriptive criticism. Carl Sandburg wrote me from Chicago, "It's hell when poets can't afford to buy each other's books." Half the people who care, only borrow. In America so few people know each other that the difficulty lies more than half in distribution. Perhaps one should make an anthology: Romains's "Un Etre en Marche" and "Prléres," Vildrac's "Visite." Retrospectively the fine wrought work of Laforgue, the flashes of Rimbaud, the hard-bit lines of Tristan Corbiére, Tailhade's sketches in "Poémes Aristophanesques," the "Litanies" of De Gourmont.

It is difficult at all times to write of the fine arts, it is almost impossible unless one can accompany one's prose with many reproductions. Still I would seize this chance or any chance to reaffirm my belief in Wyndham Lewis's genius, both in his drawings and his writings. And I would name an out of the way prose book, the "Scenes and Portraits" of Frederic Manning, as well as James Joyce's short stories and novel, "Dubliners" and the now well known "Portrait of the Artist" as well as Lewis' "Tarr," if, that is, I may treat my strange reader as if he were a new friend come into the room, intent on ransacking my bookshelf.

ONLY EMOTION ENDURES

"Only emotion endures." Surely it is better for me to name over the few beautiful poems that still ring in my head than for me to search my flat for back numbers of periodicals and rearrange all that I have said about friendly and hostile writers.

The first twelve lines of Padraic Colum s "Drover"; his "O Woman shapely as a swan, on your account I shall not die"; Joyce's "I hear an army"; the lines of Yeats that ring in my head and in the heads of all young men of my time who care for poetry: Braseal and the Fisherman, "The fire that stirs about her when she stirs"; the later lines of "The Scholars," the faces of the Magi; William Carlos Williams's "Postlude." Aldington's version of "Atthis," and "H. D." 's waves like pine tops, and her verse in "Des Imagistes" the first anthology; Hueffer's "How red your lips are" in his translation from Von der Vogelweide, his "Three Ten," the general effect of his "On Heaven"; his sense of the prose values or prose qualities in poetry; his ability to write poems that half-chant and are spoiled by a musician's additions; beyond these a poem by Alice Corbin, "One City Only," and another ending "But sliding water over a stone." These things have worn smooth in my head and I am not through with them, nor with Aldington's "In Via Sestina" nor his other poems in "Des Imagistes," though people have told me their flaws. It may be that their content is too much embedded in me for me to look back at the words.

I am almost a different person when I come to take up the argument for Eliot's poems.

31

T. S. ELIOT (1888–1965)

Thomas Stearns Eliot was born in St. Louis, Missouri, on the banks of the Mississippi River, and he later spoke of himself as a Southwesterner or Midwesterner. Even so, his deeper loyalty seems to have been to New England, where he was a Harvard student and where his family kept a summer home, and later to Old England, to which he emigrated in 1914 and stayed, taking on British citizenship in 1927.

His education was more in philosophy than in literature, and he did everything for a doctoral degree but pick up the diploma itself. He worked for some years as an officer of Lloyds Bank and then became a valued member of the directorate of the publishing firm Faber and Faber. During the 1920s Eliot established a potent international reputation as a poet and a critic, also editing the influential magazine *The Criterion* (1922–1939). Like Thomas Hardy, he was given the rare and coveted Order of Merit; like W. B. Yeats he was awarded the Nobel Prize for Literature — still, after more than fifty years, the only American-born poet to be so honored. Long after Eliot's death, Andrew Lloyd Webber turned one of Eliot's lighter works, *Old Possum's Book of Practical Cats*, into the musical show *Cats*, which ran for decades in London and New York, breaking records for longevity in both and earning billions.

At first Eliot's poetry may seem obscure and difficult, but very soon almost any reader discovers that the obscurity and difficulty serve a purpose: they are part of the poem and remind us that much of life is obscure and difficult. Experiencing Eliot's poetry is like experiencing life itself. For readers of all ages all over the world, that experience has been doing something that very little poetry has managed to do, for Eliot possessed both the subtlety and the vulgarity to find ways—images, rhythms, characters, echoes—to reach some of the hidden recesses of inner life. Eliot's poetry and Eliot's criticism are complementary in some ways but also antithetical in some ways. (Randall Jarrell predicted that the time would come when people would not believe that the same man wrote both.) Rejected and ridiculed by some of his elders, he spoke an idiom immediately familiar to many of his contemporaries and successors: Ezra Pound, James Joyce, Wyndham Lewis, John Crowe Ransom, Allen Tate, Robert Lowell, Marianne Moore, Conrad Aiken. He shaped and directed the way more than one generation read and wrote. Because of accusations of anti-Semitism and misogyny, Eliot's legacy will remain a thorny issue for some; for many more, however, the influence of his deeply emotional art—especially in the darker precincts of fear, doubt, confusion, and regret—will continue.

THE POSSIBILITY OF A POETIC DRAMA

From *The Sacred Wood: Essays on Poetry and Criticism,* (London: Methuen, 1922).

The questions—why there is no poetic drama to-day, how the stage has lost all hold on literary art, why so many poetic plays are written which can only be read, and read, if at all, without pleasure—have become insipid, almost academic. The usual conclusion is either that "conditions" are too much for us, or that we really prefer other types of literature, or simply that we are uninspired. As for the last alternative, it is not to be entertained; as for the second, what type do we prefer?; and as for the first, no one has ever shown me "conditions," except of the most superficial. The reasons for raising the question again are first that the majority, perhaps, certainly a large number, of poets hanker for the stage; and second, that a not negligible public appears to want verse plays. Surely there is some legitimate craving, not restricted to a few persons, which only the verse play can satisfy. And surely the critical attitude is to attempt to analyze the conditions and the other data. If there comes to light some conclusive obstacle, the investigation should at least help us to turn our thoughts to more profitable pursuits; and if there is not, we may hope to arrive eventually at some statement of conditions which might be altered. Possibly we shall find that our incapacity has a deeper source: the arts have at times flourished when there was no drama; possibly we are incompetent altogether; in that case the stage will be, not the seat, but at all events a symptom, of the malady.

From the point of view of literature, the drama is only one among several poetic forms. The epic, the ballad, the chanson de geste, the forms of Provence and of Tuscany, all found their perfection by serving particular societies. The forms of Ovid, Catullus, Propertius, served a society different, and in some respects more civilized, than any of these; and in the society of Ovid the drama as a form of art was comparatively insignificant. Nevertheless, the drama is perhaps the most permanent, is *capable* of greater variation and of expressing more varied types of society, than any other. It varied considerably in England alone; but when one day it was discovered lifeless, subsequent forms which had enjoyed a transitory life were dead too. I am not prepared to undertake the historical survey; but I should say that the poetic drama's autopsy was performed as much by Charles Lamb as by anyone else. For a form is not wholly dead until it is known to be; and Lamb, by exhuming the remains of dramatic life at its fullest, brought a consciousness of the immense gap between present and past. It was impossible to believe, after that, in a dramatic "tradition." The relation of Byron's *English Bards* and the poems of Crabbe to the work of Pope was a continuous tradition; but the relation of *The Cenci* to the great English drama is almost that of a reconstruction to an original. By losing tradition, we lose our hold on the present; but so far as there was any dramatic tradition in Shelley's day there was nothing worth the keeping. There is all the difference between preservation and restoration.

The Elizabethan Age in England was able to absorb a great quantity of new thoughts and new images, almost dispensing with tradition, because it had this great form of its own which imposed itself on everything that came to it. Consequently, the blank verse of their plays accomplished a subtlety and consciousness, even an intellectual power, that no blank verse since has developed or even repeated; elsewhere this age is crude, pedantic, or loutish in comparison with its contemporary France or Italy. The nineteenth century had a good many fresh impressions; but it had no form in which to confine them. Two men, Wordsworth and Browning, hammered out forms for themselves—personal forms, *The Excursion, Sordello, The Ring and the Book, Dramatic Monologues*; but no man can invent a form, create a taste for it, and perfect it too. Tennyson, who might unquestionably have been a consummate master of minor forms, took to turning out large patterns on a machine. As for Keats and Shelley, they were too young to be judged, and they were trying one form after another.

These poets were certainly obliged to consume vast energy in this pursuit of form, which could never lead to a wholly satisfying result. There has only been one Dante; and, after all, Dante had the benefit of years of practice in forms employed and altered by numbers of contemporaries and predecessors; he did not waste the years of youth in metric invention; and when he came to the

Commedia he knew how to pillage right and left. To have, given into one's hands, a crude form, capable of indefinite refinement, and to be the person to see the possibilities—Shakespeare was very fortunate. And it is perhaps the craving for some such *donnée* which draws us on toward the present mirage of poetic drama.

But it is now very questionable whether there are more than two or three in the present generation who are capable, the least little bit, of benefiting by such advantages were they given. At most two or three actually devote themselves to this pursuit of form for which they have little or no public recognition. To create a form is not merely to invent a shape, a rhyme or rhythm. It is also the realization of the whole appropriate content of this rhyme or rhythm. The sonnet of Shakespeare is not merely such and such a pattern, but a precise way of thinking and feeling. The *framework* which was provided for the Elizabethan dramatist was not merely blank verse and the five-act play and the Elizabethan playhouse; it was not merely the plot—for the poets incorporated, remodeled, adapted or invented, as occasion suggested. It was also the half-formed ὑλή [stuff, raw material—ed.], the "temper of the age" (an unsatisfactory phrase), a preparedness, a habit on the part of the public, to respond to particular stimuli. There is a book to be written on the commonplaces of any great dramatic period, the handling of Fate or Death, the recurrence of mood, tone, situation. We should see then just how *little* each poet had to do; only so much as would make a play his, only what was really essential to make it different from anyone else's. When there is this economy of effort it is possible to have several, even many, good poets at once. The great ages did not perhaps *produce* much more talent than ours; but less talent was wasted.

Now in a formless age there is very little hope for the minor poet to do anything worth doing; and when I say minor I mean very good poets indeed: such as filled the Greek anthology and the Elizabethan song-books; even a Herrick; but not merely second-rate poets, for Denham and Waller have quite another importance, occupying points in the development of a major form. When everything is set out for the minor poet to do, he may quite frequently come upon some *trouvaille*, even in the drama: Peele and Brome are examples. Under the present conditions, the minor poet has too much to do. And this leads to another reason for the incompetence of our time in poetic drama.

Permanent literature is always a presentation: either a presentation of thought, or a presentation of feeling by a statement of events in human action or objects in the external world. In earlier literature—to avoid the word "classic"—we find both kinds, and sometimes, as in some of the dialogues of Plato, exquisite combinations of both. Aristotle presents thought, stripped to the essential structure, and he is a great *writer*. The *Agamemnon* or *Macbeth* is equally a statement, but of events. They are as much works of the "intellect" as the writings of Aristotle. There are more recent works of art which have the same quality of intellect in common with those of Æschylus and Shakespeare and Aristotle: *Education Sentimentale* is one of them. Compare it with such a book as *Vanity Fair* and you will see that the labor of the intellect consisted largely in a purification, in keeping out a great deal that Thackeray allowed to remain in; in refraining from reflection, in putting into the statement enough to make reflection unnecessary. The case of Plato is still more illuminating. Take the *Theœtetus*. In a few opening words Plato gives a scene, a personality, a feeling, which color the subsequent discourse but do not interfere with it: the particular setting, and the abstruse theory of knowledge afterwards developed, co-operate without confusion. Could any contemporary author exhibit such control?

In the nineteenth century another mentality manifested itself. It is evident in a very able and brilliant poem, Goethe's *Faust*. Marlowe's Mephistopheles is a simpler creature than Goethe's. But at least Marlowe has, in a few words, concentrated him into a statement. He is there, and (incidentally) he renders Milton's Satan superfluous. Goethe's demon inevitably sends us back to Goethe. He embodies a philosophy. A creation of art should not do that: he should *replace* the philosophy. Goethe has not, that is to say, sacrificed or consecrated his thought to make the drama; the drama is still a means. And this type of mixed art has been repeated by men incomparably smaller than Goethe. We have had one other remarkable work of this type: *Peer Gynt*. And we have had the plays of M. Maeterlinck and M. Claudel. [Eliot's Note: I should except *The Dynasts*. This gigantic panorama is hardly to be called a success, but it is essentially an attempt to present a vision, and "sacrifices" the philosophy to the vision, as all great dramas do. Mr. Hardy has apprehended his matter as a poet and an artist.]

In the works of Maeterlinck and Claudel on the one hand, and those of M. Bergson on the other, we have the mixture of the genres in which our age delights. Every work of imagination must have a philosophy; and every philosophy must be a work of art—how often have we heard that M. Bergson is an artist! It is a boast of his disciples. It is what the word "art" means to them that is the disputable point. Certain works of philosophy can be called works of art: much of Aristotle and Plato, Spinoza, parts of Hume, Mr. Bradley's *Principles of Logic*, Mr. Russell's essay on "Denoting": clear and beautifully formed thought. But this is not what the admirers of Bergson, Claudel, or Maeterlinck (the philosophy of the latter is a little out of date) mean. They mean precisely what is not clear, but what is an emotional stimulus. And as a mixture of thought and of vision provides more stimulus, by suggesting both, both clear thinking and clear statement of particular objects must disappear.

The undigested "idea" or philosophy, the idea-emotion, is to be found also in poetic dramas which are conscientious attempts to adapt a true structure, Athenian or Elizabethan, to contemporary feeling. It appears sometimes as the attempt to supply the defect of structure by an internal structure. "But most important of all is the structure of the incidents. For Tragedy is an imitation, not of men, but of an action and of life, and life consists in action, and its end is a mode of action, not a quality." [Eliot's note: *Poetics*, vi. 9. Butcher's translation.]

We have on the one hand the "poetic" drama, imitation Greek, imitation Elizabethan, or modern-philosophical, on the other the comedy of "ideas," from Shaw to Galsworthy, down to the ordinary social comedy. The most ramshackle Guitry farce has some paltry idea or comment upon life put into the mouth of one of the characters at the end. It is said that the stage can be used for a variety of purposes, that in only one of them perhaps is it united with literary art. A mute theatre is a possibility (I do not mean the cinema); the ballet is an actuality (though under-nourished); opera is an institution; but where you have "imitations of life" on the stage, with speech, the only standard that we can allow is the standard of the work of art, aiming at the same intensity at which poetry and the other forms of art aim. From that point of view the Shavian drama is a hybrid as the Maeterlinckian drama is, and we need express no surprise at their belonging to the same epoch. Both philosophies are popularizations: the moment an idea has been transferred from its pure state in order that it may become comprehensible to the inferior intelligence it has lost contact with art. It can remain pure only by being stated simply in the form of general truth, or by being transmuted, as the attitude of Flaubert toward the small bourgeois is transformed in *Education Sentimentale*. It has there become so identified with the reality that you can no longer say what the idea is.

The essential is not, of course, that drama should be written in verse, or that we should be able to extenuate our appreciation of broad farce by occasionally attending a performance of a play of Euripides where Professor Murray's translation is sold at the door. The essential is to get upon the stage this precise statement of life which is at the same time a point of view, a world—a world which the author's mind has subjected to a complete process of simplification. I do not find that any drama which "embodies a philosophy" of the author's (like *Faust*) or which illustrates any social theory (like Shaw's) can possibly fulfil the requirements—though a place might be left for Shaw if not for Goethe. And the world of Ibsen and the world of Tchehov are not enough simplified, universal.

Finally, we must take into account the instability of any art—the drama, music, dancing—which depends upon representation by performers. The intervention of performers introduces a complication of economic conditions which is in itself likely to be injurious. A struggle, more or less unconscious, between the creator and the interpreter is almost inevitable. The interest of a performer is almost certain to be centered in himself: a very slight acquaintance with actors and musicians will testify. The performer is interested not in form but in opportunities for virtuosity or in the communication of his "personality";

the formlessness, the lack of intellectual clarity and distinction in modern music, the great physical stamina and physical training which it often requires, are perhaps signs of the triumph of the performer. The consummation of the triumph of the actor over the play is perhaps the productions of the Guitry.

The conflict is one which certainly cannot be terminated by the utter rout of the actor profession. For one thing, the stage appeals to too many demands besides the demand for art for that to be possible; and also we need, unfortunately, something more than refined automatons. Occasionally attempts have been made to "get around" the actor, to envelop him in masks, to set up a few "conventions" for him to stumble over, or even to develop little breeds of actors for some special Art drama. This meddling with nature seldom succeeds; nature usually overcomes these obstacles. Possibly the majority of attempts to confect a poetic drama have begun at the wrong end; they have aimed at the small public which wants "poetry." ("Novices," says Aristotle, "in the art attain to finish of diction and precision of portraiture before they can construct the plot.") The Elizabethan drama was aimed at a public which wanted *entertainment* of a crude sort, but would *stand* a good deal of poetry; our problem should be to take a form of entertainment, and subject it to the process which would leave it a form of art. Perhaps the music-hall comedian is the best material. I am aware that this is a dangerous suggestion to make. For every person who is likely to consider it seriously there are a dozen toymakers who would leap to tickle æsthetic society into one more quiver and giggle of art debauch. Very few treat art seriously. There are those who treat it solemnly, and will continue to write poetic pastiches of Euripides and Shakespeare; and there are others who treat it as a joke.

32

LAURA (RIDING) JACKSON (1901–1991)

Very few American writers have had a longer or more productive life than that of the woman who began with the name Laura Reichenthal. She was born in New York City and spent three years at Cornell University, where she met Louis Gottschalk, whom she married in 1920. Convinced that Laura Reichenthal Gottschalk was too much to say—and possibly too Germanic—she used "Laura Riding Gottschalk" as a writing name when her first poems and articles were published, beginning in 1923. Poems were published in *The Fugitive*, the periodical managed by John Crowe Ransom and others of the Fugitive group in Nashville, Tennessee. She was given an award and invited to attend a Fugitives meeting. In 1925 she and Gottschalk were divorced and she moved back to New York City, where she got to know Hart Crane and other important writers.

Robert Graves, who had admired some of her poems in *The Fugitive*, initiated a correspondence, as a result of which she went to England at the end of 1925 and began an association that lasted for more than fifteen years. In 1927 she legally changed her name to Laura Riding. In the spring of 1929 she attempted suicide; six months later she and Graves left England, eventually settling in Deyá, Mallorca, where they worked on their own individual or collaborative projects and operated the Seizin Press. (They knew Gertrude Stein, who had recommended Mallorca as a good cheap place to live.) Forced to leave Mallorca in 1936 by the Spanish Civil War, they went to England, then to

Switzerland, then to France. In April 1939 they went to the United States, where she got to know Schuyler B. Jackson. She broke off her relationship with Graves and married Jackson in 1941. In 1943 they moved to Wabasso, Florida, where they spent the rest of their lives (he died in 1968). In later years she began using "Laura (Riding) Jackson" as her writing name.

She was a productive poet until the early 1940s, when she renounced poetry as an unfit medium for telling the truth. Over the next fifty years she published a few poems but stubbornly maintained her position on the failure of poetry. She was also a productive critic, publishing two books in 1928 alone: *Contemporaries and Snobs* and *Anarchism Is Not Enough*. With Graves she collaborated on a number of important books, journals, and publishing projects.

With Schuyler Jackson she turned her interest to language itself and continued an ambitious philosophical work that she had begun during the 1930s. After her death this study was published as *Rational Meaning: A New Foundation for the Definition of Words* (1997; edited by William Harmon). It is a work of rare seriousness and depth, but is also full of incidental drama and humor. As with many other critics, Laura (Riding) Jackson was most effective on the attack, disposing of weaker critics and poets with an energy like that of Edgar Allan Poe or Ezra Pound.

POETIC REALITY AND CRITICAL UNREALITY

From *Contemporaries and Snobs*, 1928

The critical problem, then, is not so much a matter of the proper subjects or
style-modes by which to ensure the integrity of poetry, as the determining of
where the true reality of the poem lies, whether in the gross contemporary mind
of which the poet is supposed to be possessed, or in the non-contemporary
poetic mind—for *poetic* must mean non-contemporary if *contemporary* is understood as anything more than a historically descriptive phrase, if it is used,
for example, to describe the mind as shaped by contemporary influences. If the
distinction between these two minds is carefully drawn, it will be seen that, in
times when the poetic mind has been under the dictatorship of the contemporary mind, the poem has had only contemporary reality; as in the eighteenth
century, when the poem had a false poetic reality because the social dictatorship
was disguised in the literary dictatorship, and as in the Victorian period, when
the poem had a more obvious contemporary reality. In the early nineteenth
century the poem had a mixed reality; the contemporary mind, in its caprice
and inventiveness, imitating the poetic mind.

   If we observe what happens when the poem is confined to one type of reality,
to that of the contemporary mind, as in the eighteenth-century satire, or to that
of the poetic mind, as in the romantic abuse of the poetic absolute, it appears

that both of these are but half-realities and that the true reality of the poem must have a double force: a positive truth, from its origin in the poetic mind, and a negative truthfulness, from the fact that it is not made unreal when brought into contact with the contemporary mind, that is, with contemporary knowledge. When the contemporary mind, or the concrete intelligence, or whatever we please to call it, is seen to be no more, no less, than accumulated knowledge-material, it will be realized how grotesque it is that this should supply the creative origin, and hence the first reality of the poem, leaving to the poetic mind the secondary service of interpretation.

But the slaves of this knowledge-material can imagine no state of activity which shall not be dependent on it; they cannot understand that the poet can have experience of it as an independent mind reducing authoritative mass to unauthoritative ideas; that once the mass of intelligent matter is recognized as a mass of ideas about matter, every man is potentially his own scientist, though not his own poet, since only the poet is fully capable, in this way, of being his own scientist. Therefore, if the poet shows independence, if he is, indeed, not a mere mouthpiece of the contemporary mind, it is assumed by the knowledge-slaves that he cannot have an informed mind; and everything he writes is taken with a grain of scientific salt. This snobbism, which naturally appeals to criticism, because it seems another indulgence by which poetry may manage to survive, in turn drives poets who stand in fear of the knowledge-hierarchy to profess only the single reality of the poetic mind—what we may call the apologetic absolute. The result is poetry whose only subject is the psychology of the poet and whose final value is scientific; which is as it should be, since the snobbism responsible for it tries to treat poetry as if it were a science.

Poetry of this kind thus finally comes to justify itself by an analogy with mechanical reality. France and America provide numerous examples of it. In America industry itself may be said to have an imagination and so to furnish an instructive parallel to the creative mind faced with the problem of employing itself. If it cannot have poems which shall have a place in the world, perhaps it can have poems which shall have a place in themselves, which shall end where they begin; if it cannot have poetry, perhaps it can have purity. The machine is a practical symbol of automatism and may be said to create itself as the psychological poem does, to be its own product. Instead of possessing a life, such a poem possesses a mechanism, a fixed emotional routine that may be called absolute because its effect never varies. In France the analogical element is provided to poetry by the mechanical principle of other arts, by painting, principally by music. The æsthetic purity of the poem is made to consist in its behaving like a machine, in imitating its making and in maintaining an absence of meaning except as a *non-conscious* cause and instrument of a conscious effect. The history of this theory lies between Poe, in whom it was an amateur's attempt to defend the independence of the poem on the grounds of its mere pleasure-reality, and Paul Valéry and other musico-poeticians, who further develop the pleasure-reality theory by transferring the centre of the poem from its origin in the poet to its conclusion in the reader. Invention is converted into reaction, poetry into criticism. The pure poem is arrived at by subtracting the poem from itself. Only its limits remain, its points of origin and of communication. The rest is a time and space necessity between them, the place, presumably, which the poetic mind leaves to be filled in by the contemporary mind; the myth, once more, which the contemporary mind is supposed to suggest to the poetic mind, but now a blank myth, since the contemporary mind believes itself to have arrived at the all-in-all, that what is not itself is merely its shadow.

If, in spite of the present surquidry of the contemporary mind and the accidie with which the poetic mind is afflicted, it were possible to conceive of the production of a true poem, to what should we look for evidences of its reality? To those inner circumstances which make up the poetic mind and which the poem is the means of externalizing, as the poetic mind is the means of externalizing the poem, which hitherto existed only unto itself. In this mutuality lies the real clue to the double reality of the poem, its truth as a poem, its truthfulness as a demonstration of the poet's mind. For we have now come to the point where it is permissible to talk of the poetic mind as the poet's mind, and of the poet's mind as the only contemporary mind possible in the poem, its incidental reality. The poem itself is supreme, above persons; judging rather than judged; keeping criticism at a respectful distance; it is even able to make a reader of its author. It comes to be because an individual mind is clear enough to perceive it and then to become its instrument. Criticism can only have authority over the poem if the poet's mind was from the start not sufficiently clear, sufficiently free of criticism; if it obeyed an existing, that is, a past order of reality, rather than a present order of reality, that is, the order of the things which do not yet exist. How shall this true poem be recognized? By those tests of reality it imposes on the reader; perhaps, then, only by the strength of the hostility it arises and the extent of its unpopularity even with the minority cults, or by its modest contentment with itself and the obscurity to which it is consigned.

False poems, as distinguished from weak poems, are those written to respond to tests of reality imposed by the contemporary mind and are therefore able to satisfy them better than any true one. The creative history of the false poem is the age, the author sensible of the age and the set of outer circumstances involved in his delicate adjustment to the age at a particular moment, in a particular place. Nothing remains beyond this, no life, no element, as in the true poem, untranslatable except in the terms provided by the poem itself. In the true poem these terms form a measurement that hitherto did not exist, and the test of the poem's reality is: to what degree is it a new dimension of reality? Indeed, in the true poem poetry is the science of reality, so-called science itself the myth—the corpus of knowledge to which poetry has for centuries been an inspired drudge, turning it into the sensible material of a religious mysticism, a gross and flabby self-worship. Poetry, in other words, has been the divine solvent converting knowledge into truth, until knowledge, mad with its own modernity, declared itself the sole source of truth. But if knowledge can dismiss poetry, can it dismiss the poet? If the poetic mind was once the source of truth for knowledge, does it cease to have truth because the corpus of knowledge finds it no longer useful? In its primitive period of usefulness to knowledge it was a superior *knowing*; itself truth, knowledge its truthfulness: the true poem was at once truth and myth (truthfulness), knowing and knowledge, reality and test of reality. But if knowledge is, so to speak, composing its own monster-poem, has the poem as such necessarily disappeared? Can minds and their perceptions be erased by a piece of self-investigated india-rubber?

The word *poem* itself is an ever new meaning of an ever new combination of *doing* and *making* as one act, with a third inference of *being* perpetuating these in dynamic form. The only difference between a poem and a person is that in a poem *being* is the final state, in a person the preliminary state. These two kinds of realities, that of the person, that of the poem, stand at one end and the other of the poet's mind, which is but progressive experience made into a recurrent sequence circulating between one kind of reality and the other without destroying one reality in the other.

T. S. Eliot observed some time ago that 'the conditions which may be considered to be unfavourable to the writing of good poetry are unfavourable to the writing of good criticism'. This implies that the reality of poetry is externally, not internally derived. But though 'conditions' may be unfavourably disposed to good poetry, they cannot affect the *writing* of good poetry if there are poets who insist on writing it. They can, however, affect the writing of such poetry as is actually created by external contemporary conditions; poetry, in fact, that is not poetry at all but the by-product of a period's spiritual indecision. But such poetry is not a manifestation of the poetic mind but of certain unhappy formations in the contemporary mind acting as individuals whose task it is to present the signs of the times rather than poetry.

We have, then, in a period when the Zeitgeist, the Old Man of the Sea, is working particular mischief, a number of Sinbads drifting at large whose fate it is to be at the mercy of his humours. They may either be washed astride a breakwater (when their balancing gestures are called criticism) or dashed over the sea wall into the Sacred Grove, where they try to feel at home in spite of the Old Man on their back (when their balancing gestures are called poetry).

When such contemporary formations are converted into creative or critical personalities by Zeitgeist humours, a subtle strangeness will, of course, be perceived in them. First something scarcely discernible, except for the feeling of

embarrassment it conveys—a faint, but distinct foreign accent; next that disso-
ciation or snobbism which a newly converted Catholic feels toward the born
Catholic, or the cabinet-maker who has learned his trade at a school toward
one who has inherited it from his father. It is the self-conscious earnestness of
an alien doing his best to become acclimatized to his adopted country. Without
that natural endowment which makes the creative faculty indifferent to moral
justifications of itself (its moral justification being best presented in a work),
the chief preoccupation of the factitious creative personality is with the moral
values, or the legitimacy, of literature. A blend is thus made of the creative and
critical operations, resulting in much interesting self-revelation ('good criticism'), but in too much dull self-concealment in poetry, which comes to be the
martyrdom of lack-of-confidence-in-self. Mr. Eliot's axiom, therefore, which was
composed long before he was completely floored by the Zeitgeist, must be
brought up-to-date in this way: 'The conditions which may be considered favourable to the writing of good criticism may be considered favourable to the
writing of good criticism.' For in such language poetry is but an incident of
criticism. Mr. Eliot wrote several years ago: 'Every form of genuine criticism is
directed toward creation. The historical or the philosophical critic of poetry is
criticising poetry in order to create a history or a philosophy; the poetic critic
is criticising poetry in order to create poetry.' In a review of two books by two
distinguished contemporary personalities, Mr. Herbert Read and M. Ramon
Fernandez, in the October, 1926, issue of the *New Criterion* (a community of
contemporary personalities), Mr. Eliot goes still further: 'The significance of
the term critic has varied indefinitely; in our time the most vigorous critical
minds are philosophical minds, are, in short, creative of values.'

Further characteristics of this snobbism, besides its preoccupations with the
moral values of literature, are its emphasis on personal pedigree, learning and
literary internationalism. The review referred to above is so generous in examples of these that I cannot refrain from using it as a text, nor indeed this
entire number of the *New Criterion*, which includes an essay by M. Fernandez
himself beginning, 'It is pleasant for a French critic to write for the cultivated
public on the other side of the Channel'; a poem by Mr. Read himself, *The
Lament of Saint Denis* with a motto *From the Institutes of Johann Lorenz von
Mosheim, translated by Archibald Maclaine* (1764) and three foot-notes: *Inferno*
xxviii. 121–2, *Paradiso*: x. 94, and Boëthius: *De Consolatione, II., vi.*, the learned
if not the moral justifications for such lines as

> 'And then a faint rumour in the night
> An approaching murmur of enemies
> Their hearts were suddenly loud in their still bodies
> Fluttering wildly within those livid tunicles of flesh'

(poor Mr. Read, likewise floored by the Zeitgeist, who in his less contemporaneous days could write less ambitiously but more authentically:

> 'Judas was right
> In a mental sort of way;
> For he betrayed another and so
> With purpose was self-justified.
> But I delivered my body to fear—
> I was a bloodier fool than he.');

and a poem by Mr. Eliot himself, *Fragment of a Prologue*, with two mottoes, one from the *Choephoroi*, the other from St. John of the Cross, the poem itself being a kind of epilogue to *Ulysses*, or Ulysses in the Waste Land.

But the review itself is even more illuminating, especially as to the love of pedigree, learning and literary internationalism: 'Mr. Read and M. Fernandez provide an excellent example of this invalidation of the ancient classification' (critical and creative) because, the next sentence continues, 'They are of the same generation, of the same order of culture; their education is as nearly the same as that of men of different race and nationality can be. . . . Both were primarily students of literature, and animated by the desire to find a meaning and justification for literature. Mr. Read has the advantage of being European and English; M. Fernandez that of being European and American (he was born in Mexico). . . . Both are critics with international learning and international standards.' All this to prove the invalidation of that 'ancient' classification.

It is improper to advance that criticism and poetry spring from the same kind of personal impulse, unless it is made equally clear that they must diverge at an early stage toward their respective positions. Criticism and creation do not face the same way, but face each other, criticism forgoing creation in order to be able to describe it. This purpose demands learning in criticism, because it is thus the author not of one poem, let us say, but of the history of one poem and another and another (since when face to face with one poem the critic sees many others as well); but it does not mean that criticism may be substituted for creation, as would follow if that 'ancient classification' were really invalidated. The novel perhaps shows the danger of such a substitution more clearly than any other kind of writing, being avowedly critical rather than creative, historical rather than poetic: it is a description of poetic reality by contemporary reality. Wherever the novel tries to create poetic values, it becomes false art, as with Proust, Joyce, Virginia Woolf and such American poetic novelists as Waldo Frank and Sherwood Anderson. For, while the novel may suggest them or describe them, it needs to be emphasized dogmatically that there are no true creative values but poetic values—values which can be final without reference to their contemporary setting. (This does not apply to the *poetical* novel, to

Borrow or Melville, *poetical* referring only to the character of the style, not to the creative intention of the novel.) The novel may be eminently true, or truthful, but it is not truth; and no novelist who held his work in proper respect would claim it to be truth except in this relative sense of truthful. If Mr. Eliot were not so comfortably relaxing against the novel, 'a capital point for every contemporary mind (*sic*)' (to start from), evidently because it can be perverted to bring about 'this invalidation of the ancient classification', he would perhaps reject Proust with Mr. Read and M. Fernandez not so much because Proust was wanting in the moral element as because he falsified the novel—composing it synthetically of those infinitesimal morsels of poetic reality by which the connoisseur's palate has had to appear uniformly stimulated throughout that long, long from-egg-to-apple dinner.

Proust recalls the snobbism of literary internationalism, which has provided Charles Scott-Moncrieff, George Moore and Ezra Pound among others, with continuous employment. Any serious indictment of it would only assist in prolonging the sufferings of the silent populations whose palates were long ago exhausted by foreign banqueting but who go on because the connoisseurs go on, who go on because they are at the head of the table and cannot escape. Excepting rare instances of personal sympathy with a foreign language arising out of associations of circumstance or temperament; excepting also such a unique case of internationalism as that of America and England, where one is but a historical layer of the other; any persistent cultivation of a contemporary foreign literature is a snobbism inspired, apart from its association with a general programme of literary snobbism, by a romantic purpose to find relief from one dull literary scene in another—a form of literary pornography. Nothing could be more alien to Mr. Eliot's temperament, for example, than the sentiment and temperament expressed in: 'la littérature est impossible. Il faut en sorter' which he quotes from Jean Cocteau's letter to Jacques Maritain on poetry and religion. 'International standards' of literature are a degraded critical Esperanto and, like Esperanto, comprehensible only to Esperantists.

What unites *littérateurs* (the successors of the critics and creators of 'the ancient classification') in this generation is, in fact, not standards of taste or positive intellectual sympathy, but the feeling of panic occasioned by the setting adrift of literature by the time-universe. The reason why contemporary critics are so interested in inquiring into the nature of the function of literature is not, as Mr. Eliot suggests, because they do not wish 'to take for granted a whole universe', but because a whole universe has given literature its dismissal papers. Naturally endowed creative writers may protect themselves from the present Zeitgeist or remain entirely unaffected by it. But those sensitive spots in the contemporary mind to be identified as *littérateurs* can neither avoid nor revoke the Zeitgeist nor yet cancel themselves, since they are so organically of the Zeitgeist; and are thus obliged to make a religion of their own post-humousness, a religion so serious that Mr. Eliot himself calls it 'an athleticism, a *training*, of the soul as severe and ascetic as the training of the body of a runner'. The asceticism on which it is based is the deprivation of the universe which science has forced on literature; and the moral values implied are the coward's promise to keep up his courage though all is lost.

The most redeeming and yet most unfortunate characteristic of this snob-criticism is its seriousness. Unfortunate because by contrast with the complete frivolousness or inaneness of all other contemporary critical writing it is the only criticism that demands any respect from the independent writer; and in this way likely to make him, in spite of his independence, ingenuously shy of it, and of expressing his normal reactions to the awful gloom that it has cast over the whole literary scene. Such is the science of overwhelming by pomp. Even the *London Mercury* would not if it could quiz the *New Criterion*, but would on the contrary feel flattered to be counted amongst its colleagues.

The final effect of this snobbism is the deliberate cultivation of a modernity, a calculated and therefore more 'classical' quality ('We live') than mere crude romantic contemporaneousness ('I'm glad I'm alive' or 'I'm sorry I'm alive'). 'A poem which was never modern will not pass into that curious state of suspended animation by means of which the poems we call classic are preserved active to the palate', said Edgell Rickword, Editor of the *Calendar of Modern Letters*, lately next to the *New Criterion* the most serious community of contemporary personalities. Thus poetic modernism, advertised by its own uplift, reaches the poetry societies of the provinces, who by now have used up all their war and post-war subjects and are grateful for a change. 'At an evening of the Bournemouth Poetry Society', reports the *Bournemouth Echo*, 'held at Eight Bells, Christchurch, poetry enthusiasts (one came all the way from Broadstone) were well rewarded by a remarkably live and able paper by Mrs. Leslie Goodwin on "Further Aspects of Modern Poetry". Mrs. Goodwin called attention to the unappreciated importance of the Left Wing or extreme Modernist Group, who have new ideas as to what is appropriate and beautiful.' For the Old Man of the Sea must have his joke.

'Modern', however, is not a contemporary invention: it must not be forgotten that the *littérateurs* of the characteristic eighteenth century were likewise modernists and likewise invalidated 'the ancient classification'. Their poetry and criticism, although not born of the same impulse, were written from the same point of view, which gave them a mutual consistency if not a reciprocal power. Criticism became, then also, a moral measurement: arbitrary judgments for arbitrary poetic practices. Poetry was a critical convenience, criticism a poetic convenience; the offspring of this union between them had that inbred half-reality which is characteristic of present-day manifestations of the contemporary mind in criticism and poetry. The period was a 'literary' period. It had been fitting, for example, for Milton some time before, to dedicate *Samson Agonistes* to a campaign against what he called the corrupt gratification of the people with 'comic stuff', and to a classical conception and treatment of tragedy. It was fitting for Whitman, long after, to justify *Leaves of Grass* by an exactly contrary critical attitude: 'that the real test applicable to a book is entirely outside literary tests'. For, though both disregarded the meaning of poetic intention, one accepted the authority of literature, the other that of life and humanity. The authority of eighteenth-century literature was neither of these, but a working compromise between them. Literature was the rationalizing apparatus that added logic to morality; life, the literary demonstration. This code expressed the temper of the age faithfully: snobbism, or conformity of behaviour to a degree where nothing happened at all, where important poetry was prevented from happening. Such literary sterility caused a reaction in the next century, frenzied fertility resulting in an unpedigreed stock. Although a fresh creative basis was found, the preceding century furnished its literary ancestry, which could be revolted against but not cast out of the blood. So poetry was for a time a romantic misfit, until new critical values could be found to match the new poetical values. In Keats we find many Pope-ish echoes; as we find many nineteenth-century echoes in the poetry of Miss Sitwell. Torn between her inherited Wordsworthianisms and Tennysonianisms and her acquired Pope-isms, her poetry no less than Keats' bears the marks of a conflict. Her nineteenth-century-isms (as Keats' eighteenth-century-isms) it is possible to indulge because they were inherited; likewise her Gallicisms, as a decorative relief to these. But why should Miss Sitwell, with an abundantly endowed creative faculty, find it necessary to praise *The Rape of the Lock* as a beautiful example 'of the fusion of subject matter and style'? If not because prevailing critical snobbisms force the independent creative faculty to strengthen its pedigree with artificial critical values which, in turn, act as a kind of protective snobbism (as Elizabethanisms did for Keats).

Nineteenth-century poetry, after a brief period of sentimental debate, failed to develop any real critical values. Instead, it borrowed its titles from the idea of progress, the philosophical demiurge of the century, thus only changing one social god for another without the disguise this time of a literary mask. The popular mode of mysticism resulting from this religiosity was the intelligence — not the intellect. The reason why the intellect is held anti-religious is that it is an individual property rather than a social one and is therefore less likely to accept as final the generalizations of the prevailing community system of faith. Contemporary criticism is endeavouring to elevate the mass-intelligence by making it behave like an independent intellect, the effect of which is to rob the term *intellectual integrity* of all significance. While 'contemporary' eighteenth-century poetry cannot be said to have had great intellectual integrity, it did make an honest compromise between the general intelligence and the individual intellect by postulating *wit* as the common raw material of literature. However wit may be abused by being made to serve moral ends, it is in itself an intellectual competence which is bound to protect itself in some way against the uses to which it is put. *Wit* may indeed be called the subject-matter of the best of eighteenth-century poetry, as human wisdom forms the subject-matter of the worst of nineteenth-century poetry.

In the earlier period there was at least wit to act as a basis, however artificial, of critical values. In the later there was only a standard of philosophical satis-faction demanding an unrestrained flattering of every possible variety of human activity: poetry being the spiritual sign of practical prosperity and advance, the personified muse of optimism. For this later tendency Wordsworth's critical commonplaces were principally responsible; which even modern writers find it impossible to reject on the proper ground. Miss Sitwell, for example, thinks that it is time to discard the Wordsworthian tradition, not because it is funda-mentally false, but only because it has grown dull in the course of its develop-ment. It is time to leave 'the peasant and words suitable to the peasant'. That is, what poetry needs is a general correction of taste, not an independence in which creative values have a lack of conformity according to the variety of poetic minds (the use of *poetic mind* as a critical abstraction is likely to make us forget that it is *a* rather than *the* poetic mind). It is a telling piece of well-meaning literary snobbism to call Wordsworth a peasant poet. Wordsworth, like Miss Sitwell, wanted to 'interest mankind' in the proper way, 'to correct the present state of the public taste in this country'. 'Humble and rustic life was generally chosen' because it made a more fluid philosophical language for poetry: the peasant flavour is only a literary manner, as that part of Miss Sitwell's own poetry which is dedicated to taste is but the exploitation of a literary manner. Wordsworth's poetry is no more fit for reading by peasants than Miss Sitwell's is by princesses. Both have the view that poetry is a careful annotation of life. To Wordsworth, poetry is 'the spontaneous overflow of powerful feelings'; to Miss Sitwell, it brings 'new and heightened consciousness to life'. Both have a purpose to deal with what she calls the 'common movement of life', only 'the modern poet has a different stylisation.' Wordsworth, under the false mask of taste, made moral enlargements on trivial subjects. The modern poet who, like Miss Sitwell, is not overwhelmed by the world or made an instrument of the Zeitgeist, but who in spite of his contempt for its blustering demonstration of power clings to it out of an inherited and old-fashioned sense of duty, wastes himself on that sentimental, self-sacrificing office which Miss Sitwell calls 'showing the world in all its triviality'.

So that present modernism is not even literary in the eighteenth-century sense but a complex of pietist snobberies and sentimentalities.